D1561431

The Advent of Evangelicalism

Exploring Historical Continuities

Edited by
MICHAEL A. G.
HAYKIN
and
KENNETH J.
STEWART

FOREWORD BY
Timothy George

Nashville, Tennessee

Published in the USA by B&H Academic
B&H Publishing Group
One LifeWay Plaza
Nashville, Tennessee 37234

Previously published in the UK by APOLLOS (an imprint of InterVarsity Press)
Norton Street, Nottingham NG7 3HR, England
Email: ivp@ivpbooks.com
Website: www.ivpbooks.com

This collection © InterVarsity Press, 2008

All rights reserved. No part of this publication may be reproduced, stored in a retrieval system
or transmitted, in any form or by any means, electronic, mechanical, photocopying, recording
or otherwise, without the prior permission of the publisher or the Copyright Licensing
Agency.

Unless otherwise indicated, all Scripture quotations are from The Holy Bible, English
Standard Version, published by HarperCollins Publishers © 2001 by Crossway Bibles, a
division of Good News Publishers. Used by permission. All rights reserved.

Dewey Decimal Classification: 269.2
Subject Heading: EVANGELISTIC WORK—HISTORY\EVANGELICALISM—
HISTORY\CHURCH HISTORY

ISBN: 978-0-8054-4860-3

Printed in the United States of America by Versa Press

1 2 3 4 5 6 • 12 11 10 09 08

This book gathers insightful presentations on the history and development of evangelicalism with very deep historical and theological roots. It provides just the kind of constructive dialogue that is sure to help us move ever closer to a more satisfying grasp of evangelical identity, not as a mere historical curiosity, but as a matter of self-knowledge for thoughtful action to the glory of God.

Tom J. Nettles, Professor of Historical Theology,
The Southern Baptist Seminary, Louisville, Kentucky

David Bebbington is an outstanding evangelical historian and scholar of Baptist thought as well as a dedicated churchman. His work is highly respected on both sides of the Atlantic, and this assessment by colleagues of his major thesis is enlightening and informative. It is a major contribution to Christian scholarship.

Richard V. Pierard, professor emeritus,
Indiana State University and Gordon College

David Bebbington has proved himself to be one of the greatest contemporary historians of evangelicalism, providing fresh research and interpretation, stimulating able students in the subject, directing young scholars as a model and mentor of what evangelical historiography can become, and assuring evangelicalism a place among the important Christian movements in history.

After some twenty years of well-earned accolade, it is now time for another matter: an evaluation of the scholarly critiques that have been expressed of Bebbington's *Evangelicalism in Modern Britain: A History from the 1730s to the 1980s*. As a result, the editors have arranged for some eighteen scholars to express themselves on the 'emergence of evangelicalism'. It is their conviction that there is more continuity between the evangelicals and some involved in preceding awakenings of Christianity. And Bebbington, as the Christian scholar that he is, has welcomed this endeavour and himself contributed a 'Response', to further this invaluable process.

Ian S. Rennie, Emeritus Dean of Faculty,
Tyndale Seminary, Toronto, Canada

David Bebbington's characterization in 1989 of 'the Evangelical version of Protestantism' as 'created by the Enlightenment' has caught on so well, albeit comfortably simplified, in some influential quarters of UK evangelicalism as to serve as a stick to belabour as 'modernist' their least favoured varieties of the contemporary evangelical mainstream. Only the postmodernist brand, it seems, can hope to escape this baleful genetic identity. Since my (and David Bebbington's) generation of evangelicals grew up regarding 'modernism' as the rationalistic antithesis of classical biblical orthodoxy, there is urgent need for clarifying scrutiny of his thesis. This symposium, carefully constructed by its editors, will prove a significant contribution to that task. The range and quality of its chapters and their authors will surely advance our historical understanding of the manifold matrices of what Bebbington also calls 'an adaptation of the Protestant tradition through contact with the Enlightenment'.

David F. Wright, Professor Emeritus, Patristic & Reformed
Christianity, University of Edinburgh

To David Bebbington,
with deep admiration of his skill as an
evangelical historian
and with thanks to God for his friendship

CONTENTS

PART 5: RESPONSE

CONTRIBUTORS

David W. Bebbington is Professor of History, University of Stirling, Stirling, Scotland.

Joel R. Beeke is President and Professor of Systematic Theology and Homiletics, Puritan Reformed Theological Seminary, and Pastor of the Heritage Netherlands Reformed Congregation in Grand Rapids, Michigan, USA.

John Coffey is Reader in Early Modern History, University of Leicester, England.

Timothy George is founding Dean of Beeson Divinity School, Samford University, Birmingham, Alabama, USA, and a senior editor of *Christianity Today*.

Crawford Gribben is Senior Lecturer in Early Modern Print Culture, Schools of English and Histories and Humanities, Trinity College, Dublin, Ireland.

Michael A. G. Haykin is Professor of Church History and Biblical Spirituality, Southern Baptist Theological Seminary, Louisville, Kentucky, USA.

Paul Helm is a teaching fellow, Regent College, Vancouver, British Columbia, Canada.

D. Bruce Hindmarsh is the James M. Houston Professor of Theology, Regent College, Vancouver, British Columbia, Canada.

David Ceri Jones is Lecturer in the Department of History and Welsh History, Aberystwyth University.

Thomas S. Kidd is Associate Professor of History, Baylor University, Waco, Texas, USA.

Timothy Larsen is McManis Professor of Christian Thought, Wheaton College, Wheaton, Illinois, USA.

Cameron A. MacKenzie is Forrest E. and Frances H. Ellis Professor of Historical Theology, Concordia Theological Seminary, Fort Wayne, Indiana, USA.

A. T. B. McGowan is Principal of the Highland Theological College, Dingwall (UHI), and Honorary Professor of Reformed Doctrine, University of Aberdeen, Scotland.

D. Densil Morgan is Professor of Theology and Head of the College of Arts and Humanities, Bangor University, Wales.

Ashley Null is a visiting Guggenheim Fellow, the University of Cambridge and Humboldt University of Berlin, as well as Canon Theologian of the Episcopal Diocese of Western Kansas, USA.

Ian J. Shaw is Dean of Postgraduate Studies and Lecturer in the History of Christianity, International Christian College, Glasgow, Scotland.

Kenneth J. Stewart is Professor of Theological Studies, Covenant College, Lookout Mountain, Georgia, USA.

Douglas A. Sweeney is Associate Professor of Church History and the History of Christian Thought, Trinity Evangelical Divinity School, Deerfield, Illinois, USA.

Garry J. Williams is Academic Dean and Tutor in Church History and Doctrine, Oak Hill Theological College, London, England.

Brandon G. Withrow is Adjunct Professor of Church History, Beeson Divinity School, Birmingham, Alabama, USA.

FOREWORD

I first read David Bebbington's *Evangelicalism in Modern Britain: A History from the 1730s to the 1980s* in 1990, one year after it was first published in the United Kingdom. I was impressed by the narrative force of its argument, its critical apparatus with references to thousands of soundings in primary sources, its sympathetic yet critical engagement with the movement it set out to describe. While I was not entirely convinced by its interpretation of evangelical history in the modern era, I knew this was a really good book, one to which I would doubtless return again and again. At the time, however, I did not sense that this volume would become the 'classic' it is now widely recognized to be some two decades later. The status of Bebbington's book as a seminal study of great importance is born out not only by Timothy Larsen's history of the reception of the book set forth in the first chapter of this volume, but also by the fact that no one to date has yet written a more compelling account of the history of the evangelical movement from the 1730s to the 1980s.

Several years later, in 1994, I was asked to write a brief article for *Christianity Today*, 'If I'm an Evangelical, What Am I?' I referred to what was even then being widely touted as the standard definition of evangelicalism—a movement of spiritual vitality within the Protestant tradition characterized by four distinguishing marks: conversionism, activism, biblicism and crucicentrism. The most contested of these traits, *activism*, looms large in a number of the chapters in this volume, not because anyone doubts that evangelicalism indeed was (and still is) a lively movement of intense activity, but because Bebbington's linkage of activism to the doctrine of assurance has proved less than fully convincing to many scholars. Still, it is a safe bet to assume that when one thinks of the distinctive marks of the evangelical church today, the Bebbington quadrilateral more often comes to mind than the venerable ecclesial attributes of the Nicene faith—one, holy, catholic and apostolic.

It is a measure of the persuasive and enduring strength of Bebbington's book that so many historians of note still find it worthy of the kind of close analysis and critical engagement reflected in the following chapters. It is also a measure of Bebbington's stature as a leading historian and interpreter of evangelical life that he has listened well to his critics and indeed has learned from the new light they have shed on his work. In the response he makes to these chapters at the close of the volume, Bebbington both reaffirms many of his original emphases and qualifies and adjusts others. In that sense, this volume is a model of the kind of scholarly interaction that advances knowledge and opens up new horizons of interpretation.

If there is one primary undercurrent that swirls through all of these chapters, as well as Bebbington's response to them, it is the question reflected in the title and subtitle of this book: to what extent does evangelicalism of modern/postmodern times (say, from the conversion of John Wesley through to the era of Billy Graham) represent continuity or discontinuity with the preceding Christian story? Throughout history the Christian church has always been pulled toward one of two poles: *identity* or *adaptability*. This tension arises from the most central theological affirmation of the New Testament, the Word became flesh (John 1:14). The need to communicate the gospel in such a way that it speaks to the total context of the people to whom it is addressed courses through every age of church history and shapes the various disputes and controversies that have marked the development of Christian doctrine and spirituality: rigorism and laxism, orthodoxy and heresy, ecumenism and schism, reformation and retrenchment, to name only a few. Speaking of the Middle Ages, Roland Bainton once said that Christianity is wont either to conquer the world or to flee from it, and sometimes it seeks to do both at once. This same tension was certainly present in the eighteenth century as the Evangelical Awakening swept through many of the Protestant churches of Great Britain and North America. It is no less present today as Christianity in general and the world evangelical movement in particular is finding new centres of vitality in places like Nigeria, Korea, Nepal and Latin America.

When seen in the wider perspective of Christian history, evangelicalism is best understood as a renewal movement within historic Christian orthodoxy. At its heart is a theological core shaped by the trinitarian and Christological consensus of the early church, the formal and material principles of the Reformation, the missionary movement that grew out of the Great Awakening and the new movements of the Spirit that indicate 'surprising works of God' are still happening in the world today. This understanding leads me to stress the fundamental continuity the evangelical faith shares with a Great Tradition of Christian believing, confessing, worshipping and acting through the centuries, while not discounting the many local histories that must be written to explain this phenomenon in any given era.

I want to say a closing word of gratitude to David Bebbington, whose scholarly work has stimulated our reflections in this volume. Not only is he a superb historian and fine teacher; he is also a participant-observer in the movement his studies have illuminated so well. A committed person of the church, he has been a deacon in a Scottish Baptist congregation and has a record of involvement in various Christian ministries across the years. Thus this book is a tribute to one of the great scholars of our day, an extraordinary historian whose insight, character and breadth of sympathy is a model for us all.

Timothy George
Founding dean of Beeson Divinity School of Samford University
and a senior editor of *Christianity Today*

EDITORS' PREFACE

To a very considerable degree, this volume can only properly be viewed as an example of the serendipitous, that is, 'the discovery of things not sought'. Every contributor to this book has been aware to some degree that since its initial publication, David Bebbington's *Evangelicalism in Modern Britain: A History from the 1730s to the 1980s* (London: Unwin Hyman, 1989) has engendered warm discussion between those more fully and those less fully convinced of this author's contention for evangelicalism's substantially novel emergence in the 1730s. But most of the contributors initially lived and worked in settings in which they were unaware of any others who shared their own reservations about the proposal that evangelicalism began in the Whitefield and Wesley era.

One of the editors, for example, had already in 1996 read a paper on the question of evangelicalism's reputed origin in the age of the Enlightenment.[1] Yet it is likely that no other contributor to this volume knew of this at the time. In 2001, the other editor read a conference paper on the inadvisability of accepting a theory of evangelicalism's eighteenth-century origin—and he,

---

1. Michael Haykin's paper 'Evangelicalism and the Enlightenment' was first given at the Eighth International Baptist Conference, held at Jarvis Street Baptist Church, Toronto, Ontario, 21–24 Oct. 1996. It subsequently appeared under this title in Andrew M. Fountain (ed.), *Loving the God of Truth: Preparing the Church for the Twenty-first Century* (Toronto: Toronto Baptist Seminary and Bible College, 1996), pp. 47–68.

so far as he knew, was then turning over unplowed sod.[2] At this point, the pace quickened. Several of the contributors to this volume were present at the reading of the latter paper in 2001 and were led to commence their own related investigations, while yet another in the UK was already at work on a Tyndale House paper when an electronic version of the 2001 paper came into his hands.[3] By 2003, an idea had emerged that there was warrant for a revisiting of the question of evangelicalism's origins through a book of essays devoted to the subject.

This idea, when broached to David Bebbington, brought the characteristically gracious offer of the information that a number of historians had indicated to him that they too were among the unconvinced about the alleged eighteenth-century origin of evangelicalism. These were shortly recruited for the budding project. By then, it was time to stand back and ask what lacunae still existed in the survey of Protestant regions, leaders and doctrines we now proposed to undertake. Once more, we discovered what we had barely sought. We soon located esteemed writers ready and able to address aspects of our quest, which, had they been left uninvestigated, would surely have raised the question of the reason for this neglect. By November 2005, a good portion of these essays were ready to be read in a special working group of the Evangelical Theological Society meeting at Valley Forge, Pennsylvania. At this point most of the contributors were meeting face to face for the first time! Still other essays, commissioned late in the process, have been supplied subsequently.

Thanks are due to our publisher for both the endorsement of the project and the patience shown in waiting for the submission of all materials, to David Bebbington (a historian so industrious that he alone has kept nineteen of us engaged in researching his thought) and to the Lilly Foundation, which through its grants to the Kaleo Center of Covenant College, Lookout Mountain, Georgia, has materially assisted this project at some most vital points.

Michael A. G. Haykin and Kenneth J. Stewart

---

2. Kenneth J. Stewart's paper 'Does Evangelicalism Pre-date the 18th Century? An Examination of the David Bebbington Thesis' was read in the Nov. 2001 meeting of the Evangelical Theological Society, Colorado Springs, Colorado, and later published in substantially revised form in the *Evangelical Quarterly* 67.2 (2005), pp. 135–153.

3. Garry J. Williams, 'Was Evangelicalism Created by the Enlightenment?', *Tyndale Bulletin* 53.2 (2002), pp. 283–312. This essay appears reprinted in this current volume, ch. 15, under the new title 'Enlightenment Epistemology and Eighteenth-Century Evangelical Doctrines of Assurance'.

PART I: INTRODUCTION

1. THE RECEPTION GIVEN *EVANGELICALISM IN MODERN BRITAIN* SINCE ITS PUBLICATION IN 1989

Timothy Larsen

A 2005 Web visit to www.amazon.com revealed that, approaching eighteen years since it was first published, David Bebbington's *Evangelicalism in Modern Britain: A History from the 1730s to the 1980s* (1989) was still in print.[1] Moreover, this online bookshop sometimes scans the entire texts of books and, from within this e-collection, it identified no fewer than ninety-seven other books that cite Bebbington's landmark study.[2] Authors so listed include Alister McGrath, John Stott, Callum Brown, Pamela Walker, David Hempton, Sue Morgan, D. A. Carson, Bruce Hindmarsh, Hugh McLeod, Mark Noll, Doreen Rosman, Doug Sweeney, George Hunsinger, Linda Woodhead, Adrian Hastings and John

---

1. The first edition of the book was D. W. Bebbington, *Evangelicalism in Modern Britain: A History from the 1730s to the 1980s* (London: Unwin Hyman, 1989). Technically, there has been no 'second edition' in terms of a revised text, but 'first edition' is used in this chapter to refer to the original publication of the book by Unwin Hyman. The book is currently in print with Routledge, which has thus far reprinted it five times: 1993, 1995, 1999, 2000 and 2002.

2 See <http://www.amazon.com>, accessed 24 Oct. 2005. I am grateful to the students from my course in the spring 2005, BITH 677 Modern British Religious History, who helped to gather sources for this study: Anna Thompson (who did double duty as my teaching assistant), Todd Thompson, Robert Wagner and Jeremy Wells.

Wolffe. That list of ninety-seven authors does not come anywhere near to map-
ping the whole terrain to be covered when exploring this theme: the guest list
to write this article on the reception of Bebbington's *Evangelicalism in Modern
Britain* turned out to be as large as that for the reception at a royal wedding!

If we begin at the beginning, to highlight another set of germane sources, I
have also read all the reviews I could find (forty-four in total) of the first edition of Bebbington's *Evangelicalism in Modern Britain*. As reviewers are wont
to do, they make a wide range of minor complaints that accumulate across this
literature. Alan Munden, for instance, claimed to have found a misplaced footnote on page 211, although I have not been able to work out what he means.[3]
Indeed, one of the more delicious aspects of my current task is that it provides
the rare opportunity to review the reviewers, whose usual position, perched up
where they are unanswerable, is often so infuriating to authors. How solemnly
should we receive the cavils of another reviewer, for example, who persistently
refers to the author of the work under his consideration as 'Bevington'?[4] Or
who consistently has 'innerancy' for 'inerrancy'?[5] Most reviewers felt that some
aspect or other of the subject had been unjustly neglected, and therefore one
could compile quite a list of alleged lacunae from these reviews. Notably, there
were recurring concerns that David Bebbington had given insufficient attention to the providence of God and/or the principality of Wales.

Nevertheless, in general terms, the book was remarkably well received.
Derek Tidball enthused, 'This is one of the most significant books I have read
in a long time.'[6] Summary statements of admiration emphasized that it would
be an obligatory text for the foreseeable future. Callum Brown claimed that it
was 'little short of an indispensable guidebook for the social historian'.[7] Robert
Clouse pronounced in the *American Historical Review* that it should be 'required
reading', and Ian Sellers also used a similar phrase.[8] John Wolffe warned in
History that 'no one can now be regarded as a serious student of evangelicalism
unless they have read this book'.[9] Colin Matthew declared that Bebbington
had 'written what will be the standard history of the subject for many years

---

3. Alan Munden, *Anvil* 6.3 (1989), pp. 287–288.
4. Arthur Bennett, *Churchman* 103.3 (1989), pp. 276–277.
5. Dave Roberts, 'Evangelicalism in Modern Britain', *Today* (June 1990), pp. 33–34.
6. Derek Tidball, *Third Way* (June 1989), p. 27.
7. Callum G. Brown, *Scottish Economic and Social History* 10 (1990), p. 100.
8. Robert G. Clouse, *American Historical Review* 96.1 (Feb. 1991), pp. 165–166; Ian
   Sellers, *Wesley Historical Society Proceedings* 47 (Feb. 1990), pp. 133–134.
9. John Wolffe, *History* 75 (1990), pp. 346–347.

to come'.[10] And so it went on. Reviewers were universally impressed by the extensive research on display. A surprisingly high number of them observed in a staggered tone that the book had some seventy-five pages of endnotes.[11] The liberal churchman David L. Edwards found this effort not only meticulous but downright heroic, marvelling at Bebbington's ability to quote 'the tracts, the magazines and the conference reports which must have been considerably less than fascinating to read through'.[12] Despite all this, most reviewers seemed to be unaware of just how influential Bebbington's book would become. The reviewers who came just a few years later than 1989 seem to have become bolder. A review in 1991 was already referring to it as 'David Bebbington's classic study'.[13] One from 1992 pronounced, in a stronger version of Callum Brown's earlier claim, 'this book can fairly claim to have made itself indispensable'.[14] By 1993, David Bundy was using the much-coveted adjective 'magisterial'.[15] A decade on, Bebbington's 'magisterial study' was being used in the *American Historical Review* as a gauge by which to judge new works.[16]

This chapter on the reception of *Evangelicalism in Modern Britain* is the first in a volume primarily concerned with rethinking Bebbington's claim that evangelicalism began in the 1730s. This question was not a primary preoccupation of the original reviewers of *Evangelicalism in Modern Britain*, but it was a concern of a handful of them. It must be said that this point was often raised by reviewers whose own confessional commitments loomed large—indeed most reviewers who made this point were writing for the journals of theological seminaries or religious denominations. Ian Rennie wrote in *Crux*, a journal whose very name bears witness to Bebbington's crucicentrism and is published by Regent College, an evangelical institution, 'it would have been helpful if rather than being assumed, the continuities of evangelicalism with the previous ages of orthodox Christian vitality had been spelled out in even a

10. H. C. G. Matthew, *Journal of Theological Studies*, n.s., 41 (Oct. 1990), pp. 765–766.
11. Alastair Durie, e.g., observed in wonder that 'there is virtually a second book in the seventy-six pages of notes', *Scottish Journal of Religious Studies* 11.1 (spring 1990), pp. 60–62.
12. David L. Edwards, 'Evangelical Varieties', *Church Times*, 17 Feb. 1989.
13. C. Peter Williams, *Themelios* 16.3 (Apr.–May 1991), pp. 34–35.
14. M. J. D. Roberts, *Journal of Religious History* 17 (June 1992), p. 108.
15. David Bundy, *Asbury Theological Journal* 48 (autumn 1993), pp. 79–80.
16. Kenneth Brown, 'Europe: Early Modern and Modern', *American Historical Review* 108.1 (2003), p. 923.

brief page or two'.[17] That point has been made in the subsequent interaction with Bebbington's work as well. For example, Timothy George employed Bebbington's definition of evangelicalism in a 1999 article in *Christianity Today*, but with the caveat 'While such a list is helpful in pointing out major emphases, it can also obscure the basic continuities linking evangelicals with other orthodox Christians on such key doctrines of the faith as the Holy Trinity and the classic Christology of the early church.'[18] D. A. Carson had also made the same point in his 1996 book *The Gagging of God*.[19] To return to the original reviews, David Bundy suggested in the *Asbury Theological Journal* that the Caroline divines represent more of a bridge between the Puritans and the evangelical Anglicanism of Wesley than Bebbington's work indicated. Donald MacDonald warned readers of the *Monthly Record of the Free Church of Scotland* that Bebbington's presentation of a radical discontinuity between Puritanism and evangelicalism was 'controversial'.[20] Diana Butler laid particular stress on this point in her review in *Anglican and Episcopal History*:

> There are a few weaknesses as well. Most notably, one has the impression that Evangelicalism was created out of nothing in the 18th century. A brief mention of the precursors of the movement (for example, Pietism, Puritanism, and medieval reform movements) would be helpful to the reader.[21]

Other reviewers for confessional reasons emphasized continuity with what preceded evangelicalism. Thus, Gary Williams welcomes a historical account of evangelical identity that makes Wesleyanism more marginal and Reformed traditions more central.[22] Some might be tempted to contrast Bebbington's 'evenhanded scholarly approach' with such over-riding con-

---

17. Ian S. Rennie, *Crux* 25.3 (Sept. 1989), pp. 39–40.

18. Timothy George, 'If I'm an Evangelical, What Am I?', *Christianity Today* 43.9 (9 Aug. 1999), p. 62.

19. D. A. Carson, *The Gagging of God: Christianity Confronts Pluralism* (Grand Rapids: Zondervan, 1996), p. 450.

20. Donald M. MacDonald, *Monthly Record of the Free Church of Scotland* (Aug. 1992), pp. 179–180.

21. Diana Butler, *Anglican and Episcopal History* 59 (Dec. 1990), pp. 522–527.

22. Garry J. Williams, 'Was Evangelicalism Created by the Enlightenment?', *Tyndale Bulletin* 53.2 (2002), pp. 283–312 (p. 312). Reprinted in this volume. See also, from a different perspective, Roy Wallis, 'Against the Current of the Age', *The Times Higher Education Supplement* (26 May 1989), p. 19.

fessional concern.[23] However, as postmodern theorists remind us, none of us observes from a neutral vantage point, and Bebbington was ahead of the curve. The back cover of the first edition states, 'David Bebbington writes as a participant observer, for he is a Baptist deacon and lay preacher.' Deprived of this exposé, reviewers tended just to quote that sentence without comment in stunned amazement at a British Baptist with an academic position at a secular university testifying so brazenly.[24]

When surveying the reception of Bebbington's *Evangelicalism in Modern Britain* since 1989, what immediately stands out as a truly remarkable achievement is the extraordinary way that its definition of evangelicalism has become the standard one. The Bebbington quadrilateral, of course, as anyone interested in this chapter must surely already know, identifies four characteristics that mark evangelicals: *conversionism, activism, biblicism* and *crucicentrism*.[25] The reception for his book must have been exceeding abundantly above all that even Bebbington himself could have asked or imagined.

Certainly the original reviewers were not generally aware of the significance of this achievement. Many of them did not refer to it at all. Others simply cited it as delineating the scope of this particular study with no hint that it might have a more general utility. Some were actually a bit derogatory about it. Michael Watts limited his reflections on the quadrilateral to the opinion that it was expressed 'inelegantly'.[26] In a similar vein, Arthur Skevington Wood dubbed it 'ponderously'.[27] And I must confess that when I turned up in Stirling in the early 1990s as a research student, I began my reply to David's question regarding what I thought of his book with the penetrating observation that I found 'crucicentrism' to be an ugly word. John Kent, in a way that has become increasingly fashionable, wondered if 'the word "Evangelical" has become too vague to be useful'.[28] Others expressed a kind of cautious or non-committal welcome. The review in the *Churchman*, for example, merely said, 'The opening chapter

23. Bundy, *Asbury Theological Journal*, pp. 79–80.

24. See Desmond Bowen's review, *Victorian Studies* 33.3 (spring 1990), pp. 505–507.

25. Bebbington, *Evangelicalism in Modern Britain*, pp. 5–17.

26. Michael Watts, *English Historical Review* 107.424 (July 1992), pp. 747–748.

27. Arthur Skevington Wood, 'The Evangelical Factor', *Methodist Recorder*, 20 Apr. 1989. As far as I can tell, Wood has the unique distinction of having reviewed the book twice. See his review in *Evangelical Quarterly* 63.4 (Oct. 1991), pp. 360–361.

28. John Kent, 'Evangelicals and Evangelicalism', *Expository Times* 101 (Oct. 1989), pp. 24–25.

on evangelical qualities deserves close study.'[29] Donald M. MacDonald simply declared that 'we cannot quarrel' with this definition.[30] Ian Rennie conceded, 'While detailed study could point out variations within these themes, the author is undoubtedly correct in identifying these abiding themes.'[31] Out of this pool of forty-four reviews, the number of reviewers who seemed to come anywhere close to grasping what Bebbington had achieved in this area was certainly fewer than five. David Bundy is among this perceptive handful. He wrote:

> This functional definition of Evangelicalism allows Bebbington to provide an evenhanded scholarly approach to the range of phenomena normally understood as Evangelicalism and helps him avoid the ideological pitfalls into which many American scholars fall. This phenomenological approach cannot be too highly praised.[32]

A particularly insightful appreciation was made by John Wolffe in the journal *History*:

> His book is especially helpful in presenting and applying a working definition of evangelicalism that represents a satisfactory middle course between the theological innocence of some social historians and the excessive ideological rigour of party theologians. Bebbington is thus able to explore the internal diversity of the phenomenon while maintaining overall coherence.[33]

The real story of the reception of Bebbington's quadrilateral, however, comes not with the reviewers, but when others have needed a working definition of evangelicalism in order to delineate the scope of their own studies. In this area, Bebbington has developed a near monopoly position. Even those dissatisfied with the quadrilateral who wish to see it replaced approach their work as if they have taken on the Herculean task of vanquishing a hydra whose ugly heads reappear as fast as you can cut them off. D. A. Carson, for example, is well aware that Bebbington's four characteristics 'have been the most frequently quoted'.[34] Many other sources engage in much hand-wringing and hedging, emphasizing that evangelicalism is a complex and diverse

---

29. Bennett, *Churchman*, pp. 276–277.
30. MacDonald, *Monthly Record*, pp. 179–180.
31. Rennie, *Crux*, pp. 39–40.
32. Bundy, *Asbury Theological Journal*, pp. 79–80.
33. Wolffe, *History*, pp. 346–347.
34. Carson, *Gagging of God*, p. 449.

phenomenon difficult to define. Nevertheless, when one examines carefully what has been said in such discussions it is generally noticeable that, in the midst of all these declaimers, the Bebbington quadrilateral is the only definition that has actually been offered. This is the approach taken, for example, in a 1995 article by Paul Galloway.[35] This is also true of two articles that appeared in *Christianity Today*.[36]

The fact that *Christianity Today* is in the habit of reaching for Bebbington's definition (George and Yancey are both editors) is itself indicative of its astounding success. *Christianity Today*, after all, was already considered by many to be *the* authority on evangelicalism back before Bebbington had even been baptized as a believer. Such ironies abound. Ian Randall and David Hilborn, in a study of the Evangelical Alliance in Britain, published in 2001, declare at the outset that they are using the quadrilateral to define evangelicalism.[37] One presumes, however, that in its 143 years of history before the arrival of Bebbington's seminal study, the Evangelical Alliance must have had some working definition of evangelicalism of its own. Bebbington's book was sometimes reviewed alongside Kenneth Hylson-Smith's *Evangelicals in the Church of England, 1734–1984*, which also appeared in 1989. In his 1997 study, however, Hylson-Smith had accepted the quadrilateral, thus obviously finding Bebbington's 1989 study of evangelicalism more helpful on this point than his own.[38]

It would be tedious to list all of the works that have used Bebbington's definition to explain their own use of the term 'evangelical'—not to mention the fact that any boast that such a list was exhaustive would in all likelihood quickly be disproved by other scholars who identified additional titles. It is, for example, the definition accepted by the two major works of reference works containing biographies of evangelicals that have appeared since 1989, Donald Lewis's *Blackwell Dictionary of Evangelical Biography* (1995) (the fact notwithstanding that Lewis seemed to find the quadrilateral potentially problematic in some ways when he reviewed the book in *Fides et historia*) and my own *Biographical*

---

35. 'Evangelicals: Groups Defy a Simple Definition', *Post and Courier* (Charleston, S. C.), 11 June 1995.

36. George, 'If I'm an Evangelical', p. 62; Philip Yancey, 'A Quirky and Vibrant Mosaic', *Christianity Today* (June 2005), pp. 37–39.

37. Ian Randall and David Hilborn, *One Body in Christ: The History and Significance of the Evangelical Alliance* (Carlisle: Paternoster, 2001), p. 2.

38. Kenneth Hylson-Smith, *The Churches in England from Elizabeth I to Elizabeth II*, vol. 2: 1689–1833 (London: SCM, 1997), p. 183.

Dictionary of Evangelicals (2003).[39] John Wolffe identified the quadrilateral as the common, working definition for a collaborative effort he had edited (1995).[40] My former colleague Mark Noll has said in print often enough (in these precise words) that Bebbington's is 'the most serviceable general definition' of evangelicalism, but I shall not risk embarrassing him by giving a grand total.[41]

Derek Tidball affirmed in 1994 of Bebbington's definition, 'His suggestions have met with a ready response from across the spectrum of evangelicals and has quickly established itself as near to a consensus as we might ever expect to reach.'[42] Tidball is a particularly credible witness to make such a statement, since he is as well placed in British evangelicalism personally as one could hope for. In addition to his long service to the Evangelical Alliance, he is currently the chairman of its council, he is also the principal of the London School of Theology (formerly London Bible College), and has served as the chair of British Youth for Christ, as a speaker at the Keswick Convention, and much else. Other tributes to the triumph of the quadrilateral include that of the authors of *The Evangelicals: A Historical, Thematic, and Biographical Guide* (1999), who concede, 'In recent years, those with a normative bend reached a consensus around a set of convictions offered by the British scholar David Bebbington.'[43] A general, online encyclopedia also uses Bebbington's quadrilateral for its entry on evangelicalism, identifying it as 'the most common definition'.[44] Such dominance led Reg Ward to begin his 2004 chapter on 'Evangelical Identity in the Eighteenth Century' in his own inimitably arch and waggish way:

> The title which I have been given might well be thought otiose, for it is an orthodoxy among many of us that the whole matter was clarified long ago by our good friend

39. Donald M. Lewis (ed.), *The Blackwell Dictionary of Evangelical Biography 1730–1860*, 2 vols. (Oxford: Blackwell, 1995), vol. 1, p. xix; Donald M. Lewis, *Fides et historia* 22 (winter–spring 1990), pp. 103–105; Timothy Larsen (ed.), *Biographical Dictionary of Evangelicals* (Leicester: IVP, 2003), p. 1.

40. John Wolffe (ed.), *Evangelical Faith and Public Zeal: Evangelicals and Society in Britain, 1780–1980* (London: SPCK, 1995), p. 4.

41. For examples, see Mark A. Noll, *American Evangelical Christianity: An Introduction* (Oxford: Blackwell, 2001), p. 185; *America's God: From Jonathan Edwards to Abraham Lincoln* (New York: Oxford University Press, 2002), p. 5.

42. Derek Tidball, *Who Are the Evangelicals? Tracing the Roots of the Modern Movements* (London: Marshall Pickering, 1994), p. 14.

43. Robert J. Krapohl and Charles H. Lippy (Westport: Greenwood, 1999), pp. 6–7.

44. See <http://www.nationmater.com>, accessed 24 Oct. 2005.

David Bebbington; indeed the famous Bebbington Quadrilateral has become the most quoted sentence in the whole literature and was for long virtually the only beacon the suffering student had to distinguish men walking like trees in the gloom (Mark 8:24).[45]

Indeed, Bebbington's definition is now receiving the ultimate compliment of being cited without acknowledgment, as if it is not one scholar's opinion but simply the truth we all know. K. Theodore Hoppen, for example, in his 1998 volume in the influential New Oxford History of England series, simply slipped it in without a citation, 'Stressing conversion, activism, the Bible, and the atoning death of Christ upon the cross, Evangelicals . . .'[46] When *Time* magazine did its cover story on 'The 25 Most Influential Evangelicals in America' in 2005, its definition of evangelicalism was clearly recognizable as a watered-down version of the quadrilateral.[47] In one of the more interesting interactions with Bebbington's book, the Canadian sociologist Sam Reimer, following a lead set by historian George Rawlyk, has even done research that empirically verifies the validity of the quadrilateral. Having done 118 interviews in 'the evangelical subculture', Reimer discovered that 'These four components are emphatically upheld in nearly all the interviews.'[48] Bebbington's four pillars of evangelicalism have no rival anywhere near as influential or popular and are unlikely to be replaced by an alternative structure any time soon.

Now, having cleared all that ground (questions of chronological scope and definition were in fact merely necessary preliminaries), we can get on

---

45. W. R. Ward, 'Evangelical Identity in the Eighteenth Century', in Donald M. Lewis (ed.), *Christianity Reborn: The Global Expansion of Evangelicalism in the Twentieth Century* (Grand Rapids: Eerdmans, 2004), p. 11.

46. K. Theodore Hoppen, *The Mid-Victorian Generation, 1846–1886* (Oxford: Clarendon, 1998), p. 436. Hoppen does, however, cite Bebbington's *Evangelicalism in Modern Britain* at another point on the same page.

47. David Van Biema, *Time* (7 Feb. 2005), p. 34: '[I]ts members share basic commitments: to the divinity and saving power of Jesus, to personal religious conversion, to the Bible's authority and to the spreading of the Gospel'.

48. Sam Reimer, *Evangelicals and the Continental Divide: The Conservative Protestant Subculture in Canada and the United States* (Montreal: McGill-Queen's University Press, 2003), p. 43; G. A. Rawlyk, *Is Jesus Your Personal Saviour? In Search of Canadian Evangelicalism in the 1990s* (Montreal: McGill-Queen's University Press, 1996). Rawlyk uses the quadrilateral, affirming that Bebbington's arguments for it are 'persuasive' (pp. 9, 227).

to what Bebbington was actually doing in *Evangelicalism in Modern Britain*, namely offering an ambitious attempt to connect the history of evangelicalism to broader currents in intellectual and cultural history in British society as a whole. He argued that British evangelicalism had been shaped, consecutively, by the Enlightenment (as exemplified in John Wesley and the first generation of evangelicals), Romanticism (as exemplified in the Keswick Convention and the nineteenth-century Holiness movement) and modernism (as exemplified in Frank Buchman and the Oxford Group and then the charismatic movement). Many reviewers thought that some of Bebbington's evangelical readers, thinking of their movement as one that handed down doctrines unaltered from generation to generation, would find these claims regarding change over time due to wider cultural forces unsettling. Grant Wacker, for example, indicated that Bebbington's thesis might come as a shock, 'especially if one believes, as many evangelicals do, that the apostle Paul was just Billy Graham with a Greek accent'.[49] The liberal churchman David L. Edwards noted gleefully, 'That is dynamite for Evangelicals who have been accustomed to thank God that they are not as the Catholics, with their takeover of pagan ceremonies, or (even worse) the liberals, with their submission to contemporary trendiness.'[50] Yet just as when they experience Hollywood films, it seems much easier to find evangelicals who assume that other evangelicals will be offended than to find ones that feel personally affronted. For example, the review in as conservative a venue as Dallas Theological Seminary's *Bibliotheca sacra* was an entirely favourable one, with the author, John D. Hannah, declaring unapologetically, 'Bebbington's thesis that evangelicalism, despite its self-perception of antiquity, is a modern form of Christianity with its own contextualized forms, values, and perceptions, is insightful.'[51]

Unease can be found occasionally, however. David Gillet reviewed the book as a self-declared evangelical for the *Church of England Newspaper*. He apparently was persuaded by Bebbington's arguments in some measure, but his imaginings of concerns that evangelicals might have seemed to be a refracted way of expressing some of his own reactions:

> To many this will come as a surprise as evangelicals normally blame the
> Enlightenment (somewhat justifiably) for the kind of rationalism that, step by step,
> squeezes God out of humanity's view of the world. . . . Many of his conclusions will

---

49. Grant Wacker, 'A British Panorama', *Christianity Today* 34 (5 Feb. 1990), pp. 62–64.
50. Edwards, 'Evangelical Varieties', p. 6.
51. John D. Hannah, *Bibliotheca sacra* 151.602 (Apr.–June 1994), p. 256.

strike some evangelicals as startling . . . As evangelicals consider themselves to be 'biblical people' many find it uncongenial to think of secular culture having such a pronounced effect on the development of our message. . . . This book argues further that we are children of our culture to such a degree that we modify the very content and stance of our message . . . I want to say much more on the relationship between the providence of God and the meeting of gospel and culture . . .[52]

Peter Wortley, writing in the *Baptist Times*, said that these connections were 'disturbing', but he was careful to add that they might nevertheless be true.[53] Donald M. MacDonald, writing in the *Monthly Record of the Free Church of Scotland*, rather transparently accepts all the cultural connections Bebbington made for theological positions MacDonald did not adhere to, but questioned them whenever they touched upon his own beliefs. Thus, he saw Bebbington as having nailed brilliantly Edward Irving, Keswick holiness, and the nineteenth-century premillennial movement, but found him to be wrong about the discontinuity with Puritans, the way that cultural forces shaped the original evangelical revival (which is better viewed, he asserted, as 'primarily due to an outpouring of God's Spirit'), the literal, personal return of Christ, and the inerrancy of the Bible. Still, MacDonald ends his review endearingly with the observation 'No doubt the rather superficial criticism I have offered betrays my own prejudices but at least I was made to think!'[54] Likewise, the sole complaint made in a notice in the *Reformed Review* was that the charismatic movement should not be described as 'renewal'.[55] The *Criswell Theological Review*, also apparently not finding the charismatic movement and cultural modernism a happy ending, suggested that the book should have been called 'The Rise and Fall of Evangelicalism in Britain'.[56]

Scholars sometimes felt that Bebbington had linked cultural forces to the history of evangelicalism in a suffocating manner. William Sachs, in a review published in the *Journal of Religion*, claimed:

52. David Gillet, 'What Is an Evangelical?', *Church of England Newspaper*, 31 Mar. 1989.
53. Peter Wortley, 'The Story of Evangelicals—and Our Uncertain Roots ...', *Baptist Times*, 12 Oct. 1989.
54. MacDonald, *Monthly Record*, pp. 179–180.
55. Harry Buis, *Reformed Review* 46 (spring 1993), p. 246.
56. John Powell, *Criswell Theological Review* 6 (spring 1993), pp. 336–338.

Bebbington does not believe Evangelicals triumphed over their circumstances.
He endows contextual forces with the power to circumscribe religious forms.
. . . Even faithful initiative could not overcome the forces of context.[57]

Likewise Ian Sellers referred in the *Wesley Historical Society Proceedings* to
Bebbington's 'own distinctive (some would say obtrusive) philosophy of history which is a species of cultural determinism'.[58] A related critique was that
Bebbington did not demonstrate how evangelicalism had influenced the
wider culture as well as having been changed by it; this despite the fact that
he had asserted in the first paragraph of the preface, 'In the mid-nineteenth
century [evangelicalism] set the tone of British society.'[59] For example, in a
review in the *Scottish Bulletin of Evangelical Theology*, David Smith observed
after presenting Bebbington's views on the impact of wider trends on evangelicalism, 'These points are well made, although it is not altogether clear
how a movement so profoundly shaped by successive cultural waves can then
be said to have "remoulded" society in its own image.'[60] Colin Matthew, in
a very thoughtful and astute review, likewise remarked, 'Indeed the author
rather surprisingly sees the process as one way.'[61] A popular traditional British comic song is 'The Vicar of Bray'. Its lyrics recount how the vicar lives
through a whole series of contradictory policies as new monarchies implement opposing views on churchmanship, theology, politics and liturgy. The
vicar promptly adopts each one accordingly, revealing in the chorus his one
unalterable conviction: 'And this is law, I will maintain unto my dying day,
Sir. / That whatsoever King may reign, I will be the Vicar of Bray, Sir!' Does
Bebbington present evangelicalism as the Vicar of Bray? Certainly not. The
much-quoted quadrilateral is precisely intended to identify the immutable
marks of evangelicalism's core values that continue to persist while forms,
emphases and articulations change. Nevertheless, many would have liked to
have heard more from Bebbington's book about how the evangelical Vicar of
Bray denounced changes for the worse and fostered changes for the better as
well as how he adapted to changes from without.

---

57. William Sachs, *Journal of Religion* 72.1 (Jan. 1992), pp. 114–116.
58. Sellers, *Wesley Historical Society Proceedings*, pp. 133–134.
59. Bebbington, *Evangelicalism in Modern Britain*, p. ix.
60. David Smith, *Scottish Bulletin of Evangelical Theology* 8 (autumn 1990), pp. 133–134.
61. Matthew, *Journal of Theological Studies*, pp. 765–766. See also Bruce Guenther, *ARC:
     The Journal of the Faculty of Religious Studies, McGill University* 19 (spring 1991), pp.
     123–125.

Such a critique, however, must not be allowed to take on undue proportion. Many reviewers were awed by the audacity, bravery and mammoth scope of what Bebbington achieved in showing how cultural movements had influenced evangelicalism across 250 years: to ask him to have shown the reverse as well is to demand considerably more than we should expect from any one scholar, let alone one book. To allow such a critique too much room is also to forget how unfashionable both religious history and intellectual history were in British academic circles in the 1980s. As David Hempton rightly observed, 'Bebbington boldly asserts, as against a quarter of a century of Marxist scholarship, that the main agent of change within Evangelicalism is neither economic nor political, but ideological and cultural.'[62] It should also be emphasized that many reviewers were persuaded by the connections Bebbington made. A review in the *Canadian Journal of History* judged that Bebbington had made 'a compelling case' for the links with the Enlightenment.[63] Alan Sell confessed that he was persuaded in the *Calvin Theological Journal*, as did M. J. D. Roberts in the *Journal of Religious History*.[64] Albion Urdank affirmed in the *Journal of British Studies*, 'He insists convincingly that John Wesley's enthusiasm was suffused with the rationalist spirit of the Enlightenment, despite the fact that scholars have commonly thought of evangelicalism as its antithesis.'[65]

Nevertheless, some reviewers suspected that, although he was on to something, Bebbington had overplayed his hand. A review in the *Mid-America Theological Journal* spoke for many: 'The author overstates his arguments about Enlightenment and Romantic influences on evangelicalism, but they stand as his most original and provocative contributions.'[66] Several reviewers specifically pointed to John Wesley's belief in 'the power of witchcraft' as revealing that this evangelical leader was also out of sync with the Enlightenment in some ways.[67] Hugh McLeod articulated this critique in general terms in the *Journal of Modern History*:

---

62. David Hempton, *Christian Arena* (Dec. 1989), pp. 33–34. This same point was made in another review: Roger Brown, *Journal of Welsh Ecclesiastical History* 7 (1990), pp. 70–71.

63. Malcolm Greenshields, *Canadian Journal of History / Annales canadiennes d'histoire* 35 (Aug. 1990), pp. 267–270.

64. Alan P. F. Sell, *Calvin Theological Journal* 28 (Apr. 1993), pp. 200–203; M. J. D. Roberts, *Journal of Religious History*, p. 108.

65. Albion M. Urdank, *Journal of British Studies* 30.3 (July 1991), p. 341.

66. James A. Patterson, *Mid-America Theological Journal* 17 (1993), p. 114.

67. R. Brown, *Journal of Welsh Ecclesiastical History*, pp. 70–71.

My only major criticism of Bebbington's work would be that the reasons for these changes are explored too briefly and dogmatically. . . . In the nineteenth century romanticism is made to explain too much; and in the twentieth century a similarly exaggerated emphasis is placed on the repercussions of the modernist movement in literature and the arts.[68]

Weighty reviewers such as David Hempton, John Wolffe and Desmond Bowen expressed some unease that categories that are 'dangerously imprecise' such as Romanticism were being brandished about in 'somewhat monolithic fashion' or 'used very loosely'.[69]

Another interlocking critique was a sense that Bebbington had made the story too much a top-down one, thereby overemphasizing intellectual elites. Michael Watts, in comments that seem to betray a somewhat patronizing view of evangelicals, declared that Bebbington had 'exaggerated the rationality of his subject'.[70] Ian Sellers complained, 'there is a marked preoccupation here with the upper echelons of society: popular evangelicalism is virtually excluded'.[71] Hugh McLeod made the same point in more measured language: 'the more plebeian forms of Evangelicalism such as Primitive Methodism or Pentecostalism, seem a bit neglected'.[72] David Hempton went one step further by actually calling into question the degree to which popular culture is changed by elite trends, suggesting that work by some social historians indicated that popular belief and practice are 'stubbornly impervious to influence from above and from without'.[73]

Having said all that, many reviewers recognized that Bebbington had delivered so much more than one could have expected in a study of the history of evangelicalism. His book was so much more ambitious, sophisticated and intellectually rigorous than traditional church history. David Bebbington had brilliantly reconnected the history of Christianity with other historical

---

68. Hugh McLeod, 'Varieties of Victorian Belief', *Journal of Modern History* 64.2 (June 1992), pp. 321–337.

69. Hempton, *Christian Arena*, pp. 33–34; Wolffe, *History*, pp. 346–347; Bowen, *Victorian Studies*, pp. 505–507.

70. Watts, *English Historical Review*, pp. 747–748.

71. Sellers, *Wesley Historical Society Proceedings*, pp. 133–134.

72. McLeod, 'Varieties of Victorian Belief', pp. 321–337. Likewise John Briggs wanted more on the Salvation Army: 'Evangel, Evangelicals and Evangelicalism', *Baptist Quarterly* 33.7 (July 1990), pp. 297–301.

73. Hempton, *Christian Arena*, pp. 33–34; Wolffe, *History*, pp. 346–347.

subdisciplines and the wider story of the history of Britain and beyond. For myself, I can still recall the thrill that *Evangelicalism in Modern Britain* gave me. It was energizing enough to learn that church historians working on theologically conservative Protestants could talk about such exciting themes as the Enlightenment, Romanticism, and modernism. It made one positively tingle with excitement to be told that evangelicalism was not some backwater that was inevitably a generation or two behind intellectually, which even then was still attempting to fight from the losing side battles long over, but that it was actually just as much in the main story of the history of ideas as theological liberals or anyone else. *Evangelicalism in Modern Britain* was taken very seriously and treated with tremendous respect by historians outside the religious history subdiscipline and, as that was undoubtedly the game plan, it must be judged as outstandingly successful at achieving one of its own goals. To take a random example, Callum Brown enthused that Bebbington's book was evidence that church historians were 'starting to absorb the best of social history and combine it with the "inside" understanding of organised religion'.[74] As authoritative a voice of the wider culture as one could hope for, *The Times Literary Supplement* testified that the links that Bebbington had made between evangelicalism and cultural trends were 'impressive'.[75]

How historians have subsequently built upon Bebbington's work in this area of cultural and intellectual connections is a more elusive matter to track and assess. No doubt Bebbington has emboldened numerous scholars to attempt to explore the interplay between church history and other historical subdisciplines. Thinking about it now, although there are certainly no footnotes acknowledging the debt, I doubt very much that I would ever have thought to write a PhD thesis which argued that conservative evangelicals were actually on the cutting edge of political liberalism and radicalism, or a subsequent monograph with such a brash and counterintuitive subtitle as 'fundamentalism and feminism in coalition', if my doctoral supervisor at Stirling University had not given me permission to think this way with such startling juxtapositions as Wesley as an Enlightenment thinker and the charismatic movement as an expression of cultural modernism.[76]

74. C. G. Brown, *Scottish Economic and Social History*, p. 100.

75. Barbara Godlee, 'Messengers of Salvation', *Times Literary Supplement*, 27 Oct.–2 Nov. 1989.

76. Timothy Larsen, *Friends of Religious Equality: Nonconformist Politics in Mid-Victorian England* (Woodbridge: Boydell, 1999); *Christabel Pankhurst: Fundamentalism and Feminism in Coalition* (Woodbridge: Boydell, 2002).

An example of an even more direct influence, although still not acknowledged specifically on this point, would be Mark Hopkins's monograph *Nonconformity's Romantic Generation: Evangelical and Liberal Theologies in Victorian England.*[77] Hopkins cites Bebbington repeatedly, and it is unlikely that Romanticism would ever have made it into his title if it were not for *Evangelicalism in Modern Britain*. Careful discussions of the relationship between evangelicalism and the Enlightenment, such as the one offered by Mark Noll in *The Rise of Evangelicalism*, also betray a debt to Bebbington's seminal achievement.[78] An example of a popularization of Bebbington's views is Derek Tidball's *Who Are the Evangelicals? Tracing the Roots of the Modern Movements* (1994), a volume that leans heavily on *Evangelicalism in Modern Britain*, including accepting Bebbington's interpretation of the connections with the Enlightenment.[79]

In conclusion, in *Evangelicalism in Modern Britain*, David Bebbington made as significant and substantial a contribution to scholarship as the author of any book could ever hope for, in the ambitious way that he related church history to other forms of history and wider cultural developments. Along the way, he also happened to provide us with the standard definition of evangelicalism.

© Timothy Larsen, 2008

---

77. Mark Hopkins, *Nonconformity's Romantic Generation: Evangelical and Liberal Theologies in Victorian England* (Milton Keynes: Paternoster, 2004).

78. Mark A. Noll, *The Rise of Evangelicalism: The Age of Edwards, Whitefield and the Wesleys* (Leicester: IVP; Downers Grove: IVP, 2003), esp. pp. 150–151.

79. Tidball, *Who Are the Evangelicals?*

2. EVANGELICALISM AND THE ENLIGHTENMENT: A REASSESSMENT

Michael A. G. Haykin

For many of the intelligentsia of eighteenth-century Europe, theirs was a day of unparalleled advances in the realms of science and philosophical thought. Although the term 'Enlightenment' did not come into vogue until the following century,[1] they regularly invoked the image of light when speaking of their age. The Anglo-Irish philosopher George Berkeley (1685–1753), for instance, spoke of 'that ocean of light, which has broke in and made his way, in spite of slavery and superstition'.[2] The English poet Alexander Pope (1688–1744), thinking of the revolutionary contributions that Isaac Newton (1642–1727) had made to the understanding of the universe, proudly declared:

Nature and Nature's laws lay hid in night.
God said, let Newton be! and all was light.[3]

1. Owen Chadwick, *The Secularization of the European Mind in the Nineteenth Century* (Cambridge: Cambridge University Press, 1975), p. 151.
2. Cited Ulrich Im Hof, *The Enlightenment*, trans. William E. Yuill (Oxford: Blackwell, 1994), p. 4.
3. Cited Norman Hampson, *The Enlightenment* (Harmondsworth: Penguin, 1968; repr. 1982), p. 38.

Despite the biblical allusion of this couplet, the light in which Pope and other Enlightenment advocates revelled was the light cast by human reason after it had been freed from what they considered the murk of religious dogma, superstition and tradition. It was this naive 'sanctification of reason', intimately linked to an emphasis on technological progress and the 'illusion that human potential and happiness [is] unlimited',[4] that would play *the* decisive role in shaping the *mentalité* of much of western culture for the next two centuries.[5]

Now, this trust in what Alister McGrath has called the 'omnicompetence of human reason'[6] is clearly antithetical to orthodox Christianity, which affirms the ultimacy of divine revelation. Not surprisingly, this antithesis has convinced a number of historians that the Evangelical Revival of the eighteenth century, which was rooted in a devotion to the Scriptures,[7] was merely a conservative reaction to the new outlook of the Enlightenment. The influential social historian E. P. Thompson, for instance, can describe the Wesleyan Methodist wing of the revival as 'self-consciously *anti*-Enlightenment'.[8] Peter Gay's massive 1966 study of the Enlightenment echoes similar convictions when he states that the 'terrified crowds, in miserable fear of their lives, who went to hear Wesley and Whitefield preach would have been at home

---

4. Kim Ian Parker, 'John Locke and the Enlightenment Metanarrative: A Biblical Corrective to a Reasoned World', *Scottish Journal of Theology* 49 (1996), p. 57.

5. It needs to be noted that the Enlightenment was not at all a monolithic movement. Scholars now talk of 'Enlightenments' and recognize substantive differences between the Enlightenment in France and that which occurred in Scotland, for instance. See e.g. Brian Stanley, 'Christian Missions and the Enlightenment: A Reevaluation', in Brian Stanley (ed.), *Christian Missions and the Enlightenment* (Grand Rapids: Eerdmans; Cambridge: Curzon, 2001), pp. 7–8; Gertrude Himmelfarb, *The Roads to Modernity: The British, French, and American Enlightenments* (New York: Alfred A. Knopf, 2004).

6. *Christian Theology: An Introduction* (Oxford: Basil Blackwell, 1994), p. 81.

7. In the words of John Walsh, 'evangelicals ... accepted simply and firmly the strictest notions of biblical infallibility' ('Origins of the Evangelical Revival', in G. V. Bennett and J. D. Walsh [eds.], *Essays in Modern English Church History in Memory of Norman Sykes* [London: Adam & Charles Black, 1966], p. 152).

8. Cited Donald Davie, *Dissentient Voice* (Notre Dame, Ind.: University of Notre Dame Press, 1982), p. 22. In his *The Making of the English Working Class* (New York: Vintage, 1963), Thompson characterizes Methodism as 'strongly anti-intellectual' (p. 738).

in twelfth-century Chartres' and the mental universe of that era. They were clearly out of sync with the 'enlightened' paganism of leading thinkers like Voltaire (1694–1778) or David Hume (1711–76).[9]

Moreover, statements from figures involved in the revival appear at first sight to confirm this view of it as primarily a reaction to the age's emphasis on all-embracing reason. The London Baptist leader Abraham Booth (1734–1806), for instance, insisted that the gospel is 'contrary to every scheme of salvation which human reason suggests'.[10] On the other side of the Atlantic, Jonathan Edwards (1703–58), without a doubt the greatest evangelical theologian of the century, urged believers to pray fervently that God would pour out his Spirit, since the day in which they were living was 'an age, as is supposed, of great light, freedom of thought, and discovery of truth in matters of religion . . . and yet vice and wickedness did never so prevail, like an overflowing deluge'.[11]

'Permeated by Enlightenment influences': ties between evangelicalism and the Enlightenment

This perspective on the relationship between the Enlightenment and the Evangelical Revival, however,[12] has been challenged by British historian David Bebbington.[13] Not the first to notice major points of contact between these

---

9. *The Enlightenment: An Interpretation. The Rise of Modern Paganism* (New York: Alfred A. Knopf, 1966; repr. 1975), p. 254.

10. *The Reign of Grace from its Rise to its Consummation* (London, 1807[8]), p. 9.

11. Jonathan Edwards, *An Humble Attempt to Promote Explicit Agreement and Visible Union of God's People in Extraordinary Prayer for the Revival of Religion*, in Stephen J. Stein (ed.), *The Works of Jonathan Edwards*, vol. 5: *Apocalyptic Writings* (New Haven: Yale University Press, 1977), p. 359.

12. D. W. Bebbington, *Evangelicalism in Modern Britain: A History from the 1730s to the 1980s* (Boston: Unwin Hyman, 1989; repr. Grand Rapids: Baker Book House, 1992), p. 57.

13. See esp. ibid., pp. 20–74. For a more concise statement of Bebbington's position, see also his 'Evangelical Christianity and the Enlightenment', *Crux* 25.4 (Dec. 1989), pp. 29–36; and 'Revival and Enlightenment in Eighteenth-Century England', in Edith L. Blumhofer and Randall Balmer (eds.), *Modern Christian Revivals* (Urbana: University of Illinois Press, 1993), pp. 17–41.

two movements,[14] Bebbington has nevertheless synthesized previous scholarly research to produce a bold and audacious thesis: far from being intrinsically opposed to one another, eighteenth-century evangelicalism has close ties to the Enlightenment and should actually be considered its creation.[15]

Evangelicals, Bebbington is quick to point out, were as fond of the imagery of light as Enlightenment authors.[16] The image, of course, is one that evangelicals would readily have found in Scripture. Jesus, for example, is described as 'the light of the world' (John 1:4–9; 8:12; 9:5); conversion is likened to the reception of light (Acts 26:17–18; Eph. 5:14; Heb. 10:32); and to be a Christian is to be a 'son/child of light' (John 12:36; Eph. 5:8; 1 Thess. 5:5). Nevertheless, given their cultural background it is not without significance that eighteenth-century evangelicals regularly used this metaphor to describe regeneration and conversion. For Isaac Backus (1724–1806), the leader of the American Separate Baptists, when a person is converted, 'eternal rays of Light and Love shine particularly upon him to remove his darkness'.[17] Speaking of his own conversion in 1741 in the midst of the Great Awakening, Backus declares that he was 'enabled by divine light to see the perfect righteousness of Christ and the freeness and riches of His grace, with such clearness, that my soul was drawn forth to trust Him for salvation'.[18] When John Gillies (1712–96) drew up the first biography of George Whitefield (1714–70) shortly after the latter's death, he described Whitefield's mind, following his conversion, as 'being now happily enlightened'.[19] Those on both sides of the Atlantic who embraced the theology and experience of the revival were receiving 'New Light'.

There is more in common between these two movements, though, than merely a metaphor. Bebbington first of all notes that it is wrong to suppose that evangelicals were inimical to reason. John Wesley (1703–91), the indefatigable Methodist evangelist, could claim it was a 'fundamental principle' with himself and his followers that 'to renounce reason is to renounce religion, that

---

14. See e.g. William G. McLoughlin, *Isaac Backus and the American Pietistic Tradition* (Boston: Little, Brown, 1967), pp. 231–233; Roger Anstey, *The Atlantic Slave Trade and British Abolition 1760–1810* (London: Macmillan, 1975), pp. 157–164; Davie, *Dissentient Voice*, pp. 20–31.

15. *Evangelicalism in Modern Britain*, p. 74; 'Evangelical Christianity and the Enlightenment', p. 36.

16. 'Revival and Enlightenment', p. 18.

17. Cited McLoughlin, *Isaac Backus*, p. 1.

18. Ibid., p. 14.

19. Cited Bebbington, 'Revival and Enlightenment', p. 18.

religion and reason go hand in hand, and that all irrational religion is false religion'. Committed to such a union of religion and reason, Wesley had little time for what the eighteenth-century termed 'enthusiasm', that is, the claiming of special powers and revelations from the Holy Spirit. Thomas Maxfield (d. 1784), an early Methodist preacher who was sympathetic towards such claims, was told in no uncertain terms by Wesley, 'I dislike . . . overvaluing *feelings* and inward *impressions*: mistaking the mere work of *imagination* for the voice of the Spirit: expecting the ends without the means, and undervaluing *reason, knowledge* and *wisdom* in general.'[20]

Many of Wesley's fellow-evangelicals were imbued with similar convictions. Thomas Gibbons (1720–85), a Congregationalist minister, wrote a poem entitled 'A Religious, the only Reasonable Life; or Reason and Religion the Same'. Samuel Walker of Truro (1714–61), the pioneer of Cornish evangelicalism, encouraged young converts to take a course in logic. Andrew Fuller (1754–1815), the leading Baptist theologian of the late eighteenth century, informed a newly ordained minister that there were two goals towards which he should strive in his ministry, '*enlightening the minds* and *affecting the hearts* of [his] people'.[21] On another occasion, preaching on Moses' choice to embrace suffering with the people of God rather than enjoy the fleeting pleasures of Egypt (Heb. 11:24–25), Fuller noted that to 'a mind blinded by carnality, the choice of Moses will appear fanatical and foolish; but it was not so. Faith and right reason are not at variance.'[22]

---

20. Both citations are from Bebbington, *Evangelicalism in Modern Britain*, p. 52. On the limits of Wesley's commitment to reason, see the incisive remarks of Anstey, *Atlantic Slave Trade*, pp. 175–176. For a brief biographical study of Maxfield, see A. Skevington Wood, 'Maxfield, Thomas', in Donald M. Lewis (ed.), *The Blackwell Dictionary of Evangelical Biography 1730–1860*, 2 vols. (Oxford: Blackwell, 1995), vol. 2, pp. 756–757. It is noteworthy that Wesley differed from most evangelicals of his day in being thoroughly convinced that the miraculous gifts of the Spirit continued beyond the close of the New Testament era. For his position in this regard, see Lycurgus M. Starkey, Jr., *The Work of the Holy Spirit: A Study in Wesleyan Theology* (New York: Abingdon, 1962), pp. 73–77; Ted A. Campbell, 'John Wesley and Conyers Middleton on Divine Intervention in History', *Church History* 55 (1986), pp. 39–49.

21. Bebbington, *Evangelicalism in Modern Britain*, pp. 52–53; Andrew Fuller, 'Spiritual Knowledge and Love Necessary for the Ministry', in *The Complete Works of the Rev. Andrew Fuller*, rev. Joseph Belcher, 3 vols. (Philadelphia: American Baptist Publication Society; repr. Harrisonburg, Va.: Sprinkle, 1988), vol. 1, p. 479.

22. 'The Choice of Moses', in *Works of the Rev. Andrew Fuller*, vol. 1, p. 427.

Bebbington also points to various cultural characteristics shared by the two movements, of which the following are probably the most important. First, both movements were deeply permeated with the spirit of empiricism. Seventeenth-century philosophical and scientific thought had been primarily concerned with general principles and the creation of metaphysical systems that would provide a unifying web for all fields of human knowledge. John Locke (1632–1704) and Isaac Newton, respectively the most influential philosopher and scientist of the Enlightenment period, shifted the focus instead to the multiplicity and particularity of reality, since they considered particular facts to be the basis of knowledge. The observation of and experimentation with these specific phenomena, the establishment of general laws on the basis of this testing, thus became the pathway to a genuine understanding of humanity and the universe it inhabits.[23] Similarly, eighteenth- and early nineteenth-century evangelicalism was somewhat impatient with the systematizing of earlier Protestant generations, in particular, that of the Puritans. John Newton (1725–1807) represented the thinking of a goodly number of his evangelical contemporaries when he said, 'Calvinism should be, in our general religious instructions, like a lump of sugar in a cup of tea; all should taste of it, but it should not be met with in a separate form.'[24] Hannah More (1745–1832), the evangelical blue-stocking whose convictions owed much to the spiritual advice of Newton, was more blunt: 'How I hate the little narrowing names of Arminian and Calvinist. Christianity is a broad basis. Bible Christianity is what I love.'[25] This aversion to imposing a theological structure on Scripture is well summed up by a dictum of the early nineteenth-century Anglican evangelical Charles Simeon (1759–1836): 'Be Bible Christians, not system Christians.'[26] Andrew Fuller noted that 'systematic divinity, or the studying of truth in a systematic form, has been of late years much decried'.[27] Though Fuller himself did not share this attitude, it is significant that he himself never published a systematic theology.

Moreover, evangelicals were just as interested as Enlightenment scientists in conducting experiments and enquiries. They delighted in describing

23. Leonard Krieger, *Kings and Philosophers 1689–1789* (New York: W. W. Norton, 1970), pp. 139–141.
24. Cited Bebbington, *Evangelicalism in Modern Britain*, p. 63.
25. Cited James M. Gordon, Evangelical Spirituality (London: SPCK, 1991), pp. 117–118.
26. Cited Bebbington, *Evangelicalism in Modern Britain*, p. 58.
27. *The Nature and Importance of an Intimate Knowledge of Divine Truth*, in *Works of the Rev. Andrew Fuller*, vol. 1, p. 164.

biblical Christianity as an 'experimental religion', that is, one that must be tested by experience.[28] The best preaching they considered to be 'experimental preaching'—preaching that explained 'every part of the work of God upon the soul'.[29] Isaac Backus had a passion for 'tabulating, comparing, categorizing, and measuring' statistics. Like other Enlightenment figures, he was convinced that 'through the careful observation and collection of facts man could learn to know the world in which he lived'.[30] A similar passion is evidenced in the classic eighteenth-century defence of missionary endeavour, *An Enquiry into the Obligations of Christians, to Use Means for the Conversion of the Heathens* (1792). This 'business-like survey' by one of the fathers of the modern missionary movement, William Carey (1761–1834), tabulates the length, breadth, population and religious beliefs of the countries of the world in order to impress upon evangelical Protestantism the desperate spiritual state of the world outside their ranks.[31]

Second, Enlightenment thought was generally optimistic as regards the future. As Bebbington points out, eighteenth-century intellectuals were certain that 'human beings are steadily becoming wiser and therefore better'.[32] Evangelicals, however, also had high hopes for the future. Thomas Scott (1747–1821), an important Anglican evangelical author, could state in 1802 that 'more will be saved in the end than will perish'.[33] Jonathan Edwards's New Divinity disciple Joseph Bellamy (1719–90) went even further and estimated that in the final analysis the ratio of lost to saved would be 1 to 17,456 1/3![34]

Postmillennialism, which evangelicals had inherited from their Puritan forebears,[35] helped serve as a fitting channel for this optimism about the

---

28. Bebbington, *Evangelicalism in Modern Britain*, p. 57.
29. Bebbington, 'Revival and Enlightenment', p. 24.
30. McLoughlin, *Isaac Backus*, pp. 187–188.
31. Bebbington, 'Evangelical Christianity and the Enlightenment', p. 33. The description of Carey's Enquiry as a 'business-like survey' is that of W. R. Ward, 'The Baptists and the Transformation of the Church, 1780–1830', *Baptist Quarterly* 25 (1973–4), p. 170.
32. *Evangelicalism in Modern Britain*, p. 60. See also his discussion of the Enlightenment idea of progress in *Patterns in History: A Christian Perspective on Historical Thought* (Grand Rapids: Baker, 1990, rev. ed.), pp. 68–91.
33. Cited Bebbington, 'Evangelical Christianity and the Enlightenment', p. 33.
34. Ward, 'Baptists', p. 171.
35. See Iain H. Murray, *The Puritan Hope: A Study in Revival and the Interpretation of Prophecy* (Edinburgh: Banner of Truth, 1971).

future. The postmillennial perspective envisioned a time of unparalleled spiritual prosperity for the church prior to the return of Christ. The Jews would be converted, then there would follow a great ingathering of men and women from the Muslim and heathen nations. Here is the way, for instance, that Andrew Fuller developed this conviction in a sermon he preached in Edinburgh in 1799:

> The time will come when 'all the kindreds of the earth' shall worship. Ethiopia, and all the unknown regions of Africa, shall stretch out their hands to God. Arabia, and Persia, and Tartary [i.e. Russia], and India, and China, with the numerous islands in the Eastern and Southern Ocean, shall bring an offering before him. Mahomedans shall drop their delusion, papists their cruel superstition, Jews shall be ashamed of their obstinacy, deists of their enmity, and merely nominal Christians of their form of godliness without the power of it.[36]

The turmoil and upheaval of the Napoleonic Wars did little to dampen Fuller's optimism. Only a few months before his death in 1815, he finished preparing for the press his *Expository Discourses on the Apocalypse* and mentioned in the preface his expectation that his personal demise was not far distant. But, he added, 'We have seen enough, amidst all the troubles of our times, to gladden our hearts; and trust that our children will see greater things than these.'[37] Not all evangelicals were convinced that this was the way things would turn out, but postmillennial hopes were certainly widespread in evangelical circles.[38]

Third, the world view of the Enlightenment was distinctly pragmatic in temper. In the words of American historian Leonard Krieger, the philosophers of this era 'made social relevance a constant touchstone of all their thinking'.[39] This criterion of social relevance was equally important to evangelicals. Bebbington points to field preaching outside church buildings as the classic illustration in this regard.[40] It violated Anglican church order, but irrepressible evangelists like George Whitefield and John Wesley defended it on pragmatic grounds: it saved souls. Both Whitefield and Wesley were also

---

36. 'Nature and Extent of True Conversion', in *Works of the Rev. Andrew Fuller*, vol. 1, pp. 552–553.

37. *Works of the Rev. Andrew Fuller*, vol. 3, p. 202.

38. Bebbington, *Evangelicalism in Modern Britain*, pp. 62–63.

39. *Kings and Philosophers*, p. 181.

40. *Evangelicalism in Modern Britain*, p. 65; 'Revival and Enlightenment', p. 26.

unabashed supporters of lay preachers, since they reasoned that there were not enough evangelical clergymen in the Church of England to reach the masses. Although some evangelicals in the Church of England, like Samuel Walker, strongly disagreed with this pragmatic measure,[41] it eventually became a hallmark of evangelicalism.

Then, the literary taste of eighteenth-century evangelicalism was attuned to the canons of the age. Perspicuity and plainness, brevity and harmony were the qualities most sought after by writers of this period, and these criteria were also dear to evangelical authors and poets. Thomas Haweis (1734–1820), the rector of Aldwincle, Northamptonshire, is quoted by Bebbington as stating, 'The commencement of this century has been called the *Augustan age*, when purity of stile added the most perfect polish to deep erudition, as well as the *belles letters*.' Haweis especially admired the union of 'conciseness with precision' that he found in the best of eighteenth-century authors, a style he consciously tried to imitate.[42] John Wesley also approved of brevity. 'If Angels were to write books', he once declared, 'we should have very few Folios,' a remark that clearly has in view the massive tomes of the Puritan era.[43] The greatest hymn-writers of the era (Isaac Watts [1674–1748], Philip Doddridge [1702–51], Charles Wesley [1707–88], William Cowper [1731–1800] and John Newton) consciously removed anything from their hymns that would make them inaccessible to the less learned who sang them.[44] Watts, for instance, states that in his hymns he would 'neither indulge any bold metaphors, nor admit of hard words, nor tempt the ignorant worshipper to sing without his understanding'.[45] In the preface to the *Olney Hymns* (1779), Newton emphasizes that his and Cowper's hymns are 'for the use of plain people' and thus they are marked by 'perspicuity, simplicity and ease' of understanding.[46] 'The greatest monument', in Bebbington's view, of evangelicalism's use of contemporary canons of literary taste is in fact the hymnody of Charles Wesley. Such lines as 'Being's source begins to be', a reference to the Incarnation, or 'Impassive he suffers, immortal he dies', referring to

---

41. Kenneth Hylson-Smith, *Evangelicals in the Church of England 1734–1984* (Edinburgh: T. & T. Clark, 1988), pp. 22–23.

42. 'Revival and Enlightenment', p. 27.

43. Cited Bebbington, *Evangelicalism in Modern Britain*, p. 68.

44. Davie, *Dissentient Voice*, pp. 76–77.

45. Ibid., p. 74.

46. 'Preface' to the *Olney Hymns, in Three Books* (London, 1779), p. vii. A facsimile edition of this work, which has been used in this chapter, was published by the Cowper and Newton Museum, Olney, Buckinghamshire, in 1979.

Christ's crucifixion, exhibit his finest traits as a hymn-writer: 'disciplined emotion, didactic purpose, clarity, and succintness'.[47]

Finally, central to the Enlightenment and intimately linked to its optimism was an emphasis on human benevolence and philanthropy. Scottish moralist James Beattie (1735–1803) emphasized that since all human beings are 'by nature brethren . . . and equally dependent on the great author of our being', it should encourage 'the great duty of universal benevolence'.[48] Thinkers like Anthony Ashley Cooper, Earl of Shaftesbury (1671–1713), and Voltaire were convinced that men and women possessed a native benevolence that made them unique in the created realm.[49] Evangelicals robustly maintained the opposite, namely that the heart of unregenerate humanity was ruled by sinful self-love. Nevertheless, they expected genuine conversion to issue in a humanitarian spirit and acts of benevolence. Thus evangelicals were engaged in a host of philanthropic enterprises: establishing orphanages; providing organized support for the poor and destitute, war widows and immigrants; seeking the release of those imprisoned for small debts; striving to make barbarous sports like bear- and bull-baiting illegal. 'Such charitable work', Bebbington admits, 'can hardly be attributed to the Enlightenment.' It has accompanied genuine Christianity in every age and clime.[50] The 'greatest example of Evangelical humanitarianism'—the titanic struggle that evangelicals waged against slavery and the slave trade—does have, however, direct links to the Enlightenment's interest in natural rights and benevolence.

Evangelicals were initially slow to condemn the slave trade. John Newton was for a number of years after his conversion a slave trader, and, at the time, thanked God for having led him into 'an easy and creditable way of life'.[51]

---

47. 'Revival and Enlightenment', p. 27. The first hymnic fragment is cited by Davie, *Dissentient Voice*, p. 21. Davie notes that hymns from this era require 'strenuous thinking' and are frequently characterized by a 'sinewy intellectualism' (*Dissentient Voice*, pp. 38, 18).

48. Anstey, *Atlantic Slave Trade*, pp. 110–112.

49. Hampson, *Enlightenment*, p. 99.

50. Bebbington, *Evangelicalism and Modern Britain*, p. 71.

51. John Newton, *The Journal of a Slave Trader*, ed. Bernard Martin and Mark Spurrell (London: Epworth, 1962), p. xii. Newton, of course, came to have a profound change of mind regarding the slave trade. See his *Thoughts upon the African Slave Trade* (London: printed for J. Buckland and J. Johnson, 1788; repr. in Martin and Spurrell, *Journal of a Slave Trader*, pp. 97–113), where he states that to plead for 'a commerce so iniquitous, so cruel, so oppressive, so destructive, as the African Slave Trade' contradicts 'the common sense of mankind' (ibid., p. 113).

Whitefield, though publicly critical of those slave owners who ill-used their slaves, was instrumental in the introduction of slavery into the colony of Georgia and owned slaves himself.[52] The first Christian community among whom opposition to the slave trade was found were the Quakers, who began to criticize it before the end of the seventeenth century. It was through the writings of an American Quaker, Anthony Benezet (1713–84), that John Wesley became convinced in the early 1770s that the slave trade was an 'execrable sum of all villainies'.[53] From then to the end of his life, Wesley fiercely denounced, in print and from the pulpit, the slave trade and the practice of slavery.

The opposition to the slave trade that Wesley and others like William Wilberforce (1759–1833) helped to arouse in evangelical circles owed much to various Enlightenment ideals. Wesley, for instance, drew heavily on the ideal regarding inalienable rights when he declared in his *Thoughts upon Slavery* (1774), 'Liberty is the right of every human creature, as soon as he breathes the vital air; and no human law can deprive him of that right which he derives from the law of nature.'[54] The use of Enlightenment thinking about benevolence is readily seen in Abraham Booth's *Commerce in the Human Species, and the Enslaving of Innocent Persons, inimical to the Laws of Moses and the Gospel of Christ*, originally a sermon preached at Prescot Street Baptist Church, London, in 1792. Booth opened with the assertion that it is the duty of every human being 'to adore our Almighty Maker, to confide in the Lord Redeemer, and to exercise genuine benevolence toward all mankind'. Benevolence is incumbent upon men and women since they are 'social beings, surrounded with multitudes of [their] species'. On this basis Booth was prepared to take a public stand against 'the stealing, purchasing, and enslaving of innocent persons'.[55]

---

52. Arnold A. Dallimore, *George Whitefield: The Life and Times of the Great Evangelist of the Eighteenth-Century Revival*, 2 vols. (Edinburgh: Banner of Truth, 1970, 1979; repr. Westchester, Ill.: Cornerstone, 1979, 1980), vol. 1, pp. 482–483, 495–497; vol. 2, pp. 219, 367–368, 520–521.

53. *The Journal of the Rev. John Wesley, A. M.*, ed. Nehemiah Curnock, 8 vols. (London: Epworth, 1909–16), vol. 5, pp. 445–446.

54. *The Works of John Wesley*, 14 vols. (London: Wesleyan Conference Office, 1872; repr. Peabody, Mass.: Hendrickson, 1984³), vol. 11, p. 79. For Wesley's anti-slavery thought, see Irv A. Brendlinger, *Social Justice through the Eyes of Wesley: John Wesley's Theological Challenge to Slavery* (Dundas, Ont.: Joshua, 2006).

55. *The Works of Abraham Booth*, 3 vols. (London: 1813), vol. 3, pp. 185–187. For the importance of this sermon, see Ernest F. Kevan, *London's Oldest Baptist Church,*

These shared characteristics clearly indicate that there are close ties between eighteenth-century evangelicalism and the Enlightenment. The older interpretation of these two movements as intrinsically hostile to each other needs to be scrapped, as does the view that eighteenth-century evangelicalism was largely insulated from its cultural environment. Of course, there were points where evangelicals stood against their culture. For instance, the Enlightenment's commitment to the innate goodness of humans, noted above, was rejected by evangelicals, since they held fast to the biblical conviction that men and women without exception are fallen, sinful beings. Evangelical devotion to the Scriptures, also previously noted, was another area where evangelicalism thought differently from its cultural environment. As Bebbington notes, there was 'no one-to-one fit between the two movements'.[56] Nevertheless, there is clear evidence of positive cross-fertilization and interaction between our eighteenth-century evangelical forebears and their culture.

'Created by the Enlightenment'? The origin of evangelicalism and its ties to Puritanism

Central to Bebbington's discussion of eighteenth-century evangelicalism is what he terms its 'quadrilateral of priorities', four distinguishing marks that set it apart from its culture and other Christian traditions, and that Bebbington believes continue to characterize evangelicalism. First, evangelicals 'held and practised the conviction that lives have to be transformed by the gospel, that people are not naturally Christians',[57] a conviction that Bebbington terms 'conversionism'. Then, there was 'activism', which consisted 'primarily in spreading the gospel', that is, evangelism and missionary activity, but that also involved doing 'all sorts of humane works of charity'.[58] Third, evangelicalism was marked by what Bebbington calls 'biblicism'. Evangelicals showed a deep

---

Wapping 1633—*Walthamstow* 1933 (London: Kingsgate, 1933), pp. 109–110, 125–126; Ernest A. Payne, 'Abraham Booth, 1734–1806', *Baptist Quarterly* 26 (1975–6), p. 37. For an analysis of the sermon, see Michael A. G. Haykin, *Abraham Booth and His Sermon against the Slave Trade*, Strict Baptist Historical Society Bulletin (Dunstable: Strict Baptist Historical Society, 2006).

56. 'Evangelical Christianity and the Enlightenment', p. 35.
57. 'Scottish Cultural Influences on Evangelicalism', *Scottish Bulletin of Evangelical Theology* 14.1 (spring 1996), p. 23.
58. 'Evangelical Christianity and the Enlightenment', p. 29.

'devotion to the Bible', which was a 'result of their belief that all spiritual truth is to be found in its pages'.[59] Finally, evangelicals emphasized 'crucicentrism', that is, 'they . . . placed at the centre of their theological scheme the doctrine of the cross—the atoning work of Jesus Christ in his death'.[60] This 'functional definition of evangelicalism' has found widespread scholarly approval and employment.[61]

---

59. *Evangelicalism in Modern Britain*, p. 12.

60. 'Evangelical Christianity and the Enlightenment', p. 30.

61. This is the focus of Timothy Larsen's chapter in this volume. But, for acceptance of the Bebbington quadrilateral, see also Gordon, *Evangelical Spirituality*, pp. 7–8; I. Howard Marshall, 'Are Evangelicals Fundamentalists?', *Vox evangelica* 22 (1992), pp. 8–10; N. A. D. Scotland, 'John Bird Sumner, 1780–1862: Claphamite Evangelical Pastor and Prelate', *Bulletin of the John Rylands University Library of Manchester* 74 (1992), pp. 57–58; Derek J. Tidball, *Who Are the Evangelicals? Tracing the Roots of the Modern Movements* (London: Marshall Pickering, 1994), pp. 14, 99; Robert Letham, 'Is Evangelicalism Christian?', *Evangelical Quarterly* 67 (1995), pp. 4–8; Robert K. Burkinshaw, *Pilgrims in Lotus Land: Conservative Protestantism in British Columbia, 1917–1981* (Montreal: McGill-Queen's University Press, 1995), pp. 9–10, 15; John Wolffe, 'Introduction', in John Wolffe (ed.), *Evangelical Faith and Public Zeal: Evangelicals and Society in Britain 1780–1980* (London: SPCK, 1995), p. 4; Kenneth D. Brown, 'Nonconformist Evangelicals and National Politics in the Late Nineteenth century', in Wolffe , *Evangelical Faith and Public Zeal*, p. 140; G. A. Rawlyk, *Is Jesus Your Personal Saviour? In Search of Canadian Evangelicalism in the 1990s* (Montreal: McGill-Queen's University Press, 1996), pp. 9, 118–126. Especially significant is the adoption of Bebbington's quadrilateral by Lewis, *Blackwell Dictionary of Evangelical Biography*, vol. 1, p. xix.

See also the following positive reviews of Bebbington's *Evangelicalism in Modern Britain: Crux* 25.3 (Sept. 1989), pp. 39–40 (Ian S. Rennie); *Proceedings of the Wesley Historical Society* 47 (1989–90), pp. 133–134 (Ian Sellers); *Christianity Today* 34.2 (5 Feb. 1990), pp. 62–64 (Grant Wacker); *Anglican and Episcopal History* 59 (1990), pp. 522–527 (Diana Butler); *Canadian Journal of History* 25. 2 (Aug. 1990), pp. 267–270 (Malcolm Greenshields); *Fides et historia* 22.1 (winter–spring 1990), pp. 103–105 (Donald M. Lewis); *Scottish Bulletin of Evangelical Theology* 8.2 (autumn 1990), pp. 133–134 (David Smith); *Spectrum* 23.1 (spring 1991), pp. 77–79 (William K. Kay); *Themelios* 16.3 (Apr.–May 1991), pp. 34–35 (C. Peter Williams); *Enlightenment and Dissent* 10 (1991), pp. 115–118 (Alan P. F. Sell); *Asbury Theological Journal* 48.2 (autumn 1993), pp. 79–80 (David Bundy).

Now, of these four distinctive evangelical benchmarks 'activism' is especially critical to a further aspect of Bebbington's argument, namely that the
'Evangelical version of Protestantism was created by the Enlightenment'.[62]
Bebbington identifies Puritanism as the 'dominant force' within English-
speaking Protestantism prior to the emergence of evangelicalism in the
eighteenth century.[63] Puritanism and the various denominational bodies
that sought to preserve its theological vision after the Restoration of Charles
II in 1660 (the English Presbyterians, Congregationalists and Particular
Baptists, collectively known, together with the Quakers, as the 'Dissenters')
were 'undoubtedly conversionist, biblicist and crucicentric'. But, according to Bebbington, they lacked 'activism'. There were a few exceptions like
John Eliot (1604–90), who laboured among the Native Americans of eastern
Massachusetts, but by and large the Puritans and their Dissenting heirs were
not engaged in missionary endeavours to areas of the world where the gospel
was not known.[64]

Bebbington traces this failure to engage in cross-cultural missions to a particular understanding of the doctrine of assurance. According to Bebbington,
the Puritans and Dissenters 'held that assurance is rare, late and the fruit of
struggle in the experience of believers'.[65] Among the proof that he cites for
this assertion is the following text from the Westminster Confession of Faith
(1646): 'Infallible assurance doth not so belong to the essence of faith, but that
a true believer may wait long, and conflict with many difficulties before he be
partaker of it.'[66] The introspective piety fostered by this view of assurance and
the energy consumed in seeking to determine whether or not one was among

For criticism of Bebbington's definition, see, in addition to the chapters of this
book, the book review of *Evangelicalism in Modern Britain* in the *Evangelical Times*
23.12, Dec. 1989 (R. W. Oliver); and D. A. Carson, *The Gagging of God: Christianity
Confronts Pluralism* (Grand Rapids: Zondervan, 1996), pp. 449–451.

62. *Evangelicalism in Modern Britain*, p. 74. See the similar claim in 'Evangelical
    Christianity and the Enlightenment', p. 36: 'The Enlightenment actually gave rise
    to Evangelical Christianity ...'

63. 'Evangelical Christianity and the Enlightenment', p. 32.

64. *Evangelicalism in Modern Britain*, pp. 40–42; 'Evangelical Christianity and the
    Enlightenment', p. 32; 'Revival and Enlightenment', pp. 21–22. For further
    discussion of the relationship between Puritanism and evangelicalism, see the
    chapter by John Coffey in this volume.

65. *Evangelicalism in Modern Britain*, p. 43.

66. The Westminster Confession of Faith 18.3.

the elect seriously hampered Puritan and Dissenting missionary endeavours. How could they spread the gospel when they were not even sure that they were saved?

Evangelicals, by contrast, were convinced that 'assurance is the normal possession of the believer'.[67] Whitefield, reflecting on his conversion in 1735, could state in a letter he wrote to John Wesley in 1740, 'For these five or six years I have received the witness of God's Spirit; since that, blessed be God, I have not doubted a quarter of an hour of a saving interest in Jesus Christ.'[68] When Whitefield met the Welsh evangelist Howel Harris (1714–71) for the first time, he reputedly asked the Welshman, 'Do you know your sins are forgiven?'[69] And in an oft-reprinted sermon about the indwelling of the Spirit of God, Whitefield told his hearers, to 'say, we may have God's Spirit without feeling it . . . is in reality to deny the thing itself'.[70] This robust sense of assurance delivered evangelicals from the introspective piety of the Puritans and enabled them to take up the task of spreading the gospel to others with assiduity and zeal.[71]

How did this crucial shift in the doctrine of assurance come about? 'Why was there', in Bebbington's words, 'a transition from Puritanism to Evangelicalism?'[72] Bebbington finds the answer in the shift from the Baroque era, in which Puritanism had flourished, to that of the Enlightenment. The empiricism of the Enlightenment, as we have seen, was common to evangelicals of the period. Impacted by the thought of John Locke, they believed that experience and experimentation were a source of indubitable knowledge. Theologians like Jonathan Edwards and John Wesley led them to extend this assumption to the spiritual realm. Direct experiences of God became regarded as trustworthy barometers of assurance.[73] This, according to Bebbington, was 'the spark that ignited revival'.[74] And this is the reasoning that leads Bebbington to conclude that evangelicalism was 'created by the Enlightenment'[75] and that prior to the

---

67. Bebbington, *Evangelicalism in Modern Britain*, p. 45.
68. Cited Bebbington, 'Revival and Enlightenment', p. 22.
69. Dallimore, *George Whitefield*, vol. 1, p. 264.
70. 'The Indwelling of the Spirit, the Common Privilege of All Believers', in his *Sermons on Important Subjects* (London: Thomas Tegg, 1833), p. 433.
71. Bebbington, 'Revival and Enlightenment', pp. 21–22.
72. 'Evangelical Christianity and the Enlightenment', p. 33.
73. *Evangelicalism in Modern Britain*, pp. 47–50.
74. 'Revival and Enlightenment', p. 23.
75. *Evangelicalism in Modern Britain*, p. 74.

eighteenth-century revivals it simply did not exist. This claim goes far beyond what has already been established in the first part of this chapter, namely that there are clear points of cross-fertilization between eighteenth-century anglophone evangelicalism and its culture.[76] If Bebbington is correct, then evangelicalism as a product of the Enlightenment must be seen as a major purveyor of Enlightenment assumptions and be sharply distinguished from Puritanism.[77] But is he correct? A number of unresolved questions suggest that he is not.

First, were the Puritans so generally devoid of missionary zeal as he argues? Bebbington recognizes that there were some Congregationalists and Baptists who engaged in itinerant evangelism and that Richard Baxter (1615–91) longed for the conversion of the nations. But these cases and that of John Eliot he holds to be quite unusual.[78] But were they so exceptional? The Puritans, as Bebbington owns, were conversionist. Much of the immense body of sermons they preached and the literature they wrote was evangelistic in intent. Moreover, Restoration Puritan spirituality especially placed great emphasis on seeking the salvation of the lost.[79] John Janeway (d. 1657) was, in the words of Dewey Wallace, 'a paragon of soul winning'. Not long after his own conversion he was earnestly seeking that of unsaved family members and fellow students at Cambridge, 'desiring to carry as many of them as possibly he could along with him to Heaven'.[80] Joseph Alleine (1634–68), whose *Alarm to Unconverted Sinners* (1672) was a best-seller in the eighteenth-century evangelical print culture, even considered going to China to preach the gospel.[81] John Bunyan (1628–88), one of the great evangelists of the Puritan era, could describe his passion for the salvation of the lost in terms that Whitefield or Wesley would gladly have owned:

> My great desire in fulfilling my Ministry, was, to get into the darkest places in the Countrey [*sic*], even amongst those people that were furthest off of profession; yet not because I could not endure the light (for I feared not to shew my Gospel to any) but because I found my spirit learned most after awakening and converting Work, and the Word that I carried did lean itself most that way; Yea, so have I strived to preach

---

76. See Bebbington's awareness of this fact in his 'Revival and Enlightenment', p. 34.
77. Ibid.
78. *Evangelicalism in Modern Britain*, pp. 34, 40–41.
79. Dewey D. Wallace, 'Introduction' to his ed., *The Spirituality of the Later English Puritans* (Macon, Ga.: Mercer University Press, 1987), p. xv.
80. Ibid.
81. Ibid.

the Gospel, not where Christ was named, lest I should build upon another mans foundation, Rom. 15.20.

In my preaching I have really been in pain, and have as it were travelled [travailed] to bring forth Children to God; neither could I be satisfied unless some fruits did appear in my work: if I were fruitless it matter'd not who commended me; but if I were fruitful, I cared not who did condemn. I have thought of that, He that winneth souls is wise, Pro. 11.30.

It pleased me nothing to see people drink in Opinions if they seemed ignorant of Jesus Christ, and the worth of their own Salvation, sound conviction for Sin, especially for Unbelief, and an heart set on fire to be saved by Christ, with strong breathings after a truly sanctified Soul: that was it that delighted me; those were the souls I counted blessed.[82]

And the New England Puritan Cotton Mather (1663–1728) was convinced that Puritan prayers were vital for the advance of the gospel throughout the world. As he stated in *The Nets of Salvation* (1704):

Praying for souls is a main stroke in the winning of souls. If once the Spirit of Grace be poured out upon a soul, that soul is won immediately . . . Yea, who can tell, how far the prayers of the saints, & of a few saints, may prevail with heaven to obtain that grace, that shall win whole peoples and kingdoms to serve the Lord? . . . It may be, the nations of the world, would quickly be won from the idolatries of paganism, and the impostures of Mahomet, if a Spirit of Prayer, were at work among the people of God.[83]

Granted none in the Puritan era had an itinerant ministry comparable to that of Whitefield,[84] but that does not mean that the Puritans lacked a sense of mission.[85]

---

82. *John Bunyan: Grace Abounding to the Chief of Sinners*, ed. W. R. Owens (Harmondsworth: Penguin, 1987), pp. 72–73.

83. Cited Richard F. Lovelace, *The American Pietism of Cotton Mather: Origins of American Evangelicalism* (Grand Rapids: Eerdmans, 1979), p. 244.

84. J. I. Packer, 'The Spirit with the Word: The Reformational Revivalism of George Whitefield', in W. P. Stephens (ed.), *The Bible, the Reformation and the Church: Essays in Honour of James Atkinson* (Sheffield: Sheffield Academic Press, 1995), pp. 187–189.

85. John Walsh, 'Methodism at the End of the Eighteenth Century', in Rupert Davies and Gordon Rupp (eds.), *A History of the Methodist Church in Great Britain* (London: Epworth, 1965), vol. 1, p. 293. For a good treatment of the Puritan sense of mission, see J. I. Packer, 'Puritan Evangelism', in his *A Quest for Godliness: The Puritan Vision of the Christian Life* (Wheaton, Illinois: Crossway, 1990), pp. 291–308.

Moreover, why is it that eighteenth-century anglophone evangelicals did not generally engage in cross-cultural missions until the final decade of the century? There were a few like David Brainerd (1718–47), but no stream of missionaries to the world outside Protestantism until the example of William Carey galvanized English-speaking evangelicals in the 1790s. Up until that time, Whitefield, Wesley and other great evangelical preachers, like Samuel Davies (1723–61), ministered, as the Puritans did, within the bounds of their own culture. There were some tentative forerunners of the Particular Baptist Society for the Propagation of the Gospel among the Heathen, like the plan of Selina Hastings (1707–91), the Countess of Huntingdon, for work among the Georgia Indians in 1772, or the desire expressed in the 1780s by the Methodist Thomas Coke (1747–1814) to establish missionary ventures in the West Indies, Quebec, West Africa and India,[86] but nothing substantial took place until Carey went to India. If the Puritans are to be criticized for a lack of 'activism', that is, a failure to engage in cross-cultural missions, cannot the same be said of the early evangelicals in the following century? Even if one recognizes, as Andrew Walls has persuasively argued,[87] that the anglophone missionary movement in which Carey is an undoubted pioneer needs to be seen as dependent upon such earlier continental missionary ventures as those of the Pietists of Halle and the Moravians of Herrnhut, this still means that there are nearly sixty years between the first flames of revival in the British world and the Baptist mission of the 1790s. But if mission was so integral to the identity of the evangelical movement, it seems strange that there was little manifestation of what was its distinctive feature until the second or even third generation of the movement.

Moreover, can evangelical missions be explained primarily in terms of the intellectual ambience of the world of eighteenth-century evangelicalism? In an insightful essay on the relationship between evangelical missions and the Enlightenment, Brian Stanley observes that there were five key ideological features of eighteenth- and early nineteenth-century mission activity. First, western missionaries were convinced that non-occidental peoples were lost and in dire need of the salvation those missionaries had to offer them. Second, other religions besides Christianity were regarded as essentially forms of idolatry and

86. Walsh, 'Methodism', p. 299. For Coke's missionary vision, see John A. Vickers, 'Coke, Thomas', in Lewis, *Blackwell Dictionary of Evangelical Biography*, vol. 1, pp. 238–239.

87. 'The Eighteenth-Century Protestant Missionary Awakening in Its European Context', in Stanley, *Christian Missions and the Enlightenment*, pp. 22–44.

'devoid of any trace of the presence of God'. Third, there was a conviction that western culture was superior to that of the rest of the world. Fourth, there was a deep-seated belief about the importance of education as an essential corollary to gospel proclamation. Fifth, there was an emphasis on the necessity of personal and individual response to the gospel.[88] Stanley notes that of these five features, only the final two can be explained to any degree by Christianity's encounter with the Enlightenment. The other three—indeed to a certain extent all five—features are part of the inheritance from periods prior to the Enlightenment. What the Enlightenment did do, though, was to bring to the fore certain new implications of these features. For instance, the emphasis on the importance of reason as a handmaiden to Christian witness led to the assumption of the basic unity of all human beings and that all of them needed exposure to western thinking. The latter would aid both in their conversion and their 'civilization'. Stanley, while not wishing to reject totally Bebbington's belief that evangelicalism has intimate links to the environment of the Enlightenment, nonetheless does wish to qualify this belief seriously. He cannot support, he states, 'any simple ascription' of these features of evangelicalism to 'a supposedly unitary body of philosophy labeled "The Enlightenment" '.[89]

Thinking about assurance

Bebbington's thesis regarding the origins of evangelicalism especially revolves around the doctrine of assurance.[90] Specifically, he argues that Jonathan Edwards first introduced what became the evangelical attitude towards assurance during a revival that took place in the town of Northampton, Massachusetts, in 1734–5.[91] Some of those converted in the revival were actually unaware of what had happened to them. In the words of Edwards, 'many continue a long time in a course of gracious exercises and experiences, and do not think themselves to be converted, but conclude otherwise'. As the pastor of the church, however, Edwards felt it was his duty to help them to come to an assurance of what God had done for them. 'I should account it a great calamity', he wrote, 'to be deprived of the comfort of rejoicing with those of my flock who have been in

---

88. Stanley, 'Christian Missions and the Enlightenment', in Stanley, *Christian Missions and the Enlightenment*, pp. 8–16.
89. Ibid., pp. 1–21, and here and there throughout.
90. See also ch. 15 by Garry J. Williams in this volume.
91. *Evangelicalism in Modern Britain*, p. 47.

great distress, whose circumstances I have been acquainted with, when there
seems to be good evidence that those who were dead are alive, and that those
who were lost are found.'[92]

However, Bebbington's analysis at this point fails to take into account the
fact that Edwards's position on assurance changed significantly over the course
of the next few years.[93] Confronted with the fanaticism of some and the false
professions of others in the Great Awakening of 1740–2, he rethought his view
of assurance. In a very revealing letter that he wrote in 1751 to a correspondent in Scotland, a Presbyterian minister by the name of Thomas Gillespie
(1708–74), Edwards reiterated his conviction that 1734 and 1735 undoubtedly
witnessed 'a very glorious work of God wrought in Northampton, and there
were numerous instances of saving conversion'. Nevertheless, upon hindsight
he was now convinced that 'many were deceived, and deceived others' about
their true state and that 'the number of true converts was not so great as was
then imagined'.[94] Much of the problem lay in the fact that many of the congregation had wrong notions about the way of ascertaining a genuine conversion. Too much weight was placed upon 'impressions on the imagination' and
specific experiences, and not enough consideration given to what Edwards calls
'the abiding sense and temper of their hearts' and 'fruits of grace'. In other
words, Edwards came to see that perseverance is the only adequate basis for
assurance, an attitude remarkably similar to that of the Puritans.[95]

It is noteworthy that Edwards did not absolve himself of blame. He was
sensible of not having given the proper guidance and advice on occasion, and
thus some of his congregation found themselves defenceless against satanic
attack and 'spiritual calamity', even to the extent of the eternal ruination of
their souls. But so extraordinary was the Spirit's work at that time that instead
of himself, still but 'a child' in spiritual matters, Edwards told Gillespie, 'there
was want of [a] giant in judgment and discretion'.[96] In other words, far from

---

92. *A Faithful Narrative of the Surprising Work of God*, in *Jonathan Edwards on Revival*
    (London: John Oswald, 1737; repr. Edinburgh: Banner of Truth, 1984), pp. 38–39.

93. See the details in Ava Chamberlain, 'Self-Deception as a Theological Problem in
    Jonathan Edwards's "Treatise Concerning Religious Affections"', *Church History* 63
    (1994), pp. 541–556.

94. Letter to Thomas Gillespie, 1 July 1751, in C. C. Goen (ed.), *The Works of Jonathan
    Edwards*, vol. 4: *The Great Awakening* (New Haven: Yale University Press, 1972), p.
    565.

95. Chamberlain, 'Self-Deception', pp. 541–556, and here and there throughout.

96. Letter to Thomas Gillespie, in Goen, *Works of Jonathan Edwards*, vol. 4, p. 565.

seeing the advice that he gave in 1734–5 concerning assurance as a paradigm for future ministries, Edwards was later critical of its *naïveté*.

Out of this reflection on assurance Edwards produced what is the classic work on spirituality in the period of the Great Awakening, *A Treatise Concerning Religious Affections* (1746), which must also be regarded as the fruit of many years of reflection on the nature of genuine piety. In it he drew widely upon his knowledge of Anglo-American Puritanism, citing with approval such stalwarts as Richard Sibbes (1577–1635), John Preston (1587–1628), Thomas Shepard (1605–49), John Owen (1616–83) and John Flavel (1630–91).[97] He could cite such authors because his attitude towards assurance did not substantially differ from theirs. As Conrad Cherry has observed, Edwards had a 'Puritan concept of assurance'.[98]

The theological vision and spirituality of Edwards's *Religious Affections* had a profound influence on eighteenth-century evangelicalism, which would have helped to disseminate Edwards's mature reflections on the doctrine of assurance. To cite but one example, in 1790 Joseph Kinghorn (1766–1832), pastor of the Particular Baptist church in Norwich, Norfolk, asked fellow Baptist John Ryland, Jr. (1753–1825) (both of them influential figures in the revival that came to British Particular Baptist ranks in the final years of the eighteenth century), for information about the works of Edwards. Ryland was clearly all enthusiasm when he replied. 'I rejoice', he wrote, that God

> has given you a relish for the writings of that blessed man that, I think, has been more useful to me than any other. Were I forced to part with all mere human compositions but three, Edwards's *Life of Brainerd*, his *Treatise on Religious*

---

97. For a discussion of the authors whom Edwards quotes in the *Religious Affections*, see John E. Smith, 'Editor's Introduction', in John E. Smith (ed.), *The Works of Jonathan Edwards*, vol. 2: *Religious Affections* (New Haven: Yale University Press, 1959), pp. 52–73.

98. *The Theology of Jonathan Edwards: A Reappraisal* (Garden City, N. Y.: Doubleday, 1966; repr. Bloomington: Indiana University Press, 1990), p. 151. More generally, Thomas A. Schafer points out that 'Edwards not only accepted Reformed theology in its English Puritan form, he energetically defended it' (*The 'Miscellanies'* [New Haven: Yale University Press, 1994], p. 39). For a good study of Edwards's view of assurance, see Cherry, *Theology of Jonathan Edwards*, pp. 143–158, as well as the chapters by Garry J. Williams (ch. 15), and Douglas A. Sweeney and Brandon G. Withrow (ch. 12) in this volume.

Affections, and [Joseph] Bellamy's *True Religion Delineated* . . . would be the last
I should let go.[99]

Not surprisingly Ryland reproduces Edwards's teaching on the doctrine of
assurance. In a sermon entitled 'On Grieving the Holy Spirit' Ryland argues
that the seal of the Spirit, mentioned in Ephesians 4:30,

> consists in the impression of the divine image on the soul; really conforming us to
> God, in the temper of our minds. Without this, no immediate witness would be
> valid; and with it, it is unnecessary . . . This is truly a supernatural and divine work.
> It requires, indeed, the finger of God, to engrave his image on the soul, where it was
> totally effaced: to renew the resemblance of his moral perfections, and transform us
> into the likeness of his dear Son.[100]

Here Ryland understands the seal of the Spirit to be the Spirit's progressive
sanctification and transformation of the believer into the character of Christ.
Indeed where this is present, it is sufficient attestation to the reality of salvation. 'This seal', the Baptist preacher concludes, 'is the best proof of our relation to God.'[101]

The close reading by Ryland, and such friends as Andrew Fuller and John
Sutcliff (1752–1814), the pastor of Olney Baptist Church, Buckinghamshire, of
those items of the Edwardsean corpus that were available in late eighteenth-
century Great Britain was a critical factor in the profound revitalization of
many sectors of the British Particular Baptist community.[102] There were,

---

99. Cited Martin Hood Wilkin, *Joseph Kinghorn, of Norwich* (Norwich: Fletcher &
    Alexander, 1855; repr. in Terry Wolever [ed.], *The Life and Works of Joseph Kinghorn*
    [Springfield, Mo.: Particular Baptist, 1995], vol. 1, p. 183). Just as Ryland's
    somewhat eccentric father, John Collett Ryland (1723–92), had named one of his
    sons after his favourite theologian, Herman Witsius (1636–1708), so the younger
    Ryland named one of his sons Jonathan Edwards Ryland. On the younger Ryland,
    see Michael A. G. Haykin, 'John Ryland, Jr.—"O Lord, I Would Delight in Thee":
    The Life and Ministry of John Ryland, Jr. Appreciated on the 250th Anniversary
    of his Birth', *Reformation Today* 196 (Nov.–Dec. 2003), pp. 13–20.
100. *Pastoral Memorials: Selected from the Manuscripts of the Late Revd. John Ryland, D. D. of
    Bristol* (London: B. J. Holdsworth, 1828), vol. 2, pp. 157–158.
101. Ibid., p. 158.
102. For the story of this revival, see Michael A. G. Haykin, *One Heart and One Soul:
    John Sutcliff of Olney, His Friends and His Times* (Darlington: Evangelical, 1994).

however, elements of this community that put up resistance to the renewal. In the nineteenth century they would coalesce into a separate denomination, the Strict and Particular Baptists. At the heart of their opposition to their fellow Baptists Bebbington sees a loyalty to Puritan divinity and a rejection of the culture of the Enlightenment. The struggle within the Particular Baptist communion is thus understood as a clash of cultures.[103]

Ryland, Fuller and their friends, though, saw in their theological opponents an exaggerated form of Calvinism, which was actually unfaithful to the heritage of the Puritans. Their own rediscovery of an evangelical Calvinist tradition that reached back into the heart of the Puritan era (a rediscovery in which the writings of Jonathan Edwards played a key role) brought about theological renewal, which in turn led to 'a rediscovery of mission and the creation of organisations for the fulfilment of mission'.[104] This revival in the Baptist community was ultimately as profound a quickening as took place half a century or so earlier under the leadership of men like Whitefield and the Wesley brothers. And when those involved in it reflected on why it had taken place, they came up with an answer that some historians in the early twenty-first-century marketplace might reject out of hand, but which an evangelical historian can never fail to consider: it was none other than the work of God, an outpouring of the Holy Spirit.[105] F. A. Cox (1783–1853), a junior member of the circle around Fuller, looked back in his old age at what had taken place and remarked that 'copious showers of blessing from *on high* have been poured forth upon the Churches'.[106] It was a reason that earlier evangelicals like Edwards and Whitefield would have understood well.

Conclusion

There seems little doubt that eighteenth-century evangelicalism shared a goodly number of its culture's assumptions and that this cross-fertilization enabled

---

103. *Evangelicalism in Modern Britain*, pp. 55–57.

104. L. G. Champion, 'Evangelical Calvinism and the Structures of Baptist Church Life', *Baptist Quarterly* 28 (1979–80), pp. 196–197.

105. For further discussion of this point, see Tom J. Nettles, 'Iain H. Murray, *Revival and Revivalism*: A Review Article', *Baptist Review of Theology* 6.1 (spring 1996), pp. 67–79.

106. *History of the Baptist Missionary Society: From 1792 to 1842*, 2 vols. (London: T. Ward; G. & J. Dyer, 1842), vol. 1, pp. 10–11 (italics added).

evangelicals to communicate tellingly to their contemporaries. Recognition of evangelicalism's acceptance of Enlightenment ideals means that Bebbington is right to distinguish evangelicals from their Puritan predecessors. Yet, as we have seen with regard to Puritan and evangelical evangelistic activity and the doctrine of assurance, there is also a great deal of continuity between Puritanism and evangelicalism.[107] As Charles Hambrick-Stowe has pointed out in a study of evangelicalism's usage of Puritan literature, eighteenth-century evangelicals consciously sought 'to encourage the spiritual awakening and to channel it along lines congruent with the basic tenets of seventeenth-century Puritanism'. Their movement thus 'embodied tradition as well as innovation'.[108]

If the origin of evangelicalism cannot be located in a new attitude towards assurance engendered by the Enlightenment, as Bebbington claims, what then is its ultimate source? The 'mysterious suddenness' of the revival, the way that it came almost simultaneously to widely separated geographical regions of transatlantic British society, the huge crowds that gathered to listen to the preaching of the Word, the remarkable ministry of Whitefield, and the 'striking conversions' led many during the eighteenth century to view it as an outpouring of the Spirit of God. Some historians today would shy away from citing this as a way of distinguishing evangelicalism from Puritanism and would argue that this is a theological assertion that goes beyond legitimate historical analysis. But given our post-Enlightenment context, such a refusal to engage in theological reflection on the part of the historian no longer seems to carry the weight it once did when historical analysis was ruled by 'the canons of modernity'.[109]

© Michael A. G. Haykin, 2008

---

107. Bebbington does acknowledge the 'substantial legacy' that evangelicalism owed to Puritanism: *Evangelicalism in Modern Britain*, pp. 34–35.

108. 'The Spirit of the Old Writers: The Great Awakening and the Persistence of Puritan Piety', in Francis J. Bremer (ed.), *Puritanism: Transatlantic Perspectives on a Seventeenth-Century Anglo-American Faith* (Boston: Massachusetts Historical Society, 1993), pp. 280, 291.

109. For a similar conclusion, see Donald M. MacDonald, 'Book Reviews: *Evangelicalism in Modern Britain*. D. W. Bebbington', *Monthly Record* (Aug. 1992), p. 179. For the phrase 'canons of modernity', I am indebted to Stanley, 'Christian Missions and the Enlightenment', in Stanley, *Christian Missions and the Enlightenment*, p. 20.

PART 2: REGIONAL PERSPECTIVES

3. EVANGELICALISM IN SCOTLAND FROM KNOX TO CUNNINGHAM

A. T. B. McGowan

Introduction

I read Professor David Bebbington's volume *Evangelicalism in Modern Britain: A History from the 1730s to the 1980s* very soon after its initial release. I remember being tremendously impressed by the book and having a sense that I was part of an evangelical movement much wider and more significant than I had previously imagined. I learned a great deal about evangelicalism and was (and am) very grateful to Professor Bebbington for the book. There were, however, three things that troubled me then and still trouble me now. First, I found it difficult to accept that evangelicalism began in the middle of the eighteenth century. Second, I thought that an altogether too positive view of the Enlightenment was painted, with evangelicalism seemingly indebted to the Enlightenment for its origin. Third, I struggled with the author's analysis of the doctrine of assurance. It is these three concerns that I intend to address in this chapter.

The reason why I have these three concerns relates to my understanding of the history and theology of Scottish Presbyterianism. My chapter might be summarized in the following terms: first, I believe that there is an unbroken line of evangelicalism from John Knox (c. 1514–72) to William Cunningham (1805–61); second, I believe that the Enlightenment damaged evangelicalism in Scotland and elsewhere, rather than creating or promoting it; and third,

I believe that the doctrine of assurance in Scottish theology is more complex and more nuanced than Professor Bebbington allows. Now clearly it is not possible in one short chapter to analyse three hundred years of Scottish theology properly, but I hope to do enough to persuade you that my core argument is well founded.

The chapter is broken down into four sections. First, a very brief introductory section in which I highlight Professor Bebbington's definition of evangelicalism and his argument concerning its origins. Second, the main section of the chapter, examining representative theologians, documents and controversies from Scottish church history, in order to substantiate the argument for continuity of evangelicalism from 1560 to 1860. Third, an analysis of Professor Bebbington's key argument about the doctrine of assurance. Fourth, a short concluding section, summarizing the evidence and, on the basis of the evidence, challenging Professor Bebbington's thesis.

Professor Bebbington's thesis

Given that most of the chapters in this collection re-examine Professor Bebbington's core thesis, it is not necessary for each chapter to go over the same ground by providing a summary and analysis of that thesis. In order that this chapter might be read without full reference to the other chapters, however, let me summarize the specific points of the thesis, which is necessary for an understanding of this chapter.

Professor Bebbington argues that evangelicalism began in the middle of the eighteenth century and that the movement is characterized by four features. It is *biblicist, conversionist, cruciform* and *activist*. Fundamentally, I have no major disagreement with this list, except to make two general points, namely that equal weight cannot be accorded to each characteristic and that other characteristics might well have justified inclusion. I say this because it seems to me that activism, for example, is not nearly so crucial to a definition of evangelicalism as is conversionism. Also, other characteristics of evangelicalism as a movement, such as piety, prayer meetings, concern for Israel and so on, might well have been added. Nevertheless, for the purposes of this chapter, I shall accept these four characteristics and indeed shall use them as a template for the argument that Scottish Presbyterianism from 1560 to 1860 can be classified as evangelicalism.

Professor Bebbington also argues that a changed understanding of the doctrine of assurance, largely brought about by the Enlightenment, was an important factor in the creation of evangelicalism. He insists that this 'newly enhanced' doctrine of the assurance of salvation was a major factor in John

Wesley's experience and that the 'dynamism of the Evangelical movement was possible only because its adherents were assured in their faith'.[1] He argues that, whereas the Puritans believed that assurance followed saving faith, evangelicalism held assurance to be of the essence of the faith. I disagree with this analysis, both in terms of its understanding of the Enlightenment and its doctrine of assurance, as will become apparent below.

Evangelicalism in Scottish theology, 1560–1860

In this main section of the chapter, I want to demonstrate that from the time of the Scottish Reformation until the time of William Cunningham there was agreement and continuity on those marks that Professor Bebbington regards as descriptive, and indeed definitive, of evangelicalism.

We shall now consider each of Professor Bebbington's four characteristics. In each case, we shall begin with the Scots Confession before considering sample writers from each period thereafter until Cunningham.[2]

Evangelicalism emphasizes the Bible

Professor Bebbington rightly insists that the authority of the Bible is of central importance for evangelicals. It can easily be demonstrated, of course, that the Reformers held this view long before the eighteenth-century evangelicals. The Reformation is usually reckoned to have begun on 31 October 1517 when Martin Luther nailed his ninety-five theses to the Castle Church door in Wittenberg. He did so only after serious and prolonged study of the Scriptures. It was the rediscovery of the teaching of the Scriptures which provided the dynamic for all that followed, including the conviction that the authority of Scripture was supreme and that no human writing, no decision of a church council, not even

---

1. D. W. Bebbington, *Evangelicalism in Modern Britain: A History from the 1730s to the 1980s* (London: Unwin Hyman, 1989), p. 42.
2. Several books useful for a study of this nature cover the period in question, in whole or in part. They include James Walker, *The Theology and Theologians of Scotland 1560–1750* (Edinburgh: Knox, 1982); John Macleod, *Scottish Theology in Relation to Church History* (Edinburgh: Knox; Edinburgh: Banner of Truth, 1974); James Kirk, *Patterns of Reform: Continuity and Change in the Reformation Kirk* (Edinburgh: T. & T. Clark, 1989); Thomas McCrie, *The Story of the Scottish Church* (Edinburgh: Free Presbyterian, 1988); and J. H. S. Burleigh, *A Church History of Scotland* (London: Oxford University Press, 1960).

a papal bull, could be accepted if Scripture taught otherwise. The Reformation was further advanced when Calvin, again after serious and prolonged study of the Scriptures, wrote his *Institutes of the Christian Religion*. It should be no surprise, then, to learn that a strong conviction about the authority of the Scriptures was at the heart of the Reformation in Scotland also.

The Scots Confession, chapter 19, is entitled 'The Authority of the Scriptures'. Here is the statement it makes:

> As we believe and confess the Scriptures of God sufficient to instruct and make perfect the man of God, so do we affirm and avow their authority to be from God, and not to depend on men or angels. We affirm, therefore, that those who say the Scriptures have no other authority save that which they have received from the Kirk are blasphemous against God and injurious to the true Kirk, which always hears and obeys the voice of her own Spouse and Pastor, but takes not upon her to be mistress over the same.

In the previous chapter, the writers had already affirmed their convictions regarding 'the written Word of God, that is, the Old and New Testaments, in those books which were originally reckoned as canonical'. These convictions include the following:

> We affirm that in these all things necessary to be believed for the salvation of man are sufficiently expressed. The interpretation of Scripture, we confess, does not belong to any private or public person, nor yet to any Kirk for pre-eminence or precedence, personal or local, which it has above others, but pertains to the Spirit of God by whom the Scriptures were written. When controversy arises about the right understanding of any passage or sentence of Scripture, or for the reformation of any abuse within the Kirk of God, we ought not so much to ask what men have said or done before us, as what the Holy Ghost uniformly speaks within the body of the Scriptures and what Christ Jesus himself did and commanded. For it is agreed by all that the Spirit of God, who is the Spirit of unity, cannot contradict himself. So if the interpretation or opinion of any theologian, Kirk, or council, is contrary to the plain Word of God written in any other passage of the Scripture, it is most certain that this is not the true understanding and meaning of the Holy Ghost, although councils, realms, and nations have approved and received it. We dare not receive or admit any interpretation which is contrary to any principal point of our faith, or to any other plain text of Scripture, or to the rule of love.

This is certainly clear enough, but it was not only in these statements that they emphasized their convictions regarding the authority of Scripture—they

did so by their very theological method itself. When the Confession was published, the writers gave an undertaking that if anyone disputed any part of
what they had written, they would provide an answer from Scripture or would
change the part under question.[3]

John Knox himself insisted that the Scriptures were 'infallible'[4] and that the
promises of God contained in the Scriptures are infallible.[5] Elsewhere he speaks
of God's 'blessed, holy, and infallible word'.[6] Shortly before the Reformation,
Knox was tried and condemned by the Scottish Catholic bishops. In response,
he issued 'The Appellation', in which he insisted that he could provide scriptural evidence for all that he had said and done. In the course of this, he argued
that no doctor of the church should be given greater authority than Augustine,
who had insisted that 'if he plainly proves not his affirmation by God's infallible word, that then his sentence be rejected, and imputed to the error of a
man'.[7] In a letter to the Queen Dowager he argued that God had spoken 'by
his only Son . . . and after that by his Holy Spirit, speaking in his apostles'.[8]
For this reason, no one should add or take away from Scripture and no one
should introduce 'inventions' into religion that do not come from God. He
holds this point to be 'chief and principal'.[9] In the same letter he urges that
his own teaching be judged by the final authority of Scripture. He writes, 'Lay
the book of God before your eyes, and let it be judge to that which I say.'[10]
Knox throughout his writings insisted on the authority of God speaking in the
Scriptures, arguing that the message of Scripture, which he calls 'God's book',
is not to be judged by the quality of the preacher who brings it but 'shall be
held so constant and so true, as though God from the heavens had given witness to the same by the presence of his own majesty'.[11]

We could provide a great deal more evidence from Knox's writings on this
matter. For example, the detailed defence of his view that the mass is idolatry was

---

3. Thomas F. Torrance, *Scottish Theology from John Knox to John McLeod Campbell*
    (Edinburgh: T. & T. Clark, 1996), p. 130.

4. John Knox, *Selected Writings of John Knox* (Dallas: Presbyterian Heritage, 1995), p.
    179.

5. Ibid., pp. 202, 209.

6. Ibid., p. 464.

7. Ibid., pp. 530–531.

8. Ibid., p. 453.

9. Ibid.

10. Ibid., p. 465.

11. Ibid., p. 568.

based on Scripture.[12] We could also look at his many sermons and see the way in which he expounds Scripture, giving it the highest place. He even argues that, just as God is immutable, so is his word.[13] All of this is underlined in a couple of sentences from his work 'A Brief Exhortation to England'. This was written shortly after the death of Queen (Bloody) Mary and in it Knox calls the nation of England to repentance. In the course of this, he writes, 'Let God's word alone be the rule and line to measure his religion. What it commands, let that be obeyed; what it commands not, let that be execrable, because it has not the sanctification of his word, under what name or title soever it is published.'[14]

It must not be thought, however, that Knox simply saw the Bible as ammunition for theological arguments. Like any evangelical, he stressed the need to feed upon 'God's holy word' day by day in order to grow spiritually, noting that it is the 'bread of life'.[15] Perhaps the most moving example of this is a sermon he preached entitled 'A Most Wholesome Counsel', subtitled 'How to Behave ourselves in the Midst of This Wicked Generation, Touching the Daily Exercise of God's Most Holy and Sacred Word'.[16] No modern evangelistic treatise on the importance of daily reading of Scripture and prayer comes close to the power and urgency with which Knox addresses these questions. This is a sample of what we find here:

> And therefore, dear brethren, if that ye look for a life to come, of necessity it is that ye exercise yourselves in the book of the Lord your God. Let no day slip over without some comfort received from the mouth of God. Open your ears and He will speak, even pleasing things to your heart.[17]

He goes on to urge not only private devotions but also family prayers and 'assemblies of brethren' gathered for the purpose. On a practical note he encourages wide reading, combining readings in both Old and New Testaments, 'for it shall greatly comfort you, to hear that harmony and well-tuned song of the Holy Spirit'.[18]

---

12. Ibid., p. 21.

13. Ibid., pp. 307, 309.

14. Ibid., p. 595.

15. Ibid., p. 562.

16. John Knox, *Select Practical Writings of John Knox* (Edinburgh: Free Church of Scotland, 1845), pp. 173–180.

17. Ibid., p. 177.

18. Ibid., p. 179.

So much for John Knox; but those who followed him were of a similar mind in respect of the authority of the Scriptures. Robert Bruce (c. 1554–1631) was a young protégé of Andrew Melville and ultimately became Minister of Edinburgh (St Giles). His most famous legacy is his sermons on the Lord's Supper, which, as Iain Torrance notes, 'brought together Reformed doctrine and evangelical application in a way that helped to shape and become characteristic of the Scottish Reformed tradition'.[19] These sermons, first published in 1590, are full of Scripture and breathe a spirit of evangelical enthusiasm for God's holy Word.[20]

If we move on from the end of the sixteenth century into the seventeenth century, we soon encounter one of the giants of Scottish theology, Samuel Rutherford (1600–61). He too embraced a high view of the authority of Scripture, as is evidenced by his theological writings, by the way he used Scripture as a pastoral tool in his many letters and, perhaps above all, by his contributions to the discussions in the Westminster Assembly. The work of the Assembly owed a disproportionate amount to the Scottish commissioners, even though they were so few in number and had no voting rights. The *Minutes of the Assembly* bear witness to Rutherford's role in the writing of the Westminster Confession of Faith.

The Westminster Confession of Faith, once completed, was approved by the Church of Scotland in 1647. It begins with a chapter on Scripture. We are told that the former ways in which God revealed himself have now ceased and that the Scriptures have been given to us by God that we might have knowledge of God. The canonical books are named, the Apocrypha are specifically excluded and we are told that no other writings have similar authority. Indeed, the Confession goes on to affirm that even the authority by which we believe the Scriptures to be true comes from God and not from the church. There may be many reasons for believing them but ultimately the only reason is the inner testimony of the Holy Spirit, who persuades us of their truth. All that we need to know is written in the Scriptures and nothing is to be added to them. The Scriptures have a perspicuity and if there is any question of interpretation, Scripture should be compared with Scripture, the final judge in all controversy over their meaning being the Holy Spirit himself. It is hard to imagine a stronger

---

19. 'Robert Bruce', in Nigel M. de S. Cameron et al. (eds.), *Dictionary of Scottish Church History & Theology* (Edinburgh: T. & T. Clark, 1993), pp. 104–105.

20. John Laidlaw (ed. and trans.), *Robert Bruce's Sermons on the Sacrament* (Edinburgh: Oliphant, Anderson & Ferrier, 1901).

statement of what Professor Bebbington calls 'biblicism' than this confessional statement.

The year before the General Assembly of the Church of Scotland adopted the Confession, a young man by the name of Hugh Binning (1627–53) began his divinity studies. He went on to become one of the most distinguished ministers of the Church of Scotland, with significant influence at court as well as in the Kirk. After his death, some of Binning's works were published, including a catechetical work entitled *The Common Principles of the Christian Religion clearly Proved and singularly Improved, or a Practical Catechism.*[21]

In the course of this catechism, Binning preached a sermon on 2 Timothy 3:16 that holds to the same high view of Scripture articulated in the Westminster Confession of Faith. Like Calvin before him, he insists that our human reason is insufficient to enable us to find a way out of our fallen condition; hence God has given a revelation of himself and his purposes in Scripture. The authority of the Scriptures is to be accepted because 'they are given by divine inspiration'.[22] He spells out his understanding of this in some detail:

> God by his Spirit, as it were, acted the part of the soul, in the prophets and apostles; and they did no more but utter what the Spirit conceived. The Holy Ghost inspired the matter and the words, and they were but tongues and pens to speak and write it unto the people; there needed no debate, no search in their own minds for the truth, no inquisition for light, but light shined upon their souls so brightly, so convincingly, that it put it beyond all question, that it was the mind and voice of God.[23]

It is clear from the remainder of the sermon and from other sermons, that Binning held consistently to this high view of Scripture.

If we move on from the middle of the seventeenth century to the beginning of the eighteenth, we encounter the writings of the famous Thomas Boston (1676–1732). He too preached a significant sermon on 2 Timothy 3:16, entitled 'The Divine Authority of the Scriptures'.[24] He asserts that the Scriptures were 'said to be of divine inspiration, because the writers were inspired by the

---

21. James Cochrane (ed.), *The Works of the Rev. Hugh Binning*, vol. 1 (Edinburgh: William Whyte, 1839).

22. Ibid., p. 30.

23. Ibid.

24. Samuel M'Millan (ed.), *The Complete Works of the Late Rev. Thomas Boston, Ettrick*, 12 vols. (London: William Tegg, 1853), vol. 1, pp. 19–37.

Spirit, who guided their hearts and pens; he dictated and they wrote; so that it is his word and not theirs; and that is extended to the whole Scriptures'.[25] He expands on this by saying that 'The spirit of Christ drew the testament, dictating it to the holy penman.'[26] And again, 'But the principal author is the Holy Spirit, whence the scripture is called the Word of God. The penmen were but the instruments in the hand of God in writing the same. It was the Spirit that dictated them, that inspired the writers and guided them.'[27] Boston is also very specific as to the implications of this inspiration for the accuracy of the Scriptures:

> By this inspiration all of them were infallibly guided, so as they were put beyond all possibility of erring. And this inspiration was extended not only to the things themselves expressed, but to the words wherein they were expressed, though agreeable to the natural style and manner of each writer . . .[28]

In many other sermons, Boston expresses himself in similar vein. Quite apart from these specific references, however, we see in his exegetical and hermeneutical method a clear commitment to a high view of Scripture. This is also evidenced by his well-known but not well-founded argument for the inspiration of the Hebrew accents.

If we move on fifty years or so to the end of the eighteenth century, we can consult the writings of John Brown of Haddington (1722–87). Here too we see the same 'biblicism' we have seen from Knox onwards, notably in his *Systematic Theology*.[29] Chapter 3 of that work is entitled 'Of the Revealed Standard of Religion Contained in the Scriptures of the Old and New Testament, in its Possibility, Desirableness, Necessity, Propriety, Reasonableness, Credibility, Divine Authority, and Contents'.[30] His comments are very similar to Boston's, noting that the mind of God

> comes to us by the inspiration of the Holy Ghost on the penmen of the Scriptures, which infallibly taught them what they knew not before, rendered the knowledge they

---

25. Ibid., p. 19.

26. Ibid., p. 20.

27. Ibid., p. 22.

28. Ibid.

29. Joel R. Beeke and Randall J. Pederson (eds.), *The Systematic Theology of John Brown of Haddington* (Fearn: Christian Focus, 2002).

30. Ibid., pp. 39–98.

had of divine things absolutely certain, and directed them to proper words, to express their conceptions of them. While he allowed them the use of their own language and natural abilities, he instructed and directed them in a manner which transcended them.[31]

Coming finally to William Cunningham (1805–61), we find in his *Theological Lectures* adequate proof that he stood side by side with those who had gone before him, in stressing the vital importance of a high view of the authority of Scripture.[32] Here several hundred pages deal with the canon of Scripture, inspiration, hermeneutics, problems and difficulties and so on.

Were it necessary we could also adduce evidence from a younger contemporary of Cunningham, Hugh Martin (1822–85), who wrote two pamphlets on biblical inspiration in opposition to the views of Marcus Dods. I have, however, surely done enough to justify the view that, at least on this first distinctive of evangelicalism, those in the Scottish Presbyterian tradition from 1560 to 1860 were at least as committed to a high view of Scripture as the men of the eighteenth-century evangelical revival.

Evangelicalism emphasizes conversion
Once again, we begin with the Scots Confession. In chapter 3, 'Original Sin', we find the following statement, with its strong emphasis on the new birth:

> By this transgression, generally known as original sin, the image of God was utterly defaced in man, and he and his children became by nature hostile to God, slaves to Satan, and servants to sin. And thus everlasting death has had, and shall have, power and dominion over all who have not been, are not, or shall not be born from above. This rebirth is wrought by the power of the Holy Ghost creating in the hearts of God's chosen ones an assured faith in the promise of God revealed to us in his Word; by this faith we grasp Christ Jesus with the graces and blessings promised in him.

This is underlined by the mention of regeneration in chapter 13, 'The Cause of Good Works', where we read, 'For as soon as the Spirit of the Lord Jesus, whom God's chosen children receive by true faith, takes possession of the heart of any man, so soon does he regenerate and renew him, so that he begins to hate what before he loved, and to love what he hated before.'

John Knox, in his own writings, takes a similar line to the Scots Confession, as we would expect, and often emphasizes the need for true, individual

---

31. Ibid., p. 70.

32. William Cunningham, *Theological Lectures* (Greenville, S. C.: A Press, 1990).

conversion to God.[33] Interestingly, Knox also views conversion and repentance as matters requiring a national response. In his 'Brief Exhortation' to England, which I mentioned above, he writes, 'I thought it my duty (in few words) to require of you, and that in God's name, O England in general, the same repentance and true conversion unto God that I have required of those to whom before particularly I wrote.'[34]

Robert Bruce's sermons on the sacraments are concerned to ensure that those who come to the table are truly Christians, with many warnings and entreaties about the danger of communicating while not in a state of grace. Samuel Rutherford, in common with those who had gone before and those who would come after, taught that conversion is vital and that it involves transformation. He writes, 'Our believing and conversion to God doth alter and change our state before God.'[35] He describes this change in some detail, noting that before conversion a sinner is

> an unbeliever, a child of wrath, one that is disobedient, serving divers lusts; a soul unwashed, polluted in his blood before his conversion to God: but once being converted, and graced to believe, his state before God is altered and changed, even in the court of heaven; in the Lord's books he is another man, he goeth now for a fair and undefiled soul.[36]

The great desire to see men and women converted to God runs through Rutherford's writings, not least as evidenced by his personal dealings with people, by his pastoral letters and especially by his sermons. He is, however, very careful to set his understanding of conversion in the context of his wider theology, and to reject what he regards as false understandings. For Rutherford, 'Conversion is a gospel blessing, and so, must be wrought in a way suitable to the scope of the gospel.'[37] As a Calvinist he was clear that 'the promises of the gospel are not simply universal, as if God intended and purposed, that all and every one should be actually redeemed and saved in Christ, as Arminians teach'.[38]

---

33. Knox, *Selected Writings*, pp. 535, 558.
34. Ibid., p. 581.
35. Samuel Rutherford, *The Trial and Triumph of Faith* (Edinburgh: General Assembly of the Free Church of Scotland, 1845), p. 356.
36. Ibid.
37. Ibid., p. 149.
38. Ibid., pp. 151–152.

David Dickson (1583–1663) and James Durham (1622–58) in their *Sum of Saving Knowledge* outline the blessings which God pours out on believers, including that of conversion. They write, 'He doth convert or regenerate them, by giving spiritual life to them, in opening their understandings, renewing their wills, affections, and faculties, for giving spiritual obedience to his commands.'[39]

The Westminster Confession of Faith does not have a specific section on regeneration or conversion but deals with these subjects in its chapter on effectual calling:

> I. All those whom God hath predestinated unto life, and those only, He is pleased, in His appointed time, effectually to call, by His Word and Spirit, out of that state of sin and death, in which they are by nature to grace and salvation, by Jesus Christ; enlightening their minds spiritually and savingly to understand the things of God, taking away their heart of stone, and giving unto them an heart of flesh; renewing their wills, and, by His almighty power, determining them to that which is good, and effectually drawing them to Jesus Christ: yet so, as they come most freely, being made willing by His grace.[40]

Thomas Boston was clear about the vital necessity of regeneration. He writes, 'We have been once born sinners: we must be born again that we may be saints.'[41] Later he says, 'Regeneration is absolutely necessary to qualify you for heaven. None go to heaven but those who are meet for it.'[42] He makes the point very strongly when he writes, 'There is an infallible connexion between a finally unregenerate state and damnation, arising from the nature of things themselves; and from the decree of heaven which is fixed and immovable . . .'[43] Boston states his position thus: 'All men in the state of grace are born again. All gracious persons, namely such as are in favour with God, and endowed with gracious qualities and dispositions, are regenerate persons.'[44] Having stated that there are many who appear to be regenerate but are not and that there are many foolishly depending upon membership in the church for their salvation, Boston writes, 'in regeneration nature itself is changed, and we become

39. John Walter Ross (ed.), *Westminster Confession of Faith & Etc* (Edinburgh: Free Presbyterian, 1981), p. 325.
40. Westminster Confession of Faith, ch. 10.
41. M'Millan, *Thomas Boston*, vol. 8, p. 138.
42. Ibid., p. 172.
43. Ibid., p. 175.
44. Ibid., p. 139.

partakers of the divine nature; and this must needs be a supernatural change. How can we, who are dead in trespasses and sins, renew ourselves, any more than a dead man can raise himself out of his grave?'[45] Boston spells out the nature and consequences of regeneration in some detail.[46] Some sixty years later we find almost identical sentiments in the *Systematic Theology* of John Brown of Haddington, in his sections on union with Christ and effectual calling.[47] This was also the position of the Free Church of Scotland, established in 1843, and of which Cunningham was a distinguished Professor of Theology.

Evangelicalism emphasizes the cross

The Scots Confession devotes chapter 9 to 'Christ's Death, Passion, and Burial'. Here is the text of that statement:

> That our Lord Jesus offered himself a voluntary sacrifice unto his Father for us, that he suffered contradiction of sinners, that he was wounded and plagued for our transgressions, that he, the clean innocent Lamb of God, was condemned in the presence of an earthly judge, that we should be absolved before the judgment seat of our God; that he suffered not only the cruel death of the cross, which was accursed by the sentence of God; but also that he suffered for a season the wrath of his Father which sinners had deserved. But yet we avow that he remained the only, well beloved, and blessed Son of his Father even in the midst of his anguish and torment which he suffered in body and soul to make full atonement for the sins of his people. From this we confess and avow that there remains no other sacrifice for sin; if any affirm so, we do not hesitate to say that they are blasphemers against Christ's death and the ever-lasting atonement thereby purchased for us.

It is difficult to imagine a clearer statement on the centrality of the death of Christ on the cross for Christian theology. This clarity extends to the writings of Knox himself. For example, in opposition to the mass, Knox affirms the once-for-all-sacrifice of Christ on the cross,[48] insisting that only the 'eternal blood of the eternal Son of God' can take away our sins.[49] He says in one place that he would deserve damnation for his sins 'unless pardon should be granted

---

45. Ibid., p. 142.
46. See A. T. B. McGowan, *The Federal Theology of Thomas Boston* (Carlisle: Paternoster, 1997), pp. 92–122.
47. Beeke and Pederson, *John Brown*, pp. 336–358.
48. Knox, *Selected Writings*, pp. 48–49.
49. Ibid., p. 53.

to me in Christ's blood'.[50] Elsewhere, he speaks of the 'free justification which comes by faith in his blood'.[51]

In respect of the cross, Knox affirms that Christ died once for all and may die no more, having conquered death. He 'lives, and death may not prevail against him'.[52] He describes Christ as our Mediator[53] and as the 'only Saviour'.[54] He also anticipates aspects of a later, more developed Reformed theology, when he says that 'by Christ Jesus alone we have received whatsoever was lost in Adam'.[55] Even in the detailed spelling out of his atonement theology he uses language identical to that of later evangelicals, such as propitiation and redemption.[56] He also speaks of Christ's death as a sufficient sacrifice.[57] Can anyone who has read Robert Bruce doubt the centrality of Christ in his thinking, evidenced in statements like the following?

> Learn to apply Christ rightly to thy soul and thou hast won all; thou art a great theologian, if thou hast learned this well: for in the right application of Christ to the sick soul, to the wounded conscience, and diseased heart, here begins the fountain of all our felicity, and the well-spring of all our joy.[58]

Samuel Rutherford uses many expressions in his sermons to emphasize the centrality of the cross and his understanding of its significance. In a sermon dealing *inter alia* with Romans 8:1, he quotes, 'There is no condemnation to them that are in Christ Jesus,' and speaks of Christ as a 'surety' who has 'given a ransom', which he later calls the 'ransom of Christ's atonement of his dear blood'. Faith must lay hold on this ransom and thus will be freed from eternal punishment. In the same sermon, he speaks of Christ as having 'made a sufficient atonement for all that believe'.[59] The next sermon in the series deals with the non-imputation of sin and the imputation of Christ's righteousness.[60]

---

50. Ibid., p. 229.
51. Ibid., p. 351.
52. Ibid., p. 56.
53. Ibid., pp. 85–90.
54. Ibid., p. 543.
55. Ibid.
56. Ibid., p. 355.
57. Ibid., p. 473.
58. Laidlaw, *Robert Bruce's Sermons*, p. 71.
59. Rutherford, *Trial and Triumph of Faith*, pp. 214–215.
60. Ibid., pp. 217–247.

Hugh Binning, one of Rutherford's younger contemporaries, once preached a sermon on 1 Timothy 1:15: 'The saying is trustworthy and deserving of full acceptance, that Christ Jesus came into the world to save sinners . . .' In the course of that sermon he notes that all humanity stood under the sentence of divine justice because of sin, 'a sentence of death and condemnation'.[61] Then he explains how Christ came and was able

> to tread that wine-press of wrath alone, and give his life a ransom, in value far above the soul, and pay the debt of sin that we were owing to God. And, indeed, he was furnished for this purpose, a person suited and fitted for such a work;—a man, to undertake it in our name, and God, to perform it in his own strength;—a man, that he might be made under the law, and be humbled even to the death of the cross, that so he might obey the commandment, and suffer the punishment due to us,—and all this was elevated beyond the worth of created actions or sufferings, by that divine nature. This perfumed all his humanity, and all done by it, or in it. This puts the stamp of divinity upon all, and imposed an infinite value upon the coin of finite obedience and sufferings.[62]

The Westminster Confession of Faith has an excellent section on the significance of Christ's death on the cross in chapter 8, 'Of Christ the Mediator':

> IV. This office the Lord Jesus did most willingly undertake; which that He might discharge, He was made under the law, and did perfectly fulfil it; endured most grievous torments immediately in His soul, and most painful sufferings in His body; was crucified, and died, was buried, and remained under the power of death, yet saw no corruption. On the third day He arose from the dead, with the same body in which He suffered, with which also he ascended into heaven, and there sits at the right hand of His Father, making intercession, and shall return, to judge men and angels, at the end of the world.

> V. The Lord Jesus, by His perfect obedience, and sacrifice of Himself, which He through the eternal Spirit, once offered up unto God, has fully satisfied the justice of His Father; and purchased, not only reconciliation, but an everlasting inheritance in the kingdom of heaven, for those whom the Father has given unto Him.

---

61. James Cochrane (ed.), *The Works of the Rev Hugh Binning*, 3 vols. (Edinburgh: William Whyte, 1839), vol. 1, p. 251.

62. Ibid., p. 252.

If space permitted, we could consider a fine sermon by Thomas Boston on the humiliation of Christ.[63] No one who reads that sermon could doubt the centrality of the cross in his theology. Similarly, John Brown of Haddington, in the second chapter of book 4 of his *Systematic Theology*, treats the death of Christ in at least as profound and detailed a way as any modern evangelical expositor.[64] Perhaps the finest teaching on the centrality of the cross and the atonement from this later period comes from the pen of Hugh Martin. His volume *The Atonement in its Relations to the Covenant, the Priesthood, the Intercession of our Lord* is a classic.[65] In it, Martin sets the theology of the atonement in the context of covenant theology and opens up the whole heart of Reformed theology.

Evangelicalism emphasizes activism

There are two places in the Scots Confession where we might identify an emphasis upon activism. First, in chapter 14, 'The Works which Are Counted Good before God', we are told that we must live for God and for our neighbours. Then, chapter 25, 'The Gifts Freely Given to the Kirk', speaks of the need to 'speak thy Word with boldness'.

Do I need to speak of the life of John Knox to emphasize that these were not merely words but an expression of his own life of active commitment to seeking the salvation of men and women? The same is true of all the great Scottish divines, not least Samuel Rutherford. One has only to read a good biography of Rutherford to be aware of his activism. His concern for his parishioners of Anwoth, his activities in a most exciting period of the life of the church, his banishment to Aberdeen, his involvement in the great events of 1638 (surely the finest year for a Presbyterian to have been alive in Scotland), his participation in the Westminster Assembly and so on.

The life of Thomas Boston, with his great concern for reaching out to the lost with the message of Christ, surely testifies to the same spirit. Can anyone assert that Boston was less of an activist than Edwards or Wesley, even if his geographical scope was more limited? From Cunningham's era we might single out Thomas Chalmers. Think of all that he achieved in the life of the church, in the care of the poor and so on. It is hard to imagine how the man had time to do all that he did in the service of the kingdom.

---

63. M'Millan, Samuel, *Thomas Boston*, vol. 1, pp. 490–504.

64. Beeke and Pederson, *John Brown*, pp. 280–316.

65. Hugh Martin, *The Atonement* (Edinburgh: Knox, 1976).

The Enlightenment and the doctrine of assurance

Let us now turn from these four distinctive features of evangelicalism and consider the more complex problem of the Enlightenment and how it relates to the doctrine of assurance.

Professor Bebbington regards the Enlightenment as a catalyst for the creation of evangelicalism, but can this stand up to scrutiny? Immanuel Kant's combination of rationalism and idealism into a new philosophical perspective was undoubtedly a powerful agent for change, but the way in which he dealt with religion, through his espousal of the noumenal realm set apart from the phenomenal realm, did more to damage orthodox Christian theology than to support it. Indeed, Schleiermacher, Ritschl, Harnack and Hermann, in their creation of the classic liberal theology, were seeking to respond to Enlightenment philosophy in a way that ensured the continuance of Christianity rather than its demise. They believed themselves bound to accept the prevailing philosophical world view and hence to create a theological system that modified orthodoxy in such a way as to be acceptable to Kantian philosophy. The results of this move were disastrous and we are indebted to Karl Barth and others for the way in which they demonstrated the bankruptcy of the old liberal theology, although it has taken a very long time finally to expire. Barth and Van Til (never the closest of allies) separately came to the same conclusion, namely that orthodox Christian theology cannot be built on any secular philosophy but only on God's revelation to us. The Enlightenment, then, should not be regarded as a positive force for the establishment and strengthening of orthodox, evangelical theology but rather as a period of darkness, leading the church into its greatest departure from its orthodox roots and received theology.

My main focus, of course, is on Scottish theology, but even here the argument for the Enlightenment as a beneficial movement does not appear to stand up. No one is arguing surely that David Hume was a significant force in advancing Christianity! Perhaps, however, it might be argued that the work of Thomas Reid was a significant influence for good. Certainly, the influence of Scottish Realism on American evangelical theology was profound, particularly on the Princetonians, but Reid himself, a Church of Scotland minister, was no evangelical, identifying himself with the Moderate party in the Kirk.

Professor Bebbington's argument, of course, is not that the Enlightenment philosophers and thinkers were themselves evangelicals but that they helped to create a climate for thought and action that permitted and even enabled the establishment of evangelicalism. It does not seem to me, however, that he has presented sufficient evidence to sustain this aspect of his thesis.

Rather, a strong case can be made for saying that the Enlightenment has-tened the advent of secularism and seriously damaged Christianity, including evangelicalism.

If we turn specifically to the doctrine of assurance, we find that once again, Professor Bebbington's argument can be challenged. It can be demonstrated from Scottish theology that there was no change in the doctrine of assurance between the Reformers and the eighteenth century but that assurance has always had two elements: (1) assurance as being of the essence of saving faith and (2) assurance as a reflex act.

The Scots Confession, chapter 13, 'The Cause of Good Works', speaks of the Holy Spirit as bearing witness to our spirit that we are the sons of God. John Knox in 'A Godly Letter of Warning' (1553) urges his readers to seek the mercy and grace of God, and then goes on to assure them of salvation. He writes:

> I am not prejudicial to God's mercies, as that such as repent shall not find grace. No, brethren, this I most assuredly know: in whatsoever hour a sinner shall repent, God shall not remember one of his iniquities; but albeit his offences were as red as scarlet, yet shall they be made as white as snow; and albeit in multitude they were past all number, yet so shall they be blotted out, that none of them shall appear to the condemnation of the truly penitent. For such is his promise, that none truly believing in Jesus Christ shall enter into judgment; for the blood of Jesus Christ, his Son, purges them from all sin, so that how far the heaven is distant from the earth, so far does he remove the sins from the penitent.[66]

Samuel Rutherford argued strongly that assurance of salvation is compat-ible with a sorrow for sin and a bewailing of one's sinful condition. He uses Paul's comments to the Romans as an example and writes:

> Full assurance that Christ hath delivered Paul from condemnation, yea, so full and real, as produceth thanksgiving and triumphing in Christ (Rom., vii, 25, viii, 1, 2) may and doth consist with complaints and outcries of a wretched condition for the indwelling of the body of sin (Rom., vii, 14–16, 23, 24).[67]

The Westminster Confession of Faith has a section on assurance that has occasioned much debate:

---

66. Knox, *Selected Writings*, p. 191.
67. Rutherford, *Trial and Triumph of Faith*, p. 252.

I. Although hypocrites and other unregenerate men may vainly deceive themselves with false hopes and carnal presumptions of being in the favor of God, and estate of salvation (which hope of theirs shall perish): yet such as truly believe in the Lord Jesus, and love Him in sincerity, endeavouring to walk in all good conscience before Him, may, in this life, be certainly assured that they are in the state of grace, and may rejoice in the hope of the glory of God, which hope shall never make them ashamed.

II. This certainty is not a bare conjectural and probable persuasion grounded upon a fallible hope; but an infallible assurance of faith founded upon the divine truth of the promises of salvation, the inward evidence of those graces unto which these promises are made, the testimony of the Spirit of adoption witnessing with our spirits that we are the children of God, which Spirit is the earnest of our inheritance, whereby we are sealed to the day of redemption.

III. This infallible assurance does not so belong to the essence of faith, but that a true believer may wait long, and conflict with many difficulties, before he be partaker of it: yet, being enabled by the Spirit to know the things which are freely given him of God, he may, without extraordinary revelation in the right use of ordinary means, attain thereunto. And therefore it is the duty of every one to give all diligence to make his calling and election sure, that thereby his heart may be enlarged in peace and joy in the Holy Ghost, in love and thankfulness to God, and in strength and cheerfulness in the duties of obedience, the proper fruits of this assurance; so far is it from inclining men to looseness.

IV. True believers may have the assurance of their salvation divers ways shaken, diminished, and intermitted; as, by negligence in preserving of it, by falling into some special sin which wounds the conscience and grieves the Spirit; by some sudden or vehement temptation, by God's withdrawing the light of His countenance, and suffering even such as fear Him to walk in darkness and to have no light: yet are they never so utterly destitute of that seed of God, and life of faith, that love of Christ and the brethren, that sincerity of heart, and conscience of duty, out of which, by the operation of the Spirit, this assurance may, in due time, be revived; and by the which, in the mean time, they are supported from utter despair.[68]

Professor Bebbington's key argument is that there took place a change in the doctrine of assurance in the middle of the eighteenth century and that this was a key transition point, marking the origins of evangelicalism. It is paradoxical

---

68. Westminster Confession of Faith, ch. 18.

that Dr David Lachman also argued for a change in the doctrine of assurance, but he dated it in the middle of the seventeenth century.[69] Not only so but the change for which Lachman argues is precisely the opposite of that for which Bebbington argues! Lachman sought to explain the change between Calvin's apparent view that assurance is of the essence of saving faith, compared with the view of the Puritans, as expressed in the Westminster Confession of Faith (as we have just seen), that assurance follows saving faith and may not come for some long time. In my view, Lachman and Bebbington are both mistaken. There was no change in the doctrine of assurance in Reformed theology. Rather, there were always these two elements to the doctrine, assurance by a direct act of faith and assurance as a reflex act. Different scholars at different times may have put more emphasis on the one than on the other but there was no change. Indeed, the continuity of Reformed scholars on the doctrine of assurance from Calvin through to the eighteenth century divines has been well argued by William Cunningham[70] and Joel Beeke.[71] I have argued against Lachman's position elsewhere,[72] using Thomas Boston as an example of a scholar who held the two aspects of the doctrine of assurance in a healthy tension. In this context it is interesting to remember that Jonathan Edwards, one of Professor Bebbington's core models, spoke of Boston as a 'truly great divine'.[73]

Even if we argue that there was no concrete change in the doctrine of assurance in Reformed theology such as Lachman and Bebbington would maintain, it is certainly appropriate for us to ask why there was a change *in emphasis*. In this regard, I think we have to take seriously Karl Barth's assessment of the position. In his *The Theology of the Reformed Confessions*, he says that there was a change of emphasis between earlier and later Reformed Confessions, the later ones being more self-centred than God-centred. Barth speaks highly of the Scots Confession and expresses astonishment that we Scots would exchange it for the Westminster Confession of Faith. He argues that the Westminster Confession of Faith, through its emphasis on the application of redemption and the quest for assurance, focuses too much on

---

69. David C. Lachman, *The Marrow Controversy 1718–1723: A Historical and Theological Analysis* (Edinburgh: Rutherford House, 1988).

70. William Cunningham, *The Reformers and the Theology of the Reformation* (Edinburgh: Banner of Truth, 1979), pp. 111–148.

71. Joel R. Beeke, *The Quest for Full Assurance* (Edinburgh: Banner of Truth, 1999).

72. McGowan, *Federal Theology of Thomas Boston*, pp. 200–202.

73. Macleod, *Scottish Theology*, p. 146.

anthropology instead of theology.[74] Whether or not we agree with Barth, it is an argument that goes some way to explaining the different emphases at different stages of the development of Reformed theology and is certainly worthy of some careful analysis.

Summary and conclusion

In my view, the evidence does not sustain the argument of Professor Bebbington's thesis. Rather than arguing that evangelicalism began in the eighteenth century as a result of the Enlightenment, a sounder argument would be that the liberal theology created as a direct result of the Enlightenment caused a serious division within Protestant theology such that evangelicalism, which had existed since the Reformation, became more clearly identified as a separate movement. It had existed since the sixteenth century and had represented the mainstream position of orthodox Protestant Christianity for two hundred years. Only when that orthodoxy was challenged did evangelicalism begin to be viewed as a 'new movement'. In other words, I share the continuity arguments presented by Gordon Rupp[75] and G. F. Nuttall,[76] particularly in its more recent expositions by Gary Williams[77] and Kenneth Stewart.[78]

Dare I suggest that perhaps, as an English non-conformist, Professor Bebbington has not given sufficient weight in his studies to the continuity and homogeneity of the evangelicalism of Scottish Presbyterianism since the Reformation of 1560?

© A. T. B. McGowan, 2008

---

74. Karl Barth, *The Theology of the Reformed Confessions* (Louisville: Westminster John Knox, 2002), pp. 150–151.

75. Gordon Rupp, *Religion in England (1688–1791)* (Oxford: Clarendon, 1986).

76. G. F. Nuttall, *Richard Baxter and Philip Doddridge: A Study in a Tradition* (London: Oxford University Press, 1951).

77. Garry J. Williams, 'Was Evangelicalism Created by the Enlightenment?', *Tyndale Bulletin* 53.2 (2002), pp. 283–312 (reprinted in this volume, ch. 15, under the title 'Enlightenment Epistemology and Eighteenth-Century Evangelical Doctrines of Assurance').

78. Kenneth J. Stewart, 'Did Evangelicalism Predate the Eighteenth Century? An Examination of David Bebbington's Thesis', *Evangelical Quarterly* 77.2 (Apr. 2005), pp. 135–153.

4. CONTINUITY, NOVELTY AND EVANGELICALISM IN WALES, C. 1640–1850

D. Densil Morgan

The terminology of evangelicalism

The earliest mention of the adjective 'evangelical' in Welsh occurs in a work entitled *Yr Ymarfer o Dduwioldeb* (1632), a translation made by Rowland Vaughan (c. 1590–1667), the royalist squire and churchman of Caer-gai, Merionethshire,[1] of Bishop Lewis Bayly's (d. 1631) phenomenally popular *Practice of Piety*. This handbook of practical spirituality moulded generations of Anglican Christians before, during and beyond the tempestuous decades of the English Civil War and the Restoration. 'Evangelical' was used again by an equally staunch High Church Anglican, John Langford (c. 1650 to c. 1716), in his *Holl Ddeledswydd Dyn* (1672), a translation of Richard Allstree's *The Whole Duty of Man*. Like Lewis Bayly, Allstree had been an Anglican dignitary, a clergyman and, after the Restoration, Regius Professor of Divinity at Oxford, whose piety was more catholic than conversionist and for whom obedience to the precepts of discipleship as laid down in the Book of Common Prayer was a *sine qua non* of a valid Christian faith. Neither of these authors, nor their translators, would

---

1. For biographical details of all major figures mentioned in this chapter, see J. E. Lloyd and R. T. Jenkins (eds.), *Dictionary of Welsh Biography down to 1940* (London: Honourable Society of Cymmrodorion, 1959).

fit comfortably into the category of spirituality that would later come to be known as 'evangelical'.

A more promising line of continuity between the use of the word and later tradition occurs in the eighteenth century with the work of the Independent divine Jeremy Owen (fl. 1704–44), *Traethawd i Brofi ac i Gymell ar yr Holl Eglwysi y Ddyledswydd Fawr Efangylaidd o Weddïo dros Weinidogion* (A Treatise to Prove and to Encourage all the Churches [in] the Great Evangelical Duty of Praying for Ministers) (1733). No translation this, rather a work of graceful originality, its sonorous cadences expressing the high ecclesiology of the Older Dissent at its most solemn and dignified. Yet neither was this quite in the same tradition of evangelicalism as it would evolve after the Methodist Revival. The Older Dissent was too churchly, too cerebral and doctrinally precise to be wholly comfortable with the exuberance and emotionalism of the later movement. It was only when the ribald and boisterous 'Twm o'r Nant', Thomas Edwards (1739–1810), used the word 'evangelical' in one of his 'interludes' or popular plays two generations after Jeremy Owen that its sense was being standardized:

> There is no-one fit for praise or respect
> > Before an evangelical minister of the church.
> (*Nid oes un i'w ganmol na'i berchi'n gymwys*
> > *o flaen efengylaidd weinidog eglwys.*)[2]

By then the word's meaning was beginning to be transmuted from a general description of that which pertained to the Christian gospel to something nearer to the appellation that zealous nineteenth-century Protestants, whether low church Anglicans or activist Nonconformists, used of themselves. For as well as being a playwright and actor, Thomas Edwards was a Methodist whose conversion had given him a fresh appreciation for the Bible, the doctrines of the cross and a zeal to propagate the new values that, along with scores of thousands of his contemporaries, had changed his life. If '[c]onversionism, activism, biblicism and crucicentricism form the defining attributes of Evangelical religion',[3] such a religion was becoming widely accepted in Wales as embodying the essence of true Christianity. When the radical Baptist William Richards berated the Methodists and gospel clergy of the south Wales county

---

2 Twm o'r Nant, *Tri Chryfion Byd* [The World's Three Titans] (1789), ed. Norah Isaac (Llandysul: Gwasg Gomer, 1975), p. 44.

3. D. W. Bebbington, *Evangelicalism in Modern Britain: A History from the 1730s to the 1980s* (London: Unwin Hyman, 1989), p. 4.

of Pembrokeshire for their political quietism in 1798, the noun 'evangelical' was already in use: 'The aim and tendency of the clergy was well known, even that brotherhood among them that is called or nicknamed evangelicals (*y frawdoliaeth honno yn eu mysg a gyfenwir neu a lysenwir yn Efengylwyr*).'[4]

An Enlightenment rationalist and Socinian, Richards was contemptuous of classical Anglicanism, creedal Dissent and Methodist popularism in equal degrees. His ire, though, signified the triumph of a type of religion set to transform Wales startlingly in the decades to come.

Developments to the age of the Evangelical Revival

The Evangelical Revival in Wales is usually dated as having begun with the conversions of Daniel Rowland, curate of Llangeitho, Cardiganshire, and the Anglican layman Howell Harris of Trevecca, Brecknockshire, in the spring of 1735.[5] It was then that a new emphasis in Protestant spirituality, more activist and energetic than previously and very often characterized by the outward phenomena of revivalism, began to take hold. For Lewis Edwards (1809–87), principal of the Calvinistic Methodists' college at Bala, and Wales's premier intellectual of the mid-nineteenth century, the difference between post-Revival religion and the valid Christian piety which had preceded it was that the former, though expressive of a real faith, tended to the moral and cerebral, whereas the latter was directed towards experientialism and the feelings. The tendency of a doctrinally based and morally exacting faith was towards formalism, and this had been a marked characteristic of the Dissenting heirs of the Puritans. 'From a lack of new life, their religion in time tended to comprise of a series of notions in the head rather than feelings in the heart. In consequence it weakened and worsened.'[6] When revival came, it did not so much renew the intellectual content of faith,

---

4. William Richards, *Cwyn y Cystuddiedig a Griddfannau y Carcharorion Dieuog* [The Cry of the Oppressed and the Woe of the Innocent Prisoners] (Carmarthen: Ioan Evans, 1798), p. 20.

5. Eifion Evans, *Daniel Rowland and the Great Evangelical Awakening in Wales* (Edinburgh: Banner of Truth, 1985); Geraint Tudur, *Howell Harris: From Conversion to Separation, 1735–1760* (Cardiff: University of Wales Press, 2000).

6. Lewis Edwards, *Traethawd ar Hanes Duwinyddiaeth y Gwahanol Oesoedd* [An Essay on the History of the Theology of the Different Ages] (Wrexham: R. Hughes, n. d.), p. cxv.

which remained biblical and orthodox, as to ground believers' experience in the doctrines of grace and to animate their feelings. Using the word 'Methodist' as a general term signifying 'evangelical' religion more widely held, Edwards continued:

> It is obvious at once that one thing that the Methodists did was to show that true religion includes feelings, or rather that religion is grounded in the heart and not the head alone. They showed that there was such a thing that they called 'experience', that it was essential, indeed the best part of religion and without it religion ceased to be. They showed that feelings produced actions and that he who had been convicted of his own need was zealous in converting others. All this issued from one single central truth, namely the *internal effect of the work of Christ* or the ministry of the Holy Spirit on the heart. They were brought to believe that every individual needed to be converted and become a completely new creature . . . In a word, whereas the underlying truth of the Protestant Reformation was justification, the underlying truth of the Methodist Revival was regeneration.[7]

Reformation times

As in England, the Welsh brand of the Protestant Reformation can be dated from Henry VIII's breach with Rome. Although the implementation of reform was patchy and its welcome, among the people at large, was initially cool, its real impact was in Elizabeth I's appointment of resident, Welsh-speaking bishops who combined a deep commitment to traditional cultural mores with a zeal for Word-centred reform. The Welsh Prayer Book and New Testament of 1567, translated by Bishop Richard Davies (1510?–81), initially of St Asaph before his move south in 1561 to take charge of the diocese of St Davids, and the Renaissance scholar William Salesbury (1520?–84), and the Welsh Bible of 1588 translated by Bishop William Morgan (1541?–1604) of Llandaff, then of St Asaph, were exceedingly significant for the later development of the nation's life. Although a powerful group of Roman Catholic exiles kept alive the hope of reconverting Wales to the old faith, by the third quarter of the sixteenth century Reformation values had generally been accepted and the people were by then accustomed to the ministrations and liturgy of a Reformed church.[8]

---

7. Ibid., pp. cvvii–cxviii.
8. D. Densil Morgan, 'Welsh Protestantism to the Present Day', in Alister E. McGrath and Darren C. Marks, *The Blackwell Companion to Protestantism* (Oxford: Blackwell, 2004), pp. 120–122.

As scripturally and doctrinally valid as it was, this reformation remained superficial to a degree. The spiritual experience of the generality of the people, as far as we can tell, fell far short of the activism and overt zeal that would characterize the popular Protestantism of the late eighteenth and nineteenth centuries. As Glanmor Williams has said, 'There was still a prevailing tendency for the majority to look upon religion as a body of collective rites practiced by the inhabitants of the parish as a community; activities to a large extent conducted on behalf of the lay folk by their parish priests.'[9]

There is no evidence of lay religion of the Lollard type or of localized spiritual awakenings that would bring the Scriptures alive in an intimate and personal way. Indeed, Wales's sole Elizabethan Puritan, the separatist firebrand John Penry (1563–93), lamented over what he saw as the abject spiritual deadness of the people:

> For our estate is such, that we have not one in some score of our parishes, that have a saving knowledge. Thousands there be of our people that know Jesus Christ to be neither God nor man, king, priest nor prophet . . . The rest of our people are either such as never think of any religion true or false, plainly mere atheists or stark blinded with superstition.[10]

What was required was not more institutional reform but preaching of an awakening kind that would smite the conscience of the people and engender in them vital spiritual life: 'The remedy of this our grievous case is only had . . . by speedy providing unto us such pastors as may feed us with the food of life, the pure Word of God, and bring us home unto the only Lord of pastors, and shepherds, the Lord Jesus.'[11]

Penry's was a lone voice. It was a voice on behalf of Wales rather than one from within Wales. Although he was a native of Brecknockshire, he spent virtually all his adult life in Oxford, Cambridge, London and Scotland, only to be executed for sedition just after Henry Barrow and John Greenwood in 1593. His final words, in his appeal to Lord Burleigh a week before his execution, are an apt summary of his life's aim:

---

9. Glanmor Williams, *Wales and the Reformation* (Cardiff: University of Wales Press, 1997), p. 281.

10. John Penry, *The Aequity of an Humble Supplication unto her Gracious Majesty ... on the Behalf of the Country of Wales* (1578), in David Williams (ed.), *John Penry: Three Treatises Concerning Wales* (Cardiff: University of Wales Press, 1960), p. 32.

11. Ibid., p. 12.

I am a poor young man born and bred in the mountains of Wales. I am the first, since the last springing up of the Gospel in this latter age, that publicly laboured to have the blessed seed thereof sown in these barren mountains . . . And now, being to end my days before I am come to the one half of my years, in the likely course of nature, I leave the success of these my labours unto such of my countrymen as the Lord is to raise up after me.[12]

Yet the Puritans were not the only gospel-based countrymen raised up to labour towards the effective evangelization of Wales. If Penry had moved in a progressively radical direction, from the Anglicanism of his youth to Thomas Cartwright's Presbyterianism learned during his Cambridge days, thereafter from Presbyterianism to Congregationalism and from Congregationalism to separatism, thus repudiating wholly the compact between church and state, there were others who remained faithful to the established church, its ministry, liturgy, parochial and diocesan structures, and sought to make it function as a genuinely Reformed Christian body. For them the classical Reformed churchmanship of the Continent resonated better with Protestant orthodoxy than the stark biblicism of a nascent Presbyterianism. During his sojourn in Frankfort in the 1550s, Wales's leading Anglican reformer of the Elizabethan period, Bishop Richard Davies, had sided with Richard Cox's Anglicans and their polity based on the 1552 Book of Common Prayer rather than with John Knox's anti-Prayer Book Genevans.[13] Although an unyielding reformer and a staunch Protestant, staunch enough to have been forced to flee during Queen Mary's reign, Davies stands at the fountainhead of moderate rather than radical change.

Seventeenth-century developments

By the beginning of the seventeenth century, Richard Hooker's judicious rationale for the 'Ecclesia Anglicana' as a genuinely Reformed church of the middle way between what he regarded as legalistic biblicism on the one hand and the Romanist Antichrist on the other was becoming the characteristic Anglican stance. For Penry's severe biblicism and his harsh critique of the status quo, Rhys Prichard (1579?–1644), vicar of Llandovery, Carmarthenshire, was

---

12. Quoted in D. Williams, *John Penry*, p. xxvi.

13. Glanmor Williams, *Bywyd ac Amserau'r Esgob Richard Davies* [The Life and Times of Bishop Richard Davies] (Cardiff: University of Wales Press, 1953), pp. 16–24; cf. Patrick Collinson, *The Elizabethan Puritan Movement* (Oxford: Clarendon, 1967), pp. 33–34.

content to put Hooker's views into practice in the context of parochial ministry. Prichard's *Canwyll y Cymry* (The Welshpeople's Candle), a collection of easily remembered catechetical poems, grounded generations of unlearned parishioners in biblical morality and gospel truths. For the vicar of Llandovery, the Church of England was both catholic *and* Reformed. Like St Augustine of Hippo and Martin Luther he could happily affirm both baptismal regeneration *and* justification by faith alone; the need for conversion *and* liturgical worship; a personal saving faith *as well as* a Eucharistic theology that was far higher than the Presbyterians and the Congregationalists could ever countenance. Although revered universally by nineteenth-century Nonconformists as a reformer of the truest hue, Rhys Prichard was never technically a Puritan, nor should he be designated as one. His elevation to the chancellorship of St Davids Cathedral by no less an enemy of the Puritans than William Laud,[14] shows this to have been the case. Prichard was rather a Prayer Book Anglican, loyal to the Church Catechism, whose convictions were 'biblically catholic',[15] though (in his eyes) thoroughly Reformed. Apparent anomalies such as these make it difficult to trace an authentic continuity between different stands of Protestantism and the evangelicalism of a later date.

Puritanism, though, of a definite type did root itself in Wales and by the 1640s played a significant part in the nation's religious life. The exertions of such energetic Puritan evangelists and leaders as Walter Cradock (1610?–59), Vavasor Powell (1617–70), Morgan Llwyd (1619–59), John Miles (1621–83), father of the Baptist movement in Wales, and these leaders' revered senior William Wroth (1576–1641), vicar of Llanfaches in Monmouthshire and pastor of the gathered congregation there, 'which afterwards was, like Antioch, the mother church in that gentile country',[16] have been studied exhaustively and

---

14. For Laud's reign as Bishop of St Davids (1621–7), see Charles Carlton, *Archbishop William Laud* (London: Routledge & Kegan Paul, 1987), pp. 29–34.

15. The phrase was first used by D. Gwenallt Jones and remains the most appropriate designation, in D. Gwenallt Jones, *Y Ficer Prichard a 'Canwyll y Cymry'* [The Vicar Prichard and 'the Welshman's Candle'] (n. p.: Church in Wales Press, n. d. [1944?]), p. 42; cf. Nesta Lloyd (ed.), *Cerddi'r Ficer: Detholiad o Gerddi Rhys Prichard* [The Vicar's Poems: A Selection of Rhys Prichard's Verse] (n. p.: Barddas, 1994), 'Introduction'.

16. Anon., *The Life and Death of Mr Henry Jessey* (1671), cited R. Geraint Gruffydd, *'In That Gentile Country': The Beginnings of Puritan Nonconformity in Wales* (Bridgend: Evangelical Library of Wales, 1976), p. 15.

their contribution recognized widely.[17] Both the evangelical Nonconformists of the nineteenth century and, more surprisingly, the Calvinistic Methodists, whose roots were very definitely not in Puritan Dissent but in central Anglican churchmanship, looked back to the Puritans with a pride and admiration that affirmed a putative, if spirited, continuity with them. All of the characteristics of Puritan doctrine and polity are patent in the Welsh Puritans' works: the preaching of a particular, Calvinistic redemption, a morphology of conversion that includes a minute analysis of the workings of the awakened soul, a refusal to countenance the use of unnecessary externals in worship, the rejection of (even hallowed) tradition as a means of ordering the church, and a somewhat stern moralism. The Welsh Puritans were not devoid of pragmatism and were keen, on the whole, to perpetuate the link between church and state now that, under Cromwell, the church could be radically reformed along congregation-alist lines and the state was a godly commonwealth governed by the saints. Yet their main aim was effectively to spread the Pauline gospel and by so doing bring about a wholesale renewal throughout the land. The charismatic reviv-alism that sometimes accompanied their labours was strikingly described by Walter Cradock in a sermon before Parliament in 1648:

> I use not to tell stories, but let me tell you this one thing. Since I have been from you of late, I have observed and seen in the mountains of Wales the most glorious work that ever I saw in Britain, unless it were in London; the Gospel has run over the mountains between Brecknockshire and Monmouthshire, as the fire in the thatch. And who should do this? They have no ministers; but some of the wisest say there are about eight hundred godly people, and they go from one to another . . . They are filled with good news, and they tell it to others.[18]

Here we have popular religion at its most energetic, and a style of spirituality that would fit in well with the evangelicalism of a later age. Its conversionism is patent, its activism salutary, its biblicism elemental and its crucicentricism implied. But the Puritans, too, created their own norms and held to their own particularities. Their carefully structured ecclesiology, which attempted

---

17. For an excellent précis of recent scholarship on Welsh Puritanism, see Geraint H. Jenkins, *Protestant Dissenters in Wales, 1639–89* (Cardiff: University of Wales Press, 1992).

18. T. Charles and P. Oliver (eds.), *The Works of the Late Rev. Walter Cradock* (Chester: W. C. Jones, 1800), pp. 380–381.

to replicate in detail the minutiae of the New Testament church,[19] bears little resemblance to the pragmatic individualist spirituality of the Methodist Revival, while the rather oppressive introspection of the Puritan conversion process was more protracted, severe and intense than the sense of freshness and verve in which eighteenth- and nineteenth-century evangelical believers would glory.

Post-Restoration developments

It was Lewis Edwards who described the difference between Puritan experientialism and that of the Methodists and evangelicals: 'Generally they [the Reformers and Puritans] consider regeneration as a gradual restoration of the image of God, or else as the beginning of sanctification, rather than thinking of regeneration as that which makes a man in an instant a new creature.'[20] For the classic tradition according to Lewis Edwards, it was justification that was instantaneous, as the result of the individual placing his or her faith in the crucified and resurrected Christ, while regeneration was the beginning of a lifelong process whereby Christian spirituality expressed itself in the disciplined and sanctified life. For the evangelical, at least the Calvinistic Methodist faithful among whom Edwards had been raised, this procedure was reversed. Instantaneous conversion had become the norm.

Puritanism proper came to an abrupt end in England and Wales with the restoration of the monarchy in 1660, the re-establishment of Anglicanism as the state church, and the imposition of the Book of Common Prayer as the sole authority in worship in 1662. Those whose conscience prevented them from conforming with this newly triumphant and still-aggrieved Anglican establishment and its Cavalier supporters in Parliament were forced to perpetuate their witness outside the national church. Puritanism gave way to Dissent and Protestant Nonconformity was born.

These were anxious years for the Nonconformists. Some, like the learned and cautious Presbyterians Samuel Jones (1628–97) of Llangynwyd, Glamorgan, and Philip Henry (1631–96) of Hanmer, Flintshire, were reluctant Nonconformists. All their intuitions were conservative and moderate; they longed for an inclusivist

---

19. B. R. White, 'John Miles and the Structures of the Calvinistic Baptist Mission to South Wales, 1649–60', in Mansel John (ed.), *Welsh Baptist Studies* (Cardiff: South Wales Baptist College, 1976), pp. 35–76; cf. B. G. Owens, *The Ilston Book: Earliest Register of Welsh Baptists* (Aberystwyth: National Library of Wales, 1996).

20. Edwards, *Traethawd ar Hanes Duwinyddiaeth*, p. cxix.

national church and were not averse to a low episcopalianism. They deferred wholly and naturally to constituted authority in all things. It was people like them who had shuddered when the axe fell on Charles I's neck in 1649 and who had been as uneasy as the most died-in-the-wool royalist at the democratizing radicalism of the sectaries during the Civil War. But now they found themselves worshipping in conventicles alongside the radicals and sectaries, as they could not, in all conscience, approve wholesale the contents of the Book of Common Prayer. The stipulations of the Clarendon Code made scant differentiation between the most wary Presbyterian and the most reckless Quaker, while the Corporation Act (1661), the Quaker Act (1662), the First and Second Conventicle Acts (1664, 1670) and the Five Mile Act (1665) combined to deprive nonconforming Christians of their religious freedoms and their civil rights on the pain of fines, imprisonment and transportation: 'The drive to re-establish one church and to eliminate Dissent had thus begun in earnest. Welsh Dissenters were confronted by a dispiriting array of penal laws whose avowed aim was abundantly clear: to inflict upon them untold pain, suffering and humiliation.'[21]

There was something heroic in the incarceration, in Carmarthen gaol, of Jenkin Jones (1623–?) of Llanddeti, Brecknockshire, formerly captain in the parliamentary forces and zealous open-Baptist preacher, along with William Jones (d. 1700), leader of the south-west Wales Particular Baptists during the Restoration decades, both for continuing to meet for non-Prayer Book worship in contravention to the dictates of the law. The fiery Independent Vavasor Powell spent all but ten months in a series of damp and malodorous prisons between 1660 and his death, aged 53, in 1670. As for the Quakers, the most non-compliant of all the Dissenting radicals, they emigrated nearly wholesale to Pennsylvania in the 1680s, replicating in Bryn Mawr, Bala-Cynwyd, Merion and Tredyffryn (all in Philadelphia) the peaceable communities they had left behind in Montgomeryshire and in the shadow of Cadair Idris.

The irritants of persecution did not succeed in uprooting Dissent, though the Quakers' depletion did, in fact, prove fatal for their continuance. Neither did moderate Dissenters and conciliatory Anglicans wholly forget the shared Christian faith that united their divergent traditions. There occurred, in fact, 'surprising examples of fraternisation across the frontier dividing Anglican from Puritan',[22] and what R. Tudur Jones proceeded to call 'a remarkable

---

21. G. H. Jenkins, *Protestant Dissenters in Wales, 1639–89*, p. 46.

22. R. Tudur Jones, 'Relations between Anglicans and Dissenters: The Promotion of Piety, 1670–1730', in David Walker (ed.), *A History of the Church in Wales* (Penarth: Church in Wales Publications, 1976), p. 80.

experiment in religious co-operation'.[23] These Dissenters, although still out-side the bounds of the establishment and destined by conscience to remain there, worked with some powerfully influential churchmen in order to pro-mote the advancement of scriptural holiness and the verities of the Protestant faith, especially through the dissemination of soundly orthodox Christian books. In an unlikely pairing, William Thomas, the Restoration bishop of St Davids who would soon be translated to the more lucrative English see of Worcester, served as patron to Stephen Hughes (1622–88), who had vacated the parish incumbency of Meidrim at the Act of Uniformity in 1662. Hughes was a Congregationalist and leader of his co-religionists in Carmarthenshire for the duration of the penal code, but was also a most irenic and conciliatory man. Despite having suffered for his convictions at the hands of the pres-ent regime, he could still write of the clergy of the established church, 'God forbid that I should say one word against their holy calling, or against their persons, or make any suggestion in the world, to stir people up to incriminate such reverend ministers, and such as are faithful to God.'[24] The fourth part of his edition of the works of Rhys Prichard, the vicar of Llandovery, was dedicated not only to William Thomas of St Davids in appreciation of the bishop's sponsorship of his literary campaign, but to three other pious but conforming Welsh Anglican clerics along with Hughes's fellow Dissenter, the Presbyterian Samuel Jones of Llangynwyd.[25] These men had given unstinting financial support to Hughes in his mission to supply Wales with a stock of godly books. It was a remarkable example of cross-confessional goodwill dur-ing a trying time.

Another moderate Dissenter much involved in the promotion of piety through literature was Charles Edwards (1628 to after 1691), author of the *Y Ffydd Ddi-Vuant* (The Unfeigned Faith) (1667), a classic of Welsh literature and apologia for Protestantism as the catholic faith of the Christian church. Like Hughes he had been appointed to a Denbighshire incumbency dur-ing the Cromwellian period, only to leave the establishment when the Book of Common Prayer was made compulsory in 1662. Though the moderate and courteous Edwards had endured harsh circumstances for his refusal to conform to the new administration, he would have nothing said against the

23. Ibid., p. 83.
24. Stephen Hughes, *Cyfarwydd-deb i'r Anghyfarwydd* [A Help to the Uninitiated] (London: Thomas Dawks, 1677), introduction.
25. *Gwaith Mr. Rees Prichard* [The Works of Mr. Rees Prichard] (London: Thomas Dawks, 1672), dedication.

Anglican Church. It was the Church, after all, through its parish-based min-istrations and biblically sound liturgy, that was best placed to provide wor-ship for the people and enlighten them in the Christian faith. Both Edwards and Hughes became instrumental in administering the so-called Welsh Trust, a venture instigated by Thomas Gouge, a London philanthropist, to distrib-ute further Welsh language Bibles, prayer guides and spiritual literature. As well as further popularizing the already well-known works of the churchman Rhys Prichard, the Trust was responsible for steering through the press those staunchly Anglican works mentioned at the outset of this chapter, *Yr Ymarfer o Dduwioldeb*, a later translation of Lewis Bayly's *Practice of Piety*, and *Holl Ddeledswydd Dyn*, a version of Richard Allstree's *The Whole Duty of Man* along with more markedly Puritan works such as Perkins's Catechism and books by Richard Baxter. Hughes and Edwards also collaborated in 1667–8 on produ-cing a new edition of the Welsh Bible replete with the Apocrypha, the Book of Common Prayer and Archdeacon Edmund Prys's metrical psalms.[26]

This was not a cynical ploy on their part to curry favour with the pow-ers that be, but an expression of genuine Christian missionary concern. These Dissenters could not only appreciate the scriptural if catholic nature of Anglican piety, but were happy to affirm it. They were not in the least worried that the non-Puritan elements contained therein would somehow threaten the salvation or the sanctification of the common people. There is nothing here of the anti-Anglican polemic of a John Penry or a Vavasor Powell in times past or the extreme anti-establishment antipathy of the nineteenth-century campaign to disendow the Church in Wales. What was displayed, unexpect-edly, was zeal for 'a pietism nurtured at its roots by the godly tradition which was to be found in the Anglican church and in the puritan sect'.[27] However, despite its irenic biblicism, its doctrinal orthodoxy and its sincere desire to impart a saving knowledge of Christ, it is difficult to claim a convincing con-tinuity between this venture and the evangelical movement of a later time. Post-Cromwellian Dissent possessed characteristics of its own, more in keep-ing with the quiet Reformed Protestantism of the past than with the overt revivalism of the future.

With the accession of William and Mary to the throne in 1688 and the institution of the Act of Toleration a year later, there occurred a parting of the ways. Unlike the Welsh Trust, the Society for the Propagation of Christian

---

26. Geraint H. Jenkins, *Literature, Religion and Society in Wales, 1660–1730* (Cardiff: University of Wales Press, 1978), pp. 55–60.

27. R. T. Jones, 'Relations between Anglicans and Dissenters', p. 89.

Knowledge, set up in 1699, was a solely Anglican body with much antipathy towards Dissent. As for the Dissenters themselves, now that they were afforded more obvious liberties, they used the opportunity to develop their own churchly communities, while the establishment chose, for the most part, to keep to itself. At last tolerated by the law, Nonconformists registered their congregations, began building plain but handsome chapels in the Augustan style, and consolidated their presence. Such was the context for the flourishing of the Older Dissent, that blend of churchliness, doctrinal exactitude and sober, undemonstrative piety that would eventually yield to the rather noisy individualism of the Evangelical Revival.

Existing dissent responds to the new evangelicalism

For the Older Dissent, the right ordering of the church was as essential to the gospel as the concept of the believer's assurance of his or her own salvation. The Baptist Enoch Francis's clear and dignified treatise *Gwaith a Gwobr Ffyddlon Weinidog yr Efengyl* (The Labour and Reward of a Faithful Minister of the Gospel) (1729) portrayed an unashamedly high concept of the ordained ministry: 'The Church remains a Church when it possesses a true ministry and faithful discipline, despite the corruptions of the godly and the presence of hypocrites.'[28] Here the ordained ministry is no optional extra nor is the church a chance gathering of pious souls; rather it is God's specific ordinance for the perpetuation of his saving presence in the world. In *Social Religion Exemplify'd* (1737) the Congregationalist Matthias Maurice (1684–1738) set forth a covenant-bound ecclesiology that was as definite as that of Geneva's in Calvin's day. The eucharistic teaching of orthodox Dissent went well beyond the insipid Zwinglian memorialism that became so acceptable among Victorian Nonconformists, while the doctrinal seriousness of the tradition was patent to all.[29]

It was not that the evangelical note, or the conversionist impulse, was muted. On the contrary, both Baptists and Congregationalists were zealous missionaries ever alert for the opportunity to call sinners to repentance and to

---

28. Enoch Francis, *Gwaith a Gwobr Ffyddlon Weinidog yr Efengyl*, reissued in *Transactions of the Welsh Baptist Historical Society* (1911–12), pp. 25–44 (30).

29. See R. Tudur Jones, 'Yr Hen Ymneilltuwyr, 1700–40' [The Older Dissent, 1700–40], in D. Densil Morgan (ed.), *Grym y Gair a Fflam y Ffydd: Ysgrifau ar Hanes Crefydd yng Nghymru* [The Power of the Word and the Flame of Faith: Essays on Welsh Religious History] (Bangor: Centre for the Advanced Study of Religion in Wales, 1998), pp. 126–152; R. Tudur Jones, *Congregationalism in Wales*, ed. Robert Pope (Cardiff: University of Wales Press, 2004), pp. 79–109.

expand the boundaries of the kingdom of Christ. Enoch Francis (1688–1740) and his fellow Baptist Morgan Griffiths (1669–1738)[30] were perhaps the most effective Dissenting preachers of their generation, while a younger cohort of Independent pastor-evangelists of whom Edmund Jones (1702–93) reigned supreme, were equally successful in consolidating the Dissenting cause. But the cause remained a minority affair, select, exclusivist and somewhat middle class, and their leaders sober and reserved.

It is interesting to note that the most able theological treatise which the Older Dissent produced, Timothy Thomas's *Y Wisg Wen Ddisglair* (The Shining White Garment) (1759), was on the doctrine of justification by faith alone; it placed regeneration in the context of justification and emphasized the objective facts of the gospel and their appropriation through faith rather than through subjective religious experience.[31] This lends credence to Lewis Edwards's opinion that the Reformation's doctrine of justification, the *articulus stantis et cadentis ecclesiae* (the article by which the church stands and falls), was, by the late-eighteenth century, being eclipsed by the evangelicals' conviction concerning the need to be born again.

The history of orthodox Dissent between the 1770s and the late nineteenth century was that of the victory of evangelicalism over a church-centred confessionalism of the older type. The gains were obvious for the churches as well as for the nation itself. Nonconformity would no longer be a small, introverted, somewhat diffident body, but would become the most powerful force in the land, overwhelming the established church and a uniquely active engine for social change.[32] 'Perhaps there is no other nation relative to the size of its population who have been brought over so wholly to heed the gospel, as the Welsh,' wrote the revivalist preacher Christmas Evans in the 1820s. 'Meeting houses have been built throughout the land, and the common people, for the most part, in fact nearly all of them, press in to listen.'[33]

---

30. Griffiths is not listed in the *Dictionary of Welsh Biography*, but see Thomas Rees, *History of Protestant Nonconformity in Wales* (London: John Snow, 1861), pp. 336–338.

31. Timothy Thomas, *Y Wisg Wen Ddisglair, Gymmwys i fyned i lys y Brenhin Nefol* [The Shining White Garment, Enabling an Approach to the Court of the Heavenly King] (Carmarthen: E. Powell, 1759), pp. 192–195.

32. See D. Densil Morgan, 'Christmas Evans (1766–1838) and the Birth of Nonconformist Wales', *Baptist Quarterly* 34 (1991), pp. 116–124.

33. Owen Davies (ed.), *Gweithiau Christmas Evans* [The Works of Christmas Evans], 3 vols. (Caernarfon: Gwenlyn Evans, 1898), vol. 2, p. 13.

Wales would become one of the most highly Christianized parts of Europe, and it was evangelicalism that would drive the process along. But not all, even of the faithful, were comfortable with what was about to occur. Philip David (1709–87), the Independent minister of Penmaen, Monmouthshire, expressed his qualms in a diary entry of 22 March 1775:

> Ministers' Meeting, as it was termed, in a place called New Inn, but I seldom or ever spent a day in publick worship with so little satisfaction . . . two other persons who are rank Methodists, screaming with some hideous noises and unbecoming gestures, and yᵉ people well liking these things.[34]

If the staid Congregationalist hardly knew where these disturbing trends would lead, the following generation witnessed how the Older Dissent would be swallowed whole. In 1821 J. R. Jones (1765–1822), a contemporary of Christmas Evans and leader of the Scotch Baptist secession in Merionethshire, wrote:

> The Welsh Baptists of former days especially their preachers were an infinitely superior people to anyone of their ilk among the current generation, especially the current popular peripatetic preachers. About 50 years ago the Baptists began to lose all semblance of sobriety and simplicity in their religion, and with wild and lunatic passion began to follow the despicable example of the Methodists.[35]

'The despicable example of the Methodists'; 'yᵉ people well liking these things'. By the first decade of the nineteenth century a sea change was occurring in Welsh religious life.

Methodist self-understanding: the role of Griffith Jones

If later Nonconformist evangelicals traced a continuity between their populist movement and the Puritanism of Dissent, the Methodists tended to look back to the remarkable contribution of Griffith Jones, rector of Llanddowror, as the spring from which their renewal had risen. From humble beginnings, Griffith

---

34. Quoted in R. T. Jenkins, *Yng Nghysgod Trefeca: Ysgrifau ar Hanes Crefydd a Chymdeithas yng Nghymru yn y Ddeunawfed Ganrif* [In the Shadow of Trevecca: Essays on the History of Religion and Society in Eighteenth-Century Wales] (Caernarfon: Calvinistic Methodist Bookroom, 1969), p. 36.

35. Quoted in David Williams, *Cofiant J. R. Jones, Ramoth* [A Biography of J. R. Jones, Ramoth] (Carmarthen: Morgan Evans, 1913), p. 824.

Jones (1684–1761) had been ordained into the established church in 1708 and was drawn into the educational work of the Society for the Propagation of Christian Knowledge (SPCK). While serving different curacies in south-west Wales he became known for the mighty effects of his popular preaching, and by the time of his institution to the incumbency of Llanddowror, Carmarthenshire, through the sponsorship of his brother-in-law, Sir John Philipps, in 1717, his reputation as a spiritual authority was complete.

He perpetuated the sort of ministry Stephen Hughes had championed during the Restoration; he was passionate for the dissemination of Bibles, prayer books and catechisms, and was deeply involved in the spreading of literacy and religious knowledge through the SPCK. His system of 'Welsh schools' superseded the network the SPCK had overseen and became ultimately much more successful, quickly spreading throughout the length of Wales. They were cheap, simple and hugely effective, not least because the medium of instruction was the vernacular Welsh. By the time of Jones's death in 1761 some 250,000 people, adults as well as children and youth, had been taught to read their Bible, Church Catechism and Prayer Book, in a network of 3,325 schools throughout the land.[36]

When the Evangelical Revival began, its leaders, all of whom were committed Anglicans, felt a natural affinity with Griffith Jones; indeed Daniel Rowland had been converted through his preaching. The rector of Llanddowror, though, was never comfortable in the role of Welsh Methodism's morning star. Although, as a curate, he had more than once fallen foul of diocesan law, Jones was much too enamoured of ecclesiastical authority and vigilant that his educational ventures should not be drawn too close to a potentially disruptive and enthusiastic movement. Moreover, his own piety, though obviously conversionist, activist and rooted in the biblical message of redemption through the cross, bore all the marks of the Anglicanism of the golden age. His vast output of literary works was practical in nature and didactic in tone; they included a series of guides to prayer and numerous expositions of the Church Catechism and the Apostles' Creed. The influence of Richard Hooker although unstated was obvious: the episcopal ministry as a divine ordinance, the validity of hallowed tradition in governing the church, baptismal regeneration as an inference of the concept of justification by faith alone and a high ideal of eucharistic grace. Like Rhys Prichard a century before, Griffith Jones was a Prayer Book Anglican;[37]

36. Geraint H. Jenkins, *The Foundations of Modern Wales: Wales 1642–1780* (Oxford: Clarendon, 1987), pp. 370–381.

37. D. Ambrose Jones, *Griffith Jones Llanddowror* (Wrexham: Hughes & Son, 1923).

it would be both anachronistic and somewhat misleading to define him as proto-evangelical as such.

Evangelicalism's ascendancy

Evangelicalism proper can be said to have taken the ascendency in Wales from the mid-1770s onwards. The Revival of 1762, which brought together the two previously estranged factions within the Methodist movement, the one led by Howell Harris and the other by Daniel Rowland, also rekindled a blaze that had not burned so brightly since the 1740s; Methodism was now becoming the most popular religious option among a majority of the people. Thousands of new converts were finding a spiritual home in the movement's *seiadau* (fellowship meetings), which ran in parallel with, but not in opposition to, the parish structures of the established church.[38] Whereas, apart from some early signs in the late 1730s, Nonconformity had been mostly impervious to the energies of renewal, by the mid-1770s first the Baptists and then the Independents began to experience revivalist activity that would revolutionize their respective communions.[39]

By the turn of the century a new breed of preacher was coming to the fore, populist, unrestrained, little wedded either to decorum or tradition, but exceedingly skilled in gaining the confidence and commitment of the common folk. 'No nation in Christendom has . . . been blessed with a succession of abler and more effective preachers than the Welsh,' recounted the Independent historian Thomas Rees in 1866. Their characteristics of sound doctrine, richness of thought, clarity of style, animated delivery, earnestness, solemnity and directness of appeal, most powerfully exemplified by Christmas Evans (1766–1838) for the Baptists, John Elias (1774–1841) among the Calvinistic Methodists and the Independent William Williams of Wern (1781–1840), was the reason why the greater part of the people were within the chapels and not without.

---

38. Gomer M. Roberts (ed.), *Hanes Methodistiaeth Galfinaidd Cymru*, cyfrol 1: *Y Deffroad Mawr* [A History of Welsh Calvinistic Methodism, vol. 1: The Great Awakening] (Caernarfon: Calvinistic Methodist Bookroom, 1974); Derec Llwyd Morgan, *The Great Awakening in Wales* (London: Epworth, 1981).

39. T. M. Bassett, *The Welsh Baptists* (Swansea: Ilston, 1977), pp. 87–95; D. Densil Morgan, '"Smoke, Fire and Light": Baptists and the Revitalization of Welsh Dissent', *Baptist Quarterly* 32 (1988), pp. 224–232; R. T. Jones, *Congregationalism in Wales*, pp. 110–131.

While it appears that the bulk of working classes of England never attend the means of grace, and that a large proportion of them are avowed infidels, fully ninety per cent of the corresponding classes in Wales . . . are frequent or constant attendants at one or other of our places of worship.[40]

With the secession of the Methodists from the Anglican Church in 1811 (an inevitability given the ecclesiastical ambiguity within the Welsh Methodist movement from the beginning and the loosening bonds with the establishment since the deaths of Howell Harris in 1773, Daniel Rowland in 1790 and William Williams of Pantycelyn in 1791) evangelical Nonconformity had become the principal manifestation of Christianity within Wales, while Wales itself was becoming progressively more religious. 'The Welsh is now one of the most religious nations on the face of the earth,' Thomas Rees had stated in 1850.[41] Hyperbole or not, it was certainly true that popular evangelicalism, fed by the religious revivals that would culminate in the awakening of 1859, had seemingly brought the bulk of the population into the chapels. Attendance at worship was unparalleled, the all-age Sunday schools were full to overflowing, and the thirst for religious literature, especially through a host of denominational magazines, was unprecedented. 'Nine-tenths of the middle and working classes', continued Rees, 'are either professors of religion or constant attenders at the means of grace. Evangelical religion in Wales has the public opinion decidedly in its favour.'[42] By this he meant evangelical Nonconformity, though following the 1811 secession evangelical Anglicanism, albeit a minority choice, would also perpetuate its witness within some of the parishes of the established church in Wales.[43]

However one assesses the elements of continuity between the activist movement of the mid-eighteenth and nineteenth centuries and the Anglicanism, Puritanism and confessional Dissent that flourished before, the evidence marshalled above can be said to support David Bebbington's contention that 'Evangelical religion is a popular Protestant movement that has existed in Britain since the 1730s.'[44] It was the novelty, the startling effectiveness and

40. Thomas Rees, 'The Working Classes of Wales and Religious Institutions' (1866), in his *Miscellaneous Papers on Subjects Relating to Wales* (London: Thomas Snow, 1867), p. 24.

41. Rees, 'The Great Revival in South Wales in 1849' (1850), ibid., p. 96.

42. Ibid.

43. See Roger Lee Brown, *The Welsh Evangelicals* (Tongwynlais: Tair Eglwys, 1986).

44. Bebbington, *Evangelicalism in Modern Britain*, p. 1.

unprecedented appeal of the revivalist energies that were most remarked upon at the time and that created frankly a new state of affairs within a Welsh Christianity which stretched back to the sixth century 'Age of the Saints'.[45] The four 'marks' of the movement, conversionism, activism, biblicism and crucicentricism, along with a pragmatic genius for adapting to the exigencies of the age, became the hallmark of Welsh religion during the nineteenth century, and found an outlet in the astounding nationwide revival of 1904–5.[46] If there were, at times, many resonances with the classic orthodoxy of the earlier centuries, it was only latterly that evangelicalism as a specific movement came into its own.[47]

© D. Densil Morgan, 2008

45. See D. Densil Morgan, 'Wales', *Theologische Realenzyklopädie* (Berlin: de Gruyter, 2003), vol. 35, pp. 402–408.

46. R. Tudur Jones, *Faith and the Crisis of a Nation, Wales 1890–1914*, ed. Robert Pope (Cardiff: University of Wales Press, 2004), pp. 283–369.

47. In an earlier assessment of the Bebbington thesis, R. Tudur Jones depicted 1800–50 as being Welsh Evangelicalism's 'high noon'; see his 'Awr anterth Efengylyddiaeth yng Nghymru, 1800–1850' [The High Noon of Evangelicalism in Wales], in Morgan, *Grym y Gair a Fflam y Ffydd*, pp. 285–308.

5. CALVINISTIC METHODISM AND THE ORIGINS OF EVANGELICALISM IN ENGLAND

David Ceri Jones

In a review of David Bebbington's *Evangelicalism in Modern Britain: A History from the 1730s to the 1980s* (1989), Hugh McLeod observed that for a book which 'purports to be about Britain; there seems a disproportionate emphasis on England'.[1] While Bebbington certainly discusses the origins and development of evangelicalism in Scotland, Wales and Ireland at appropriate points in his narrative, admitting at the outset that the Evangelical Revival actually had its origins in Wales,[2] the central arguments of the book rest largely on evidence drawn from an English context. Were Bebbington to be writing his book today, then perhaps its balance might be different. The 'new' British history has challenged Anglocentric interpretations of 'British' history,[3] and there has been a

---

1. Hugh McLeod, 'Varieties of Victorian Belief', *Journal of Modern History* 64.2 (June 1992), p. 336.

2. D. W. Bebbington, *Evangelicalism in Modern Britain: A History from the 1730s to the 1980s* (London: Unwin Hyman, 1989), p. 20.

3. The original case for a four-nations approach to the study of the British archipelago was made in J. G. A. Pocock, 'British History: A Plea for a New Subject', *Journal of Modern History* 47 (1975), pp. 601–628. For a critique of its achievements and weaknesses, see Paul O'Leary, 'Historians and the "New" British History', in Peter Lambert and Phillipp Schofield (eds.), *Making History: An*

renaissance in the study of the history of evangelical religion in the constituent nations of the British Isles thanks, in no small part, to the lead given by David Bebbington himself. An integrative four-nations approach could, therefore, be a particularly appropriate tool to adopt for the study of evangelicalism, particularly in its early decades, when the movement spilled over many of the traditional boundaries of state, society and culture.[4]

The extent to which Bebbington's contentions are borne out by evidence from other parts of the British archipelago is not the primary concern here. His synthesis of an impressive amount of English religious history, while providing plenty of latitude to analyse his arguments, makes the task of responding to the Bebbington thesis from the perspective of evangelicalism in England somewhat daunting. It is not my intention here to engage with his analysis of English evangelicalism from its purported beginning in the 1730s right up until the 1990s, but rather to focus on the eighteenth century, and particularly on the crucial early decades when what began as a fluid evangelical revival slowly solidified to become an evangelical movement. This chapter will begin with an examination of some of the areas where there was obvious continuity between eighteenth-century evangelicalism and previous expressions of English Protestantism, by looking at the ongoing debate over the origins of the Evangelical Revival. It will then go on, in the second place, to examine how eighteenth-century evangelicalism marked a break with the past, and use English Calvinistic Methodism as a case study.

Continuities in the origins of English evangelicalism

For many the most startling, even contentious, sentence in the whole of Bebbington's book has been the one that opens the first chapter: 'Evangelical religion is a popular Protestant movement that has existed in Britain since the 1730s.'[5] This new popular Protestant movement, born in the evangelical revivals of the 1730s, and based around the quadrilateral of theological concepts combining *conversionism*, *activism*, *biblicism* and *crucicentrism*, represented in Bebbington's own words, a 'sharp discontinuity'

Introduction to the History and Practices of a Discipline (London: Routledge, 2004), pp. 215–226.

4. G. M. Ditchfield, *The Evangelical Revival* (London: University College London, 1998), pp. 3–4.

5. Bebbington, *Evangelicalism in Modern Britain*, p. 1.

between the variants of Protestantism that had preceded it and those that followed.[6] Bebbington's *Evangelicalism in Modern Britain* can, therefore, be read as a further, albeit much more far-reaching, contribution to the debate concerning the origins of the Evangelical Revival. Historians of Methodism, both of the Wesleyan and Calvinistic variety, have long been accustomed to thinking through issues relating to the beginnings of their respective movements. But the Methodist movement was only one element, albeit the most vibrant, of the religious revivals that affected many parts of England after 1737; it would be only natural to assume that some of the reasons adduced to explain the birth of Methodism could also be seconded to account for the rise of the broader and more expansive eighteenth-century evangelical movement.

The questions that have concerned historians of the origins of Methodism are, of course, very familiar. Why did individuals from countries as diverse as England, Wales, Scotland, parts of central Europe and the American colonies all pass through dramatic conversion experiences, apparently unbeknown to one other, at roughly the same time? How and why did these scattered individuals lead revivals that coalesced into something resembling a religious movement, at first Methodist, but then more broadly evangelical? Why did the evangelicals succeed when others before them had found it so difficult to attract committed supporters in significant numbers?

These were some of the questions uppermost in the mind of French historian Elie Halévy in his essay 'La Naissance du Méthodisme en Angleterre' (The Birth of Methodism in England), which first appeared in 1906.[7] Halévy attributed the birth of Methodism, by which he almost exclusively meant Wesleyan Methodism, to the latent Protestant fervour of the English people, a hangover, he suggested, from the Puritan era.[8] This was tapped into by Pietists like the Moravians and the Welsh Methodists, whose dramatic open-air preaching inspired others to exploit the crisis following the economic slump of the late 1730s and the political instability that eventually brought about the fall of Robert Walpole in 1742, to champion religious revivals in their own localities.

---

6. Ibid., p. 74.

7. For an English edition, see Elie Halévy, *The Birth of Methodism in England*, trans. and ed. B. Semmel (Chicago: University of Chicago Press, 1971). See also Gerald Wayne Olson (ed.), *Religion and Revolution in Early Industrial England: The Halévy Thesis and Its Critics* (Lanham, Md.: University Press of America, 1990).

8. J. D. Walsh, 'Elie Halévy and the Birth of Methodism', *Transactions of the Royal Historical Society* 25 (1975), pp. 2–3.

Halévy's thesis actually raised many more questions than it answered, and its implications have been vigorously debated ever since; but his thesis does have at least two advantages. In the first place, Halévy suggested that there was significant continuity between Methodism and earlier Protestant traditions, especially Puritanism and Pietism. But he also went beyond a simple evolutionary interpretation of Methodist origins by suggesting that it was in the combination of elements of both Puritanism and Pietism that something different, even new, came into existence.[9]

However, it was John Walsh's essay 'Origins of the Evangelical Revival', published in 1966, that cast the longest shadow over studies of the birth of Methodism and, by extension, evangelicalism. With obvious echoes of Halévy, Walsh approached the problem of Methodist origins by identifying three taproots that, he argued, created the circumstances necessary for the outbreak of religious revival in the 1730s. These were the tradition of High Church piety, so influential in the Church of England during the decades between 1660 and 1730, the residual stirrings of Puritanism and the disturbing, not to say intimidating, threat of rationalism; these three factors led some Christians, particularly of the more enthusiastic and practical bent, to seek out alternative patterns of religious belief.[10]

As with Halévy, Walsh's interpretation showed how the early evangelicals were nurtured in the piety of English Puritanism, and moulded by the demanding discipline of pietistic spirituality. John Wesley was the arch systematizer; drawing on the Reformed, Arminian and High Church traditions to fashion what Herbert McGonigle has called Evangelical Arminianism.[11] On the Calvinist side, George Whitefield drew upon Puritan devotional and theological writings and was frequently 'charged with being a Dissenter',[12] but was shaped just as much by the pietistic spirituality imbibed as a member of the Holy Club at Oxford, where he learned the necessity of a devout and

9. Bernard Semmel, *The Methodist Revolution* (London: Heineman Educational, 1974), pp. 10–13.

10. John Walsh, 'Origins of the Evangelical Revival', in G. V. Bennett and J. D. Walsh (eds.), *Essays in Modern Church History: In Memory of Norman Sykes* (London: A. & C. Black, 1966), pp. 132–162.

11. Herbert B. McGonigle, *Sufficient Saving Grace: John Wesley's Evangelical Arminianism* (Carlisle: Paternoster, 2001).

12. Iain H. Murray (ed.), *George Whitefield's Journals* (London: Banner of Truth, 1960), p. 222.

holy life.[13] His deputy in the leadership of Calvinistic Methodism in England, the Welsh evangelist Howel Harris, loved to stress that the Methodists had revived the spirituality of the 'good old orthodox Reformers and Puritans',[14] but the contents of his library reveal that he was also conditioned by the writings of Boehme and Francke as well as those from the English High Church tradition.[15]

The debt the eighteenth-century evangelicals owed the Puritans has been confirmed by a considerable amount of other research published in the same decade as Bebbington's *Evangelicalism in Modern Britain*. Geoffrey Nuttall, in his work on Methodism and the English Dissenting tradition spoke of 'Evangelicals before the Revival',[16] while Leigh Eric Schmidt has traced the origins of community-based revivals, not to the 1730s or to Northampton, Massachusetts, but to the communion seasons of mid-seventeenth-century Scotland.[17] In the context of spirituality, Charles Hambrick-Stowe has stressed the persistence of Puritan piety within early evangelicalism,[18] while Bruce Hindmarsh has adumbrated some of the similarities between evangelical notions of religious conversion and those of earlier generations of English Protestants, both Puritans and from the broader Reformation tradition.[19]

It is now impossible to study the birth of evangelicalism in England without reference to the European context. John Wesley's debt to a group of

13. Arnold A. Dallimore, *George Whitefield: The Life and Times of the Great Evangelist of the Eighteenth Century Revival*, 2 vols. (London: Banner of Truth, 1970, 1980), vol. 1, pp. 66–72.

14. Gomer Morgan Roberts, *Selected Trevecka Letters (1742–1747)* (Caernarvon: Calvinistic Methodist Bookroom, 1956), p. 166.

15. Geoffrey F. Nuttall, *Howell Harris, 1714–1773: The Last Enthusiast* (Cardiff: University of Wales Press, 1965), pp. 63–64; Eifion Evans, 'Howel Harris and the Printed Page', *Cylchgrawn Hanes* 23 (1999), pp. 33–62.

16. Geoffrey F. Nuttall, 'Methodism and the Older Dissent: Some Perspectives', *Journal of the United Reformed Church Historical Society* 2.18 (Oct. 1981), p. 261.

17. Leigh Eric Schmidt, *Holy Fairs: Scottish Communions and American Revivals in the Early Modern Period* (Princeton: Princeton University Press, 1989).

18. Charles Hambrick-Stowe, '"The Spirit of the Old Writers": The Great Awakening and the Persistence of Puritan Piety', in Francis J. Bremer (ed.), *Puritanism: Transatlantic Perspectives on a Seventeenth-Century Anglo-American Faith* (Boston: Massachusetts Historical Society, 1993), pp. 277–291.

19. D. Bruce Hindmarsh, *The Evangelical Conversion Narrative: Spiritual Autobiography in Early Modern England* (Oxford: Oxford University Press, 2005).

Moravians on his way to Georgia in 1735 is, of course, the stuff of Methodist legend,[20] but its familiarity can mask the extent of the early evangelical's debt to Pietism. W. R. Ward has demonstrated how the origins of many of the characteristics of what later became evangelicalism are to be found in central and southern Germany at the end of the seventeenth and beginning of the eighteenth centuries. These included such staples as field preaching, heart religion, class meetings, the circulation of devotional texts and camp meetings, championed by groups such as the Huguenots, the Salzbergers and the Moravians.[21] These groups had come under intense persecution from Europe's Catholic monarchies following the revocation of the Edict of Nantes in 1685.[22] The crisis of confidence that ensued brought about the dispersal of pietistic Christians, many of whom fled Europe for the American colonies, some settling in England en route. The dispersal of their distinctive spirituality has led Ward to argue in his latest work that the history of evangelicalism should not begin in the mid-1730s, as Bebbington has insisted, but in the 1670s,[23] the decade in which Philip Jakob Spener published his *Pia desideria* (1675).[24]

Pietistic ideas were picked up in England in the second half of the seventeenth century largely by Anglicans whose religious monopoly in England had been curtailed in the aftermath of the Glorious Revolution. Through organizations like the Society for Promoting Christian Knowledge, the Society for the Reformation of Manners and the Society for the Propagation of the Gospel, as well as a large number of private devotional societies, many Anglicans tried to raise the spiritual temperature through voluntary means like education, the publication of devotional literature and the inculcation

---

20. Henry D. Rack, *Reasonable Enthusiast: John Wesley and the Rise of Methodism* (London: Epworth, 1989), pp. 114–115.

21. W. R. Ward, *The Protestant Evangelical Awakening* (Cambridge: Cambridge University Press, 1992).

22. W. R. Ward, *Christianity under the Ancien Régime, 1648–1789* (Cambridge: Cambridge University Press, 1999), pp. 14, 17.

23. W. R. Ward, *Early Evangelicalism: A Global Intellectual History, 1670–1789* (Cambridge: Cambridge University Press, 2006).

24. Richard L. Gawthrop, *Pietism and the Making of Eighteenth-Century Prussia* (Cambridge: Cambridge University Press, 1993), pp. 104–120; W. R. Ward, 'Evangelical Awakenings in the North Atlantic World', in Stewart J. Brown and Timothy Tackett (eds.), *The Cambridge History of Christianity: Enlightenment, Reawakening and Revolution, 1660–1815* (Cambridge: Cambridge University Press, 2006), pp. 329–331.

of godly standards of behaviour.[25] The Oxford Holy Club, from which both Whitefield and the Wesley's graduated in the mid-1730s, was merely another expression of this desire to recapture the spirit of primitive Christianity through a rigorous lifestyle of ascetic piety and good works.[26] It was within these religious societies that the influence of the Moravians was first felt in England, especially the Fetter Lane Society, where the Wesley brothers first learned about genuine heart religion. The Evangelical Revival started out as a renewal movement within these religious societies, its headquarters being firmly located within Fetter Lane, although this was quickly to prove too restricting for the competing egos of Whitefield, Wesley and some of the leading Moravians.[27]

However, neither of these two streams, Puritanism or Pietism, led by some sort of inevitable succession into evangelicalism. John Wesley, George Whitefield and Howel Harris, to a greater or lesser degree, exhausted, or were exhausted by, the demands of High Church spirituality. The inheritors of the Puritan tradition, particularly within English Dissent, tended, with a few notable exceptions, to keep the early evangelicals at arm's length.[28] Evangelicalism was indebted to both streams of spirituality and drew a considerable amount from each of them, but neither stream was sufficient on its own to bring about a religious revival in England.

The reasons for the beginning of the revival during the mid-1730s must, therefore, lie elsewhere. For the early evangelicals, of course, explaining their origins was not a problem. They looked no further for an explanation than the Spirit of God, who, they thought, was being poured out on the church as in the days of the apostles. Contemporary historians, whether writing from a position of faith or not, need to appreciate the evangelicals' understanding of themselves, but strictly providentialist interpretations can mask the degree

25. Henry D. Rack, 'Religious Societies and the Origins of Methodism', *Journal of Ecclesiastical History* 38.4 (Oct. 1987), pp. 582–584.

26. Eamon Duffy, 'Primitive Christianity Revived: Religious Renewal in Augustan England', in Derek Baker (ed.), *Renaissance and Renewal in Christian History: Papers Read at the 15th Summer Meeting and the 16th Winter Meeting of the Ecclesiastical History Society*, Studies in Church History 14 (Oxford: Basil Blackwell, 1977), pp. 290–291.

27. Colin Podmore, *The Moravian Church in England, 1728–1760* (Oxford: Oxford University Press, 1998), pp. 67–71.

28. Nuttall, 'Methodism and the Older Dissent', pp. 268–274; Michael Watts, *The Dissenters: From the Reformation to the French Revolution* (Oxford: Oxford University Press, 1978), pp. 434–445, 450–455.

to which the Evangelical Revival began in response to other, more mundane, changes in the social, cultural and intellectual milieu of the mid-eighteenth century.[29] John Walsh and David Bebbington have both been sensitive to this and have accorded particular significance to the cultural mood created by the Enlightenment.

Walsh takes a traditional view of the Enlightenment, arguing that the challenge of rationalism and the spectre of deism created a crisis of confidence within English Christianity. The evangelicals, he argues, reacted against the predominantly atheistic spirit of the Enlightenment by championing a faith-based and experience-led religious movement. By contrast, Bebbington has suggested that evangelicalism and the Enlightenment enjoyed a much more fruitful relationship. He singles out the writings of John Locke, who had argued that personal experience was the foundation for obtaining true knowledge; evangelicals echoed Locke in their conviction that a genuine knowledge of God could be accessed only through a personal encounter with the divine.[30] The contrast between 'head knowledge' (an intellectual assent to Christian teachings) and 'heart knowledge' became, for evangelicals almost everywhere, the difference between genuine and spurious religion. This had an impact on the doctrine of assurance; evangelicals wanted to know for certain that they were children of God, and Jonathan Edwards taught them that the way to achieve this was through the identification of signs, or evidences, of God's grace in one's life. This interpretation has not been without its critics,[31] but Bebbington was not arguing that there was any new theological insight here; what was different was the importance that the evangelicals attached to the doctrine of assurance, particularly their emphasis on its realistic attainability.[32]

The dramatic conversions Whitefield, the Wesley brothers and many others experienced in the mid-1730s became the catalyst for the revival itself. Whitefield's experience, remarkable only for the fame it subsequently achieved through the written account printed in his *Journal*, was typical of that experienced by so

---

29. Mark A. Noll, *The Rise of Evangelicalism: The Age of Edwards, Whitefield and the Wesleys* (Leicester: IVP, 2004), pp. 129–131.

30. Bebbington, *Evangelicalism in Modern Britain*, pp. 48–50.

31. See Garry J. Williams, 'Was Evangelicalism Created by the Enlightenment?', *Tyndale Bulletin* 53.2 (2002), pp. 283–312. The article is reprinted in this volume (ch. 15) as 'Enlightenment Epistemology and Eighteenth-Century Evangelical Doctrines of Assurance'.

32. Noll, *Rise of Evangelicalism*, p. 141.

many others at this time. After a period of intense conviction of sin throughout the winter of 1734 and 1735, the crisis point was reached during Lent when the emaciated Whitefield was confined to his bed for seven weeks by his doctor. It was at this point, exhausted and desperate, that

> God was pleased to remove the heavy load, to enable me to lay hold of His dear Son by a living faith, and by giving me the Spirit of adoption, to seal me even to the day of everlasting redemption . . . a full assurance of faith, broke in upon my disconsolate soul! Surely it was the day of mine espousals—a day to be had in everlasting remembrance![33]

John Wesley's experience was broadly similar. After having his heart 'strangely warmed' at Aldersgate Street, he confessed that 'One thing I know: I was blind, but now I see.'[34] Having passed through such life-changing experiences, evangelicals like Wesley and Whitefield emerged confident and secure in their spiritual standing; this freed them from protracted bouts of morbid introspection to concentrate on ambitious schemes of evangelism, reformation and revival. For Whitefield this meant Anglican ordination in June 1736, and then two months deputizing at the Chapel at the Tower of London, during which time the 'boy parson'[35] became a star attraction in the city. By the time he departed for his first visit to Georgia in early 1738, many London clergymen had already barred him from their pulpits on account of his preaching the new birth. The Evangelical Revival was under way.

As well as emerging in the age of Enlightenment, evangelicalism was birthed in a period of profound social, economic and commercial change. It coincided with, indeed even fed off, a significant increase in the population of the British Isles, the disjunction created by the first stirrings of the Industrial Revolution, the rise of the commercial middle classes and the rapid expansion of Britishness, first throughout the British Isles, but then right across the first British Empire.[36] In England and Wales, at least, evangelicalism attracted men

33. Murray, *George Whitefield's Journals*, p. 58.
34. John Telford (ed.), *The Letters of the Rev. John Wesley*, 8 vols. (London: Epworth, 1931), vol. 2, p. 384.
35. Murray, *George Whitefield's Journals*, p. 77.
36. Some of these changes can be best traced in Paul Langford, *A Polite and Commercial People: England, 1727–1783* (Oxford: Oxford University Press, 1989). For their relationship to the rise of evangelicalism, see David Hempton, *Methodism: Empire of the Spirit* (New Haven: Yale University Press, 2005), ch. 1.

and women from the middling orders of society,[37] literate individuals who had also acquired sufficient economic independence to enable them to exercise a measure of autonomy over the direction of their lives. They thrived in the extra space that had been created for individual initiative and they fuelled the popularity of voluntary associations in both politics and religion. The Church of England, so often cumbersome and unwieldy, found it almost impossible to adapt to these new circumstances, and so hybrid religious movements like evangelicalism gladly took full advantage, making provision for marginalized groups like the Kingswood colliers or the inhabitants of the sprawling parishes of Yorkshire and Cornwall.[38] It would be inconceivable to assume that this social, cultural and economic context did not impinge, to a greater or lesser degree, on the English Protestant tradition during the middle decades of the eighteenth century.[39]

The creation of an evangelical movement

Bebbington's case for the discontinuity between evangelicalism and previous forms of Protestantism does not rest on the evidence of theology and spirituality alone; it also relies on the innovativeness of evangelicalism as a social and cultural movement. The heavy emphasis placed on activism within Bebbington's quadrilateral definition of evangelicalism is indicative of this. With a rudimentary theological core, around which orthodox Protestants of many different hues could happily congregate, evangelicals were able to mobilize the energies of their followers towards spreading vital heart religion, and, once established, venture into the uncharted waters of more radical social action. W. R. Ward recognized this and commented that the Evangelical Revival combined 'theological conservatism with practical innovation'.[40] The evangelicals drew on a diverse heritage of Protestant belief and spirituality, but devised new ways, new techniques, and even a new movement, by means of which they could promote and spread experiential religion.

---

37. See Clive D. Field, 'The Social Composition of English Methodism to 1830: A Membership Analysis', *Bulletin of the John Rylands University Library of Manchester* 76.1 (spring 1994), pp. 153–169.

38. Michael J. Crawford, *Seasons of Grace: Colonial New England's Revival Tradition in Its British Context* (New York: Oxford University Press, 1991), p. 14.

39. Bebbington, *Evangelicalism in Modern Britain*, p. 19.

40. Ward, *Protestant Evangelical Awakening*, p. 355.

Evangelicalism was, by definition, an international movement—the presence of religious awakenings in diverse national settings is testimony to that. But it does not necessarily follow that those awakenings automatically constituted a coherent movement. What turned the activities of a relatively small group of evangelicals into evangelicalism were the networks of communication and influence that brought these individual awakenings together.[41] As Bebbington has said elsewhere, on this occasion in conjunction with Mark Noll and George Rawlyk, 'Innovative networks of communication have sustained the transnational character of evangelicalism and given it much of its distinctive shape.'[42]

These networks were multiform, and included the evangelists themselves (who often acted as *loci* around whom people congregated), associations, books, magazines, techniques of ministry, perceptions and chains of influence.[43] Some of these techniques were to become so central as to be defining characteristics of the evangelical movement itself.

George Whitefield and the Calvinistic revival

The majority of interrevival networks were established between 1735 and 1740, undoubtedly the most fluid and creative years of the Evangelical Revival. In England, at this stage, most of the key evangelical leaders (George Whitefield, John Wesley and the Moravian leadership within the Fetter Lane Society) were still pulling in a broadly similar direction—not until the spring of 1741 did the English revival finally splinter into its three factions.[44] It would be no exaggeration to say that the Calvinistic expression of the Evangelical Revival was the mainstream version of the English awakening during this early period.

---

41. This is the argument Frank Lambert has developed in his *'Pedlar in Divinity': George Whitefield and the Transatlantic Revivals, 1737–1770* (Princeton: Princeton University Press, 1994), and his *Inventing the 'Great Awakening'* (Princeton: Princeton University Press, 1999).

42. 'Introduction', in Mark A. Noll, David W. Bebbington and George W. Rawlyk (eds.), *Evangelicalism: Comparative Studies of Popular Protestantism in North America, the British Isles, and Beyond* (New York: Oxford University Press, 1994), p. 9.

43. Noll, *Rise of Evangelicalism*, pp. 15–16.

44. The circumstances of these splits are discussed in David Ceri Jones, '"The Lord Did Give Me a Particular Honour to Make [Me] a Peacemaker": Howel Harris, John Wesley and Methodist Infighting, 1739–1750', *Bulletin of the John Rylands University Library of Manchester* 82.2, 82.3 (summer–autumn 2003), pp. 73–88.

It was focused, disproportionately so, on the ministry of George Whitefield.[45] This is an obvious element of discontinuity with earlier Protestant movements; the reliance on a charismatic individual, which developed from the evangelicals' use of lay preachers and itinerants, would become characteristic of much subsequent evangelicalism in England and beyond.[46] Whitefield had begun preaching in London in 1736; by 1739 John Cennick had founded societies in Wiltshire and taken on Methodist leadership in Bristol; Benjamin Ingham had done the same at Ossett in Yorkshire, and Jacob Rogers and Francis Okely had gathered some societies together in Bedford and Nottingham respectively.[47] But at the same time as he was extending the boundaries of the English revival, Whitefield had also begun to move on a much larger stage. He had spent most of 1737 in Georgia, making important connections in the American colonies. On his return to England he had written to Howel Harris and had visited Wales in person during March 1739, when both leaders committed themselves to closer collaboration.[48]

Whitefield returned to America once more at the end of 1739, and during his fifteen-month visit undertook a punishing intercolonial itinerary that effectively linked up a series of local revivals, creating the Great Awakening.[49] During his absence John Wesley took control of the English evangelical movement, stepping into the power vacuum Whitefield had carelessly created.[50] When he returned to England, Whitefield was forced to enter into public controversy with Wesley over predestination, a clash that led to the permanent division of the English evangelical community.[51] Almost by way of reaction,

---

45. See e.g. Harry S. Stout, 'George Whitefield in Three Countries', in Noll, Bebbington and Rawlyk, *Evangelicalism*, pp. 58–72.

46. Mark A. Noll, 'National Churches, Gathered Churches and the Varieties of Lay Evangelicalism, 1735–1859', in Deryck W. Lovegrove (ed.), *The Rise of the Laity in Evangelical Protestantism* (London: Routledge, 2002), pp. 142–143. For more detail, see D. W. Lovegrove, *Established Church, Sectarian People: Itinerancy and the Transformation of English Dissent, 1780–1830* (Cambridge: Cambridge University Press, 1988); and for the American experience, see Nathan O. Hatch, *The Democratization of American Christianity* (New Haven: Yale University Press, 1989).

47. Podmore, *Moravian Church in England*, pp. 34–36.

48. David Ceri Jones, '*A Glorious Work in the World': Welsh Methodism and the International Evangelical Revival, 1735–1750* (Cardiff: University of Wales Press, 2004), pp. 113–124.

49. For Whitefield and the colonial revivals, see Frank Lambert, 'George Whitefield and the Great Awakening', *Journal of American History* 77 (1990), pp. 812–837.

50. Rack, *Reasonable Enthusiast*, pp. 212–213.

51. Jones, 'The Lord Did Give', pp. 85–89.

Whitefield headed north to Scotland where his preaching fuelled the revival already in progress in the parishes of Cambuslang and Kilsyth, and encouraged the nascent evangelical movement within the Church of Scotland.[52] By the summer of 1741, therefore, Whitefield had woven together a Calvinistic evangelical movement; sympathetic evangelicals in England, Wales, Scotland and the American colonies had been introduced to one another and had begun to dream that perhaps they represented the first intimation of the start of the millennial reign of Christ.[53]

It is hard to overestimate the role Whitefield's personality and dynamic revivalism played in the creation of this network, but recent scholarship has demonstrated how commercially savvy Whitefield actually was. Utilizing the marketing techniques of the burgeoning consumer revolution, Whitefield hawked the gospel about as a religious commodity, especially to those middling sorts who, having become economic consumers, now became spiritual consumers too.[54] His strategy was doubly successful because, as Carla Gardina Pestana has shown, the relative dearth of institutional structures in the British Atlantic world tended to favour those spiritualities that could function well in an institutionally simplified environment.[55] The rudimentary spirituality of evangelicalism, eminently adaptable in different cultures and contexts, therefore provided an alternative organizational structure, however basic, that bound evangelicals from diverse backgrounds together into something resembling a coherent evangelical movement. The sinews of this movement were put in place by Whitefield himself, who, in addition to visiting other awakenings and giving them his enthusiastic support, set about forging tangible links between

52. See Arthur Fawcett, *The Cambuslang Revival: The Scottish Evangelical Revival of the Eighteenth Century* (Edinburgh: Banner of Truth, 1971).

53. For evangelical millenarianism more generally, see David Hempton, 'Evangelicalism and Eschatology', *Journal of Ecclesiastical History* 31.2 (Apr. 1980), pp. 179–194.

54. Lambert, *'Pedlar in Divinity'*, pp. 25–36. For the wider context of the transatlantic consumer revolution, see Neil McKendrick, 'The Consumer Revolution of Eighteenth-Century England', in Neil McKendrick, John Brewer and J. H. Plumb, *The Birth of a Consumer Society: The Commercialisation of Eighteenth-Century England* (London: Europa, 1982), pp. 9–33; John Brewer, *The Pleasures of the Imagination: English Culture in the Eighteenth Century* (London: HarperCollins, 1997).

55. Carla Gardina Pestana, 'Religion', in David Armitage and Michael J. Braddick (eds.), *The British Atlantic World, 1500–1800* (Houndmills: Palgrave Macmillan, 2002), p. 74.

them, and created what Susan O'Brien has called 'a transatlantic community of saints'.[56]

Whitefield would not have been able to create this network without the assistance of a group of loyal printers and booksellers in London who devoted their professional expertise, often sacrificially, to overseeing its day-to-day administration. Initially, he relied on James Hutton, the Moravian bookseller and founding member of the Fetter Lane Society,[57] and on William Seward, a former stockbroker, who became Whitefield's principal secretary, chief reporter and press agent[58] between 1737 and his untimely death at the hands of a mob in Wales during 1740.[59] By careful use of the media, Whitefield ensured that positive accounts of his activities appeared in the pages of the most widely read newspapers and periodicals of the day. Seward sent glowing accounts of Whitefield's preaching to places next on his itinerary, heightening expectations and thereby encouraging the revival's spread from place to place. After Seward's death, Whitefield came to rely on a small group of secretaries, printers and booksellers, which included Hutton, Samuel Mason,[60] John Syms,[61] John Lewis[62] and later Thomas Boddington, who combined his duties with the co-leadership of the

---

56. Susan O'Brien, '"A Transatlantic Community of Saints": The Great Awakening and the First Evangelical Network, 1735–1750', *American Historical Review* 91 (1986), p. 811.

57. John A. Vickers (ed.), *A Dictionary of Methodism in Britain and Ireland* (Peterborough: Epworth, 2000), p. 172; J. E. Hutton, *A History of the Moravian Church* (London: Moravian Publication Office, 1909), pp. 283–288.

58. Lambert, *'Pedlar in Divinity'*, p. 57.

59. See George L. Fairs, 'Notes on the Death of William Seward at Hay, 1740', *Journal of the Historical Society of the Presbyterian Church of Wales* 58.1 (Mar. 1973), pp. 12–18.

60. For Mason, see H. R. Plomer (ed.), *A Dictionary of the Printers and Booksellers Who Were at Work in England, Scotland, and Ireland from 1726 to 1775* (London: Bibliographical Society, 1968), p. 164; Graham C. G. Thomas, 'George Whitefield and Friends: The Correspondence of Some Early Methodists', *National Library of Wales Journal* 26 (1990), pp. 251–264.

61. For Syms, see Dallimore, *George Whitefield*, vol. 1, p. 395; vol. 2, pp. 142, 154, 155, 213.

62. David Ceri Jones, 'John Lewis and the Promotion of the International Evangelical Revival, 1735–1756', in E. Dyfed Roberts (ed.), *Revival, Renewal and the Holy Spirit* (Carlisle: Paternoster, forthcoming).

Tabernacle Society during Whitefield's extended absences in the American colonies in the later 1740s.[63]

A Calvinistic evangelical community

The foundation of the network was correspondence. Letter-writing was the means by which the pioneer evangelists made initial contact with one another, but once that first contact had been made, it could then be put to more sophisticated uses. For the rank-and-file converts of the revival, hearing the latest letters read aloud publicly, reading correspondence themselves and writing their own letters were often the chief way they interacted with the wider evangelical movement. There had, of course, been a transatlantic correspondence network in the seventeenth century,[64] and the triangular correspondence between English Dissenters like Philip Doddridge and Isaac Watts, a small number of colonial ministers and some Scottish Presbyterians, although severely attenuated, still survived.[65] It had been through this last network that news of Jonathan Edwards's awakening at Northampton, Massachusetts, in 1735, first reached the ears of sympathetic onlookers in England; and it was this same network that Whitefield had used to publicize his own ministry in the early months of the revival. Once he had begun to establish his own networks of friends and correspondents, though, it was not long until a more sophisticated evangelical network was called for. Letters were written between evangelicals in many regions of the revival; particularly edifying examples were circulated among local communities of saints, and by the early 1740s special 'Letter Days' were being held regularly at Whitefield's Tabernacle in London at which the latest revival news was relayed to enthusiastic congregations.[66]

What sort of material was included in these letters? Most of them were journalistic in tone, carrying the latest news of the progress of the gospel throughout the British Atlantic world. Yet the letters also served other equally

---

63. For Boddington's role, see National Library of Wales, Aberystwyth, Calvinist Methodist Archive (Trevecka Group), 'The Trevecka Letters, 1674, Thomas Boddington to Mrs Doyle (29 June 1747)'; Lambert, *'Pedlar in Divinity'*, pp. 91–92.

64. David Cressy, *Coming Over: Migration and Communication between England and New England in the Seventeenth Century* (Cambridge: Cambridge University Press, 1987), pp. 213–234.

65. Francis J. Bremer, *Congregational Communion: Clerical Friendship in the Anglo-American Puritan Community, 1610–1692* (Boston: Northwestern University Press, 1994), pp. 249–256; Hambrick-Stowe, 'Spirit of the Old Writers', pp. 277–291.

66. O'Brien, 'Transatlantic Community of Saints', pp. 825–826.

important purposes. They became a means for rank-and-file evangelicals to articulate their religious experiences, particularly in the form of conversion narratives. By recounting their experiences in a letter to one of the pioneer evangelists, or a prominent lay leader at least, converts could seek verification of their experiences from those who were experts in matters of the soul. The letter-writing network also came to be used as a kind of self-help forum in which converts could air their problems, seek answers to those that were most disturbing, and even in some instances offer advice to individuals with whom they felt some affinity. Then, when the early evangelical movement was facing damaging internal divisions during the early 1740s, the letter-writing network became a forum in which issues could be discussed and compromises hammered out. What all this activity did, of course, was to create a sense of communal identity and belonging. Converts were presented with compelling evidence that they were not just scattered individuals belonging to local awakenings, but part of a far-reaching movement, inextricably bound together by their shared experiences and their access to a common group of personalities.

Despite the creativity of the evangelical leaders, both nationally and locally, there was inevitably a limit to the number of individuals who could access this material. A new medium was required, capable of reaching a larger number of people. The mid-eighteenth century witnessed the beginnings of mass forms of communication, and evangelicals like Whitefield were acutely aware of the opportunities such means provided. Following his return to England in 1741, Whitefield fortuitously discovered that *The Christian's Amusement*, a struggling evangelical periodical edited by the London-Welsh printer and bookseller John Lewis, was in serious financial difficulty and running short of appropriate material to fill its pages. Whitefield assumed editorial control, rebranded it *The Weekly History*, and stated in its first issue that it would now 'be furnished with various accounts, which doubtless will be useful and edifying to the reader'.[67] In its new incarnation, the magazine appeared more regularly: every week at the height of the revival during 1741 and 1742. It was printed cheaply on four folio pages and, in its earliest stages, was filled with vibrant and exciting letters charting the progress of the gospel throughout the British Atlantic world.

The magazine enjoyed a respectable circulation throughout its eight-year run. Precise figures for the whole of its life are not available, but Frank Lambert

---

67. John Lewis (ed.), *The Weekly History or an Account of the Most Remarkable Particulars Relating to the Present Progress of the Gospel, by the Encouragement of the Rev. Mr Whitefield* 1 (n. d.), p. 4.

has estimated that Calvinistic Methodist preachers must have delivered at least 500 copies on their regular circuits.[68] The minutes of Whitefield's Tabernacle Society contain some indication of circulation figures towards the end of its print run, where it appears that bundles of the latest issues were delivered to the various Calvinistic Methodist outposts. In July 1747, for example, 150 were sent to Exeter and Plymouth, 80 to Gloucester, 40 to Portsmouth, 50 to Essex and 50 to Staffordshire.[69] The English magazine was supplemented by two sister periodicals. In Scotland, William McCulloch edited *The Glasgow Weekly History* for a year between December 1741 and 1742, before *The Christian Monthly History* superseded it in November 1743; while in the American colonies, Thomas Prince printed the first edition of *The Christian History* in March 1743.[70]

There was considerable overlap in the content of the three magazines. While they each concentrated on events in their own constituency, each version printed and reprinted letters from other revival communities, and at certain times the same material was published in all three versions virtually simultaneously. Like the letter network, the contents of the magazine mirrored the mood of the revival. When things were going well its pages were packed with exciting news, as for example when Whitefield went to Cambuslang in the summer of 1742 and John Lewis had to issue a special double issue.[71] At other times the magazine reflected the issues of most concern to the leaders of the revival. Its pages included discussions of theological issues, particularly the rival merits of Calvinism and Arminianism during the early 1740s; later divisions over Christian Perfection and aspects of the Moravians 'blood and wounds' theology also featured.[72] The magazine also became a forum in which problems were discussed and solutions to spiritual difficulties were offered.[73]

---

68. Lambert, *'Pedlar in Divinity'*, p. 70.

69. Edwin Welch (ed.), *Two Calvinistic Methodist Chapels, 1743–1811: The London Tabernacle and Spa Fields Chapel* (London: London Record Society, 1975), p. 13.

70. J. E. van de Wetering, '*The Christian History* of the Great Awakening', *Journal of Presbyterian History* 44 (1966), pp. 122–129.

71. *Weekly History* 66 (10 July 1742).

72. 'The Copy of a Letter from Mr Humphreys to the Rev Mr Wesley (5 April 1741)', in Lewis, *Weekly History* 11 (n. d.); 'Letter from a Friend', in John Lewis (ed.), *The Christian's Amusement* 12 (n. d.); Jones, *'Glorious Work'*, pp. 273–280.

73. 'A Letter to a Person whom God Hath Wounded, but He Hath since Apply'd to the Devil to Be Cured', in Lewis, *Christian's Amusement* 19 (n. d.); Jones, *'Glorious Work'*, pp. 270–273.

Ironically, though, the very success of the magazine became the reason for
its premature demise. It was most popular when the Evangelical Revival was
experiencing one of its periodic bursts of expansion, as had happened during
the summer of 1742. But when circumstances were less propitious, circulation
figures could fall away quite dramatically.

By the time the English magazine eventually folded in 1748, the Calvinistic
Methodist movement was in a pretty sorry state. Whitefield was eager to
shed his leadership role, and Howel Harris's leadership had become increasingly erratic and controversial on account of his adoption of elements of
the Moravians' patripassianism.[74] John Lewis, for his part, had become
entangled with a prostitute and was almost bankrupted by the dwindling of
support for the magazine.[75] But this is not to suggest that *The Weekly History*
was a failure. For eight years it acted as the official mouthpiece of English
and Welsh Calvinistic Methodism, drawing together Calvinists throughout
England, Wales and, for a time, much further afield. Growing out of the
letter-writing network, it was another of the means by which Whitefield
and his co-evangelists created and sustained an evangelical, or at least a
Calvinistic, evangelical identity in the later 1730s and throughout much of
the 1740s.

The extent to which the early evangelical movement was defined and sustained by the publication of godly literature has been demonstrated at length
in the writings of Susan O'Brien.[76] The early evangelicals were expert journal-
ists, producing their own accounts of the progress of the revival in letters and
magazines; but they also took full advantage of the transatlantic book trade,
which had mushroomed following the repeal of the Licensing Act in 1695.[77]
Adopting the latest commercial techniques, including cheap print, popular
advertising and aggressive mass-marketing, booksellers placed the latest literature into the hands of people of relatively modest means, many of whom

74. Geraint Tudur, *Howell Harris: From Conversion to Separation, 1735–1750* (Cardiff:
    University of Wales Press, 2000), pp. 163, 171–172.
75. Jones, 'John Lewis and the Promotion'.
76. Susan O'Brien, 'Eighteenth-Century Publishing Networks in the First Years of
    Transatlantic Evangelicalism', in Noll, Bebbington and Rawlyk, *Evangelicalism*, pp.
    38–57.
77. Michael Treadwell, 'The Stationers and the Printing Acts at the End of the
    Seventeenth Century', in John Barnard, D. F. McKenzie and Maureen Bell (eds.),
    The Cambridge History of the Book in Britain, vol. 4: *1557–1696* (Cambridge:
    Cambridge University Press, 2000), pp. 755–776.

had only recently learned to read. There had been a transatlantic book trade since the early seventeenth century,[78] but it had never been called upon to bear the volume of material the evangelicals now began to produce. A flavour and indication of the range of this material can be gauged by examining some of the book adverts included in John Lewis's magazine during the 1740s. Here Whitefield's innovative booksellers came into their own. They were keen to publish his and other evangelical works, and were committed to doing so in as inexpensive a format as possible. Books and pamphlets were put on sale in their bookshops, hawked around the country by Whitefield and his fellow evangelists, and advertised in imaginative ways. Utilizing the vogue for inexpensive subscriptions, these works satisfied the appetite of those middling sorts for whom access to godly literature had become an integral part of their economic, social and cultural identity.[79]

Initially, the most popular literary productions were Whitefield's own journals. Whitefield released regular instalments of his journal, after the appearance of the first issue in 1737. When collected, they became a substantial autobiographical narrative, ensuring that literature of this kind quickly established itself as one of the dominant modes of evangelical expression. Wesley followed Whitefield's example and began issuing his own journal shortly after, but there were also other published journals by lesser-known figures, including that produced by William Seward,[80] and the many shorter conversion narratives collected by Charles Wesley and William McCulloch[81] or that were written in the form of familiar letters and printed in *The Weekly History*.[82]

---

78. David D. Hall, 'Learned Culture in the Eighteenth Century', in Hugh Amory and David D. Hall (eds.), *A History of the Book in America*, vol. 1: *The Colonial Book in the Atlantic World* (Cambridge: Cambridge University Press, 2000), pp. 411–415.

79. For the rise in literacy levels in early modern England, see Keith Thomas, 'The Meaning of Literacy in Early Modern England', in Gerd Baumann (ed.), *The Written Word: Literacy in Transition* (Oxford: Oxford University Press, 1986), pp. 97–131. The religious implications of the acquisition of literacy may be further explored in Ian Green, *Print and Protestantism in Early Modern England* (Oxford: Oxford University Press, 2000), pp. 24–27; Leonore Davidoff and Catherine Hall, *Family Fortunes: Men and Women of the English Middle Class, 1780–1850* (London: Routledge, 2002, rev. ed.), pp. 90–91.

80. William Seward, *Journal of a Voyage from Savannah to Philadelphia, and Philadelphia to England in 1740* (London: J. Oswald, 1740).

81. See Hindmarsh, *Evangelical Conversion Narrative*, chs. 4, 6.

82. David Ceri Jones, 'Narratives of Conversion in English Calvinistic Methodism', in

Whitefield also ensured that his best sermons, those he preached repeatedly, were rushed into print in the later 1730s, which in many respects were a manifesto of the early revival. The most popular included his most famous sermon on the new birth[83] and his sermon on the importance of religious society, or of Christians meeting together in small groups to stir up the gifts of the Spirit among themselves.[84] These publications summarized the early Methodists' evangelistic strategy;[85] conversion was key, as was assurance of one's salvation; new converts were encouraged to join a small cell group where pastoral oversight could be guaranteed. These societies were part of an accountability structure that ultimately reported to the Joint Association of English and Welsh Calvinistic Methodism following its establishment in 1743.

These converts were serviced by a flourishing publication programme: the recommendations that appeared in *The Weekly History* bear eloquent testimony to this. Calvinistic leaders initially turned to writers from the past to support their position; in 1740, for example, John Lewis advertised a new edition of the Henrician martyr Robert Barnes's work on justification by faith, which included a commendatory preface by John Wesley.[86] Wesley's recommendations disappeared from *The Weekly History* by the early 1740s, to be replaced by adverts for works by Whitefield and other contemporary sympathetic Calvinists. However, perhaps the most enthusiastic recommendation to be included in Lewis's magazine appeared in April 1742, when he inserted a lengthy section drawing attention to a new edition of Jonathan Edwards's *The Distinguishing Marks of a Work of the Spirit of God*.[87]

Kate Cooper and Jeremy Gregory (eds.), *Revival and Resurgence in Christian History*, Studies in Church History 44 (London: Boydell & Brewer, forthcoming).

83. George Whitefield, *The Nature and Necessity of our New Birth in Christ Jesus, in Order to Salvation* (London: C. Rivington, 1737).

84. George Whitefield, *The Nature and Necessity of Society in General and Religious Society in Particular* (Bristol: Felix Farley, 1740).

85. W. R. Ward, 'Was There a Methodist Evangelistic Strategy in the Eighteenth Century?', in Nicholas Tyacke (ed.), *England's Long Reformation, 1500–1800* (London: University College London, 1998), pp. 285–304.

86. Robert Barnes, *Two Treatises; The First on Justification by Faith Only ... The Second on the Sinfulness of Man's Natural Will ... To which Is Prefix'd, a Preface, Containing Some Account of the Life and Death of Dr Barnes: Extracted from the Book of Martyrs. By John Wesley* (London: John Lewis, 1739).

87. London: Samuel Mason, 1741.

Edwards's significance as the chief apologist of the evangelical movement is becoming increasingly evident. In a recent volume of essays discussing his international significance, Bruce Hindmarsh has shown how Edwards's works exerted an enormous influence upon evangelicals and Methodists, at least until the publication of Charles Finney's *Lectures on Revivals* (1835). Following the publication of *A Faithful Narrative of Surprising Conversions* in England in 1737, Edwards's theology of revival became widely accepted, but his narrative account of the revival at Northampton also played an important psychological role. According to Hindmarsh, it gave English evangelicals 'hope—hope that they might see revival, too'.[88] When those revivals duly arrived time and time again throughout the eighteenth century, successive generations turned afresh to his writings in order to make sense of them. What this did was provide the evangelical movement with a remarkably settled sense of what genuine revival actually was: how it originated and how it was to be managed once underway. As Charles Goen has perceptively observed, 'when [Edwards] gave his narrative to the world, the simple fact is that no revival could ever be a surprise again'.[89] The longing for revival, characteristic of so many evangelicals since the middle of the eighteenth century,[90] is in large measure due to the epistemological work carried out by Edwards in the heat and immediate aftermath of the revivals in which he himself participated. This common understanding of the way in which the Holy Spirit actually operated had a remarkably unifying effect on the revivals in England, Wales, Scotland and the American colonies, making it possible to trace common characteristics.

Expressing evangelical unity

While the revivals in England, Wales, Scotland and the American colonies were clearly generically part of the same movement, there was no administrative structure to bind them together. The most successful attempt to

---

88. D. Bruce Hindmarsh, 'The Reception of Jonathan Edwards by Early Evangelicals in England', in David W. Kling and Douglas A. Sweeney (eds.), *Jonathan Edwards at Home and Abroad: Historical Memories, Cultural Movements, Global Horizons* (Columbia: University of South Carolina Press, 2003), p. 202.

89. C. C. Goen, 'Introduction', in his *The Works of Jonathan Edwards*, vol. 4: *The Great Awakening* (New Haven: Yale University Press, 1972), p. 27.

90. One need only look at the range of chapters in Andrew Walker and Kristin Aune (eds.), *On Revival: A Critical Examination* (Carlisle: Paternoster, 2003), to appreciate the hold the concept of revival has had on generations of evangelicals since the middle of the eighteenth century.

establish such a structure was that which George Whitefield and Howel Harris attempted to put in place between the Welsh revival and the English Calvinistic movement. Following their first meeting in early 1739, Harris and Whitefield had begun to collaborate in an ad hoc fashion, discussing issues of mutual concern. In the aftermath of the splintering of the English revival in the early 1740s, Whitefield was eager to formalize the relationship between the two awakenings, largely in order to secure the long-term future of his own English converts. As a result, England and Wales were split into a number of regions, with superintendents appointed to oversee each, who reported to Quarterly Association meetings. The Quarterly meeting reported to an annual General Association, which became the chief decision-making forum of the movement. The first of these meetings was held at Watford near Caerphilly in South Wales in January 1743, where Whitefield and John Cennick representing England, together with Howel Harris, Daniel Rowland and William Williams, Pantycelyn, established the Joint Association of English and Welsh Calvinistic Methodism. Whitefield was appointed Moderator, and Harris General Superintendent, with the acknowledgment that he would have responsibility for the English revival during Whitefield's prolonged absences in the American colonies.[91]

They established what was, in essence, a connexional system of government, albeit still within the Established Church, and in the early days of the revival it served its purpose well. However, it was gradually undermined by Whitefield's lack of commitment, particularly during his four-year absence in the American colonies between 1744 and 1748, and was then irreparably damaged by Harris's excommunication from the movement in 1750 on the grounds of theological error and rumours of sexual immorality.[92] There remained a relationship of sorts between the two movements throughout the 1750s, but it took Harris's reintegration into the revival in 1763 for further collaboration to take place.[93] The Countess of Huntingdon, who by this stage had replaced Whitefield as the dominant figure in English Calvinistic Methodism, decided to locate her training college for preachers at Trevecca,[94] and then

91. Jones, 'Glorious Work', p. 215.

92. Tudur, Howell Harris, chs. 7–8.

93. R. Geraint Gruffydd, 'The Revival of 1762 and William Williams of Pantycelyn', in Emyr Roberts and R. Geraint Gruffydd, Revival and Its Fruit (Bridgend: Evangelical Library of Wales, 1981), p. 23.

94. Edwin Welch, Spiritual Pilgrim: A Reassessment of the Life of the Countess of Huntingdon (Cardiff: University of Wales Press, 1995), ch. 7; Boyd Stanley Schlenther, Queen of

came increasingly to rely on Welsh preachers to fill the pulpits of her chapels from the 1770s onwards.[95]

Considerable effort was also expended to ensure that relations between Calvinists in England and Wales and those in the American colonies were given practical expression. In the early days of the revival, the most tangible demonstration of this connection was a mutual interest in the spread of the gospel in the New World, chiefly via George Whitefield's orphanage project at Bethesda in Georgia. Whitefield had first visited the colony in 1738, and established his Orphan House in response to the endemic poverty he witnessed there.[96] In characteristic evangelical fashion, Whitefield turned the Orphan House into a faith mission, funding it by the voluntary contributions of evangelicals in the northern colonies and back home in the British Isles. Whitefield was, consequently, forced to give the Orphan House a prominent place in his ministry, concluding most sermons of his with appeals for funds and filling the pages of *The Weekly History* with accounts of events at Bethesda, especially during the periods when its religious temperature was raised. Through these accounts, Whitefield was able to control the news regarding the Orphan House that reached the ears of potential supporters in the British Isles. This became all the more important as rumours began to circulate that the regime at Bethesda was not particularly enlightened, and its management not always carried out according to the highest principles of conduct.[97]

While it would be too much to claim that the early evangelicals' commitment to the Orphan House project was pioneer missionary activity, it is not too much to assert that a commitment to the spreading of the gospel overseas characterized evangelicalism from its earliest days. The so-called modern missionary movement is usually dated to the end of the eighteenth century, but recent scholarship has shown how the optimistic ethos of the Enlightenment lent itself to the promotion of overseas Christian missions far earlier in the century.[98] Andrew Porter has attributed this to a lessening of the rigours of

the Methodists: The Countess of Huntingdon and the Eighteenth Century Crisis of Faith and Society (Bishop Auckland: Durham Academic Press, 1997), ch. 5.

95. Alan Harding, *The Countess of Huntingdon's Connexion: A Sect in Action* (Oxford: Oxford University Press, 2003), pp. 348–349.

96. Murray, *George Whitefield's Journals*, p. 156.

97. Neil J. O'Connell, 'George Whitefield and Bethesda Orphan-House', *Georgia Historical Quarterly* 54 (1970), pp. 53–54.

98. Brian Stanley, 'Christian Missions and the Enlightenment: A Re-evaluation', in Brian Stanley (ed.), *Christian Missions and the Enlightenment* (Grand Rapids:

predestinarian Calvinism, which fuelled the conviction that missionary activity was not futile, since the ultimate destiny of humankind was not predetermined.[99] For many evangelicals commitment to missionary endeavour was wrapped up in ambitious millennial speculations. Here the writings of Jonathan Edwards proved influential once again. In *The Distinguishing Marks of a Work of the Spirit of God* (1741), Edwards argued that the Great Awakening was 'the commencement of that last and greatest outpouring of the Spirit of God, that is to be in the latter ages of the world'.[100] By contributing to Whitefield's Georgia Orphan House, a genuinely transatlantic philanthropic venture, many first-generation evangelicals felt that they were claiming a tangible stake in this worldwide expansion of the evangelical faith, and hastening the second coming of Jesus Christ.

By the mid-1740s, as the initial fervour associated with the revival receded, the minds of its leaders naturally turned to ways in which they could recapture their earlier dynamism. For a brief period it seemed as though the English Calvinistic movement, the Welsh revival and the evangelicals in Scotland and the American colonies were going to come together in a remarkable show of unity through a plan to inaugurate special seasons of prayer for a fresh outpouring of the Spirit. This initiative originated in Scotland, where a group of 'awakened' ministers had begun to set aside special times each week for intercessory prayer. Evangelicals in England were invited to join, including even the otherwise ostracized John Wesley,[101] as were the colonial evangelicals Gilbert Tennant and Jonathan Edwards. But it was Edwards himself with his *A Humble Attempt to Promote Explicit Agreement and Visible Union of God's People in Extraordinary Prayers* (1747) who transformed the idea from a private agreement between like-minded ministers into an international solution to the problems dogging the evangelical movement. Edwards argued that extraordinary seasons of prayer were inextricably linked to new revivals, and that the unified commitment of God's people to pray for revival was a sure indica-

Eerdmans, 2001), pp. 1–22. For an example of this early missionary activity, see J. C. S. Mason, *The Moravian Church and the Missionary Awakening in England, 1760–1800* (London: Royal Historical Society, 2001).

99. Andrew Porter, *Religion versus Empire? British Protestant Missionaries and Overseas Expansion, 1700–1914* (Manchester: Manchester University Press, 2004), pp. 32–33.
100. In Goen, *Works of Jonathan Edwards*, vol. 4, p. 230.
101. Frank Baker (ed.), *The Works of John Wesley*, vol. 26: *Letters II: 1740–1755* (Oxford: Oxford University Press, 1982), p. 128.

tion that God would be inclined to respond favourably.[102] That the plan did not really take off is not necessarily a sign of any lack of enthusiasm, but an indication of the extent to which Whitefield's converts in England were feeling embattled and dejected, particularly once it became clear that Whitefield wished to relinquish the leadership of the Tabernacle Society, and therefore that of Calvinistic Methodism in England and Wales, altogether.[103] What the 'Concert for Prayer' demonstrates is the extent to which an evangelical movement had begun to emerge, even within a decade of the original outbreak of revival in the late 1730s. The 'Concert for Prayer' was a realistic attempt to give concrete expression to evangelical unity, drawing together Anglicans, Methodists, Presbyterians and Congregationalists and others from two continents who were concerned to revive the flagging fortunes of their movement. While it would be precipitous to argue that it was a precursor of organizations like the Evangelical Alliance, founded almost exactly a century later in 1846,[104] the 'Concert for Prayer' was at least an attempt to express unity in an organizational, rather than merely spiritual, way.

What this analysis has attempted to do is demonstrate, almost solely in relation to English Calvinistic Methodism, how a collection of widely scattered individuals, who found themselves at the vanguard of a religious revival during the middle years of the eighteenth century, turned themselves into a religious movement that cut across the old denominational and national boundaries. The Bebbington thesis has undoubtedly been pressed too far in some circles; there is no question that Bebbington himself recognizes the substantial degree of continuity between the first generation of evangelicals and their Protestant forerunners.[105] But the existence of these continuities does not necessarily jeopardize his thesis. The first generation of English evangelicals were innovators. Through the international itinerant ministry of the 'Grand Itinerant', George Whitefield, the forging of networks of communication via letters, magazines and books, and ambitious efforts to give visible expression to the commonality felt by communities of geographically dispersed evangelicals who shared a commitment to a moderate Calvinistic theology, something resembling an interdenominational, transnational and transatlantic movement was

102. George M. Marsden, *Jonathan Edwards: A Life* (New Haven: Yale University Press, 2003), pp. 334–335.

103. Dallimore, *George Whitefield*, vol. 2, pp. 256–259.

104. Ian Randall and David Hilborn, *One Body in Christ: The History and Significance of the Evangelical Alliance* (Carlisle: Paternoster, 2001), pp. 20–21.

105. Bebbington, *Evangelicalism in Modern Britain*, pp. 1, 34–35.

brought into existence. Evangelicalism did not run exclusively along existing lines of Protestant belief and practice; by its reliance on a diverse mix of individuals, ideas, books and spiritualities, a different religious configuration was brought into being. This recasting, not to say re-energising, had far-reaching consequences for the subsequent British Protestant community, so that by the nineteenth century, to use David Bebbington's own words, evangelicalism had become 'a vital force in modern Britain'.[106]

© David Ceri Jones, 2008

---

106. Ibid., p. 276.

6. 'PRAYER FOR A SAVING ISSUE': EVANGELICAL DEVELOPMENT IN NEW ENGLAND BEFORE THE GREAT AWAKENING

Thomas S. Kidd

David Bebbington has defined evangelicalism with his famous quadrilateral: *conversionism* ('the belief that lives need to be changed'), *activism* ('the expression of the gospel in effort'), *biblicism* ('a particular regard for the Bible') and *crucicentrism* ('a stress on the sacrifice of Christ on the cross'). In *Evangelicalism in Modern Britain*, Bebbington notes both continuities and discontinuities between evangelicalism and movements that preceded it, including Puritanism. On balance, however, he prefers to emphasize the discontinuity of evangelicalism from its predecessors.[1]

A close look at the years between Puritanism and evangelicalism in New England reveals the finer texture of the transition between the two. Evangelicalism did, no doubt, inaugurate a new emphasis on the discernible moment of an individual's conversion, with assurance confirming that experience. Certain kinds of activism, biblicism and crucicentrism characterized both Puritanism and evangelicalism. Bebbington's definition does not account for the most striking discontinuity between Puritanism and evangelicalism, however. New England evangelicalism was most markedly distinguished from earlier forms of Protestantism by new expectations for seasons of revival, or outpourings of the Holy Spirit. During those seasons, large numbers of

---

1. David Bebbington, *Evangelicalism in Modern Britain: A History from the 1730s to the 1980s* (London: Unwin Hyman, 1989), pp. 2–3, 34–74.

sinners would experience the convicting presence of the Spirit and convert almost simultaneously. One begins to see signs of a new emphasis on mass conversions precipitated by an outpouring of the Spirit as early as the late seventeenth century in New England.[2]

To expect revival, one had to experience despair, a mood in which the New England Puritans specialized. Puritan church leaders had famously begun lamenting the decline of their godly experiment begun in the 1660s and 1670s, and calls for moral reformation seemed not to help the perceived flood of immorality and divine judgments. In the 1670s certain New England leaders began publicly calling for prayers for an outpouring of the Holy Spirit to revive the languishing churches, while some also began trying new measures that raised the possibility of corporate renewal of individual churches and towns.

In terms of the theology of revival, Samuel Torrey, pastor of Weymouth, Massachusetts, might be considered the first evangelical in New England. Torrey was the son of William Torrey, a Puritan with significant interests in eschatology, who moved his family to Massachusetts in 1640 when Samuel was eight. Samuel attended but did not graduate from Harvard, because of a disagreement about degree requirements, and in 1666 he became the minister at Weymouth. There he rose to a sufficiently prominent position to be offered the presidency of Harvard in 1682 and 1684, which he declined both times. In 1757, Samuel Torrey's *A Brief Discourse Concerning Futurities* was posthumously published in Boston, including a preface by Thomas Prince, Sr., who recalled Samuel Torrey as a powerful, emotional speaker: 'His Sermons were very scriptural, experimental, pathetical, sensibly flowing from a warm and pious Heart. When He treated on awful Subjects, it was with most awakening Solemnity.' Prince, himself one of the leaders of the Anglo-American evangelical movement, presented Torrey in the evangelical style, and given Torrey's public rhetoric it is plausible to consider him the earliest evangelical spokesman in New England.[3]

---

2. Bebbington, *Evangelicalism in Modern Britain*, pp. 5–10; Jerald C. Brauer, 'Conversion: From Puritanism to Revivalism', *Journal of Religion* 58.3 (July 1978), pp. 238–243; Michael J. Crawford, *Seasons of Grace: Colonial New England's Revival Tradition in Its British Context* (New York: Oxford University Press, 1991), pp. 22–23; D. Bruce Hindmarsh, *The Evangelical Conversion Narrative: Spiritual Autobiography in Early Modern England* (New York: Oxford University Press, 2005), pp. 53–54, 61–62.

3. Samuel Torrey, *A Brief Discourse Concerning Futurities* (Boston, 1757), pp. i–ii; John Sibley (ed.), *Biographical Sketches of Graduates of Harvard University* (Cambridge, Mass.: Charles William Sever, 1873), vol. 1, pp. 564–567; Kenneth Murdock, *Handkerchiefs from Paul* (Cambridge, Mass.: Harvard University Press, 1927), p. xxxix.

In three election sermons in Boston, delivered in 1674, 1683 and 1695, Torrey raised doubts as to whether the churches' efforts to reform could ever succeed without an effusion of the Holy Spirit leading to large numbers of conversions. Certainly, Torrey continued to emphasize the 'Work of Reformation', but thought what the work truly needed was 'Heart-reformation, or making of a new heart'. The churches would not revive through their moral effort, Torrey argued, but only when God poured 'out abundance of converting grace, and so revive and renew the work of Conversion'. The problem with the churches was that too many congregants had no vital experience of the Spirit, and 'if ever these Churches be thoroughly recovered, it will be, it must be by such a dispensation of converting grace, unto an unconverted generation'. By 1674 Torrey was already proclaiming the need for revival among pastors and congregations, arguing that 'If God make this Ministry a Converting Ministry, the Work of Reformation will be again revived.' He called for 'Prayer unto God for a dispensation of Converting grace by their Ministry, that the Work of Conversion, and so the Work of Reformation, may be revived.' In Torrey's mind, the work of reformation began with the work of conversion.[4]

Torrey and Josiah Flint wrote the preface to William Adams's 1678 fast sermon *The Necessity of the Pouring out of the Spirit from on High upon a Sinning Apostatizing People* and continued to call for revival. The mood in New England following King Philip's War (1675–6) was bleak and raw, and Torrey and Flint thought it obvious that 'we are a people in extream danger of perishing, in our own sins and under Gods Judgements'. Moreover, 'all ordinary means' of promoting moral reformation had failed, making them wonder whether 'our degeneracy and apostacy may not prove Judicial, and so perpetual'. Perhaps, they thought, God had condemned New Englanders to damnable sinfulness because of their intransigence. If so, then no one could reverse the downward slide, except for God. The only answer was for God to pour out a spirit of revival. 'Truly then it is high time for all orders, degrees & societies of men in New-England, by faith in prayer, to seek the Lord until he come and rain righteousness upon us.' Evangelicals like Torrey always held out a proactive role for the people in revival, but this role was for them to seek God often in prayer.[5]

Torrey continued these pleas in his 1683 and 1695 election sermons. He thought that if only New England would mourn for its sins, God would revive pure religion. In fact, he thought godly mourning would be a sign of the coming

---

4. Samuel Torrey, *An Exhortation unto Reformation* (Cambridge, Mass., 1674), pp. 10, 34; Crawford, *Seasons of Grace*, p. 19.
5. William Adams, *The Necessity of the Pouring out of the Spirit* (Boston, 1679), A2–A5.

revival: 'We must follow God mourning . . . this is the way wherein God prom-
iseth to revive his People . . . Such a Mourning is the certain effect of the saving dispensation of the Spirit and converting Grace.' In the greatest of Torrey's
sermons promoting revival, his 1695 *Mans Extremity, Gods Opportunity*, he argued
that New England's sin was so severe that hope for ordinary reformation was
gone. Providential history offered hope, however, because 'there are certain
times, and extraordinary cases, wherein God . . . Saves his People by Himself'.
The Puritan colonies had once been godly showcases for the Reformation, but
had forgotten their first love. Their sins were many, but they were not grieved by
them. Torrey thought that God would reclaim New England, and 'O when God
comes to Save New-England by himself, we shall see and feel wonderful effects
& changes.' Hearkening back to John Winthrop's vision for New England in *A
Model of Christian Charity* (1630), Torrey assured his audience that God

> will magnifie New-England again before the world . . . God will glorifie himself
> before all people in us, when he shall thus Save us from our sins & apostacy, by the
> power of his Spirit, in a general work of Conversion and Reformation; and by a
> glorious resurrection of Religion.[6]

God indeed had a controversy with New England because of its unrepentant
hearts, but God himself would set New England right when he sent the revival.

It is one thing, of course, to discuss revival, and another to see it happen.
When did the evangelical revivals begin? The clearest antecedents to the revivals of the 1720s to 1740s were the periodic covenant renewals in New England.
Historian Perry Miller once argued that the Great Awakening was 'nothing
more than an inevitable culmination' of the covenant renewals.[7] These renewals
had roots in English Puritanism. After King Philip's War, increasingly desperate
ministers held a Reforming Synod of 1679, calling for repentance. Soon New
England saw what one might call a revival of renewals: a great new interest in
corporate commitments to God and the covenant. As promoted by Boston's

---

6. Samuel Torrey, *A Plea for the Life of Dying Religion* (Boston, 1683), p. 25; Samuel
   Torrey, *Mans Extremity, Gods Opportunity* (Boston, 1695), pp. 10, 36, 59; Crawford,
   Seasons of Grace, pp. 34–35; Stephen Foster, *The Long Argument: English Puritanism and
   the Shaping of New England Culture, 1570–1700* (Chapel Hill, N. C.: Published for the
   Institute of Early American History and Culture, Williamsburg, Va., by the
   University of North Carolina Press, 1991), pp. 271–272.

7. Perry Miller, 'Jonathan Edwards and the Great Awakening', in his *Errand into the
   Wilderness* (Cambridge, Mass.: Harvard University Press, 1956), p. 160.

Increase Mather, the covenant renewal usually featured the pastor reminding all church members, including 'halfway' church members not yet admitted to the Lord's Supper, of their covenant promises to God and each other. A major reform, the Halfway Covenant of 1662, had allowed growing numbers of those New Englanders who were baptized and moral, but not converted, to have their own children baptized. Normally only full members had received this privilege prior to 1662, so the Halfway Covenant extended the right of baptism, but not the Lord's Supper, to many of the unregenerate. The Halfway system ensured that the churches would be filled with substantial numbers of pseudo-members waiting for their conversion. That situation set the stage for outbreaks of spiritual fervour, precipitating mass numbers of conversions.

The renewal presented an opportunity for all to consider whether they were right before God, and also for halfway members to seek conversion and full admission into church membership. The covenant renewal ceremony would often be followed by weeks of preaching on salvation and conversion, which led to many conversions in a number of churches. Pastor James Fitch of Norwich, Connecticut, led the first of these covenant renewal ceremonies in March 1676, and his was followed by hosts of others over the next four years. Thomas Prince later recalled these renewals as the first 'Instances of the transient REVIVAL of Religion in some particular Places in the Midst' of New England's declension.[8]

During King Philip's War, John Cotton, Jr., of Plymouth, Massachusetts, also led his congregation through covenant renewal. He began by addressing the

---

8. Thomas Prince, Jr., *The Christian History* (4 June 1743), vol. 1, pp. 106–107; Perry Miller, 'Jonathan Edwards and the Great Awakening', in his *Errand into the Wilderness* (Cambridge, Mass.: Harvard University Press, 1956), p. 160. On covenant renewals, see Foster, *Long Argument*, pp. 223–230, 239; Mark Peterson, *The Price of Redemption: The Spiritual Economy of Puritan New England* (Stanford, Calif.: Stanford University Press, 1997), p. 48; Mark Peterson, 'The Plymouth Church and the Evolution of Puritan Religious Culture', *New England Quarterly* 66.4 (Dec. 1993), pp. 581–582, 587–588; Charles Hambrick-Stowe, *The Practice of Piety: Puritan Devotional Disciplines in Seventeenth-Century New England* (Chapel Hill, N. C.: Published for the Institute of Early American History and Culture, Williamsburg, Va., by the University of North Carolina Press, 1982), pp. 130–132, 248–253; Harry S. Stout, *The New England Soul: Preaching and Religious Culture in Colonial New England* (New York: Oxford University Press, 1986), pp. 96–99; Richard Gildrie, *The Profane, the Civil, and the Godly: The Reformation of Manners in Orthodox New England, 1679–1749* (University Park, Pa.: Pennsylvania State University Press, 1994), pp. 26–27, 38.

ways that the church had forsaken their covenant with God, and pleading with
the 'children of the church' (members who had been baptized but not admitted
to the Lord's Supper) to come to full ownership of the covenant, and to come to
the Lord's Table. On 18 July 1676, Cotton addressed the whole church and pled
with all to consider their commitment to the Lord, and made a special plea for
halfway members to own the covenant and further secure the rising generation's
fidelity. In coming years, Cotton bolstered the renewal by hosting catechetical
small-group meetings for fathers in the church, and by these means successfully
brought much of the next generation into full church communion.[9]

Likewise, in 1680, covenant renewals occurred in the North and Old
South Churches in Boston, and in Salem and Haverhill. The Salem church
acknowledged that they could not 'perform any spiritual duty unless the Lord
enable us thereunto by the Grace of his Spirit', but they were 'awfully sensible
that in these times by the loud voice of his judgments both felt and feared, the
Lord is calling us all to Repentance and Reformation'. They recognized the
Reforming Synod's promotion of the covenant renewals, and responded to the
Synod's catalogue of New England's sins with a cry for 'pardoning mercy'.[10]
The Reforming Synod's call for massive repentance was doing its work.

Samuel Willard, one of the leaders of the Reforming Synod, led the Old
South Church in covenant renewal in 1680. Early that year a number of children of the church approached Willard about publicly embracing the responsi-
bilities of their baptismal covenant. That summer, Willard led the whole church
through the renewal, and more than a hundred eventually owned the baptismal covenant, with many of those also eventually becoming full communicant
members. 1680 proved to be the greatest harvest time of Willard's distinguished
ministry. The revival of 1680 'soon pass'd away', according to Prince, and the
pastors were left again to worry over the provoking sins of New England.[11]

The key covenant renewal in New England, however, and the most
publicized, was the ceremony at Taunton (in south-eastern Massachusetts) in
1705 led by Samuel Danforth, Jr. Danforth's covenant renewal received attention in the 1706 *A Help to a National Reformation*, printed in London, England,
and Danforth published his sermon at the renewal and the renewal covenant

---

9. Peterson, 'Plymouth Church', pp. 587–588.

10. Foster, *Long Argument*, p. 229; *A Copy of the Church-Covenants which Have Been Used
    in the Church of Salem* (Boston, 1680), pp. 5, 7.

11. Peterson, *Price of Redemption*, p. 48; Seymour Van Dyken, *Samuel Willard, 1640–1707:
    Preacher of Orthodoxy in an Era of Change* (Grand Rapids: Eerdmans, 1972), pp.
    39–40; Prince, *Christian History*, vol. 1, p. 108.

itself in *Piety Encouraged*, in Boston in 1705. Thomas Prince presented the Taunton renewal as 'a second Instance' of revival following the 1680 renewals, and reprinted in his revivalist newspaper *The Christian History* a passage from *A Help to a National Reformation* and letters from Danforth giving accounts of the renewal. Taunton's church had held a covenant renewal during King Philip's War in 1676, and now Danforth used the renewal again as a means to awaken his congregation, and especially those who had not become full members. Danforth had received accounts of reformation societies meeting in England, and thought that these might prove useful for the promotion of conversions and true piety in Taunton. So in 1704 he began meeting monthly with lay leaders in the church 'to consult what might be done to promote a Reformation of Disorders there'. This group began organizing fathers in the town for regular family worship. Danforth also began organizing young people's meetings, following ones in London and the recently established model by Cotton Mather in Boston. Danforth, like future evangelicals, saw reforming his town's youth as a top priority of revival, and the meetings put 'an End to & utter Banishment of their former disorderly and profane Meetings to drink, &c'.[12]

Danforth reported in February 1705 that 'we are much encouraged by an unusual and amazing Impression, made by GOD'S SPIRIT on all Sorts among us, especially on the young Men and Women'. The young people had become sober as a result of the meetings and some 'awful Deaths and amazing Providences'. He hoped that their sobriety was not temporary, and asked for 'Prayer, that these Strivings of the SPIRIT, may have a saving Issue'. On 1 March 1705, Danforth led the covenant renewal itself. The covenant of 1676 was read aloud, and 'We gave Liberty to all Men and Women Kind, from sixteen Years old and upwards to act with us; and had three hundred Names given in to list under Christ, against the Sins of the Times.' He thought perhaps a hundred more who could not attend that service would soon submit their names. Danforth also noted a number of new full memberships, as well as some adult baptisms. Later that month Danforth reported that he had no time for his regular pastoral duties because of his constant visits from young people seeking their salvation. He thought that this commotion might be a sign of something greater yet to come: 'I think sometimes that the Time of the pouring out of the SPIRIT upon all Flesh, may be at the Door. Lets be

---

12. Cotton Mather, *Methods and Motives for Societies to Suppress Disorders* (Boston, 1703); *Private Meetings Animated and Regulated* (Boston, 1706); Gildrie, *Profane, the Civil, and the Godly*, pp. 202–208; Prince, *Christian History* (4 June 1743), vol. 1, pp. 108–109; Crawford, *Seasons of Grace*, pp. 46–47.

earnest in Prayer that CHRIST's Kingdom may come.' For his part, Cotton
Mather noted that 'the Spirit of Grace has of late been doing wondrously in
our Taunton', and commended the late 'astonishing Harvest' led by Danforth.
Mather cautioned against satanic excesses, and though it is not clear whether
Mather had already heard of such excesses, he wrote in his diary that he
thought it fitting to warn the Taunton renewers against the devil's schemes
to hurt 'a glorious work of God which has lately been done, in bringing that
popular and vicious Town to a wonderful Reformation'.[13]

Taunton's renewal was only one of many 'revivals' before the 'First' Great
Awakening. In the 1710s and 1720s, these occurrences became more frequent in
New England.[14] Much of the earliest revival activity, in the form of covenant
renewals, was in eastern Massachusetts, but the trend towards revivalism was
also growing in the Connecticut River Valley, particularly under the ministry
of Solomon Stoddard of Northampton, Massachusetts, the grandfather and
ministerial predecessor of Jonathan Edwards. Stoddard passed on a considerable revivalist heritage to Edwards, as Edwards noted in his *A Faithful Narrative
of the Surprising Work of God* (1737). He described Stoddard as 'renowned for his
gifts and grace; so he was blessed, from the beginning, with extraordinary success in his ministry in the conversion of many souls. He had five harvests, as he
called them.' These 'harvests' came in 1679, 1683, 1690, 1712 and 1718. Stoddard
himself told his congregation in 1687, 'I have made it my business to gain Souls
to Christ,' and in this business he may have been the most successful of any
New England preacher in his generation. Stoddard relied on the Lord's Supper
as a 'converting ordinance', or a preparatory ritual that could lead unconverted
seekers to Christ. On this point Stoddard significantly differed from his eastern
New England colleagues, who believed that the Supper was only meant for the
converted.[15] Stoddard had to defend his policy of open communion against

13. Prince, *Christian History*, vol. 1, pp. 109–112; Samuel Danforth, *Piety Encouraged*
     (Boston, 1705), A2, A5; Cotton Mather, *The Diary of Cotton Mather* (New York:
     Frederick Ungar, n. d.), p. 513.

14. Among the New England revivals noted by contemporaries, beyond those I shall
     discuss here, there were revivals in Lynn, Mass.,1712 (Jeremiah Shepard, pastor);
     East Windsor, Conn., 1712–13, 1715–16 (Timothy Edwards, pastor); Preston, Conn.,
     1716 (Salmon Treat, pastor); Norwich, Conn., 1718 (Benjamin Lord, pastor);
     Woodbury, Conn., 1726–7 (Anthony Stoddard, pastor). List mainly derived from
     Crawford, *Seasons of Grace*, p. 108.

15. John E. Smith, Harry S. Stout and Kenneth Minkema (eds.), *A Jonathan Edwards
     Reader* (New Haven: Yale University Press, 1995), p. 58; Solomon Stoddard, *The Safety*

various attacks from the eastern establishment, and argued that he would not hesitate to 'clear up a Truth that has not been received, whereby a door is opened for the revival of Religion'. Edwards was particularly impressed that during each harvest 'the bigger part of the young people in the town seemed to be mainly concerned for their eternal salvation'.[16] Here was a key feature of the evangelical style of ministry: getting young people to turn away from their silly frolics and think about their eternal destinies.

Stoddard developed the most extensive evangelical theology of conversion prior to Edwards. As an orthodox Calvinist, Stoddard firmly believed that the Spirit of God drew sinners to salvation, but he also believed that powerful preaching was often the means that God used to draw people. Thus Stoddard promoted a Calvinist view of evangelism by powerful preachers who warned of the threat of damnation on one hand and offered the hope of salvation through Christ's grace on the other. This view no doubt heavily influenced his grandson Edwards. Stoddard argued that the dread of damnation was the most, and perhaps the only, effective means to lead sinners to true 'humiliation', or a sense that their sin was grievous and awful in the light of God's holiness. God

---

of Appearing (Boston, 1687), A4; Thomas A. Schafer, 'Solomon Stoddard and the Theology of the Revival', in Stuart C. Henry (ed.), *A Miscellany of American Christianity: Essays in Honor of H. Shelton Smith* (Durham, N. C.: Duke University Press, 1963), pp. 332–340. On Stoddard, and his influence on Jonathan Edwards and evangelicalism generally, see also Ralph J. Coffman, *Solomon Stoddard* (Boston: Twayne, 1978); Paul R. Lucas, '"The Death of the Prophet Lamented": The Legacy of Solomon Stoddard', in Stephen J. Stein (ed.), *Jonathan Edwards's Writings: Text, Context, Interpretation* (Bloomington: Indiana University Press, 1996), pp. 69–84; 'An Appeal to the Learned: The Mind of Solomon Stoddard', *William and Mary Quarterly* 3rd ser., 30.2 (Apr. 1973), pp. 257–292; Perry Miller, 'Solomon Stoddard, 1643–1729', *Harvard Theological Review* 34 (1941), pp. 277–320; E. Brooks Holifield, 'The Intellectual Sources of Stoddardeanism', *New England Quarterly* 45.3 (Sept. 1972), pp. 373–392; James Walsh, 'Solomon Stoddard's Open Communion: A Reexamination', *New England Quarterly* 43.1 (Mar. 1970), pp. 97–114; Patricia J. Tracy, *Jonathan Edwards, Pastor: Religion and Society in Eighteenth-Century Northampton* (New York: Hill & Wang, 1980), pp. 13–50; Norman Pettit, *The Heart Prepared: Grace and Conversion in Puritan Spiritual Life* (Middletown, Conn.: Wesleyan University Press, 1989²), pp. 200–207; Crawford, *Seasons of Grace*, pp. 47–50, 71–76; George M. Marsden, *Jonathan Edwards: A Life* (New Haven: Yale University Press, 2003), pp. 11–14, 114–127.

16. Solomon Stoddard, *An Appeal to the Learned* (Boston, 1709), A3; Smith, Stout and Minkema, *Jonathan Edwards Reader*, p. 58.

awakened conviction of sin, to be followed by the hope that Christ's grace was sufficient to deliver them from the judgment of God. The brutal wars that plagued the Connecticut River Valley through the length of his ministry in Northampton no doubt coloured Stoddard's preaching on judgment and damnation. The families there knew precisely how immediate the judgment could be, in the light of episodes like the Deerfield raid of 1704 that had decimated Northampton's neighbours to the north. Northamptonites, faced with the ever-present threat of French Catholic and Native American attacks, could easily accept Stoddard's reminders of the threat of judgment.[17]

Following ideas similar to those of his contemporary Samuel Torrey, Stoddard insisted that conversions would not happen without the presence of the Holy Spirit. Stoddard noted in his 1713 *The Efficacy of the Fear of Hell, to Restrain Men from Sin* that in times of languishing piety, 'there are means that are serviceable for the reviving of it: And this is one special means, when the Ministers have the Spirit of the Lord upon them. The Spirit of the Lord must be poured out upon the People, else Religion will not revive.' Apparently, Stoddard had just seen such a pouring out, as one of his 'harvests' had occurred in 1712. Notice that in Stoddard's model, the Spirit poured through the ministers. His was still very much a church and community-based theology of conversion, different from some of the more individualistic and anti-clerical tendencies some evangelicals would later embrace. Stoddard argued that the Spirit allowed ministers to preach powerfully the threat of God's judgment, and 'if the Consciences of Men be terrified, that makes way for their Conversion'.[18]

Stoddard also posited that the church should expect seasons of revival to come, characterized by special outpourings of the Spirit. In times of revival, the Spirit would quicken the believers' faith, convert grieving sinners and make careless sinners more interested in things of God. Stoddard thought that revival could be general or particular. For instance, he saw the Reformation as a general revival, 'when some Nations broke off from Popery, and embraced the Gospel'. He also believed, however, that revival sometimes came to individual towns or congregations, as it had to Northampton in his church's harvests. God determined the time and extent of revivals, but God also chose to respond to people's prayers for revival. Thus, Stoddard insisted, 'we should beg of God, that Religion may revive in this Land'. Stoddard, with the endorsement of his old nemesis Increase Mather, also helped build the foundation for evangelicalism when he

---

17. Schafer, 'Solomon Stoddard', pp. 335–346; Lucas, 'Death of the Prophet', p. 79.

18. Solomon Stoddard, *The Efficacy of the Fear of Hell, to Restrain Men from Sin* (Boston, 1713), pp. 34, 40.

wrote *A Guide to Christ* in 1714, which became a standard treatise on evangelical conversion in Anglo-American evangelical circles through to the nineteenth century. George Whitefield, for one, thought highly of Stoddard's work and especially recommended *A Guide to Christ* as a solid evangelical text.[19]

Stoddard's evangelical theology ultimately promoted the evangelization of North America's Native American societies and the expansion of the gospel across the globe. If religion languished among the Christian churches of New England, then who would bring the message of Christ to the pagan Indians? Stoddard knew the answer: the Roman Catholics, and specifically the Jesuits, would enter the vacuum and lead the Indians astray with their false gospel. He expressed public embarrassment about New England's near-total failure to evangelize Native Americans. In *An Answer to Some Cases of Conscience Respecting the Country* (1722) and *Question Whether God Is not Angry with the Country for Doing so Little towards the Conversion of the Indians?* (1723), as new war raged with northern Wabanakis and their Jesuit supporter, Father Sebastien Rale, Stoddard chastised New Englanders for their failures to evangelize the Indians. Appended to *An Answer* was a hopeful poem he had penned in 1701, which asked God to 'Give the poor INDIANS Eyes to see, / The Light of Life: and set them free'. He anticipated the millennial day in which 'ASIA, and AFRICA, EUROPA, with AMERICA: / All Four, in Consort join'd, shall Sing, / New Songs of Praise to CHRIST our KING'. For this day to come, and for the Roman Catholic powers to be destroyed, Protestants needed a great outpouring of the Holy Spirit. This hope Stoddard passed on to many Anglo-American evangelicals who for the next 150 years would read his works. Not least among these successors were Stoddard's son-in-law Timothy Edwards, and his grandson Jonathan Edwards.[20]

Like Stoddard, many early evangelicals believed that they participated in a great global expansion of the gospel. Some thought this expansion might

19. Ibid., pp. 190, 197; George Whitefield, *George Whitefield's Journals* (Carlisle, Pa.: Banner of Truth, 1962), pp. 462, 476. *A Guide to Christ* saw these American editions: Boston, 1714, 1735, 1742; New York, 1751; Newburyport, Mass., 1801; New York, 1813; Northampton, Mass., 1816; and these British editions: Yarmouth, 1819; London, 1825; Edinburgh, 1848.

20. Solomon Stoddard, *An Answer to Some Cases of Conscience Respecting the Country* (Boston, 1722), pp. 10–13, 16; Stoddard, *Question Whether God Is not Angry* (Boston, 1723), pp. 9–12; Thomas S. Kidd, *The Protestant Interest: New England after Puritanism* (New Haven: Yale University Press, 2004), pp. 104–106, 160–161; Lucas, 'Death of the Prophet', pp. 75–76. On Stoddard's relationship to Timothy and Jonathan Edwards, see Marsden, *Jonathan Edwards*, pp. 23, 29–33, 112–125.

end in the destruction of Roman Catholicism and Islam, the mass conversion of the Jews to Christianity, and the coming of the millennium. No one was more interested in these eschatological developments than Increase and Cotton Mather, who received every piece of news of successful evangelism from overseas as a sign of the approaching last days. For instance, in Increase Mather's 1710 *A Discourse Concerning Faith and Fervency*, he called for fervent prayer in response to the news that Dutch missionaries were winning converts in the East Indies, and continued reports of Jewish conversions in Europe. Though he thought that the Spirit alone brought conversions, he believed that God chose to send the Spirit in response to believers' prayers. The more news became available about missions, as well as the persecution of European Protestants, the more urgently writers like Mather called for prayers supporting the expansion of the global church and the hastening of the last days. 'We should therefore Pray that there may be a plentiful Effusion of the Holy Spirit on the world. Then will Converting work go forward among the Nations.' He dreamed of the last days, expedited by prayers: 'Oh that the Jewish Nation were Converted! Oh that the fullness of the Gentiles were come in! Oh that our Lord Jesus Christ would Come and take possession of the World for himself.'[21] Following writers like Mather, early evangelicals thought a great deal about global, national, regional and local effusions of the Spirit.

Stoddard helped foster a sense that churches along the Connecticut and Thames Rivers in western New England could help begin a great new revival of religion, and a number of his younger colleagues began to promote revival in the 1710s and 1720s. This was especially true of the key early evangelical minister in Connecticut, Eliphalet Adams of New London. Though later a target of radical evangelical attacks because of his moderation and opposition to unrestrained itinerancy, Adams became in the 1710s and 1720s a great proponent of both the new revivalism and increased clerical authority. One historian has suggested that his zeal for promoting revival was an 'obsession'. Obsessive or not, Adams surely became one of the most vocal proponents of the need for a massive outpouring of the Holy Spirit in Connecticut.[22] He thought that a revival in Connecticut could spark a larger revival fire, which

---

21. Increase Mather, *A Discourse Concerning Faith and Fervency* (Boston, 1710), pp. 65, 84. This book, which seems to have been sold by at least five Boston booksellers in the 1710s, was also printed in London in 1713 and Ireland in 1820. Michael Hall, *The Last American Puritan: The Life of Increase Mather* (Middletown, Conn.: Wesleyan University Press, 1988), p. 325.

22. Lucas, 'Appeal to the Learned', p. 290, n. 83.

might ultimately consume the globe. Adams, along with East Windsor's Timothy Edwards, Norwich's Benjamin Lord, Windham's Samuel Whiting and Windsor's Jonathan Marsh formed the most activist contingent yet of evangelical ministers in New England. This group helped lead a series of local and regional revivals in the Connecticut River Valley in the 1710s and 1720s.

Timothy Edwards, husband of Stoddard's daughter Esther, was 'an expert on the science of conversion', according to historian George Marsden. Unlike Stoddard, Edwards still required applicants for full membership to give a public conversion 'relation', some of which have survived as testimony to his revival ministry. He led four or five revivals in his East Windsor congregation before the 1734–5 Northampton awakening, according to Jonathan Edwards's adult memory. At least two of these took place in the 1710s and profoundly affected Jonathan. In 1716, the young Jonathan wrote to his sister Mary that 'there hath in this place been a very remarkable stirring and pouring out of the Spirit of God . . . About thirteen have been joined to the church.'[23] Edwards's awakenings were followed by more regional revivals in the coming years, punctuated especially by a large regional revival in towns along the Connecticut and Thames Rivers from 1720 to 1722.

Samuel Whiting's Windham church saw one of the largest awakenings in 1721, with eighty people joining the church in about six months. Eliphalet Adams gave a thanksgiving sermon at the church in July 1721 to commend Whiting's ministry and celebrate the 'greater Stirring than Ordinary among the dry bones'. He hoped that the Windham revival might inspire others: 'Oh! That the same Good Spirit from on High were poured out upon the rest of the Country . . . May the Lord Please to revive his own work.' Adams also used the imminence of the last days as a motivation for revival: 'WHO can tell but that as he hath begun to pour out of His good Spirit, so he may please to perfect the good work and cause the Good favour of his Knowledge to spread far and wide . . . seeing the Times are drawing near.' He exhorted Christians to 'Pray for the Success of the Gospel in other Places & for the Peace of Jerusalem.' Lay prayer was key to the revival of piety in New England, and the coming of the great revivals of the last days. Therefore, he called on them to 'Pray that the Spirit may be poured out from on High upon every part of the Land, that the work of Religion may not die among Us where it once so remarkably flourished.'[24] Early

---

23. Kenneth Minkema, 'The East Windsor Relations, 1700–1725', *Connecticut Historical Society Bulletin* 51 (1986), pp. 3–63; Marsden, *Jonathan Edwards*, pp. 25–26, 33.

24. Eliphalet Adams, *A Sermon Preached at Windham, July 12th, 1721* (New London, 1721), pp. ii–vi, 39–40.

evangelicals celebrated current revival activity, but never saw it as complete, because they knew that a greater revival always remained on the horizon.

The Connecticut revival of 1720–2 was the first major revival of the evangelical era in New England. It touched congregations in Windham, Preston, Franklin, Norwich, and Windsor, Connecticut, and seems to have resulted in several hundred new memberships, and perhaps more conversions. However, its significance has been obscured because of the lack of printed publicity surrounding the revival. Revivals had begun in force, but the print trades did not yet fully service the creation of the awakenings. Thus, not only has the Connecticut revival been largely forgotten, but it also remained a limited regional revival and did not extend to other parts of New England or the rest of the colonies.[25]

The most significant awakening before Jonathan Edwards's 1734–5 Northampton awakening, however, came in response to a 1727 earthquake in New England. It was this revival that began the trend of publicizing awakenings on a massive scale in order to promote further revivals. No doubt the dramatic and frightening nature of the event fed into its marketability in print, and some thirty sermons were eventually published concerning the earthquake.[26]

On Sunday evening, 29 October, a terrible earthquake shook New Englanders' homes, waking many up both physically and spiritually. This was followed by a long series of aftershocks that kept the threat fresh in the minds of penitents. Immediately, the churches filled with seekers anxious to secure their salvation, lest they be caught unprepared for their own death, or the last days. Jonathan Pearson, a layman in the Lynn End, Massachusetts, church, reported that

> God has by the late amazing Earth-quake Layd open my neglect before me that I see no way to escape. But by fleeing to Christ for refuge. God in that hour Set all my Sins before me. When I was Shaking over the pit looking every moment when the earth would open her mouth and Swallow me up and then must I have been miserable for ever & for ever.[27]

25. Crawford, *Seasons of Grace*, pp. 108–110.

26. Ibid., pp. 114–117; Erik Seeman, *Pious Persuasions: Laity and Clergy in Eighteenth-Century New England* (Baltimore: Johns Hopkins University Press, 1999), pp. 149–154; Stout, *New England Soul*, pp. 177–179.

27. Kenneth Minkema, 'The Lynn End "Earthquake" Relations of 1727', *New England Quarterly* 69.3 (Sept. 1996), p. 490.

His experience seems to have been common in 1727 and 1728, as the pastors preached up revival with a most striking object lesson at hand: an earth that seemed ready to open up and swallow the people. The earthquake helped spark revival in the Merrimac Valley towns of Haverhill, Hampton, Newbury, Bradford and Andover, Massachusetts, where the earthquake had been centred. Andover and Malden, Massachusetts, both held covenant renewal services on 21 December in response to the earthquake.[28]

Haverhill's church in particular witnessed a large revival after the earthquake, as documented by Pastor John Brown in a 20 November letter to Newton's John Cotton. Brown told Cotton that his church, often joined by the Bradford, Massachusetts, church, met in a series of fervent services after the first earthquake. Many came to Brown seeking full membership, baptism or renewal of their baptismal covenant: 154 people in all. Brown noted that most of these were young people. He also wrote that many gross sinners had come under deep conviction and now sought salvation. 'There seems to be in the Town, a General Reformation,' he wrote. He had heard that the revival had spread to Exeter also, with forty baptized there since the earthquake. Someone also told him that at Almsbury 'they were willing to spend their whole time in the Worship of God'.[29]

Although Brown thought that God had sent the earthquake to help precipitate the revival, he did not believe that the earthquake alone precipitated it. He remembered that since the spring of 1727 he had seen a new religious interest in his congregation, and the earthquake had only served to sharpen that already existing appetite. Brown wanted to correspond with Cotton in order to hear of the revival's extent elsewhere, and hear 'what are the thoughts of the most Judicious about the Signs of the Times'. Eschatological speculations were never far in the background when awakenings came. He asked for Cotton to send him 'the best accounts and communicate this where you think proper'.[30] Brown here suggested methods of promoting revival that would become critical in the 1730s and 1740s. Ministerial correspondence and printers would publicize and help drive the revivals, making what formerly might have remained localized stirs into regional, continental and transoceanic explosions of revivalist religion. Cotton responded to his friend's request by arranging for Brown's letter to be published along with Cotton's own sermon

---

28. *On a Day of Public Fasting and Prayer* (Boston, c. 1727); Samuel Phillips, *Three Plain Practical Discourses, Preach'd at Andover* (Boston, 1728).

29. John Cotton, *A Holy Fear of God* (Boston, 1727), appendix, pp. 5–7.

30. Ibid., p. 6.

A Holy Fear of God: Brown would lead his congregation in a covenant renewal on 21 March 1728, like the church had done in 1680.

The leading pastors of New England responded to the earthquake with calls for repentance, and argued that the trembling earth was a divine providence that God might pair with a new outpouring of the Spirit to bring revival. At the opening of the General Court in Boston, three weeks after the initial earthquake, Thomas Foxcroft tried to show how God spoke through the earthquake. He thought 'it is a hopeful Symptom of the Spirit's co-operating with Divine Providence, that we hear so many, in great fear & concern for their Souls, crying out with the Jaylor, What must I do to be saved?' It was a special opportunity for New Englanders to promote reformation and revival. He believed that God brought both a punishing and a winsome message in the earthquake. The punishment was against the provoking sins of New England. He particularly noted people's waste and overindulgence, 'the Superfluities of their voluptuous Tables', sexual immorality, lying, Sabbath-breaking, financial oppression and extortion as the worst iniquities. These 'expose the Land to shaking Dispensations'. But the Lord also sent a message of hope in the earthquake. No one had died, and thus it was not too late to find salvation in Christ. Foxcroft called on the ministers to seize the moment of spiritual receptivity. 'After Men have been so terrify'd by Earthquake and great Noise, what more likely to melt and charm their Souls, than the still small Voice of the preached Gospel?' He prayed that God would 'pour out his Spirit upon us, that we may give ourselves wholly to these things' and see New England revive.[31]

Thomas Prince of the Old South Church thought that the earthquake was worth the damage caused, if accompanied by revival. After noting the course of the earthquake in the appendix to his *Earthquakes the Works of God* (1727), he rejoiced that the terrible shaking had led to a 'wonderful Reformation'. People had abandoned their grievous sins, and had 'vastly thronged' the churches. Many hundreds had come forward for baptism, covenant renewal, or admission to communion. The terror of the earthquake had become the delight of revival: 'What a Joy is There, even as the Joy of the Harvest, and as Men rejoice when they divide the spoil! What an happy Effusion of the HOLY SPIRIT!' Later, as the revival cooled, the ministers may have felt slightly embarrassed that the first major awakening in the evangelical era had been prompted by a natural disaster. Prince gave little attention to the earthquake revival in *The Christian History*, citing only the Boston ministers' introduction to the third edition of Edwards's *Faithful Narrative*, where they noted that God

---

31. Thomas Foxcroft, *The Voice of the Lord* (Boston, 1727), pp. 37–38, 41–44.

in 1727 was 'present to awaken many'. However, the fear of the earthquake did not last, and 'there has since been great Reason to complain of our speedy Return to our former Sins, notwithstanding some Hopes given of a more general Reformation'. This became a familiar cycle for evangelicals: bursts of revival would invariably be followed by a waning of fervour and a waxing of worldliness. Nevertheless, they never gave up hope that a greater, or even the final, revival of religion might soon appear. According to Prince, the next New England awakening was 'more remarkable' than the earthquake revival, for it came in a 'Time of great Security; when there was no terrible Dispensation of Providence'. This was the Northampton revival led by Solomon Stoddard's bookish grandson, Jonathan Edwards. Despite its limitations, the earthquake revival got New England's growing evangelical cohort thinking collectively about the potential for massive, publicized revival.[32]

As we have seen, many revivals and covenant renewals preceded the revivals usually associated with the First Great Awakening. Compared to Puritanism, evangelicalism in New England carried a heightened emphasis on conversion as the *raison d'être* of the movement and the defining experience of a believer's life. However, the most profound disjunction between the movements lay in the new evangelical emphasis on the outpouring of the Holy Spirit for revival. In these seasons of grace, the Spirit would precipitate the conviction and conversion of many sinners at one time. In retrospect, the 1734–5 'work of God in the conversion of many hundred souls in Northampton' that Jonathan Edwards elatedly described as 'surprising' may not have been that surprising after all.[33] Some New Englanders had been praying for and witnessing such outpourings of the Spirit for sixty years.[34]

© Thomas S. Kidd, 2008

32. Thomas Prince, *Earthquakes the Works of God* (Boston, 17272), appendix; Prince, *Christian History*, vol. 1, p. 114; Stout, *New England Soul*, p. 179.

33. Jonathan Edwards, *A Faithful Narrative of the Surprising Work of God in the Conversion of Many Hundred Souls in Northampton* (Boston, 1738).

34. A version of this chapter appeared in Thomas S. Kidd, *The Great Awakening: The Roots of Evangelical Christianity in Colonial America* (New Haven: Yale University Press, 2007), pp. 1–12.

7. EVANGELICALISM AND THE DUTCH FURTHER REFORMATION

Joel R. Beeke

Many of us who read David Bebbington's groundbreaking *Evangelicalism in Modern Britain: A History from the 1730s to the 1980s* in the early 1990s felt a bit overwhelmed by the breadth of his scholarship. And yet, some are also convinced that the book's very strengths also revealed its weaknesses.

Having at that time recently completed a doctoral dissertation on assurance of faith,[1] I remember how amazed I was to read Bebbington's generalizations and caricatures of the Puritan views on assurance of faith. I found myself thinking, *It's almost as if he's regurgitating the historical inaccuracies of Robert T. Kendall.*[2] I quickly turned to Bebbington's endnotes, curious about his sources, and was not surprised to find that his most serious caricatures were dependent on Kendall's now largely discredited book.[3]

---

1. Later published as Joel R. Beeke, *Assurance of Faith: Calvin, English Puritanism, and the Dutch Second Reformation* (New York: Peter Lang, 1991); then in a revised form as *The Quest for Full Assurance: The Legacy of Calvin and His Successors* (Edinburgh: Banner of Truth, 1999).

2. Robert T. Kendall, *Calvin and English Calvinism to 1649* (New York: Oxford University Press, 1979).

3. E.g. Paul Helm, *Calvin and the Calvinists* (Edinburgh: Banner of Truth, 1982); Richard A. Muller, *Christ and the Decree* (Grand Rapids: Baker, 1988). For review

While I have great respect for Bebbington, I find his view of the Puritan doctrine of assurance of faith problematic. That viewpoint plays a central role in his promoting a high degree of discontinuity between the Puritans and the post-1730 evangelicals. That, in turn, feeds into Bebbington's positing a closer continuity between those evangelicals and the Enlightenment. I am convinced that a close, scholarly look at the doctrine of assurance (not to mention his other evangelical characteristics of conversionism, activism, biblicism and crucicentrism)[4] in the Reformers and in the Puritans (whether in England, New England, Scotland, or on the Continent, particularly the Netherlands) will reveal that Bebbington's attempt at this radical discontinuity proves little more convincing than Kendall's attempt to promote a radical discontinuity between Calvin and the Calvinists.

I shall examine Bebbington's hypothesis by looking at how the seventeenth- and early eighteenth-century Dutch pietistic movement called the *Nadere Reformatie* (most accurately translated as 'Dutch Further Reformation') relates to his definition of evangelicalism. This will show how the Dutch Further Reformation exhibits nearly all of Bebbington's defining attributes for eighteenth-century evangelicalism, thereby confirming that he is mistaken in arguing that evangelicalism first took form in the 1730s.

The Dutch Further Reformation

Dutch Calvinism did not flower profusely until the seventeenth century. It was cultivated by the Synod of Dort (1618–19) and fortified by the Dutch Further Reformation, a movement paralleling English Puritanism in both time and substance. The Dutch Further Reformation began with Willem Teellinck (1579–1629), often called the father of the movement, and concluded with the writings of Alexander Comrie (1706–74) and Theodorus van der Groe (1705–84).[5]

---

articles opposing Kendall's dissertation, see Beeke, *Quest for Full Assurance*, p. 3, n. 6.

4. David W. Bebbington, *Evangelicalism in Modern Britain: A History from the 1730s to the 1980s* (London: Unwin Hyman, 1989; repr. Grand Rapids: Baker, 1992), p. 3.

5. For a concise introduction to the leading Dutch Further Reformation divines, see B. Glasius (ed.), *Godgeleerd Nederland: Biographisch Woordenboek van Nederlandsche Godgeleerden* [Dutch Divines: Biographical Dictionary of Dutch Divines], 3 vols. ('s-Hertogenbosch: Gebr. Muller, 1851–6); Sietse Douwes van Veen, *Voor tweehonderd jaren: Schetsen van het leven onzer Gereformeerde Vaderen* [For Two Hundred Years: Sketches of the Lives of our Reformed Fathers] (Utrecht: Kemink & Zoon, 1905); J. P.

de Bie and J. Loosjes (eds.), *Biographisch Woordenboek Protestantische Godgeleerden in Nederland* [Biographical Dictionary of Protestant Divines in the Netherlands], 5 vols. ('s-Gravenhage: Martinus Nijhoff, 1907–43); *Christelijke Encyclopedie* [Christian Encyclopedia], 6 vols. (Kampen: J. H. Kok, 1959); K. Exalto, *Beleefd Geloof: Acht schetsen van gereformeerde theologen uit de 17e Eeuw* [Experiential Faith: Eight Sketches of Reformed Theologians from the Seventeenth Century] (Amsterdam: Ton Bolland, 1974); *De Kracht der Religie: Tien schetsen van Gereformeerde 'Oude Schrijvers' uit de 17e en 18e Eeuw* [The Power of Religion: Ten Sketches of Reformed 'Old Writers' from the Seventeenth and Eighteenth Centuries] (Urk: De Vuurtoren, 1976); H. Florijn (ed.), *Hollandse Geloofshelden* [Dutch Heroes of Faith] (Utrecht: De Banier, 1981); W. van Gorsel, *De Ijver voor Zijn Huis: De Nadere Reformatie en haar belangrijkste vertegenwoordigers* [The Zeal for His House: The Further Reformation and Its Most Significant Representatives] (Groede: Pieters, 1981); C. J. Malan, *Die Nadere Reformasie* [The Further Reformation] (Potchefstroom: Potchefstroomse Universiteit vir CHO, 1981); H. Florijn, *100 Portretten van Godgeleerden in Nederland uit de 16e, 17e, 18e Eeuw* [A Hundred Portraits of Dutch Divines from the Sixteenth, Seventeenth and Eighteenth Centuries] (Utrecht: Den Hertog, 1982); D. Nauta et al., *Biografisch Lexicon voor de Geschiedenis van het Nederlandse Protestantisme* [Biographical Dictionary of the History of Dutch Protestantism], 3 vols. (Kampen: Kok, 1978–88); W. van't Spijker et al., *De Nadere Reformatie: Beschrijving van haar voornaamste vertegenwoordigers* [The Further Reformation: A Description of its Most Distinguished Representatives] ('s-Gravenhage: Boekencentrum, 1986); W. van't Spijker, *De Nadere Reformatie en het Gereformeerd Pietisme* [The Further Reformation and Reformed Pietism] ('s-Gravenhage: Boekencentrum, 1989); Joel R. Beeke, 'Biographies of Dutch Second Reformation Divines', *Banner of Truth* 54.2 (1988) through to 56.3 (1990): a series of twenty-five articles representing the major divines of the movement.

For bibliographies of the Dutch Further Reformation, see P. L. Eggermont, 'Bibliographie van het Nederlandse Pietisme in de zeventiende en achttiende eeuw' [Bibliography of Dutch Pietism in the Seventeenth and Eighteenth Century], *Documentatie-blad 18e eeuw* 3 (1969), pp. 17–31; W. van Gent, *Bibliotheek van oude schrijvers* [Library of the 'Old Writers'] (Rotterdam: Lindebergs, 1979); J. van der Haar, *Schatkamer van de Gereformeerde Theologie in Nederland (c.1600–c.1800)*, Bibliografisch Onderzoek [A Treasury of Reformed Theology in the Netherlands (c. 1600–c. 1800): A Bibliographical Examination] (Veenendaal: Antiquariaat Kool, 1987).

Cf. F. Ernest Stoeffler, *The Rise of Evangelical Pietism* (Leiden: E. J. Brill, 1971), pp. 109–168, covering twelve Further Reformation divines in varying depth and quality; Cornelis Graafland, *De Zekerheid van het Geloof: Een onderzoek naar de*

Scholars responsible for the periodical *Documentatieblad Nadere Reformatie*[6] offer the following definition of the Dutch Further Reformation:

> The Dutch Further Reformation is that movement within the Nederduits Gereformeerde Kerk (Dutch Reformed Church) during the seventeenth and eighteenth centuries, which, as a reaction to the declension or absence of a living faith, made both the personal experience of faith and godliness matters of central importance. From that perspective the movement formulated substantial and procedural reformation initiatives, submitting them to the proper ecclesiastical, political, and social agencies, and/or in conformity therewith pursued in both word and deed a further reformation of the church, society, and state.[7]

---

geloofsbeschouwing van enige vertegenwoordigers van reformatie en nadere reformatie [The Assurance of Faith: An Examination of the Consideration of the Doctrine of Faith by Some of the Most Prominent Representatives of the Reformation and Further Reformation] (Wageningen: H. Veenman & Zonen, 1961), pp. 138–244, concentrating on the doctrine of faith and assurance in fourteen Further Reformation theologians; Johannes de Boer, *De Verzegeling met de Heilige Geest volgens de opvatting van de Nadere Reformatie* [The Sealing of the Holy Spirit according to the Views of the Further Reformation] (Rotterdam: Bronder, 1968), which examines the soteriological thought of fourteen Further Reformation divines.

Monographs have also been published in Dutch on the following divines of Dutch Further Baudartius (Roelofs); Bogerman (van Itterzon; van der Tuuk); W. Brakel (Los); Colonius (Hoek); Comrie (Honig; Verboom); Dathenus (Ruijs); Gomarus (van Itterzon); Haemstedius (Jelsma); Helmichius (Hania); Hommius (Wijminga); Hoornbeeck (Hofmeyr); Junius (de Jonge, Reitsma, Venemans); Koelman (Janse, Krull); Lodenstein (Proost; Slagboom); Lubbertus (van der Woude); Marnix (van Schelven); Maresius (Nauta); Rivetus (Honders); Saldenus (van den End); Schortinghuis (Kromsigt; de Vrijer); Smytegelt (de Vrijer); Taffin (van der Linde); Teellinck (Engelberts; Bouwman); Trigland (ter Haar); Voetius (Bouwman, Duker, Janse, McCahagan, Steenblok); Udemans (Meertens, Vergunst); Walaeus (van Wijngaarden); Wittewrongel (Groenendijk). For bibliographical information on these studies, see Beeke, *Assurance of Faith*, pp. 451–500.

6. These scholars have an officially organized society in the Netherlands, *Stichting Studie der Nadere Reformatie*, with the goal of promoting in-depth study of the Dutch Further Reformation.

7. *Documentatieblad Nadere Reformatie* 19 (1995), p. 108, trans. Bartel Elshout in his

The Dutch Further Reformation has also been called 'Dutch Puritanism'. At first glance, that seems reasonable, since the link between the Dutch movement and English Puritanism is historically and theologically strong.[8] Keith Sprunger says seventeenth-century Holland was home to tens of thousands of English and Scottish believers of Puritan persuasion. Those believers represented about forty congregations and 350 ministers.[9]

The leaders of English Puritanism and the Dutch Further Reformation had much respect for one another. Their fellowship was enriched through personal contact and writings such as their Latin treatises and the many books translated from English into Dutch.[10] More Reformed theological books were printed in the seventeenth century in the Netherlands than in all other countries combined.[11]

English Puritan and Dutch Further Reformation divines also had simi-

---

The Pastoral and Practical Theology of Wilhelmus à Brakel (Grand Rapids: Reformation Heritage, 1997), p. 9.

8. Cf. Keith Sprunger, *Dutch Puritanism: A History of English and Scottish Churches of the Netherlands in the Sixteenth and Seventeenth Centuries* (Leiden: E. J. Brill, 1982); *The Learned Doctor William Ames: Dutch Backgrounds of English and American Puritanism* (Chicago: University of Illinois Press, 1972); Douglas MacMillan, 'The Connection between 17th Century British and Dutch Calvinism', in his *Not by Might nor by Power* ([London]: Westminster Conference, 1988), pp. 22–31.

9. Willem op't Hof points out the influence of Dutch refugee congregations in England, noting that 'it can be justifiably concluded that it is chiefly the Dutch congregations in England which are in the background of the Puritanization of spiritual life in the Netherlands' (*Engelse pietistische geschriften in het Nederlands, 1598–1622* [English Pietistical Writings in the Dutch Language] [Rotterdam: Lindenberg, 1987], p. 639).

10. Speaking of English Puritan writings translated into Dutch from 1598 to 1622, op't Hof says, 'A total of 114 editions were issued of a total of 60 translations. These 60 translations concerned works by ... twenty-two English authors ... Two authors are numerically preeminent among them: Cowper (18 editions of 10 translations) and Perkins (71 editions of 29 translations). Indeed, Perkins alone eclipses all the others taken together ... Auction catalogues show that Udemans possessed 20 Puritan books in Latin and 57 in English. Similarly, Voetius possessed 30 Puritan works in Latin and 270 in English ... A rough estimate for the period from 1623 to 1699 gives 260 new translations, 580 editions and 100 new translators' (op't Hof, *Engelse pietistische geschriften*, pp. 636–637, 640, 645).

11. Sprunger, *Dutch Puritanism*, p. 307.

lar ideals: to foster God-glorifying experiential piety and ethical precision
in individuals, churches and nations. Only England, however, under Oliver
Cromwell, had the opportunity to implement those ideals.

But despite similar outlooks, English Puritanism and the Dutch Further
Reformation developed distinctive identities. English Puritanism was a primary influence on the Dutch Further Reformation, particularly in its emphasis
on the need for a personal and congregational life of practical godliness,[12] but
not an exclusive influence. Non-English factors also contributed.[13] In some
respects, the Dutch movement was more Puritan than English Puritanism
itself. As Jonathan Gerstner says:

> In England from an orthodox Reformed perspective, for all but a short period under
> Cromwell, there were always grossly unbiblical things to fight: the presence of
> bishops, superstitious rites in the Book of Common Prayer, vestments, etc. In the
> Netherlands none of those were present, and the task was all the more subtle.
> Defenders of the *status quo* were not so clearly unreformed as in England. In this
> context the true spirit of Puritanism came to the fore.[14]

Divines of the Dutch Further Reformation were less interested in reforming the government and church than were their English brethren. Then too,
the Dutch were more inclined to emphasize theology as a science; the English
emphasized the practical aspects of theology.[15] Nevertheless, the essence of
the Dutch Further Reformation is similar to English Puritanism's emphasis
on Reformed spirituality. S. van der Linde, a leading scholar on the Dutch
Further Reformation, says the goal of the movement, like that of Puritanism,
was to wed doctrine to daily life.[16] He notes, 'The Further Reformation sides

---

12. Op't Hof, *Engelse pietistische geschriften*, pp. 583–597, 627–635, 645–646. Cf. Cornelis
    Graafland, 'De Invloed van het Puritanisme op het Ontstaan van het Reformeerd
    Pietisme in Nederland', *Documentatieblad Nadere Reformatie* 7.1 (1983), pp. 1–19.
    Graafland also details influences on preaching, the art of meditation, casuistry,
    covenanting, the administration of the Lord's Supper, and eschatology.

13. Graafland, 'Invloed van het Puritanisme', pp. 2, 15–16.

14. Jonathan N. Gerstner, *The Thousand Generation Covenant: Dutch Reformed Covenant
    Theology and Group Identity in Colonial South Africa* (London: E. J. Brill, 1991), pp.
    77–78.

15. Cornelis Pronk, 'The Dutch Puritans', *Banner of Truth* 154–155 (July–Aug. 1976),
    p. 6.

16. S. van der Linde, 'De Godservaring bij W. Teellinck, D. G. à Brakel en A. Comrie',

entirely with the Reformation and levels criticism not so much against the *reformata* (the church which is reformed), but rather against the *reformanda* (the church which needs to be reformed).'[17]

The Dutch Second Reformation, like Puritanism, was evangelical in character. Though eighteenth-century evangelicalism had different emphases at various times (particularly on its tendency to reduce spirituality almost exclusively to the 'new birth'), it was hardly the beginning of a new movement. Even the differences that Bebbington singles out are not sufficient to substantiate his case that evangelicalism was a new movement; there are simply too many similarities even in these areas between the Dutch Further Reformation and eighteenth-century evangelicalism.

The issues at stake

In his second chapter, Bebbington acknowledges that three of the four marks of evangelicalism 'had been as much a part of Puritanism as they were of Methodism'. These include 'conversionism, biblicism, and crucicentrism'.[18] Those marks are true of the Dutch Further Reformation as well, as we see by examining Wilhelmus à Brakel's classic *The Christian's Reasonable Service*. This book was reprinted scores of times and became as popular in eighteenth-century Dutch circles as Bunyan's *Pilgrim's Progress* was in seventeenth-century England. The typical eighteenth-century Dutch farmer would read 'a piece' (*een stukje*) of 'Father Brakel', as he was fondly called, every evening during family worship.

Brakel's *Reasonable Service* emphasizes the need for conversion. In an intriguing section on regeneration, he explains that sinners are often converted in different ways. Some are converted suddenly, like the Philippian jailer; some are brought to conversion via the Spirit's application of the condemning power of the law, like the crowd of three thousand at Pentecost; and others are converted 'in a very evangelical manner', like Zacchaeus, receiving Jesus with such joy that 'they have no time to think upon their sins with terror'. Still others are converted in a quiet manner 'by granting them a view of

---

    Theologia reformata 16 (1973), p. 205.

17. S. van der Linde, 'De betekenis van de Nadere Reformatie voor Kerk en Theologie', *Kerk en Theologie* 5 (1954), p. 216.

18. David Bebbington, *Evangelicalism in Modern Britain: A History from the 1730s to the 1980s* (London: Unwin Hyman, 1989), p. 35.

the truth' about their sins and deliverance in Christ, Brakel says. They do not experience 'much grievous sorrow or ecstatic joy, but find delight in the truth' and in 'a sweet approbation of it'. Interestingly, Brakel says that 'these are generally the most consistent and steadfast Christians'. Finally, some people are converted gradually, often vacillating in the process between joy and sorrow, faith and unbelief, strife and victory.[19]

Most commonly, Brakel says, sinners are converted by being convicted of sin and brought to need and then find salvation outside themselves in Jesus Christ.[20] Nevertheless, no one needs to trouble himself if he was converted in a less common way. 'If your conversion is a reality, all is well,' Brakel says.[21]

As for biblicism, Brakel stresses the inspiration and authority of the Scriptures in a traditional Reformed manner. He defends the perfection, completeness and perspicuity of the Word, and argues that the Old and New Testaments are one organic and harmonious whole.[22] Holy Scripture is the only rule of doctrine and life, he says.[23] He provides guidelines for reading Scripture and explains why it must be read regularly by everyone, from the beginner in grace to the most advanced.[24] With a touch of reverent humour, he concludes that the Scriptures are 'a brook from which a lamb may drink and an ocean in which an elephant may drown'.[25]

Ministers should know the original languages of Scripture, be equipped with hermeneutical skills, and never wrest the Word of God from its context, Brakel writes.[26] Brakel followed his own advice: throughout his work, he fortifies his points with scriptural proof. This is typical of the writings of the Dutch Further Reformation divines. Like the Puritans, they were men of the living Book. They loved, lived and breathed Scripture, relishing the power of the Spirit that accompanies the Word.[27]

---

19. Wilhelmus à Brakel, *The Christian's Reasonable Service* [originally pub. as *Redelijke Godsdienst*, 1700], trans. Bartel Elshout and ed. Joel R. Beeke, 4 vols. (Grand Rapids: Reformation Heritage, 1992–5), vol. 2, pp. 238–239.

20. Ibid., pp. 239–243.

21. Ibid., p. 239.

22. Brakel, *Christian's Reasonable Service*, vol. 1, pp. 27–41.

23. Ibid., vol. 2, pp. 653, 657.

24. Ibid., vol. 1, pp. 67–69, 77–79.

25. Ibid., p. 73.

26. Ibid., p. xxxiv.

27. See Joel R. Beeke and Ray B. Lanning, 'The Transforming Power of Scripture', in Don Kistler (ed.), *Sola Scriptura: The Protestant Position of the Bible* (Morgan, Pa.: Soli

Also typical of the Dutch Further Reformation divines, Brakel's theology is centred on the cross. All the suffering of Christ is atoning in nature, he asserts.[28] He focuses on the veracity of Christ's satisfaction, expounds the surety of Jesus and answers a host of objections raised by those who doubt Jesus' satisfaction of God's justice for sin.[29] Brakel maintains that Christ's atonement is perfect and complete.[30] Typical of evangelical writers of the early eighteenth century, Brakel promotes 'conversionism, biblicism and crucicentrism'.

Activism

In *Evangelicalism in Modern Britain*, Bebbington argues for the uniqueness of evangelicalism because of a fourth major mark, which he calls 'activism'. In his section titled 'Discontinuity with the Reformed Tradition', Bebbington describes how that mark is exhibited: belonging to religious societies, engaging in rigorous self-examination, pursuing holiness, imbibing mystical tendencies, assimilating influences from continental Protestantism (particularly German Pietism) and emphasizing missions. All of these behaviours, Bebbington concludes, 'are bound together by an underlying factor, a shift in the received doctrine of assurance with all that it entailed'.[31] To test Bebbington's thesis, let us compare the Dutch Further Reformation and evangelicalism in their teachings on activism and on the doctrine of assurance.

Belonging to religious societies
According to Bebbington, the 'religious society' was pioneered by Anthony Horneck in 1678, and then developed under Wesley and his 'The Holy Club'. Yet that society resembles 'the gatherings of the godly' that the Dutch Further Reformation developed to encourage intimate Christian fellowship and action, explain the Scriptures and share personal leadings of God. These groups were called *gezelschappen* (literally, 'societies') in the Netherlands, and were, as Clair Davis at Westminster Seminary used to say, 'the granddaddy of the Holy Club'. Fellowship, however, does not fully convey the meaning of *gezelschap*, which is usually translated as 'conventicle', the term ascribed to parallel meetings in

---

Deo Gloria, 1995), pp. 221–276.

28. Brakel, *Christian's Reasonable Service*, vol. 1, pp. 584–586.

29. Ibid., pp. 586–594.

30. Ibid., pp. 594–598.

31. Bebbington, *Evangelicalism in Modern Britain*, p. 42.

Scotland. (Similar meetings in English Puritanism were called 'prophesyings' and in German Pietism, *collegiae pietatis*.)[32]

Conventicles were more successful in Scotland than anywhere else (including the Netherlands), due in part to closer supervision by the teaching and ruling presbyters. In the Netherlands, *gezelschappen* were supervised for a time, but on occasion they turned into unsupervised, elitist groups that criticized sermons and promoted introspective spirituality.[33] Certain leaders, such as Jacobus Koelman (1633–95)[34] and Gisbertus Voetius (1589–1676), however, developed traditions of *gezelschappen* in which believers helpfully assisted each other through spiritual problems and encouraged one another to be active in God's service. Voetius, for example, who was to the Dutch Further Reformation what John Owen was to English Puritanism, organized fellowships and action programmes consisting of friends and students that became known as the 'Utrecht Circle' or the 'Voetian Circle' (*De Voetsiaanse Kring*).[35] Members of this group spread Voetius' convictions throughout the Netherlands. By the time Voetius died in 1676, dedicated Voetians, consisting of scholars, pastors and other leaders who were committed to a Further Reformation within the Dutch Reformed Church, were in every university and ecclesiastical province in the Netherlands.[36]

The religious societies of the Further Reformation, however, were not as organized as those of Wesley in that there was no 'connection' or federation of them. Though Koelman, Voetius and a few others established movements throughout the Netherlands, most divines of the Further Reformation stressed the necessity of reform primarily to their own parishioners, that is, their reformation was a movement within, not outside, the churches. The contours

---

32. Cf. Clair Davis, 'History of Small Groups' (audio tape available from Westminster Media, P. O. Box 27009, Philadelphia, Pa., 19118).

33. Van't Spijker, 'De Nadere Reformatie', in Van't Spijker et al., *De Nadere Reformatie: Beschrijving*, p. 14; Fred A. Van Lieburg, 'Het gereformeerde conventikelwezen in de classis Dordrecht in de 17e en 183 eeuw', *Holland, regional-historisch tijdschrift* 23 (1991), pp. 2–21; Stoeffler, *Rise of Evangelical Pietism*, p. 160; M. Eugene Osterhaven, 'The Experiential Theology of Early Dutch Calvinism', *Reformed Review* 27 (1974), p. 189.

34. C. J. Meeuse, 'De visie van Koelman op de puriteinen' [Koelman's Assessment of the Puritans], *Documentatieblad Nadere Reformatie* 20 (1996), pp. 44–61.

35. Fred A. Lieburg, *De Nadere Reformatie in Utrecht ten tijde van Voetius* [The Further Reformation in Utrecht at the Time of Voetius] (Rotterdam: Lindenberg, 1989).

36. Joel R. Beeke, *Gisbertus Voetius: Toward a Reformed Marriage of Knowledge and Piety* (Grand Rapids: Reformation Heritage, 1999), p. 17.

of this call to reform naturally took on distinctive shapes in various localities and generations.[37]

In short, though the Holy Club took on nuances and developments of its own under his leadership, Wesley borrowed the concept of religious societies from already existing groups. Belonging to a religious society was not a unique development of the 'new evangelicals' in the mid-eighteenth century.

Self-examination

Bebbington rightly stresses that Oxford Methodism often took self-examination 'to an extreme': to the point of very frequent tests on various aspects of devotion.[38] Those extremes surfaced in the Dutch Further Reformation as well. Willem Teellinck's most extensive work, *Sleutel der Devotie* (The Key of Devotion), offers nearly eight hundred pages on devotion and self-examination, which, for Teellinck, were important aspects of sanctification. He explains many marks of grace for self-examination. Like later evangelicals, Teellinck rooted devotion and self-examination in the believer's commitment to God in Christ, which is man's highest calling.[39]

Another prominent Dutch Further Reformation writer, Bernardus Smytegelt (1665–1739), published 145 sermons on Matthew 12:20 ('a bruised reed he will not break, / and a smouldering wick he will not quench'). Throughout these sermons, he called on his readers to examine themselves continually.[40]

Puritan works that stressed the minutiae of self-examination in somber and searching tones were translated into Dutch early on and reprinted often. Matthew Mead's *The Almost Christian Discovered* (1662) was translated into Dutch in 1682 as *Byna een Christen ontdekt*, and reprinted seven times by 1750. Thomas Shepard's most searching books, *The Sincere Convert* (1641), *The Sound Believer* (1645) and *The Parable of the Ten Virgins* (1660), were translated into Dutch and reprinted one or more times by the 1740s.[41]

---

37. Cornelis Graafland, 'Kernen en contouren van de Nadere Reformatie' [Marks and Contours of the Further Reformation], in Van't Spijker et al., *De Nadere Reformatie: Beschrijving*, p. 350.

38. Bebbington, *Evangelicalism in Modern Britain*, p. 37.

39. Cf. Willem Teellinck, *The Path of True Godliness*, trans. Annemie Godbehere, ed. Joel R. Beeke (Grand Rapids: Baker, 2003), p. 23.

40. Bernardus Smytegelt, *Het Gekrookte Riet* [The Bruised Reed], 2 vols. (Amsterdam, 1744).

41. J. VanderHaar, *From Abbadie to Young: A Bibliography of English, Mostly Puritan Works,*

Pursuit of holiness

Bebbington duly notes that Wesley's focus on personal holiness and 'religion of the heart' was deeply influenced by Thomas à Kempis's *Imitation of Christ* and Jeremy Taylor's *Holy Living and Dying* (1650–1). His section 'Continuity with the Past' properly emphasizes that 'the fifty-volume *Christian Library* published by Wesley contains far more Puritan-like literature than of any other ecclesiastical genre'.[42] According to Robert C. Monk, 'Puritan materials constitute some 7,200 pages, whereas Church of England materials make up only 3,900 pages.'[43] This fact should be stressed, given the influence that this set of books had on Wesley, who intended that the entire set would 'form a complete body of Practical Divinity'.[44]

Interestingly, Wesley printed approximately fifty works, twenty of which are from the Puritan tradition. In these reprinted books, he often eliminated or changed substantial sections of material that related to the doctrines of predestination, effectual calling and perseverance, but on holiness he seldom abridged the material, unless it impinged on the extent of the believer's perfectability. Obviously, the Puritan pursuit of holiness resonated with Wesley, except when his perfectionistic tendencies took matters farther than the Puritans were willing to go.[45]

Most of the books on holiness Wesley selected had previously been translated into Dutch. Surprisingly, he did not include Lewis Bayly's *The Practice of Piety* (1611), which was translated into Dutch in 1620 and reprinted at least thirty-one times in the seventeenth century alone.[46]

Dutch Further Reformation writers also focused on the theme of pursuing holiness. Willem Teellinck's first love was promoting the Puritan ideal of the sanctification of life in all its aspects, nurtured by heartfelt devotion. His *Sleutel der Devotie* explains *devotion* as commitment to God in Christ to pursue holiness. The first section covers communion with and love for Christ. The believer will be humble and volunteer 'to suffer the Christian life';[47] he will

    translated i/t Dutch Language (Veendendaal: Kool, 1980), pp. 86, 119–120.

42. Bebbington, *Evangelicalism in Modern Britain*, pp. 35, 37.
43. Robert C. Monk, *John Wesley: His Puritan Heritage* (Nashville: Abingdon, 1966), p. 38, n. 24.
44. Ibid., p. 36.
45. Ibid., pp. 47–61.
46. VanderHaar, *From Abbadie to Young*, pp. 12–13; cf. Lewis Bayly, *The Practice of Piety* (Morgan, Pa.: Soli Deo Gloria, 1996).
47. Willem Teellinck, *Sleutel der Devotie ons openende de Deure des Hemels* [The Key of

serve the Lord alone, meditate on eternity, and have communion with Christ. In the second section the importance of self-denial is stressed. 'How we must use all spiritual means . . . in order really to deny ourselves, and to be one with Christ'[48] is the focus of the third section. The fourth section explains the 'modesty and lowliness, which one must observe in the use of the means to receive the gracious gifts of God',[49] while the fifth section shows how faith can discern the many errors of the day. The sixth section speaks about divine grace, without which the Christian life is impossible.

Teellinck's best work on pursuing holiness, however, is *Noord-Sterre, aanwijzende de juiste richting van de ware godsaligheid* (translated into English in 2003 as *The Path of True Godliness*). This Puritan-style manual on how to practise godliness offers nine sections called 'books', which can be summarized as follows.

Book 1. Since many people boast of their faith but have no saving knowledge of the truth, Teellinck addresses three matters: (1) what true godliness is; (2) how believers should conduct themselves in practising godliness; and (3) why the exercise of true godliness is of utmost importance.

Book 2. Here Teellinck discusses the realm of darkness that opposes the practice of godliness. The three main powers of this realm are our depraved flesh, the world and the devil. Our depraved flesh is active through our carnal mind, our evil desires and our depraved consciences. The evil world works through sinful customs, wrong role models and an erroneous premise of reward and recompense. The devil is active through evil temptations, false doctrines and fierce persecutions. Teellinck's point is that we must be on guard against the realm of darkness.

Book 3. Teellinck shows how the kingdom of grace, in contrast to the realm of darkness, promotes godliness. The kingdom of grace also has three powers: the renewed spirit, which wars against the depraved flesh; the church of God, which fights against the world; and the Spirit of God, who opposes the devil. Each of these powers possesses three gifts that oppose and overcome its enemy in the realm of darkness.

Book 4. Teellinck focuses on how to respond to these two realms. We must at all times keep life's three major purposes before us: glorifying God, the salvation of our own souls and promoting the salvation of others.

True Devotion Opens Heaven's Door] (Utrecht: Johannes van Someren, 1656), p. 19.

48. Ibid., p. 80.

49. Ibid., p. 243.

Book 5. This book describes the means of achieving the true purposes of life: God's holy ordinances, God's works and God's promises. Believers should help each other to live holy lives and edify each other with godly conversation in fellowship gatherings.

Book 6. Teellinck outlines how Christians must attain the right purposes of life through the means described in the last book, while living consistently, watching diligently and struggling against every hindrance. Consistent living involves establishing fixed times for all our duties, assigning priority to those duties that are most critical, and daily examining how we are practising godliness. Watching diligently means knowing what to guard against, being aware of the deceitfulness of one's heart, and staying alert to what may be approaching. Struggling against every hindrance involves diligently using the Christian armour of Ephesians 6:10–20.

Book 7. Teellinck provides God-centred motivations for practising godliness. These include the Father's wisdom, omnipotence and lovingkindness; the Son's incarnation, exemplary life and kind invitations to come to him; and the Spirit's promise to give new hearts, to overlook weaknesses and graciously to reward the practice of godliness.

Book 8. This book contains motivations for practising godliness. It is divided into three major sections: our natural condition, the manifold blessings of God and the promises we make to God.

Book 9. The last book presents motivations for practising godliness, including the glorious God we serve, the glorious work accomplished and the glorious fruits that result; the misery of the godless life, including the awful master served, the detestable work accomplished and the shameful fruits that result; and the emptiness of material things with regard to this life, to death and to life after death.

Throughout the volume, Teellinck insists on the need for personal religious experience and disciplined Christian conduct in life, especially in prayer, fasting, Christian education and Sabbath observance, but also in mealtimes, clothing, dancing, carnivals and card playing.

The Netherlands, however, may not have been as ready for Teellinck's comprehensive call for the pursuit of holiness as England had been for William Perkins's. Some of his peers found Teellinck's call for renewal and holiness in church, school, family, government and society too intense. Yet in all of this, Teellinck showed how serious he was to pursue holiness in all areas of life.[50]

---

50. The comments in this section are condensed from my introduction in Teellinck,

Mystical character

'Evangelicals were drawn back towards the mystical,' writes Bebbington, 'especially the forms propagated by [William] Law (1686–1761) in his later years, for the Evangelical and the mystic shared a common attachment to experiencing the divine.'[51] Bebbington footnotes John Walsh's 'The Cambridge Methodists' in *Christian Spirituality*, edited by Peter Brooks, for support.

Walsh, however, shows that mystical tendencies influenced only segments of evangelicalism. He uses Francis Okely as a case study to show how those segments often espoused a kind of love–hate relationship between mysticism and evangelicalism. Okely joined Wesley's cause for a time, but then confessed doubts about the spiritual depths of many Methodists. He ended up abandoning Wesley and supporting William Law.[52]

William Law can scarcely be relegated to any category. At best, he transmitted the spirituality of seventeenth-century forms of piety into the eighteenth century with an accent on the mystical.[53] Though Law's writings influenced a goodly number of evangelicals, the mystical inclinations of many English Puritans and many Dutch Further Reformation divines (though more tightly tied to the Scriptures than that of most eighteenth-century evangelicals)[54] differed little from them in practice.

Mysticism was present nearly from the beginning of the Dutch Further Reformation movement. It was rooted in Bernard of Clairvaux's strong emphasis on the emotional love experienced in communion with God.[55] Reminiscent of the writings of Bernard of Clairvaux, Teellinck's later writings, such as *Soliloquium* (Soliloquy) and *Het Nieuwe Jerusalem* (The New Jerusalem [1635]), revealed a mystical emphasis that had surfaced only occasionally in his earlier writings. Feelings and emotions are accented more than faith; the believing soul becomes one with Christ in tender communion. Gisbertus

Path of True Godliness, pp. 23–26.

51. Bebbington, *Evangelicalism in Modern Britain*, p. 38.
52. John Walsh, 'The Cambridge Methodists', in Peter Brooks (ed.), *Christian Spirituality: Essays in Honour of Gordon Rupp* (London: SCM, 1975), pp. 274–283.
53. Isabel Rivers, 'William John Law', in H. C. G. Matthew and Brian Harrison (eds.), *Oxford Dictionary of National Biography* (Oxford: University Press, 2004), vol. 32, p. 771.
54. E.g. Richard Sibbes and Thomas Goodwin (see Beeke, *Quest for Full Assurance*, pp. 205, 263, nn. 93–94).
55. See Arie de Reuver, *Sweet Communion: Trajectories of Spirituality from the Middle Ages through the Further Reformation*, trans. James A. de Jong (Grand Rapids: Baker, 2007), pp. 281–283.

Voetius says that in this book Teellinck 'could rightly be regarded as a second Thomas à Kempis', albeit Reformed in his theology.[56]

In *Het Nieuwe Jerusalem*, Teellinck typically has 'Mary' address Jesus when she feels close to him as 'the God of my total delight and joyfulness'.[57] Teellinck affirms that when the believer communes with God 'in stillness and in solitude',[58] he can expect Jesus' refreshing presence. In *Soliloquium*, Teellinck says that when he personally clung to the Lord Jesus and worshipped him for an entire day, he would most likely 'feel great joy' by evening. All of this is dependent on a 'continuous movement toward God' through Spirit-worked prayer, he says.[59] The Spirit's movements in prayers are sovereignly distributed from the hands of Jesus to the believer. Such stirrings enliven prayer and, 'like the wind of heaven',[60] enable us to grow in grace.

Believers should do their utmost, Teellinck says, to 'cultivate susceptibility to these stirrings' and divine visitations, 'so that they are not the exception but become the rule and do not wither but flourish'.[61] The best means to awaken these movements of the Spirit is the Holy Scriptures: reading, preaching, meditation and discussion. When believers fill their lives with the Word, the breath of the Spirit permeates them and lifts them up to focus on both the earthly Christ crucified and the heavenly Christ exalted at the Father's right hand, thereby enabling them to be transformed into and conformed to 'the mannerisms, virtues, and qualities' of Christ.[62] Teellinck preserves himself from a rudderless mysticism here and elsewhere by correlating Word and Spirit in the revelations of Christ to the soul, and by conjoining his ethics to his mysticism, so as to keep it practical for daily life.[63]

---

56. Gisbertus Voetius, *Te asketika sive Exercitia Pietatis* (Gorinchen: Vink, 1654), p. 74; cf. de Reuver, *Sweet Communion*, p. 117.

57. Willem Teellinck, *Het Nieuwe Jerusalem Vertoont in een t'samensprekinge, tusschen Christum en Mariam, sittende aensign voeten* [The New Jerusalem Disclosed in the Dialogue between Jesus and Mary while She Was Sitting at His Feet] (Utrecht, 1652) 1.4.33.

58. Cited in de Reuver, *Sweet Communion*, p. 114.

59. Willem Teellinck, *Soliloquium, ofte alleensprake eens zondaers, in den angst zijner wedergeboorte* [Soliloquies: The Monologue of a Sinner, Expressing the Traumatic Nature of His New Birth] (Erfstadt: Lukassen, 1984), dedicatie, p. 2.

60. Teellinck, *Nieuwe Jerusalem*, p. 151.

61. DeReuver, *Sweet Communion*, p. 117.

62. Teellinck, *Sleutel der Devotie*, 1.2.2.

63. DeReuver, *Sweet Communion*, pp. 105–162; 'Een mystieke ader in de Nadere

Later Dutch Further Reformation writers, such as Godefridus Udemans (c. 1580–1649), Theodorus à Brakel (1608–69), Jodocus van Lodensteyn (1620–77), Guiljelmus Saldenus (1627–94), Bernardus Smytegelt (1665–1739) and Wilhelmus Schortinghuis (1700–50), show similar strains of mysticism in emphasizing spiritual experiences, cross-bearing and meditation on the life to come.[64] However, other Dutch Further Reformation divines, like many eighteenth-century evangelicals, were more objective in their writing (e.g. Gisbertus Voetius and Johannes Hoornbeeck).[65]

While the eighteenth-century evangelicals on the whole were more mystical than the Dutch Further Reformation divines, the degree of difference, though attributable in part to William Law, is minimal. The major distinction is not in the quantity of mysticism in the two groups, but in the quality of it: the mysticism of the Dutch Second Reformation was more tightly tied to Scripture.

Continental Protestantism and Pietism

Bebbington rightly stresses the influence of continental Protestantism, particularly German Pietism, on evangelicalism. Little additional comment is needed here, as this only lends support to the point that evangelicalism was alive and well in late seventeenth- and early eighteenth-century Europe. Though later evangelicalism developed nuances of its own through Wesley's thinking and a variety of other influences, we should not exaggerate the differences between movements such as German Pietism and the Dutch Further Reformation.

Some scholars, such as Heinrich Heppe, James Tanis and F. Ernest Stoeffler, list the Dutch movement under the title of 'Pietism'.[66] That is a mistake for several reasons. First, the Dutch Further Reformation predates Philip

---

Reformatie' [A Mystical Vein in the Further Reformation], *Documentatieblad Nadere Reformatie* 21 (1997), pp. 12–18.

64. S. van der Linde, 'De betekenis van de Nadere Refomatie voor Kerk en Theologie', *Kerk en Theologie* 5 (1954), p. 218; cf. DeReuver, *Sweet Communion*, pp. 163–230.

65. See Gisbertus Voetius and Johannes Hoornbeeck, *Spiritual Desertion*, trans. John Vriend and Harry Boonstra and ed. M. Eugene Osterhaven (Grand Rapids: Baker, 2003).

66. Heinrich Heppe, *Geschichte des Pietismus und der Mystik in der Reformierten Kirche, namentlich der Niederlande* [The History of Pietism and Mysticism in the Reformed Churches, especially the Netherlands] (Leiden: E. J. Brill, 1879); James Tanis, *Dutch Calvinistic Pietism in the Middle Colonies: A Study in the Life and Theology of Theodorus Jacobus Frelinghuysen* (The Hague: Martinus Nijhoff, 1967); Stoeffler, *Rise of Evangelical Pietism*.

Spener's (1635–1705) appeal for reform by nearly half a century. The Dutch Further Reformation became a more extensive movement than German Pietism. Second, Pietism in German Lutheranism was more concerned with the believer's inner life than with transforming society, whereas most divines of the Further Reformation were very much concerned with both.[67] Third, Pietism is usually regarded as a protest against Protestant scholastic theology and doctrinal precision, whereas many Further Reformation divines helped formulate Reformed orthodoxy and doctrine while they pursued a lifestyle of piety.[68] Finally, using Stoeffler's work as a guide, Pietism had more emphasis on practical matters: Bible study, extemporaneous preaching, cross-bearing and personal sacrifice, the minimization of differences, the importance of felicity, the need for revivals, and spiritual journalling.[69]

Nevertheless, the influence of German Pietism and the Dutch Further Reformation on each other is undeniable. Both movements were deeply rooted in the sixteenth-century Reformation and longed for more thorough reform. Both developed similar forms of religious experience. Both stressed the Scriptures as a textbook for godly living, prayer, spiritual fellowship groups, an experimental relationship with Christ, regeneration and repentance, an experienced conversion, a devotional life, spiritual songs, concern for outreach and missions, strict monitoring of the Lord's Supper, family worship, obedience to the Ten Commandments, the invisible church, self-denial and catechizing the laity. Most of these emphases were simply passed on to eighteenth-century evangelicals.[70]

---

67. S. van der Linde, *Vromen en Verlichten: Twee eeuwen Protestantse Geloofsbeleving 1650–1850* [Pietism and the Enlightenment: Two Centuries of Protestant Praxis of Faith] (Utrecht: Aarsbisschoppelijk Museum, 1974), p. 2.

68. Gerstner, *Thousand Generation Covenant*, p. 76; S. van der Linde, 'Jean Taffin: eerste pleiter voor "Nadere Reformatie" in Nederland' [Jean Taffin: The First Advocate for Further Reformation in the Netherlands], *Theologia reformata* 25 (1982), p. 7.

69. Stoeffler, *Rise of Evangelical Pietism*, pp. 9–23.

70. Ibid. and his *German Pietism during the Eighteenth Century* (Leiden: E. J. Brill, 1973).

Missions

Even in the case of missions, where Bebbington has some cause for making a distinction between seventeenth- and eighteenth-century evangelicals, he still feels obliged to mention great Puritan missionaries, such as Richard Baxter, John Eliot and Jonathan Edwards. Sidney Rooy's newly reprinted *The Theology of Missions in the Puritan Tradition* provides a masterful examination of the Puritans' support of missions and their passionate desire to seek the salvation of the lost. Through the writings of five notable Puritans (Richard Sibbes, Richard Baxter, John Eliot, Cotton Mather and Jonathan Edwards) Rooy explores Puritan missiology's theological foundation, development, establishment and progress.[71]

Many leaders of the Dutch Further Reformation, including Willem Teellinck and Gisbertus Voetius, had the same heart for missions as their Puritan counterparts. Teellinck was an early proponent of foreign missions in the Netherlands. This is particularly shown in his *Ecce Homo, ofte ooghen-salve voor die noch sitten in blintheydt des ghemoedts* (Behold the Man, or Eye-salve for Those Whose Hearts Are Still Blinded) and *David's danckbaerheyt voor Gods weldadicheyt* (David's Thankfulness for God's Lovingkindness), which stress the Reformed Church's duty to bring Christianity to all the pagans with whom the Dutch East and West India companies traded. Teellinck tells the directors of these companies that God did not give the discovery of new continents for them to obtain earthly treasure so much as to send his eternal treasures to those continents.

While pastoring in Heusden, Voetius persuaded various trading companies to send missionaries with the Dutch ships to distant parts of the world. As H. A. Van Andel points out, 'Voetius attempted not only to sketch the outlines of a solid theology of missions, but he was also the first who attempted seriously to give missiology a legitimate scientific place in the whole of theology.'[72] It is remarkable that the greatest Dutch scholastic of Reformed orthodoxy developed the first comprehensive Protestant theology of missions. Jan Jongeneel says:

> [Voetius'] Protestant theology of mission properly subordinated all concrete missionary activity to the praise, honor and adoration of God and precisely for this reason was able to develop a broad vision which makes possible a world-wide, non-

---

71. Sidney H. Rooy, *The Theology of Missions in the Puritan Tradition* (Grand Rapids: Eerdmans, 1965; repr. Laurel, Miss.: Audubon, 2006).

72. H. A. Van Andel, *De Zendingsleer van Gisbertus Voetius* [The Missiology of Gisbertus Voetius] (Kampen: Kok, 1912), p. 19.

coercive mission to convert people from every race and plant the church of Christ everywhere.[73]

The Dutch Further Reformation divines were mission-minded but lacked many of the opportunities the eighteenth-century evangelicals had for reaching overseas. Nevertheless, there were some substantial results, such as the establishing of the Reformed Church of Sri Lanka.

Assurance

Finally, Bebbington exaggerates the difference between seventeenth-century Puritanism and eighteenth-century evangelicalism on personal assurance of faith. His presentation is simplistic: the doctrine of assurance in Puritan and Dutch Further Reformation theology, which influenced Edwards, the Great Awakening and later eighteenth-century evangelicalism, is more nuanced than Bebbington allows.[74] Here let us examine a few areas in which Bebbington confuses those differences.

Bebbington claims that the eighteenth-century evangelicalism transformed the content of the doctrine of assurance. He writes, 'Whereas the Puritans had held that assurance is rare, late and the fruit of struggle in the experience of believers, the Evangelicals believed it to be general, normally given at conversion and the result of simple acceptance of the gift of God.'[75] Though assurance was admittedly more *commonly claimed* in eighteenth-century evangelicalism, it is not certain that it was *more common*—with the exception of times of remarkable revival. Assurance is known by its fruits. The main fruits of assurance, such as increased desire for fellowship with God, God-centred and Christ-extolling thinking and living, a godly walk of obedience, intercession for missions and revival, and yearning for God's glory and heaven, do not appear, for the most part, to be stronger in the eighteenth century than in the seventeenth.

To illustrate, compare seventeenth-century assurance in the English Puritan and Dutch Further Reformation traditions with assurance among evangelicals today. When I was contemplating doing my doctoral dissertation on the subject of assurance, one professor responded, 'Why would you do that? Everyone has assurance today.' My conviction is the opposite. I believe that

---

73. Jan Jongeneel, 'The Missiology of Gisbertus Voetius: The First Comprehensive Protestant Theology of Missions', *Calvin Theological Journal* 26.1 (1991), p. 79.

74. See Beeke, *Quest for Full Assurance*.

75. Bebbington, *Evangelicalism in Modern Britain*, p. 43.

genuine, full assurance of faith has been waning among true Christians since the seventeenth century.

Claiming to have assurance and actually possessing assurance, which can be seen by its fruits of godliness, are often two different things. Whereas many Puritans were too reticent to claim the assurance that was theirs for fear of deceiving themselves, the fruits of their lives often showed more assurance than people of later centuries who so easily claim to possess it.

Bebbington does not seem to recognize that the seventeenth-century Puritans and Dutch Further Reformation evangelicals meant something more by 'full assurance' than what eighteenth-century evangelicals meant by 'assurance'. Contrary to what Bebbington says, the former asserted that the seed of assurance lies in every act of saving faith and that it is normal for believers to have some measure of assurance.[76] But they also emphasized the need to grow into 'full assurance', which they defined as a hearty personal persuasion that Jesus Christ has accepted and forgiven me for my sins, that God loves me and will bring me to heaven, that I am free from the guilt and dominion of sin as is evidenced in my godly walk of life, and that I have great liberty in knowing God as my Father so that I can rejoice in my salvation in a full and experiential manner.

This full assurance, says James W. Alexander, 'carries with it the idea of fullness, such as of a tree laden with fruit, or of a vessel's sails when stretched by a favouring gale'.[77] This deep, intimate relationship with God, associated with full assurance though not emphasized in later eighteenth-century evangelicalism as it was in seventeenth-century Puritanism and the Dutch Further Reformation, was nevertheless fully advocated by men such as Jonathan Edwards and George Whitefield. We can conclude then the opposite of what Bebbington asserts: the fuller and more robust doctrine of assurance was presented in the seventeenth and first half of the eighteenth century rather than the latter half of the eighteenth century when assurance was based more on the new birth than on its evidences.[78]

---

76. Beeke, *Quest for Full Assurance*, pp. 102–103, 114, 230.

77. James W. Alexander, *Consolation on Select Topics, Addressed to the Suffering People of God* (New York: Scriber, 1853; repr. Ligonier, Pa.: Soli Deo Gloria, 1992), p. 138.

78. 'Robust' is Bebbington's word choice (*Evangelicalism in Modern Britain*, p. 45). I am using it here in the sense of its given definitions of 'having or exhibiting strength; firm in purpose or outlook; strongly formed or constructed; requiring strength or vigor' (*Webster's New Collegiate Dictionary* [Springfield, Mass.: G. & C. Merriam, 1977], under 'robust').

Further on, Bebbington wrongly distances Jonathan Edwards from the Puritans on assurance. He claims that if Edwards was satisfied that parishioners who explained their conversion to him were truly converted, he would assure them that they were real Christians. But, Bebbington adds, 'received Puritan practice would have been to encourage them to wrestle through their own doubts and fears over a protracted period'.[79] Actually, Edwards (often called the last Puritan), the Puritans and the Dutch Further Reformation ministers were doing something different that fell between these extremes. Instead of telling people they were Christians and instead of encouraging them to doubt their conversion, these pastors would set the marks and fruits of saving grace before their congregants and tell them that if they truly trusted in the promises of God and could say that, by God's grace, some of these marks of faith were evident in their hearts and lives, they could then conclude that they were children of God. That conclusion had to be reached, however, not by pastoral proclamation, but by personal self-examination, in dependency on the Holy Spirit.

Bebbington also reads too much into Jonathan Edwards's statement that people get assured when they 'have been better instructed'. Two sentences later, Bebbington admits that Edwards 'sets out a checklist of signs that conversion had been valid'.[80] That is precisely what the Puritans and Further Reformation divines were doing! They wrote numerous treatises on assurance and set checklists of signs and marks of conversion in front of their people so that the people might be 'better instructed', knowing that when that instruction would be blessed by the Holy Spirit, they would grow in assurance. Edwards's 'Evangelical framework for interpreting Christian experience' differs little from that of mainstream Puritanism.[81]

Emphases on the doctrine of assurance may have changed in eighteenth-century evangelicalism by evangelicals gravitating more towards the idea of sudden or easy conversions, but the doctrine itself remained the same. Depending on the tradition in which they were immersed, late eighteenth-century evangelicals continued to rely on the codified statements on assurance as set forth by the Westminster Confession of Faith (ch. 18) and the Canons of Dort (head 5), both of which maintain that the primary ground of assurance is the promises of God, and the secondary grounds are the evidences of grace and the witnessing testimony of the Spirit.

---

79. Bebbington, *Evangelicalism in Modern Britain*, p. 47.
80. Ibid.
81. Ibid.

Conclusion

Though Bebbington's book highlights some aspects of discontinuity in evangelical history, it seriously discounts its continuity. The history, theology and activism of the Dutch Further Reformation divines do not support Bebbington's assertion that evangelicalism emerged as a new entity through transatlantic evangelical revivals in the 1730s. Divines such as Willem Teellinck, Wilhelmus à Brakel and Gisbertus Voetius are proven evangelicals in the broadest sense of Bebbington's definition.

The position of radical discontinuity in evangelicalism in the 1730s cannot be historically confirmed and is theologically dangerous, for it leaves us with the impression that Jonathan Edwards and John Wesley are the fathers of evangelicalism. The result of this controversial position is that Wesley's Arminianism could then no longer be viewed as aberrational theology within a solidly Reformed movement. Instead, Reformed and Arminian theology would be given equal status in the origins of evangelicalism, as is often done today.

Evangelicalism would be better served if Bebbington labelled evangelicalism as Carter Lindberg labelled the Reformation when he titled his text *The European Reformations*. Indeed, it would be wiser to speak of Reformation evangelicalism, Puritan evangelicalism, Dutch Further Reformation evangelicalism, Pietistic evangelicalism, Methodist evangelicalism and so on. To be accurate, we should say that new strains developed within eighteenth-century evangelicalism that diminished the previous century's emphasis on assurance and helped augment its emphasis on missions and revivals. Then too, I submit, it would be profitable to undertake an in-depth study of different emphases within evangelical history, such as experimental evangelicalism, activistic evangelicalism and revivalistic evangelicalism.

© Joel R. Beeke, 2008

PART 3: ERA PERSPECTIVES

8. THE EVANGELICAL CHARACTER OF MARTIN LUTHER'S FAITH

Cameron A. MacKenzie

Martin Luther was an evangelical. Although he was certainly the heir of a catholic tradition, what was new about his faith and the movement he initiated was his understanding of the gospel, the *Evangelium* in both of Luther's languages, German and Latin.[1] 'Evangelical' (German *evangelisch*; Latin *evangelicus*), therefore, is a term Luther employed positively to describe true Christianity;[2] and

---

1. Just how 'new' Luther's faith was is a matter for debate. As far as he was concerned, it was a return to the teachings of Paul and the New Testament; for his opponents it was a departure from what the church had always taught. In either case, however, what Luther taught about salvation marked a significant departure from contemporary scholastic theologians. See Heiko A. Oberman, '"*Iustitia Christi*" and "*Iustitia Dei*": Luther and the Scholastic Doctrines of Justification', in his *The Dawn of the Reformation: Essays in Late Medieval and Early Reformation Thought* (Edinburgh: T. & T. Clark, 1986), pp. 104–125; Alister E. McGrath, *Iustitia Dei: A History of the Christian Doctrine of Justification*, 2 vols. (Cambridge: Cambridge University Press, 1986), vol. 2, pp. 1–20; and the title essay in George Yule (ed.), *Luther: Theologian for Catholics and Protestants* (Edinburgh: T. & T. Clark, 1985), pp. 1–22.

2. E.g. as early as the Leipzig Debate (1519), Luther said that among the articles of John Hus and the Bohemians, 'many were plainly most Christian and evangelical [*evangelicos*]', cited Otto Seitz (ed.), *Der authentische Text der Leipziger Disputation*

very early it was associated with the Protestant Reformation as a whole.[3] Of course, the mere label does not mean that evangelicals of the eighteenth century or of today, for that matter, have anything in common with Luther. But if we

---

(Berlin: C. A. Schwetschke & Son, 1903), p. 87. Similarly, in the Galatians lectures of the same year, Luther uses the expression 'evangelical truth' for Paul's message. In this chapter, citations of the original text of Luther's works are from the critical edition, D. Martin Luthers Werke: Kritische Gesamtausgabe, vols. 1– (Weimar: Hermann Böhlaus Nachfolger, 1883–) (hereafter cited as WA). The Galatians citation is WA 2:451.26. Unless otherwise noted, the English language Luther quotations in this chapter are from Jaroslav Pelikan and Helmut T. Lehmann (eds.), Luther's Works, 55 vols. (St. Louis: Concordia; Philadelphia: Fortress, 1955–86) (hereafter cited as LW). Later in his career, in the Genesis lectures (1535–45), Luther still employs the Latin term positively as e.g. 'evangelical freedom' (WA 43:322.38, 323.21; and WA 44:178.18) and 'evangelical hymn' (WA 43:219.38). For Luther's use of the German term, see Ph. Dietz, Wörterbuch zu Dr. Martin Luthers deutschen Schriften (Hildesheim: Georg Olms, 1961²), under 'Evangelisch'. In his New Testament (1522), Luther used evangelisch in 2 Tim. 4:5, 'Do the work of an evangelical preacher' (D. Martin Luthers Werke: Kritische Gesamtausgabe, Die Deutsche Bibel, 12 vols. [Weimar: Hermann Böhlaus Nachfolger, 1906–61], vol. 7, p. 280; hereafter WADB); and in his introduction to the New Testament, he complained that the book of James had 'no evangelical form' in it (WADB 6:10.34). The next year, when he began to publish the Old Testament, he described Genesis as 'an exceedingly evangelical book' (WADB 8:12.33).

3. Luther referred to the 'party of the gospel' among the Augustinians in a letter to John Lang in 1521 (D. Martin Luthers Werke: Kritische Gesamtausgabe, Briefwechsel, 18 vols. [Weimar: Hermann Böhlaus Nachfolger, 1930–85], vol. 2, p. 413.4–5). In sermons on the Gospel of John that Luther preached in the 1530s, he referred to his faction as those called 'evangelical' in contrast to the papists, but he was also highly critical of them (WA 46:656.6–10; see also WA 47:94.13–19, and 33:672.3–42); e.g. 'You merely cover and embellish yourselves with the name and title of church and Christians' (LW 23:419). According to the Oxford English Dictionary, 13 vols. (Oxford: Clarendon, 1933), under 'evangelical', Thomas More used 'evangelical' as a label for the Protestants William Tyndale and Robert Barnes, in 1532. In 1524, Erasmus wrote a letter to Gerard de la Roche in which he complained about two factions in the church, one of them the 'Lutheran faction'. Of these, Erasmus says that 'they boast they are now "evangelicals" (Evangelicos) although they are not at all', cited P. S. Allen (ed.), Opus epistolarum Des. Erasmi Roterodami, 12 vols. (Oxford: In Typographeo Clarendoniano, 1906–58), vol. 5, p. 421.

examine the content of Luther's faith, we shall soon see that there are important continuities between the beliefs of the Reformer and later evangelicals. After all, Whitefield and Edwards saw themselves in fundamental agreement with Luther and sixteenth-century Protestants.[4] And they were not wrong.

Of course, one must recognize at the outset that Luther was a sixteenth-century evangelical and not an eighteenth-century one; and thus there are important differences between him and those who came later. Indeed, even in his own times, Luther differed significantly from those whom we call 'Reformed'.[5] But neither the differences then nor now should obscure the evangelical character of Luther's faith. For basic to Luther's understanding of Christianity were the following: (1) an exclusively biblical basis for the truths of Christianity; (2) the centrality of justification by grace through faith in the atoning work of Christ; (3) the need to oppose those errors in the church that militate against the truth of the gospel; (4) the agreement of this faith with the beliefs of the true church through the ages; and (5) the necessity of good works as the fruit of faith. Obviously, these characteristics are not precisely the same as those David Bebbington has used to describe the modern evangelical movement;[6] but, as I shall demonstrate in this chapter, there is certainly enough overlap between Luther and the subjects of Bebbington's study to justify employing the same 'evangelical' label.

---

4. Jonathan Edwards, *A History of the Work of Redemption*, ed. John F. Wilson (New Haven: Yale University Press, 1989), pp. 421–422; and Arnold A. Dallimore, *George Whitefield: The Life and Times of the Great Evangelist of the Eighteenth-Century Revival*, 2 vols. (Westchester: Cornerstone, 1979), vol. 2, pp. 366, 563. John and Charles Wesley, of course, were both 'converted' in part by Luther's writings. See Mark A. Noll, *The Rise of Evangelicalism: The Age of Edwards, Whitefield, and the Wesleys* (Downers Grove: IVP, 2003), pp. 95–97.

5. Hans J. Hillerbrand (ed.), *The Oxford Encyclopedia of the Reformation* (hereafter *OER*), 4 vols. (New York: Oxford University Press, 1996), under 'Protestantism: An Overview'. See also Mark U. Edwards, Jr., *Luther and the False Brethren* (Stanford: Stanford University Press, 1975).

6. At the outset of his work *Evangelicalism in Modern Britain: A History from the 1730s to the 1980s* (Grand Rapids: Baker Book House, 1992) Bebbington identifies four characteristics as the identifying marks of modern evangelicalism (p. 3): '*conversionism*, the belief that lives need to be changed; *activism*, the expression of the gospel in effort; *biblicism*, a particular regard for the Bible; and what may be called *crucicentrism*, a stress on the sacrifice of Christ on the cross'.

Statements of Luther's faith

Since Luther wrote so voluminously, it would not be difficult to discover quotations from his works that support each of the five characteristics mentioned above; and there are a host of secondary works that treat each of them as well.[7] So the challenge is not to find them in Luther but to show that they were significant for Luther. To that end, this chapter examines specific works in which the Reformer himself identifies the essential teachings of Christianity, that is, in a very deliberate way, presents his own understanding of what it means to be a Christian. The following are four such statements of Luther's faith: Part 3 of his *Confession Concerning Christ's Supper* (1528), the Small Catechism (1529), the Marburg Articles (1529) and the Smalcald Articles (1537). In each of these, Luther was concerned with making a public record of what it meant to be a Christian. Although these works differ in circumstance and in detail, they nonetheless are in substantial agreement and together demonstrate that Luther was an evangelical.

The first two in the list, the 1528 *Confession*[8] and the Marburg Articles,[9] are mirror opposites of each other in terms of context while remarkably similar in terms of content. The first is Luther's final treatise in his argument

7. Two excellent surveys of Luther's theology in English are Paul Althaus, *The Theology of Martin Luther* (Philadelphia: Fortress, 1966); and Bernhard Lohse, *Martin Luther's Theology: Its Historical and Systematic Development* (Minneapolis: Fortress, 1999). Lohse, *Martin Luther's Theology*, pp. 347–380, has compiled a topical bibliography. But see also Donald K. McKim (ed.), *The Cambridge Companion to Martin Luther* (Cambridge: Cambridge University Press, 2003), pp. 304–312, for a Luther bibliography, including online sources.

8. The 1528 *Confession* can be found in *LW* 37:161–372 and *WA* 26:261–509. For the background to its composition and a summary of its contents, see Martin Brecht, *Martin Luther*, 3 vols. (Philadelphia: Fortress, 1985–93), vol. 2, pp. 314–324. The sixth International Congress for Luther Research (1983) organized a seminar on Luther's personal confession in his *Confession* of 1528. The *Lutherjahrbuch* 52 (1985), p. 296, gives a one-page summary of the seminar's activities.

9. The Marburg Articles can be found in *LW* 38:85–89 and *WA* 30[III]:160–171. The Weimar edition actually prints three versions, two based on manuscripts (German and Swiss) and one based on a printed version of the Swiss. Unless otherwise noted, references in this chapter are to the German version. For background to the articles, see Brecht, *Martin Luther*, vol. 2, pp. 325–334; for background to the various versions, see 'Handschriften der "Artikel"', in *WA* 30[III]:101–109.

with Huldrych Zwingli over the presence of Christ's body and blood in the Eucharist;[10] and, as a result of this argument, Luther pronounces a very harsh judgment against his fellow-evangelicals who disagree with his views on the Real Presence.[11] Moreover, he attaches a personal confession of faith in Part 3 of this work because he does not trust his opponents to describe his beliefs fairly especially after his death:

> Lest any persons during my lifetime or after my death appeal to me or misuse my writings to confirm their error . . . I desire with this treatise to confess my faith before God and all the world, point by point. I am determined to abide by it until death and (so help me God!) in this faith to depart from this world and to appear before the judgment seat of our Lord Jesus Christ.[12]

The Marburg Articles, however, constitute a statement of faith that Luther wrote up at the Marburg Colloquy in order to demonstrate as much unity as possible with the very people he had denounced in the earlier work: Zwingli and his allies! Although the articles themselves acknowledge continuing disagreement over 'whether the true body and blood of Christ are bodily present'

---

10. Zwingli (1484–1531) was the principal reformer of Zurich in the first years of the Reformation. For his basic biography, see G. R. Potter, *Zwingli* (Cambridge: Cambridge University Press, 1976); and for his theology, see W. P. Stephens, *The Theology of Huldrych Zwingli* (Oxford: Clarendon, 1986). For the differences between Zwingli and Luther especially concerning the Eucharist, see Hermann Sasse, *This Is My Body: Luther's Contention for the Real Presence in the Sacrament of the Altar* (Adelaide, Australia: Lutheran, 1977, rev. ed.).

11. E.g. 'I have declared that I write not against flesh and blood ... but against the devil and his followers ... Shall I now become so timid for the sake of these delicate, highly spiritual, profoundly holy fanatics, that I must avoid mentioning my enemy? I am quite willing to be called blasphemous and mad when I attack the devil pungently and pointedly in his messengers' (*LW* 37:270 [*WA* 26:402.8–14]).

12. *LW* 37:360 (*WA* 26:499.3–10). M. U. Edwards, *Luther and the False Brethren*, pp. 91–92, discusses the basis for Luther's fears in works by Martin Bucer and Leo Jud from 1526. Interestingly, in his answer to Luther's 1528 *Confession*, Zwingli used Luther's earlier writings to correct his later Christology. See his *Über D. Martin Luthers Buch, Bekenntnis genannt* in *Huldreich Zwinglis sämtliche Werke*, ed. E. Egli et al., 14 vols., *Corpus reformatorum* edition (Berlin: C. A. Schwetschke & Son, 1905–), 6[II]:136.11–137.6; 138.5–17; 144.4–31; 148.24–149.23.

in the Eucharist, they nevertheless express a remarkable degree of unity on basic Christian beliefs.[13]

The third of the documents, the Small Catechism,[14] has an entirely different origin because Luther prepared it for the instruction of the young. Accordingly, he describes its contents as the basics of the faith, what everyone who calls himself a Christian must know. 'Those who are unwilling to learn the catechism', Luther writes, 'should be told that they deny Christ and are not Christians.' Using a form inherited from the medieval church, Luther joined his own explanations to three chief parts of Christian doctrine that were often part of medieval instructional manuals (Ten Commandments, Apostles' Creed and Lord's Prayer). He then added two more parts of doctrine (Baptism and the Lord's Supper) as well as a form of confession of sins, prayers and a 'Table of Duties' for the instruction of Christians in various walks of life. The result is a brief but comprehensive description of Christianity according to Martin Luther.[15]

The fourth document, the Smalcald Articles,[16] is again a confession of faith—in some ways like Luther's statement of faith in the 1528 *Confession*,

---

13. *LW* 38:88 (*WA* 30^{III}:170.6–8).

14. The Small Catechism (cited hereafter as SC) belongs to the Lutheran Confessions as compiled in the *Book of Concord*. In this chapter, citations are from *Concordia: The Lutheran Confessions* (St. Louis: Concordia, 2005). At the same time that Luther prepared the Small Catechism, he also published a significantly larger version for pastors, known as the Large Catechism (cited hereafter as LC). Because of its size as well as its more specialized intended audience, I have not analysed it in this chapter. However, from time to time I have found it useful for explicating something in the SC. I have checked all citations of both the Large and Small Catechisms against the critical edition of the *Book of Concord*—*Die Bekenntnisschriften der evangelisch-lutherischen Kirche* (Göttingen: Vandenhoeck & Ruprecht, 1986^{10}). For background to the composition of the catechisms, see Brecht, *Martin Luther*, vol. 2, pp. 273–280; and *OER*, under 'Catechisms'. See also M. Reu, *Dr. Martin Luther's Small Catechism: A History of Its Origin, Its Distribution and Its Use* (Chicago: Wartburg, 1929).

15. SC Preface 11.

16. Like the Small Catechism, the Smalcald [also spelled 'Schmalkald'] Articles (cited as SA) are a part of the *Book of Concord*. William R. Russell, *Luther's Theological Testament: The Schmalkald Articles* (Minneapolis: Fortress, 1995), offers a very fine analysis of this document. Russell's article in the *OER* under 'Schmalkald Articles' provides a useful introduction, as does Brecht, *Martin Luther*, vol. 3, pp. 178–193.

although written in an entirely different context. The first three documents were all written within a relatively brief span of time in Luther's life, but the Reformer composed this one several years later. The Smalcald Articles, therefore, offer an opportunity to test the consistency of Luther's views over time. On the one hand, what Luther says about the composition of these articles is reminiscent of what he had said about Part 3 of his *Confession*, in that he wished to prevent people from misinterpreting his teachings after his death. Complaining of 'poisonous people' who 'want to dress up their poison with my labor' and so by Luther's name 'mislead the poor people', Luther presents the Smalcald Articles: 'If I die, those who are alive and those who come after me will have my testimony and confession . . . I have remained in this confession up to now, and by God's grace, I will remain in it.' On the other hand, Luther also intended these articles to serve a public purpose in that his prince and protector, Elector John Frederick of Saxony, requested them as a list of non-negotiables if the evangelicals ever decided to participate in the church council Pope Paul III had recently announced. For both reasons, as a theological testament and as a platform for discussions with Rome, Luther's Smalcald Articles offer insight into what Luther considered essential for the Christian faith.[17]

Biblical authority[18]

Although differing significantly from each other regarding the circumstances of their composition, the four documents under consideration here are remarkably similar in content. First, in each of the four documents, Luther presented his doctrine as the teaching of the Scriptures.[19] Describing the content of his

---

17. SA Preface 3–4. See also SA 3.15.3, and Russell, *Luther's Theological Testament*, pp. 18–19, 23–42.

18. This characteristic of Luther's faith corresponds very nicely to Bebbington's 'Biblicism', in his *Evangelicalism in Modern Britain* (pp. 12–14): 'The third main feature of Evangelicals, their devotion to the Bible, has been the result of their belief that all spiritual truth is to be found in its pages.'

19. Richard P. Bucher, *The Ecumenical Luther: The Development and Use of His Doctrinal Hermeneutic* (St. Louis: Concordia, 2003), has summarized Luther's use of Scripture to prove doctrine this way (p. 28): 'A necessary doctrine of the Christian faith must be based on Scripture alone, the right Scripture, and the right Scripture rightly interpreted.'

confession of faith in the earliest of the four, the 1528 *Confession*, Luther wrote, 'I have most diligently traced all these articles through the Scriptures, [and] have examined them again and again in the light thereof'; and at the very end, Luther summarized his confession with these words: 'This is my faith, for so all true Christians believe and so the Holy Scriptures teach us.' Likewise, in the last of the documents, the Smalcald Articles, Luther presented scriptural authority in the form of a rule: 'God's Word shall establish articles of faith and no-one else, not even an angel can do so.' Luther also viewed the traditional catechism as nothing but a summary of the Bible: 'For in these three parts [Ten Commandments, Creed and Lord's Prayer], everything that we have in the Scriptures is included in short, plain, and simple terms.' Of the four documents, only the Marburg Articles contain little explicit Scripture, but still the thirteenth article presents the Word of God as the church's standard: 'What is called tradition or human ordinances in spiritual or ecclesiastical matters, *provided they do not plainly contradict the word of God*, may be freely kept or abolished' (emphasis mine).[20]

Beyond general statements of biblical authority, Luther fills these documents with references to the Scriptures in order to prove his doctrine, especially regarding topics he knows are controversial.[21] Even in the Marburg Articles with its paucity of references, Article 8 invokes Romans 10 and Article 9 quotes God's command ('Go, baptize') from Matthew 28 and God's promise ('he who believes') from Mark 16.[22] In contrast to the Marburg Articles, the Small Catechism is heavily biblical. Two of the traditional parts are biblical texts themselves. Luther also offers Bible passages to prove his statements about the meaning, benefit, power and significance of baptism, while his discussion of the sacrament of the altar is simply an explication of the instituting words of Jesus, recorded in the Synoptic Gospels and Paul (1 Corinthians). The 'Table of Duties' in the Small Catechism consists of Bible passages attached to various vocations.[23]

---

20. *LW* 37:360, 372 (*WA* 26:499.13–500.2; 509.19–20); SA 2.2.15; LC Short Preface 18; and *LW* 38:88 (*WA* 30^{III}:168.2–7).

21. E.g. in the Smalcald Articles, as Russell points out (*Luther's Theological Testament*, pp. 70–72), Luther does not use Scripture to prove his statements regarding the Trinity, which he knew his opponents accepted, but did use Bible passages to prove his doctrine of the forgiveness of sins through faith in Christ alone, because this was a matter of dispute.

22. *LW* 38:87 (*WA* 30^{III}:165.6, 12, 14).

23. SC 4.4, 8, 10, 14; 6.4–10; 9.1–15.

Luther's *Confession* of 1528 also contains many specific biblical references as proof of his doctrines. Sometimes the references point to a particular place in the Bible (e.g. Gen. 1; Rom. 3; 1 Tim. 4);[24] at other times they refer directly to the sacred penmen (e.g. 'St. Luke describes', or 'St. Paul says'); and sometimes they occur in combination (e.g. 'David says in Psalm 51').[25] Luther can also generalize about biblical teaching, such as his statement about the basic social structures established by God, namely church, family and government: 'These three religious institutions or orders are found in God's Word and commandment; and whatever is contained in God's Word must be holy, for God's Word is holy and sanctifies everything connected with it and involved in it.' Beyond this generality and unlike the 'Table of Duties', Luther does not offer specific Bible passages in support of the three estates.[26] Luther also uses the Scriptures negatively to reject purgatory ('Nor have we anything in Scripture concerning purgatory. It too was certainly fabricated by goblins'); the invocation of saints ('Of the invocation of saints nothing is said in Scripture; therefore it is necessarily uncertain and not to be believed'); and monasticism ('I reject and condemn . . . all such things devised and instituted by men beyond and apart from Scripture').[27]

The Smalcald Articles employ the Scriptures in a similar fashion. Once again Luther adduces particular passages to demonstrate his doctrine either by referring to a book and chapter (e.g. Rom. 3; John 1; Isa. 53) and/or by naming the source (e.g. 'St Paul says', 'St Peter says' and 'Christ declares').[28] He also uses the Scriptures in a more general way to reject a particular doctrine or practice (e.g. 'the Mass is dangerous, fabricated and invented without God's will and Word'). He does the same thing regarding private masses, pilgrimages, relics, the invocation of saints, the papacy, papal teachings, and external dress and ceremonies.[29]

---

24. *LW* 37:361, 364 (*WA* 26:500.14; 504.22, 29).

25. *LW* 37:361, 363 (*WA* 26:501.3; 503.10, 12).

26. For Luther's theology of created 'orders', see Paul Althaus, *The Ethics of Martin Luther* (Philadelphia: Fortress, 1972), pp. 36–42.

27. *LW* 37:365, 369, 370, 363 (*WA* 26:505.7–10; 508.6–7, 15–16; 503.17–504.1). Similarly, Luther asserts (*LW* 37:362 [*WA* 26:502.6–9]) that he can prove original sin 'from Scripture' but does not offer specific references.

28. SA 2.1.1, 2, 4, 5; 2.2.2.

29. SA 2.2.5. See also 2.2.8–9, 18, 22, 25; 2.4.1, 14; and 3.12.3. For Russell's discussion of Luther's use of Scripture in the SA, see his *Luther's Theological Testament*, pp. 70–72.

But in addition to the essential similarity of the Smalcald Articles to the previous documents in their approach to scriptural authority, there is a sharpening of Luther's reliance upon the Word on account of his rejection of those whom he calls 'enthusiasts': those who, Luther charges, 'boast that they have the Spirit without and before the Word'.[30] For Luther, the Scriptures are important precisely because the Holy Spirit works through them. He identifies Thomas Müntzer[31] as one of the 'enthusiasts' he has in mind but also charges the pope with the same vice since he too claims that 'whatever he decides and commands within his church is from the Spirit and is right, even though it is above and contrary to Scripture and the spoken Word'. Luther even identifies the primal sin as 'enthusiasm': 'The old devil and old serpent . . . turned Adam and Eve into enthusiasts. He led them away from God's outward Word to spiritualizing and self-pride.'[32]

Now, clearly Luther has in mind the oral proclamation of God's Word as well as the written Scriptures when he speaks of the external, objective Word of God; and an important part of Luther's approach to the Bible is that it needs to be preached.[33] For example, in his introduction to the New

---

30. SA 3.8.3. Luther encountered 'enthusiasts' early in the Reformation in the so-called 'Zwickau Prophets', who had appeared in Wittenberg by the time Luther returned from the Wartburg in 1522. Luther rejected their claim to be speaking under direct inspiration of the Holy Spirit. Not long before Luther composed the SA, other 'enthusiasts' had been ousted from their control of the city of Münster in which they had hoped to establish the 'Kingdom of God'. See Brecht, *Martin Luther*, vol. 2, pp. 34–38, and vol. 3, pp. 34–38. For Luther's theological concerns about the attitude of 'enthusiasts' toward the Scriptures, see Lohse, *Martin Luther's Theology*, pp. 190–191.

31. Thomas Müntzer (d. 1525) was a one-time follower of Luther who relied on special revelations of the Spirit in addition to the Scriptures for guidance as a preacher of the end times. During the Peasants' War, he encouraged his followers to take up arms against ungodly authorities; but when they were defeated at Frankenhausen, Müntzer was captured and executed. For Luther, he remained a symbol of what enthusiasm could lead to. See *OER*, under 'Müntzer, Thomas'; and M. U. Edwards, *Luther and the False Brethren*, pp. 35–39, 66–70.

32. SA 3.8.3–5.

33. Though preaching is not singled out by Bebbington, *Evangelicalism in Modern Britain*, as one of his four characteristics of modern evangelicalism (pp. 2–3), he nonetheless entitled his first chapter 'Preaching the Gospel: The Nature of Evangelical Religion', and appropriately so, since, as he himself acknowledges (p. 5), 'preaching the gospel was [for evangelicals] the chief method of winning converts'.

Testament that accompanied his translation of it into German, Luther first described the New Testament as 'a book in which are written the gospel and the promises of God, together with the history of those who believe and of those who do not believe them'. But as he elaborated on his explanation, he emphasized the oral character of the gospel; for example, 'this gospel of God or New Testament is a good story and report, sounded forth into all the world by the apostles' and 'Christ, before his death, commanded and ordained that his gospel be preached after his death in all the world.' The task of the church, then, is to *preach* the gospel.[34]

But such preaching is not independent of the written Word. Although the apostles first preached the gospel and only later did some of them write the books of the New Testament, they did so in order to guarantee the authenticity of the gospel that was being preached. In a sermon published in 1522, Luther explained:

> When heretics, false teachers, and all manner of errors arose in the place of pious preachers giving the flock of Christ poison as pasture, then every last thing that could and needed to be done, had to be attempted . . . they began to write in order to lead the flock of Christ as much as possible by Scripture into Scripture. They wanted to ensure that the sheep could feed themselves and hence protect themselves against the wolves.[35]

So when Luther writes about the spoken Word, one needs to understand it as founded on the written Word, not as something new or extra. Luther provides examples of what he means in the Smalcald Articles. In referring to the spoken word that adults who are baptized 'must first have heard', he quotes a scriptural text: 'Whoever believes and is baptized will be saved' (Mark 16:16). So they hear what is in the Bible. Similarly, Cornelius 'heard' from the Jews about the coming Messiah, and he heard from Peter that the Messiah had now come. But in each instance, what Cornelius heard was what was already in the Scriptures or would be when the New Testament was finally written.[36]

---

34. *LW* 35:358–359 (*WADB* 6:2.18–21; 4.3–5, 15–17). For the significance of preaching in Luther's thought, see Fred W. Meuser, 'Luther as Preacher of the Word of God', in McKim, *Cambridge Companion to Martin Luther*, pp. 136–148. For the relationship between the spoken and the written Word, see Althaus, *Theology of Martin Luther*, pp. 72–73.
35. *LW* 52:206 (*WA* 10¹:627.3–9).
36. SA 3.8.7–8.

Luther's point, then, in emphasizing the spoken Word is not to set it against the written Word but to stress that God wants his Word to be preached. People are to rely on God's objective revelation in the Scriptures or on the proclamation (something outside themselves) and not on their own thoughts and ideas, which they confuse with the work of the Holy Spirit.

Justification by faith[37]

Of course, what Luther has especially in mind when he talks about the necessity of the Word is the gospel. For Luther, this is absolutely the heart and soul of the Scriptures, and so, in each of the four documents under consideration, the gospel is at the centre.[38] Indeed, in the Smalcald Articles, Luther identifies the gospel as the 'first and chief article'. About this article, he says, '*nothing can be yielded or surrendered,* even though heaven and earth and everything else falls' (emphasis mine). So important is this article that Luther maintains that everything he teaches 'depends' on it, 'in opposition to the pope, the devil, and the whole world'. 'Therefore,' he concludes, 'we must be certain and not doubt this doctrine. Otherwise, all is lost, and the pope, the devil, and all adversaries win the victory and the right over us.'[39]

Luther specifies precisely what he means by the 'first and chief article'. Significantly, he bolsters every part of his description by direct references to the Bible. Therefore, the gospel that must be preached is the gospel the Scriptures teach. Biblical authority remains basic to Luther's understanding of the Christian religion.

But just what does Luther mean by the 'gospel'? Quite simply, the work of Jesus Christ on behalf of sinners in which people must trust for their salvation. Although Luther confesses the Trinity and the person of Christ,[40] when

---

37. With this characteristic, Luther lays the theological foundations for what Bebbington, *Evangelicalism in Modern Britain*, identifies as 'conversionism' (p. 5): 'The call to conversion has been the content of the gospel. Preachers urged their hearers to turn away from their sins in repentance and to Christ in faith.'

38. For the relationship of the gospel to the Scriptures in Luther's thought, see Althaus, *Theology of Martin Luther*, pp. 74, 79–81. Lohse, *Martin Luther's Theology*, p. 258, calls justification 'the heart and soul' of Luther's theology.

39. SA 2.1.1, 5.

40. Althaus, *Theology of Martin Luther*, pp. 179–200.

it comes to the 'chief article' in the Smalcald Articles, Luther focuses not on who Jesus is but on what he has done:

> Jesus Christ, our God and Lord, died for our sins and was raised for our justification (Romans 4:24–25).
>
> He alone is the Lamb of God who takes away the sins of the world (John 1:29), and God has laid upon Him the iniquities of us all (Isaiah 53:6).
>
> All have sinned and are justified freely, without their own works or merits, by His grace, through the redemption that is in Christ Jesus, in His blood (Romans 3:23–25).[41]

Since these statements are virtually quotations from the Bible, it would be difficult for any Christian to gainsay them. What is significant, however, is that Luther identifies them as the most important part of the entire Scriptures: Christ's death and resurrection on behalf of sinful humanity.[42] Clearly, Christ's work is important to Luther on account of his sense of the significance of sin, and elsewhere in these articles he discusses the total depravity of man's nature.[43] But the remedy for sin is more significant yet. Likewise, it is not incidental to his theology that Jesus is both God and man, but the real importance of the incarnation is that it enabled 'our God and Lord' to rescue humanity from sin. The saving work of Jesus is at the heart of Luther's faith.[44]

But there is one thing more: an answer to the question 'How does the sinner appropriate this work of Christ for himself?' So Luther continues:

---

41. SA 2.1.1–3. Of course, Luther's original biblical references include only book and chapter, since verse numbers had not yet been developed.

42. This emphasis in Luther dovetails very nicely with what Bebbington, *Evangelicalism in Modern Britain*, calls 'crucicentrism' in modern evangelicalism (pp. 14–17). The terminology 'theology of the cross' derives from Luther's own work and has been used by modern theologians to characterize Luther's theology. See e.g. Alister E. McGrath, *Luther's Theology of the Cross* (Grand Rapids: Baker, 1990). Although Bebbington indicates (p. 15) that 'the standard view of Evangelicals was that Christ died as a substitute for sinful mankind', Althaus, *Theology of Martin Luther*, pp. 202–211, shows that Luther taught not only that Christ, by his suffering and death, assuaged the wrath of a righteous God but also that he overcame the powers of hell. In either case, however, Christ on the cross is a central element in Luther's soteriology.

43. See SA 3.1.1–10.

44. SA 1.4; 2.1. For the role of Christ in human salvation, see Lohse, *Martin Luther's Theology*, pp. 223–228.

This is necessary to believe. This cannot be otherwise acquired or grasped by any work, law, or merit. Therefore, it is clear and certain that this faith alone justifies us. As St. Paul says:

For we hold that one is justified by faith apart from works of the law. (Romans 3:28)
   That He might be just and the justifier of the one who has faith in Jesus. (Romans 3:26)

One grasps the work of Christ solely by faith. Since Jesus has paid the complete penalty, there is nothing that humans can add to it. Therefore, Luther repudiates any personal contribution to salvation. It is all God's grace; it is all Christ's work; and therefore, it is all by faith. This too is a part of the chief article.[45]

As one might expect, Luther confesses the same doctrine in each of the earlier confessions. In none of the others, however, does he call it the 'first and chief article'. Nonetheless, in each case, Luther describes it and indicates its importance. For example, in the Marburg Articles, already in the fourth article on original sin, Luther adds as an aside, 'And if Jesus Christ had not come to our aid by his death and life, we would have had to die eternally.' Then in Article 5, Luther affirms justification by faith:

We believe that we are saved from such sin and all other sins as well as from eternal death, if we believe in the same Son of God, Jesus Christ, who died for us, etc., and that apart from such faith we cannot free ourselves of any sin through any kind of works, station in life or [religious] order, etc.

In Article 7, Luther elaborates even more on the significance of faith:

Such faith is our righteousness before God, for the sake of which God reckons and regards us as righteous, godly, and holy apart from all works and merit, and through which he delivers us from sin, death, and hell, receives us by grace and saves us, for the sake of his Son, in whom we thus believe.[46]

In the Small Catechism, Luther provides this eloquent description of the gospel as an explanation of the Second Article of the Creed:

---

45. SA 2.1.4–5. For the meaning of 'faith' in Luther's theology, see Lohse, *Martin Luther's Theology*, pp. 200–203, 260–261.

46. *LW* 38:86 (*WA* 30^{III}:162.8–11, 14–163.5; 164.2–10).

[Jesus Christ] has redeemed me, a lost and condemned creature, purchased and won me from all sins, from death, and from the power of the devil. He did this not with gold or silver, but with His holy, precious blood and with His innocent suffering and death, so that I may be His own, live under Him in His kingdom, and serve Him in everlasting righteousness, innocence, and blessedness, just as He is risen from the dead, lives, and reigns to all eternity.[47]

Whereas the text of the Creed itself is simply a recitation of the work of Christ from his incarnation to his second coming, Luther's explanation emphasizes the saving significance of that work for 'me', the sinner.

The same idea is prominent in Luther's *Confession* of 1528. This entire confession is really an affirmation and expansion of the Creed. Instead of distinguishing text and explanation as in the Small Catechism, Luther integrates the two. So in confessing the work of Christ, Luther includes its saving significance: 'I believe also that this Son of God and of Mary, our Lord Jesus Christ, suffered *for us poor sinners*, was crucified, dead, and buried, *in order that he might redeem us from sin, death, and the eternal wrath of God by his innocent blood*' (emphasis mine). Similarly, Luther also affirms the vicarious atonement in his discussion of sin, 'All men . . . would necessarily be guilty of eternal death if Jesus Christ had not come to our aid and taken upon himself this guilt and sin as an innocent lamb, paid for us by his sufferings, and if he still did not intercede and plead for us.'[48]

Although Luther does not include a separate statement regarding faith in his 1528 *Confession*, it is still explicitly present in his statement regarding the saints of the church who had become monks. 'Although many great saints have lived in them [monasteries]', Luther writes, 'and as the elect of God are misled by them even at this time, yet finally *by faith in Jesus Christ* [they] have been redeemed and have escaped' (emphasis mine). 'Faith alone' is also implicit in Luther's rejection of human ability to contribute to salvation: 'There is no power or ability, no cleverness or reason, with which we can prepare ourselves for righteousness and life or seek after it.' Once again, Luther rejects any human contribution to salvation, 'It is impossible that there should be more saviors, ways, or means to be saved than through the one righteousness which our Savior Jesus Christ is and has bestowed upon us.'[49]

Therefore, in all four of Luther's creedal statements, we find the same basic doctrine of salvation. It begins with man's need, his inherent and inescapable

---

47. SC 2.2.
48. *LW* 37:362 (*WA* 26:501.18–502.2, 7–14).
49. *LW* 37:363–364 (*WA* 26:504.2–4; 503.2–4; 504.19–21).

sinfulness that renders him totally incapable of saving himself, as Luther writes in the Marburg Articles:

> We believe that original sin is innate and inherited by us from Adam and is the kind of sin which condemns all men. And if Jesus Christ had not come to our aid . . . we would have had to die eternally as a result of it and could not have received God's kingdom and salvation.[50]

But God has provided a way of salvation in his Son, Jesus, who died for man's sin in order to satisfy the wrath of God and thus rescue all people from the power of Satan and the destiny of hell. God offers this salvation to all who believe.

Obviously, Luther's view of salvation is rigorously monergistic. Man does nothing. God does it all. This suggests a doctrine of predestination. However, in spite of the fact that Luther held to predestination,[51] that doctrine is not mentioned in any of the four documents under consideration here. Nevertheless, Luther is clear that salvation is entirely at God's initiative, for faith is purely the work of the Holy Spirit, as Luther attests in the Marburg Articles, 'Such faith is a gift of God which we cannot earn with any works or merit that precede, nor can we achieve it by our own strength, but the Holy Spirit gives and creates this faith in our hearts as it pleases him.'[52] Similarly, in the Small Catechism, Luther confesses, 'I cannot by my own reason or strength believe in Jesus Christ, my Lord, or come to Him. But the Holy Spirit has called me by the Gospel, enlightened me with His gifts, sanctified and kept me in the true faith';[53] and in the 1528 *Confession*, Luther says:

> Because this [saving] grace would benefit no one if it remained so profoundly hidden and could not come to us, the Holy Spirit comes and gives himself to us also, wholly

---

50. *LW* 38:86 (*WA* 30^{III}:162.4–12). See also *LW* 37:362–363 (*WA* 26:503.1–6); SC 2.2, 3; and SA 3.2–11.

51. In his preface to Romans that accompanied his 1522 New Testament (*LW* 35:378; *WADB* 7:22.26–29), Luther writes that '[Paul] teaches of God's eternal predestination [*Versehung*]—out of which originally proceeds who shall believe or not, who can or cannot get rid of sin—in order that our salvation may be taken entirely out of our hands and put in the hand of God alone'. Both Althaus, *Theology of Martin Luther*, pp. 274–286, and Lohse, *Martin Luther's Theology*, pp. 165–168, discuss this doctrine especially in relation to Luther's *Bondage of the Will*.

52. *LW* 38:86 (*WA* 30^{III}:163.6–13).

53. SC 2.3.

and completely. He teaches us to understand this deed of Christ which has been manifested to us, helps us receive and preserve it, use it to our advantage and impart it to others, increase and extend it.[54]

But there is an interesting shift in emphasis regarding the Holy Spirit between 1528 and 1537. Although the earlier confession connects the work of the Spirit to the means of grace, it also refers to the inner testimony of the Spirit; for example:

> [The Holy Spirit] does this both inwardly and outwardly—inwardly by means of faith and other spiritual gifts, outwardly through the gospel, baptism, and the sacrament of the altar, through which . . . he comes to us and inculcates the sufferings of Christ for the benefit of our salvation.

So the Spirit uses means, but we can also rely on his work within, 'This is our assurance if we feel this witness of the Spirit in our hearts that God wishes to be our Father, forgive our sin, and bestow everlasting life on us.'[55]

However, reflecting his hostility to the enthusiasts, by the time Luther writes again about the Spirit in 1537, his emphasis is entirely on connecting the Spirit to the external Word:

> In issues relating to the spoken, outward Word, we must firmly hold that God grants His Spirit or grace to no one except through or with the preceding outward Word (Galatians 3:2, 5). This protects us from the enthusiasts (i.e., souls who boast that they have the Spirit without and before the Word). They judge Scripture or the spoken Word and explain and stretch it at their pleasure.

What Luther wants is just the opposite: the Word is to stand in judgment over the opinions of men, especially the enthusiasts. As he says, 'Whatever is praised as from the Spirit—without the Word and Sacraments—is the devil himself.'[56]

---

54. *LW* 37:366 (*WA* 26:506.3–7).

55. *LW* 37:366 (*WA* 26:505.35–37; 506.7–12).

56. SA 3.8.3, 10. Lohse, *Martin Luther's Theology*, pp. 237–238, comments on Luther's shift in emphasis regarding the 'inner testimony' of the Spirit; but even in the early years, Lohse insists (p. 237), 'Luther never conceived the activity of the Spirit as independent of external means.' See also Althaus, *Theology of Martin Luther*, pp. 35–42. Obviously, at this point, Luther's attitude contrasts with many later

This quotation, however, suggests another characteristic of Luther's soteriology that later evangelicals might find problematical, and this is his insistence on the sacraments as real means of grace. Nevertheless, Luther's treatment
of the sacraments is entirely evangelical.[57] He rejects any idea that baptism or
the Eucharist save apart from faith. Instead, like the Word, they are means
the Holy Spirit employs to create and nurture faith in the saving work of
Christ. In his 1528 *Confession*, Luther affirms the sacraments as means, along
with the gospel, by which the Holy Spirit 'comes to us and inculcates the sufferings of Christ for the benefit of our salvation'. Beyond that, Luther does
not elaborate much in this confession about either sacrament. He affirms one
baptism, presumably of infants, and rejects those who rebaptize; and regarding the Eucharist, he insists that 'the true body and blood of Christ are orally
eaten and drunk in the bread and wine'.[58]

The discussion of the sacraments in the Marburg Articles that Luther signed
along with Zwingli is more elaborate and even more evangelical. The two
men affirmed that baptism 'is not merely an empty sign or watchword among
Christians but, rather, a sign and work of God by which our faith grows and
through which we are regenerated to [eternal] life'. Likewise, regarding the
Eucharist, the two men explain that 'like the Word', it 'has been given and
ordained by God Almighty in order that weak consciences may thereby be
excited to faith by the Holy Spirit', even though they could not agree on

evangelicals who, according to Noll, *Rise of Evangelicalism* (p. 267), 'were not at all
reluctant to rely on dreams, visions and special words of counsel from the Holy
Spirit'. Nevertheless, Noll continues, 'these sources of divine knowledge were
usually subordinated to broader understandings of the Bible'.

57. Bebbington, *Evangelicalism in Modern Britain*, pp. 9–10, shows that baptismal
regeneration was a perennial issue for evangelical Anglicans because the Prayer
Book affirmed it, while evangelicals generally held to 'conversion' as the way in
which a person becomes a Christian. Luther would definitely have sided with the
Prayer Book champions. For Luther on the sacraments, see Althaus, *Theology of
Martin Luther*, pp. 345–403; and Lohse, *Martin Luther's Theology*, pp. 298–313. An
excellent and thorough treatment of Luther's theology of baptism that shows how
it developed through the years is Jonathan D. Trigg, *Baptism in the Theology of
Martin Luther* (Leiden: E. J. Brill, 2001).

58. *LW* 37:366–367 (*WA* 26:506.11–12, 21–23). It is worth remembering, of course, that
Luther's brief statement here regarding the Real Presence comes at the end of a
major work in which he has defended this doctrine against Zwingli and others.

whether the body and blood of Jesus were bodily present in the bread and wine.[59]

Probably the best explanation of the two sacraments occurs in Luther's Small Catechism. For each of them, he offers a brief definition, grounded in the Word of God, and shows that at the heart of each is God's promise that is received by faith. For example, regarding baptism, after stating that it works forgiveness of sins, life and salvation, Luther asks, 'How can water do such great things?' His answer:

> It is not the water indeed that does them, but the Word of God, which is in and with the water, and faith, which trusts this Word of God in the water. For without the Word of God, the water is simple water and no Baptism. But with the Word of God it is a Baptism, that is, a gracious water of life and a washing of regeneration in the Holy Spirit. As St. Paul says in Titus chapter three, 'He saves us . . . by the washing of regeneration and renewal of the Holy Spirit, whom He poured out on us richly through Jesus Christ our Savior, so that being justified by His grace we might become heirs according to the hope of eternal life.'[60]

Therefore, the strength of baptism is not in the outward element or in the ritual act but in the promises that God has attached to baptism for Christ's sake in the Scriptures, and it is on these promises that faith relies.

The same thing is true with respect to the Eucharist. Again, Luther affirms the benefits of the sacrament, 'forgiveness, life, and salvation', before raising the question 'How can bodily eating and drinking do such great things?' And again Luther explains that it is not the outward activity that accomplishes anything; it is the promise that God attaches to the sacrament, in this case, right in the words of institution, 'given . . . and shed for you, for the forgiveness of sins'. 'The person', Luther writes, 'who believes these words has what they say and express, namely the forgiveness of sins.' The essence of the gospel is God's promise that one receives by faith. For Luther, this is as true of the sacraments as it is of the Word itself.[61]

In comparison with the Small Catechism, Luther's discussion of the sacraments in the Smalcald Articles is limited, but it is still evangelical. In an article entitled 'The Gospel', Luther points out that God 'does not give us . . . aid against sin in only one way'. Instead, he 'is superabundantly generous in His

---

59. *LW* 38:87, 88 (*WA* 30III:165.14–166.2, 170.1–5).

60. SC 4.9–10.

61. SC 6.7–8.

grace'; and so he comes to us first of all by the preaching of the forgiveness of sins but then also through baptism and the 'Sacrament of the Altar'. Beyond this general statement, Luther also insists regarding baptism that its power is in God's Word in the water and nowhere else and that children should be baptized, since they too have been redeemed by Christ. Regarding the Eucharist, Luther once more insists 'that the bread and wine in the Supper are Christ's true body and blood', while rejecting papal practice, communion in one kind and the papal doctrine of transubstantiation. Thus, Luther bases his doctrine of the sacraments on the Scriptures and regards it as integrally connected to the gospel of God's free grace in Christ.[62]

Luther's polemics[63]

Even a casual reading of Luther quickly reveals still another characteristic of his faith, namely a concern to identify what he does not believe as well as what he does. For Luther, confessing the faith includes also repudiating falsehood. For one thing, if the Scriptures establish doctrine, then what is unscriptural must not be taught. As noted above, Luther uses the Bible to reject a number of practices and beliefs of the late medieval church. But even more important to Luther than the scriptural principle is the evangelical principle, that is, using the gospel itself as a criterion of judgment. Since salvation is at stake, Luther decisively rejects any alternative to the gospel. While the truth of God saves, its opposite damns.[64]

---

62. SA 3.4; 3.5.1–4; 3.6.1. See Russell, *Luther's Theological Testament*, pp. 99–111.

63. To a certain extent, Luther's polemics distinguish him from later evangelicals who often preferred to emphasize a common centre in the gospel, while ignoring certain doctrinal differences. E.g. Noll, *Rise of Evangelicalism*, p. 162, points out that the Anglican Whitefield willingly preached from Independent and Baptist pulpits. Bebbington, *Evangelicalism in Modern Britain*, pp. 65–66, locates such attitudes in the pragmatism of the eighteenth century. However, in their opposition to Roman Catholicism, many later evangelicals would be in complete agreement with Luther. See Bebbington, pp. 101–102, 133–134, 194. Moreover, as champions of truth, evangelicals sometimes debated among themselves about correct doctrine, e.g. the Arminians vs. the Calvinists. See Noll, *Rise of Evangelicalism*, pp. 267–273; but even at this point, argues Bebbington, pp. 16–17, common agreement on the 'cruciality of the cross' helped to bring the sides together in the nineteenth century.

64. For the gospel as theological criterion of true and false doctrine, see Lohse, *Martin Luther's Theology*, pp. 258–260; and Russell, *Luther's Theological Testament*, pp. 80–84,

This is evident already in 1528 and is even more prominent in the Smalcald Articles. The Small Catechism does not include Luther's rejections, probably because its intended audience was the young and uneducated. The Marburg Articles do not include many condemnations, but they do include a few. In Article 12, both 'papists' and 'Anabaptists' are condemned by name for rejecting temporal authority, 'secular laws, courts, and ordinances'. In three other articles, particular practices of the medieval church are condemned (monasticism, clerical celibacy and the mass as a meritorious work), but these condemnations occur only in the Swiss version of the original manuscripts. Luther certainly agreed with these additions and signed the Swiss version, but they are not present in the German version and were not a part of his original composition.[65]

However, in his two personal testaments, Luther clearly uses the gospel as a criterion for evaluating doctrine and practice. In Part 3 of the 1528 *Confession*, Luther rejects and condemns 'all doctrines which glorify free will, as diametrically contrary to the help and grace of our Lord Jesus Christ'. Similarly, Luther rejects monasticism because it teaches 'ways and work' by which 'men may seek and win salvation'. But this amounts to 'abominable blasphemy and denial of the unique aid and grace of our only Savior and Mediator, Jesus Christ'. Likewise, Luther condemns papal pardons and indulgences as something additional to the gospel and also for basing satisfaction for sins in the works of men, 'whereas only Christ can make and has made satisfaction for us'. Finally, since 'Christ alone should be invoked as our Mediator', Luther disavows the invocation of saints.[66]

The Smalcald Articles are even clearer than the earlier *Confession* in using the gospel as a test for truth. Once Luther has established justification by faith as the 'first and chief article', he proceeds to use it directly as a criterion

---

who explains that Luther used it especially against the papal teachings regarding salvation. Hans-Werner Genischen, *We Condemn: How Luther and 16th-Century Lutheranism Condemned False Doctrine* (St. Louis: Concordia, 1967), pp. 45–51, shows that however much Luther can acknowledge articles of faith that can be treated independently of justification by faith, they still have no independent validity. All Christian truth is directed toward human salvation.

65. *LW* 38:86, 88 (*WA* 30^{III}:167.5–10). For the differences between the two sets of articles, cf. *WA* 30^{III}:164.12 and 164.29–31; 168.11 and 168.26–27; and 169.9 and 169.26–29. See William P. Russell, 'Translator's Note', 'The Marburg Articles', in Robert Kolb and James A. Nestingen (eds.), *Sources and Contexts of the Book of Concord* (Minneapolis: Fortress, 2001), pp. 91–92.

66. *LW* 37:362–363, 364, 369, 370 (*WA* 26:502.14–503.1; 504.5–8; 507.33–34; 508.14–15).

for judging contemporary church practice. On eight separate occasions he rejects something explicitly because it conflicts with the 'chief article'. These include the sacrifice of the mass, purgatory, indulgences, invocation of saints, monasticism and the papacy.[67] For Luther, Christianity is all about Christ the Saviour. Any doctrine or practice that obscures this reality or turns one's attention toward someone or something else besides Christ is *ipso facto* non-Christian.

Unity with the early church[68]

By means of his condemnations, Luther can also make another point, and that is that his evangelical faith is the faith of the true church through the ages but especially of the early church since he rejects the same heresies that the Fathers fought.[69] In his 1528 *Confession*, Luther makes it clear that he condemns the ancient heresies. Sometimes he is content to say that he rejects what 'certain heretics have taught'. But at other times he mentions the heretics by name: the Arians, Macedonians, Sabellians, Nestorians, Pelagians, Donatists and Novatians.[70]

   In the other documents, Luther does not mention these heretical groups, but does unite himself with the early church by laying a trinitarian and Christological foundation for his confession in each of the documents in spite of the fact that he did not see this as a point of difference between him and the papal church.[71] Luther writes in the 1528 *Confession*:

---

67. SA 2.2.1, 7, 12, 24, 25; 2.3.2; 2.4.3; 3.14.1.

68. Although this was clearly something that concerned Luther more than later evangelicals, the latter accepted the traditional trinitarian and Christological doctrines as the basis for their doctrine of justification, as did Luther. See Noll, *Rise of Evangelicalism*, pp. 49, 151, 267.

69. Luther did not use the Church Fathers as a norm for doctrine and practice in addition to the Scriptures. They were, instead, a witness to scriptural truth; and if they slipped from the truth at times, Luther was willing to say so. See John M. Headley, *Luther's View of Church History* (New Haven: Yale University Press, 1963), pp. 162–181.

70. *LW* 37:361, 362, 363, 366, 368 (*WA* 26:500.13; 501.4–5, 13–14; 503.7; 506.20; 507.15).

71. The fact that Luther insists on mentioning these traditional doctrines when they were not a matter of dispute shows how important he thought they were.

First, I believe with my whole heart the sublime article of the majesty of
God, that the Father, Son, and Holy Spirit, three distinct persons, are by nature
one true and genuine God . . . All this has been maintained up to this time
both in the Roman Church and among Christian churches throughout the
whole world.

Luther then adds a statement of traditional Christology, 'This man became
true God, as one eternal, indivisible person, of God and man, so that Mary the
holy Virgin is a real, true mother not only of the man Christ, but also of the
Son of God.'[72]

The Marburg Articles also begin with an affirmation of the Trinity 'exactly
as was decided in the Council of Nicaea and as is sung and read in the Nicene
Creed by the entire Christian church throughout the world'. Luther then confesses the incarnation and personal union ('this same Son of God and of Mary,
undivided in person, Jesus Christ'). In the Smalcald Articles, Luther again
begins with the Trinity and the person of Christ and refers to the 'Apostles'
and Athanasian Creeds' in support. Here again, he maintains that 'concerning
these articles there is no argument or dispute'.[73]

Only in the Small Catechism does Luther avoid an explicit statement of
traditional trinitarian doctrine. Nevertheless, in the Large Catechism Luther
shows his trinitarian intentions in the Small Catechism, especially in his treatment of the Creed. As he says:

In the first place, the Creed has until now been divided into twelve articles . . . But
to make the Creed most easily and clearly understood as it is to be taught to children,
we shall briefly sum up the entire Creed in three chief articles, according to the
three persons in the Godhead. Everything that we believe is related to these three
persons . . . I believe in God the Father, who has created me; I believe in God the
Son, who has redeemed me; I believe in the Holy Spirit, who sanctifies me. One
God and one faith, but three persons.[74]

Clearly, then, Luther understands himself as teaching nothing new. He stands
with the early church in its doctrine of God and of Christ; and it is this God

---

See Lohse, *Martin Luther's Theology*, pp. 207–210. Russell, *Luther's Theological
Testament*, p. 59, describes this as 'the Catholic pillar of Luther's theology'.

72. *LW* 37:361–362 (*WA* 26:500.10–15; 501.10–14).

73. *LW* 38:85–86 (*WA* 30^{III}:160.14–17, 161.14–16); SA 1.1–4.

74. LC 2 Preface 5–7.

and Christ who have acted for man's salvation. The chief article rests upon the right understanding of the Trinity.

But what is especially noteworthy about Luther's trinitarian doctrine is how he relates this traditional teaching to the individual Christian. Already in the *Confession* of 1528 Luther explains the work of the Trinity as it pertains to the believer:

> These are the three persons and one God, who has given himself to us all wholly and completely, with all that he is and has. The Father gives himself to us, with heaven and earth and all the creatures, in order that they may serve us and benefit us. But this gift has become obscured and useless through Adam's fall. Therefore the Son himself subsequently gave himself and bestowed all his works, sufferings, wisdom, and righteousness, and reconciled us to the Father . . .
>
> But because this grace would benefit no one if it remained so profoundly hidden and could not come to us, the Holy Spirit comes and gives himself to us also wholly and completely. He teaches us to understand this deed of Christ . . . helps us receive and preserve it, use it to our advantage and impart it to others.[75]

Then, in the Small Catechism, Luther transforms the Apostles' Creed from a general statement about God's activities into a personal statement of what God has done for the individual believer. Luther begins his explanation of the First Article (which deals with creation) this way: 'I believe that God has made *me* and all creatures. He has given *me* my body and soul, etc.' (emphasis mine). Similarly, the Second Article (about Christ and his work) becomes a statement of what he has done for 'me': 'He has redeemed *me*, a lost and condemned creature, purchased and won *me* from all sins, from death, and from the power of the devil, etc.' (emphasis mine). And finally, in the Third Article (about the Holy Spirit) Luther confesses, 'The Holy Spirit has called *me* by the Gospel, enlightened *me* with His gifts, sanctified and kept *me* in the true faith' (emphasis mine).[76]

In this way, Luther shows that his chief article not only rests upon the traditional doctrine of God but that it also transforms the way in which the traditional doctrine is understood, for Luther shifts the focus away from the three persons of the Trinity in themselves and toward each of the persons in relationship to the believer. Thus, the true God is also a gracious God, a giving and a forgiving God, to all the faithful.

---

75. *LW* 37:366 (*WA* 26:505.38–506.7).

76. SC 2.1–6.

Christian activism[77]

The doctrine of justification by faith also had a powerful impact upon Luther's understanding of the Christian life. Not only did the chief article overthrow traditional piety (pilgrimages, monasticism, votive masses and other ecclesiastically approved rites and ceremonies), but it also became the foundation of Christian activity in the world and on behalf of the neighbour.[78] Article 10 of the Marburg Articles states, 'Such faith, through the working of the Holy Spirit, and by which we are reckoned and have become righteous and holy, performs good works through us, namely love toward the neighbor, prayer to God, and the suffering of persecution.'[79]

In the Smalcald Articles, Luther makes it clear that saving faith and good works are two different things, and that the latter makes absolutely no contribution to salvation:

> Such faith, renewal, and forgiveness of sins are followed by good works. What is still sinful or imperfect in them will not be counted as sin or defect, for Christ's sake . . . Therefore, we cannot boast of many merits and works, if they are viewed apart from grace and mercy.

So Christ's work always comes first, and one grasps it solely by faith. But Luther adds, 'We say, besides, that if good works do not follow, the faith is false and not true.' In short, faith alone saves, but it is never alone. It inevitably produces good works.[80]

But these works are not the works of the medieval church. Luther directs much of his polemic against false works primarily, it is true, because people believed they could contribute to salvation. Thus, he condemns not only the mass but trafficking in masses; not only purgatory but all the rites related to it;

---

77. Compared to later evangelicals, Luther's activism was quite conservative; nonetheless, the basis of evangelical activism (good works as a response to the gospel) was also basic to Luther's faith. See Bebbington, *Evangelicalism in Modern Britain*, pp. 6, 10–12, 16, 22 et al.

78. See Althaus, *Ethics of Martin Luther*, pp. 3–24; and William H. Lazareth, *Christians in Society: Luther, the Bible, and Social Ethics* (Minneapolis: Fortress, 2001), pp. 198–234, for the significance of justification in the sanctified life of a Christian.

79. *LW* 38:87 (*WA* 30^{III}:166.4–10).

80. For the 'necessity' of good works in Luther's theology, see Althaus, *Theology of Martin Luther*, pp. 245–250.

the cult of the saints, relics and pilgrimages; indulgences; clerical celibacy; and monasticism. He condemns the notion that true sanctity derives 'from albs, tonsures, long gowns, and other ceremonies' and describes the 'consecration of wax candles, palm branches, cakes, oats, spices, and such' as 'sheer mockery and fraud'.[81]

Besides, however, condemning the Roman church for investing such works with saving significance, Luther also rejects them in the Smalcald Articles for detracting from truly good works. For example, in rejecting pilgrimages, Luther points out:

> So why do they leave behind their own callings, their parishes, their pastors, God's Word, their wives, their children, and such? These *are* ordained and commanded. Instead, they run after unnecessary, dangerous illusions of the devil.

Similarly, Luther condemns monasticism for detracting from the 'offices and callings ordained by God' and celibacy of the clergy for its denigrating God's institution of marriage.[82]

In contrast to false works, Luther spends time describing truly good works in both the Small Catechism and his 1528 *Confession*. Luther makes two basic points: good works are those that God has established and are motivated by love. For example, in explaining each of the Ten Commandments in the catechism, Luther begins by saying, 'We should fear and love God so that . . .', and only then indicates what the specific requirement is, for example, 'help and befriend [our neighbour] in every bodily need' (Fifth Commandment) or 'help him to protect his property and business' (Seventh Commandment). For Luther, the motivation behind the work is as important as the work. Even unbelievers can do works that look 'good';[83] but the Christian does them for the love of God. As Luther says in the Large Catechism, 'But do good to all men. Help them and promote their interest—in every way and wherever you can—purely out of love for God and to please Him.'[84]

---

81. SA 3.12.3; 3.15.5.

82. SA 2.2.18; 2.3.2; 3.11.1–3. See also the 1528 *Confession*, LW 37:371 (WA 26:509.1–8).

83. *LW* 37:365 (WA 26:505.20–21): 'Even the godless may have much about them that is holy without being saved thereby.' See Lazareth, *Christians in Society*, pp. 167–173, for Luther's positive evaluation of 'civil righteousness' for this life even though it is of no use at all in justification.

84. SC 1.10, 14; LC 1.328.

So the love of God leads to the love of neighbour that is to characterize the Christian life. Luther can describe this in general terms as 'the common order of Christian love . . . [which] serves every needy person in general with all kinds of benevolent deeds'. But he also understands that God has established human society and that Christians carry out their obligations of love very specifically through the created orders in which God has placed them. In his 1528 *Confession*, Luther identifies three such orders: church, family and civil government. Regarding the first, Luther says, 'All who are engaged in the clerical office or ministry of the Word are in a holy, proper, good and God-pleasing order and estate.' But Luther does not mean only the ordained clergy but also 'sextons and messengers or servants who serve such persons'. Likewise, with respect to the family, Luther includes fathers, mothers and children but also servants. This estate too is 'a holy order'. And finally, 'princes and lords, judges, civil officers, state officials, notaries, male and female servants and all who serve such persons, and further, all their obedient subjects—all are engaged in pure holiness and leading a holy life before God'.[85]

What makes Luther so confident that works done by Christians in these circumstances are 'good' is the fact that these 'orders are found in God's Word and commandment'. Luther does not demonstrate this in his 1528 *Confession*, but does so in the Small Catechism, since the last part of this work is the 'Table of Duties', which he describes as 'certain passages of Scripture for various holy orders and positions, by which these people are to be admonished, as a special lesson, about their office and service'. Luther directs his first section of biblical admonitions to the ecclesiastical order: 'for bishops, pastors, and preachers'. The next section applies to the political order: 'concerning civil government'. The next several relate to marriage and the family: husbands, wives, parents, children, servants and labourers, masters and mistresses, young people and widows. Luther concludes the entire list with two Bible passages for 'all in common': 'The commandments . . . are summed up in this word, "You shall love your neighbor as yourself"' (Rom. 13:9) and 'First of all, then, I urge that supplications, prayers, intercessions, and thanksgivings be made

85. *LW* 37:364–365 (*WA* 26:505.11–13; 504.31–35; 504.35–505.5; 505.5–7). According to Bernd Wannenwetsch, 'Luther's Moral Theology', in McKim, *Cambridge Companion to Martin Luther*, p. 130, Luther 'conceived these estates as "con-creatures" of humankind ... created together with man in order to provide the social spheres that are necessary for a flourishing and obedient life'. See also Lohse, *Martin Luther's Theology*, pp. 322–324.

for all people' (1 Tim. 2:1).[86] When Christians perform their works of love in accordance with God's Word, they can be certain they are pleasing him.

Conclusion

In Luther's concern for the obligations of love in daily life as well as in his emphasis on justification by faith in Christ, the German Reformer was stepping away from medieval Christianity and into modern Protestantism. In statements that Luther intended as general descriptions of what it means to be Christian, he articulated an evangelical faith: Bible-based, Christ-centred and active in love. To be sure, Luther was not a modern-day evangelical. He possessed, for example, no strong evangelistic commitment to convert the world;[87] and his sacramental theology distinguishes him from most evangelical leaders in the modern period. But at the heart of Luther's faith were basic convictions about a gracious God, a sinful humanity and a Saviour, Jesus Christ, who paid for sins and offers salvation to all who believe. You can't get more evangelical than that!

© Cameron A. MacKenzie, 2008

---

86. *LW* 37:365 (*WA* 26:505.7–8); SC Table of Duties.

87. David J. Bosch, *Transforming Mission: Paradigm Shift in Theology of Mission* (Maryknoll: Orbis, 1991), pp. 243–248, contends that the theology of Luther (and of Calvin) was 'fundamentally missionary' (p. 245) in nature, but unlike the Anabaptists, the magisterial Reformers 'could not conceive of a missionary outreach into countries in which there was no Protestant ... government' (p. 246).

9. CALVIN, A. M. TOPLADY AND THE BEBBINGTON THESIS

Paul Helm

Introduction: the suffix

David Bebbington's thesis is that evangelicalism is a phenomenon beginning in the early decades of the eighteenth century.[1] He offers four essential qualities that together 'form a quadrilateral of priorities that is the basis of Evangelicalism': *conversionism, activism, biblicism* and *crucicentrism*.[2] Each of these features was present in earlier eras of Christianity, but in a novel development they come together in the early part of the eighteenth century, in the British Isles, to form 'evangelicalism'.

The suffix 'ism' on each of these terms adds to the exactness of the thesis and as a result both exposes it to empirical refutation and also protects it against such refutation. It adds precision, because according to the thesis not only are each of these features essential to evangelicalism (another term that also shares the suffix), indeed form the essence of evangelicalism, but also each of these features is capable of being stated, if not by an exact definition, then by a set of necessary conditions that come close also to being sufficient

---

1. David W. Bebbington, *Evangelicalism in Modern Britain: A History from the 1730s to the 1980s* (London: Routledge, 1993), ch. 2.
2. Ibid., p. 3.

conditions. Like vegetarianism, liberalism and cubism, Bebbington's four features embody an expectation of precisely characterizable, if not exactly defin-
able, conditions. They also suggest, what Bebbington may not intend, the
presence of a strong self-awareness on the part of the new evangelicals that
they are in the vanguard of a novel Christian movement. We need to keep
in mind both these features, the possible overexactness of the thesis, and the
issue of self-awareness, in what follows.

Rather surprisingly, as Garry Williams points out,[3] despite the prominence of the four 'isms', Bebbington reckons that it is a fifth factor, the more
optimistic and introspection-free doctrine of assurance that he believes is
characteristic of the Revival, that is the new element, and that this gave rise
to activism, the only really distinctive feature of 1730s evangelicalism when
compared with its earlier relatives.[4] No evidence is offered as to why such
assurance leads inevitably to activism. Perhaps the connection is regarded as
being self-evident. But it is far from being that. After all, it could be claimed
a priori, in a parallel fashion to Bebbington's claim that such confident
assurance could lead to an 'I'm all right, Jack' attitude, to complacency and
indifference towards those who lack it. In what follows, I shall ignore this
slimmed-down version of his thesis and keep the four 'isms' in mind. In any
case, I reckon that there is plenty of evidence of eighteenth-century evangelical saints wrestling with their doubts and fears; we shall touch on some of
this evidence later.

Paradoxically, the suffix also fortifies the thesis against empirical refutation.
For it denotes a step change. To anticipate a little of our discussion, it is not
at all difficult to show that John Calvin believed in religious conversion. He
believed that he himself was converted, and that others needed conversion. He
tells us (see below), in his characteristically modest and self-effacing way, how
he himself came to be converted and how important it was. In his preaching
and teaching he told his hearers of the need for conversion. It is true that for
Calvin *conversio* was a term used not to denote a bounded, shortish period of
radical religious change but a lifelong reorientation of the self. We must not,
however, confuse the word and the thing. Calvin believed both in the need
for conversion and in the need for *conversio*. But did he believe in conversion-
ism? Or (not quite the same question, as we have learned), was he a case of

---

3. Garry J. Williams, 'Was Evangelicalism Created by the Enlightenment?', *Tyndale
    Bulletin* 53.2 (2002), p. 286 (reprinted in this volume, ch. 15, as 'Enlightenment
    Epistemology and Eighteenth-Century Evangelical Doctrines of Assurance').
4. *Evangelicalism in Modern Britain*, p. 74.

conversionism without believing it? Either question is a much harder one to answer, at least as Bebbington presents it. While Bebbington recognizes the presence of continuities between evangelicalism and earlier Protestant trad-itions,[5] the presence of the suffixes make it easier for him to stress discontin-uity than might otherwise be the case.

A scholar is entitled to regiment his field of enquiry as he wishes if he believes that what he is doing will yield explanation and illumination. Nonetheless, one might complain that Bebbington's approach is a rather unhelpful one, if not an unfair one. For in the field of religion, and of religious belief, and particularly in the study of changes in religious belief, almost invariably we are dealing not with step changes but with gradual, incremental shifts. When does a belief in the need for conversion become a case of conversion*ism*? Clearly there are many important differences between John Calvin and, say, George Whitefield. Yet each believed in the need for conversion. What made Whitefield a conversionist and Calvin not one?

Does David Bebbington tell us? It is not clear to me that he does. For his answer to that question has to indicate that there has been a stepwise change between Calvin and Whitefield. What would the evidence for that be? It becomes a relatively easy task to discover that a person believes it is important for him not to eat meat. But is this vegetarian*ism*? It is relatively easy to show that a person believes in the need for conversion. But is this conversion*ism*? Bebbington's claim that it is not, or may not be, insulates his thesis (it seems to me) from empirical refutation.

What lies ahead

In this chapter I shall attempt to discuss some of these questions further by doing two things. First, I shall look, fairly briefly, at the case of John Calvin (1509–64) in the light of Bebbington's four 'isms'. And then I shall examine, at a little greater length, the case of Augustus Montague Toplady (1740–78), an undoubted 'Calvinist'. Had we more space it would be interesting to look at the intervening period: English Puritanism in its Elizabethan and Commonwealth expressions, Reformed Scholasticism, the Covenanters and their successors in Scotland, the New England Puritan predecessors of Jonathan Edwards, the antecedents of the great Welsh preachers of the Revival and so on.

---

5. Ibid., p. 3.

John Calvin

I shall briefly review some evidence in favour of the claim that Calvin exemplified the four 'isms', though because his life was very largely an interweaving of these elements, we shall find that the four are often merged, though not in the self-conscious way implied by the suffixes.

Scripture

The centrality of Scripture for Calvin hardly needs establishing. He is paramount among the Reformers in emphasizing the principle of *sola scriptura* in the faith of the church. He is engaged in a constant polemic against the practice of the Roman Catholic Church of both obscuring the Word of God with her traditions and of nullifying its effect in practice. Calvin's voluminous commentaries bear witness to the single-minded way in which he wished to display the riches of Scripture to the pastors and laypeople in the emerging Reformed churches.

Scripture is necessary for clear understanding of God and ourselves. It gives its own evidence of its God-inspiredness:

> Let this then stand as a fixed point, that those whom the Spirit has inwardly taught rest firmly upon Scripture, and that Scripture is self-authenticated, and that it is not right for it to be made to depend upon demonstration of reasoning, for it is by the Spirit's witness that it gains in our minds the certainty that it merits.[6]

A Christian's faith should rely on the promises of God's Word (*Institutes* 3.2.6–7), being governed by them, and the church should be subject to its authority (*Institutes* 4.8). Scripture functions as divinely given spectacles (*Institutes* 1.6.1); through its teaching God accommodates himself to us, lisping to us like children (*Commentary* John 3:12).[7]

Scripture is not to be speculated over, but to be understood and applied. It is both necessary and sufficient for faith and life. Scripture is the school of the Holy Spirit, in which, as nothing is omitted that is needful and useful to know, so nothing is taught but what is expedient to know (*Institutes* 2.21.3). It is therefore to be approached with reverence, with a prayer for the help of the enlightening and enabling Spirit.

---

6. *Institutes of the Christian Religion*, trans. F. L. Battles (London: SCM, 1961), 1.7.5.

7. All references to Calvin's *Commentaries* are to those of the Calvin Translation Society, Edinburgh, 1843–55; repr. Grand Rapids: Baker, 1979.

Conversion

As already noted, Calvin was converted, an event in his life he regarded as pivotal. This fact and its importance for Calvin must be set against the views of commentators such as Lane, who see little emphasis in Calvin on the need for personal conversion.[8] Whatever might be true of Calvin's attitude to the phenomenology of conversion, he is clear that men and women need regenerating: they need to receive life from the dead.

In his preface to his *Commentary* on the Psalms, comparing himself to the psalmist David, he writes:

> And first, since I was too obstinately devoted to the superstitions of Popery to be easily extricated from so profound an abyss of mire, God by a sudden conversion subdued and brought my mind to a teachable frame, which was more hardened in such matters than might have been expected from one at my early period of life. Having thus received some taste and knowledge of true godliness, I was immediately inflamed with so intense a desire to make progress therein, that although I did not altogether leave off other studies, I yet pursued them with less ardour.[9]

Whether or not Calvin is reading features back into his conversion of twenty-five years before, he is clearly endorsing the possibility of an instantaneous conversion, and giving it some importance. And beneath it lies a more profound idea. For Calvin, sin has brought spiritual death. No one can raise himself to life, but divinely imparted regeneration is required.[10] This is, in the nature of things, an instantaneous change, though it may manifest itself in a variety of ways at the level of conscious experience. So perhaps it is important to stress, for Calvin, the distinction between the inception of new life (regeneration in a narrow sense) and the conscious expression of the effects of this in repentance, faith and love (a conversion experience).

As we have seen, Calvin employs two senses of conversion, one as the beginning of new life in Christ, which occurs often suddenly, and (whatever its other characteristics) in a once-for-all manner, and the other as the process of lifelong renewal of which conversion in the narrow sense is the beginning, the coming of new life to the soul. He characterizes lifelong *conversio* in the following terms:

---

8. A. N. S. Lane, 'Conversion: A Comparison of Calvin and Spener', *Themelios* 13.1 (1987), pp. 19–21.

9. John Calvin, *Commentary on the Psalms*, preface, pp. xl–xli.

10. See e.g. *Commentary* on Ps. 81:14.

[T]hrough continual and sometimes even slow advances God wipes out in his elect the corruptions of the flesh, cleanses them of guilt, consecrates them to himself as temples, renewing their minds to true purity that they might practice repentance throughout their lives and know that this warfare will end only in death.[11]

Pete Wilcox has noted these senses, and shown how, though distinct, they are connected in Calvin's thought by his teaching of the 'double grace' of justification and sanctification that flows from a person's union with Christ.[12]

By partaking of [Christ] we principally receive a double grace: namely, that being reconciled to God through Christ's blamelessness, we may have a gracious Father in heaven, instead of a Judge; and secondly, that sanctified by Christ's Spirit, we may cultivate blamelessness and purity of life.[13]

Christ
The person and work of Christ is central to Calvin's understanding of theology, and therefore of the Christian message, as in this typical passage from the *Institutes*:

It was his task to swallow up death. Who but the Life could do this? It was his task to conquer sin. Who but very Righteousness could do this? It was his task to rout the powers of world and air. Who but a power higher than world and air could do this? Now where does life or righteousness, or lordship and authority of heaven lie but with God alone? Therefore our most merciful God, when he willed that we be redeemed, made himself our Redeemer in the person of his only-begotten Son.[14]

It is principally to Calvin that we owe our understanding of the threefold work of Christ as *prophet, priest* and *king*, and of the twofold grace of justification and sanctification that proceeds from our union with him. And it is our union with him that lies at the heart of Calvin's understanding of the relation between justification, sanctification and the sacraments. By baptism, we are united with Christ in his death and resurrection. By faithful partaking of the

---

11. *Institutes* 3.3.9.
12. Peter Wilcox, 'Conversion in the Thought and Experience of John Calvin', *Anvil* 14.2 (1997), pp. 113–128.
13. *Institutes* 3.11.1.
14. *Institutes* 2.12.2.

elements of the Lord's Supper our union with Christ is confirmed with visible signs as Christ comes to us by his Spirit. Christ was at the heart of his theology, and the cross at the heart of his understanding of Christ's work.[15]

Evangelism

Calvin did not see himself as a missionary or evangelist in a narrow sense. He was a Reformer and called by God, he believed, to lead and support the work of making Geneva into a Christian city, and of equipping pastors and teachers for the hoped-for Reformation in his native France. His sermons and lectures, his published works and his correspondence reflect the many-sided nature of the task. Nevertheless, in them are many expressions of the need for his hearers to be converted where this typically involved, for Calvin, the renunciation of any hope of salvation by merit and a reliance upon Christ for justification and sanctification.

Here are some typical expressions, from his sermons and commentaries. They could be multiplied many times:

> [The meaning of this metaphor] is, that an opportunity of promoting the gospel had presented itself. For as an opportunity of entering is furnished when the door is opened, so the servants of the Lord make advances when an opportunity is presented. The door is shut, when no prospect of usefulness is held out. Now as, on the door being shut, it becomes us to enter upon a new course, rather than by farther efforts to weary ourselves to no purpose by useless labour, so where an opportunity presents itself of edifying, let us consider that by the hand of God a door is opened to us for introducing Christ there, and let us not withhold compliance with so kind an indication from God.[16]

In his Isaiah commentary he states:

> [Isaiah] shows that it is our duty to proclaim the goodness of God to every nation. While we exhort and encourage others, we must not at the same time sit down in indolence, but it is proper that we set an example before others; for nothing can be more absurd than to see lazy and slothful men who are exciting other men to praise God.[17]

---

15. For a recent treatment of Calvin's Christology, see Stephen Edmondson, *Calvin's Christology* (Cambridge: Cambridge University Press, 2004).

16. *Commentary* on 2 Cor. 2:12.

17. *Commentary* on Isa. 12:5.

In commenting on Genesis 17 he says:

> So, at this day, God seems to enjoin a thing impossible to be done, when he requires his gospel to be preached every where in the whole world, for the purpose of restoring it from death to life. For we see how great is the obstinacy of nearly all men, and what numerous and powerful methods of resistance Satan employs; so that, in short, all the ways of access to these principles are obstructed. Yet it behooves individuals to do their duty, and not to yield to impediments; and, finally, our endeavours and our labours shall by no means fail of that success, which is not yet apparent.[18]

To five missionaries to France who had been arrested at Lyons and were facing death by martyrdom, Calvin wrote on 15 May 1553:

> Since it pleases him [i.e. God] to employ you to the death in maintaining his quarrel [with the world], he will strengthen your hands in the fight, and will not suffer a single drop of your blood to be spent in vain. And though the fruit may not all at once appear, yet in time it shall spring up more abundantly than we can express. But as he hath vouchsafed you this privilege, that your bonds have been renowned, and that the noise of them has been everywhere spread abroad, it must needs be, in despite of Satan, that your death should resound far more powerfully, so that the name of our Lord be magnified thereby. For my part, I have no doubt, if it please this kind Father to take you unto himself, that he has preserved you hitherto, in order that your long-continued imprisonment might serve as a preparation for the better awakening of those whom he has determined to edify by your end. For let enemies do their utmost, they never shall be able to bury out of sight that light which God has made to shine in you, in order to be contemplated from afar.[19]

Compassion for the lost condition of people also should drive Christians to witness. 'If we have any kindness in us,' he declared in a sermon on Deuteronomy 33, 'seeing that we see men go to destruction until God has got them under his obedience: ought we not to be moved with pity, to draw the silly souls out of hell, and to bring them into the way of salvation?'[20] In fact,

---

18. *Commentary* on Gen. 17:23.

19. *Letters* of John Calvin, ed. Jules Bonnet, trans. David Constable (Philadelphia: Presbyterian Board of Publication, 1858; repr. Grand Rapids: Baker Book House, 1983), pt. 2, 1545–53, p. 406.

20. John Calvin, *Sermons on Deuteronomy*, trans. Arthur Golding (London, 1583; facsimile repr., Edinburgh: Banner of Trust Trust, 1987), p. 1219.

a Christian who is not involved in witness is really a contradiction in terms. As Calvin remarks:

> [T]he godly will be filled with such an ardent desire to spread the doctrines of religion, that every one not satisfied with his own calling and his personal knowledge will desire to draw others along with him. And indeed nothing could be more inconsistent with the nature of faith than that deadness which would lead a man to disregard his brethren, and to keep the light of knowledge choked up within his own breast.[21]

Calvin was concerned not only for France, but also for the reformation of the church in such places as Scotland and England, Spain and Poland, Hungary and the Netherlands. He even encouraged a mission to Brazil in 1555, which turned out, though, to be a failure.[22]

Pete Wilcox offers a fine exposition of the theme of evangelization in Calvin's thought and practice. Characteristically, Calvin's ideas about the expansion and worldwide character of the kingdom of God, and particularly with the calling of the Gentiles, arise from his attention to Scripture, particularly to the Old Testament. According to Wilcox, Calvin developed these ideas from 1557 onwards, at a time when many hundreds of preachers and teachers were being sent back to France from Geneva. The same emphasis is not to be found in the *Institutes*, though it is there in seed form: 'We must daily desire that God gather churches unto himself from all parts of the earth; that he spread and increase them in number, that he adorn them with gifts; that he establish a lawful order among them . . .'[23] At this time Calvin published his revised *Commentary on Isaiah* as well as lectures on other Old Testament prophetic books, including his *Commentary* on the book of Psalms, which Calvin treated as prophetic.[24]

Part of a prayer after the sermon uttered a few years before he died brings together all the themes I have touched on:

---

21. *Commentary* on Isa. 2:3.
22. Amy Glassner Gordon, 'The First Protestant Missionary Effort: Why Did It Fail?', *International Bulletin of Missionary Research* 8.1 (Jan. 1984), pp. 12–18. R. P Beaver, 'The Genevan Mission to Brazil', in John H. Bratt (ed.), *The Heritage of John Calvin* (Grand Rapids: Eerdmans, 1973), pp. 55–73.
23. *Institutes* 3.20.42. See also *Institutes* 1.9.12.
24. Peter Wilcox, 'Evangelisation in the Thought and Practice of John Calvin', *Anvil* 12.3 (1995), pp. 201–217. I am grateful to Dr Ashley Null for drawing attention to the two fine articles by Wilcox.

Since you desire all men to acknowledge you as Saviour of the world, through the redemption by our Lord Jesus Christ, may those who do not know him, being in darkness and captive to ignorance and error—may they by the light of your Holy Spirit and the preaching of your gospel, be led into the way of salvation, which is to know you, the only true God, and Jesus Christ whom you have sent.[25]

Augustus Montague Toplady

In the case of Toplady we move into the years of the alleged formation of a new phenomenon, 'evanglicalism'. My argument regarding Toplady is as follows: I shall try to establish that he is in all relevant respects an 'evangelical',[26] that he fulfils the necessary criteria. Nevertheless, although he kept the company of 'evangelicals', and may be said to have been in the thick of the Evangelical Revival, Toplady's self-understanding is not that of an 'evangelical' at all, if by that is intended one who saw himself as a member of a distinct religious movement or tendency or spirit that had begun about nine years before his own birth. He has no awareness of being an 'evangelical' in this sense, nor of a step change among himself and his co-religionists when compared with the Protestantism that preceded. Rather, he understood himself, and his spiritual lineage, and that of the Church of England, as deriving from Calvin and the later Calvinism.

So I do not intend to show that Toplady, while a contemporary of the Evangelical Revival, nonetheless stood apart from it. Rather, I intend to show that he understood the movement of which he was a part not as giving birth to 'evangelicalism' but rather as (in its fullest and purist expression) the resurgence of Calvinism, a Calvinism that was for him optimally expressed in the historic doctrinal stance of the Church of England.

This review of Toplady does not offer any opinion on whether what Toplady says about himself, Calvinism and the Church of England is in fact either accurate or true. My claim does not require this. It suffices to establish, if possible, that Toplady understood himself not as an 'evangelical' in a distinct sense but as a Calvinist. My claim will appear better established, of course, if it can be shown that his understanding of Calvin and of Calvinism,

---

25. *Sermons on the Beatitudes*, trans. Robert White (Edinburgh: Banner of Truth, 2006), p. 84.

26. In what follows, 'evangelical' within quotation marks signifies the use of that term in David Bebbington's sense.

as a historical movement, involves him saying positive things about the central importance of conversion, about preaching and missionary work, of the supremacy and sufficiency of Holy Scripture, and exhibits Christ-centredness. We shall find that it does. I shall conclude with some remarks about Toplady and the Bebbington thesis. My case is that if Toplady had been confronted by the Bebbington thesis he would have countered by arguing that there is a better explanation: the Revival is better understood as a reawakening of the Calvinism of the Church of England.

Educated at Westminster School and Trinity College, Dublin, Toplady was converted in 1755 in a barn through hearing the words of a preacher, James Morris, and 'led into a full and clear view of the doctrines of grace' (i.e. of Calvinism) three years after. (Some years later, in 1768, he caught up with Morris and hearing of his decision to cease preaching writes movingly to persuade him to continue.)[27] Ordained in 1762, after a short spell at Fen Ottery (1766–8) he was Vicar of Broad Hembury, Devon, 1768–76 (a rural parish with a church building that could hold over 600 people).[28] He moved to London to be preacher at the French Calvinist Chapel in Orange Street, which had recently (in 1776) become an Anglican place of worship, and died of consumption less than three years later, in 1778. He is immortalized as the author of 'Rock of Ages', but little scholarly work has been done on him.[29]

Toplady's eighteenth-century characteristics
Bebbington claims that evangelicalism in the 1730s was *inter alia* the product of the Enlightenment, and sketches a number of distinctive features characteristic

---

27. *The Whole Works of Augustus M. Toplady* (London: J. Cornish & Sons, 1869), p. 830. All quotations from Toplady in this chapter are from this edition. This is a 'New Edition' (although the editor's name is not given) of the first edition (2 vols., 1774).
28. Ibid., p. 832.
29. There is a biography by Thomas Wright, *The Life of Augustus M. Toplady* (London: Farncombe, 1911). Wright evidently had access to unpublished materials of Toplady's but their present whereabouts are unknown. Two other popular treatments are George Lawton, *Within the Rock of Ages: The Life and Work of Augustus M. Toplady* (Cambridge: James Clarke, 1983); and George M. Ella, *Augustus Montague Toplady, a Debtor to Mercy Alone, Biography and Anthology* (Eggleston, Co. Durham: Go, 2000). Probably the best-known piece on Toplady is a chapter by J. C. Ryle, 'Toplady and His Ministry', in J. C. Ryle, *Christian Leaders of Last Century* (London: T. Nelson, 1880).

of that period.[30] He cites the influence of Isaac Newton and John Locke,[31] of the scientific method,[32] the prominence of the theme of happiness,[33] an interest in literature and politics, sympathy with the American colonists[34] and 'ridicule as the test of truth'.[35] It is interesting to measure Toplady against these. He exhibits many of the characteristics of an educated eighteenth-century English gentleman, influenced by the writers and writings of the Enlightenment.

Toplady was active in evangelism, preaching for conversion. His ministry, like his best-known hymns, exhibits a Christ-centredness. In 1774 he told the Countess of Huntingdon that in the first four years of his ministry he 'preached of little else but of justification by faith only in the righteousness and atonement of Christ; and of that personal holiness, without which no man shall see the Lord'.[36] He had numerous connections among the leaders and participants in the Evangelical Awakening, for example with William Romaine,[37] who preached for him in Devon, other luminaries such as John Berridge, the Curate of Everton in Bedfordshire,[38] and the Countess of Huntingdon.[39] He was a frequent correspondent of Ambrose Serle, who became Secretary to Lord Howe, and who was the author of *Americans against Liberty*, defending the legitimacy of British rule of the American Colonies.[40] He knew Richard Hill, the brother of Rowland Hill; and corresponded with Martin Madan[41] and the John Rylands, father and son, Baptist ministers.[42] For a short time Toplady edited the newly founded *Gospel Magazine*.

Possibly his indifferent health and certainly his strong Anglican convictions regarding the parish ministry kept Toplady in Devon for most of his life, where he often preached to crowded churches. He records Whitefield asking him, 'My good sir, why do you not come out? You might be abundantly more useful, were

30. *Evangelicalism in Modern Britain*, pp. 57ff.
31. Ibid., p. 48.
32. Ibid., p. 60.
33. Ibid.
34. Ibid., p. 73.
35. Ibid., p. 67.
36. *Works*, p. 862.
37. Ibid., pp. 848, 854, 858.
38. Ibid., p. 874.
39. Ibid., pp. 862, 872.
40. Ibid., pp. 834, 837, 839, 850, 851, 852, 853, 859, 867.
41. Ibid., pp. 858.
42. Ibid., p. 866.

you to widen your sphere, and preach at large, instead of restraining your ministry to a few parish churches.' He replied, 'The same Providence which bids others roll at large seems to have confined me to a particular orbit.'[43] Nevertheless,
he repeatedly writes of large, attentive congregations. He was involved on at least
one occasion, in 1776, in preaching in Wales, perhaps at Trevecca, with several
other ministers, to a crowd of thousands.[44] Here is part of his account:

> On the Anniversary Day in Wales, the congregation was so large that the chapel
> would not have contained a fourth part of the people, who were supposed to amount
> to three thousand. No fewer than one thousand, three hundred horses were turned
> into one large field adjoining the College; besides what were stationed in the
> neighbouring villages. [He proceeds to give an account of how the scaffold on which
> six or seven ministers preached partly collapsed, and then continues as follows.] Such
> was the wonderful goodness of the Lord to me, that I was not in the least
> disconcerted on this dangerous occasion; which I mention to the praise of that grace
> and providence without which a much smaller incident would inevitably have
> shocked every nerve I have. About half a minute after the interruption had
> commenced, I had the satisfaction to inform the people that no damage had ensued;
> and removing for security to a lower step, I thanked the Lord, with the rejoicing
> multitude, for having so undeniably given his angels charge concerning us. Prayer
> ended, I was enabled to preach; and great grace seemed to be upon us all.[45]

This seems the regular Revival style of things.

He published a laudatory memorial sketch of George Whitefield, which
includes this:

> I deem myself happy in having an opportunity of thus publicly avowing the
> inexpressible esteem in which I held this wonderful man; and the affectionate
> veneration, which I must ever retain, for the memory of one whose acquaintance and
> ministry were attended with the most important spiritual benefit to me, and to tens
> of thousands beside. . . . He was a true and faithful son of the Church of England,
> and invincibly asserted her doctrines to the last; and that not in a merely doctrinal
> way (though he was a most excellent systematic divine) but with an unction of power
> from God, unequalled in the present day.[46]

---

43. Ibid., p. 863.
44. Ibid., p. 875.
45. Ibid., pp. 875–876.
46. Ibid., p. 494.

Note here what Toplady writes about Whitefield's relation to the Church of England and her doctrines.

He spoke in a similarly exalted way of the Countess of Huntingdon ('the most precious saint of God I ever knew'),[47] though his opinion of her 'Connexion' is not recorded. He quotes John Newton of Olney with approval,[48] and makes use of the work of Jonathan Edwards in his own writings in defence of determinism.[49] Conversions, Christ-centredness, great activity in the pulpit and (as we shall see) with the pen, and Bible-centredness, were all characteristics of Toplady's ministry.

And what of those other eighteenth-century features Bebbington draws our attention to? Take for example the idea of happiness. Among numerous Christocentric hymns written by Toplady is the moving 'Happiness, thou lovely name'. 'Happiness' is mentioned twice more in the hymn:

> Object of my first desire,
>   Jesus, crucified for me,
> All to happiness aspire.
>   Only to be found in thee:
>
> Let me but thyself possess,
>   total sum of happiness!
> Real bliss I then shall prove;
>   Heav'n below, and heav'n above.[50]

If for Wesley 'holiness is happiness',[51] for Toplady, Christ is its 'total sum'.

The influence of John Locke,[52] Robert Boyle[53] and Isaac Newton[54] are evident. There is a more direct connection with the Unitarian Joseph Priestley, the discoverer of oxygen, with whom he corresponded.[55] Priestley's influence is perhaps found more prominently in Toplady's work on necessity, *The*

---

47. Ibid., p. 876.
48. Ibid., p. 668, n.
49. Ibid., p. 864.
50. Ibid., p. 909.
51. Bebbington, *Evangelicalism in Modern Britain*, p. 60.
52. Toplady, *Works*, p. 95.
53. Ibid., p. 825.
54. Ibid., p. 791.
55. Ibid., pp. 863, 880.

Scheme of Philosophical Necessity (1775). Here Toplady argues not for the materialistic determinism of Priestley, however, but for a dualistic determinism. Toplady was rather keen on souls: he believed that non-human animals possessed an 'immaterial principle',[56] though these were not, perhaps, immortal souls. Nevertheless Toplady evidently believed in the resurrection of the entire animal kingdom.[57] It is possible that he took the idea of non-human animals having souls from Pierre Bayle.

He had a considerable interest in literature. Rather surprisingly, he had a number of good things to say about *Letters to his Son*, by Philip Dormer Stanhope (the fourth Earl of Chesterfield),[58] though recognizing the basic immorality of the work. According to Thomas Wright, Toplady was distantly related to the Stanhopes.[59] Toplady refers a number of times to Pierre Bayle,[60] and Dr Johnson was an acquaintance, if not a friend,[61] as were James Boswell and Oliver Goldsmith.[62] He was full of praise for Johnson, though not for his temper, nor of his high opinion of himself. In all such respects Toplady is typical of an educated gentleman of his time. Most prominently among these characteristics, he fulfilled the test of ridicule being a test of truth.[63] Not, in Toplady's case, only receiving ridicule (though he was certainly on the receiving end of John Wesley's invective) but engaging in a great deal of it himself. As well as the writings against Wesley, he has a number of amusing short pieces, on 'Female Education' and 'Christianity Reversed', a satire on Chesterfield's principles.[64]

Although a convinced Anglican, which in those days implied adherence to the doctrines of the Thirty-Nine Articles, in common with many leaders of the Evangelical Revival he had sympathies with and a high estimate of several Calvinistic dissenters. The learned Baptist John Gill was a favourite.[65] Though given his Anglicanism, these friendships and the high regard he had for many

56. Ibid., p. 792.
57. Wright, *Life of Augustus M. Toplady*, p. 213.
58. *Works*, pp. 607, 858, 868.
59. *Life of Augustus M. Toplady*, p. 13. For further connections with Chesterfield, see ibid., p. 40.
60. *Works*, p. 792.
61. Ibid., p. 867.
62. Wright, *Life of Augustus M. Toplady*, p. 128.
63. Bebbington, *Evangelicalism in Modern Britain*, p. 67.
64. *Works*, p. 607.
65. Ibid., pp. 3, 4, 7, 72.

Dissenting ministers put him in a difficult position. He gives interesting advice to a rather disenchanted Anglican about attending 'gospel preaching'.[66]

As a writer, Toplady was something of a paradox. For besides his seraphic hymns and meditations he had (as already noted) a sharp and amusing pen, and became a fierce and unrelenting critic of John Wesley's intention to advance Arminianism as a legitimate theological position into the Church of England. Indeed, his interest in Wesley borders on the obsessive. It might even have *been* obsessive.

The critical year seems to have been 1769. In that year Toplady published a lengthy pamphlet against Thomas Nowell (1730–1801), the Public Orator of Oxford University, *The Church of England Vindicated from the Charge of Arminianism*. Six undergraduates had been expelled from Oxford University for holding Calvinistic views; the students had been supported by Richard Hill in a pamphlet entitled *Pietas Oxoniensis*, to which Nowell replied with *Answer to the Author of Pietas Oxoniensis* (1767). Around the same time, Toplady published a translation of writings of the Reformed theologian Jerome Zanchius (1516–90) on predestination, together with some of his own comments. He then encountered Wesley's abridgment of Zanchius in the form of a twelve-page pamphlet (1770), to which he replied in an open letter to Wesley, *A Letter to the Rev. Mr. Wesley, Relative to his Abridgement on Zanchius on Predestination* (1770). To a further tract from Wesley in 1771, *The Consequence Proved*, he replied with *More Work for Mr Wesley, or a Vindication of the Decrees and Providence of God* (1771), a 'tract' of about 40,000 words. To Toplady's intense annoyance, Wesley delegated to his lieutenant Walter Sellon the task of defending Arminianism. To Sellon's *The Doctrine of General Redemption Considered* (1769), Toplady replied with his major work *Historical Proof of the Doctrinal Calvinism of the Church of England* (1774), in which his learning is sprinkled with anti-Wesleyan invective.

With the bit now firmly between his teeth, Toplady widened his attacks on Wesley by controverting his views on liberty and necessity in *The Scheme of Philosophical Necessity* (1775),[67] with an essay of a markedly Lockean character, *The Sensible Qualities of Matter*, attached. Wesley's views on American independence were expressed in *A Calm Address to our American Colonies* (1775), much of which was borrowed without acknowledgment from Samuel Johnson's *Taxation no Tyranny* (1775). Toplady could not resist drawing attention to the plagiarism in *An Old Fox Tarr'd and Feather'd* (1775). Among these

---

66. Ibid., pp. 878–879. For his view of Dissent, see p. 831.

67. Ibid., p. 784.

writings, the most important for present purposes are the two works on the Calvinistic character of the Church of England. Toplady saw Wesley's outspoken Arminian views as intrusive into the Calvinistic Church of England, an intrusion not without precedent, but serious for all that. What made matters worse in Toplady's eyes was Wesley's bungling attempt to justify his position, as well as the unwarranted charges he and his circle levelled against the Calvinists. Wesley may have commended Jonathan Swift's rapier-like literary style,[68] but he found himself repeatedly on the receiving end of something similar from Toplady.

Bebbington's treatment of the Calvinism–Arminianism debate in the years of the Revival is curious. He notes that the Revival was riven by this controversy,[69] and that Wesleyan Arminianism became a distinctive body of thought,[70] observing that 'methodism' was organized on different theological lines, by Whitefield and Wesley respectively, and with different church polities. These organizations also enjoyed very different fates. Whitefield's largely collapsed, Wesleyan Methodism went from strength to strength, and in England the Calvinistic wing of the Revival found expression within existing denominations, the Church of England, English Dissent and, for a time, the Countess of Huntingdon's Connexion. Things went differently in Wales and very differently in Scotland, of course.[71] Perhaps because he wishes to stress that the Evangelical Revival was a novel development, united by its four 'isms', Bebbington does not dwell on the significance of this rift. But the participants certainly did not think that what united them was greater than what divided them. The occurrence of Calvinist–Arminian division was very serious, fairly permanent, and sad. How accurate the personal charges are that Toplady makes against Wesley (and vice versa) may be left to further research.

So Toplady's sentiments in defence of Calvinism and especially the Calvinism of the Church of England were not unique to him. What prompted him to keep up this sustained barrage against the Methodist leader was fairly clear. Not only Toplady's genuine love and jealousy for the Church of England and its Reformed constitution, and his hatred and fear of Arminianism, but also a desire to cut Wesley down to size propelled him. For Wesley offered the public not only his theological opinions but advice on many other matters, including

---

68. Bebbington, *Evangelicalism in Modern Britain*, p. 67.

69. Ibid., pp. 1–7.

70. Ibid., pp. 27–28.

71. Ibid.

political, scientific and philosophical ideas.[72] Toplady also seems to have been intensely irritated with the man himself, and by his refusal to debate the issues fairly and squarely.

Perhaps the roots of his attitudes to Wesley lie deep in Toplady's personality, and in Wesley's too. It may be that Toplady's early loss of his father, his consequent dependence on his mother (he never married), and the fact that he was virtually an only child (his elder brother, Francis, died after a few days), together with his ill-health, hold part of the key. Another factor may have been Toplady's intense loyalty to institutions, to his friends (Chesterfield, Serle, Hill) and to the Church of England's formularies. I shall not attempt here to go down these murky paths. J. C. Ryle, in his rather pompous episcopal way, said of the controversial aspect of Toplady's output that he would not stain his paper nor waste his readers' time by supplying proofs of Toplady's bitterness. It has to be said that in a culture hamstrung by political correctness, Toplady's quaintly worded, fierce invective is amusing and refreshing. He made it clear that he was not being malicious,[73] but (as he put it), 'It is not necessary to be timid in order to be meek.'[74]

However, the *motives* Toplady had for writing so strongly in defence of the Church of England (whatever they were) should not be confused with the *grounds* he cites within his writings for the Calvinistic character of the Church of England, and the importance of the issue for him and for others. Its importance for us is that it provides good evidence of Toplady's religious self-understanding. We shall spend the remainder of our examination of Toplady on this theme: Toplady's Calvinism and his self-understanding.

Toplady's Calvinism

Toplady's Calvinism was undoubtedly strong and distinctive and always to the forefront of his mind. Distinctively Calvinistic themes form the substance of much of his preaching, diary-keeping, and letter and hymn-writing. He called it 'doctrinal Calvinism' to indicate that it was distinct from the polity of the various denominations in which Calvinists were found, himself holding tenaciously to the polity of the Church of England. Such Calvinism was, in essence, the soteriology of Calvin (aspects of which we touched on earlier) as it had been affected by the Arminian conflict and the Puritan movement in

---

72. Bebbington mentions Wesley's publication of a book on the curative powers of electricity, ibid., p. 57.

73. *Works*, p. 46.

74. Ibid., p. 48.

England. The themes of the bondage of the will to sin, free and unmerited election, the particular or definite character of Christ's atonement, the imputation of Christ's righteousness, the effectual call by grace and the grace of perseverance in the faith were prominent. In Toplady's case, at least, the definite character of the atonement did not imply that only a few were to be redeemed.[75] It is a big question how such Calvinism relates to the theology of Calvin himself, and this is not the place even to touch this thicket of issues. It is sufficient to say, perhaps, that Toplady certainly thought that the relation was very close, for he makes no difference between the Calvinism of Calvin and that of later Calvinists.

Equally important in understanding Toplady's religious character was the experimental or experiential character of his religion. Christian doctrine was not for him a dry system, but a framework of understanding in terms of which one had daily 'dealings' with God, as the Lord gave his grace to bless, or witheld it, or at least witheld the signs of it, in order to warn or to chastise. These givings and witholdings registered themselves in Toplady's feelings, or perhaps consisted in these feelings and the beliefs he had about them. His diary, as well as his hymns, record the fluctuating state of his consciousness. His diary and some of his hymns record the experience of doubt and the absence of the presence of God, as do those of the Olney hymn-writers, John Newton and William Cowper, and many of Newton's letters, a number of collections of which were published.[76] On the evidence provided by Iain Murray, Wesley himself seemed to change his view on the nature of assurance, coming to think that faith and the assurance of faith are distinct, and hence that faith is compatible with doubt.[77]

From the quotations Toplady gathered (he seems to have been a great squirrel), it is clear that he was familiar with Westminster divines such as John Arrowsmith, Puritans such as John Owen and Thomas Manton, and Anglican Calvinists such as William Gurnall and Ezekiel Hopkins. Reading Thomas Manton on John 17 was instrumental in Toplady coming to adopt Calvinistic views. Citations from the Puritan Tobias Crisp, and an adherence to the doctrine of eternal justification,[78] may suggest a 'high Calvinism' verging on hyper-Calvinism, but it would be a mistake to tar Toplady with this particular brush. For he is strong on the indiscriminate preaching of the gospel to all and

---

75. Ibid., p. 863.

76. John Newton (1727–1807) published *Omicron* (1774) and *Cardiphonia* (1781).

77. *Wesley and Men Who Followed* (Edinburgh: Banner of Truth, 2003), p. 50, n.

78. *Works*, p. 7.

sundry, to making the 'free offer' of Christ, as it is sometimes called.[79] And he believed, with the mainstream Calvinist tradition, that although Christ by his death has abolished the law as the believer's ground of justification, it is nevertheless to be observed as a rule of life.[80] Besides the Puritans, Toplady seems to have read widely continental Reformed divines such as Herman Witsius and of course Jerome Zanchius, as well as his contemporary John Gill, whom he greatly admired.

However, the Calvinism he defended in his writings on the Church of England was not his 'experimental' Calvinism but rather the doctrinal framework in which such religious experience, the 'tasting' of God's grace in its various workings, could occur and be understood. Rather surprisingly, in his work on the doctrinal Calvinism of the Church of England, Toplady does not typically defend it in doctrinal terms, by expounding the Articles and Liturgy in Calvinistic vein, as one might expect. (He adopted this approach in other writings, e.g. his published sermon 'Clerical Subscription no Grievance; or the Doctrines of the Church of England Proved to Be the Doctrines of Christ' [1772].)[81] He was intent upon showing the de facto influence of the Reformers on the formulating of the Articles and the preparation of the Prayer Book.

His argument seems to be: since many of the Reformers were invited to give advice on these matters, and willingly did so, the presumption must be that their natural sense is not simply consistent with Calvinism, but has a meaning that excludes an Arminian interpretation. One might think that, expressed in this way, this is a somewhat anachronistic thesis.

Whatever questions might be raised about the accuracy or fairness of the evidence Toplady marshalls, questions that no doubt would reward further investigation, the point is that he understands these formularies of the Church of England in an exclusively Calvinistic way, believing that because they are the product of Calvinistic belief both in England and on the continent of Europe this is their natural, intended sense. Thus understood, in Toplady's view they provided a formidable weapon against Wesley's attempts to advance Arminianism within the Church of England. More significantly for us, they offer the clue to Toplady's self-understanding as an eighteenth-century evangelical, which he shares with Romaine, Berridge, Hervey, Madan, John Newton and, as time went on, an increasing number of others.

---

79. Ibid., p. 543.
80. Ibid., pp. 367, 310.
81. Ibid., p. 340.

Calvin, Toplady and the Bebbington Thesis

Calvin seems obviously 'evangelical' even though he naturally enough tended to define his position in terms of the abuses prevalent in the Church of Rome. We must bear in mind that he held a very different view of church and state from that which came to prevail in post-1688 Britain.

Toplady also presses most of the right Bebbingtonian buttons. He exemplifies the four 'isms', though not self-consciously, and most if not all of the characteristics of the English Protestant religious life of the eighteenth century, influenced as it was by the Enlightenment. But he also presses another button, historic Calvinism, at least as he himself (and his peers among evangelical Anglicanism and Dissent) understood this term. For Toplady, this Calvinism was the way to understand the 'isms' of the Bebbington quadrilateral.

In the 750,000 words or so that Toplady has left us, while the term 'evangelical' is certainly used, I am unaware of any explicit reference to the four Bebbingtonian 'isms'. And almost certainly the suffixes are entirely absent. Of course he could have exemplified these without being aware of them, even while believing that he was not exemplifying them. All this is possible. But the Bebbington thesis only has a hope of empirical support if we make the reasonable supposition that the four 'isms' registered in the consciousness of those who are claimed to exemplify them, so that they might write about them, for example, or publicly express them in other ways, and in such ways make them historically identifiable. Otherwise, if we search for evidence favourable to the Bebbington thesis, we are driven to claim that while at one level of their psyche evangelicals of the eighteenth century, such as Toplady, were ignorant of such 'isms' and how they were reflected in their lives, at another level they were driven by their subconscious to live as 'evangelicals' of the 1740s. The thesis then becomes more psychological, even psychoanalytic, than historical.

On historical grounds, the evidence is that Toplady, through his controversies with John Wesley and nascent Wesleyan Methodism, avowedly distanced himself from the very idea of the pan-evangelicalism so explicit a part of the Bebbington thesis. Or perhaps it is more accurate to say that he saw such evangelicalism within a broader and more discriminating framework, as expressions (at their best) of the Christian gospel as understood and exemplified by John Calvin and the Calvinists who followed. The position was different only because of the way they believed that their understanding of the gospel had benefited from the extraordinary impetus of George Whitefield's personality and preaching. Whichever way we interpret the significance of his ministry, Toplady's short life is a clear piece of historical counter-evidence to the Bebbington thesis, and for obvious reasons a more significant counter-instance than that of John Calvin himself. Whether or not there are many more such cases, as I suspect there are, is a matter 'for further research' (as they say). But perhaps no instance will prove to be clearer than that of Augustus Toplady.

© Paul Helm, 2008

10. THOMAS CRANMER AND TUDOR EVANGELICALISM

Ashley Null

'All the world's a stage, / And all the men and women merely players.' With these famous words Shakespeare concisely captured the sixteenth century's 'self-fashioning' approach to life. Although human beings had to play a role in society which was largely predetermined, they were still expected to perform their part with as much insight and artifice as possible. The challenge was to discern the right model to imitate, the best script to follow. For Jaques, Shakespeare's libertine-turned-philosopher who uttered those memorable lines in *As You Like It*, his goal in life was to find the true way of discharging the foul infections, both corporeal and spiritual, which he had acquired on his many world travels. At the end of the play, Jaques pinned his hopes for a return to wholeness on meeting the former persecuting Duke Frederick who had abandoned the pomp of court life to become a monastic penitent: 'To him will I. Out of these convertites / There is much matter to be heard and learn'd.'[1]

Of course, in Shakespeare's England none of those in his audience who wished to purge themselves of the world could actually avail themselves of

---

1. William Shakespeare, *As You Like It*, Act II, Scene 7, lines 139–140; Act V, Scene 4, lines 184–185. For the theme of 'self-fashioning' in the English Renaissance, see Stephen Greenblatt, *Renaissance Self-Fashioning: From More to Shakespeare* (Chicago: University of Chicago Press, 1980).

Jaques's solution, for English converts no longer congregated in monasteries. The reason lay in changes beginning much earlier during the reign of Henry VIII in the 1520s and 1530s. At that time courtiers like Sebastian Newdigate and Sir John Gage could still convert in the traditional medieval meaning of the word by turning from a life lived in this world to the retreat of a monastic way station in preparation for admittance to heaven after death.[2] Yet other options were beginning to present themselves. Influenced by the rise of Catholic humanism, Thomas More attempted to hold together both a life lived at court and that of a monastic penitent. Fashioning a secular career for himself that culminated in becoming Henry VIII's Lord Chancellor in 1529, More played the role of a wise and witty man of wealth and power before his king. Yet on Fridays he retreated to his manor in Chelsea, where he visited his personal chapel and purged himself of the ills of his worldly career through weeping in confession before Christ's wounded corpus on the cross. Grieving at having inflicted such pains on Jesus, More trusted that his self-tormenting penances would mitigate the punishments his sins in this world merited at God's hand in the next.[3]

Others, however, took the Catholic humanist revival in a completely different direction. Concerned that the medieval emphasis on human effort obscured the sufficiency of Christ's redeeming work on the cross, they sought to cleanse themselves of their sins by rejecting much of the church's established belief and practice. Returning to the fountainhead of the Christian faith, they found a new model to follow for forgiveness, a script based only on the plain sense of the Bible, as read through the prism of the writings of St Paul. These dissenters from both the world and the church insisted that a true Christian should give priority to this radically new script over everything else in shaping one's life:[4] priority over culturally hegemonic beliefs like purgatory, pardons and penance; priority over universally cherished devotional practices like praying to saints and burning lights before their images; priority over time-honoured 'unwritten verities' and centuries of well-reasoned biblical interpretation that authorized such practices; priority over even the ancient institutional authority of the church itself that had notoriously endorsed them. After the sword of scriptural authority had cut away centuries of error, what remained, these reformers believed, was the simple message of salvation by faith in Christ

---

2. Peter Marshall, *Religious Identities in Henry VIII's England* (Aldershot: Ashgate, 2006), p. 27, n. 40.

3. Greenblatt, *Renaissance Self-Fashioning*, pp. 11–73, esp. at pp. 11–13, 45–46, 51–52.

4. Ibid., pp. 93–105.

alone. This 'fervent biblicism' was the coat-of-arms by which they presented themselves on the doctrinal battlefield and by which they recognized their comrades-in-arms.[5]

Cranmer's conversion

Born on 2 July 1489, Thomas Cranmer spent his formative years as a son of the late medieval English church. Initially schooled by the parish priest, Cranmer eventually studied from 1503 at Jesus College, Cambridge, during the thirty years of John Fisher's chancellorship. Under the influence of the future saint's reforming programme, Cranmer was trained to combine scholastic reasoning with humanist learning in order to promote the renewal of traditional Catholic faith and practice. Having proceeded to his doctor of divinity degree in 1526, Cranmer demonstrated his own commitment to humanist reform by stressing the importance of scriptural knowledge as a university don.

According to John Foxe, Cranmer put candidates for the Bachelor of Divinity degree through such a 'severe examination' on 'the story of the Bible' that members of religious orders 'were commonly rejected by him', because they had been trained in the 'study of school authors without regard had to the authority of Scriptures'.[6] In other words, by the 1520s Cranmer had decided to follow Erasmus more than Fisher and demand that in expounding the Bible candidates should give priority to the humanist principles of philology and historical development over the received tenets of scholastic theology. Yet, like Erasmus, there is no indication that during his university career Cranmer ever stepped outside the parameters of medieval orthodoxy by espousing controversial doctrines like justification by faith.[7] Although he insisted on the primary authority of Scripture for faith and practice, Cranmer continued to believe that only the institutional church, not individual theologians like Luther, could decisively determine its interpretation.

---

5. Marshall, *Religious Identities*, p. 7.

6. John Foxe, *Ecclesiasticall History Contaynyng the Actes and Monumentes of Thynges Passed in Euery Kynges Tyme in this Realme* (London: John Day, 1570), p. 2033. Spelling has been modernized in all quotations from this text.

7. Diarmaid MacCulloch has persuasively argued that Cranmer was not a participant in the reformist theological discussions held at the White Horse Tavern (*Thomas Cranmer: A Life* [London: Yale University Press 1996], pp. 24–33).

Significantly for his future, however, Cranmer also declined to invest a single individual with the authority to make such pronouncements on behalf of the whole church. Once again following Erasmus rather than Fisher, Cranmer argued that the ultimate power for defining Christian truth lay with general councils rather than the papacy.[8] Hence, as the dispute over Henry VIII's desire for a 'divorce' grew more intractable in 1529, the king realized that Cranmer was just the sort of scholar he needed. Like Henry, Cranmer was willing to challenge papal authority based on biblical exegesis, but not the received teachings of the church on justification or transubstantiation. When Cranmer left Cambridge at the age of 40 to enter the king's service, he was clearly a reformer, but one who still used his humanist scholarship in the service of the essentials of the faith that had formed him from birth.

Less than a decade later, however, the situation had radically changed. Cranmer had been the Archbishop of Canterbury since 1533. The Church of England had operated independently of the papacy since the declaration of royal supremacy one year later. In 1536 Henry's campaign to close the monasteries had begun. Within four years none would exist in England. In 1537 the bishops of the English church had tried to establish the new entity's doctrinal standards by publishing the *Institution of a Christian Man*, commonly known as the Bishops' Book. And by January 1538, Cranmer was no longer promoting merely a reformation of morals arising from the knowledge of Scripture. He was using his biblical scholarship to lobby the king directly to accept justification by faith as outlined in a passage from the *Institution of a Christian Man*.

According to the Bishops' Book, for a Christian to believe in God the Father meant that

> I believe also and profess, that he is my very God, my Lord, and my Father, and that I am his servant and his own son by adoption and grace, and the right inheritor of his kingdom; and that it proceedeth and cometh of his mere goodness only, without all my desert . . .[9]

Upon his review of the book after its publication, Henry decided that the phrase 'the right inheritor' needed a qualifier: 'as long as I persevere in his precepts and laws'. Cranmer responded:

---

8. Ashley Null, *Thomas Cranmer's Doctrine of Repentance: Renewing the Power to Love* (Oxford: Oxford University Press, 2000), pp. 94–98.

9. J. E. Cox, *Miscellaneous Writings and Letters of Thomas Cranmer* (Cambridge: Parker Society, 1846), p. 84.

This book speaketh of the pure Christian faith unfeigned, which is without colour, as well in heart, as in mouth. He that hath this faith, converteth from his sin, repenteth him . . . and applieth himself wholly to please [his heavenly Father] again, and trusteth assuredly, that for Christ's sake he will and doth remit his sin, withdraweth his indignation, delivereth him from hell, from the power of the infernal spirits, taketh him to his mercy, and maketh him his own son and his own heir: and he hath also the very Christian hope, that after this life he shall reign ever with Christ in his kingdom. For St Paul saith: *Si filii sumus, et haeredes; haeredes quidem Dei, cohaeredes autem Christi* [Now if we are sons, then we are heirs, indeed heirs of God and joint heirs with Christ].[10]

In this text Cranmer makes no mention of saving faith needing first to be formed by love. He makes no room for human works to play any role in delivering a sinner from judgment. He refers only to Christ's work. Indeed, human merit was explicitly denied in the original passage, and here salvation is attributed exclusively to divine mercy. Now repentance is the fruit of saving faith, not part of its grounds. Finally, because of St Paul's teaching, a person who has been justified by saving faith should trust that he will also inherit eternal life. Clearly, Cranmer has crossed the Rubicon, but in his case away from Rome towards the German-speaking lands of the north.

What makes a man in middle age turn his back on lifelong beliefs so he can stand alongside those he previously argued were heretics? Unlike Luther, Cranmer has given us no *Turmerlebnis* (tower experience) to attempt to explain his change of heart.[11] If English reformers like Thomas Bilney and Katherine Parr attempted to shape a more public presentation of their private conversion so as to have an evangelizing effect on others, Cranmer was not among them. Like his peer Thomas More, Cranmer carefully shaped his self-presentation on the stage of public life so as to conceal as completely as possible the state of his private world.

---

10. Ibid.

11. Luther's *Turmerlebnis* derives its name from Luther's account that his 'Reformation breakthrough' came while pondering Rom. 1:17 in the tower of the Black Cloister in Wittenberg (*Table Talk*, ed. Theodore G. Tappert, in *Luther's Works*, ed. Helmut T. Lehman, 55 vols. [Philadelphia: Fortress, 1955–86], vol. 45, pp. 193–194). Cf. Luther's autobiographical fragment from 1545 (*Career of the Reformer IV*, ed. Lewis W. Spitz, in *Luther's Works*, ed. Helmut T. Lehmann [Philadelphia: Fortress, 1960], vol. 34, pp. 336–338).

If More's self-fashioned persona was as a Renaissance worthy with easy wit and worldly wisdom in equal measure, Cranmer's model, as befitting a spiritual rather than temporal magnate, was public monastic self-mortification. According to Ralph Morice, his principal secretary,

> he was a man of such temperature of nature, or rather so mortified, that no manner of prosperity or adversity could alter or change his accustomed conditions: for, being the storms never so terrible or odious, nor the prosperous estate of the time never so pleasant, joyous, or acceptable, to the face of [the] world his countenance, diet, or sleep commonly never altered or changed, so that they which were most nearest and conversant about him never or seldom perceived by no sign or token of countenance how the affairs of the prince or the realm went. Notwithstanding privately with his secret and special friends he would shed forth many bitter tears, lamenting the miseries and calamities of the world.[12]

Alexander Alesius, one of Cranmer's 'secret and special friends', confided to Elizabeth I that those tears were shed on at least two occasions by severe setbacks for his gospel of justification by faith, namely the death of Anne Boleyn and the Act of Six Articles.[13] While More hid the intense traditional piety of his mortifying hair shirt under the fine robes of his high worldly status, Cranmer wore mortification on his face to hide his hopes and fears for the new piety that had captured his heart.

Defining Tudor evangelicalism

What shall we call reformers like Thomas Cranmer who clearly wanted to change England's script in the 1520s and 1530s, yet were only gradually clear about exactly what they wanted to change? Although convenient, to describe them as 'Protestants' at this stage would be anachronistic. The term was first coined in Germany only in 1529 and then as a term of reproach by the enemies of those princes who issued a joint *protestatio* against the Diet of Speyer's revocation of religious privileges. Consequently, in England throughout the reign of Henry VIII, 'Protestant' referred to Germans of the Lutheran states allied

---

12. John Gough Nichols (ed.), *Narratives of the Days of the Reformation* (London: Camden Society, 1859), pp. 244–245. Spelling has been modernized in this quotation.

13. MacCulloch, *Cranmer*, pp. 159, 251.

against Charles V in the Schmalkaldic League.[14] During Edward VI's reign, the English reformers began to be called 'Protestant', but this practice become standard only during Mary's reign.[15] Even then, however, Nicholas Ridley, the former Bishop of London and soon-to-be martyr, still recognized its origin as a term of abuse.[16]

Yet, if to call them 'Protestants' would be an anachronism, to refer to them as 'Lutherans' would be equally inappropriate. Although the latter term was the 'catch-all' epithet for religious dissent used by English traditionalists, the first reformers were actually influenced by a wide variety of sources, including the monastic pursuit of holiness, Erasmian scholarship, French court circles associated with Anne Boleyn, remnants of native English Lollardy as well as South German and Swiss reformed theologians, in addition to Luther himself. Given the fluid nature of the new religious identities gradually developing during Henry's reign, using terms with clearly fixed doctrinal associations like 'Lutheran' or 'Protestant' would be to apply 'premature precision'.[17]

Like Cranmer, the first reformers were as much late medieval Christians as they were initiators of a new religious movement.[18] They never saw themselves as anything other than true Catholics who were simply returning to the

---

14. Thus, the plans for Henry VIII's funeral and Edward VI's coronation refer to the representatives from the Schmalkaldic League as 'the Protestants' (Diarmaid MacCulloch, *Tudor Church Militant: Edward VI and the Protestant Reformation* [London: Allen Lane, 1999], p. 2).

15. Diarmaid MacCulloch, 'Henry VIII and the Reform of the Church', in Diarmaid MacCulloch (ed.), *The Reign of Henry VIII: Politics, Policy and Piety* (Basingstoke: Macmillan, 1995), p. 168; *Cranmer*, p. 2; Peter Marshall and Alec Ryrie, 'Introduction: Protestantisms and Their Beginnings', in Peter Marshall and Alec Ryrie (eds.), *The Beginnings of English Protestantism* (Cambridge: Cambridge University Press, 2002), p. 5.

16. 'I will frankly and freely utter my mind ... And yet I will do it under this protestation, call me a Protestant who listeth [chooses], I pass not thereof [do not care]' (Henry Christmas [ed.], *The Works of Nicholas Ridley* [Cambridge: Parker Society, 1843], p. 14).

17. Greg Walker, *Persuasive Fictions: Faction, Faith and Political Culture in the Reign of Henry VIII* (Aldershot: Scolar, 1996), pp. 136–138; MacCulloch, *Reign of Henry VIII*, pp. 167–170. Cf. John F. Davis, 'The Trials of Thomas Bylney and the English Reformation', *Historical Journal* 24 (1981), pp. 775–790.

18. Brad S. Gregory, *Salvation at Stake: Christian Martyrdom in Early Modern Europe* (Cambridge, Mass.: Harvard University Press, 1999), p. 141.

authentic, original script for their centuries-old faith, the Bible.[19] Reflecting this claim, Luther called the reformation movement in Germany *evangelisch*, a generic description derived from *euangelion*, the New Testament's word for 'good news' or 'gospel', and the adjective is still used today to describe general Protestantism in Germany.[20] Likewise, the original terms for such people in English were 'evangelicals' and its cognate 'gospellers'.[21] Because the designation is 'vague', reflecting only 'fervent biblicism' and not specific doctrinal content, it is now becoming 'normative' among Tudor historians to refer to the English reformers as 'evangelicals'.[22]

Yet, the practice is not without its critics. Cognizant of the German distinction between *evangelisch* (Protestant) and *evangelikal* (modern evangelical), Peter Matheson, a historian of the German Reformation, ended his review of a recent monograph on Thomas Cranmer with a final query: 'Does it further the debate about Cranmer's sixteenth-century stance to describe his theology as "evangelical", given the specific connotation of that term in our own time?'[23] Matheson's concern is understandable. As a former principal of the Uniting Theological College in Melbourne, he is only too familiar with the assertive evangelicalism of the Anglican Diocese of Sydney and its training centre, Moore Theological College. Noted for its steadfast advocacy of biblical

---

19. Andrew Pettegree, *Reformation and the Culture of Persuasion* (Cambridge: Cambridge University Press, 2005), pp. 1–2.

20. E.g. the umbrella organization for Germany's twenty-three Lutheran, Reformed and United *Landeskirchen* is called the *Evangelische Kirche in Deutschland*.

21. For Thomas More's hostile use of these labels, see his *The Confutacyon of Tyndales Answere* (London: William Rastell, 1532), sigs. Dd2v, Dd4r; *The Apologye of Syr Thomas More Knyght* (London: William Rastell, 1533), sig. B2r.

22. MacCulloch, *Reign of Henry VIII*, pp. 168–169; *Cranmer*, p. 2; Marshall, *Religious Identities*, pp. 5, 7. Cf. Kenneth Hylson-Smith, *Christianity in England from Roman Times to the Reformation*, 3 vols. (London: SCM, 2001), vol. 3, pp. 156–164; Susan Wabuda, *Preaching during the English Reformation* (Cambridge: Cambridge University Press, 2002), p. 18; Felicity Heal, *Reformation in Britain and Ireland* (Oxford: Oxford University Press, 2003), pp. 226–242; Alec Ryrie, *The Gospel and Henry VIII: Evangelicals in the Early English Reformation* (Cambridge: Cambridge University Press, 2003), pp. xv–xvi. However, for a scholar who takes a different approach, see Catharine Davies, *A Religion of the Word: The Defence of the Reformation in the Reign of Edward VI* (Manchester: Manchester University Press, 2002), pp. xx–xxii.

23. Peter Matheson, book review of 'Thomas Cranmer's Doctrine of Repentance', *Journal of Theological Studies* 54 (2003), p. 827.

supremacy, personal conversion and lay presidency, the diocese is clearly out of sync with what much of the rest of Australia understands as Anglicanism and, indeed, out of sync with what the other main Australian denominations understand as Christianity. Whereas Sydney Anglicans vigorously defend their beliefs as being faithful to the biblical principles of the Reformed Church of England, for Australia's Uniting Church the Reformation's legacy is more appropriately a mandate for peace and justice.

Of course, Matheson is not the only Reformation scholar who would wish to make a distinction between the Protestant reformers and the later transatlantic evangelistic tradition. David Steinmetz has sought to distinguish Luther and Calvin's understanding of conversion as a lifelong process of repentance as well as learning from the historic American evangelical emphasis on 'the initial moment of faith in which one passes from death to life, from darkness to light'.[24] Speaking from the English context, Anthony Lane concurs, insisting that the model of 'instantaneous conversion' normative for most contemporary evangelicals must be clearly distinguished from 'Calvin's concept of conversion as a process'.[25] Finally, in seeking to explain the dearth and, therefore, what she considers to be the relative unimportance of conversion narratives for sixteenth-century Protestants, Judith Pollmann has come to the same conclusion. She argues that Protestants were reluctant to appear as theological innovators; consequently, they rejected as a template for their own era the ideal of a dramatic ' "moment" of conversion' derived from the stories of Paul and Augustine. Rather, for sixteenth-century Protestants, conversion was a process 'of learning old truths and of unlearning bad habits, not as one of changing personality',[26] a conclusion Bruce Hindmarsh incorporates into his recent monograph on spiritual autobiography in early modern Britain.[27]

---

24. David C. Steinmetz, 'Reformation and Conversion', *Theology Today* 35 (1978), p. 30.

25. A. N. S. Lane, 'Conversion: A Comparison of Calvin and Spener', *Themelios* 13 (1987), p. 20.

26. Judith Pollmann, 'Different Road to God: The Protestant Experience of Conversion in the Sixteenth Century', in Peter van der Veer (ed.), *Conversion to Modernities: The Globalization of Christianity* (London: Routledge, 1996), pp. 48, 54–55. For the sixteenth-century use of tales of martyrdom to bring about conversion, see Gregory, *Salvation at Stake*, pp. 7–8, 163 (English Protestants), pp. 283–285 (English Catholics).

27. D. Bruce Hindmarsh, *The Evangelical Conversion Narrative: Spiritual Autobiography in Early Modern England* (Oxford: Oxford University Press, 2005), pp. 26–28.

Still, since the late 1980s the most influential voice in stressing the dissimilarity between the sixteenth-century English reformers and the evangelists of
the eighteenth century has been that of a noted scholar of modern evangelicalism, David Bebbington.[28] In his classic work *Evangelicalism in Modern
Britain: A History from the 1730s to the 1980s*, Bebbington argues that the new
experiential emphasis of Enlightenment epistemology encouraged evangelicalism's uniquely emotive character, thus making it a 'new phenomenon of
the eighteenth century'. Although he recognizes 'much continuity with earlier
Protestant traditions', he insists that the movement associated with Wesley
and Whitefield represents such a clear break from the past that its beginnings cannot be said to date from any earlier than the 1730s.[29] Therefore,
Bebbington distinguishes between 'evangelical', which he accepts as an appropriate description of the English reformers, and 'the term "Evangelical", with
a capital letter', which he applies exclusively to advocates of experiential conversion from the eighteenth century onwards.

Tudor historians today have no quarrel with such an approach. Having
adopted 'evangelical' as the preferred term precisely because of its very vague-
ness, they have no intention thereby of implying a theological consistency
between the English Reformation and the 'experiential and emotional form
of Christianity which belongs more to the eighteenth century than the
sixteenth'.[30] At best, for Diarmaid MacCulloch, the generic use of 'evangelicalism' in the Reformation era is intended to 'liberate' the term from its
nineteenth-century associations with a specific party within Protestantism in
general and the Church of England in particular.[31] For Peter Marshall, however, the term is simply 'the least-worst label'.[32]

Evangelical conversion in the English Reformation

It is worth noting, however, that the adoption of a new terminology
among current Tudor historians is part of a much larger re-evaluation of their

---

28. See Timothy Larsen, 'The Reception Given *Evangelicalism in Modern Britain* Since
    Its Publication in 1989', ch. 1 in this volume.
29. D. W. Bebbington, *Evangelicalism in Modern Britain: A History from the 1730s to the
    1980s* (London: Unwin Hyman, 1989), p. 1.
30. Ryrie, *Gospel and Henry VIII*, p. xvi.
31. MacCulloch, *Cranmer*, p. 2.
32. Marshall, *Religious Identities*, p. 20.

understanding of the English Reformation. When Bebbington was preparing *Evangelicalism and Modern Britain* in the 1980s, the standard authority on the subject was A. G. Dickens.[33] Although he was beginning to be seriously challenged,[34] the scholarly consensus still largely accepted his approach of focusing on the 'theme of Protestant conversion'.[35] And for Dickens, such conversion was primarily a moment of intellectual insight,[36] rather than an experience of an existential inner resonance, including Luther's own tower experience.[37] Hence, Dickens argued that the religious alterations in England were brought about fairly rapidly by a popular movement arising as a natural response to the 'rational appeal of a Christianity based upon the authentic sources of the New Testament'.[38] With the advent of an increasingly educated populace, Protestantism's book-based faith was inevitably more persuasive than the medieval church's affective ritualism.[39] If one accepts Dickens's

---

33. A. G. Dickens, *The English Reformation* (London: Batsford, 1989²).

34. Christopher Haigh, *Reformation and Resistance in Tudor Lancashire* (Cambridge: Cambridge University Press, 1975); J. J. Scarisbrick, *The Reformation and the English People* (Oxford: Blackwell, 1984); Christopher Haigh, *The English Reformation Revised* (Cambridge: Cambridge University Press, 1987).

35. A. G. Dickens, 'The Shape of Anti-clericalism and the English Reformation', in E. I. Kouri and Tom Scott (eds.), *Politics and Society in Reformation Europe: Essays for Sir Geoffrey Elton on His Sixty-Fifth Birthday* (London: Macmillan, 1987), p. 380.

36. 'Luther declared war between bible-Christianity and churchly, scholastic Christianity. Within this intellectual context, by 1530 widely apparent, we should also locate the core of the English Reformation' (*English Reformation*, p. 21).

37. 'Whatever the importance of the tower-experience, it should not be regarded as a "religious experience" as one applies this term either to medieval mystics or modern revivalists … The tower-experience was something different; it taught [Luther] what he believed to be the true sense of the Scriptures, the understanding of something objective, of something God had long ago thrown open to the insight of men' (A. G. Dickens, *Martin Luther and the Reformation* [London: English Universities Press, 1967], p. 30).

38. Dickens, 'The Shape of Anti-clericalism and the English Reformation', p. 380.

39. This thesis is, of course, as old as John Foxe himself: '[A]s printing of books ministered matter of reading: so reading brought learning: learning showed light, by the brightness whereof blind ignorance was suppressed, error detected, and finally God's glory, with truth of his word, advanced' (*Actes and Monuments*, p. 838). Cf. Ethan H. Shagan, *Popular Politics and the English Reformation* (Cambridge: Cambridge University Press, 2003), pp. 2–3.

view that evangelical conversion in the sixteenth century was more a matter
of mind than heart, then the experiential emphasis of the eighteenth century
would seem very novel indeed.

Yet it is precisely this whiggish assumption of the inherent superiority of
a 'rational' Protestantism that has been so successfully challenged by revisionist Tudor historians since the 1980s.[40] On the one hand, Eamon Duffy
has illuminated how traditionalist religious beliefs and practices were just as
appealing to members of the educated classes as they were to rural labourers.[41]
Indeed, Richard Rex has helpfully shown that English humanism, the force
that Dickens posited as leading inevitably to Protestant thought, was in fact
originally a flowering of late medieval Catholic learning in support of traditionalist belief that then fuelled the Counter-Reformation as much as the
Reformation.[42] On the other hand, Alec Ryrie has found little evidence for
Dickens's grassroots movement of Protestant conversions. According to Ryrie,
'most English people never experienced a dramatic, individual conversion;
Protestant England was formed by pragmatic gospellers'.[43] Consequently,
Ethan Shagan has recently sought to offer a new interpretative model for
the English Reformation based on popular pragmatism rather than conversion. He finds the eventual advent of Protestant England to be the result of a
process of mutual cultural accommodation between the Tudor regimes, who
were pushing religious alterations, and the populace, who gradually agreed
to changes for their own non-religious reasons, even as they modified them
along the way according to their own interests.[44]

Since so much of the revisionist fire has been directed at Dickens's negative
assessment of late medieval Catholicism, little scholarly attention has been paid

---

40. Shagan, *Popular Politics*, pp. 4–5. Cf. Hebert Butterfield, *The Whig Interpretation
of History* (London: G. Bell, 1931).

41. Eamon Duffy, *Stripping of the Altars: Traditional Religion in England c. 1400–1570*
(London: Yale University Press, 1992); *The Voices of Morebath: Reformation and
Rebellion in an English Village* (London: Yale University Press, 2001).

42. Richard Rex, 'The Role of English Humanists in the Reformation up to 1559',
in N. S. Amos, A. Pettegree and H. van Nierop (eds.), *The Education of a Christian
Society: Humanism and Reformation in Britain and the Netherlands* (Aldershot: Ashgate,
1999), pp. 19–40.

43. Alec Ryrie, 'Counting Sheep, Counting Shepherds: The Problem of Allegiance in
the English Reformation', in Marshall and Ryrie, *Beginnings of English Protestantism*,
p. 105.

44. Shagan, *Popular Politics*.

to the second half of his thesis, namely his understanding of Protestantism as the rational alternative. After all, those scholars who would argue that the communal and cultic rhythms of late medieval Catholicism were superior to the Protestantism that followed can easily assume that evangelicalism's apparent lack of large-scale appeal was precisely because of its purported intellectualism. Such a one-sided approach to religious faith would seem to have held genuine appeal only for a narrow band of linear-thinking idealists.

Yet if current Tudor scholarship has shown that late medieval traditionalists held both heart and head together, why should early English evangelicals, as late medieval Christians themselves, not have done likewise? It is an important question. For even if it is accepted that there were far fewer genuine converts to the Protestant faith than Dickens thought, it still remains crucial for Tudor historians to understand what motivated those life-changing decisions that rendered some previously earnest Catholics true believers in evangelicalism.[45] Surely in that pre-Enlightenment era there was no inherent need for a bifurcation of human faculties. Recognizing the continuing influence of Dickens's work on our understanding of evangelicalism, Peter Marshall has cautioned against the 'tendency to perceive the rise of Protestantism in terms of the triumph of intellect over emotion, of the controlled and printed Word over the affective, ritual, and mimetic religion of the Middle Ages'.[46]

Instead, Marshall counsels historians to 'consider more closely the symbiotic relationship between an existential or emotional experience, and the internalisation of a profoundly theological and intellectual proposition'.[47] We would be wise to heed his advice. As Diarmaid MacCulloch has succinctly summarized the situation:

> The old Church was immensely strong, and that strength could only have been overcome by the explosive power of an idea . . . Monarchs, priests, nuns, merchants, farmers, labourers were seized by ideas which tore through their experiences and memories and made them behave in new ways . . .[48]

---

45. Richard Rex has helpfully noted that the leading English reformers uniformly came from 'highly orthodox' Catholic backgrounds; consequently, the 'key to the success of the English Reformation lies not in the conversion of Lollards, but in the conversion of Catholics' (*The Lollards* [Basingstoke: Palgrave, 2002], p. 142).

46. Marshall, *Religious Identities*, p. 29.

47. Ibid., p. 27.

48. Diarmaid MacCulloch, *Reformation: Europe's House Divided, 1490–1700* (London: Allen Lane, 2003), p. 110.

Conversion as a 'process of persuasion'

In his recent study of the methods by which Protestantism took hold in the lands of the Reformation, Andrew Pettegree has offered a helpfully nuanced approach to the matter of conversion.[49] On the one hand, he cites the classic autobiographical fragments from both Luther and Calvin to argue that the reformers chose to follow in the footsteps of Paul and Augustine, their chief theological authorities, by offering their personal stories of a moment of sudden reorientation as an 'inspiration' for others. On the other hand, he acknowledges that the reformers came to their mature religious commitments by a gradual process that was certainly more complicated than their telescoped reflections in hindsight suggested.

From these observations Pettegree draws two significant conclusions. First, whereas Pollmann discounts the importance of Calvin's account of his 'sudden conversion' (*subita conversio*) precisely because it was an artificial construct, Pettegree shrewdly recognizes that such a self-fashioned narrative only proves that even the great Calvin himself felt constrained by 'the very powerful strength of the conversion paradigm' during the Reformation era.[50] Second, as a result, the Reformation teaching on conversion has coherence only if two different aspects are given their due:

> [The reformers] had a complex and refined sense of the process of Christian conversion. On the one hand, there was the dramatic moment of acceptance; then again, the creation of a Christian people required a process of long, hard unrelenting struggle . . . A people had to be led to right understanding and right living.[51]

Therefore, Pettegree outlines a four-stage 'process of persuasion' by which people in the sixteenth century came to embrace the new Protestant 'dialectic of belonging and rejection': awareness of the new teachings, self-identification with them, growing understanding of their implications for the Christian life

---

49. Pettegree, *Reformation*, pp. 2–7. For a concise description of how many of the leading reformers came to hold their Protestant convictions, see Euan Cameron, *The European Reformation* (Oxford: Clarendon, 1991), pp. 168–185.

50. Pollmann, 'Different Road to God', p. 49; Pettegree, *Reformation*, p. 4.

51. Pettegree, *Reformation*, p. 5. Cf. Peter Wilcox's thoughtful arguments for Calvin holding to both an initial conversion experience and a subsequent need for ongoing repentance as the Christian norm, 'Conversion in the Thought and Experience of John Calvin', *Anvil* 14 (1997), pp. 113–128.

and commitment to activism on their behalf.[52]

Certainly, awareness through learning played an important role in the conversions of early English evangelicals. Rejecting the charge of novelty, the sixteenth-century reformers understood their open break with many of the beliefs
and customs of the medieval church to be a recovery of the authentic way of
being a Christian as outlined in the ancient writings of the apostles.[53] Hence,
for Katherine Parr, Henry VIII's widow, coming to know Scripture was the decisive difference between stark alternatives: between darkness and light, ignorance
and perfect knowledge, superstition and holiness, worldly vanities and truth; in
short, the difference between the way to hell and the way to heaven.[54]

Despite being baptized a Christian, Katherine felt that she had lived many
years no better than 'the heathen', although she tried to cover her sins with a
'pretence of holiness'. 'And no marvel it was that I so did, for I would not learn
to know the Lord and his ways', having 'regarded little God's Word'. When
Katherine finally listened to God's 'many pleasant and sweet words', she came
to understand the crux of her error. She had never truly looked to Christ as
her Saviour, since she had not accepted that his blood was 'sufficient for to
wash me from the filth of my sins'. Repenting of being a 'proud Pharisee' who
'went about to set forth mine own righteousness', she came to 'ripe and sea-
sonable knowledge': 'This is the life everlasting, Lord, that I must believe thee
to be the true God, and whom thou didst send, Jesu Christ.'[55]

Thomas Bilney came to the same conclusion upon reading Erasmus' new
Latin translation of the Bible while at Cambridge.[56] 'After this, the Scripture

---

52. Pettegree, *Reformation*, p. 6.

53. Pollmann, 'Different Road to God', pp. 52–54; Bruce Gordon, 'The Changing Face of
    Protestant History and Identity in the Sixteenth Century', in his *Protestant History and
    Identity in Sixteenth-Century Europe*, 2 vols. (Aldershot: Scolar, 1996), vol. 1, pp. 1–23.

54. Katherine Parr, *The Lamentacion of a Sinner* (London: Edward Whitchurch, 1547),
    sigs. A2v, A4r. Spelling has been modernized in all quotations from this text. For
    decidedly different views of Katherine's theological development, see William P.
    Haugaard, 'Katherine Parr: The Religious Convictions of a Renaissance Queen',
    Renaissance Quarterly 22 (1969), pp. 346–359; Susan E. James, *Kateryn Parr: The
    Making of a Queen* (Aldershot: Ashgate, 1999), esp. pp. 115–118. Cf. MacCulloch,
    Cranmer, pp. 326–327.

55. Parr, *Lamentacion*, sigs. A2v, A4v, A5v, A6v, B3v.

56. Bilney's description of his conversion is contained in correspondence to Bishop
    Cuthbert Tunstal during Bilney's 1527 heresy trial. See Davis, 'Trials of Thomas
    Bylney'; Walker, *Persuasive Fictions*, pp. 143–165.

began to be more pleasant unto me than the honey' because there 'I learned that, all my travails [in penitential works]' were 'a hasty and swift running out of the right way' but that sinners could 'obtain quietness and rest' when 'they believed in the promise of God'. As Bilney 'began to taste this heavenly lesson', his greatest desire became to share this life-changing insight from Scripture with others.[57] When he did so with Hugh Latimer under the guise of confession, the result was, according to Latimer, that 'God called me to knowledge . . . So from that time forward I began to smell the word of God, and forsook the school-doctors and such fooleries.'[58] As Richard Rex has shown, the very phrase 'new learning' was coined, not to describe the academic direction represented by humanism per se, but rather the use of humanism to justify an interpretation of Scripture that rejected the medieval way of salvation.[59]

Thomas Cranmer also wrote that his conversion was the result of a process of enlightenment: 'From time to time as I grew in knowledge of [Jesus Christ], by little and little I put away my former ignorance.'[60] In his portrait of 1545 Cranmer has left us an important indication of how humanism could play a leading role in convincing an essentially traditionalist Cambridge don gradually to embrace the 'new learning'. In the same year in which Luther wrote his famous autobiographical fragment, Gerlach Flicke painted Cranmer. Very much a typical Renaissance programmatic work, the painting depicts Cranmer seated, holding a copy of St Paul's epistles in his hands, while a copy of Augustine's *De fide et operibus* (On Faith and Works) lies on a table in front of him. A product of Augustine's later affective theology, *De fide et operibus* outlined his mature understanding of the relationship between faith and works—the issue in dispute between Cranmer and the king over the Bishops' Book.

On the one hand, Augustine clearly stated that Paul's teaching on justification by faith meant that good works did not precede justification, but followed

57. Foxe, *Actes and Monuments*, pp. 1141–1143. Foxe has given two versions, the original Latin and an English translation. All citations are based on Foxe's translation, but altered as needed for more precision and clarity in contemporary English against the Latin original.

58. George Elwes Corrie (ed.), *Sermons of Hugh Latimer* (Cambridge: Parker Society, 1844), pp. 334–335.

59. Richard Rex, 'The New Learning', *Journal of Ecclesiastical History* 44 (1993), pp. 26–44.

60. J. E. Cox (ed.), *Writings and Disputations of Thomas Cranmer ... Relative to the Sacrament of the Lord's Supper* (Cambridge: Parker Society, 1844), p. 374.

it, because only people who had received the Holy Spirit could perform works out of love for righteousness. On the other hand, once Christ dwelt in the believer's heart by faith, this living faith necessarily produced good works performed out of love for God. In short, a good life was inseparable from faith, because a life could not be good without faith, and true faith could not but bear the fruit of a good life. If Erasmus awoke Cranmer to the authority of the Scriptures over the tenets of scholastic theology, the Flicke portrait suggests that Cranmer's reading of Augustine led him to consider justification by faith to be the true Pauline doctrine.

At first consideration, this emphasis on conversion through learning might seem to confirm Dickens's assessment of the essential intellectualism of Reformation Protestantism. Yet there is a surprisingly sensuous dimension to these early English descriptions. Katherine called the words of Scripture 'pleasant and sweet'.[61] Bilney claimed that through reading Scripture he 'felt' in himself a 'change from the most Highest'. For when he 'began to savour of this heavenly lesson', he, too, found its message 'most sweet'.[62] Latimer went so far as to describe his doctrinal volte-face as coming 'to smell the Word of God'.[63] As Brad Gregory has noted:

> Tasting, imprinting, grafting, piercing, engraving, running, holding, rooting, cleaving, embracing—these terms do not reflect dispassionate encounter with a text . . . They reflect the experience of people who not only read scripture, but made it part of their being.[64]

Even the notoriously circumspect Cranmer seems to have permitted a cryptic reference to passion in his portrait. Although clerical marriage in England was still officially outlawed in 1545, the female carving next to the window-jamb would appear to be a very sophisticated reference to his clandestine spouse.[65] As Henry VIII's ambassador to Germany, Cranmer wed in 1532 the niece of the wife of Andreas Osiander, the Lutheran reformer of Nuremburg. It is highly unlikely that the notoriously difficult Osiander would have allowed Cranmer to marry into his family, unless Cranmer had already adopted solifidianism (justification by faith, from *sola fide* [by faith alone]). Nor would the

---

61. Parr, *Lamentacion*, sig. A2v.

62. Foxe, *Ecclesiasticall History*, pp. 1141–1143.

63. Corrie, *Sermons of Hugh Latimer*, pp. 334–335.

64. Gregory, *Salvation at Stake*, p. 160.

65. See Null, *Cranmer's Doctrine of Repentance*, pp. 106–115.

cautious Cranmer probably have been willing to violate such a clear tradi-tionalist taboo, unless he had come to accept the new doctrinal standards that authorized him to do so.

Consequently, the most likely period for Cranmer's conversion is during his ambassadorship to Germany. A reference to this marriage in a portrait docu-menting his path to eventual Protestantism suggests that Cranmer's decision to embrace the 'new learning' involved more than just intellectual considerations. To understand the conversions of early English evangelicals we need to look beyond merely analysing the doctrinal dimensions of justification by faith and also examine how its message moved the affections of its true believers. Here was the source of their powerful self-identification with this new doctrine.

Christian authenticity as an alteration of the affectations

One could hardly find a greater proponent of the importance of moving the affections than Erasmus himself. His scathing critique of scholastic theology and many medieval cultic practices was but the bitter fruit of his deep-rooted conviction that they had failed to touch the hearts of the people sufficiently to inspire them to love God and do good.[66] Hence, Erasmus was one of the chief architects of the Renaissance's academic revolution that restored rheto-ric to the heart of the university curriculum.[67] With its tripartite mission to educate, to please, to move (*docere, delectare, movere*), the persuasive power of rhetoric was essential to the humanists' aim of bettering society through the moral improvement of its people.

---

66. See J. Laurel Carrington, 'Desiderius Erasmus (1469–1536)', in Carter Lindberg (ed.), *The Reformation Theologians* (Oxford: Blackwell, 2002), pp. 34–48; Erika Rummel, 'The Theology of Erasmus', in David Bagchi and David C. Steinmetz (eds.), *The Cambridge Companion to Reformation Theology* (Cambridge: Cambridge University Press, 2004), pp. 28–38.

67. Erasmus was the author of several textbooks on rhetoric including *De duplici copia verborum ac rerum* (Foundations of the Abundant Style), the most influential book on rhetoric in the sixteenth century; Peter Mack, 'Humanist Rhetoric and Dialectic', in Jill Kraye (ed.), *The Cambridge Companion to Renaissance Humanism* (Cambridge: Cambridge University Press, 1996), p. 88. For a survey of modern assessments of Erasmus and rhetoric, see Bruce Mansfield, *Erasmus in the Twentieth Century: Interpretations c. 1920–2000* (Toronto: University of Toronto Press, 2003), pp. 151–183.

Naturally, Erasmus felt this emphasis on transformation through the power of words must be the chief aim of the church's appropriation of Scripture.[68] In the *Paraclesis* (Invitation), a preface to his Greek–Latin New Testament of 1516 that so moved Bilney, Erasmus delighted in contrasting the superfluity of scholastic subtleties to the absolute necessity of biblical morality for true Christian identity:

> Neither think I that any man will count himself a faithful Christian because he can dispute with a craft and tedious perplexity of words of relations, quiddities and formalities, but in that he acknowledgeth and expresseth in deeds those things which Christ both taught and accomplished.[69]

Of course, only the inherent moral persuasion of the Scriptures could bring about a Christian people who would 'not differ only in title and certain ceremonies from the heathen and unfaithful, but rather in the pure conversation of our life'.[70] For Jesus spiritually indwelt its message, since 'the Evangely [gospel] doth represent and express the quick and living image of his most holy mind, yea, and Christ himself speaking, healing, dying, raising again and, to conclude, all parts of him'.[71] Consequently, using the same sensuous language we have already encountered in the writings of the English evangelicals, Erasmus urged Christians to devote themselves passionately to the Word of God:

> Let us, therefore, all with fervent desire thirst after these spiritual springs. Let us embrace them. Let us be studiously conversant with them. Let us kiss these sweet

---

68. For Erasmus' rhetorical theology, see Marjorie O'Rourke Boyle, *Erasmus on Language and Method in Theology* (Toronto: University of Toronto Press, 1977); Manfred Hoffmann, *Rhetoric and Theology: The Hermeneutic of Erasmus* (Toronto: University of Toronto Press, 1994).

69. Erasmus, *An Exhortation to the Diligent Studye of Scripture* (Antwerp: J. Hoochstraten, 1529), sig. A2. I have elected to quote from English reformer William Roye's contemporary translation of Erasmus' Latin original. Spelling has been modernized in all quotations from this text. For the background of this translation, see the recent critical edition, Douglas H. Parker (ed.), *William Roye's An Exhortation to the Diligent Studye of Scripture; and, An Exposition in to the Seventh Chapter of the Pistle to the Corinthians* (Toronto: University of Toronto Press, 2000), pp. 28–36.

70. Ibid., fol. [8]r.

71. Ibid., sig. A6r.

words of Christ with a pure affection. Let us be new transformed into them, for such are our manners as our studies be.[72]

Two years later Erasmus wrote a treatise on his rhetorical approach to the study of theology, the *Ratio seu methodus compendio perveniendi ad veram theologiam* (Method of Attaining True Theology).[73] In its opening columns, he makes even more explicit the inherent connection between a personal affective response to Scripture and the humanist's desideratum of individual moral transformation: 'This is your first and only goal; perform this vow, this one thing: that you be changed, that you be seized, that you weep at and be transformed into those teachings which you learn.'[74] Having themselves been changed from the inside out, 'the special goal of theologians' was so to expound the Scriptures in order to elucidate the faith (rather than 'frivolous questions') that they could likewise in their students 'wring out tears' and 'inflame spirits to heavenly things'.[75] Not surprisingly, Erasmus inserted a copy of this treatise as a foreword to the second edition of his New Testament in 1519.

As the author of one of the most influential textbooks on Renaissance rhetoric, second only to Erasmus himself,[76] it was natural that Philip Melanchthon would explain Luther's soteriology in a manner consistent with that discipline's emphasis on the moving of the affections.[77] In his *Loci communes* (Commonplaces) (1521), Melanchthon argued that the affections of the heart determined the choices of the will. Hence, after the fall, both human reason

---

72. Ibid., sig. A5v.

73. Erasmus, *Opera omnia Desiderii Erasmi Roterodami*, ed. J. Leclerc, 10 vols. (Leiden: Pieter van der Aa, 1703–6), vol. 5, cols. 73–138. See Hoffmann, *Rhetoric and Theology*, pp. 32–39, 55–60; O'Rourke Boyle, *Erasmus on Language*, pp. 59–127.

74. 'Hic primus et unicus tibi sit scopus, hoc votum, hoc unum age, ut muteris, ut rapiaris, ut affleris, ut transformeris in ea quae discis' (Erasmus, *Opera omnia*, vol. 5, col. 77B; O'Rourke Boyle, *Erasmus on Language*, p. 73).

75. 'At praecipuus Theologorum scopus est, sapienter enarrare Divinas litteras: de fide, non de frivolis questionibus rationem reddere: de pietate graviter atque efficaciter disserere: lacrymas excutere, ad coelestia inflammare animos' (Erasmus, *Opera omnia*, cols. 83F–84A; O'Rourke Boyle, *Erasmus on Language*, p. 73).

76. See Philip Melanchthon, *Elementa rhetorices / Grundbegriffe der Rhetorik*, trans. Volkhard Wels (Berlin: Weidler, 2001), pp. 443–461; Kees Meerhoff, 'The Significance of Philip Melanchthon's Rhetoric in the Renaissance', in Peter Mack (ed.), *Renaissance Rhetoric* (New York: St. Martin's, 1994), pp. 46–62.

77. For a fuller account, see Null, *Cranmer's Doctrine of Repentance*, pp. 98–101.

and the will were held captive by the affection of self-love, that is, the concupiscence of the flesh. Therefore, moral transformation could come about only through the intervention of an outside force, the Holy Spirit. When the good news of justification by faith was proclaimed, the Spirit, working through God's Word, assured believers of their salvation. This new confidence in God's gracious goodwill towards them reoriented their affections, calming their turbulent hearts and inflaming in them a grateful love in return. These new godly affections would continually have to fight to restrain the ever-present stirrings of the concupiscence of the flesh. Nevertheless, because of the renewing work of the Holy Spirit believers now had the necessary desire and ability to live a life of deepening repentance. Seen in this light, accepting Luther's Reformation insight was the key to experiencing the affective transformation demanded by Erasmus' rhetorical theology. Little wonder it became proverbial that Luther hatched the egg Erasmus laid.

The conversion narratives of both Bilney and Katherine read like textbook case studies of solifidianism, producing new, Spirit-infused affections in its adherents. According to their accounts, when they accepted that justification by faith was the gospel truth, they sensed a radically new and life-changing spiritual power at work within them. In his relatively compact description, Bilney compared his experience to the story of the chronically ill woman in Luke 8:43–48. She had spent twelve years seeking a remedy for her ongoing bleeding without success. Yet when she managed in faith to touch the hem of Jesus' garment, 'she was so healed that immediately, she felt it in her body'.[78] Likewise, Bilney had worn himself out in trying to satisfy his scrupulous conscience with years of penitential activities. Yet in the moment he first trusted that Jesus freely offered full forgiveness to sinners like himself, he experienced a perceptible inner change: 'immediately, I felt a marvellous comfort and quietness, in so much, *that my bruised bones leapt for joy*'.[79]

Significantly, Bilney stated that he had felt this sensible spiritual healing 'more than once'.[80] Clearly, his evangelical inner wholeness could still be wounded. Now, however, when fresh sins weighed upon his conscience, Bilney considered himself armed with gospel knowledge. He knew to approach Christ in faith once again for immediate pardon rather than resorting to priestly confession and a further round of increasingly inadequate penitential offerings as in the

---

78. Note that Foxe translated *statim* with 'by and by', a sixteenth-century usage for 'immediately' (*Actes and Monuments*, pp. 1141–1142).

79. Ibid., pp. 1141, 1143.

80. Ibid., p. 1141.

past. Here was the motivation for Bilney's activism. He engaged in evangelistic campaigns in order to share with others the same pastoral strategy for inner affective wholeness that he himself had found through justification by faith.

Here also was the reason why Bilney was at pains to portray his initial acceptance of solifidianism in Damascene terms. Anything less than a convincing account of instantaneous forgiveness would not have addressed what he considered to be the root of the church's pastoral misdirection—the medieval insistence on the necessity of a significant period of preparation for pardon. Not surprisingly, nothing seemed to Bilney more clearly the work of Antichrist than one famous preacher's warning:

> Thou hast lain rotting in thine own lusts, by the space of these sixty years, even as a beast in his own dung, and wilt thou presume in one year, to go forward toward heaven, and that in thine age, as much as thou wentest backwards from heaven towards hell in sixty years?[81]

If Bilney had been plagued with anxiety about his spiritual state before his conversion, Katherine Parr suffered from the opposite danger: 'great confidence' in the pope's 'riff-raff' remedies for her sins. Although she had only a 'certain vain, blind knowledge, both cold and dead', she saw no need to inquire more closely into gospel matters. Indeed, turning the standard slogan of medieval penitential teaching on its head, Katherine wrote of her previous piety: 'I did as much as was in me to obfuscate and darken the great benefit of Christ's passion.' Content to follow the crowd in matters of religion, she was not concerned that the good news about the cross of Christ was 'never truly and lively printed' in her heart.[82]

Then God opened her eyes to what true faith was—not a

> dead human, historical faith, gotten by human industry, but a supernal lively faith, which worketh by charity, as [St Paul] himself plainly expresseth. This dignity of faith is no derogation to good works, for out of this faith springeth all good works.[83]

Of course, it was standard medieval penitential teaching to insist that faith was not justifying until it was formed by the divine gift of charity. Yet Katherine made clear that this was not what she meant. She insisted that the gift of

---

81. Foxe, *Actes and Monuments*, p. 1145.

82. Parr, *Lamentacion*, sigs. A4v, A5r, A6r, A7v.

83. Ibid., sig. B4r.

indwelling charity, as well as the good works it produced, were the fruit of living faith, not its grounds.

According to Katherine, the divine gift of living faith first opened her eyes to the truth that her salvation was totally dependent on 'Christ crucified'. 'Then I began (and not before) to perceive and see mine own ignorance and blindness.' Realizing how stubborn and ungrateful she had been to refuse to rely on Christ alone earlier, 'all pleasures, vanities, honour, riches, wealth, and aides of the world began to wear bitter unto me'. This alteration in her affections was the turning point for Katherine: 'Then I knew it was no illusion of the devil, nor false, [nor] human doctrine I had received: when such success came thereof, that I had in detestation and horror, that which I [formerly] so much loved and esteemed.'[84]

By the light of living faith Katherine now recognized that her 'sins in the consideration of them to be so grievous and in the number so exceeding' that she deserved eternal damnation. Yet she saw that her prior penitential works had only been a 'hindrance'. The more she had sought 'means and ways to wind' herself out of her sinful state, the more she had in fact become 'wrapped and tangled therein'. Consequently, she now put all her hope in one thing only: the promise of full, free and immediate pardon in God's 'own Word'. 'Saint Paul saith, we be justified by the faith in Christ, and not by the deeds of the law.' Therefore, 'by this faith I am assured: and by this assurance, I feel the remission of my sins'. Experiencing assurance brought the 'inward consolation' of having imputed right standing with God: 'I feel myself to come, as it were in a new garment, before God, and now by his mercy, to be taken just, and rightwise.' Hence, 'all fear of damnation' was gone for those who with justifying faith 'put their whole hope of salvation in his hands that will and can perform it'. Katherine admitted that true believers would still fall into sin because of their human 'frailty'. Yet they needed only to humble themselves and return to God by trusting in his goodness. Now freed from all fear because of the love of God in bringing her to salvation, Katherine began to love and serve him in gratitude. Thus, from justifying faith 'sprang this excellent charity' in her heart.[85]

Katherine's account of her conversion makes clear that she adopted solifidianism not as a repudiation of her late medieval emotive piety, but precisely because she found its grace-and-gratitude theology much more effective in moving her affections than the traditional medieval means. Indeed, her active patronage of an English translation of Erasmus' *Paraphrases* of the Gospels

---

84. Ibid., sigs. B5r–B6r.
85. Ibid., sigs. A8r, B1r–B2v, B3v–B4v, B6v, C5v, F7r.

and Acts, finally published just two months after the story of her conversion,[86] suggests she understood her mature soteriology to be the true means of fulfilling the expectations of Erasmian humanism, not its betrayal. For, according to Katherine's account, only the ever-present hope associated with justification by faith had imprinted on her heart the assurance of benefiting from the cross, thereby redirecting her desires and enabling her at last to experience the indwelling presence of divine love. As a result, she agreed with those who said 'by their own experience of themselves that their faith doth not justify them'. For 'true it is, except they have this faith the which I have declared here before, they shall never be justified . . . because so many lack the true faith'.[87]

The life-changing 'lively faith' experienced by Katherine Parr was exactly the sort that Thomas Cranmer wanted the formularies of the Church of England to encourage. As early as July 1536, the description of contrition in the Ten Articles stressed the classic evangelical narrative of an initial heartfelt struggle with fear of damnation, which then gave way to certain hope of eternal salvation through faith in Christ:

> The penitent and contrite man must first acknowledge the filthiness and abomination of his own sin (unto which knowledge he is brought by hearing and considering of the will of God declared in his laws) and feeling and perceiving in his own conscience that God is angry and displeased with him for the same. He must also conceive not only great sorrow and inward shame that he hath so grievously offended God, but also great fear of God's displeasure towards him, considering he hath no works, or merits of his own, which he may worthily lay before God as sufficient satisfaction for his sins. Which done, then afterward with this fear, shame and sorrow must needs succeed and be conjoined . . . a certain faith, trust, and confidence of the mercy and goodness of God, whereby the penitent must conceive certain hope and faith, that God will forgive him his sins, and repute him justified, and of the number of his elect children, not for the worthiness of any merit or work done by the penitent, but for the only merits of the blood and passion of our Saviour Jesus Christ.

A year later the text was wholly incorporated into the Bishops' Book.[88]

---

86. John Craig, 'Forming a Protestant Consciousness? Erasmus' *Paraphrases* in English Parishes, 1547–1666', in Hilmar M. Pabel and Mark Vessey (eds.), *Holy Scripture Speaks: The Production and Reception of Erasmus' Paraphrases on the New Testament* (Toronto: University of Toronto Press, 2002), pp. 316–322.

87. Parr, *Lamentacion*, sig. B7r.

88. *The Institution of a Christen Man* (London: Thomas Berthelet, 1537), fol. 37r. Spelling has been modernized in this quotation.

Significantly, this description of contrition had already abandoned the medieval teaching that Christians should face the future with a sober uncertainty about their eternal fate, striving to lead a godly life in a constant state of both hope and fear. But Cranmer wanted the Church of England formularies to go even further. In his response to Henry VIII over the Bishops' Book, Cranmer, in good Melanchthonian fashion, sought to make clear that assurance of salvation was not only a necessary part of true faith but also the true source of indwelling love:

> But, if the profession of our faith of the remission of our own sins enter within us into the deepness of our hearts, then it must needs kindle a warm fire of love in our hearts towards God, and towards all other for the love of God,—a fervent mind to seek and procure God's honour, will, and pleasure in all things,—a good will and mind to help every man and to do good unto them, so far as our might, wisdom, learning, counsel, health, strength, and all other gifts which we have received of God, will extend,—and, *in summa*, a firm intent and purpose to do all that is good, and leave all that is evil.[89]

Cranmer had to wait until the reign of Edward VI to produce a set of formularies for the Church of England that fully expressed his mature evangelical soteriology. Required to be read on a regular basis in parishes from 1547, his three homilies on salvation, faith and good works made solifidianism normative for the English church.[90] First, Christians were reputed just, not because of anything within them, but only because of their trust in Christ's redeeming work on the cross.[91] Second, justifying faith was more than just intellectual assent to dogmatic statements. Since demons also acknowledged Christian doctrine to be true, saving faith was not merely accepting the teachings of Scripture but also always included assurance of the believer's own salvation.[92] Third, indwelling love sprang from this assurance: 'For the right and true Christian faith is . . . to have sure trust and confidence in God's merciful promises, to be saved from everlasting damnation by Christ: whereof doth follow a loving heart to obey his commandments.'[93] Finally, saving faith was

---

89. Cox, *Miscellaneous Writings*, p. 86.
90. For an extended analysis of 'A Homily of the Salvation of Mankind', 'A Short Declaration of the True, Lively and Christian Faith' and 'A Homily of Good Works Annexed unto Faith', see Null, *Cranmer's Doctrine of Repentance*, pp. 213–234.
91. Cox, *Miscellaneous Writings*, pp. 128–130.
92. Ibid., p. 133.
93. Ibid.

a 'lively faith', that is, a faith that showed its love for God by doing good works.[94] When the benefits of God's merciful grace were considered, unless they were 'desperate persons' with 'hearts harder than stones', people would be moved to give themselves wholly unto God and the service of their neighbours.[95] Thus, assurance brought about an inner change in the justified—a loving, living faith that purified the heart from sin's poison and made 'the sinner clean a new man'.[96]

In sum, although Thomas Bilney and Katherine Parr had different pastoral issues, both came to the same conclusion: that accepting justification by faith enabled them to experience true biblical conversion away from sin towards a lifelong service of God and greater godliness. As Steinmetz has rightly argued, the deep-seated nature of human self-centredness meant that the new power both Bilney and Katherine felt working within them would always be provoking them to further conformity to Christ.[97] Yet their loving desire to continue to repent was the direct result of the freedom from fear of damnation they experienced at the moment they first trusted Christ's atoning sacrifice on the cross to win for them eternal salvation, as Pettegree's multistep description of the conversion process has suggested. This renewal of their affections was the source of their powerful self-identification with the evangelical cause. Here was the inner impetus for Bilney's activism and Katherine's publishing projects. This grateful love for God was also the new internal motivation for the Christian life that Thomas Cranmer attempted to inculcate in everyone in the country through his shaping of the evolving formularies of the Church of England. Thus, the first generation of English reformers turned to the evangelicals' new script for forgiveness, not as an alternative to the affective piety of their medieval upbringing, but in their view as its true fulfilment.

The Wesleyan recovery of Tudor evangelical assurance

If the effective moving of the affections was integral to the conversion of England's sixteenth-century evangelicals, then the distance between them and their eighteenth-century namesakes is not nearly so great as modern scholars have

---

94. Ibid., p. 136.
95. Ibid., p. 134.
96. Ibid., p. 86.
97. Steinmetz, 'Reformation and Conversion', p. 30.

supposed. Indeed, the role of affective experience in the English Reformation has particular consequences for David Bebbington's work, since he has based his argument for the uniqueness of modern evangelicalism squarely on the newness of its doctrine of assurance. According to Bebbington, 'the Puritans had held that assurance is rare, late and the fruit of struggle in the experience of believers', whereas 'the Evangelicals believed it to be general, normally given at conversion and the result of simple acceptance of the gift of God'.[98] Hence, the 'novelty of Evangelical religion . . . lay precisely in claiming that assurance normally accompanies conversion'.[99]

In the case of John Wesley, Bebbington attributes this supposed shift in the received doctrine of assurance to specific 'symptoms of discontinuity' from seventeenth-century Puritanism. First, Wesley was an Enlightenment thinker who believed that knowledge was a matter of sense experience. Second, his 'High church quest for holiness' left him with nagging doubts about his salvation. Third, his acceptance of contemporary Continental Protestant teaching via the Moravians led him to look for an inner witness of assurance to assuage his anxieties. Consequently, his religious experience at Aldersgate simply confirmed his empiricist epistemology. According to Bebbington, the result was evangelicalism's dynamism, for 'without assurance, the priority for the individual in earnest about salvation had to be its acquisition; with it, the essential task was the propagation of the good news that others, too, could know the joy of sins forgiven'.[100]

It is beyond the purview of this chapter to determine whether Bebbington's characterization of seventeenth-century Puritan doctrine is accurate.[101] However, it must be immediately noted that *Evangelicalism in Modern Britain* never actually discusses England's Reformation era. As a result, Bebbington has no awareness of the English reformers' own doctrine of joyous assurance accompanying conversion. Far more surprisingly, however, neither does Bebbington ever examine John Wesley's own clear and consistent claim to be following the Reformation understanding of assurance as enshrined by Cranmer in the founding formularies of the Church of England. When modern Anglican evangelicals like those of the Diocese of Sydney maintain that their adherence to the Thirty-Nine Articles gives them a recognized position

---

98. Bebbington, *Evangelicalism in Modern Britain*, p. 43.

99. Ibid., p. 7.

100. Ibid., pp. 42–43, 48–50.

101. See ch. 15 in this volume, Garry J. Williams, 'Enlightenment Epistemology and the Eighteenth-Century Evangelical Doctrines of Assurance'.

in the Church of England and its wider Communion,[102] they are merely following in the footsteps of John Wesley.

In mid-November 1738, a little more than six months after his life-changing experience at Aldersgate, Wesley recorded in his journal that he began 'more narrowly to inquire what the doctrine of the Church of England is concerning the much controverted point of justification by faith; and the sum of what I found in The Homilies I extracted and printed for the use of others'. The result was *The Doctrine of Salvation, Faith, and Good Works, Extracted from the Homilies of the Church of England*, a short pamphlet of twelve pages that went through at least nineteen editions during Wesley's lifetime.[103] Since the Book of Homilies had been given official doctrinal status by the Thirty-Nine Articles, Wesley sought to use these selections to prove that both his teaching on justification by faith and the necessity of personal assurance were not novel at all but merely the true received teaching of the Church of England.

In particular, Wesley highlighted with italics the following passage from Cranmer's 'Homily on Salvation':

> *The right and true Christian faith is not only to believe that Holy Scripture and the articles of our faith are true, but also to have a sure trust and confidence to be saved from everlasting damnation by Christ, whereof doth follow a loving heart to obey his commandments.*[104]

Wesley also included the following passage from Cranmer's 'Homily on Faith':

> Another faith there is in Scripture which is not idle [or] unfruitful but (as St. Paul declares) 'worketh by love' . . . so this may be called a quick or [living] faith. This is not only a belief of the articles of our faith but also a 'true trust and confidence of the mercy of God through our Lord Jesus Christ and a steadfast hope of all good things at God's hand' called by St. Paul, 'The full assurance of faith'; a confidence [that though we should] fall from him by sin, yet if we return to him by true repentance, he will forgive our offences for his Son's sake and make us his inheritors of his everlasting Kingdom.[105]

102. Report of the Archbishops' Commission on Christian Doctrine, *Subscription and Assent to the 39 Articles* (London: SPCK, 1968), p. 32.

103. Albert C. Outler (ed.), *John Wesley* (New York: Oxford University Press, 1964), pp. 16, 121.

104. Ibid., p. 128.

105. Ibid., p. 130. Brackets indicate Wesley's interpolations. Outler's additional references to Scripture verses have been deleted.

In a footnote to this paragraph, Wesley added, 'It is the doctrine of the Church of England to which every minister of our Church hath subscribed, in subscribing the Thirty-fifth Article, that "without or before this [faith] can no good work be done".'[106] Time and again John and Charles Wesley would refer to the Homilies to prove the essential Anglican orthodoxy of their teaching on assurance.[107] So successful were such claims that the Anglican divine Theophilus Lindsey became a Unitarian, since he concluded that only the Methodists truly preached the doctrine of the Thirty-Nine Articles, and he could not subscribe to their views. Anglican divine Thomas Scott eventually concurred with Lindsey's assessment, but decided to take the opposite approach, converting to Methodism himself.[108]

Of course, such doctrinal comparisons across centuries are always fraught with difficulties. Every dogmatic point is always intertwined in both a wider theological system and a specific cultural view of the world, both of which reflect as well as express the human assumptions and experiences of a particular historical era. It is not possible, therefore, that John Wesley simply repristinated the pure teachings of Thomas Cranmer's formularies. Since Methodism was a conscious synthesis of both Laudian and Reformation strains of Anglicanism, there were significant doctrinal differences between its adherents and the English reformers. At the very least, Wesley's emphasis on free will was at odds with the Reformed doctrine of predestination taught by Cranmer and the sixteenth-century Church of England, as Augustus Toplady was at pains to point out.[109] Consequently, Cranmer taught an assurance of salvation because of the perseverance promised to the justified.[110] Wesley, however, interpreted

---

106. Ibid., p. 130, n. 19.

107. Frank Baker, *John Wesley and the Church of England* (London: Epworth, 1970), pp. 54–56, 70, 92–93, 104, 249, 327–328; Richard P. Heitzenrater, 'Great Expectations: Aldersgate and the Evidences of Genuine Christianity', in Randy L. Maddox (ed.), *Aldersgate Reconsidered* (Nashville: Kingswood, 1990), pp. 69–70, 77–78, 83–84; Hindmarsh, *Evangelical Conversion Narrative*, p. 141.

108. Ibid., pp. 277–282.

109. Augustus Montague Toplady, *Historic Proof of the Doctrinal Calvinism of the Church of England* (London: George Keith, 1774). Cf. B. G. Felce, 'Toplady's View of Doctrinal Continuity after the Reformation', in D. N. Samuel (ed.), *The Evangelical Succession in the Church of England* (Cambridge: J. Clarke, 1979), pp. 30–39.

110. 'And [the true faithful man's] trust is so much in God, that he doubteth not in God's goodness toward him, but that, if by fragility and weakness he fall again, God will not suffer him so to lie still, but put his hand to him and help him up

the Homilies as teaching only assurance of present pardon, since Wesley never ceased to believe that the justified could refuse, when fallen into sin, to 'return to [God] by true repentance'.[111] Equally, there were significant cultural differences between them, including that the sixteenth century's division between an individual's self-fashioned public role and the privacy of his interior life before God had greatly diminished by the eighteenth. We have no direct knowledge of Thomas Cranmer's inner life. We have the many volumes of John Wesley's journals, specifically edited for public dissemination. Finally, the intellectual assumptions of the two historical eras were also greatly different. Erasmus' realist rhetorical theology as adapted and harnessed to interpret and expound the Lutheran understanding of Christian anthropology lies behind Cranmer's formularies. David Bebbington is surely correct to insist on the influence of empiricist epistemology in helping Wesley to interpret his religious experience and to inculcate the same in others of his day.[112]

Despite these notable differences, however, we must not overlook the marked similarities. Bebbington's own description of Wesley's life leading up to Aldersgate in fact reflects a classic Reformation conversion narrative. Driven by anxiety produced by a traditionalist Catholic pursuit of holiness,[113] but holding out hope for a sensible pardon as promised by Continental Protestantism,[114] John Wesley personally encountered the kind of religious experience and subsequent motivation in the Christian life that were the

---

again, and so at the last he will take him up from death unto the life of glory everlasting' (Cox, *Miscellaneous Writings*, p. 93).

111. 'We speak of an assurance of *our present pardon*, not (as he does) *of our final perseverance*', John Wesley, 6 October 1738, *Journal*, in *The Works of John Wesley*, editor-in-chief, Frank Baker (Nashville: Abingdon, 1984–), vol. 19, p. 15; Frederick Dreyer, 'Faith and Experience in the Thought of John Wesley', *American Historical Review* 88 (1983), pp. 16, 22; Heitzenrater, 'Great Expectations', p. 72.

112. Cf. Dreyer, 'Faith and Experience', pp. 21–30.

113. Wesley even cited as indicative of his own thinking the classic medieval scholastic maxim 'Fac quod in te est, et Deus aderit bonae tuae voluntati', which he translated as 'Do what lieth in thy power, and God will assist thy good will'; Heitzenrater, 'Great Expectations', p. 61. Yet, Wesley's diaries also record his frustration with relying on sincerity for assurance. According to Heitzenrater, 'the closer [Wesley] kept track of himself, the more he became aware of his shortcomings, doubted his sincerity, and feared lest he should fall short of the mark of his calling' (ibid., p. 58).

114. Cf. ibid., pp. 61–65.

stated ideals of the Edwardian reformers.[115] He then looked to both the philosophical assumptions of his era and the received teachings of his church to understand his experience as well as to give him the language needed to pass it on to others of his era. In short, Wesley's doctrine of assurance was at the same time both the recovery of an authentic aspect of the affective tradition in the English Reformation as well as an Enlightenment innovation in the means of its interpretation and presentation for an eighteenth-century audience. Having learned much from both past Cranmerian 'convertites' and his era's own *philosophes*, Wesley, unlike Shakespeare's Jaques, was a highly pertinent role model for those in his audiences seeking to purge themselves of their spiritual and social ills. Perhaps herein lies the greatest difference between the Edwardian and Wesleyan teachings on conversion—not their equally emotive dimension as previously thought, but rather how much more popular Wesley's explanation was in its eighteenth-century English cultural context than Cranmer's was in its sixteenth.

© Ashley Null, 2008

---

115. Wesley would, however, spend a lifetime reflecting upon this experience and refining his interpretation of its significance; ibid., pp. 65–91.

11. PURITANISM, EVANGELICALISM AND THE EVANGELICAL PROTESTANT TRADITION

John Coffey

Historians of eighteenth-century evangelicalism are in two minds when it comes to Puritanism. On the one hand, they readily acknowledge the continuity between Puritanism and evangelicalism. Thus David Bebbington emphasizes the affinity between Puritans like Richard Baxter and evangelicals like Philip Doddridge and George Whitefield. He suggests that 'in many respects Evangelical religion prolonged existing lines of development'. 'Even Methodism', he explains, 'had roots in the Puritan tradition.' 'Three characteristic marks of evangelicalism, conversionism, Biblicism and crucicentrism, had been as much a part of Puritanism as they were of Methodism.'[1] Mark Noll lays even greater emphasis on the Puritan roots of evangelicalism. 'In England', he tells us,

> the Puritan movement featured many themes that eighteenth-century evangelicals would later promote as well, especially intense preaching about the need for a saving Christ and calculated opposition to the merely formal religion that Puritans saw infecting the Church of England.

---

1. D. W. Bebbington, *Evangelicalism in Modern Britain: A History from the 1730s to the 1980s* (London: Unwin Hyman, 1989), pp. 34–35.

Puritans promoted 'grace-centred Protestantism that would rise again in the evangelical revival'. Although 'aggressive heart religion' was widely discredited by its association with the Puritan Revolution, key figures like Baxter, Joseph Alleine, John Bunyan, Cotton Mather, Thomas Boston and Isaac Watts kept alive 'the traditions of experiential Calvinism' with their 'evangelical emphases'. Their books were read with appreciation by evangelicals, and when the revival of the 1730s flickered into life, the news about it was spread across the English-speaking world by a well-established network of Calvinist divines.[2]

But as well as noting continuities, Noll and Bebbington are also keen to identify key differences between Puritanism and evangelicalism. Noll argues that 'even as it pushed towards a more personal and more internal practice of the Christian faith, Puritanism still remained a traditional religion of traditional European Christendom'. Although the content of this traditionalism is not fully unpacked, Noll seems to have several elements in mind. First, Puritans retained '*the ideal of a comprehensive, unified society*'. They 'promoted coercive plans for the comprehensive reform of society' and held 'state-church assumptions'. Evangelicals, by contrast, endorsed a profound shift from concern with godly order to godly fellowship, from religious uniformity to toleration, and from communalism to voluntarism.[3] 'Where the Puritans worked for purified state-church establishments,' Noll explains elsewhere, 'most modern evangelicals have been independent-minded people delighted with the separation of church and state.'[4] Second, Noll implies that Puritans were 'doctrinal precisionists', confessional Protestants 'committed to high standards of doctrinal orthodoxy' such as those set out in the Westminster Confession. Evangelicals, by contrast, were shaped by the shift 'from Christian faith defined as correct doctrine towards Christian faith defined as correct living'. They were less inclined to let theological differences impede spiritual fellowship.[5] Third, Noll claims that 'where Puritanism retained an *exalted role for the clergy* and great respect for formal learning, evangelicals since the eighteenth century have been powered by lay initiative and in the twentieth century have been wary of formal scholarship'.[6]

For his part, Bebbington highlights three significant 'symptoms of discontinuity': the stimulus of High Church Anglicanism, the influences of continental

---

2. Mark A. Noll, *The Rise of Evangelicalism* (Leicester: IVP, 2004), p. 48.

3. Ibid., pp. 49–50.

4. Mark A. Noll, *American Evangelical Christianity: An Introduction* (Oxford: Blackwell, 2001), p. 13.

5. Noll, *Rise of Evangelicalism*, pp. 47, 50.

6. Noll, *American Evangelical Christianity*, pp. 13–14.

Pietism, and the new emphasis on mission. Evangelical 'activism', he suggests, stood in 'stark contrast' to the 'pitiably weak' missionary effort of previous generations of Protestants. Underlying these symptoms of change was a fundamental cultural shift associated with the Enlightenment. Slipping into hyperbole, Bebbington declares that 'The Evangelical version of Protestantism was created by the Enlightenment.' Eighteenth-century evangelicals, he argues, displayed a series of characteristic Enlightenment traits: empiricism, reasonableness, optimism, pragmatism, tolerance and humanitarianism. Above all, they were distinguished from their Puritan forebears by a much more emphatic promise of assurance, something that produced 'a metamorphosis in the nature of popular Protestantism'. Evangelicalism was 'a new movement and not merely a variation on themes heard since the Reformation'. 'The Evangelical Revival', he concludes, 'represents a sharp discontinuity in the Protestant tradition.'[7]

It is worth noting the difference of emphasis between these two accounts of 'the rise of evangelicalism'. Noll argues that eighteenth-century evangelicalism constituted a 'revival' of Puritan 'heart religion', though not of 'Puritanism as a complete social movement'. Puritans had discredited their experiential 'grace-centred Protestantism' by associating it with revolution, enthusiasm, antinominianism, doctrinal wrangling and intolerance; it took seven decades after the Restoration for 'evangelical movements' to recover and gather 'critical mass'. Released from the drag of revolutionary politics, state-church assumptions and doctrinal correctness, evangelical religion was finally able to take off. But the essence of 'grace-centred Protestantism', Noll seems to imply, remained unchanged. If I am reading him right, Noll offers us a 'weak' discontinuity thesis.[8] Bebbington, however, explicitly makes the case for 'sharp discontinuity'. His language is unusually emphatic. Evangelicalism was the product of 'a revolution in taste' and was 'created' by the Enlightenment. It was 'a new movement', a 'metamorphosis'. The implication is that even if evangelicalism evolved from Puritanism, the two are nevertheless different species.[9]

Noll and Bebbington are among the finest historians of English-speaking Protestantism. They have done more than anyone else to revive the study of evangelical history, and their recent volumes in 'The History of Evangelicalism' series are exceptionally rich and learned.[10] But I want to suggest that they

7. Bebbington, *Evangelicalism in Modern Britain*, pp. 35–74.

8. Noll, *Rise of Evangelicalism*, pp. 48–54.

9. Bebbington, *Evangelicalism in Modern Britain*, pp. 43, 74.

10. Noll, *Rise of Evangelicalism*; D. W. Bebbington, *The Dominance of Evangelicalism: The Age of Moody and Spurgeon* (Leicester: IVP, 2005).

each exaggerate the differences between seventeenth-century Puritanism and eighteenth-century evangelicalism, and that Bebbington's strong discontinuity thesis is particularly problematic. The problem arises, I argue, because both Noll and Bebbington make questionable assumptions about Puritanism, and fail to appreciate its dynamism and diversity. Once we understand the varieties of Puritanism, it becomes more difficult to make hard and fast distinctions between Puritans and evangelicals.

Defining Puritanism

Before we can explore the relationship between Puritanism and evangelicalism in more detail, we need to define 'Puritanism'. Historians of evangelicalism tend to assume that Puritanism is an unproblematic category. In reality, it is a rather artificial construct, and historians have agonized over its definition.

In recent years, Patrick Collinson has addressed this problem with new rigour and sophistication. Collinson reminds us that in the sixteenth and seventeenth centuries, the word 'Puritan' was largely used as a term of abuse rather than an objective label. Although some Protestants eventually talked with nostalgia of 'the old English Puritan', few used it as a term of self-description. 'Puritan' was analogous to modern pejoratives like bigot, killjoy or extremist. 'Puritans' were zealous Protestants whose behaviour aroused the irritation or even anger of their contemporaries. Nonconformist clergy provoked the vitriol of ecclesiastical officials and monarchs; godly critics of the theatre incurred the wrath of playwrights; pastors or parishioners who attacked traditional festive culture were stigmatized by their neighbours; and fervent pietists who loved extempory prayer and fiery preaching alienated those who preferred a more formal religion. Thus the term 'Puritan' was hurled in fraught situations at a wide variety of people. As a consequence, the concept is necessarily imprecise. It belongs to the realm of early modern polemic rather than modern social science.[11]

Collinson also emphasizes that 'Puritans' are often hard to distinguish from other committed Protestants. Recent scholarship has emphasized that

---

11. See P. Collinson, *The Puritan Character: Polemics and Polarities in Early Seventeenth-Century English Culture* (Los Angeles: Clark Memorial Library, 1989); 'Ecclesiastical Vitriol: Religious Satire in the 1590s and the Invention of Puritanism', in J. Guy (ed.), *The Reign of Elizabeth I: Court and Culture in the Last Decade* (Cambridge: Cambridge University Press, 1995), ch. 7.

the Church of England was a self-consciously Reformed church. Its foundational documents (including Cranmer's Book of Common Prayer and the Thirty-Nine Articles) expressed an evangelical Calvinist theology. Although a new High Church party started to emerge from the 1590s, archbishops like Parker, Grindal, Whitgift and Abbott were firmly Reformed in their outlook and were not plotting a *via media* between Rome and Geneva. The majority of bishops and many of the clergy were devoted to preaching an evangelical Protestant gospel, with its emphasis on the authority of Scripture and justification by faith. As a result, it is difficult to tell where evangelical Calvinism ends and 'Puritanism' begins. Many so-called 'Puritans' were well integrated into the Church of England and worked closely with conformist clergy. The old dichotomy between a subversive Puritanism and an Anglican establishment has been broken down.[12]

Despite problematizing Puritanism, Collinson does not dispense with it. Like another leading historian, Peter Lake, he suggests that while there was much common ground between conformist Calvinists and Puritans, Puritans were nonetheless distinctive; although the image of the 'Puritan' was polemically constructed, it bore eloquent testimony to the angular presence of the godly.[13] Borrowing a striking phrase from an Elizabethan observer,

12. See P. Collinson, *The Religion of Protestants: The Church in English Society, 1559–1625* (Oxford: Oxford University Press, 1982). See also N. Tyacke, *Anti-Calvinists: The Rise of English Arminianism, c. 1590–1640* (Oxford: Oxford University Press, 1987); K. Fincham, *Pastor as Prelate: The Episcopate of James I* (Oxford: Oxford University Press, 1990); A. Milton, *Catholic and Reformed: The Roman and Protestant Churches in English Protestant Thought, 1600–1640* (Cambridge: Cambridge University Press, 1995). N. Tyacke, *Aspects of English Protestantism, c. 1530–1700* (Manchester: Manchester University Press, 2001), p. 302, points out that as late as the 1680s Calvinist theologians occupied both the Lady Margaret and Regius Chairs of Divinity at Oxford University. Neither could be considered as Puritan.

13. See e.g. his *The Elizabethan Puritan Movement* (Cambridge: Cambridge University Press, 1967); *English Puritanism* (London: Historical Association, 1983); *Godly People: Essays on English Protestantism and Puritanism* (London: Hambledon, 1983); *The Birthpangs of Protestant England* (London: Macmillan, 1988), chs. 4–5; 'Puritan Emmanuel', in S. Bendall, C. Brooke and P. Collinson (eds.), *A History of Emmanuel College, Cambridge* (Woodbridge: Boydell & Brewer, 1999), ch. 6. Collinson's policy, which is to problematize the term and then carry on using it, is nicely showcased in his short article 'Puritans', in H. Hillerbrand (ed.), *The Oxford Encyclopedia of the Reformation*, 4 vols. (Oxford: Oxford University Press, 1996), vol. 3, pp. 364–370.

Collinson has famously (and loosely) defined Puritans as 'the hotter sort of Protestants'.[14] Distinguished by the zeal and intensity of their evangelical Protestantism, they were different in degree rather than in kind from the conformist Calvinists who held all the best bishoprics and deaneries in England until the rise of the Laudians.

Despite sharing much common ground with other evangelical Protestants, 'the godly' (as they liked to call themselves) formed a distinctive subculture centred on a vigorous voluntary religion of Bible study, prayer, fasting, sermon consumption and strict sabbatarianism.[15] Although they were far from being the only purveyors of the Protestant gospel, they were its most ardent and uncompromising carriers. Puritans were 'forward Protestants', 'super-Protestants', 'perfect Protestants', 'the militant tendency' of English Protestantism.[16] As another historian explains, Collinson has taught us that 'Puritanism' is 'an extremely convenient shorthand term' for 'the hotter sort of Protestants', but one that 'is unavoidably a contextual, imprecise term, not an objective one, a term to use carefully but not take too seriously in itself'.[17]

Lake has vigorously defended the distinctiveness of Puritanism in a series of important works: *Moderate Puritans and the Elizabethan Church* (Cambridge: Cambridge University Press, 1982); 'Puritan Identities', *Journal of Ecclesiastical History* 35 (1984), pp. 112–123; *Anglicans and Puritans? Presbyterian and Conformist Thought from Whitgift to Hooker* (London: Unwin Hyman, 1988); 'Defining Puritanism—Again?', in F. Bremer (ed.), *Puritanism: Trans-atlantic Perspectives on a Seventeenth-Century Anglo-American Faith* (Boston: Massachusetts Historical Society, 1993), pp. 3–29; *The Boxmaker's Revenge: 'Orthodoxy', 'Heterodoxy' and the Politics of the Parish in Early Stuart England* (Stanford: Stanford University Press, 2001); *The Antichrist's Lewd Hat: Protestants, Papists and Players in Post-Reformation England* (New Haven: Yale University Press, 2002).

14. *Elizabethan Puritan Movement*, p. 27.

15. P. Collinson, 'Elizabethan and Jacobean Puritanism as Forms of Popular Religious Culture', in C. Durston and J. Eales (eds.), *The Culture of English Puritanism* (Basingstoke: Macmillan, 1996), pp. 32–57.

16. Phrases used by Collinson in *English Puritanism*, p. 16; 'Elizabethan and Jacobean Puritanism', p. 46; 'The Sherman's Tree and the Preacher: The Strange Death of Merry England in Shrewsbury and Beyond', in P. Collinson and J. Craig (eds.), *The Reformation in English Towns* (Basingstoke: Macmillan, 1998), pp. 215–216.

17. M. Winship, 'Were There Any Puritans in New England?', *New England Quarterly* 74 (2001), pp. 137–138.

This emphasis on heat or zeal as a key characteristic of Puritans dovetails with another stream of scholarship focused on Puritan spirituality. In what remains the finest analysis of Puritan practical divinity, Geoffrey Nuttall highlights the central place in Puritan writing of the doctrine and work of the Holy Spirit, and shows how this produced intense piety and a longing for communion with God.[18] The same stress on the passionate spirituality of the Puritans can be found in the essays of Nuttall's best-known student, J. I. Packer.[19] Another scholar, Charles Hambrick-Stowe, writes that 'at its heart . . . Puritanism was a devotional movement, rooted in religious experience' and committed to 'heart religion'.[20] Most recently, Dwight Bozeman has argued that English Puritans developed 'the first Protestant pietism' in the late sixteenth century, combining a passion for inward, introspective piety with 'a rich complex of communal and private exercises . . . Bible reading, meditation, flocking to sermons, private meetings of saints . . . for worship and mutual edification, family devotions and catecheses, Sabbath and fast days exercises . . .'[21] Indeed, English Puritans became famous throughout Calvinist Europe for their affectionate, practical divinity, and their writings were a major stimulus to the emergence of Pietism elsewhere.[22]

The heat and intensity of the godly is emphasized by another group of scholars, those concerned to explain the factiousness of Puritanism. Recent studies have depicted English Puritanism as a dynamic, unstable and fissiparous religious subculture. Historians like Peter Lake and David Como explore the 'tensions and potential contradictions' within early Stuart Puritanism and the resultant diversity of the godly. They highlight tensions between legalism and antinomianism, lay activism and clerical authority, the godly community and the national church, charismatic experientialism and doctrinal orthodoxy. If mainstream moderate Puritanism involved a careful balance between these

---

18. G. F. Nuttall, *The Holy Spirit in Puritan Faith and Experience* (1946; repr., Chicago: University of Chicago Press, 1992).

19. See J. I. Packer, *Among God's Giants: The Puritan Vision of the Christian Life* (Eastbourne: Kingsway, 1991).

20. C. Hambrick-Stowe, *The Practice of Piety: Puritan Devotional Disciplines in Seventeenth-Century New England* (Chapel Hill: University of North Carolina Press, 1982), p. vii.

21. T. D. Bozeman, *The Precisianist Strain: Disciplinary Religion and Antinomian Backlash in Puritanism to 1638* (Chapel Hill: University of North Carolina Press, 2004), p. 65.

22. See P. Benedict, *Christ's Churches Purely Reformed: A Social History of Calvinism* (New Haven: Yale University Press, 2002), pp. 518–526.

poles, radicals within the Puritan milieu were often keen to press one at the expense of the other.

Even before 1640, English Puritanism was troubled by prophets and prophetesses, antinomian controversies, sectarianism, lay preaching and heresy.[23] The godly community had become the spawning ground for a variety of radical sects, including separatists and Baptists (both Calvinist and anti-Calvinist). Similar problems erupted in New England, where intensely pious figures like Roger Williams and Anne Hutchinson challenged conventional Puritan positions. These individuals cannot be lightly dismissed as unrepresentative mavericks. The 'free grace controversy' divided the Massachusetts establishment in the mid-1630s, pitting its leading preacher (John Cotton) and governor (the youthful Henry Vane) against the majority of the clergy and magistrates (including John Winthrop). Vane returned to England in disgrace, but in the 1640s was to become a close friend of Williams and one of the central figures in the Puritan Revolution.[24]

Indeed, it was during the Revolution that the fissiparous potential of Puritanism was fully realized. Although Puritans agreed on the need for 'further reformation', they soon found themselves bitterly divided over what that entailed. By the mid-1640s, Presbyterians who supported a uniform national church were at odds with Independents who favoured religious toleration and self-governing congregations. Backed by Cromwell's New Model Army, the Independents were able to seize control of the Revolution. Radical sects organized openly, especially in London, and promoted all kinds of heterodox ideas. By the early 1650s, the community of the godly had splintered into numerous factions. Presbyterians and Congregationalists made up the respectable majority, but they had to compete with Separatists, General Baptists, Particular Baptists, Seekers, Diggers, Fifth Monarchists, Quakers, Mugabeologists, Socinians and (wildest of all) Ranters.[25]

23. Lake, *Boxmaker's Revenge*; D. Como, *Blown by the Spirit: Puritanism and the Emergence of an Antinomian Underground in Pre-Civil-War England* (Stanford: Stanford University Press, 2004); 'Women, Prophecy and Authority in Early Stuart Puritanism', *Huntingdon Library Quarterly* 61 (1998), pp. 203–222; I. Atherton and D. Como, 'The Burning of Edward Wightman: Puritanism, Prelacy and the Politics of Heresy in Early Modern England', *English Historical Review* 120 (2005), pp. 1215–1250.

24. See M. Winship, *Making Heretics: Militant Protestantism and Free Grace in Massachusetts, 1636–1641* (Princeton: Princeton University Press, 2002).

25. The classic study of the ideological turmoil of the Revolution is Christopher Hill's *The World Turned Upside Down: Radical Ideas in the English Revolution* (London:

Some of these groups were very small. But by 1660, the Baptists and Quakers together accounted for approaching 100,000 people, and many more had been involved in the radical sects at some point during the Revolution.[26] Diggers, Muggletonians, Socinians and Ranters had moved beyond the bounds of evangelical Protestantism, and Quakers were widely accused of downgrading both Scripture and Christ's atonement.[27] But all these sects had emerged from *within* the Puritan subculture. If they had left traditional Protestant religion far behind, they had done so by taking characteristic Puritan emphases to extremes (the presence of the Spirit within, freedom from the law, the restoration of primitive Christianity, *sola scriptura* versus churchly traditions). It is understandable, then, that various historians discuss all of these groups under the rubric of 'radical Puritanism'.[28]

Of course, most of the godly clung to more traditional forms of Protestant religion. A clear majority affirmed trinitarianism, Calvinist predestinarianism, religious establishment and uniformity, tithes, clerical authority and infant baptism. But 'mainstream' Puritanism was under constant pressure

---

Temple Smith, 1972). But see also M. Tolmie, *The Triumph of the Saints: The Separate Churches of London* (Cambridge: Cambridge University Press, 1977); J. F. Macgregor and B. Reay (eds.), *Radical Religion in the English Revolution* (Oxford: Oxford University Press, 1984); P. Mack, *Visionary Women: Ecstatic Prophecy in Seventeenth-Century England* (Berkeley: University of California Press, 1992); Mark R. Bell, *Apocalypse How? Baptist Movements during the English Revolution* (Macon, Ga.: Mercer University Press, 2000); A. Hughes, *Gangraena and the English Revolution* (Oxford: Oxford University Press, 2004).

26. MacGregor and Reay, *Radical Religion*, pp. 33, 141.
27. See T. L. Underwood, *Primitivism, Radicalism and the Lamb's War: The Baptist–Quaker Conflict in Seventeenth-Century England* (New York: Oxford University Press, 1997).
28. See e.g. P. Gura, *A Glimpse of Sion's Glory: Puritan Radicalism in New England* (Middleton, Conn.: Wesleyan University Press, 1984); N. Smith, *Perfection Proclaimed: Language and Literature in English Radical Religion, 1640–1660* (Oxford: Oxford University Press, 1989); R. J. Acheson, *Radical Puritans in England, 1550–1660* (Harlow: Longman, 1990); W. Lamont, *Puritanism and Historical Controversy* (London: UCL Press, 1996); D. Loewenstein, *Representing Revolution in Milton and His Contemporaries: Religion, Politics and Polemics in Radical Puritanism* (Cambridge: Cambridge University Press, 2001). Geoffrey Nuttall's classic study *The Holy Spirit in Puritan Faith and Experience* also makes a strong case for Quakerism as the culmination of tendencies central to mainstream Puritanism.

from a more 'radical' Puritanism that claimed to be just as godly and more emphatically biblical. Following the Restoration of the monarchy in 1660, even the Presbyterians found that they too had become Dissenters. Excluded from the Established Church, they started to rethink their traditional belief in religious uniformity, and reinvent themselves as voluntary gathered churches.[29] Puritanism was an evolving, protean phenomenon. It is hardly surprising that one leading historian has spoken of 'Puritanisms'.[30]

Comparing Puritanism and evangelicalism

The Puritanism that emerges from recent scholarship is rather different from the Puritanism familiar to modern evangelicals. The evangelical picture of Puritanism has been powerfully shaped by conservative Reformed publishers like the Banner of Truth. The Banner has published a wide range of important Puritan texts, by Presbyterians like Richard Baxter, Congregationalists like John Owen, Baptists like John Bunyan, and even conformists like William Gurnall. But what is omitted from this canon of Puritan literature is just as revealing as what is included.

Missing are the doctrinal works of Richard Baxter that promote a 'neonomian' doctrine of justification, a Grotian theory of atonement, and a minimalist, ecumenical creed; the writings of Roger Williams, who believed that the restoration of true churches would have to await the emergence of end-times apostles; the works of John Milton, the great Puritan poet, who defended divorce, freedom of the press and regicide, and was almost certainly Arminian and anti-trinitarian in his later life; the political writings of the Levellers, including the separatist John Lilburne and the Baptist Richard Overton; the Arminian works of John Goodwin, one of London's leading Puritan pastors in the mid-seventeenth century; the visions of prophetesses like Anna Trapnel; the antinomian tracts of influential figures like Tobias Crisp and John Eaton; and scores of books published by the General Baptists.

All of these figures were involved in the subculture of the godly. Their exclusion from the canon of Puritan literature means that whole swathes of Puritan writing and experience have been left untouched by Calvinist publishers. Radical

29. See M. Sutherland, *Peace, Toleration and Decay: The Ecclesiology of Later Stuart Dissent* (Carlisle: Paternoster, 2003).

30. A. Hughes, 'Anglo-American Puritanisms', *Journal of British Studies* 39 (2000), pp. 1–7.

Puritans (like Goodwin and Lilburne) who were famous in their own day are now virtually unknown (and unread) within evangelicalism.[31] That this is so is due to the great success of conservative Calvinists in constructing an image of Puritanism as a solid, cohesive movement of impeccable Reformed orthodoxy.

Ironically, both Bebbington and his critics tend to work with this rather dated image of Puritanism as sober, stable and doctrinally sound. Garry Williams, for example, takes it for granted that Puritans were staunchly committed to Calvinist orthodoxy. He fears that by dating the origins of evangelicalism to the 1730s, 'Bebbington's analysis serves to give a strong foothold to Arminianism within the evangelical movement by making foundational one of its most noted proponents' (i.e. John Wesley). By contrast, the long view of evangelicalism's origins entails that 'Reformed theology becomes the authentic Evangelical mainstream of three centuries [sixteenth to eighteenth], and the historical case for the foundational status of Arminianism is undermined.'[32]

Yet once we examine the theological situation on the ground in the sixteenth and seventeenth centuries, things start to look more complicated. It is true that a majority of early modern Protestants held to absolute predestination, but alternative (conditional) accounts of predestination were favoured by Melanchthon and his followers within Lutheranism, by evangelical Anabaptists and Mennonites, by 'Freewillers' in mid-Tudor England (including some of Foxe's martyrs), by Arminians in the Dutch republic, by the earliest English Baptists (the General Baptists), and by a small number of Puritan divines including John Goodwin, John Horn and Thomas Moore.[33] Moreover,

---

31. On Goodwin, see my book *John Goodwin and the Puritan Revolution: Religion and Intellectual Change in Seventeenth-Century England* (Woodbridge: Boydell & Brewer, 2006). Goodwin's most famous work has, however, recently been republished: *Redemption Redeemed: A Puritan Defense of Unlimited Atonement*, ed. J. Wagner (Eugene, Oreg.: Wipf & Stock, 2004²).

32. Garry J. Williams, 'Was Evangelicalism Created by the Enlightenment?', *Tyndale Bulletin* 53 (2002), pp. 283–312 (reprinted in this volume, ch. 15, under the title 'Enlightenment Epistemology and Eighteenth-Century Evangelical Doctrines of Assurance').

33. See D. Bagchi and D. Steinmetz (eds.), *The Cambridge Companion to Reformation Theology* (Cambridge: Cambridge University Press, 2004), pp. 74–75, 165–169, 203–205; M. Watts, *The Dissenters: From the Reformation to the French Revolution* (Oxford: Oxford University Press, 1978), pp. 41–50; Coffey, *John Goodwin*, ch. 7; G. F. Nuttall, 'John Horne of Lynn', in P. Brooks (ed.), *Christian Spirituality: Essays in Honour of Gordon Rupp* (London: SCM, 1975), ch. 10.

Puritan 'Calvinism' itself was profoundly variegated: high Calvinists like John Owen were deeply unhappy with the watered-down Calvinism of Baxter and the antinomian Calvinism of Crisp. Rather than speaking of a singular 'Calvinism', we should perhaps talk about rival Reformed theologies.[34] In theology, as well as ecclesiology, the diversity of modern evangelicalism has roots in the sixteenth and seventeenth centuries. Appealing to the 'aboriginal' era to discredit current expressions of evangelical religion ignores the heterogeneity of early Protestantism and Puritanism.

If critics of 'the Bebbington thesis' work with a one-dimensional picture of Puritanism, the same can be said of its supporters. Indeed, it is partly this static image of Puritanism that has led historians to draw such sharp contrasts with eighteenth-century evangelicalism. Take Mark Noll's description of Puritanism as 'a traditional religion of traditional European Christendom'.[35] Each of the three features of this 'traditional religion' that Noll mentions were certainly present in mainstream Puritanism. The majority of the godly worked for 'purified state-church establishments', valued confessional orthodoxy and 'retained an exalted role for the clergy and great respect for formal learning'.[36] But there were powerful counter-currents within Puritanism.

During the Puritan Revolution, many radicals followed Roger Williams and John Goodwin in condemning state-church establishments and promoting voluntarist religion. Although the Westminster Confession of Faith (and its Congregationalist and Baptist derivatives) was endorsed by most of the godly, a substantial minority denied significant teachings of the Confession or (like Richard Baxter) questioned the need for new creeds to add to the Apostles' Creed and the Scriptures. Even within the Westminster Assembly itself, a surprising number of divines were opposed to the imposition of man-made creeds on the grounds of Scripture sufficiency.[37] And within the Puritan subculture, there was a potent strain of anti-clericalism that fostered lay preaching, sectarianism and anti-intellectualism, and reached its apogee

---

34. The full range of Puritan opinion is surveyed in D. Wallace, *Puritans and Predestination: Grace in English Protestant Theology, 1525–1695* (Chapel Hill: University of North Carolina Press, 1982).

35. *Rise of Evangelicalism*, p. 49.

36. *American Evangelical Christianity*, p. 14.

37. See C. van Dixhoorn, 'A New Taxonomy of the Westminster Assembly (1643–52): The Creedal Controversy as Case Study', *Reformation and Renaissance Review* 6 (2004), pp. 82–106.

in the assault on the Presbyterian clergy during the late 1640s.[38]

Moreover, if one considers the three features of modern evangelicalism highlighted by Noll, all three are applicable to Puritanism as well.[39] First, Puritanism (like evangelicalism) was 'an extraordinarily complex phenomenon . . . diverse, flexible, adaptable, and multiform'. Indeed, perhaps the single most striking thing about seventeenth-century Puritanism was its fissile character. The Presbyterian, Congregationalist, Baptist and Quaker movements all sprang from Puritanism, not evangelicalism. Second, like evangelicalism, Puritanism was 'profoundly affected by its popular character'. Monarchs and bishops associated 'Puritanism' with the dreaded spectre of 'popularity'; Puritanism formed a popular religious culture in its own right; and Puritan radicals were purveyors of a populist, anti-intellectual style of charismatic 'enthusiasm'.[40] Third, 'innovative but informal networks of communication . . . sustained the transnational character' of Puritanism as much as evangelicalism and gave it 'much of its distinctive shape'. Already in the middle of the seventeenth century, we can see evangelical Protestants establishing networks of communication across the Atlantic.[41]

There are, to be sure, differences of degree. One could argue that evangelicalism was *more* diverse than Puritanism, though there is a case for saying that Richard Baxter in the 1640s had to face a more anarchic religious scene than George Whitefield in the 1740s. In any case, the continuities are just as striking as the discontinuities. Although Mark Noll offers us an unusually subtle and nuanced account of the rise of evangelicalism, the contrasts he identifies are still overdrawn.

Bebbington's attempt to drive a wedge between Puritanism and evangelicalism is more problematic. He is quite right to assert that there are 'symptoms of discontinuity', in particular the influence of High Church Anglicanism and continental Pietism. But High Church Anglicanism was hardly a significant source for Scottish or North American evangelicals, and continental Pietism owed a good deal to the devotional writings of the English Puritans. Moreover, when one looks at the leading Calvinist preachers of the Evangelical

38. See MacGregor and Reay, *Radical Religion*; L. F. Solt, 'Anti-intellectualism in the Puritan Revolution', *Church History* 25 (1956), pp. 306–316.

39. Noll, *American Evangelical Christianity*, pp. 14–15.

40. See Collinson, 'Elizabethan and Jacobean Puritanism'; D. Lovejoy, *Religious Enthusiasm in the New World* (Cambridge, Mass.: Harvard University Press, 1985).

41. See F. Bremer, *Congregational Communion: Clerical Friendship in the Anglo-American Puritan Community, 1610–1692* (Boston: Northeastern University Press, 1994).

Revival (Jonathan Edwards, George Whitefield and Gilbert Tennent), one is
struck by how much they were consciously reviving the doctrine and piety
of the Puritans. Although many scholars have stressed Edwards's debt to the
Enlightenment, others have argued persuasively that he was 'first and last a
Puritan theologian'.[42] In the case of the Presbyterian 'New Lights', Leonard
Trinterud maintains that the Tennents and their allies were reviving 'evangelical Puritanism' and following in the footsteps of earlier Puritan 'experimental'
divines.[43] The most recent assessment of Whitefield tells us that he was in
many ways 'a puritan redivivus' who 're-energized the Calvinist message'.[44]

Bebbington, however, claims that evangelical Calvinists differed decisively
from earlier Calvinists on the doctrine of assurance. He writes that 'Whereas
the Puritans had held that assurance is rare, late and the fruit of struggle in
the experience of believers, the evangelicals believed it to be general, normally given at conversion and the result of simple acceptance of the gift of
God.'[45] Other scholars have demonstrated that this dichotomy imposes a
black-and-white grid on a complex and messy reality.[46] As my own account of
Puritanism suggests, we should be wary of pronouncing on *the* Puritan view
of any given topic. To do so is to beg the question, which Puritans? On the
doctrine of assurance, we can be quite sure that there was no single line among
the godly. While mainstream Puritans did teach that assurance was hard won,
their teaching fostered a powerful 'antinomian backlash' from preachers who
insisted that assurance was readily available.[47] It was this 'free grace' account
of assurance that was to influence early Scottish evangelicals via *The Marrow of
Modern Divinity*, a mid-seventeenth-century Puritan tract whose republication

42. C. Cherry, *The Theology of Jonathan Edwards: A Reappraisal* (Garden City, N. Y.:
    Doubleday Anchor, 1966), p. xxiii. For compelling supporting evidence, see H. S.
    Stout, 'Edwards and the Puritans', in N. O. Hatch and H. S. Stout (eds.), *Jonathan
    Edwards and the American Experience* (New York: Oxford University Press, 1988), ch.
    9; B. Walton, *Jonathan Edwards, Religious Affections and the Puritan Analysis of True
    Piety, Spiritual Sensation and Heart Religion* (Lewiston, N. Y.: Edwin Mellen, 2002).
43. See L. Trinterud, *The Forming of an American Tradition: A Re-Examination of Colonial
    Presbyterianism* (Philadelphia: Westminster, 1949), pp. 57–60.
44. Boyd Stanley Schlenther, under 'George Whitefield', *Oxford Dictionary of National
    Biography* (Oxford: Oxford University Press, 2004).
45. Bebbington, *Evangelicalism in Modern Britain*, p. 43.
46. J. Beeke, *The Quest for Full Assurance: The Legacy of Calvin and His Successors*
    (Edinburgh: Banner of Truth, 1998); G. J. Williams, 'Was Evangelicalism Created?'
47. See esp. Bozeman, *Precisianist Strain*.

in 1718 sparked 'the Marrow controversy'.[48] Even if evangelicals were unanimous on assurance (which may be doubted), we cannot draw a sharp contrast between 'the Puritan view' and 'the Evangelical view'.[49]

The suggestion that Puritanism did not display the fourth characteristic of evangelicalism, namely activism, is also highly questionable. Carl Trueman is surely right to insist that all four elements of Bebbington's evangelical quadrilateral are 'rooted in the Reformation' and manifestly present within Puritanism.[50] Bebbington concedes that the Puritans were biblicist, crucicentric and conversionist, but doubts their activism. Yet Puritan lives were characterized by a ceaseless round of prayer, fasting, Bible reading, family worship, conferences and sermons. Godly divines like Richard Baxter were phenomenally productive in their writing, preaching, catechizing, correspondence and counselling. Puritans were at the cutting edge of the drive to evangelize early modern England, and spread the gospel of evangelical Protestantism.[51] Indeed, they were notorious for their activism—why else did the playwright Ben Jonson in his *Bartholomew Fair* (staged 1614 and published 1631) name his most famous Puritan character 'Zeal-of-the-Land-Busy'?

Bebbington is on firmer ground when he points to the relative absence of cross-cultural mission in the Puritan era. The Protestant missionary effort did not compare well to that of the Catholics, or even the early Quakers. However, many Puritans encouraged the readmission of the Jews to England in the 1650s with a view to their conversion, and strongly supported John Eliot's mission to the New England Indians.[52] David Brainerd and Jonathan Edwards were consciously treading in Eliot's footsteps. It has also been argued that Puritan

---

48. See D. C. Lachman, *The Marrow Controversy* (Edinburgh: Rutherford House, 1988).

49. If Nathan Cole's experience is anything to go by, evangelical conversions could be just as agonized and protracted as those of some Puritans. See Cole's narrative describing his hearing of Whitefield and subsequent inner turmoil in M. Crawford, 'The Spiritual Travels of Nathan Cole', *William and Mary Quarterly*, 3rd ser., 33 (1976), pp. 89–126.

50. C. R. Trueman, 'Reformers, Puritans and Evangelicals: The Lay Connnection', in D. Lovegrove (ed.), *The Rise of the Laity in Evangelical Protestantism* (London: Routledge, 2002), pp. 31–32.

51. See Christopher Hill's famous chapter 'Puritans and the Dark Corners of the Land', in his *Change and Continuity in 17th-Century England* (London: Weidenfeld & Nicolson, 1974), pp. 3–47.

52. See R. Cogley, *John Eliot's Mission to the Indians before King Philip's War* (Cambridge, Mass.: Harvard University Press, 1999).

postmillennialism laid the groundwork for later missionary endeavours by fostering an expectation that the latter days would witness the conversion of the nations.[53] Most importantly, it is far from clear that the 'pitiable' missionary effort of sixteenth- and seventeenth-century Protestants was due to an absence of 'activism'.

Early modern Protestants were preoccupied with securing the Reformation, by withstanding the grave threat from counter-Reformation Catholicism and tackling the daunting task of turning nominal Protestants into real Protestants. As recent scholarship on 'England's long Reformation' has emphasized, the English *state* became Protestant decades before the English *people*, and for generations Protestant energies were sunk into evangelizing their own populations.[54] The fact that Protestants had no equivalent to the Catholic religious orders was another major hindrance to cross-cultural mission: Protestant clergy were expected to minister to existing congregations, and even John Eliot had to combine his mission to the Indians with his ordinary ministry. What changed the situation was not the injection of a hitherto absent activist zeal, but the expansion of empire and the rise of the voluntary society in the eighteenth century. Even then, it was not until the 1790s (half a century after the outbreak of revival) that evangelicals followed the Moravian example by sending significant numbers of missionaries overseas.

If Bebbington's claims about assurance, activism and mission are dubious, what should we make of his suggestion that evangelicalism was 'created' by the Enlightenment? It is undeniable that eighteenth-century evangelicals were influenced by the culture of Enlightenment, just as seventeenth-century Puritans were shaped by the culture of scholasticism and Renaissance humanism. But Bebbington tends to attribute certain features of evangelicalism to Enlightenment influence when more plausible candidates lie close to hand. Take the evangelical stress on 'experimental religion'. There was nothing novel about this vocabulary and there is no need to invoke 'the Enlightenment' to explain it. The language of 'inward', 'experimental', 'vital' and 'heart' religion

53. See J. D. De Jong, *As the Waters Cover the Sea: Millennial Expectations in the Rise of Anglo-American Missions 1640–1810* (Amsterdam: Kampen, 1970); I. H. Murray, *The Puritan Hope: A Study in Revival and the Interpretation of Prophecy* (London: Banner of Truth, 1971).

54. See N. Tyacke (ed.), *England's Long Reformation, 1500–1800* (London: UCL Press, 1997).

can be traced to seventeenth-century Puritans.[55] Seventeenth-century Baptists admitted people to membership on 'a declaration of an experiential work of the spirit upon the heart'.[56]

Other features of Enlightenment Christianity identified by Bebbington also have clear precedents in seventeenth-century Puritanism. Take their optimism, their conviction that 'humanity enjoyed great potential for improvement'. As Bebbington realizes, evangelical optimism was often underwritten by postmillennialism.[57] But this postmillennialism had its roots in the seventeenth century, when many Reformed theologians had come to believe that a great era of 'latter day glory' lay ahead, and would be ushered in by the conversion of the Jews, the fall of Roman Catholicism, and the triumph of Protestant religion.[58] Significantly, such millennial optimism was not restricted to 'religious' matters. Leading Puritan intellectuals also shared Francis Bacon's belief that Europeans were on the verge of 'a great instauration'. Had not the prophet Daniel predicted that in the last days knowledge would increase, and men would travel to and fro? Puritans like John Milton, John Goodwin and Samuel Hartlib were imbued with millennial optimism, and anticipated great advances in theology, learning, science, politics and social reform.[59]

If 'optimism' was emerging before the Enlightenment, so was moderate Calvinism. Bebbington writes that 'in its refusal to subordinate free inquiry to the authority of one man, in its repudiation of mysterious dogma, in its very moderation, [moderate Calvinism] was a typical product of the eighteenth century'.[60] It would be truer to say that moderate Calvinism was a product of the seventeenth century. Divines like Amyraut, John Davenant, James Ussher, Richard Baxter and John Howe had softened Calvinism in exactly the same ways as Bebbington's evangelicals. They insisted on the necessity of obedience to God's law and rejected antinomianism; they denounced fatalism; and

55. See Walton, *Jonathan Edwards*. See also A. Taves, *Fits, Trances and Visions: Experiencing Religion and Explaining Experience from Wesley to James* (Princeton: Princeton University Press, 1999), pp. 16–18; Nuttall, *Holy Spirit*, pp. 7–8; Bozeman, *Precisianist Strain*, pp. 82, 128.

56. *Association Records of the Particular Baptists in England, Wales and Ireland to 1660*, ed. B. R. White (London: Baptist Historical Society, 1971–4), p. 56.

57. Bebbington, *Evangelicalism in Modern Britain*, pp. 60, 62–63.

58. See Murray, *Puritan Hope*.

59. See the classic study of Charles Webster, *The Great Instauration: Science, Medicine and Reform, 1626–1660* (London: Duckworth, 1975).

60. Bebbington, *Evangelicalism in Modern Britain*, p. 63.

they argued that all men had a duty (and even the ability) to repent and believe.[61] Enlightenment sensibilities may have bolstered the growth of moderate Calvinism, but it had been on the rise since the 1620s.

Bebbington suggests that 'the abandonment of exclusive denominationalism' reflected 'the spirit of the age—flexible, tolerant, utilitarian'.[62] This may be true, but rejection of party spirit had also been at the heart of the vision of both Oliver Cromwell and Richard Baxter. Cromwell himself prioritized basic Protestant piety over mere 'forms', and the Cromwellian state church brought together Presbyterians, Congregationalists and Baptists.[63] Even the staunchly Calvinist John Owen was willing to forge a doctrinal consensus that would satisfy godly Arminians while excluding Socinians.[64] Although Baxter was no fan of Cromwell or Owen, he shared their passion for unity among the godly. A self-styled 'reconciler', he never tired of promoting what Bebbington calls 'the catholic spirit'.[65] Of course, hopes for ecumenical brotherhood may have been more fully realized in the eighteenth century than in the seventeenth, but here again the difference is one of degree.

Bebbington is surely right to detect the influence of Enlightenment in evangelical support for the American Revolution and religious toleration, but even the politics of evangelicalism owed much to Puritanism. The American Revolution received overwhelming support from Presbyterians, Congregationalists and Baptists, the very groups that had formed the backbone of Parliamentarianism during the English Civil War. Reformed preachers turned again to Calvinist resistance theory and millenarianism to justify revolt, and even invoked the earlier English Revolution as a noble precedent.[66] If

---

61. See J. Moore, '"Christ Is Dead for Him": John Preston (1587–1628) and English Hypothetical Universalism' (PhD thesis, University of Cambridge, 2000); D. Field, *Rigide Calvinism in a Softer Dresse: The Moderate Presbyterianism of John Howe* (Edinburgh: Rutherford House, 2004).

62. Bebbington, *Evangelicalism in Modern Britain*, pp. 65–66.

63. On Cromwell's ecumenical 'antiformalism', see J. C. Davis, 'Cromwell's Religion', and A. Fletcher, 'Oliver Cromwell and the Godly Nation', in J. Morrill (ed.), *Oliver Cromwell and the English Revolution* (Harlow: Longman, 1990), chs. 7–8.

64. See Coffey, *John Goodwin*, pp. 233–235.

65. Baxter's 'catholic' vision is ably analysed in P. Lim, *In Pursuit of Purity, Unity and Liberty: Richard Baxter's Puritan Ecclesiology in its Seventeenth-Century Context* (Leiden: E. J. Brill, 2004).

66. See K. Phillips, *The Cousins' Wars: Religion, Politics, and the Triumph of Anglo-America* (New York: Basic, 1999); K. Griffin, *Revolution and Religion: The American*

evangelical support for toleration reflected Enlightenment influence, it should be pointed out that numerous radical Puritans had championed toleration and liberty of conscience.[67] Politically, there was significant continuity between radical Puritanism and evangelical Dissent. When eighteenth-century evangelicals spoke the language of 'civil and religious liberty', they were echoing, sometimes consciously, the revolutionary writings of John Milton.

None of this is to deny that eighteenth-century evangelicalism differed from seventeenth-century Puritanism, or that the difference was due in part to the influence of the Enlightenment (though historians today are all at sea when it comes to defining 'the Enlightenment').[68] It is simply to suggest that Puritanism and evangelicalism were not nearly as dissimilar as Bebbington maintains. Once we appreciate the dynamism and diversity of seventeenth-century Puritanism, the contrasts with evangelicalism become much more blurred. In place of the strong discontinuity thesis, we require a subtler account of continuity and change.

Continuity and change in the evangelical Protestant tradition

Let us begin with the continuities. As Mark Noll recognizes, evangelicalism revived both 'grace-centred Protestantism' and 'aggressive heart religion'. Evangelical religion, as defined by Whitefield's *Journals* (surely one of the key texts of the Awakening), was a combination of Reformation doctrine and Pietist fervour, both of which were present in seventeenth-century Puritanism. Whitefield became worried whenever either of these was missing.

On the one hand, many Dissenters preached 'the doctrines of grace', but having not 'experienced the power of them in their hearts' they shied away from revivalist ardour. On the other hand, Quakers shared the evangelicals' longing for 'heart religion', but often downplayed 'Christ crucified'. Whitefield's fellow Anglicans frequently combined the worst of both worlds, since they

---

    Revolutionary War and the Reformed Clergy (New York: Paragon House, 1993); R. Bloch, *Visionary Republic: Millennial Themes in American Thought, 1756–1800* (Cambridge: Cambridge University Press, 1985).

67. See J. Coffey, 'Puritanism and Liberty Revisited: The Case for Toleration in the English Revolution', *Historical Journal* 41 (1998), pp. 961–985; *Persecution and Toleration in Protestant England, 1558–1689* (Harlow: Longman, 2000), ch. 3.

68. See J. Robertson, *The Case for the Enlightenment* (Cambridge: Cambridge University Press, 2005), ch. 1.

lacked the doctrine of the Dissenters and the passion of the Quakers. He lamented, 'how sadly are our Church ministers fallen from the doctrines of the Reformation'. But he also knew that most Anglicans instinctively recoiled at any hint of 'enthusiasm'. By contrast, evangelical religion was about both 'the fundamentals of Christianity' and 'inward feelings'.[69]

Doctrinally, Whitefield's evangelicalism was far from innovative. It was deeply rooted in the Reformation. John Wesley had significant disagreements with Reformed orthodoxy, but he too was a profoundly Protestant preacher, who proclaimed man's depravity, Christ's atoning sacrifice, justification by faith, and regeneration. His conversion, after all, came through reading Luther on Romans.[70] Generations of evangelicals were moulded by their reading of such key post-Reformation texts as the Book of Common Prayer and the Westminster Confession of Faith. Evangelicalism, then, like Puritanism before it, cannot be understood unless it is firmly placed within the longer and broader history of the evangelical Protestant tradition.

As Hans Küng argues in his major work on the history of Christianity, movements like Puritanism, Pietism, evangelical revivalism and fundamentalism all fit within the 'Protestant evangelical paradigm of the Reformation' alongside traditional Lutheran and Reformed religion.[71] Küng notes that in the Evangelical Revival one finds that

> the characteristic concerns of the Reformation stand at the centre: justification by faith and the rebirth of the new person in the spirit of Christ. Here a fundamental role is played on the one hand by being overwhelmed with God's grace and on the other by the believing trust of sinful men and women.[72]

The truth is that while the 1730s and 40s were a turning point in church history, they do not compare with the fracture created by the earliest Reformers

---

69. *George Whitefield's Journals: A New Edition*, ed. I. Murray (London: Banner of Truth, 1960), pp. 351, 353, 350, 356.

70. See *The Journal of John Wesley: A Selection*, ed. E. Jay (Oxford: Oxford University Press, 1987), pp. 34–35. For an excellent treatment of Wesley's theology, see H. B. McGonigle, *Sufficient Saving Grace: John Wesley's Evangelical Arminianism* (Carlisle: Paternoster, 2001).

71. Hans Küng, *Christianity: The Religious Situation of Our Time* (London: SCM, 1995), pt. 4.

72. Ibid., pp. 633–634.

in the 1510s and 20s.[73] Even Luther was not *sui generis*, of course, and recent scholarship has rediscovered the medieval roots of Reformation theology.[74] But Luther redefined Western Christianity far more profoundly than Whitefield, Edwards and Wesley. Luther and his allies effectively inaugurated a new theological tradition, evangelical Protestantism, founded on the supreme authority of Scripture and centred on intense preoccupation with salvation through faith in Christ's atoning sacrifice. The basic theological convictions of the early Reformers were defended and elaborated in what Philip Schaff called 'the creeds of the Evangelical Protestant Churches'.[75] Eighteenth-century evangelicals stood within this broader evangelical Protestant tradition and defended the common core of its creeds. Theologically, evangelicalism was essentially (and self-consciously) derivative.[76] To a remarkable degree, this continues to be the case.[77]

Yet evangelicalism was not simply a matter of doctrinal truth. It was also about revivalist fervour. As Whitefield, Edwards and the Wesleys made abundantly clear, their work entailed a 'revival', 'awakening' or 'quickening' of a well-established religious tradition that had grown somewhat drowsy.[78] Like the founder of Pietism, Philipp Jakob Spener, they had a 'hearty desire for an improvement of the true Evangelical Churches'.[79] Above all, improvement was about putting the fire back into Protestant hearts. Whitefield's *Journal* abounds with references to blazing hearts, melted souls, tearful faces, liberty of spirit, enlargement of heart, inward feelings, and experimental religion. This is not

---

73. Mark A. Noll, *Turning Points* (Grand Rapids: Baker, 1997), chs. 7 and 10, discusses both turning points, but does not assess which was the more profound.

74. See A. E. McGrath, *The Intellectual Origins of the European Reformation* (Oxford: Oxford University Press, 2004²).

75. See P. Schaff, *Creeds of the Evangelical Protestant Churches* (London: Hodder & Stoughton, 1877).

76. This is not to deny that some evangelicals (e.g. Wesleyans and Moravians) had distinctive and even novel doctrines, but it is to suggest that most of their theology was inherited from earlier evangelical Protestants.

77. See J. I. Packer and T. Oden (eds.), *One Faith: The Evangelical Consensus* (Downers Grove: IVP, 2004). This is a useful anthology and analysis, even if Packer and Oden sometimes exaggerate the area of theological consensus among evangelicals.

78. This is emphasized in W. R. Ward, *The Protestant Evangelical Awakening* (Cambridge: Cambridge University Press, 1992).

79. The phrase is found in the German title of Spener's classic work *Pia desideria* (1675). See Küng, *Christianity*, p. 625.

the language of Enlightenment; it is the language of Puritanism. Evangelicals like Whitefield were steeped in classic Puritan texts, from Bunyan's *Pilgrim's Progress* (1678) to Watts's *Hymns and Spiritual Songs* (1707). Anglican critics of evangelicalism were in no doubt that it represented a return of Puritan zeal. William Warburton complained of 'the old Puritan fanaticism revived under the new name of Methodism'. Horace Walpole feared that the New Light was 'a revival of all the folly and cant of the last age' (the seventeenth century). James Hervey had to tell his fellow evangelicals, 'Be not ashamed of the name Puritan.'[80]

Like Puritans before them, evangelicals were 'the hotter sort of Protestants'. Both movements reproduced the spiritual intensity we find in Luther's own conversion experience, but they did so more successfully than the often rather formal state churches of Protestant Europe. They were marked out by their zeal for the promotion of the Protestant Gospel. For Puritans and evangelicals, identity formation worked in much the same way. They defined themselves over against rival 'others', especially Roman Catholics and Protestant 'formalists'. Their religion was both anti-popish and anti-nominal, both Protestant and intense. Evangelicals and Puritans saw themselves, and were seen by others, as 'hot gospellers'.[81] Evangelicalism, like Puritanism, was defined not just by its 'reformational convictions' but also its 'pietistic priorities'.[82]

If evangelicalism rehabilitated Reformation doctrine and revived Puritan piety, should we simply see it as a return to 'old-time religion'? Should we, like E. J. Poole-Connor, begin our history of *Evangelicalism in England* (1951) with Tyndale rather than with Whitefield? Doing so would have certain advantages. Current evangelical historiography runs the risk of obscuring evangelicalism's place within the older and broader tradition of evangelical Protestantism. The terms 'Puritanism' and 'evangelicalism' force us to chop the history of the tradition into separate slices, breaking up the flow of the story. But again and again, one finds that it is simply impossible to account for key features of modern evangelicalism without reference to their roots in the sixteenth and seventeenth centuries.

A number of examples serve to illustrate the point. If we want to tell the story of Protestant revivalism, we need to go back to the seventeenth-century communion festivals of Presbyterians in Scotland and Ulster, which are themselves

---

80. A. S. Wood, *The Inextinguishable Blaze: Spiritual Renewal and Advance in the Eighteenth Century* (London: Paternoster, 1960), p. 29.

81. A phrase noted by Collinson, *English Puritanism*, p. 12.

82. Packer and Oden, *One Faith*, p. 172.

part of the revival lore of the Ulster-Scots.[83] If we wish to give an account of the evangelical conversion narrative, we need to begin with the emergence of the genre among mid-seventeenth-century Puritans.[84] If we want to know when evangelical Protestants started using study Bibles, we shall have to talk about the Geneva Bible.[85] If we want to witness the birth of the English evangelical hymn, we have to go back to the Puritans Keach and Watts.[86] If we want to find the origins of evangelical fascination with the conversion of the Jews and an imminent millennium, we have to turn to the early modern Calvinist theologians who first promoted Protestant millenarianism.[87] If we want to place recent controversies over the imputation of Christ's righteousness in historical context, we need to see how they emerged within seventeenth-century Puritanism.[88] If we want to examine the evangelical itch to campaign for moral

---

83. See M. Westerkamp, *The Triumph of the Laity: Scots–Irish Piety and the Great Awakening* (New York: Oxford University Press, 1988); L. E. Schmidt, *Holy Fairs: Scottish Communions and American Revivals in the Early Modern Period* (Princeton: Princeton University Press, 1989); M. Crawford, *Seasons of Grace: New England's Revival Tradition in its British Context* (New York: Oxford University Press, 1991). See also J. Gillies, *Historical Collections of Accounts of Revival* (Glasgow, 1754).

84. See D. B. Hindmarsh, *The Evangelical Conversion Narrative: Spiritual Autobiography in Early Modern England* (Oxford: Oxford University Press, 2005).

85. See D. Daniel, *The Bible in English* (New Haven: Yale University Press, 2003), ch. 17.

86. See J. R. Watson, *The English Hymn* (Oxford: Oxford University Press, 1997), chs. 6–8.

87. See H. Hotson, 'The Historiographical Origins of Calvinist Millenarianism', in B. Gordon (ed.), *Protestant History and Identity in Sixteenth-Century Europe*, 2 vols. (Aldershot: Ashgate, 1996), vol. 2, pp. 159–181; Murray, *Puritan Hope*; D. Katz, *Philosemitism and the Readmission of the Jews to England, 1603–55* (Oxford: Oxford University Press, 1982).

88. See Lake, *Boxmaker's Revenge*, pp. 221–246; Coffey, *John Goodwin*; C. van Dixhoorn, 'Reforming the Reformation: Theological Debate at the Westminster Assembly' (PhD thesis, University of Cambridge, 2004), ch. 5. When the Westminster Assembly itself was divided over whether justification involved the imputation of Christ's active righteousness to the believer, it is hardly surprising that modern evangelicals have been split on the issue as well. The debate resurfaced in disputes between Wesley and his Calvinist critics in the eighteenth century, and between Robert Gundry and Thomas Oden in 2001: Robert H. Gundry, 'Why I Didn't Endorse "The Gospel of Jesus Christ: An Evangelical Celebration" ... Even though

reform, we would do well to go back to Calvin's Geneva, Knox's Scotland, Winthrop's Massachusetts and Cromwell's England.[89] If we want to trace the history of sabbatarianism, to which most evangelicals were devoted until recent times, we have to start once again with sixteenth-century Britain.[90] Historians of evangelicalism are right to stress the innovatory nature of the movement, but they sometimes underplay its traditionalism. Evangelicals (at least in the eighteenth and nineteenth centuries) were extraordinarily effective at conserving and transmitting the doctrines and practices of early modern Protestantism.

However, there are two reasons for continuing to speak of 'modern evangelicalism' as a religious movement born in the eighteenth century. The bad reason is that this thoroughly conventional usage is too well established to be uprooted. David Bebbington is hardly alone in seeing a new movement being born out of the mid-eighteenth-century awakening, and he certainly did not invent the idea.[91] The better reason is that there was something genuinely new about the eighteenth-century revivals.

The difficulty comes when we try to identify exactly what was new. There are, I would suggest, two distinctive features that came to mark out the evangelical movement as a new movement. First, there was the *language of 'revival'*, popularized by men like Whitefield, Edwards and Erskine. The theological convictions and ardent piety of these men were also present within Puritanism. What is new is their passion for what they call 'revival'.[92] Not all evangelical Protestants shared the enthusiasm for revival, but those who did were marked

---

I Was Asked to', *Books & Culture* 7.1 (Jan.–Feb. 2001), pp. 6–9; Thomas Oden, 'A Calm Answer ... to a Critique of "The Gospel of Jesus Christ: An Evangelical Celebration"', in the same issue, pp. 6–9; Robert H. Gundry, 'On Oden's Answer', *Books & Culture* 7.2 (Mar.–Apr. 2001), pp. 14–15, 39.

89. The continuity of the Protestant drive for moral reform is emphasized by J. A. Morone, *Hellfire Nation: The Politics of Sin in American History* (New Haven: Yale University Press, 2003).

90. See K. Parker, *The English Sabbath* (Cambridge: Cambridge University Press, 1988); Todd, *The Culture of Protestantism in Early Modern Scotland* (New Haven: Yale University Press, 2002), pp. 41–42, 342–343.

91. See e.g. G. R. Balleine, *A History of the Evangelical Party in the Church of England* (London: Longmans, 1908); L. E. Elliott-Binns, *The Evangelical Movement in the Church of England* (London: Methuen, 1928); K. Hylson-Smith, *Evangelicals in the Church of England, 1734–1984* (Edinburgh: T. & T. Clark, 1989).

92. Here I concur with Thomas Kidd (ch. 6 in this volume), who helpfully shows how the idea of 'revival' had been developing for some decades. Packer, *Among God's*

out as 'evangelicals'. Modern evangelicals, one could argue, are people who tell stories about past revivals and pray for future ones. For this reason, they constitute a distinct community of discourse.

Second, the novelty lay in the *practical methods* of the new evangelicalism. As W. R. Ward suggests, the Awakening combined 'theological conservatism with practical innovation'.[93] Whitefield and his contemporaries had found new ways to promote the old-time religion. They established what Noll calls 'organised evangelical movements'.[94] These international and interdenominational movements were devoted to propagating vital evangelical religion, and they coalesced around dynamic itinerant evangelists like Whitefield, Wesley, Harris and Tennent. Whitefield himself was the first modern revivalist preacher, the first mass evangelist.[95] For the first time in the history of Protestantism, the pace was set not by theologians or settled pastors, but by a travelling evangelist who merrily worked across denominational boundaries. The evangelical Protestant world had never seen anything quite like it before.

Whether this turning point was any more significant than others in the history of evangelical Protestantism is open to debate. From the day Luther took his stand at Worms in 1521, evangelical Protestantism has been a dynamic, evolving tradition. Its current manifestations are the product of wave after wave of reform, renewal and restructuring.

Among the most important were the rise of Reformed Protestantism and Anabaptism in the 1520s and 1530s; the emergence of Puritan pietism in Elizabethan England; the splintering of English Protestantism in the seventeenth century; the rise of continental Pietism and anglophone evangelicalism in the early eighteenth century; the birth of missionary societies in the 1790s; the American 'democratic' revivals of the early nineteenth century; the upsurge of Pentecostalism in the 1900s; the formation of the 'neo-evangelical' movement in the 1940s; and the emergence of the charismatic movement in the 1960s. Each of these developments involved a reconfiguration of the tradition,

---

Giants, ch. 3, argues that Puritanism was 'a movement of revival', but admits that seventeenth-century Puritans spoke of 'reform' rather than 'revival'.

93. Ward, *Protestant Evangelical Awakening*, p. 355.

94. *Rise of Evangelicalism*, p. 66.

95. The case is made by both H. S. Stout, *The Divine Dramatist: George Whitefield and the Rise of Modern Evangelicalism* (Grand Rapids: Eerdmans, 1991), and F. Lambert, *Pedlar in Divinity: George Whitefield and the Transatlantic Revivals, 1737–1770* (Princeton: Princeton University Press, 2002).

even if the underlying principles of evangelical Protestantism (biblicism, cruci-centrism, conversionism and activism) remained in place. Eighteenth-century evangelicalism, like seventeenth-century Puritanism before it, was the latest expression of the evangelical Protestant tradition.

Nevertheless, the awakening was explosive and deeply controversial. Indeed, it divided the heirs of seventeenth-century Calvinism. Some, like the Tennents and Edwards, became leading figures in the new evangelicalism. Others, like the Congregationalist Old Lights in New England, the Presbyterian Old Sides in the Middle Colonies, and many conservative Presbyterians in Scotland and Ireland, sternly opposed Whitefield.[96] Both the awakeners and their opponents had a reasonable claim to be upholding seventeenth-century Puritan ideals. Proponents of revival shared the conviction of many Puritans that inward piety mattered more than forms. Critics of the revival perpetuated the insistence of many Puritans on the necessity of correct ecclesiastical order and discipline. Both groups subscribed to mainstream Reformation doctrine. Strange as it might seem, 'the Evangelical Revival' both renewed and divided evangelical Protestants.

What we call 'modern evangelicalism' has roots in both the sixteenth-century Reformation and the eighteenth-century Revival. As a result, evangelicals have something of an identity crisis. For some, 'evangelical' denotes sound-ness: evangelicals are the orthodox party within Protestantism (not the 'liber-als') who hold to Reformation teachings about biblical authority and salvation by grace through faith. For others, 'evangelical' denotes fervour: evangelicals are the pietist party within Protestantism (not the 'formalists'), who promote experiential heart religion and long for revival. Both definitions make some historical sense, though they make better sense when put together. At their best, evangelicals (like the Puritans before them) combined the strengths of the Reformers and the Pietists.

© John Coffey, 2008

---

96. On Calvinist critics of the revival, see E. Morgan, *The Gentle Puritan: A Life of Ezra Stiles, 1727–1795* (New Haven: Yale University Press, 1962), chs. 1–2; Trinterud, *Forming of an American Tradition*; E. B. Holifield, *Theology in America: Christian Thought from the Age of the Puritans to the Civil War* (New Haven: Yale University Press, 2003), pp. 149–156; A. L. Drummond and J. Bulloch, *The Scottish Church, 1688–1843* (Edinburgh: St Andrews, 1973), pp. 48–56; I. R. McBride, *Scripture Politics: Ulster Presbyterians and Irish Radicalism in the Late Eighteenth Century* (Oxford: Oxford University Press, 1998), pp. 63–65.

12. JONATHAN EDWARDS: CONTINUATOR OR PIONEER OF EVANGELICAL HISTORY?

Douglas A. Sweeney and Brandon G. Withrow

The man whom Samuel Hopkins praised for calling 'no Man, Father' is today honoured as the father of many American evangelicals. Jonathan Edwards's Christianity could be defined as the passionate pursuit of 'true religion', a spirituality that resonates with the evangelical mind. In 1989, David Bebbington did a great service to evangelicals by giving them a glimpse into their history, connecting them in significant ways to many important figures, such as George Whitefield (1715–70), John Wesley (1703–91) and, most notably, Edwards. George Whitefield preached more, usually to much larger crowds. John Wesley did far more to organize revival forces. But Edwards made the best sense of spiritual 'signs and wonders', interpreting them in relation to traditional Protestant thought.[1]

As the greatest theological mind behind the revivals, Edwards set the agenda for evangelical theology. Bebbington's famous quadrilateral, the 'defining qualities' of evangelical revivalists, boils that agenda down to

---

1. Samuel Hopkins, *The Life and Character of the Late Reverend Mr. Jonathan Edwards, President of the College of New Jersey. Together with a Number of His Sermons on Various Important Subjects* (Boston: S. Kneeland, 1765), p. 41; D. W. Bebbington, *Evangelicalism in Modern Britain: A History from the 1730s to the 1980s* (London: Unwin Hyman, 1989), p. 74.

conversionism, the belief that lives need to be changed; *activism*, the expression of the gospel in effort [e.g. missions and evangelism]; *biblicism*, a particular regard for the Bible; and what may be called *crucicentrism*, a stress on the sacrifice of Christ on the cross.

While these characteristics may be assumed simply to follow the Reformed Protestant tradition, Bebbington argues that there are 'sharp discontinuities' between evangelical revivalism and the Protestant Reformation. 'There can be no doubt', says Bebbington, 'that Edwards was the chief architect of the theological structures erected by evangelicals in the Reformed tradition. That was sufficient to ensure that they were built on Enlightenment foundations.' As Hopkins recalls, Edwards once held up a copy of Locke's *Essay Concerning Human Understanding* and said that 'he had more Satisfaction and pleasure in studying it, than the most greedy Miser in gathering up handfuls of Silver and Gold from some new discovered Treasure'.[2] While still owing much to Bebbington's work, current scholarship is undergoing an evolution of perspective, arguing that these discontinuities are not as sharp as they once appeared.

This chapter will re-examine Bebbington's thesis in the light of Edwards's use of his Reformed theological tradition. Important questions will be asked, such as how did Edwards understand his own role as an evangelical leader? Is evangelical activism founded upon an Enlightenment epistemology? And if not, what explains the explosion of evangelism and missions under the evangelical leadership of the eighteenth century? In concluding this chapter, the question as to whether Edwards was a continuator or pioneer of evangelical history will be answered.

Edwards in his time

Much has been made of Edwards's claim that he would 'not take it all amiss, to be called a Calvinist, for distinction's sake', while at the same time declaiming a 'dependence on Calvin', so that he could not be 'charged with believing in every thing just as he [Calvin] taught'.[3] Bebbington notes that evangelicals

---

2. Hopkins, *Life and Character*, p. 4; D. W. Bebbington, 'Revival and Enlightenment in Eighteenth-Century England', in Edith L. Blumhofer and Randall Balmer (eds.), *Modern Christian Revivals* (Urbana: University of Illinois Press, 1993), p. 21; Bebbington, *Evangelicalism in Modern Britain*, pp. 2–3, 74, 65.
3. Jonathan Edwards, *The Works of Jonathan Edwards*, vol. 1: *Freedom of the Will*, ed. Paul Ramsey (New Haven: Yale University Press, 1957), p. 131. Hereafter, all references to

harboured a 'certain reserve' when it came to an 'allegiance' to Calvinism.[4] Much the same, Hopkins painted a picture of a man whose 'Principles were Calvinistic', but who was 'truly very much of an Original'. Perry Miller saw Edwards as a man 'so much ahead of his time that our own can hardly be said to have caught up with him', but there have also been contrary voices. Vernon Parrington saw Edwards as one who 'followed a path that led back to an absolutist past, rather than forward to a more liberal future'.[5] There is no end to the many portraits of Edwards.

Today, scholarship is returning Edwards to his Anglo-American context. In 2001, Bruce Kuklick confessed that though he had viewed Edwards as 'noteworthy' as a 'powerful philosophical theologian', he now acknowledges that 'crucial to Edwards is something that is located not in Locke's *Essay Concerning Human Understanding*', but in 'works like Matthew Poole's 1669, five-volume *Synopsis Critocorum Aliorumque Sacrae Scripturae Interpretum*'.[6] The most 'fruitful path' to reading Edwards 'is one that will look at his role in a popular religious tradition, one that will place him more centrally in the provincial theological culture of premodern New England'.[7] In 2002, Robert Brown demonstrated in his *Jonathan Edwards and the Bible* that Edwards was on the cutting edge of scholarly activity and biblical culture, aggressively collecting the latest theological volumes from across the sea with the purpose of engaging early proposals by deists.[8]

---

volumes in this series will have a full first citation, after which they will follow the abbreviated citation *WJE*.

4. Bebbington, *Evangelicalism in Modern Britain*, p. 63.

5. Hopkins, *Life and Character*, p. 41; Perry Miller, *Jonathan Edwards* (Amherst: University of Massachusetts Press, 1981), p. xiii; Vernon Louis Parrington, *Main Currents in American Thought: An Interpretation of American Literature from the Beginnings to 1920*, 3 vols. in one (New York: Harcourt, Brace, 1930), pp. 162, 158.

6. Bruce Kuklick, 'A Review Essay: An Edwards for the Millennium', *Religion and American Culture* 11 (winter 2001), p. 115.

7. Ibid., p. 117.

8. Robert E. Brown, *Jonathan Edwards and the Bible* (Bloomington: Indiana University Press, 2002). See also Douglas A. Sweeney, 'Longing for More and More of It'? The Strange Career of Jonathan Edwards's Exegetical Exertions', in Harry S. Stout, Kenneth P. Minkema and Caleb J. D. Maskell (eds.), *Jonathan Edwards at 300: Essays on the Tercentenary of His Birth* (Lanham, Md.: University Press of America, 2005), pp. 25–37.

Bebbington readily acknowledges the existence of continuities between evangelicals and the past. When discussing the Methodists he notes that 'three characteristic marks of Evangelicalism, conversionism, biblicism, and crucicentrism, had been as much a part of Puritanism as they were of Methodism' and that 'Methodists inherited a substantial legacy from the Puritans'. But the emphasis falls foremost on elements of discontinuity between evangelicals and the Puritans in the area of 'activism': 'The Evangelical revival nevertheless does represent a break with the past.'[9]

A better understanding of Edwards takes into account his own perspective. He saw himself as simultaneously continuing the great Reformed tradition and standing at the dawn of a new age. It is too much to say that Edwards was making a firm break from the past, and too little to say that he merely carried on in the same ebb and flow of Reformed theology. This comes out clearly in his apocalyptic expectations, writings that tell us something about how Edwards saw his own position in history.

Viewing history as a grand cosmic battle between the church and the antichristian world, Edwards knew which side was righteous. His apocalyptic interpretation of Scripture, especially the book of Revelation, provided a lens through which he could interpret the purpose of divine providence in history, discerning both God's and Satan's side, as well as his own role in playing out that real history. Reformation theology, especially justification by faith alone, is the 'highest glory of the gospel', according to Edwards, and often the target of antichristian attacks in his eschatological scheme. And as he remarks in his Masters *Quaestio* in 1723, it is no 'slight glory to guard' this 'central' Christian doctrine.[10] To strike too dissonant a chord between Edwards and this tradition, therefore, would be to misunderstand how important Reformation theology was for Edwards and possibly to place him on a side he equated with Satan himself.

The Reformation, which Edwards equated with the 'fifth vial' of the book of Revelation, was the first important sign of the demise of the kingdom of the Antichrist. Originally, Edwards associated the historical event of the Reformation with that of the 'second vial'. It was his reading of Moses Lowman's (c. 1679–1752) commentary on the apocalypse, *A Paraphrase and Notes on the Revelations of St. John* (1737), that was largely responsible for changing his mind.

---

9. Bebbington, *Evangelicalism in Modern Britain*, p. 35.

10. Jonathan Edwards, *The Works of Jonathan Edwards*, vol. 14: *Sermons and Discourses, 1723–1729*, ed. Kenneth P. Minkema (New Haven: Yale University Press, 1997), p. 60.

Revelation 16:10–11 reads in Edwards's Authorized (King James) Version: 'And the fifth angel poured out his vial upon the seat of the beast, and his kingdom was full of darkness, and they gnawed their tongues for pain, and blasphemed the God of heaven, because of their pains and their sores, and repented not of their deeds.'[11] This passage carried significant meaning for Edwards's view of history and his place in it: 'This was the reformed religion, and the gospel of Jesus Christ.'[12] When the writer of the Apocalypse says, 'they repented not of their deeds', Edwards interprets this as the 'obstinacy' of the Church of Rome, an obstinacy manifested in their convening of the Council of Trent. But there are more vials in Revelation 16 and Edwards looked for the fulfilment of the 'sixth vial'. The Reformation itself began the work of God 'to weaken it and to diminish' the kingdom of the Antichrist 'both in extent and degree', but it would not finish it off.[13] That would be left for another generation, one that begins in Edwards's time.

If there were only five vials in Revelation, the emphasis of God's workings in history, for Edwards, would probably have fallen only on the Reformation. But there are more vials to be interpreted, and in understanding Edwards's explanation of the sixth vial, a properly balanced perspective of Edwards's thought in history is found. While dedicated to the Reformed tradition, Edwards believed that God's work continued until his day: 'Thus their kingdom hath actually been filled with darkness; and they have been confounded in their devices and attempt to overthrow the Protestant church, from the first Reformation till their great frustration by King William and Queen Mary.'[14] This work of God in the sixth vial, according to Edwards, begins in his time and is manifested in the revivals of the First Great Awakening. He saw every sermon preached and every soul saved in New England as contributing to the cause of redemptive history and the struggle against the dogma of Rome.

---

11. Unless otherwise noted, all Scripture citations are from the Authorized Version. For more on Edwards's apocalyptical views, see C. C. Goen, 'Jonathan Edwards: A New Departure in Eschatology', *Church History* 28 (Mar. 1959), pp. 25–40; Brandon Withrow, 'An Empty Threat: Jonathan Edwards on Y2K and the Power of Preaching', *Reformation and Revival Journal* 9 (winter 2000), pp. 69–92; 'A Future of Hope: Jonathan Edwards and Millennial Expectations', *Trinity Journal* 22 (spring 2001), pp. 75–98.

12. Jonathan Edwards, *The Works of Jonathan Edwards*, vol. 5: *Apocalyptic Writings*, ed. Stephen J. Stein (New Haven: Yale University Press, 1977), p. 199.

13. Ibid., pp. 199, 193.

14. Ibid., p. 195.

From Edwards's perspective, the rise of the redemptive-historical work occurring in New England was marked by several factors. 'And 'tis worthy to be noted that America was discovered about the time of the Reformation, or but little before,' he wrote in *Some Thoughts Concerning Revival* (1742),

> which Reformation was the first thing that God did towards the glorious renovation of the world, after it had sunk into the depths of darkness and ruin under the great antichristian apostasy. So that as soon as this new world is (as it were) created, and stands forth in view, God presently goes about doing some great thing to make way for the introduction of the church's latter-day glory, that is to have its first seat in, and is to take its rise from that new world.[15]

In America, Edwards saw the revivals as events fulfilling the prophecy of the sixth vial of Revelation. Revelation 16:12 says that 'the sixth angel poured out his vial upon the great river Euphrates; and the water thereof was dried up, that the way of the kings of the east might be prepared'. He interpreted this passage to mean that Rome would lose its power and influence and he immediately began recording any evidence that demonstrated this point in his notes titled 'An Account of Events Probably Fulfilling the Sixth Vial', and 'Events of an Hopeful Aspect of the State of Religion'.[16] According to Edwards, this vial is not to be equated with the millennium; rather, it is a precursor to the latter-day glory. As he writes in his *An Humble Attempt to Promote Explicit Agreement and Visible Union of God's People in Extraordinary Prayer* (1747):

> All the seven vials bring terrible judgments upon Antichrist; but there seems to be something distinguishing of the three last, the fifth, the sixth, and the seventh, viz., that they more directly tend to the overthrow of his kingdom, and accordingly each of 'em is attended with a great revival of religion . . . . It seems as though the sixth vial should be much more so; for 'tis the distinguishing note of this vial, that it is the *preparatory* vial, which more than any other vial prepares the way for Christ's coming to destroy the kingdom of Antichrist, and set up his own kingdom in the world.[17]

---

15. Jonathan Edwards, *The Works of Jonathan Edwards*, vol. 4: *The Great Awakening*, ed. C. C. Goen (New Haven: Yale University Press, 1972), p. 353.

16. *WJE* 5:251–284, 285–297.

17. Ibid., 426.

The sixth vial is accompanied with a 'great outpouring of the Spirit', that is, the revivals of the Great Awakening. The fifth vial also included 'glorious outpouring of the Spirit of God', but was followed by 'an exceeding great decay of vital piety', a problem to be rectified by the sixth vial.[18]

Edwards sees another parallel between the two vials, one tied closely to the question of whether he is a continuator or pioneer of evangelical history. During the time before the fifth vial, the 'world seemed overrun with barbarous ignorance', but the Reformation brought with it the printing press and therefore increased learning. Likewise, in conjunction with the special outpouring of the sixth vial are new advances in science and learning, and 'the unraveling intricacies, and removing difficulties attending Christian doctrines . . .'[19] While his apocalyptic interpretations gave him reason to embrace and defend the doctrines of the Reformation, he was not without the belief that these same doctrines, by virtue of the progress of redemptive history, would find fuller explanation during the time of the sixth vial. He understood himself as both continuator of Reformation theology and a pioneer of new, creative expressions of that same doctrine. The unfurling of Edwards's creative mind in explaining the affections and the will were justified by this interpretation, and should be understood within that framework for a balanced historical view of his thought. The emphasis was on 'unraveling intricacies' and 'removing difficulties', not making a clean break or starting from scratch. In his own time, Edwards sees himself as standing between two eras, the foundation of which is the Reformation. So, while Edwards lived in two worlds, the question is, how much or little discontinuity is there between Edwards and his Reformed forefathers?

Activism and epistemology

All four characteristics of evangelicalism (conversionism, activism, biblicism and crucicentrism) defined the 'qualities of those associated with revival', says Bebbington, and 'of these qualities, activism was new'. What is activism? Activism is the playing out of these doctrines practically, as evident in, but not limited to, evangelism and missions. 'The Puritans of the seventeenth century had been conversionist, crucicentric, and biblicist', writes Bebbington, 'but

18. Jonathan Edwards, *The Works of Jonathan Edwards*, vol. 9: *A History of the Work of Redemption*, ed. John F. Wilson (New Haven: Yale University Press, 1989), p. 438.

19. *WJE* 5:426; 9:440–441.

rarely had they devoted themselves to spreading the gospel where it was not yet known.'[20]

If not Puritanism, what inspired missions and evangelism? An epistemological transformation moved evangelicals towards activism, writes Bebbington:

> The transition from Puritan introspection to evangelical activism was founded on an altered attitude to the knowledge of God. It was a shift in the doctrine of assurance. Puritans held that certainty of being in a state of grace, though desirable, is normally late in the experience of believers and attained only after struggle . . . Evangelicals, by contrast, held that assurance is usually given to all believers at conversion.[21]

Evangelical confidence in their spiritual knowledge, according to Bebbington's thesis, comes from their Enlightenment epistemology, particularly the empiricism of John Locke (1632–1704), as found in his *Essay Concerning Human Understanding* (1690). Human reason makes judgments about truth through experience, says Locke:

> Reason therefore here, as contradistinguished to *Faith*, I take to be the discovery of the Certainty and Probability of such Propositions or Truths, which the Mind arrives at by Deductions made from such *Ideas*, which it has got by the use of its natural Faculties, *viz.* by Sensation or Reflection.[22]

Only through empirical data could knowledge be gained. The question became, what does this do for matters above the five senses, those things that are spiritual? How are they verified? What warrant do human beings have for believing them if they cannot be touched or tasted? According to early studies in Edwards's thought, since Locke's empiricism lacked the necessary tools for evaluating spiritual knowledge, Edwards offered a corrective. He posited another sense, one that is spiritual and therefore raises the experience of the spiritual to the level of knowledge. 'For Locke,' writes Bebbington, 'knowledge derived from the senses is certain . . . Edwards was simply extending the range

---

20. Bebbington, 'Revival and Enlightenment', p. 21. See also Mark A. Noll, *The Rise of Evangelicalism: The Age of Edwards, Whitefield and the Wesleys* (Leicester: IVP; Downer's Grove: IVP, 2003), p. 19.

21. Bebbington, 'Revival and Enlightenment', p. 22.

22. John Locke, *An Essay Concerning Human Understanding* 4.18.2, ed. Peter H. Nidditch (Oxford: Clarendon, 1975), p. 688.

of sense available to a human being,' and assurance was founded upon this new sense.[23]

It is here that Bebbington is both on to something and missing something very important for understanding Edwards. While many of Locke's concerns are picked up by Edwards, simply tying his new sense to Locke's empiricism misses the bigger picture. By writing *A Faithful Narrative of the Surprising Work of God* (1737), *The Distinguishing Marks of a Work of the Spirit of God* (1741), *Some Thoughts Concerning Revival* (1742) and *The Religious Affections* (1746), Edwards provided evangelicals with an invaluable tool for examining revivals and conversion, as well as a way to establish their validity and find personal assurance in spiritual experiences. While these books were written in the Enlightenment climate, their content was not dictated by Enlightenment conclusions.

Words like 'idea' and 'sense' do fill Edwards's notebooks, sermons and books. Bebbington is careful to point out the very Lockean phrase 'new simple idea' found in Edwards's *Religious Affections*.[24] In 1981, Norman Fiering warned that it was 'erroneous' to conclude that the use of 'idea' or other similar terms 'reveals the hidden presence of Locke'.[25] The use of Locke's terminology, according to Fiering, was to 'satisfy empiricist critics', not to imitate Locke: 'Edwards's spiritual sense has little resemblance to anything in Locke, and the English philosopher, had he been alive, would undoubtedly have dismissed Edwards's idea of a special sensation of divine things as "enthusiastic nonsense."'[26] Fiering's point is overstated. Edwards's understanding of the spiritual sense is not his attempt to correct Locke's empiricism as Bebbington writes, nor is Locke's empiricism entirely opposed to the idea of a spiritual illumination by the Spirit.

Robert E. Brown, interacting with Fiering in his *Jonathan Edwards and the Bible*, seeks a solid middle ground: 'But it would appear that while Edwards may not have been a thoroughgoing empiricist, his appropriation of Locke's terminology was more than merely conventional.'[27] Edwards did not need

23. Bebbington, *Evangelicalism in Modern Britain*, p. 48. On Edwards's relationship to the Enlightenment, see also Leon Chai, *Jonathan Edwards and the Limits of Enlightenment Philosophy* (New York: Oxford University Press, 1998).

24. Bebbington, *Evangelicalism in Modern Britain*, p. 48; Jonathan Edwards, *The Works of Jonathan Edwards*, vol. 2: *Religious Affections*, ed. John E. Smith (New Haven: Yale University Press, 1959), p. 205.

25. Norman Fiering, *Jonathan Edwards's Moral Thought and Its British Context* (Chapel Hill: University of North Carolina Press, 1981), p. 37.

26. Ibid., p. 125.

27. Brown, *Jonathan Edwards and the Bible*, p. 40.

to make up for Locke's lack of a spiritual sense, says Brown. The idea of a spiritual sense was not denied by Locke; rather, 'he explicitly allowed for it'.[28] Locke admits in his *Essay*:

> In what I have said I am far from denying, that GOD can, and doth sometimes enlighten Mens Minds in the apprehending of certain Truths, or excite them to Good Actions by the immediate influence and assistance of the Holy Spirit, without any extraordinary Signs accompanying it. But in such Cases too we have Reason and the Scripture, unerring Rules to know whether it be from GOD or no.[29]

Locke received plenty of criticism for giving too many tools to the deists, but he never divorced himself from the possibility of spiritual sight. While matters of faith are 'above Reason', they are not hostile to it. '*Faith* gave the Determination, where *Reason* came short,' Locke argues. Faith and reason are not opponents, rather faith is given a different 'Dominion', which does not offer any 'violence, or hindrance to *Reason*', in that reason 'is not injured, or disturbed but assisted and improved, by new Discoveries of Truth, coming from the Eternal Fountain of all Knowledge'.[30] Edwards would not have needed to correct Locke in the manner suggested by Bebbington. And since Locke did not dismiss a form of spiritual knowledge, he appears comfortable writing commentaries on Scripture (which Edwards used frequently). It is no wonder then that while Edwards does interact with Locke's philosophy, Locke the biblical commentator is often of greater use for him. It is worth noting, however, that Locke's recognition of the limitations of human knowledge keeps him firmly planted in the older paraphrase tradition, one that left speculation to a minimum and at times merely restated the biblical text for clarity.[31]

---

28. Ibid., p. 38.

29. Lock, *Essay* 4.19.16. See also Nicholas Wolterstorff, *John Locke and the Ethics of Belief* (New York: Cambridge University Press, 1996), pp. 118–133.

30. Locke, *Essay* 4.18.9, 10.

31. According to Brown's thesis, Edwards did at least make one late adjustment to Locke's thought, which is related to evangelical epistemology and certainty. According to Locke's *Essay*, knowledge is 'the perception of the connexion and agreement, or disagreement and repugnancy of any of our Ideas' (4.1.2). Faith falls short of certainty, rising to the level of probability, and therefore is not properly equal to knowledge. It is not required that something rise to the level of knowledge or certainty for one to assent to it. Matters of faith, for example, have a high degree of probability, bordering 'so near upon Certainty, that we make no doubt at all

Though Edwards was not addressing Locke's empiricism, he was keenly aware of the issues of the Enlightenment, and even worked comfortably within its terminology. As with much of his reading, Edwards's interest was to plunder the Egyptians while remaining guarded against Enlightenment extremes. That watchful approach is largely due to Edwards's own perception of his place in history. He is standing on the foundation of the Reformation doctrines, living out the history of redemption, and this means, from his perspective, that he is entrusted with the protection of those doctrines. At the same time, he is looking forward and seeking out new ways of 'unraveling' the intricacies of those doctrines, with each new book published being a potential source, as is evidenced by his copious copying of sources into his notebooks. He did engage the Enlightenment sources, even using their expressions, but was also just as eager to bring Scripture and his Reformed Calvinism to bear upon their excesses, especially in his latter years as he prepared to tackle the deist threat.

Beyond the question of Locke, Edwards's explanation of the religious affections cannot be fully appreciated outside a theological context. By design *A Treatise Concerning the Religious Affections* not only restricts excesses, but also

---

about them; but *assent* to [i.e. have faith in] them as firmly, and act according to that Assent, as resolutely, as if they were infallibly demonstrated, and that our Knowledge of them was perfect and certain' (4.15.655).

Matthew Tindal took Locke's definition of knowledge to new heights. He did not want to 'quit certainty', for that which 'is not pretended to amount to more than Probability' (Matthew Tindal, *Christianity as Old as Creation* [London, 1730], p. 330). Edwards's concern over Tindal's definition was due to its implications for religious knowledge, specifically as it related to divine revelation. Edwards, as Brown establishes, countered Tindal by subtly changing Locke's definition of knowledge in his notebook 'The Mind' (Brown, *Jonathan Edwards and the Bible*, pp. 83–86). Here Edwards softens the qualifications for knowledge by saying that 'KNOWLEDGE is not the perception of the agreement or disagreement of ideas, but rather the perception of the union or disunion of ideas, or the perceiving whether two or more ideas belong to one another' (Jonathan Edwards, *The Works of Jonathan Edwards*, vol. 6: *Scientific and Philosophical Writings*, ed. Wallace E. Anderson [New Haven: Yale University Press, 1980], p. 385). This of course provides a greater sense of assurance for religious sense knowledge, but in terms of Edwards's development of the spiritual sense, this adjustment of Locke's definition occurs nearly two years after *The Religious Affections*.

responds to the claims of revival opponents, such as Charles Chauncy, that the radical experiences in revivals were merely the contrivance of the lower faculties of the human soul, and not the movement of the Spirit upon the affections. 'He mistakes the workings of his own passions for divine communications', wrote Chauncy, 'and fancies himself immediately inspired by the SPIRIT of GOD, when all the while, he is under no other influence than that of an over-heated imagination.'[32] On one hand, Edwards agreed with Chauncy: 'There must be light in the understanding, as well as an affected fervent heart, where there is heat without light, there can be nothing divine or heavenly in that heart.' It was this absence that posed a problem for the enthusiasts. Nevertheless, 'True religion, in great part, consists in holy affections,' argues Edwards,

> so on the other hand, where there is a kind of light without heat, a head stored with notions and speculations, with a cold and unaffected heart, there can be nothing divine in that light, that knowledge is no true spiritual knowledge of divine things.[33]

What makes this human experience more than giving in to the passions, as claimed by Chauncy? According to Edwards, it is the outworking of the union a Christian has with Christ in justification through the bond of the Spirit. 'Affections that are truly spiritual and gracious, do arise from those influences and operations on the heart, which are *spiritual*, *supernatural* and *divine*,' writes Edwards.[34] In other words, epistemological certainty is founded upon a divine relationship.

Edwards's examination of the divine influences on the soul began with his own conversion, which did not fit the traditional pattern of Puritan preparationism taught to him by his father, Timothy, and his grandfather, Solomon Stoddard. Preparationism was a twofold or threefold process including a 'conviction' or 'awakening', followed by 'humiliation' and ending in 'repentance'.[35]

---

32. Charles Chauncy, *Enthusiasm Described and Caution'd Against* (Boston: S. Eliot Cornhill & J. Blanchard, 1742), p. 3.

33. *WJE* 2:120.

34. Ibid., 95, 96, 197. See also George M. Marsden, *Jonathan Edwards: A Life* (New Haven: Yale University Press, 2003), pp. 268–290.

35. See Solomon Stoddard, *The Safety of Appearing at the Day of Judgement, in the Righteousness of Christ* (Boston: Samuel Phillips, 1687), p. 205; *A Guide to Christ or, the Way of Directing Souls that Are under the Work of Conversion, Compiled for the Help of Young Ministers, and May be Serviceable to Private Christians, who Are Enquiring the Way*

His search for conversion was, at first, acts of 'miserable seeking', futile attempts that Edwards believed were mere self-deception.[36] He 'returned like a dog to his vomit', he recalls, 'and went on in ways of sin'.[37] When Edwards actually did encounter conversion, he found something very different from fear and humiliation:

> From about that time I began to have a new kind of apprehensions and ideas of Christ, and the work of redemption, and the glorious way of salvation by him. I had an inward, sweet sense of these things, that at times came into my heart; and my soul was led away in pleasant views and contemplations on them.

He was raptured into thoughts of the beauty of the divine. Whether he saw the 'blue sky', the sun, moon, flowers or trees, he saw only the 'divine glory'. Even thunderstorms, which previously terrified him, now led him to 'sweet contemplations' of his 'great and glorious God'.[38] That this experience was very different from what he expected left him less convinced of the validity of his own conversion. Even more, it pushed him to examine the very nature of conversion and whether his own experience was valid:

> The chief thing, that now makes me in any measure to question my good estate, is my not having experienced conversion in those particular steps, wherein the people of New England, and anciently the Dissenters of Old England, used to experience it. Wherefore, now resolved, never to leave searching, till I have satisfyingly found out the very bottom and foundation, the *real reason, why they used to be converted in those steps* [emphasis mine].[39]

---

to Zion (Northampton: Andrew Wright, 1816; repr. Morgan, Pa.: Soli Deo Gloria, 1993), p. xv; *A Treatise Concerning the Nature of Saving Conversion* (Boston: James Franklin for D. Henchman, 1719; repr. Morgan, Pa.: Soli Deo Gloria, 1999).

36. See John H. Gerstner, *Steps to Salvation: The Evangelistic Message of Jonathan Edwards* (Philadelphia: Westminster, 1950); Kenneth Pieter Minkema, 'The Edwardses: A Ministerial Family in Eighteenth-Century New England' (PhD diss., University of Connecticut, 1988), p. 82; Jonathan Edwards, *The Works of Jonathan Edwards*, vol. 16: *Letters and Personal Writings*, ed. George S. Claghorn (New Haven: Yale University Press, 1998), p. 791.

37. *WJE* 16:790, 791.

38. Ibid., 93–794.

39. Ibid., 779.

It was against a theological background that Edwards began working out his understanding of conversion and the true nature of the 'sweet sense'. Edwards's answer, in part, would come in the form of an extensive study of the Reformed divines, eventually leading to his master's *Quaestio* and a doctrine of justification.

The union of Christ with the believer in justification by the power of the Holy Spirit provided an answer for Edwards. Through faith, Christ is united or 'one' with sinners, and their sins are 'put on his account . . . to bear the punishment himself'.[40] Edwards also concludes that in this union, the soul of the Christian receives more than a forensic declaration. 'The soul is united to Christ', wrote Edwards in his sermon *Living to Christ* (1722/1723) over twenty years before *The Religious Affections*, 'and therefore partakes of his life: he lives in Christ and Christ lives in him, yea, not only lives in him but is his life. He is invigorated with him, with his Holy Spirit which is diffused as new life all over his soul.'[41] When one is regenerated, there is a 'very principle of spiritual life' in the soul, said Edwards, echoing his Reformed tradition and the *Theoretico-practica theologia* (1699) of his favorite theologian, Peter van Mastricht (1630–1706). 'For regeneration, strictly so called, finds a man spiritually dead', wrote van Mastricht, 'into whom it infuses the first act or principle of spiritual life, by which he has a power or ability to perform spiritual exercises.' Similarly, the Anglican Calvinist John Edwards (1637–1716), whose *Theologia reformata* (1713) Jonathan Edwards read early on, writes that the Holy Spirit 'shines into the Soul with bright Beams of Knowledge, and sufficiently illuminates the Understanding'. The soul is ignited with '*Desires* of Knowledge and goodness', and the Christian's '*Affections* are wrought upon by the Influence of the Holy Ghost'. More precisely, the Spirit 'irresistibly insinuates himself into our Souls, thus he moves and acts upon our Hearts, and effecteth that in us by his Secret, but Almighty Power, which we could never attain to by our own natural Strength, or by the Influence of any Created Power whatsoever'.[42]

---

40. Jonathan Edwards, *The Works of Jonathan Edwards*, vol. 13: *The 'Miscellanies' (Entry Nos. a–z, aa–zz, 1–500)*, ed. Thomas A. Schafer (New Haven: Yale University Press, 1994), pp. 164, 165; ('Misc.' b).

41. Jonathan Edwards, *The Works of Jonathan Edwards*, vol. 10: *Sermons and Discourses, 1720–1723*, ed. Wilson H. Kimnach (New Haven: Yale University Press, 1992), p. 570. See also Robert W. Caldwell III, *Communion in the Spirit: The Holy Spirit as the Bond of Union in the Theology of Jonathan Edwards* (Milton Keynes: Paternoster, 2006), pp. 101–165.

42. Peter van Mastricht, *A Treatise on Regeneration*, ed. Brandon Withrow (Morgan, Pa.: Soli Deo Gloria, 2002), p. 7; John Edwards, *Theologia reformata*, 2 vols.

With the new invigorating presence of the Holy Spirit, there comes a new understanding of spiritual things, a new sense of holiness and a new relationship to the natural world. In Miscellanies V entitled 'Union with Christ' (1722/1723), Edwards writes that 'by virtue of the believer's union with Christ, he doth really possess all things'. And by 'all things', Edwards means as follows:

> God three in one, all that he is, and all that he has, and all that he does, all that he has made or done—the whole universe, bodies and spirits, earth and heaven, angels, men and devil, sun moon [and] stars, land and sea, fish and fowls, all the silver and gold, kings and potentates as well as mean men—are as much the Christian's as the money in his pocket, the clothes he wears, or the house he dwells in, or the victuals he eats; yea more properly his, more advantageously, more *his*, than if he [could] command all those things mentioned to be just in all respects as he pleased at any time, by virtue of his union with Christ . . .[43]

(London: John Lawrence, John Wyat & Ranew Robinson, 1713), vol. 1, p. 499. While there are many sources for *The Religious Affections*, John Edwards and his *Theologia reformata* have long been overlooked. Jonathan Edwards's catalogue is replete with references to John Edwards's books—a source he found invaluable from his earliest days at Yale. There are many allusions to John Edwards in *The Religious Affections*. Both Edwardses emphasized the unity of the human mind. When Jonathan Edwards writes, 'the will and the affections of the soul are not two faculties; the affections are not essentially distinct from the will' (*WJE* 2:97), it sounds much like John Edwards: 'To the Will belong the *Affections* ... we should not speak amiss, if we said, that the Affections are the same with the Will ...' (John Edwards, *Theologia reformata*, vol. 1, p. 17). Both Edwardses appealed to the union of the body and soul: '*Affections*, for it hath this name from the Souls *affecting* the Body by due and orderly moving and agitating of the Spirits', says John Edwards, 'and likewise from the Body's moving and affecting the Soul by the different Objects presented to the bodily Senses, which is produced from the Union of the Body and Soul' (John Edwards, *Theologia reformata*, vol. 1, p. 18). Likewise, Jonathan Edwards appeals to the 'laws of the union of the body and soul' to argue that 'there never is any case whatsoever, any lively and vigorous exercise of the will or inclination of the soul, without some effect upon the body, in some alteration of the motion of its fluids [blood], and especially of the animal spirits' (*WJE* 2:98).

43. *WJE* 13:183–184; 'Misc.' ff.

Edwards's conversion experience could now make sense against this background. His experience and heightened senses were different, but not out of line with the nature of union and justification. The Christian, by virtue of this union to Christ through the Spirit, can sit back and 'enjoy' all of creation 'with surprising, amazing joy'.[44] His conversion and new 'sweet sense' of the reality of the divine beauty in nature was the natural result of his new relationship in union with Christ. He was now co-owner of the universe itself, albeit one whose will it is to leave the 'trouble of managing it' to Christ alone.[45]

In his Miscellanies 'a', titled 'Of Holiness' (1722), the word 'sweet' appears to describe the new vision of the spiritual gained by this new principle of life. Holiness is 'sweet and ravishingly lovely', a 'sweet calmness', and 'a sweet, humble nature', and not the 'melancholy, morose, sour, and unpleasant thing' Edwards thought it might be. Holiness makes the soul a 'sweet and delightful image of the blessed Jehovah'.[46] Similarly in his sermon fragment titled 'Application on Love to Christ' (1723), Edwards exudes enthusiasm for the new nature of the soul and its sense of the spiritual:

> [L]ove to Christ has a tendency to fill the soul with an inexpressible sweetness. It sweetens every thought and makes every meditation pleasant; it brings a divine calm upon the mind, and spreads a heavenly fragrance like Mary's box of ointment. It bedews the soul with the dew of heaven, begets a bright sunshine, and diffuses the beginnings of glory and happiness in embryo. All the world smiles upon such a soul as loves Christ: the sun, moon and stars, fields and trees, do seem to salute him. Such a mind is like a little heaven upon earth.[47]

It is this theological background, much more than his reading of Locke, that Edwards has in mind in his *Religious Affections*:

> Holiness, which is as it were the beauty of sweetness of the divine nature, is as much the proper nature of the Holy Spirit, as heat is the nature of fire, or sweetness was the nature of that holy anointing oil, which was the principal type of the Holy Ghost in the Mosaic dispensation.

---

44. Ibid., 185–186; 'Misc.' gg.
45. Ibid., 184; 'Misc.' ff.
46. Ibid., 163; 'Misc.' a.
47. *WJE* 10:617.

The presence of the Holy Spirit in the soul is a 'seed or spring of life', he writes, and the Spirit 'communicates himself, in this his sweet and divine nature'.[48] This theological background supplies the fuller context of Edwards's spiritual sense. The spiritual sense, which Edwards casually refers to as a 'new simple sense', is really first and foremost about the Christian's relationship to the divine being and the joy and assurance gained from it. The certainty of assurance could not be found in an Enlightenment epistemology fraught with problems, but rather in a vibrant relationship with God. More importantly, this position of assurance or certainty of knowledge as a testimony of the Spirit comes from the Calvinist tradition. Commenting on Romans 8:16, which reads, 'The Spirit itself beareth witness with our spirit, that we are the children of God,' Calvin says:

> Paul means that the Spirit of God affords us such a testimony that our spirit is assured of the adoption of God, when He is our Guide and Teacher. Our mind would not of its own accord convey this assurance to us, unless the testimony of the Spirit preceded it . . . for while the Spirit testifies to us that we are the children of God, He at the same time pours this confidence into our hearts, so that we dare invoke God as our Father.[49]

Edwards used this theology to provide criteria for verifying the work of the Spirit in revival and this did help to promote the cause of revival and its kin, evangelism and missions. However, the greatest influence of Edwards over evangelical activism comes from something with more ingenuity, his view of the will and his understanding of missions.

Activism: evangelism and missions

Is Bebbington overstating his point that 'evangelical revivalism . . . represents a break with the past'? The eighteenth century did see an explosion of activism exemplified by both evangelism and missions. Evangelism, especially in the form of revivalism, however, was not new in the eighteenth century. A tradition

---

48. *WJE* 2:201.
49. John Calvin, *Calvin's Commentaries*, vol. 8: *The Epistles of Paul the Apostle to the Romans and to the Thessalonians*, trans. Ross Mackenzie and ed. David W. Torrance and Thomas F. Torrance (Edinburgh: Oliver & Boyd, 1973; repr. Grand Rapids: Eerdmans, 1973), p. 170.

of itinerant ministers can be found as far back as the Scottish Reformed martyr George Wishart (c. 1513–46), who was mentor to John Knox (c. 1513–72). His fame was highlighted by Knox in his *The Historie of the Reformation of the Church of Scotland* and Wishart provided a model for Knox's own itinerancy in Scotland upon his return.[50] Antecedents with a closer relationship to the revivals of the First Great Awakening were the sacramental revivals of Scotland in the centuries following Knox.

Published in the same year as *Evangelicalism in Modern Britain*, Leigh Eric Schmidt's *Holy Fairs: Scotland and the Making of American Revivalism* (1989) demonstrates that Presbyterian awakenings in Scotland were present early in the seventeenth century. Joined to the sacramental service, these awakenings were often described as having the same type of enthusiasm that was often used to portray the awakenings of the eighteenth century. 'Fair days' in Scotland were family opportunities for farmers to sell and buy crops and other goods, and were, in many ways, a vestige of medieval times. When they were combined with the sacrament, they became something else entirely. 'Sacramental occasions in Scotland were great festivals,' writes Schmidt, 'an engaging combination of holy day and holiday. They were, as one divine said, "fair-days of the gospel," festal events in a Reformed calendar otherwise dominated by week-to-week observance of the Sabbath.'[51] These Holy Fairs were accompanied by tent meetings and revivals of religion. In the 1620s and 30s Presbyterian minister John Livingston led a string of fervent and fiery revivals in the kirk of Schotts:

> Schotts was indeed a high point in an extensive Presbyterian awakening, but the rituals performed there were not spontaneous creations of the moment. With roots in the growing Presbyterian and Episcopalian struggles of post-Reformation Scotland, sacramental occasions burgeoned in the 1620s into great evangelistic events.[52]

---

50. John Knox, *The Historie of the Reformation of the Church of Scotland* (London: John Raworth, Eorge Thomason & Octavian Pullen, 1644), vol. 1, pp. 67ff. See also Lord Eustace Percy, *John Knox* (Richmond, Va.: John Knox, 1965), pp. 21–40; W. Stanford Reid, *Trumpeter of God: A Biography of John Knox* (New York: Charles Scribner's Sons, 1974), pp. 27–53.

51. James G. Leyburn, *The Scotch-Irish: A Social History* (Chapel Hill: University of North Carolina Press, 1962), p. 28; Leigh Eric Schmidt, *Holy Fairs: Scotland and the Making of American Revivalism* (Grand Rapids: Eerdmans, 1989), p. 3.

52. Schmidt, *Holy Fairs*, p. 22.

Similar stirrings occurred in 1638 when ministers used their pulpits to preach on the moral and biblical necessity of the National Covenant (1638). By one account, during the nationwide fast day intended to raise support for the Covenant, Minister John Chairtres of the Currie parish church in Lothian oversaw an 'extraordinary influence of Gods Spirit' leading to 'sobs, tears, promises and voues'.[53] Revival activity during this century, while having peaks and valleys, was far from being a series of isolated incidents; rather, it supplied the following century with a model for the First Great Awakening.

The implementation of the Woollens Act of 1698 and the enforcement of the Test Act (1672) under Anne gave the Scots-Irish both religious and economic reasons to leave the Ulster colony for the American colonies, bringing along with them the Holy Fairs. In America, revival theology was popular among the Scottish Presbyterian immigrants such as William Tennent of Neshaminy Creek, Pennsylvania, whose Log College was closely aligned with the New Side of the Great Awakening. It was his son, Gilbert Tennent, who brought the Scottish tradition of joining sacrament and revival together in his *Sermons on Sacramental Occasions* (1739).[54] Under leaders like these, revival theology thrived in the colonies like never before.

When revival broke out at Jonathan Edwards's Northampton church in the mid-1730s, he entered the revival scene with more than conversion stories to tell—he had an enduring theology that led to an explosion of evangelical activity. His hope of 'unraveling intricacies, and removing difficulties attending Christian doctrines' during the time of the sixth vial finds its supreme expression in his theological achievements after this period.

---

53. Quoted in Margaret Steele, 'The "Politick Christian": The Theological Background to the National Covenant', in John Morrill (ed.), *The Scottish National Covenant in its British Context* (Edinburgh: Edinburgh University Press, 1990), p. 31; originally from the *Diary of Archibald Johnston of Wariston, 1632–1639*, 2 vols., ed. G. M. Paul (Edinburgh: the university press by T. & A. Constable for the Scottish History Society, 1911), vol. 1, pp. 327–328.

54. Gary E. Schnittjer, 'The Ingredients of Effective Mentoring: The Log College as a Model for Mentorship', *Christian Education Journal* 15.1 (autumn 1994); Marilyn J. Westerkamp, *The Triumph of the Laity: Scots-Irish Piety and the Great Awakening, 1625–1760* (New York: Oxford University Press, 1988), p. 161. For the only extensive study on William Tennent's life and the Log College, see Gary E. Schnittjer, 'William Tennent and the Log College: A Common Man and an Uncommon Legacy' (ThM thesis, Dallas Theological Seminary, 1992).

Building on the theology of sin and grace found in the Reformation, Edwards's work on the doctrine of the *Freedom of the Will* (1754) exerted the greatest force on evangelical theology.[55] Outside Wesleyan circles (which were comparatively slow to form in Britain's American colonies), Calvinistic evangelicals usually led revival efforts. Some of them held forbiddingly strict views of the scope of Christ's atonement for the sins of fallen humanity, views that, early in the revival, placed a drag on spiritual outreach. To like-minded Calvinists harbouring qualms about the Awakening and its use of what was then called 'indiscriminate' evangelism (i.e. the revivalists' practice of extending the gospel promises to everyone, without stressing that God redeems only those elected for salvation) Edwards provided an analysis of the freedom of the will that distinguished between a non-elect sinner's 'natural ability' (or constitutional capacity) to repent and turn from sin, and his or her 'moral inability' (or ineradicable unwillingness) to do the same. Everyone gets what he or she wants, Edwards's treatise told its readers. The problem is that hardened sinners never *want* to submit to God. They *will not* kneel at the foot of the cross (unless God draws them by his grace). They have themselves to blame, therefore, for their refusal to convert.

It may seem strange to say that Christian conservatives hindered the revivals, that there were Calvinists at the time whose views of election and predestination kept them from preaching to people outside their own communities. But by the time of the Awakening, there was a long and hallowed tradition, in Great Britain especially, whose adherents thought it presumptuous to suggest to perfect strangers that it was possible for any of them to repent and be reborn.[56] Edwards's doctrine cleared the way for many such people to preach revival and to evangelize outside their own churches and ethnic groups. It helped them share the gospel freely without suggesting in the process that non-Christians had the power to save themselves.

---

55. The best treatment of this doctrine and its roles in American history is Allen C. Guelzo, *Edwards on the Will: A Century of American Theological Debate* (Middletown, Conn.: Wesleyan University Press, 1989).

56. In Edwards's day, there were English Dissenters, such as the Calvinistic Baptists John Gill (1697–1771) and John Brine (1703–65), who taught that this could be said with confidence only in the confines of a rightly ordered, covenanted community. For a helpful recent discussion of Edwards's impact on such ministers, see D. Bruce Hindmarsh, 'The Reception of Jonathan Edwards by Early Evangelicals in England', in David W. Kling and Douglas A. Sweeney (eds.), *Jonathan Edwards at Home and Abroad* (Columbia: University of South Carolina Press, 2003), pp. 207–212.

In New England, Edwards's colleagues, known as New Divinity preachers, did the most to spread this doctrine of natural ability. By the time the Awakening ended, they were but one of several groups who sought control of New England's churches. But by the early nineteenth century, these Edwardseans would win the hearts and minds of most of their peers, enculturating the region with their leader's New Divinity.[57] Led at first by Edwards's colleagues Joseph Bellamy and Samuel Hopkins, they soon attracted the brightest college students at Yale. They promoted church renewal and evangelical conversion, all on the basis of Edwards's notion of natural ability.

Edwards also laid a foundation for evangelical missions. The Puritans, as Bebbington noted, had not 'devoted themselves to spreading the gospel where it was not yet known', but the evangelicals of the eighteenth century would change all that. As Stuart Piggin has claimed, 'Jonathan Edwards was massively constitutive of modern Protestant missions.'[58] Not only did his writings inspire numerous Calvinist ministers to promote 'indiscriminate', or cross-cultural, evangelism. His example as a missionary (and missionary biographer) inspired a surge of intercultural ministries. In 1747, Edwards promoted a transatlantic, evangelical Concert of Prayer 'for the revival of religion and the advancement of Christ's kingdom'.[59] In 1736, his congregation in Northampton had helped to found a frontier Indian mission in Stockbridge, Massachusetts. Then in 1751, Edwards moved to Stockbridge himself, becoming the leading missionary in the colonies.

Most significant of all for the rapid spread of Protestant missions was Edwards's *Life of David Brainerd* (1749), the best-selling book to come from his pen. Brainerd ministered as a missionary to Indians in New Jersey (as well

---

57. On the notion of an Edwardsean enculturation of Calvinist New England, see Douglas A. Sweeney, *Nathaniel Taylor, New Haven Theology, and the Legacy of Jonathan Edwards* (New York: Oxford University Press, 2003), pp. 13–65; 'Nathaniel William Taylor and the Edwardsian Tradition: A Reassessment', in Stephen J. Stein (ed.), *Jonathan Edwards's Writings: Text, Context, Interpretation* (Bloomington: Indiana University Press, 1996), pp. 139–158.

58. Stuart Piggin, 'The Expanding Knowledge of God: Jonathan Edwards's Influence on Missionary Thinking and Promotion', in Kling and Sweeney, *Jonathan Edwards*, p. 266.

59. Jonathan Edwards, *An Humble Attempt to Promote Explicit Agreement and Visible Union of God's People in Extraordinary Prayer for the Revival of Religion and the Advancement of Christ's Kingdom on Earth, Pursuant to Scripture-Promises and Prophecies concerning the Last Time* (Boston: D. Henchman, 1747). Available in *WJE* 9:307–436.

as New York and Pennsylvania). He was a protégé of Edwards, and represented to Edwards, as to millions ever since, 'a remarkable instance of true and eminent Christian piety': the ideal, outward-reaching, gospel-driven evangelical.[60] Brainerd died of tuberculosis at the age of 29, drawing his final breath from a bed in the Edwards parsonage. But he had kept a strikingly intimate spiritual diary for years. Edwards organized his *Life* around selections from the diary and, though Brainerd served for fewer than five years on the mission field, Edwards's *Life* transformed him into a Christian hero. His rather ordinary tombstone in Northampton's cemetery became a virtual Protestant shrine, attracting pilgrims far and wide. His name was hallowed through the halls of the early missions institutions. His legendary example of personal sacrifice for Christ—some have called it martyrdom—inspired multitudes to missionary service.[61]

Eighteenth-century Americans were not the first Protestants to enter the mission field. Europeans had dabbled in missions from the time of the Reformation: the British Puritans founded the first formal missions to Native Americans; Moravian Pietists proved the first global force in Protestant missions; and the English founded the early international sending agencies. But American evangelicals have commissioned the most missionaries. It took them a while to begin. But by the antebellum period, their ministries were burgeoning, thanks in large part to the legacy of Edwards.

Conclusion

By calling historians to recognize the theological advances made by evangelicals during the revival activity of the eighteenth century, Bebbington gives them a better picture of the immediate historical context. However, by placing that activism on 'Enlightenment foundations', he has overstated his case and severed the link with the past far too much. There is a sense in which Edwards is both a continuator and pioneer of evangelical history. Indeed, Edwards saw himself as one of many ministers fulfilling the sixth vial and therefore having a great mission to remove the difficulties and unravel the intricacies of doctrine. But he also understood that he was living out the great

---

60. Jonathan Edwards, *The Works of Jonathan Edwards*, vol. 7: *The Life of David Brainerd*, ed. Norman Pettit (New Haven: Yale University Press, 1985), p. 96.

61. Joseph Conforti, 'David Brainerd and the Nineteenth-Century Missionary Movement', *Journal of the Early Republic* 5 (autumn 1985), pp. 309–329.

programme of redemption and therefore was burdened with a great responsibility to continue the doctrines of the Reformation. Thus, he did not mind being called a Calvinist, as long as he was not seen as holding to everything Calvin taught in exactly the same way. While calling Edwards a man 'caught between two worlds' (Enlightenment and Reformed), Peter Thuesen notes that there is definitely a favoured position:

> In the end, though, what can be said about the relative proportions of 'polite' versus 'impolite' books in his working library? As we have seen, the 'Account Book' provides a rough index of works that mattered to Edwards and his acquaintances. Of the approximately seventy-seven strictly theological works mentioned in the document, two in seven are 'polite' (Anglican, latitudinarian, or Enlightenment) volumes, while the rest may be classified broadly as Nonconformist or Reformed.[62]

Edwards's understanding of the affections and the spiritual sense first and foremost are a part of his Reformed Protestant heritage, and in this way he is a continuator. From that trajectory, Edwards interacted with the Enlightenment. The criteria for judging experience are rooted in Edwards's own conversion and his understanding of a relationship with the divine through union in justification. The presence of the Spirit in the soul of the person brought about a vital principle of life, one that changed a person's perspective on the world to see the beauty of the Creator.

In his attempt to unravel the intricacies of doctrine, Edwards is in one sense also a pioneer. His work on the freedom of the will, while founded on Calvinism, offered unique solutions to the problem of calling sinners to repent and exerted the greatest force on evangelical theology. Edwards's doctrine became a practical tool for evangelists and missionaries. He provided a way for the gospel to be offered without compromising a Reformed understanding of depravity. And going beyond the theoretical, Edwards applied this conviction to his own missionary and publishing efforts, laying a foundation for an explosion of evangelical activity. From Edwards came the highly influential New England theology. As distinguished from the rest of the theology of New England, 'the New England Theology' was uniquely Edwardsean. A tradition of variations on certain key Edwardsean themes, it represented the

---

62. Peter J. Thuesen, 'Edwards' Intellectual Background', in Sang Hyun Lee (ed.), *The Princeton Companion to Jonathan Edwards* (Princeton: Princeton University Press, 2005), p. 26.

nation's first indigenous theological movement; and it represents one who longed for the 'church's latter-day glory'.[63]

Edwards is no mere mythological chimera, pulling together unrelated pieces of theology and philosophy into one strange animal. For Edwards, the question as to whether he was a continuator or a pioneer was an either–or that he would have found irrelevant. To be Reformed is to carry out God's plan of redemption and to perfect our understanding of doctrine; it is not to be a continuator or pioneer, but is the substantive union of both.

© Douglas A. Sweeney and Brandon G. Withrow, 2008

---

63. Scholarly literature on the New England Theology is vast and contentious. For a historiographical summary, see Douglas A. Sweeney, 'Edwards and His Mantle: The Historiography of the New England Theology', *New England Quarterly* 71 (Mar. 1998), pp. 97–119. Cf. The 'Select Bibliography', in Douglas A. Sweeney and Allen C. Guelzo (eds.), *The New England Theology: From Jonathan Edwards to Edwards Amasa Park* (Grand Rapids: Baker, 2006), pp. 279–317; *WJE* 5:426.

13. THE EVANGELICAL REVIVAL THROUGH THE EYES OF THE 'EVANGELICAL CENTURY': NINETEENTH-CENTURY PERCEPTIONS OF THE ORIGINS OF EVANGELICALISM

Ian J. Shaw

'The hundred years or so before the First World War', according to David Bebbington, 'deserve to be called the Evangelical Century'.[1] Therefore, a consideration of the nature and origins of evangelicalism viewed from the perspective of the century in which it was so firmly established, and from a period at such close proximity to the Evangelical Revival, must be of particular significance. It allows for an exploration of events through the eyes of the immediate heirs of the eighteenth century, some of whom were directly influenced by key players in the revival. Their testimony and thinking may get us much closer to an understanding of the mentality of the eighteenth century itself. This chapter seeks to explore whether David Bebbington's contention that the 'Evangelical version of Protestantism was created by the Enlightenment'[2] finds resonance in the writings of nineteenth-century English evangelical historians and biographers, both Anglican and Dissenting. Their work was highly significant in formulating and maintaining issues of evangelical self-identity and continuity. This is a field ripe for exploration, and could easily be extended by looking at

---

1. D. W. Bebbington, *Evangelicalism in Modern Britain: A History from the 1730s to the 1980s* (London: Unwin Hyman, 1989), p. 149.
2. Ibid., p. 74.

material from other parts of Britain, Europe or the United States, or by drawing on perspectives from those outside the evangelical tradition.

This chapter takes us into the very rich, but often highly subjective, fields of nineteenth-century autobiography, biography and early evangelical historical discourse. Much of the material is strongly coloured by denominational preferences and confessional perspectives; the writings reflect the multichrome nature of evangelicalism. In his discussion of the nineteenth century, David Bebbington continues his thesis beyond a consideration of influence of the Enlightenment, to argue that the popular Protestantism that was evangelicalism continued to be remoulded by contemporary cultural influences such as Romanticism, or modernism.[3] If a common historical hermeneutic arises in such a changing context, and from such a variety of materials, it should prove to be of positive significance. This would not be proof to the twenty-first-century historian that nineteenth-century interpreters were in fact right, but would be an indicator that their perspective should be considered in contemporary discussions.

The heirs of the Evangelical Revival

Among the immediate heirs of the eighteenth-century revival, Charles Simeon was highly significant. He became the leading spokesman of Anglican Evangelicals, and a mentor to many Evangelical ordinands at Cambridge from 1783 to 1836.[4] He was a strong admirer of the Anglican liturgy, placing the Prayer Book second only to the Bible.[5] When accused of Calvinism, Simeon argued that he preached only what was 'in harmony with the Articles, the Homilies, and the Liturgy of the Church of England'. In *The Excellency of the Liturgy*, a series of sermons preached in 1811 before the University of Cambridge, he was at pains to claim that the Church of England was a Reformation church: the Liturgy set out 'the views of our Reformers', whom Simeon believed were true interpreters of the inspired Bible. As an Evangelical,[6] therefore, Simeon saw himself as standing where the Reformers had done, and in continuity with

---

3. Ibid., pp. 74, 273.

4. Bebbington, *Evangelicalism in Modern Britain*, pp. 8, 31.

5. C. Smyth, *Simeon and Church Order* (Cambridge: Cambridge University Press, 1940), p. 291.

6. In this chapter 'Evangelical' is used to refer to 'evangelicals' within the Anglican tradition, and 'evangelical' for those in the Dissenting tradition, or when the word is being used generically.

their tradition.[7] He adopted a moderate Calvinist position, affirming in 1822 'though strongly Calvinistic in some respects, I am as strongly Arminian in others. I am free from all the trammels of human systems.'[8] Above the Reformers he looked to the Bible, preferring Scripture above system: 'the Scripture system, be it what it may, is of a broader and more comprehensive character than some very exact and dogmatical theologians are inclined to allow'.[9]

Another highly significant figure among Anglican Evangelicals was Thomas Scott, who held non-trinitarian views early in his ministry. In 'The Force of Truth', his account of his conversion to evangelicalism, he rejected suggestions that he had come to evangelical convictions through the influence of other evangelicals, but insisted it was through study of the Bible, and the Anglican articles, homilies and liturgy, together with 'authors of allowed reputation of the Church of England', citing among others Tillotson, Hooker and Joseph Hall. He believed that the closer the writers were towards the 'fountain of the blessed Reformation', the more power flowed from them. By the time he read from Dissenting and Methodist sources, his 'system' was nearly complete. He later came to the conviction that those dismissed as Methodists were in fact zealously preaching the doctrines of the first English Reformers, who laid the foundation of the church and 'gave their bodies to be burned in confirmation of their doctrine'.[10]

Evangelical Anglican historians

Thomas Haweis, the vicar of Aldwincle, chaplain to the Countess of Huntingdon and a child of the Evangelical Revival, in an early venture into evangelical

---

7. W. Carus, *Memoirs of the Life of the Rev. Charles Simeon* (London: J. Hatchard & Son, 1848[3]), pp. 210–219.

8. Letter to Rev. T. Thomason, 26 Apr. 1822, in ibid., p. 393. See also p. 429: 'Sometimes I am a high Calvinist, at other times a low Arminian, so that if extremes will please you, I am your man; only remember, it is not to one *extreme that we are to go to, but* both *extremes*.'

9. C. Simeon, *Horae homileticae: Expository Outlines on the Whole Bible*, vol. 1 (London: Holdsworth & Ball, 1832; repr. Grand Rapids: Zondervan, 1951), 'Preface', pp. xxiii–xxiv.

10. T. Scott, 'The Force of Truth: An Authentic Narrative', in J. Scott (ed.), *Works of the Late Rev. Thomas Scott* (1812[9]; repr. London: L. B. Seeley & Son, 1823), pp. 98–103. Scott's account is also summarized in Bebbington, *Evangelicalism in Modern Britain*, p. 30.

historiography, confessed the difficulty of writing of the eighteenth century with impartiality, and expressed his openness to 'receive rebuke and correction'. Far from believing that evangelicalism owed a debt to the Enlightenment, he presented a robust polemic against its effects.[11] Throughout Europe, 'the infidel philosophy had too generally diffused its fatal miasmata, and had affected the mass of literati'. Weishaupt and Kant had seen it as their 'object to exterminate the Christian name and worship', and had 'terrified mankind with the monsters bread from this hebridous race of philosophers and theosophists'. Rousseau was 'the arch-infidel'; Voltaire spread 'the poison of his scepticism'.[12] Enlightenment rationalism had a similarly devastating effect on Britain. For all its excellencies, the work of Hume and Gibbon contained 'the concentrated virus of infidelity, couched under the most able faculties, and most engaging style'. Thinkers from the age of reason

> summoned revelation to their unhallowed bar and condemned it. Insensibility to God, and carelessness about a judgement to come, no longer believed or feared, have opened the floodgates to ungodliness . . . the general departure from all religious principle is glaringly evident, in the universal neglect of all divine ordinances.[13]

The Evangelical Revival was, to Haweis, not an embracing of the influences of the age of the Enlightenment, but a return to the great truths and spiritual heights of the Reformation. The German Pietists had maintained the 'life of true religion' of the Reformation, and the Moravians had served to 'call their Lutheran brethren to the Augsburg confession, to the essential doctrines of revelation, and to a life of greater purity than was generally in vogue'.[14] George Whitefield is likened to the great German reformer: 'Perhaps no man since the days of St Paul, not even Luther himself, was ever personally blest to the call and conversion of so many souls from darkness to light.' Haweis particularly believed that the Evangelical Revival stood in continuity with the Reformed side of the Reformation: 'all our subscriptions are strongly Calvinistic . . . this is the true and natural sense of the church and its articles'. To this pattern Whitefield's theology conformed.[15]

---

11. J. Milner and T. Haweis, *A History of the Church of Christ, with a Continuation to the Present Time by Rev. T. Haweis* (Edinburgh: Peter Brown, 1837), p. 773.

12. Ibid., pp. 786–787, 814.

13. Ibid., p. 797.

14. Ibid., pp. 787–788.

15. Ibid., pp. 810, 797, 799.

In his *Memoir of the Rev. George Whitefield*, Samuel Drew similarly identified Whitefield with a 'revival of genuine religion', based particularly on the principles of the Reformation. Both his 'experimental' and 'practical' approaches were rooted in the sixteenth century, not in the Enlightenment or the eighteenth century. These historic roots were then built upon during the Evangelical Revival, and promised 'to introduce a new epoch in the morals of the human race'. This too Drew describes as a 'reformation'.[16]

The perspective of Simeon, Scott and Haweis was maintained by J. C. Ryle later in the nineteenth century. Particularly interested in evangelical self-identity, Ryle sought to defend the legitimacy of the Evangelical heritage within Anglicanism in the face of the continued strength of the Broad Church, and the advances of Anglo-Catholicism.[17] Ryle emphasizes the steep religious decline after the era of the Reformers and the Puritans: 'as for the weighty truths for which Hooper and Latimer had gone to the stake, and Baxter and scores of Puritans had gone to jail, they seemed clean forgotten and laid on the shelf'; the nation became morally and religiously 'barren of all that is really good . . . Christianity seemed to lie as one dead'.[18] The transformation brought by the eighteenth-century revival was, to Ryle, profound: 'Both in religion and morality the country gradually went through a complete revolution.' It was indeed a surprising work of God, 'without previous concert, scheme, or plan'.[19]

Despite seeing it as a new work of God, Ryle stresses the continuity between the Evangelical Revival and the sixteenth century: 'Who, in a word, were the instruments that God employed in bringing about the great English Reformation of the eighteenth century?' The methods of these evangelists, or 'spiritual reformers' were not new: their preaching 'revived the style of sermons in which Luther and Latimer used to be so eminently successful'. Stressing that their doctrine was classic Reformation teaching, Ryle introduces each point (notably the sufficiency of Scripture and justification by

---

16. S. Drew, *Memoir of the Rev. George Whitefield*, in G. Whitefield, *Sermons on Important Subjects* (London: William Tegg, 1854), pp. iii–v.

17. J. C. Ryle, 'Evangelical Religion', in his *Knots Untied: Being Plain Statements on Disputed Points in Religion from the Standpoint of an Evangelical Churchman* (London: William Hunt, 1874), p. 23.

18. J. C. Ryle, *The Christian Leaders of the Last Century* (London, 1868; repr. in shortened form as *Five Christian Leaders of the Eighteenth Century*, London: Banner of Truth, 1960), pp. 11–12.

19. Ibid., pp. 17–18.

faith alone) with the formula 'the reformers of the eighteenth century taught constantly'.[20]

Ryle believed that the doctrines of 'an Evangelical Churchman' were simply to be found 'in Holy Scripture, in the Thirty-nine Articles, in the Prayer-book fairly interpreted, in the works of the Reformers, or in the writings of the pre-Caroline divines'.[21] 'Evangelical' religion was the authentic, historic teaching of the Church of England:

> We appeal boldly to the Thirty-nine articles of our own Church, and assert
> unhesitatingly that they are on our side—We appeal boldly to the writings of our
> leading Divines, from the Reformation down to the time of Archbishop Laud, and
> invite any man to compare our teaching with theirs.[22]

He was particularly anxious to 'repudiate with scorn the vulgar charge of novelty'.[23] While recognizing the 'Evangelical Revival' as a distinctly eighteenth-century phenomenon, and avoiding discussion of the genesis of the term 'the Evangelical Party' ('When it began first to be called by this name, and why it was so called, are points into which it is not worth while now to inquire'),[24] during his consideration of key sources for evangelical teaching, Ryle gives decided emphasis to the Reformers, although he also draws the Puritans into this heritage: Ridley, Jewel, Usher, Davenant, Owen, Baxter, Manton and others are all named. Ryle adds, with a pointed question, 'To what school do they belong, I should like to know, if not to the Evangelical?' Only three names are added from the 'Egyptian darkness of last century'.[25] His rallying cry is that Evangelicals should not depart from the ' "faith once delivered to the saints," or from the worship handed down to us by the Reformers'.[26]

Ryle's view maintains a continuity of Anglican historical interpretation that the origins of evangelical thinking and practice lay in the Reformation, a line that reached from Simeon, Scott and Haweis, which continued into the early twentieth century, although he is more explicit about the debt to the Puritans

---

20. Ibid., pp. 17–20, 21–23. A very similar list is given in Ryle, 'Evangelical Religion',
    pp. 8–9.

21. Ryle, *Knots Untied*, preface, pp. vii–viii.

22. Ibid., pp. 22, 10.

23. Ibid., p. 10.

24. Ibid., p. 2.

25. Ibid., p. 11.

26. Ibid., p. 25.

than others. Even G. R. Balleine, writing in 1908, argued that, although the Evangelical party in the Church of England dated from the eighteenth century, they traced their pedigree to 'the Puritans, the Reformers, and the Lollards'. He believed that they did not invent any new theology, but 'simply taught the old doctrines of the Reformation', rooted in the Thirty-Nine Articles.[27]

English Dissenters

Among English Dissenters of the nineteenth century a more ambivalent attitude to the Evangelical Revival can be found. Alongside clear disapproval of some of the events of the Evangelical Revival, there was an acceptance that 'Old Dissent' had derived fresh vitality and strength from it, but also a firm conviction that this was in fact a revival of the power and spiritual reality of the Puritan era. Itinerancy had received a new boost, church planting moved forward, yet there was a concern that the enthusiasm of the revival had introduced elements that fell below the standards of historic Puritanism and Nonconformity.

In their *History of the Dissenters*, David Bogue and James Bennett acknowledged the achievement of the reformers in rescuing Britain from 'popery', but believed that about them there was 'remaining darkness', from which the Puritans were increasingly freed. Puritanism reached its high point in the Great Ejection of 1662: 'Ecclesiastical history furnishes no finer instance of a noble army of confessors at one time; it is an honour peculiar to the English Dissenters.'[28] Bogue and Bennett signified their approval of the eighteenth century where they discerned points of continuity with the Puritan era. Here, they believed, the true spirit of Old Dissent lay, although they discountenanced other aspects of the revival and New Dissent, particularly the excesses and emotionalism of some of its preachers. They believed that the theology of George Whitefield, 'a judicious scriptural Calvinist', was moulded by late Puritan and early Nonconformist thinking,[29] especially Matthew Henry's *Commentary*, a work shaped by the creed of 'the Westminster Assembly of Calvinistic divines'. To this Whitefield owed his 'serious evangelical train of thinking, and that simple popular mode of instruction from which he afterwards became so deservedly renowned'. This

---

27. G. R. Balleine, *A History of the Evangelical Party in the Church of England* (London: Longmans, 1908³; repr. London: Church Book Room, 1951), pp. 1, 106–107.

28. D. Bogue and J. Bennett, *History of the Dissenters from the Revolution in 1688 to the Year 1808*, 4 vols. (London: Williams & Smith, 1808–12), vol. 1, pp. 47, 99.

29. Ibid., vol. 3, pp. 77, 85–86.

Calvinism was reinforced by Whitefield's contact with the heirs of the Puritans in America.[30] However, Bogue and Bennett lamented that John Wesley did not benefit from this 'pure' Reformation heritage: if he had studied Matthew Henry rather than William Law 'how much benefit might he have derived to his own religion'.[31]

The undoubted direct benefits enjoyed by the Nonconformists in the aftermath of the Evangelical Revival could not be discounted by Bogue and Bennett: they acknowledged accessions to membership through a mixture of 'proselytes from the Established Church', as well as those who had not previously attended church.[32] However, they also emphasized the contribution of an increased number of evangelical Nonconformist preachers, inspired by the work of Philip Doddridge and others, who preached 'evangelical doctrines in a plain, spiritual, experimental, and affectionate way',[33] together with their 'diligent perusal of the writings of the nonconformists and Puritans'. David Bebbington has questioned the activism of Puritanism,[34] but such sentiment was not shared by Bogue and Bennett, who saw the Reformation and Puritan heritage as being more than simply theological: it was also practical and spiritual. Although 'most Calvinists in England' had adopted Whitefield's preaching style, this was in fact a return to the 'straightforward, pointed, address to consciences' of 'a Baxter, a Flavel, and their fellow labourers'. The influence of the Arminian John Wesley was firmly downplayed, being 'confined chiefly within the limits of his own sect'.[35]

Independent ministers of the early nineteenth century similarly sought to affirm that their evangelical heritage lay truly with the Reformers and Puritans. William Jay (1769–1853), who was to become a notable Independent minister at Bath, became a convert of eighteenth-century evangelicalism through attending a Methodist meeting as a teenager in the 1780s.[36] Although one of a

---

30. Ibid., pp. 17, 31.

31. Ibid., pp. 18, 77.

32. Ibid., p. 315.

33. Ibid., p. 323.

34. Bebbington, *Evangelicalism in Modern Britain*, pp. 40–42; and D. W. Bebbington, 'Revival and Enlightenment in Eighteenth-Century England', in E. Blumhofer and R. Balmer (eds.), *Modern Christian Revivals* (Urbana: University of Illinois Press, 1993), p. 22.

35. Bogue and Bennett, *History of the Dissenters*, vol. 4, pp. 312–313.

36. G. Redford and J. A. James (eds.), *Autobiography of William Jay* (London: Hamilton Adams, 1854; repr. Edinburgh: Banner of Truth, 1974), pp. 22–23.

group of eminent Independents who had been directly or indirectly influenced by the 'religious zeal which, had been kindled amongst the Methodists',[37] he rooted his theological understanding in the Puritan era. Reading the works of Puritans such as Baxter, Alleine, Flavel and Owen, 'the prince of divines', was foundational to his doctrinal convictions, and even for 'private and pious use' he 'never found anything comparable to Henry'.[38] Jay was of the opinion that it was with the Calvinistic scheme of divinity that his 'principles accorded generally more than any other', although certain parts of that scheme 'I could never admit'. The moderated Calvinism of John Newton held an attraction, but he particularly likened his views to those of John Bunyan in the sixteenth century.[39]

In the later nineteenth century, Dissenting historians continued to assert that evangelicalism was not a product of the eighteenth century. To John Stoughton it was 'Christianity as taught in the New Testament, plain, spiritual, practical—all gathering around the Life and Death of our blessed Lord.'[40] The theology of the revival leaders was that of the Reformers: Wesley's 'heart strangely warmed' experience was 'the same as that of Luther', a fact confirmed by its occurrence while Luther on Galatians was being read, which also linked Wesley to the apostle Paul. Stoughton found in Wesley 'much spiritual feeling of the Puritan cast', although he had reservations about Wesley's emphasis on 'certain phases of feeling'.[41] George Whitefield's work is compared to that of Bunyan, Baxter, the London Reformers and Luther at Wittenberg, together with preachers in the early church at Antioch and Constantinople. Although applauding Whitefield's zeal, Stoughton had

37. R. W. Dale, 'The Theology of John Wesley' (preached 4 Mar. 1891), in his *Fellowship with Christ and Other Discourses Delivered on Special Occasions* (London: Hodder & Stoughton, 1902), p. 225. Dale lists along with William Jay, Thomas Raffles, John Leifchild and his own one-time colleague John Angell James, who was taken to Methodist meetings on Sunday nights by his mother: 'there was a touch of Methodism in him to the very last' (ibid.).
38. Redford and James, *Autobiography of William Jay*, pp. 122–124.
39. Ibid., pp. 169–170. On the developing pattern of Newton's Calvinistic views, see D. B. Hindmarsh, *John Newton and the English Evangelical Tradition* (Oxford: Clarendon, 1996), pp. 156–168.
40. J. Stoughton, *History of Religion in England, from the Opening of the Long Parliament to the End of the Eighteenth Century*, vol. 6: *The Church in the Georgian Era* (London: Hodder & Stoughton, 1881), p. 441.
41. Ibid., pp. 117, 120–121.

reservations over his emotionalism, and believed his language 'violated rules of taste'.[42]

Stoughton certainly believed that Methodism helped change the religious temper of England during the eighteenth century, bringing a demise of 'Old-fashioned scholars, dryasdust antiquaries in parsonage and manse, cosy, respectable, ease-loving teachers'; evangelical religion had laid hold of Englishmen 'with a firmer grasp, and in a greater number of instances than ever', with the spirit of philanthropy more widely spread, and popular preaching, and new religious societies, following. However, this was not something new, but a 'revival of evangelical religion', and a reaction against the 'neglect of doctrines dear to Reformers and Puritans'.[43] The revival was therefore essentially a return to previous emphases; indeed, Doddridge was an early encourager of Whitefield, and an example that Nonconformity had not lost its evangelical vitality.[44] Evangelical Anglicans of the later eighteenth century, such as Venn, Romaine, Scott and Cecil, were, to Stoughton, 'disciples of the Puritans', their distinctive doctrines owing to 'Protestant works of the sixteenth and Nonconformist works of the seventeenth century', although he believed that they 'dangerously treated Christian experience'.[45]

The Baptist preacher C. H. Spurgeon was more than willing to rank the work of Whitefield and Wesley among God's 'mighty acts': through their work, 'England was permeated with evangelical truth'. Spurgeon believed that the story of God's mighty acts was written on a seamless, unfolding canvas, stretching from the exodus to Pentecost, through to the work of Chrysostom, Wycliffe, Luther and Calvin. The revival of the eighteenth century stood in continuity with what had gone before, as supremely a work of God:

> God has done his mightiest works by the meanest instruments: that is a fact most true of all God's works—Peter the fisherman at Pentecost, Luther the humble monk at the Reformation, Whitefield the potboy of the Old Bell Inn at Gloucester in the time of the last century's revival; and so it must be to the end.[46]

---

42. Ibid., pp. 124–128, 243.

43. Ibid., pp. 441, 443–446, 427.

44. Ibid., pp. 130–131.

45. Ibid., pp. 207, 217.

46. C. H. Spurgeon, 'The Story of God's Mighty Acts', preached at Surrey Gardens Music Hall, 17 July 1859, Sermon 263, in *New Park Street Pulpit*, vol. 5 (London: Alabaster, Passmore & Sons 1860; repr. London: Banner of Truth, 1964), p. 308.

Spurgeon believed his own theology was part of this unbroken lineage: 'what is commonly called Calvinism' was neither more nor less than the 'good old gospel of the Puritans', which was also the gospel of 'the Martyrs, and the Apostles of our Lord Jesus Christ'. At the inaugural services for the opening of the Metropolitan Tabernacle in 1861, Spurgeon stressed the longevity of his doctrinal heritage:

> 'Calvinism' did not spring from Calvin; we believe that it sprang from the founder of all truth. Perhaps Calvin himself derived it mainly from the writings of Augustine. Augustine obtained his views, without doubt, through the Spirit of God, from the diligent study of the writings of Paul; and Paul received them from the Holy Ghost, from Jesus Christ the great founder of the Christian dispensation.[47]

Indeed, Spurgeon rooted his 'evangelical' Calvinism not in the Evangelical Revival, but in the work of the Puritans and Reformers: 'Did not Bunyan plead with sinners? Charnock, Goodwin, Howe?' He mentions Edwards and Whitefield as worthy exemplars in the lineage of faithful gospel preachers: Augustine, Wycliffe, Hus, Luther, Calvin, Wishart, Bradford. His teaching was also that of the Reformers, particularly Calvin, although Luther's 'On the bondage of the will' was 'as strong a book upon the free grace of God as Calvin himself could have written'. Spurgeon does not see his Calvinism as being transformed by the Enlightenment; rather, it transcends it: 'It is a system which was practically acknowledged on high philosophic grounds by such men as Bacon, Leibnitz, and Newton, and yet it can charm the soul of a child and expand the intellect of a peasant.'[48]

Writing from a different theological perspective to Spurgeon, Luke Tyerman, in his 1876 biography of Whitefield, rooted the origins of the Methodist revival in the teachings of the Reformation. He believed that the doctrine which 'created the Methodism that now exists' was 'the doctrine of justification *by faith only*. This is one of the great doctrines of the Word of God. It was pre-eminently one of the doctrines of Luther and of the Reformation.'[49]

---

47. C. H. Spurgeon, *New Park Street Pulpit*, vol. 1 (London: Passmore & Alabaster, 1856; repr. London: Banner of Truth, 1963), preface, p. ii; 'Exposition of the Doctrines of Grace', at Inaugural Ceremonies for Metropolitan Tabernacle, London, Thursday 11 Apr. 1861, Sermon 385, in *Metropolitan Tabernacle Pulpit*, vol. 7 (London: Passmore & Alabaster, 1861; repr. Pasadena: Pilgrim, 1969), p. 298.

48. Ibid., pp. 302, 303.

49. L. Tyerman, *The Life of the Rev. George Whitefield, B. A., of Pembroke College, Oxford,*

Tyerman summarized Whitefield's theological convictions by quoting his 1739 sermon 'The Indwelling of the Spirit': 'Blessed be God! There are some left among us who dare maintain the doctrines of the Reformation, and preach the truth as it is in Jesus. But the generality of the clergy are fallen from our Articles, and do not speak agreeable to them.'[50] Tyerman argued that John Wesley concurred with this viewpoint, and quoted his 1770 sermon preached on the occasion of Whitefield's death, in which he summed up the theology of the first Methodists as the '*new birth*, and *justification* by faith'.[51] Wesley had preached this Reformation doctrine of justification by faith, 'salvation by faith', from the time of his conversion.[52] The sentiment was echoed in Henry Venn's 1770 sermon on the same occasion: 'Mr Whitefield's doctrine was the doctrine of the Reformers, of the Apostles, and of Christ.'[53]

Whitefield's spiritual debt to the Puritans is also noted by Tyerman. He quotes Whitefield's 1767 statement:

> For these thirty years past, I have remarked that the more true and vital religion has revived, either at home or abroad, the more the good old Puritanical writings, or the authors of a like stamp, who lived and died in the communion of the Church of England, have been called for.[54]

Tyerman was, however, unsympathetic towards Whitefield's Calvinism, questioning whether he 'ever fully understood the Calvinism which he preached'.

---

2 vols. (London: Hodder & Stoughton, 1876–7), vol. 1, p. 102.

50. G. Whitefield, *The Indwelling of the Spirit, the Common Privilege of all Believers* (London, 1739), quoted in Tyerman, *George Whitefield*, vol. 1, p. 242.

51. J. Wesley, *A Sermon on the Death of the Rev. Mr. George Whitefield. Preached at the Chapel in Tottenham Court Road, and at the Tabernacle near Moorfields, on Sunday, November 18, 1770* (London: G. Keith, 1770), quoted in Tyerman, *George Whitefield*, vol. 2, p. 615.

52. L. Tyerman, *The Life and Times of the Rev. John Wesley, M. A.* (London: Hodder & Stoughton, 1890⁶), p. 183.

53. H. Venn, *A Token of Respect to the Memory of the Rev. George Whitefield, A. M. Being the Substance of a Sermon Preached on his Death at the Right Hon. the Countess of Huntingdon's Chapel at Bath, the 18th of November 1770* (London, 1770), quoted in Tyerman, *George Whitefield*, vol. 2, p. 625.

54. G. Whitefield, *The Works of That Eminent Servant of Christ Mr John Bunyan* (London: W. Johnston & E. C. Dilly, 1767), preface, quoted in Tyerman, *George Whitefield*, vol. 2, p. 508.

He believed that much of it came from the 'Scottish Presbyterians and the Independents of America' whom Whitefield had encountered.[55]

A late nineteenth-century perspective on the origins of evangelicalism is found in the Birmingham Congregationalist R. W. Dale's sermon 'The Evangelical Revival'. He emphasized the achievement of the revival in rescuing England 'from the peril of atheism', believing it to be one of the 'brightest and most sacred periods of the history of Christendom'.[56] It came at a time when Dissent had lost the courage, earnestness and fervour of Puritanism: 'Latitudinarianism and religious indifference were spreading through the English Church and the Evangelical Nonconformists suffered from the infection.'[57] Yet Dale roots the 'great positive truths which were incessantly reiterated by the Evangelical leaders' in the teachings of St Paul, and the Reformers. The theology of the Evangelical Revival 'was substantially the theology of the Reformation. The Puritans of the seventeenth century and the Evangelicals of the eighteenth were the legitimate descendants of the Reformers.' Dale in fact questioned the merit of retaining traditional doctrinal views, believing that the work of the Reformers, informed by renaissance approaches, was of a 'provisional character'. In the nineteenth century, the 'intellectual revolution' was finally 'approaching its term', only to be 'gone through again'. Dale called the evangelicals of the late nineteenth century to the work of theological reconstruction, clearly believing that although the Evangelical Revival was significant, it had in fact added little new to the Reformation legacy.[58] Although the late eighteenth century had seen an easing of the 'severe and rigid lines of Calvinism', first observed in the work of Andrew Fuller and Edward Williams, Dale believed this was due to the 'influence of Methodism', particularly the Arminianism of Wesley who had 'asserted the moral freedom of man' and 'the universality of the atonement', rather than being a product of the Enlightenment. Yet this was no eighteenth-century creation, for Dale argued that English Arminianism and the Calvinism of the post-1662 Nonconformists were both rooted in the Puritan era, especially the reigns of James I and Charles I. The theological roots of both Whitefield and Wesley lay in the Reformation and Puritan periods.[59]

---

55. Tyerman, *George Whitefield*, vol. 1, pp. 274, 102.

56. R. W. Dale, *The Evangelical Revival and other Sermons* (London: Hodder & Stoughton, 1880), pp. 2, 40.

57. Ibid., pp. 12–13.

58. Ibid., pp. 6–8, 18, 20, 23–24.

59. Ibid., pp. 20–21.

Dale shared Bogue and Bennett's suspicion of the excesses and emotionalism of the preachers of New Dissent, many of whom were untrained: 'the zeal of many of them was out of all proportion to their knowledge'. He notes how Whitefield's 'passion and his tears, his vehemence, his popular eloquence, his audacity' had shocked some Nonconformists at the time. While Dale acknowledges that the fresh vitality of the 'Evangelical Nonconformists' owed much to the Evangelical Revival, he still affirmed that this surge of eighteenth-century life was building on foundations that long predated this: 'We existed and were strong before the movement began, and among us the movement assumed a form which was partly determined by our previous history.' However, the Evangelical Revival was to be credited with decisively carrying forward the moral reformation that Protestantism had only begun.[60]

In 1891, Dale was invited to preach at services in City Road Chapel, London, in connection with the centenary of Wesley's death. He stressed how Wesley's upbringing blended the 'external institutions and aids of the religious life' of the 'great Anglicans' with 'the traditions of Puritanism'. He also rooted Wesley's teaching of justification by faith, and the 'complete certainty' that a Christian was 'no longer a "child of wrath," but a child of God', in the Reformation. Wesley was 'of one mind with Luther'; indeed, in him this 'great evangelical truth . . . which had been for many years well-nigh lost and forgotten' was recovered. Wesley was therefore completing the unfinished work of Luther.[61]

The perspective of English high Calvinists

A different source for nineteenth-century perceptions of the Evangelical Revival can be found among the small, but notable, group of nineteenth-century English high Calvinists. Drawing on the work of Calvin, and English Puritans such as John Eaton and Tobias Crisp, high Calvinism stressed free grace to the elect, a focus upon eternal justification, with some espousing a form of doctrinal antinomianism. It was furthered by the publication of Joseph Hussey's *God's Operations of His Grace but No Offers of His Grace* in 1707.[62] The Baptist

---

60. Ibid., pp. 13–14, 17.

61. R. W. Dale, 'The Theology of John Wesley', in Dale, *Fellowship with Christ*, pp. 219, 238–239.

62. For a discussion of the native English roots of high Calvinism, see Peter Toon, *The Emergence of Hyper-Calvinism in English Nonconformity, 1689–1765* (London: Olive Tree, 1967).

John Gill (1697–1771) did much to develop the native English tradition of high Calvinism in the eighteenth century,[63] which became widespread in Particular Baptist circles. High Calvinism was a theological subculture developed by individuals who, on the whole, stood formally apart from the Evangelical Revival.

However, in the late eighteenth and early nineteenth century, a number of high Calvinists do appear to have come under the influence of the Evangelical Revival. The strong experimentalism of William Huntington (1745–1813), with his emphasis on felt assurance and extensive itinerancy, is one such example.[64] Although he confessed that the first time he had heard the 'Bible alone' preached was by the Methodist Torial Joss, Huntington argued that his high Calvinism sprang from his own experience and reading of the Bible, together with his study of the Thirty-nine Articles, especially the tenth and seventeenth.[65] High Calvinists remained convinced that their views were ultimately derived from their own experience and understanding of Scripture. The Strict Baptist John Warburton clearly knew the work of Gill, Doddridge, Goodwin and Hawker, but when preparing to preach looked to the Bible alone for help: 'I cannot carry another man's line of things into the pulpit.'[66]

If they were pressed to identify a historical root for their views, high Calvinists steadfastly looked to the Reformers and the Puritans. Robert Hawker (1753–1827), the Anglican high Calvinist, had a conversion experience influenced by both John Wesley and William Romaine. Although he was involved in the early pan-evangelical movement, including the London Missionary Society and the Religious Tract Society, he asserted his high Calvinism was founded on the Articles of the Church of England dating from the Reformation.[67] To the Strict Baptist James Wells, the five points of Calvinism were the 'order of

63. On Gill, see R. W. Oliver, 'John Gill (1697–1771)', in M. A. G. Haykin (ed.), *The British Particular Baptists*, 2 vols. (Springfield, Mo.: Particular Baptist, 1998–2000), vol. 1, pp. 145–165; M. A. G. Haykin (ed.), *The Life and Thought of John Gill (1697–1771): A Tercentennial Appreciation* (Leiden: E. J. Brill, 1997).

64. On early nineteenth-century high Calvinists, see I. J. Shaw, *High Calvinists in Action: Calvinism and the City, Manchester and London, c. 1810–60* (Oxford: Oxford University Press, 2002).

65. T. Wright, *Life of William Huntington, S. S.* (London: Farncombe & Son, 1909), p. 24.

66. Quoted in J. R. Broome, *John Warburton: Servant of a Covenant God* (Harpenden: Gospel Standard Trust, 1996), pp. 116–117.

67. J. Williams, *Memoir of the Life and Writings of the Rev. Robert Hawker, D. D.* (London, 1831), pp. 24, 126.

truth, the line of life, the line of eternal mercy'.[68] His associates claimed that his Calvinism was 'in fact no different from that of Calvin, or the English Puritans John Owen and Thomas Goodwin'.[69] Yet Wells did not draw an exact correspondence between his views and those of Calvin: 'He was a good man, and so were a good many others who had a good deal of error about them.' He spoke instead of the deep historic roots of his thinking: 'that truth existed before Calvin was ever thought of . . . we do not subject the Bible to him, but we subject him to the Bible'.[70]

The influence of the Evangelical Revival on some dimensions of nineteenth-century high Calvinism seems clear, such as extensive itinerancy and strong experimentalism, but any overt acknowledgment of theological or spiritual dependence was firmly rejected. Andrew Fuller's *The Gospel Worthy of All Acceptation* has been called by David Bebbington 'the classic statement of eighteenth-century evangelical Calvinism'.[71] The Manchester Strict Baptist William Gadsby had no time for this, believing that Fuller's Arminianizing of Calvinism made him the 'greatest enemy the church of God ever had, as his sentiments were so much cloaked with the sheep's clothing'.[72]

Conclusion

David Bebbington has argued that 'the Evangelical Revival represents a sharp discontinuity in the Protestant tradition'.[73] However, the nineteenth-century sources surveyed in this chapter do not appear to be aware of such a sharp discontinuity, and rather understood events as a renewal, or restoration, of what had gone before in the Reformation and Puritan eras. Nor is there evidence of a consciousness that evangelicalism was 'created by the Enlightenment'.

68. J. Wells, 'The Three Birthrights', in *Surrey Tabernacle Pulpit*, vol. 6, sermon 276 (London: G. J. Stevenson, 1864), p. 110.

69. T. Jones and W. Crowther, *Services in Connection with the Decease and Funeral of the late Mr James Wells* (London: G. J. Stevenson, 1872), p. 18.

70. J. Wells, 'A Good Hope', in *Surrey Tabernacle Pulpit*, vol. 2, sermon 69 (London: Robert Banks, 1860), pp. 75–76; and J. Wells, 'Trouble Ended', *Surrey Tabernacle Pulpit*, vol. 10, sermon 488 (London: G. J. Stevenson, 1868), p. 87.

71. Bebbington, *Evangelicalism in Modern Britain*, pp. 64–65.

72. J. Gadsby, *Memoir of the Late Mr William Gadsby* (London: J. Gadsby, 1847²), p. 27.

73. Bebbington, *Evangelicalism in Modern Britain*, p. 74.

In some ways, this evidence is unsurprising because, as Brian Stanley has pertinently observed, the majority of nineteenth-century evangelicals would have been 'totally mystified' by discussion of the influence of the Enlightenment upon evangelicalism. The English rendering of the German term Aufklärung as 'Enlightenment' did not appear until 1865, and the phrase 'the Age of Enlightenment' was first used only in 1889.[74] Thomas Haweis's association of the period with the religious scepticism and extreme rationalism of Voltaire or Rousseau is not untypical. He and others believed that Enlightenment thinking stood in sharp discontinuity with earlier religious progress. Stanley notes how 'the Enlightenment' has been used as an interpretative device to explain mutually contradictory trends, and rightly warns of the danger of applying a term that now encompasses 'a far broader and more diverse spectrum of intellectual and cultural trends' to a period in history that understood that term as having a far more precise, and negative, meaning.[75] Indeed, Richard Bernstein has questioned the value of using the term 'Enlightenment': 'There is no single platform, no set of substantive claims, no common essence that thinkers of the age of Enlightenment share.'[76] Suffice it to say, in the nineteenth century we are dealing with people who were largely unfamiliar with the term 'Enlightenment', and it should not come as a surprise if we search in vain for it in their writings.

Among nineteenth-century evangelicals we find individuals who were acutely conscious of their self-identity, and who sought to explain their historical roots. As they did this they looked to the Reformation and Puritan eras. This was a risky business, for in the eyes of many it was identifying with the enthusiasm and fanaticism of the Civil War, and the Commonwealth period with its regicide, upheaval in the Established Church and tendencies towards doctrinal antinomianism.[77] The historic links between Puritanism

---

74. B. Stanley, 'Christian Missions and the Enlightenment: A Re-evaluation', in B. Stanley (ed.), *Christian Missions and the Enlightenment* (Grand Rapids: 2001), p. 6, citing O. Chadwick, *The Secularization of the European Mind in the Nineteenth Century* (Cambridge: Cambridge University Press, 1975), p. 151.

75. Stanley, 'Christian Missions and the Enlightenment,' p. 7.

76. R. Bernstein, 'Are we beyond the Enlightenment Horizon?', in W. M. Shea and P. A. Huff (eds.), *Knowledge and Belief in America: Enlightenment Traditions and Modern Religious Thought* (Cambridge: Cambridge University Press, 1995), p. 338, quoted in Stanley, 'Christian Missions and the Enlightenment', p. 7.

77. J. Walsh, 'The Yorkshire Evangelicals in the Eighteenth Century with Especial Reference to the Methodists' (PhD thesis, University of Cambridge, 1956), pp. 11ff.

and Nonconformity render such claims by the Dissenters understandable, but it would be an unlikely association for Establishment men like Ryle to make if they were not convinced it was true. And convinced they apparently were, although Anglicans tended to appeal beyond the Puritans to the Anglican Reformers, and to claim that Anglicanism was in fact Calvinist by origination and in its formularies.

How, then, is this interpretation of nineteenth-century writers that their evangelical roots lay in the sixteenth and seventeenth centuries, rather than in the eighteenth, to be explained? It may be that they were simply mistaken in their historical understanding. John Walsh has questioned the narrative, likening the decline of Puritanism to the retreat of a great wave, which as it receded left 'innumerable rock pools of piety' behind it, often leaderless Nonconformist groupings that clung to the Reformation faith when their pastors slid into Arianism, or Huguenot immigrants who had escaped persecution in Europe. Many were left with a knowledge of the need for regeneration that Puritanism had taught them, but without the preaching or understanding by which to experience it.[78] When revival came, it was not in fact to the Calvinist Dissenters who had longed for it, and had preserved the Puritan 'doctrines of grace', but to 'an Arminian Church of England in which the old Puritan Calvinism was virtually extinct', and that had 'reneged spectacularly on much of the Reformed theology of its Thirty-nine Articles'. Indeed, it took decades for the Dissenters to profit fully from the evangelical movement. Yet, part of the success of the revival lay not only in its ability to attract converts, but also its capacity to draw to itself those who were maintaining the traditions of the Reformers and the Puritans, some of whom were meeting with the Dissenters, others in praying societies. As John Newton observed, the preaching of the gospel drew out and attracted God's already faithful people, as 'a standard erected, to which they may repair, and thereby become known to each other'.[79]

John Walsh observed a similar appeal to Calvin and the Reformation among eighteenth-century Evangelical Anglicans. He argued that this owed

---

78. J. Walsh, 'Methodism and the Origins of English-Speaking Evangelicalism', in M. A. Noll, D. W. Bebbington and G. A. Rawlyk (eds.), *Evangelicalism: Comparative Studies of Popular Protestantism in North America, the British Isles, and Beyond 1700–1990* (Oxford: Oxford University Press, 1994), pp. 29–30.

79. Walsh, 'Methodism and the Origins', p. 22; and J. Newton, *The Works of Rev. John Newton* (London, 1816²), vol. 4, p. 313, quoted in Walsh, 'Methodism and the Origins', p. 29.

less to conscious study of the tradition of Calvin, and more to their experience of sin and spiritual need, and a consequent quest for assurance, which
they chose to understand in terms of Calvinistic and Reformation doctrine.[80]
He also believed that their sense of identity with the Puritans was only moderate, and included a firm rejection of its excesses. Disliking systems, they
preferred to attribute their views to the Articles and homilies of the church,
to Augustine, and supremely to the Bible. Calvin's teaching on reprobation
and his supralapsarian scheme were disavowed as going beyond the English
Reformers.[81] Walsh therefore discerns a distinctive historical hermeneutic
among eighteenth-century Anglican Evangelicals, who should not be seen
as simply a Methodist offshoot, and should be treated separately from the
Arminian Methodists and the Calvinists associated with George Whitefield
and the Countess of Huntington.[82]

It has been seen that, on the whole, nineteenth-century evangelical historians did separate out the Wesleyan Arminian tradition, but possibly conflated
the Whitefield tradition with that of the Anglican Evangelicals, and so over-
stressed the sense of continuity with the Calvinistic Reformers and the Puritans.
Nonetheless, this cannot entirely explain the common historical understanding of a Reformation origination for evangelicalism shared by writers from
Simeon or Thomas Scott to Ryle, Tyerman or the Dissenting historians.

J. C. Ryle was well aware of the charges being raised against the Puritans,
but was unrepentant in his claims. While accepting that they were not fault-
less, he argued that

> The man who tells the world that there is any disgrace in being 'a Puritan' is only
> exposing his own ignorance of plain facts, or shamefully presuming on that wide-
> spread ignorance of English Church history which marks the nineteenth century.[83]

He argued that the Puritans were not enemies of the monarchy, or the Church
of England, nor were they unlearned or ignorant men. Ryle applauds their
bold Protestantism, and their 'clear, sharply-cut, distinct *Evangelicalism*'. The
Reformers were the 'genuine prototypes and predecessors' of the '*Evangelical
School*'; the distinctive views of Evangelical Churchmen were 'neither more nor

---

80. Walsh, 'Yorkshire Evangelicals', p. 50.

81. Ibid., p. 27.

82. Ibid., p. 56.

83. J. C. Ryle, *Light from Old Times* [1890] (London: Charles J. Thynne & Jarvis, 1924⁵),
    p. xv.

less than the views of the Reformers'—to condemn them was to condemn those who 'reformed the Church of England'. Evangelicals are rightly to be called 'Successors of the Reformers'; their supreme achievement was 'the Thirty-nine Articles, to which all clergy are required to solemnly give their assent'.[84]

Another reason directing the nineteenth-century narrative of evangelical origins towards the Calvinistic side of the Reformation and the Puritan era was the suspicion of some authors towards Arminian Methodism, with its emphasis on emotions, and its distinctive teaching of Christian perfection and holiness that was becoming resurgent after the middle of the nineteenth century, a particular concern to Ryle. Anglican and Dissenting evangelicals were suspicious of Wesley's Arminianism, and his looking to the early church, and were more comfortable with the Reformation and Puritan tradition.[85] Dissenting historians attributed only modest positive benefits to Wesley's side of the Evangelical Revival. Yet, the Arminian–Calvinist divide cannot be pushed too far. Luke Tyerman, writing from the Methodist camp, is quite clear that the teaching of the Evangelical Revival leaders, whether from Wesley or Whitefield, sprang from the Reformation.

The influence of the growing fear of Catholicism, whether in Anglican or Roman forms, on the production of consciously Protestant narratives in the nineteenth century should not be ignored; certainly this was the case with J. C. Ryle. The strength of anti-Catholicism as a feature of nineteenth-century Protestant evangelical identity has been shown by John Wolffe, who found the four defining characteristics of evangelicalism (conversionism, activism, biblicism and crucientrism) replicated in nineteenth-century evangelical anti-Catholic activity.[86] Allowance should also be made for David Bebbington's observation of the disillusionment with evangelicalism itself among some evangelicals in the early decades of the nineteenth century, together with a growing yearning 'after the primitive convictions of the divines'.[87] A number who were unable to reconcile the principles of the Church of England with their desire for a purer form of Calvinism were to leave the Establishment in the years after the 'Western Schism' of 1815, when a number of West Country

---

84. Ibid., pp. xvii, xviii, xxi–xxii, xxvi.

85. K. Hylson-Smith, *Evangelicals in the Church of England, 1734–1984* (Edinburgh: T. & T. Clark, 1988), p. 12.

86. J. Wolffe, 'Anti-Catholicism and Evangelical Identity', in Noll, Bebbington and Rawlyk, *Evangelicalism*, pp. 179–184. See also J. Wolffe, *The Protestant Crusade in Great Britain 1829–60* (Oxford: Clarendon, 1991).

87. Bebbington, *Evangelicalism in Modern Britain*, p. 78.

clergymen seceded.[88]

David Bebbington has ensured that evangelicalism can no longer be dismissed as an anti-intellectual or irrational response to the Enlightenment. Nineteenth-century evangelicals would have concurred with his views. His exploration of the further development of Reformation and Puritan thinking in the eighteenth century cannot be discounted. The direct impact of the Evangelical Revival on many of the authors discussed must also be recognized, for a number owed their conversion directly to it. Even those who adhered to high Calvinism could not entirely escape its influence.

This confluence of Puritan and eighteenth-century contexts is seen in the upbringing and early ministry of Andrew Reed, Independent minister in Stepney, London, from 1811 to 1861. He was to become a strong evangelical Calvinist who knew great success in his preaching and philanthropic work. Presented by his mother with a copy of the Westminster Shorter Catechism at the age of seven, his was a Nonconformist home steeped in the thinking of the Reformers and Puritans.[89] His parents owned a small library of volumes from the Puritan era, including authors such as Howe, Manton, Baxter, Poole and Boston. *Pilgrim's Progress* featured heavily in his early reading.[90]

Coming under conviction of sin and judgment as a teenager, it was the Puritan Joseph Alleine's *Alarm to Unconverted Sinners* that brought Reed spiritual relief. He was early inclined towards high Calvinism,[91] but contact with Matthew Wilks, one of Whitefield's successors at the Moorfields Tabernacle, London, and studies at Hackney College, helped soften his views into evangelical Calvinism. A defining moment was reading a biography of George Whitefield.[92] Both Puritan and eighteenth-century influences on Reed are clear, but he would not have seen as something new his eventual emphasis on the 'rich and spontaneous grace of God', and his balance between limited atonement and a sense of imperative duty that 'we should

---

88. On the 'Western Schism', see G. Carter, *Anglican Evangelicals: Protestant Secessions from the Via Media, c. 1800–50* (Oxford: Oxford University Press, 2001), pp. 105–151.

89. I. J. Shaw, *The Greatest Is Charity: Andrew Reed (1787–1862), Preacher and Philanthropist* (Darlington: Evangelical Press, 2005), p. 23.

90. A. Reed and C. Reed, *Memoirs of the Life and Philanthropic Labours of Andrew Reed, D. D., with Selections from his Journals* (London: Strahan, 1863), pp. 18, 21.

91. Ibid., pp. 14–15.

92. Ibid., p. 22.

proclaim the will of God to all men'. It was rather a return to the proper sense of Calvin's system.[93]

The views of nineteenth-century evangelicals were not expressed uniformly. The sense of continuity with the Puritan era is stronger with the Dissenting historians, but is not absent from the Anglicans, and both emphasize the Reformation continuity. The shaping influence of individual churchmanship and confessional stances upon their interpretations cannot be ignored. Yet the weaknesses of nineteenth-century evangelical historiographers, or wider contextual factors, are unable to explain entirely the inability of this wide range of writers to recount their story without tracing evangelicalism's historic roots to the Reformation and the Puritan rediscovery of a biblical gospel, and ultimately to the pages of the New Testament. They believed that something new, a 'mighty act of God' had occurred in the eighteenth century, and many acknowledged that to this they owed a great debt, but they persisted in speaking of it in terms of continuity with what had gone before, rather than discontinuity.

From high Calvinist to Arminian, Anglican to Dissenter, they believed it was a time of renewal, and re-emphasis, but not of origination. David Bebbington does acknowledge elements of continuity between the Reformation and Puritan era, and the eighteenth century revival, but when it comes to proving what he admits is 'so inherently a likely hypothesis' as a direct thread linking the Reformed tradition with the Evangelical, he finds 'scant evidence'.[94] Writers in the 'Evangelical Century' came to different conclusions, and believed that eighteenth-century evangelicals had known such success because they stood on the doctrinal and spiritual shoulders of Reforming and Puritan giants.

© Ian J. Shaw, 2008

---

93. A. Reed, *The Revival of Religion: A Narrative of the State of Religion at Wycliffe Chapel during the Year 1839* (London: Thomas Ward, 1840[6]), pp. 21–22.

94. Bebbington, *Evangelicalism in Modern Britain*, pp. 34–36. See also M. A. Noll, *The Rise of Evangelicalism: The Age of Edwards, Whitefield and the Wesleys* (Leicester: IVP, 2004), pp. 48–54, for a more positive assessment of the continuity between Puritanism and the Evangelical Awakening.

PART 4: EVANGELICAL DOCTRINES

14. THE ANTECEDENTS OF EVANGELICAL CONVERSION NARRATIVE: SPIRITUAL AUTOBIOGRAPHY AND THE CHRISTIAN TRADITION*

D. Bruce Hindmarsh

David Bebbington argues that evangelical religion in Britain originated as a popular non-denominational movement among Protestants in the 1730s, and acknowledges that there was some continuity with earlier Protestant traditions, but says, nevertheless, 'Evangelicalism was a new phenomenon of the eighteenth century.'[1] Bebbington expounds the distinctive and defining characteristics of this movement, characteristics he argues that have persisted throughout the history of the movement even while evangelicals adapted to cultural change in other ways. Bebbington's thesis is thus concerned to interpret evangelical religion within a framework of 'Christianity and culture'

---

1. David W. Bebbington, *Evangelicalism in Modern Britain: A History from the 1730s to the 1980s* (London: Unwin Hyman, 1989), p. 1.

*This chapter is a revised and edited version of my article "The Antecedents of Evangelical Conversion Narrative: Spiritual Autobiography and the Christian Tradition', *Crux* 38 (2002), pp. 4–13. I also survey the history of conversion in the introduction and first chapter of my *The Evangelical Conversion Narrative: Spiritual Autobiography in Early Modern England* (Oxford: Oxford University Press, 2005), pp. 16–60.

and his argument is structured in terms of continuities and discontinuities in history.[2]

In order to demonstrate that modern evangelicalism appeared as a *new* phenomenon in the eighteenth century, Bebbington needs to establish certain features of the movement as distinctive, and the hallmarks he settles upon are the characteristically evangelical preoccupations with conversion, the cross, the Bible and activism. He acknowledges, however, that three of these characteristics were not particularly *new*: 'Three characteristic marks of Evangelicalism, conversionism, biblicism and crucicentrism, had been as much a part of Puritanism as they were of Methodism.'[3] What was therefore the most 'distinguishing mark' (to borrow a phrase from the period) of modern evangelicalism was its new dynamism or expansive energy for mission and service: its *activism*. Much as R. T. Kendall sees changes in the doctrine of assurance in the seventeenth century as the crux that distinguished the later Calvinists, such as the Westminster Divines, from Calvin, so also Bebbington sees changes in the experience of assurance a century later as the one thing, above all others, that sets evangelicalism apart from its Puritan and Reformed antecedents.[4] A more robust assurance among evangelicals was the source of the tremendous energy they expended in mission.

Other chapters in this volume explore Bebbington's thesis about assurance, probing the continuities and discontinuities of evangelical experience in the modern period with earlier traditions, as well as the variety and range of

---

2. Bebbington summarizes his particular view of evangelicalism and culture, ibid., pp. 271–276; see also David W. Bebbington, 'Gospel and Culture in Victorian Nonconformity', in Jane Shaw and Alan Kreider (eds.), *Culture and the Nonconformist Tradition* (Cardiff: University of Wales, 1999), p. 43, for a more general discussion of the Christianity-and-culture paradigm.

3. Bebbington, *Evangelicalism in Modern Britain*, p. 35.

4. Ibid., pp. 42–45 (and notes) on the contrast between the Westminister divines and the early evangelicals; cf. R. T. Kendall, *Calvin and English Calvinism to 1649* (Oxford: Oxford University Press, 1979), pp. 200, 203–205, on the contrast between the Westminister divines and Calvin. Joel R. Beeke, *Assurance of Faith: Calvin, English Puritanism, and the Dutch Second Reformation* (New York: Peter Lang, 1991), pp. 366–371, takes issue with Kendall and argues for greater continuity between Calvin and the later Calvinists on the doctrine of assurance. David Bebbington also contrasts seventeenth- and eighteenth-century understandings of assurance in his 'Evangelical Conversion, c. 1740–1850', *Scottish Bulletin of Evangelical Theology* 18 (2000), pp. 122–124.

experiences of assurance within modern evangelicalism itself. In this chapter I would like to focus narrowly on conversionism as a distinctive evangelical characteristic. By offering a short history of conversion narrative and spiritual autobiography, I hope to show that evangelical conversion did in fact emerge in history as a new, distinctive and identity-giving mark of Christian experience in the modern period, but that it did so about a century *before* the revivals of the 1730s and 40s, which are often taken to mark the beginning of 'modern evangelicalism'. By stressing the novelty of evangelical conversion as it appears in the seventeenth century, as compared with the preceding eras, I hope the extent to which the Puritan and early evangelical experience of conversion ought to be understood in the early modern period as a story of relative continuity will become clear. Another way to put this is to say that evangelical conversion ought not to be overperiodized as beginning with the Evangelical Revival.

David Bebbington and I have both used the Methodist Sampson Staniforth as a classic example of evangelical conversion. Staniforth was a 25-year-old soldier in the English army who was converted in about 1743. He described the experience in an autobiography written for the *Arminian Magazine*:

> From twelve at night until two it was my turn to stand sentinel at a dangerous post.
> . . . As soon as I was alone, I kneeled down, and determined not to rise, but to
> continue crying and wrestling with God, till He had mercy on me. How long I was
> in that agony I cannot tell; but as I looked up to heaven I saw the clouds open
> exceeding bright, and I saw Jesus hanging on the cross. At the same moment these
> words were applied to my heart, 'thy sins are forgiven thee.' My chains fell off; my
> heart was free. All guilt was gone, and my soul was filled with unutterable peace.[5]

My question in this chapter concerns the prehistory of this kind of evangelical conversion narrative. Just how far back can we trace the pattern? Some would claim a long pedigree for evangelical conversion. Matthew Arnold held that the conversion of Sampson Staniforth was of 'precisely the same order' as the conversion of St Paul.[6] William James linked the Nova Scotian evangelical Henry Alline with Augustine, describing them both as similar cases of sin-sick souls who were 'twice-born'.[7] For some evangelicals

---

5. John Telford (ed.), *Wesley's Veterans*, 7 vols. (London: Robert Culley, 1912), vol. 1, pp. 74–75.

6. Matthew Arnold, *St. Paul and Protestantism* (London: Smith, Elder, 1870), p. 36.

7. William James, *The Varieties of Religious Experience* (London: Longman, Green, 1929), pp. 166–175.

the apostle Paul, Augustine, Luther and Wesley have likewise been understood together in a tradition of crisis conversion across the ages.[8] Yet for all the similarities, the Damascus road encounter, the child's voice in the garden at Milan, the tower experience at Wittenberg and the strangely warmed heart at Aldersgate Street took place in very different religious and cultural contexts.

A few examples from modern scholarship illustrate this by establishing the different historical horizons within which climactic conversion has appeared and been understood. In a landmark essay in 1961 Krister Stendahl critiqued the view that St Paul's conversion was identical with the evangelical pattern of conversion in which relief for a plagued conscience is found through the message of justification by faith. Stendahl argued that the plagued conscience is the product of centuries of penitential discipline in the West and should not be read back into the apostle's experience on the Damascus road, an experience better understood in its context as something like the calling of a Hebrew prophet through a vision at noonday prayer.[9] Since Stendahl, several competing interpretations of the apostle's Damascus road experience have appeared. Larry Hurtado concludes a review of these studies by stating that 'the research of the last few decades has demonstrated the tendentious and misleading nature of more traditional portraits of Paul's Damascus road experience as a cathartic resolution of a guilty soul or the renunciation of Jewish "legalism" '.[10]

Likewise, the conversion of Augustine and Luther ought not to be accommodated too hastily to modern viewpoints. Henry Chadwick argues that the form of Augustine's narrative in the *Confessions* is indebted to the Neoplatonic

8. On evangelical traditions of conversion, see e.g. Hy. Pickering, *Twice-Born Men* (London: Pickering & Inglis, n. d.). Erik Routley refers to Paul, Augustine and Wesley as 'classic conversions' in his *Conversion* (Philadelphia: Muhlenberg, 1960), pp. 19–23. On readings of John Wesley's conversion, see Randy L. Maddox, 'Aldersgate: A Tradition History', in Randy L. Maddox (ed.), *Aldersgate Reconsidered* (Nashville: Abingdon, 1990), pp. 133–146.

9. Krister Stendahl, 'The Apostle Paul and the Introspective Conscience of the West', in Krister Stendahl (ed.), *Paul among the Jews and Gentiles and Other Essays* (London: SCM, 1976), pp. 78–96.

10. Larry W. Hurtado, 'Convert, Apostate or Apostle to the Nations: The "Conversion" of Paul in Recent Scholarship', *Studies in Religion* 22.3 (1993), pp. 283–284; cf. Richard N. Longenecker (ed.), *The Road from Damascus* (Grand Rapids: Eerdmans, 1997).

pattern of the ascent of the soul. Augustine's quest was to achieve union with the God from whom all beauty, truth and goodness derives, and his crisis of conversion was a crisis of the philosopher who could see the nature of the good life in ascetic self-denial and contemplation, but who had not the moral power to achieve it.[11] Marilyn Harran contends that Luther's conversion, too, must not be telescoped into a climactic either/or experience in the tower but should be interpreted as the culminating insight of a biblical scholar wrestling with close exegesis of Scripture.[12]

It is safe to say that however much evangelicals owed to the theology of Paul, Augustine and Luther, not many of the evangelical conversions in the eighteenth century or since owed much to Palestinian Judaism or Plotinus, nor have they come as a result of a fine syntactical decision about a genitive in Romans. To understand climactic religious experiences and spiritual narratives in the course of Christian history, we must pay close attention to the immediate milieu and larger cultural context of the convert.

It is my aim, then, to trace some of the antecedents to the evangelical conversion narrative in the spiritual autobiography of the premodern church. Despite my use of the adjective 'evangelical' to characterize this form of conversion narrative, and the example I have given from Sampson Staniforth, the roots of the genre were not in the evangelical revivals of the eighteenth century but in the movements of experiential Protestant piety in the seventeenth century, which we call Puritan and Pietist. It was in the mid-seventeenth century that conversion narrative emerged as a truly popular oral and literary form. As with so much else, the early evangelical experience of conversion and the practice of personal narration were a revival of seventeenth-century piety. I hope simply to point up something of the novelty of the Puritan-evangelical genre by describing the alternative forms of spiritual autobiography that preceded it. I shall begin with Augustine, and take the story as far as the Puritan Richard Baxter, since this takes us to within a generation of Sampson Staniforth and beginnings of modern evangelicalism.

---

11. Augustine, *Confessions*, ed. Henry Chadwick (Oxford: Oxford University Press, 1991), introduction, pp. ix–xxviii; Henry Chadwick, *Augustine* (Oxford: Oxford University Press, 1986), pp. 66–74. See also Peter Brown, *Augustine of Hippo: A Biography* (Berkeley: University of California Press, 1969), pp. 158–181.

12. Marilyn J. Harran, *Luther on Conversion* (Ithaca: Cornell University Press, 1983), p. 185.

From Augustine to the high Middle Ages: spiritual autobiography and 'the summit of the blessed life'

It is perhaps surprising that Augustine's magisterial example in the late fourth century of what could be done with the confessional form of religious autobiography was so little explored in the Christian centuries that followed. In the early Middle Ages the new situation north of the Alps, with the entry of the barbarian tribes into Christianity, certainly created a vastly different sort of conversion from the experience of private interiority in Augustine. The difference is epitomized in the contrast between the *Confessions* of Augustine and the *Confession* of St Patrick, despite the fact that these two autobiographies were separated by no more than a century. Augustine wrote at the end of one Christian civilization; Patrick wrote at the beginning of another. Augustine wrote about an inward journey prompted by keen theological questions; Patrick's account was principally of his outward vocation as a charismatic missionary, and he wrote in part to correct false accusations and misrepresentations about his mission.

Indeed, Patrick's *Confession* is something of a foundation legend for Irish Christianity.[13] In this sense it is similar to the royal conversion narratives of Clovis of the Franks in the fifth century, Ethelbert of Kent in the sixth century and Edwin of Northumbria in the seventh century.[14] These latter narratives were not autobiographical, however, and the form of Patrick's *Confession* stands out in this way as exceptional.[15] In proselyte conversions and other national conversions in early medieval Europe, right up to the conversion of the Lithuanians in the fourteenth century, there is little that we would recognize as spiritual autobiography. Somehow, the conditions and questions that would prompt an answer in the form of a retrospective interpretation of one's life from a religious perspective did not arise.

If early medieval converts were, so to speak, not Christian enough to write a conversion narrative such as Augustine's, later medieval spiritual

---

13. John Skinner (ed.), *The Confession of St. Patrick and Letter to Coroticus* (New York: Image, 1998).

14. Richard Fletcher, *The Barbarian Conversion: From Paganism to Christianity* (New York: Henry Holt, 1997), pp. 97–129.

15. The autobiographical ending to Bede's *Historica ecclesiastica*, written in the eighth century, was more a curriculum vitae than a spiritual autobiography in any significant sense. See *Bede's Ecclesiastical History of the English Nation*, trans. John Stevenson (London: J. M. Dent & Sons, 1954), pp. 283–285.

autobiographers (as they appear beginning in the twelfth century) are, on the contrary, too Christian. Christendom has become so expansive that conversion can no longer be the proselyte experience of conversion from paganism that it was for early medieval Christians or for Augustine. Indeed, the word *conversio* comes to denote not principally the transition from pagan to Christian, but the passage of a Christian into the life of a religious, taking up the *vita apostolica*, or vowed life. Bernard of Clairvaux's sermon 'On Conversion', preached at Paris in 1140 (a powerful piece of rhetoric if ever there was one), led more than twenty men to offer themselves to the Cistercian order.

Within monastic theology, this understanding of *conversio*, which for Bernard still also meant a conversion of the heart, is further developed so that conversion comes to denote not just initiation but final transformation, as the spiritually minded Christian strives from *initium conversationis* to *perfectionem conversationis*, from the beginning to the perfection of conversion (as it is put at the end of the Rule of St Benedict). In consequence, spiritual autobiography in the Middle Ages is typically structured less by the experience of Christian initiation than by the pursuit of compunction and the vision of God.[16]

Just as Augustine's contribution comes late in the antique period, when Christianity could be grafted on to the stock of classical culture with the maturing of Mediterranean Christian civilization, so also medieval spiritual autobiography comes into its own late in the period, with the maturing of European Christian civilization.[17] The first conscious imitations of Augustine's *Confessions* appear in the eleventh century with a German monk, Othloh, and in the twelfth century with the *De vita sua* (Concerning One's Life) of Guibert de Nogent.[18] Guibert's memoirs have been described as the

---

16. Bernard of Clairvaux, *Sermons on Conversion*, trans. Marie-Bernard Saïd (Kalamazoo, Mich.: Cistercian, 1981). See also Gillian R. Evans, 'A Change of Mind in Some Scholars of the Eleventh and Early Twelfth Centuries', in Derek Baker (ed.), *Religious Motivation: Biographical and Sociological Problems for the Church Historian* (Oxford: Basil Blackwell, 1978), pp. 27–38.

17. Cf. Georges Gusdorf, 'Conditions and Limits of Autobiography', in James Olney (ed.), *Autobiography: Essays Theoretical and Critical* (Princeton: Princeton University Press, 1980), pp. 28–48.

18. Wayne Shumaker, *English Autobiography: Its Emergence, Materials, and Form* (Berkeley: University of California Press, 1954), p. 13; *A Monk's Confession: The Memoirs of Guibert of Nogent*, trans. with an introduction by Paul J. Archambault (University Park: Pennsylvania State University Press, 1996).

first comprehensive medieval autobiography, treating the course of the author's life from birth onwards.[19]

Guibert is preoccupied with his recurring struggles with sin and his repeated recoveries by the grace of God, but the 'conversion' it recounts is really the decision to take up the religious life of a monk at the monastery of Saint Germer. He had lived a rowdy and irreverent life, and his mother arranged for him to be received into the monastery. When he visited, he found his first longings for the monastic life.[20] After trying to resist this inner goading for some time, he says, 'So I went back to the abbot . . . I fell at his feet and tearfully implored him to receive me, sinner that I was.' And he received his habit the next day.[21]

For the fourteenth-century Italian laymen Petrarch and Dante, spiritual autobiography was cast in the form of allegory, whose spiritual meaning had to do not with monastic conversion but with the ends of the devout life. The pursuit of spirituality meant embracing the 'affirmative way' through courtly love and the celebration and transcendence of the unconsummated love of a woman: Dante's love for Beatrice and Petrarch's for Laura. This earthly desire became an allegory of the love between a human person and God, a God for whom one longs but whom one cannot finally reach.

In Dante's autobiographical *La vita nuova* (The New Life) he recounted how his love for Beatrice led after her death to a spiritual vision, one that would reach its acme in the *Divine Comedy*.[22] Petrarch was greatly influenced

---

19. Georg Misch, *A History of Autobiography in Antiquity*, trans. E.W. Dickes (London: Routledge & Keegan Paul, 1950). p. 109.

20. Says Guibert, 'You are my witness, O Lord, you who had arranged all this ahead of time, that the moment I entered the church of that monastery and saw the monks sitting side by side, there welled up within me at the sight of this spectacle such a yearning for the monastic life that my fervor could not be abated nor my soul find its peace until its prayer was granted' (*A Monk's Confession*, p. 48).

21. Ibid., p. 49. Peter Abelard's concerns to defend himself against his enemies makes his *Historia calamitatum* (The Story of my Misfortunes) another remarkable autobiography in the twelfth century, but while it reflects a distinctive piety and heightened individualism, it would stretch our categories too far to consider it a spiritual autobiography in the mode of Augustine's great work.

22. Dante Alighieri, *The New Life*, trans. Charles Eliot Norton (Boston: Houghton Mifflin, 1909). Cf. James Collins, who discusses Dante's fusion of the traditions of courtly love (*amor*) with mystical love (*charitas*) in *Pilgrim in Love: An Introduction to Dante and His Spirituality* (Chicago: Loyola University Press, 1984), pp. 19–33.

by Augustine's *Confessions* and his autobiographical *Secretum* is a dialogue with Augustine over whether or not to withdraw from the world. In this and in his letters, we learn of how he climbed Mount Ventoux and how this became another allegory of spiritual pilgrimage and longing for the summit of the blessed life.[23]

In contrast to these most learned fourteenth-century poets is the anchorite Julian of Norwich, who wrote some decades later. But the themes that shaped Julian's autobiographical writings had likewise to do with 'the summit of the blessed life', for it was of her spiritual ecstasy that she wrote in her *Showings*, seeking to understand the visions given to her when she was in her early thirties.[24] Her contemporary the laywoman Margery Kempe likewise wrote about her vision of Christ and her attempt to live a contemplative life with many tears in the midst of foreign travel and pilgrimage.[25]

---

23. Francesco Petrarca, *Petrarch's Secret: or, The Soul's Conflict with Passion: Three Dialogues between Himself and S. Augustine*, trans. William H. Draper (London: Chatto & Windus, 1911; repr. Norwood, Pa.: Norwood Editions, 1975); cf. his letter to Father Dionigi De Roberti of Borgo San Sepolcro, dated 26 Apr. 1336, describing his ascent of Mount Ventoux in *Letters from Petrarch*, trans. Morris Bishop (Bloomington: Indiana University Press, 1966).

24. *The Revelations of Divine Love of Julian of Norwich*, trans. James Walsh (Wheathampstead, Hertfordshire: Anthony Clark, 1961); Denise Nowakowski Baker, *Julian of Norwich's Showings: From Vision to Book* (Princeton: Princeton University Press, 1994). Cf. also the experience of Margaret Ebner who was a religious for many years before she was provoked to more seriousness in her spiritual life by a severe illness that began to afflict her in the year 1312. The illness and suffering lasted at least thirteen years, but through this she was brought to greater spiritual resignation, and her sense of God's love and consolation increased. In 1335, she had a profound mystical experience, her heart grasped by an ineffable divine power, and this led to ecstatic speech. Thus even within the monastic life, it seems, one could be 'converted'. The preoccupation here is also, however, with final conversion and beatitude. See further, *Margaret Ebner: Major Works*, trans. and ed. Leonard P. Hindsley (New York: Paulist, 1993). Further examples of medieval spiritual autobiography in the vernacular and shaped by spiritual preoccupations may be found among the thirteenth-century Beguines (religious laywomen) and fourteenth-century Dominican nuns. See Jill Rait (ed.), *Christian Spirituality: High Middle Ages and Reformation* (New York: Crossroad, 1987), pp. 140–143, 155–158.

25. Margery Kempe, *The Book of Margery Kempe*, trans. Barry Windeatt (London: Penguin, 1994).

If these writings by Dante, Petrarch, Julian and Margery Kempe can be considered conversion narratives (and in a sense of course they are), then they are conversion narratives of a very different kind from those that emerge in the later Protestant tradition. Like the later spiritual autobiographies, these late medieval examples were occasioned variously by confessional, apologetic, hortatory and doxological concerns, but in narrative terms they were shaped most profoundly by the desire for final conversion rather than the experience of initial conversion.

Jean Delumeau's provocative reinterpretation of Christian history in this period is that on the eve of the Reformation, Europe was only superficially Christianized. The process of late medieval reformation was in fact one process of primary evangelization. The masses were still Christian in name only and the reformations of the early modern period were in fact a process of spiritualizing religion and Christianizing the common people. This movement began in the cities and was carried on into the rural world in the seventeenth century and afterward. If true, it would help to account for the reappearance of spiritual autobiography in a few precocious examples in the Renaissance and then with increasing regularity in the vernacular in the early modern period as this process of 'Christianizing' and 'spiritualizing' advanced.[26]

From Luther to the Puritans: *apologia* and the beginnings of conversion narrative

While we have autobiographical writings from Ignatius Loyola and Teresa of Avila in the sixteenth century, it is noteworthy that the Protestant magisterial reformers did not, as a rule, write their spiritual memoirs or the narrative of their initial conversion experiences. The reformers wrote tracts, treatises and catechisms, but they did not write spiritual autobiographies. We have to go to an autobiographical fragment written in 1545 in the prologue to the Wittenberg edition of Luther's Latin writings to find his famous 'tower experience'.[27]

---

26. Jean Delumeau, *Catholicism between Luther and Voltaire: A New View of the Counter-Reformation*, trans. Jeremy Moiser (London: Burns & Oates; Philadelphia: Westminster, 1977), pp. 175–231.

27. Heiko A. Oberman, *Luther: Man between God and the Devil*, trans. Eileen Walliser-Schwarzbart (New Haven: Yale University Press, 1989), pp. 164–166; Harran, *Luther on Conversion*, pp. 174–188.

Luther describes his spiritual breakthrough as something that occurred while studying the book of Romans. He recalled the sense of personal guilt under which he laboured, saying, 'Although I lived a blameless life as a monk, I felt that I was a sinner with an uneasy conscience before God.' As he meditated on the meaning of the 'righteousness of God' in Romans 1, he came to understand this in a new way as the righteousness by which God mercifully justifies the sinner by faith. Luther recalls the effect this had on him: 'This immediately made me feel as though I had been born again, and as though I had entered through open gates into paradise itself.' Many scholars now argue that Luther, looking back as an old man, telescoped a much longer process of growing insight into that alleged breakthrough some twenty years earlier, and that it may be problematic in any case to construe it as his 'conversion'.[28] Moreover, it is a fragment only.

Our knowledge of John Calvin's conversion is even slighter, and it comes likewise from a document written at a much later stage in his life. At a distance of some twenty-five years Calvin wrote about his 'sudden conversion', but again, to find this passing reference you have to squint hard at his preface to his *Psalms Commentary* (1557).[29] 'When I was too firmly addicted to the papal superstitions to be drawn easily out of such a deep mire, by a sudden conversion He brought my mind (already more rigid than suited my age) to submission.' This is a very cryptic allusion in the course of a short description of his timid beginnings as a reformer, amid much trouble and persecution. The reference has occasioned much debate as to what exactly Calvin meant by a sudden conversion (*subita conversio*) to submission (*docilitas*). But Calvin's interest in spiritual autobiography itself is very much accidental. His reflections are called forth by his desire to demonstrate how the psalms may be of comfort to those who are in a situation similar to David.

The same may be said about the Reformation as a whole. Judith Pollmann writes, 'There is a peculiar gap in the long tradition of the conversion narrative. The tens of thousands of Europeans who in the course of the sixteenth

---

28. See further Harran, *Luther on Conversion*, who reviews the primary sources and the range of interpretations of Luther's conversion. Harran's own view is that Luther's conversion was a 'culminating insight' (ibid., p. 185).

29. On Calvin's conversion, see Peter Wilcox, 'Restoration, Reformation and the Progress of the Kingdom of Christ: Evangelisation in the Thought and Practice of John Calvin, 1555–1564' (DPhil, University of Oxford, 1993), pp. 177–209; Peter Wilcox, 'Conversion in the Thought and Experience of John Calvin', *Anvil* 14.2 (1997), pp. 113–128.

century turned to Protestantism left very few accounts of their experiences of conversion.'[30] We may speak of the evangelical conversion narrative in the eighteenth century or the Puritan conversion narrative in the seventeenth century, but there is no genre of sixteenth-century Reformation conversion narrative.[31]

As a reason for this lacuna Pollmann reminds us of the enormous effort of the Reformers to emphasize the antiquity of their doctrines rather than the novelty of their ways. Innovation was widely unacceptable and to distance yourself from your past could be perceived as a sin against filial piety. Typically, the Reformers spoke not of changes in their personalities but of learning and understanding old truths and unlearning bad habits.[32] David Steinmetz likewise stresses the fact that for the Reformers conversion was understood principally as a continuous and lifelong process of learning faith within the context of the church, often described as a school.[33]

Thus, while the secular autobiography followed its own course during this period as a memoir of outward achievements, the first forms of specifically religious autobiography among Protestants in the sixteenth and seventeenth centuries took the form of religious *apologia* (narratives of suffering and martyrdom), reflecting the religious and political strife of the period.[34] Conversion features in passing in these narratives, but it is not the central theme it will be in the seventeenth century.

For example, Calvin's successor in Geneva, Theodore Beza, wrote of his conversion experience in a letter to a friend in 1560. This then served as a

---

30. Judith Pollmann, 'A Different Road to God: The Protestant Experience of Conversion in the Sixteenth Century', in Peter van der Veer (ed.), *Conversion to Modernities: The Globalization of Christianity* (New York: Routledge, 1996), pp. 47–48.

31. Cf. the comments of W. R. Ward, *The Protestant Evangelical Awakening* (Cambridge: Cambridge University Press, 1992), p. 2: 'The movements of renewal and revival of the eighteenth century sought their legitimation in the hand of God in history; their characteristic achievement was not, like the Reformers of the sixteenth century, to offer a confession of faith for public discussion, but to accumulate archives which would support their understanding of history.'

32. Pollmann, 'Different Road to God,' pp. 52–54.

33. David C. Steinmetz, 'Reformation and Conversion', *Theology Today* 35.1 (1978), p. 30.

34. For a description of the memoir or impersonal autobiography as distinct from spiritual autobiography in this period, see Donald A. Stauffer, *English Biography Before 1700* (Cambridge, Mass.: Harvard University Press, 1930), pp. 175–216. See also e.g. *The Life of Sir Thomas Bodley* in *Trecentale Bodleianum* (Oxford: Clarendon, 1913).

preface to his *Confessio christianae fidei* (Confession of the Christian Faith). He commented upon his experience in 1548:

> Behold [God] inflicted a very serious illness on me, so that I almost despaired of my life. What should I do in this wretched state, when nothing stood before my eyes beyond the horrific judgment of a just God? After endless torments of mind and body, God, taking pity on his fugitive slave, so consoled me that I no longer doubted that I had been granted forgiveness. Thus in tears I cursed myself, I sought forgiveness and I renewed my vow to openly embrace His true worship and finally I dedicated myself wholly to Him. And so it came about that the image of death placed before me in earnest aroused in me the slumbering and buried desire for the true life, and that this disease for me was the beginning of true health . . . And as soon as I could leave my bed, having severed all my ties and gathered my possessions, I once and for all abandoned my country, parents and friends to follow Christ, and together with my wife I retired into voluntary exile in Geneva.[35]

Judith Pollmann (whose translation of Beza I have quoted here) argues that this 'conversion narrative' was an exception in the sixteenth century. Moreover, it was written not for the doxological or hortatory motives that induced Bunyan to write, nor certainly for the celebration of individuality that appears in Cellini, but rather for wholly apologetic reasons. Beza's Catholic adversaries had accused him of having lived an unrighteous life as a young man. He offered this narrative as an explanation of the contrast between his past shortcomings and his present status.[36] It was *apologia* not *confessio*. The same was true of Hugues Sureau, a French Calvinist minister, who converted to Catholicism and was pressed by officials to write a confession. A year later he reconverted to Calvinism and so wrote a new conversion narrative to explain his decision and to recant his earlier confession. Again it is the apologetic motive that comes to the fore.[37]

For the most part, sixteenth-century religious autobiographical reminiscences were fragmentary and unpublished, collected and printed only posthumously. *The Bloody Theater, or, Martyrs' Mirror* is a collection of accounts of Anabaptist suffering compiled from various chronicles, memorials and testimonies by Thieleman J. van Braght, originally published in Dutch in 1660. It bears the subtitle *Of the Defenceless Christians who Baptized only upon Confession of Faith, and who Suffered and Died for the Testimony of Jesus, their Saviour, from the Time*

---

35. Pollmann, 'Different Road to God', pp. 49–50.
36. Ibid.
37. Ibid., pp. 50–51.

of Christ to the year A. D. 1660. The English edition is a large volume of closely printed text laid out in double columns, over a thousand pages of which recount the details of Anabaptist martyrdoms during the sixteenth century.

Most of the documents drawn upon in these accounts were official court documents and letters written by the martyrs while in prison awaiting execution. The letters are typically cast in the distinctive form of a spiritual last will and testament (recalling the original sense of the Greek word *martys*). Most include a confession of faith and a strongly worded admonition to the faithful who remain, exhorting family members and church members to stand firm. The autobiographical narrative is typically limited to an account of the arrest, trial and imprisonment, and there is almost no extended religious autobiography. Apparently, the Anabaptist martyrs did not feel the need to offer up a religious narrative of their lives as a whole.

One exception to this appears in the account of Joriaen Simons, an Anabaptist weaver and bookseller burned at the stake as a heretic at Haarlem in Holland on 26 April 1557. Simons was martyred in the persecution that followed the rise to power of Phillip II as king of Spain and his attempt to stamp out Protestantism in his dominions in the Netherlands. While in prison Simons wrote a 'testament' to leave behind for his young son, and in this he recounts some details of his own spiritual autobiography. His narrative has the shape of conversion, with its contrast between his life before and after choosing to follow Christ. He begins:

> The beginning of my life was unprofitable, proud, puffed-up, drunken, selfish, deceitful, and full of all manner of idolatry. And when I attained maturity, and began to be my own master, I sought nothing but what pleased my flesh, an indolent and luxurious life.

He adds that he was greedy and refers cryptically to his seeking to 'bring my neighbour's daughter to a fall'. He continues, introducing his change of life:

> But, my dear child, when I betook myself to the Scriptures, and searched and perused them, I found that my life tended to eternal death, yea, that the everlasting woe was hanging over me, and that the fiery pool which burns with brimstone and pitch was prepared for me.

Simons evaluated his life and determined it was better

> to suffer affliction with the people of God for a little while, than to live in every luxury with the world, which will perish. Thus I abandoned my ease, voluntarily and

uncompelled, and entered upon the narrow way, to follow Christ, my Head, well knowing that if I should follow Him unto the end, I should not walk in darkness.

He concludes this brief narrative by returning to his present situation in prison:

> Now, when I had partly forsaken and cast from me the old damnable practices, and wanted to be a new divine creature, and to lead a pious, penitent, godly life, I was immediately, like all the pious that had been before me, hated, yea, imprisoned in Haarlem, in St. John's gate.[38]

Thus, within the larger form of 'last will and testament', Simons offers a spare and unembellished conversion narrative as part of an admonition, which he hopes his son will read when old enough to understand such matters. The narrative is of outward actions only and contrasts with later Puritan and Pietism narratives by the complete absence both of any sense of moral or spiritual inability or of a troubled introspective conscience.

Moreover, the piety is that of the *imitatio Christi* (imitation of Christ), not of the penal, substitutionary atonement. Simons exhorts his son that he can escape the impending wrath of God 'in no better way than by looking to Jesus Christ, the Son of the Almighty and eternal Father, who is the Head and Pattern of all believers', and warns him to avoid the 'sects' of the Lutherans and Zwinglians. He concludes by urging his son to a costly obedience, saying, 'You must be born again, and converted, if you would enter the kingdom of God.' The language is similar to that of later evangelicals, but the piety is very different.

John Foxe's *Acts and Monuments* was first published in English in 1563, and this also drew upon autobiographical documents. Like the *Martyrs' Mirror* it was compiled to extol the heroic faith of martyrs, though its chief focus was on the English Protestants who were martyred under Queen Mary. And just as the *Martyrs' Mirror* was written with apologetic intentions to defend Anabaptists and denounce Roman Catholic and Protestant persecutors, so also Foxe's *Acts and Monuments* was designed as a polemic for English Protestantism and a demonstration of papist tyranny. It is impossible to understand the documents in these collections outside the context of intense religious polemic fostered by the determined efforts of state bureaucracies to enforce uniformity and achieve the ideals of the confessional state.

---

38. Thieleman J. van Braght and Joseph F. Sohm, *The Bloody Theater, or, Martyrs' Mirror* (Scottdale, Pa.: Herald, 1987[17]), p. 565.

In all of this, however, is the beginning of a kind of spiritual autobiography. As in the case of the *Martyrs' Mirror*, the examples are very few. One comes from a letter recorded by John Foxe, written in 1527 by Thomas Bilney (c. 1495–1531) to Cuthbert Tunstall, Bishop of London. It contains an eloquent conversion narrative of sorts. The occasion that calls forth Bilney's personal narrative is again emphatically adversarial. Indeed, the letter forms part of the legal records of Bilney's trial for heresy before the bishop, who was acting on behalf of Cardinal Wolsley. In this letter, Bilney explains how he procured a Latin edition of Erasmus' New Testament because of his interest in Erasmus' Latin style. But upon his very first reading he was struck by the 'sweet and comfortable' sentence in 1 Timothy 1:15, 'It is a true saying, and worthy of all men to be embraced, that Christ Jesus came into the world to save sinners; of whom I am the chief and principal.' Bilney describes what passed within him:

> This one sentence, through God's instruction and inward working, which I did not then perceive, did so exhilarate my heart, being before wounded with the guilt of my sins, and being almost in despair, that immediately I felt a marvellous comfort and quietness, insomuch 'that my bruised bones leaped for joy'.[39]

These were early days in the reform movement and Lutheran ideas had only just begun to penetrate England. Condemned as a heretic, Bilney was burned at the stake under Henry VIII three years before the Act of Supremacy. But this passing autobiographical reference anticipates the most significant formal element of conversion narrative that will later emerge among the Puritans, namely conviction under the law ('wounded with the guilt of my sins') and relief under the promises of the gospel ('a marvellous comfort and quietness'). The larger document, and collection of documents, forms an *apologia* for an accused Protestant or Lollard, but within this is a more private psychological narrative of conversion.

Throughout the Tudor period and well into the early Stuart period in England, conversion was understood as a matter of true belief and allegiance to the true institutional church, whether that be the Roman Catholic Church or the Church of England. However, it was also understood, within this framework, as a matter of inward salvation. Michael Questier argues that the political and religious motives for conversion in this period were in constant tension in the minds of individual converts:

---

39. *The Acts and Monuments of John Foxe*, 8 vols. (London: Seeley, Burnside & Seeley, 1843–9; repr. New York: AMS, 1965), vol. 4, p. 635.

Conversion refers primarily to the way in which sinful man is made regenerate by grace. Nevertheless, the theology of conversion raises certain imperatives about the sort of Church to which the regenerate man should adhere. This promotes the second type of conversion, namely between ecclesiastical institutions, which takes on a political character.[40]

The State could demand, and often achieve, politico-ecclesiastical obedience, but the innermost religious beliefs of people could not be ignored. Clergymen on both sides of the religious divide sought to influence proselytes towards a deeper sense of conversion, one that transcended politico-ecclesiastical boundaries. Catholics were not satisfied with mere recusancy; Protestants were not happy with mere conformity. Both Jesuit and Puritan evangelists aimed for an ecclesiastical obedience that issued from a deeper conversion from sin to grace.[41]

The late seventeenth-century Puritan Richard Baxter reflected a similar insight in his comments on conversion in his memoirs. First he recognized the category of proselyte conversion in which people turn to 'the profession of Christianity' from outside the Christian religion altogether. He was astonished to think that 'so small a part of the world hath the profession of Christianity in comparison with heathens, Mahometans and other infidels'. But then he makes a further distinction, astonished also that 'among professed Christians there are so few that are saved from gross delusions and have but any competent knowledge'. This distinction between 'gross delusions' and 'competent knowledge' went to the heart of politico-ecclesiastical attempts at reformation.

But Baxter's astonishment goes one step further as he expresses his wonder that among those with competent knowledge 'there are so few that are seriously religious and truly set their hearts on heaven'.[42] Like peeling back the layers of an onion, Baxter had at last reached the innermost sense of conversion, the conversion of the heart. In the seventeenth century, this concept

---

40. Michael C. Questier, *Conversion, Politics and Religion in England, 1580–1625*, Cambridge Studies in Early Modern British History (Cambridge: Cambridge University Press, 1996), pp. 3–4.

41. Ibid., pp. 168–202.

42. Richard Baxter, *Reliquiae Baxterianae; or, Mr. Richard Baxter's Narrative of the Most Memorable Passages of his Life and Times ... Published from his own Original Manuscripts by Matthew Sylvester* (London: T. Parkhust, J. Robinson, J. Lawrence & J. Dunton, 1696). Richard Baxter, *The Autobiography of Richard Baxter*, ed. Ernest Rhys, Everyman's Library (London: J. M. Dent & Sons, 1931), p. 117.

of inward conversion would in fact provide the theological framework for the emergence of conversion narrative as a truly popular genre. Baxter's own paranetic works, such as his *Treatise on Conversion* (1657), *Directions and Persuasions to a Sound Conversion* (1658) and particularly his much reprinted *Call to the Unconverted* (1658), did much to stimulate this concern for inward conversion of the heart.

As a popular genre, evangelical conversion narrative emerged especially during the Commonwealth and among the gathered churches in the context of testimonies required for admission to membership. In 1653, two substantial collections were published: *Spirituall Experiences of Sundry Believers* (most likely edited by the London Independent Henry Walker) and John Rogers' *Ohel and Beth-shemesh: A Tabernacle for the Sun*. Since the mid-seventeenth century the genre of conversion narrative has persisted in English religious life and untold variations have been composed on the theme. But in Baxter's own lifetime, when he began to observe formal similarities in the narratives of conversion he heard from respected ministers and to worry whether he himself was truly converted, he came to realize with some relief what we too can see from this brief survey of spiritual autobiography 'that God breaketh not all men's hearts alike'.[43] This continued, I think, to be true in the 1730s and 1740s when pastors began writing of the new and 'surprising work of God in the conversion of many hundred souls'.[44]

© D. Bruce Hindmarsh, 2008

---

43. Ibid., p. 11.
44. My allusion is to the title of Jonathan Edwards's famous *Faithful Narrative of the Surprising Work of God in the Conversion of Many Hundred Souls* (London: printed for John Oswald, 1737).

15. ENLIGHTENMENT EPISTEMOLOGY AND EIGHTEENTH-CENTURY EVANGELICAL DOCTRINES OF ASSURANCE

Garry J. Williams

The task of identifying the enduring essence of particular religious movements is one of the perennial challenges the church historian faces. From time to time brave individuals propose definitions that claim to function sufficiently well to allow the discussion of a particular movement to continue, or even to take a significant step forward. With similar frequency, gainsayers protest that the movement in question is actually undefinable and should in fact no longer be thought of as a movement. The debate grinds on, the whole process resembling a war in the paralysis of attrition, while every so often someone sitting in safety far from the front lines wins a prize for writing the best summary of the struggle so far. Notorious examples abound. In the second century it might be Gnosticism, in the sixteenth, Radicalism. Both have been defined and redefined, and both have been denied. Gnosticism, we are told, needs to be rethought out of existence, the Radical Reformation scarcely deserves the title. Probably each century has its own example. In the eighteenth century, it is evangelicalism.

The definition of evangelicalism

One of the more successful of such historical definitions has been the account of evangelicalism offered by David Bebbington in *Evangelicalism in Modern*

Britain: A History from the 1730s to the 1980s (1989). This history of evangelical-ism was rightly hailed for its liveliness, breadth and light touch in deploying an impressive range of detailed evidence from primary sources. Bebbington defines the four essential evangelical characteristics as conversionism, activ-ism, biblicism and crucicentrism.[1] His definition has been widely accepted. It is almost true that wherever one turns in recent writing on evangelicalism in its British forms these characteristics are employed.

Writing in 1994, Derek Tidball notes that the fourfold definition 'has quickly established itself as near to a consensus as we might ever expect to reach'.[2] A 1990s transatlantic study notes that even though Bebbington was writing about British history, his categories have been found to have 'a defini-tional virtue' that has carried them beyond Britain to America.[3] In a compara-tive treatment Bebbington himself has stated that 'the defining characteristics were the same in Britain and the United States'.[4] Some voices have been raised in dissent at different levels. In his personal sketch of the history of evangeli-calism from 1935 to 1995, Oliver Barclay argues that the four terms need to be reordered and given more precise definition.[5] D. A. Carson raises various problems, including the fact that the characteristics emphasize evangelical distinctives at the expense of those creedal areas on which evangelicals may agree with others.[6] Further criticisms have been, and no doubt will be, made of the definition qua definition.

---

1. D. W. Bebbington, *Evangelicalism in Modern Britain: A History from the 1730s to the 1980s* (London: Unwin Hyman, 1989), pp. 1–17. This is Bebbington's most significant work on the subject and is the basis of his other presentations of the same argument, to which reference will be made below where appropriate.

2. D. J. Tidball, *Who Are the Evangelicals?* (London: Marshall Pickering, 1994), p. 14.

3. R. H. Krapohl and C. H. Lippy, *The Evangelicals: A Historical, Thematic, and Biographical Guide* (Westport, Conn.: Greenwood, 1999), p. 7. Though it is important to note that the American discussion of evangelicalism is capable of proceeding without reference to Bebbington; e.g. G. Dorrien, *The Remaking of Evangelical Theology* (Louisville: Westminster John Knox, 1998).

4. 'Evangelicalism in Modern Britain and America', in G. A. Rawlyk and M. A. Noll (eds.), *Amazing Grace: Evangelicalism in Australia, Britain, Canada, and the United States* (Grand Rapids: Baker, 1993), p. 185.

5. O. Barclay, *Evangelicalism in Britain: 1935–1995* (Leicester: IVP, 1997), pp. 10–12.

6. D. A. Carson, *The Gagging of God: Christianity Confronts Pluralism* (Leicester: Apollos, 1996), pp. 449–451.

The Enlightenment origins of evangelicalism

Here, however, my interest is not so much in the defining characteristics themselves as in the way in which Bebbington uses them to date the origins of
evangelicalism (though I shall raise some broad questions about his account
of activism below). While earlier writers such as J. C. Ryle and E. J. Poole-
Connor turned to the Reformers or even to John Wyclif for their starting point
for evangelical history, Bebbington opens his book with the declaration that
'Evangelical religion is a popular Protestant movement that has existed in Britain since the 1730s.'[7] He grants that the movement did not emerge *ex nihilo*,
but it was nonetheless something that had not been seen before: 'There was
much continuity with earlier Protestant traditions, but . . . Evangelicalism was
a new phenomenon of the eighteenth century.'[8] Without wanting to deny the
many good reasons for which Bebbington's treatment has proved seminal, I
shall seek to show that the case made for this dating does not hold. It is not my
purpose here to propose an alternative dating. I am seeking simply to reopen
the case for seeing Puritanism and the Reformation as themselves authentically
evangelical movements.

In substantiating his opening declaration, Bebbington offers a distinctive
detailed argument for the origins of evangelicalism. He dates the origins to the
1730s because he holds that the movement was a child of the Enlightenment.
The evidence here rests on the role the second characteristic plays:

> The activism of the Evangelical movement sprang from its strong teaching on
> assurance. That, in turn, was a product of the confidence of the new age about the
> validity of experience. The Evangelical version of Protestantism was created by the
> Enlightenment.[9]

This is a telling argument, since it shows that despite the fourfold definition,
the decisive emphasis for Bebbington is on the single feature of activism. As he
himself allows, 'Three characteristic marks of Evangelicalism, conversionism,

---

7. Bebbington, *Evangelicalism in Modern Britain*, p. 1. For examples of the earlier
   dating, see E. J. Poole-Connor, *Evangelicalism in England* (London: Fellowship of
   Independent Evangelical Churches, 1951), which begins in the fifteenth century,
   and J. C. Ryle, *Knots Untied* (London: William Hunt, 1874), where Ryle repeatedly
   treats a host of Reformation writers as evangelicals.

8. *Evangelicalism in Modern Britain*, p. 1.

9. Ibid., p. 74.

biblicism and crucicentrism, had been as much a part of Puritanism as they were of Methodism.'[10] It is activism that marks the step from the Puritans to the evangelicals. The link from activism to the Enlightenment is made by the evangelical doctrine of assurance. Bebbington explains that 'the dynamism of the evangelical movement was possible only because its adherents were assured in their faith'.[11] Earlier Protestants had been concerned with assurance, but now 'the content of the doctrine was transformed'.[12] The novelty lay in the expected *timing* and *ground* of an individual's sense of assurance: 'Whereas the Puritans had held that assurance is rare, late and the fruit of struggle in the experience of believers, the Evangelicals believed it to be general, normally given at conversion and the result of simple acceptance of the gift of God.'[13]

The final phrase here is significant: all that was needed for assurance from the start of the Christian life was 'simple acceptance of the gift of God'. Bebbington paints a picture in which this early assurance arising from simple acceptance stands in sharp contrast to the Puritan emphasis on late assurance arising from close self-examination. In the Puritan context, 'the ignorance of the believer about his future destiny would drive him to scrutinise himself for signs of grace'.[14] The Puritans even had lists of the signs of grace for which the believer should search. Against this picture of introspective gloom, Bebbington depicts the evangelical position as one of robust confidence in which early assurance is the norm. There might, he states, be a momentary self-examination, but 'the process was, as it were, non-recurrent: it was expected that the verdict would be favourable'.[15] Self-examination was for the Puritans, while 'Eighteenth-century Evangelicals, by contrast, turned their attention from their own state to the message that was to be proclaimed.'[16]

Bebbington precisely identifies the 1734–5 revival in Northampton under Jonathan Edwards as the point at which this shift took place. From here it is a small step from the confidence of Edwards in assuring converts back to the Enlightenment origins of evangelicalism:

---

10. Ibid., p. 35.

11. Ibid., p. 42.

12. Ibid., p. 43.

13. Ibid.

14. Ibid.

15. Ibid., p. 46.

16. D. W. Bebbington, 'Revival and Enlightenment in Eighteenth-Century England', in E. L. Blumhofer and R. Balmer (eds.), *Modern Christian Revivals* (Urbana: University of Illinois Press, 1993), p. 21.

How could he be so bold? It was because he was far more confident than his Puritan forefathers of the powers of human knowledge. A person, he held, can receive a firm understanding of spiritual things through a 'new sense' which is as real as sight or smell.[17]

Edwards reached this epistemic confidence because he drank deeply from the waters of the English Enlightenment, in particular from the works of John Locke. Edwards was merely 'postulating a capacity for religious knowledge acceptable to philosophers of his era'.[18] To put it simply, where Locke's empiricism said 'you can trust your senses', Edwards counselled, 'you can trust your spiritual sense'.

According to Bebbington, John Wesley was also decisively influenced by Locke via Peter Browne's *The Procedure, Extent, and Limits of Human Understanding* (1728). Wesley agreed with the empiricists that knowledge is based on the senses, but where this left the empiricists with at best indirect knowledge of God, Wesley added a sixth sense.[19] This sense operates through faith: 'Faith in the spiritual world is what sight is in the natural.'[20] Faith is thus as reliable a source of knowledge as sight. Bebbington's precise point here is that the decisively new element in early evangelicalism was the 'understanding of faith in terms of self-validating sense impressions'.[21]

It was thus under philosophical influences that the Revival leaders engaged in what Bebbington terms the 'remoulding of the doctrine of assurance according to empiricist canons'.[22] Thus the confident activism of evangelicalism was born from the epistemology of the Enlightenment.

Many accept this dating for the emergence of evangelicalism. Derek Tidball finds that 'no one is quite sure where the beginning is' (which is hardly true of Bebbington), but despite the difficulty, he agrees that 'evangelicalism became a much more easily identified stream within the British church in the eighteenth century'.[23] Tidball is also convinced by Bebbington's detailed arguments: 'David Bebbington has persuasively argued that the "evangelical

---

17. *Evangelicalism in Modern Britain*, pp. 47–48.
18. Ibid., p. 48.
19. Ibid., p. 50.
20. Ibid., p. 49.
21. 'Revival and Enlightenment', p. 24.
22. *Evangelicalism in Modern Britain*, p. 54.
23. *Who Are the Evangelicals?*, p. 32.

version of Protestantism was created by the Enlightenment".'[24]

Others appear to accept the conclusion without always commenting on the detail. Writing before Bebbington, Kenneth Hylson-Smith stated circumspectly that evangelicals could 'trace their history back to the Puritans, the Reformers and the Lollards' and that it was simply in its 'modern phase' that the story began in the eighteenth century.[25] Writing later, he quotes Bebbington with approval: 'It was in the 1730s that the English-speaking world experienced what has been declared as "a more important development than any other, before or after, in the history of Protestant Christianity: the emergence of the movement that became Evangelicalism".'[26]

The dating as well as the definition has crossed the Atlantic. Bebbington himself has co-edited a collection of comparative studies on international evangelicalism from 1700 to 1900. The introduction to the book sets out the four characteristics and states that 'Evangelical' is the 'best word available to describe a fairly discrete network of Protestant Christian movements arising during the eighteenth century in Great Britain and its colonies'.[27]

The idea that evangelicalism was created by the Enlightenment may be questioned in a number of ways. My present aim is a discrete one, to scrutinize the crux of Bebbington's case, his argument that a new evangelical doctrine of assurance arose from Enlightenment epistemology and grounded a distinctive activism.[28] I shall proceed by testing the claim against the evidence we find in selected writings of John Wesley, Jonathan Edwards and John Newton, and by questioning the type of activism Bebbington requires to discern the presence of evangelicalism.

---

24. Ibid., p. 36.

25. K. Hylson-Smith, *Evangelicals in the Church of England: 1734–1984* (Edinburgh: T. & T. Clark, 1988), p. vii.

26. K. Hylson-Smith, 'Roots of Pan-Evangelicalism: 1735–1835', in S. Brady and H. Rowdon (eds.), *For Such a Time as This* (London: Scripture Union, 1996), pp. 137–138, quoting from Bebbington, *Evangelicalism in Modern Britain*, p. 20.

27. M. A. Noll, D. W. Bebbington and G. A. Rawlyk (eds.), *Evangelicalism: Comparative Studies of Popular Protestantism in North America, the British Isles, and Beyond, 1700–1990* (New York: Oxford University Press, 1994), p. 6.

28. Kenneth J. Stewart has recently asked some important broader questions of Bebbington's account in his article 'Did Evangelicalism Predate the Eighteenth Century? An Examination of David Bebbington's Thesis', *Evangelical Quarterly* 77.2 (Apr. 2005), pp. 135–153.

John Wesley on self-examination

Wesley does speak of a direct and immediate assurance normally given on conversion. In *Sermon 10* on the witness of the Spirit (1746), he seeks to defend
from the extremes of either enthusiasm or scepticism the view that assurance is
a gift given to ordinary Christians. In his definition of the witness of the Spirit
he argues against identifying it with a rational process of reflection:

> The testimony of the Spirit is an inward impression on the soul, whereby the Spirit of
> God directly 'witnesses to my spirit that I am a child of God'; that Jesus Christ hath
> loved me, and given himself for me; that all my sins are blotted out, and I, even I, am
> reconciled to God.[29]

Nonetheless, in the same text Wesley also argues that there is a subsequent
conjoined rational testimony from the believer's *own* spirit. He remarks that
the Spirit does not extinguish but perfects reason, citing a number of texts
from 1 John that explain the process of rational inference. This shows that
while both witnesses are dependent on the work of the Spirit, the second
is unlike the first in that it is an indirect witness mediated through rational
reflection. Welsey then concludes in syllogistic form, 'It all resolves into this:
those who have these marks, they are the children of God. But we have these
marks: therefore we are children of God.'[30] Such is the evidence provided for
the believer by his conscience.

What is the relation between these two witnesses? In *Sermon 11* (1767),
Wesley holds that upon conversion the witness of the Spirit exists on its own
without the witness of the believer's spirit, there having been no time for the
believer to perform evidentiary good works. There is a '*total absence* of the fruit
of the Spirit' at the time 'when the direct witness is first given'.[31] As soon as
time has passed, however, every believer must ascertain that he is not deluded
by the devil, and he must continue to do so. Wesley writes, 'let none ever pre-
sume to rest in any supposed testimony of the Spirit which is separate from
the fruit of it'.[32] Such separation may occur again only under temptation so

---

29. *The Works of John Wesley*, ed. A. C. Outler (Nashville: Abingdon, 1984–), vol. 1, p. 274.

30. Ibid., p. 272.

31. Ibid., p. 294. *Sermon 11* contains some differences of emphasis from *Sermon 10*.
    On change in Wesley's doctrine of assurance, see K. J. Collins, *The Scripture Way
    of Salvation* (Nashville: Abingdon, 1997), pp. 131–152.

32. *Works of John Wesley*, vol. 1, p. 297.

strong that it clouds the appearance of the fruit to the believer's eye.[33] Apart from these two cases, both witnesses 'testify conjointly' and are to be heard together since 'while they are joined we cannot be deluded'.[34]

In *Sermon 10*, Wesley goes so far as to specify self-examination as a universal Christian duty: 'it highly imports all who desire the salvation of God to consider it with the deepest attention, as they would not deceive their own souls'.[35] Wesley instructs the believer to do this by turning to the witness of his own spirit. Here the self-deceived will be exposed, since Scripture defines marks 'which a little reflection would convince him, beyond all doubt, were never found in his soul'.[36] He must have experienced repentance. He must have experienced a dramatic rebirth from death to life. The one who vainly presumes will see that he has not done this.[37] Or he may look to his present state to find the fruits of the spirit and obedience to the commandments of God; from failing to find them it follows 'with undeniable evidence' for the self-deceiver that 'he has not the true testimony of his own spirit'.[38] The language Wesley uses here is unambiguous: this universal Christian duty which proves to the individual that he is not self-deceived is a process of rational reflection on evidence. This witness of the human spirit is not an immediate sense experience.

Wesley can speak eloquently of the witness of the Spirit and he believes that it is discerned by 'spiritual senses'.[39] Indeed, he is concerned to defend such a direct, unmediated sense. But for all his asseverations, Wesley still has to urge the believer to come back to the process of rational enquiry to confirm that he is not self-deceived in his spiritual sense. For example, he pictures a man hearing the voice of God saying, 'Thy sins are forgiven thee.'[40] This voice is known by the spiritual sense. Wesley can see the next question coming: 'But how shall I know that my spiritual senses are rightly disposed?' He answers:

> Even by the 'testimony of your own spirit'; by 'the answer of a good conscience
> toward God'. By the fruits which he hath wrought in your spirit you shall know the

---

33. Ibid., pp. 294, 297–298.
34. Ibid., p. 295.
35. Ibid., p. 277.
36. Ibid., p. 278.
37. Ibid., pp. 278–279.
38. Ibid., p. 81.
39. Ibid., p. 282.
40. Ibid.

'testimony of the Spirit of God'. Hereby you shall know that you are in no delusion; that you have not deceived your own soul. The immediate fruits of the Spirit ruling in the heart are 'love, joy, peace'; 'bowels of mercies, humbleness of mind, meekness, gentleness, long-suffering'. And the outward fruits are the doing good to all men, the doing no evil to any, and the walking in the light—a zealous, uniform obedience to all the commandments of God.[41]

This test which all believers must apply to themselves to check that they are rightly perceiving the witness of the Spirit is the rational scrutiny of their own works.

In sum, for all but the newest believer or the believer under the strongest temptation, Wesley urges self-examination and the confirmation of the witness of the Spirit by syllogistic reasoning applied to the evidence of an attentive conscience. He looks to correct not only those who denied the witness of the Spirit, but also those who 'have mistaken the voice of their own imagination for this "witness of the Spirit" of God, and thence idly presumed they were the children of God while they were doing the works of the devil!'[42] Nor is this a one-off check for the fruit of the Spirit, since both witnesses operate conjointly. The believer must, normatively and persistently, look for the fruit of the Spirit.

The resulting Wesleyan appeal to self-examination is a real problem for the thesis that Wesley's carefree doctrine of assurance is the explanation of evangelical activism. The Christian could be free from self-scrutiny only at the very outset of the Christian life or in the worst of times, as Wesley himself knew in his own experience. Such brief times without scrutiny will not suffice to explain the activism of evangelicals. This is not to deny that assurance was more widely experienced by Wesleyans, but it is to counter Bebbington's argument that the Methodists were freed for their activism by leaving the self-examination of the Puritans behind them.

John Wesley on spiritual sense

From Bebbington's account we would expect to find Wesley casting spiritual sense in terms of physical sense. In this piece he does something more subtle. When he speaks of the witness of the believer's own spirit, Wesley readily draws

---

41. Ibid., p. 283.
42. Ibid., p. 269.

such comparisons. Hence he says that the believer has an 'immediate consciousness' that he obeys God in the same way as he has an immediate consciousness that he is alive or is at ease and not in pain.[43] Such consciousness
entails the believer's reflection on himself, a conception amenable to Locke.
The comparison here is one of manner; both are alike rational processes of
reflection. But Wesley then accents not the similarity but the contrast with the
witness of the Spirit of God:

> The *manner* how the divine testimony is manifested to the heart I do not take upon
> me to explain. 'Such knowledge is too wonderful and excellent for me; I cannot
> attain unto it'. 'The wind bloweth; and I hear the sound thereof'; but I cannot 'tell
> how it cometh, or whither it goeth'. As no one knoweth the things of a man save the
> spirit of the man that is in him, so the *manner* of the things of God knoweth no one
> save the Spirit of God.[44]

With this witness Wesley will indeed allow a simple comparison with sense
experience in saying that the testimony of the Spirit is no more doubtful than
the shining of the sun. But the comparison here is a comparison pertaining
to the *degree* of certainty, not to the *manner* of certainty. The manner of the
two witnesses is beyond comparison since one relies on human reflection and
the other on the direct work of the unfathomable Spirit of God. This means
that Wesley is careful to avoid the epistemic step from Enlightenment views
of knowledge based on the senses to the doctrine of assurance. The spiritual
sense is radically different from the other senses. That, of course, is why many
Enlightenment thinkers rejected it.

Moreover, writers on Wesley frequently point out that he found his idea of
spiritual sense in diverse sources, most of them predating the Enlightenment.
As Theodore Runyon notes, 'there is a long tradition in the Scriptures and in
Christian history which speaks of spiritual *senses*'.[45] The following text that
Runyon cites from the patristic Macarian Homilies provides an excellent
example of the antiquity of the tradition:

> Our Lord Jesus Christ came for this very reason, that he might change, and renew,
> and create afresh this soul that had been perverted by vile affections, tempering it

---

43. Ibid., p. 273.
44. Ibid., p. 276.
45. T. Runyon, *The New Creation: John Wesley's Theology Today* (Nashville: Abingdon,
    1998), p. 74.

with his own Divine Spirit. He came to work a new mind, a new soul, and new eyes, new ears, a new spiritual tongue.[46]

Here, long before the Enlightenment and in a text read by Wesley, we find the doctrine of spiritual senses created anew in the believer. If this much of the doctrine was available to Wesley in the pre-Enlightenment texts he was reading, it is a serious overstatement to say that the Wesleyan doctrine of assurance was in fact created by the Enlightenment. We cannot even posit a rediscovery of the idea of spiritual sense in the 1730s, since, as Randy Maddox notes, it had survived in Puritan writers.[47] To take one example, the Puritan John Owen in his *Pneumatologia* (Spiritual Things) can speak of a unique 'spiritual sense of the defilement of sin' and a 'gracious view' of the cleansing power of the blood of Christ that is worked in the believer by the Holy Spirit and is impossible in a natural man.[48] Even the idea of a self-validating knowledge of God through faith in his Word remained an unbroken tenet of Reformed theology from the sixteenth century. Calvin gave memorable expression to it in the *Institutes of the Christian Religion* 1.7, and was closely followed by the Puritans. John Owen in *The Reason of Faith* (Book 6 of *Pneumatologia*) uses the language of the senses to describe the way in which the Scripture 'evinceth this its divine efficacy by that *spiritual saving light* which it conveys into and imparts on the minds of believers'. Through Scripture the Holy Spirit gives a self-validating knowledge to believers:

> God by his Holy Spirit doth secretly and effectually persuade and satisfy the minds and souls of believers in the divine truth and authority of the Scriptures, whereby he infallibly secures their faith against all objections and temptations whatsoever.[49]

I do not for a moment want to deny that Wesley shaped his idea of spiritual sense in the language of, and relevant to, his times. The leitmotif of Bebbington's work is the claim that evangelicalism has always been fashioned by its contexts. In principle that is an unobjectionable claim, but it is quite

---

46. Ibid., p. 75.

47. R. L. Maddox, *Responsible Grace: John Wesley's Practical Theology* (Nashville: Abingdon, 1994), pp. 27–28, cites as possible sources for the idea of spiritual sense John Norris, the Macarian Homilies, western spiritual, Pietist and Puritan writers.

48. *The Works of John Owen*, ed. W. H. Goold, 16 vols. (Edinburgh: Banner of Truth, 1965–8; repr. 1994), vol. 3, p. 443.

49. Ibid., vol. 4, pp. 99–100.

another step to say that evangelicalism was 'created by' one of its contexts. A shared vocabulary is not sufficient to demonstrate an intellectual origin, especially when there are obvious alternatives available to account for the provenance of the substance of Wesley's ideas. We shall return to this point in consideration of Edwards.

Jonathan Edwards on spiritual sense

From his early works onwards Edwards, like Wesley, held to a high view of the new sense given to the believer by the Holy Spirit. His sermon *A Divine and Supernatural Light*, delivered in 1733 and published the following year, argues from Matthew 16:17 for the necessity of a Spirit-given revelation of God. This is not the same as a moral conviction of sin, an impression on the imagination, a merely speculative knowledge or an instance of being affected by the things of religion. Rather, it is a direct, unmediated sense of divine excellency that affects the 'heart', the term Edwards uses for the entire 'cognitive-volitional-affective complex' of the human person.[50] As Edwards puts it, 'The evidence that they that are spiritually enlightened have of the truth of the things of religion, is a kind of intuitive and immediate evidence.' Such evidence might suggest that Edwards did indeed preach and write about an immediate, early assurance for Christians. That conclusion, however, can be reached only if we do not pause to investigate the content of the assurance thus given to the believer. *Divine and Supernatural Light* is a sermon concerned exclusively with the objective truth of the Gospel, and not with the truth of the claim that any individual is saved. In other words, Edwards advocates a direct, immediate assurance that there is such an excellent being as the gospel proclaims. He does not advocate an immediate sense in the Christian that he or she is saved. This is a traditional distinction within Reformed theology, and it is no surprise to find that when Edwards comes to explain how any individual can find assurance of salvation the answer is quite different, as we

---

50. This helpful definition of the 'heart' in Edwards is given by Brad Walton in *Jonathan Edwards, Religious Affections and the Puritan Analysis of True Piety, Spiritual Sensation and Heart Religion* (Lewiston, N. Y.: Edwin Mellen, 2002), e.g. p. 209. For the arguments from *A Divine and Supernatural Light*, see *The Works of Jonathan Edwards*, vol. 17: *Sermons and Discourses, 1730–1733*, ed. M. Valeri (New Haven: Yale University Press, 1999), pp. 410ff. All references to volumes in this series will have a full first citation, after which they will follow the abbreviated citation *WJE*.

shall see below. For now the point is that when in such texts Edwards speaks of an immediate certainty, he is not speaking about the certainty of salvation that fuels confident action.

Having granted that there is a real emphasis on immediate spiritual sense in Edwards, it is also necessary to consider the provenance of this emphasis. The 1746 *Treatise Concerning Religious Affections* is often said to be his most revealingly Lockean text at this point. In it, Edwards delineates the marks of religious affections that accompany a saving work of the Spirit. When he discusses the first of his twelve signs of genuine affections, he again defends the concept of a new spiritual sense against its detractors:

> in those gracious exercises and affections which are wrought in the minds of the saints, through the saving influences of the Spirit of God, there is a new inward perception or sensation of their minds, entirely different in its nature and kind, from anything that ever their minds were the subjects of before they were sanctified.[51]

Edwards is happy to cast this spiritual sense in language favourable to philosophers: he acknowledges that it is 'what some metaphysicians call a new simple idea'.[52] The exact relation between Edwards and such metaphysicians is, however, a matter of great and lively contention. Perry Miller emphasized the Lockean identity of Edwards. Norman Fiering countered by emphasizing his debt to Nicolas Malebranche, and writing of Miller's work as 'rhetorically brilliant but utterly misleading in content[,] . . . an unaccountable lapse in the scholarship of one of the greatest of American historians'.[53] Conrad Cherry identified Edwards as 'first and last a Puritan theologian' rather than an Enlightenment thinker.[54] The disagreement over Edwards as philosopher or Puritan has raged on in the literature, but it is beyond the scope of this

---

51. *The Works of Jonathan Edwards*, vol. 2: *Religious Affections*, ed. J. E. Smith (New Haven: Yale University Press, 1959), p. 205.

52. Ibid.

53. For Miller, see esp. 'Jonathan Edwards on the Sense of the Heart', *Harvard Theological Review* 41 (1948), pp. 123–145; *Jonathan Edwards* (New York: William Sloane Associates, 1949). The Fiering quotation is from Norman Fiering, *Jonathan Edwards's Moral Thought and Its British Context* (Chapel Hill: University of North Carolina Press, 1981), p. 373.

54. Conrad Cherry, *The Theology of Jonathan Edwards: A Reappraisal* (Bloomington: Indiana University Press, 1966; repr. 1990), p. xxiii.

chapter to deal with it thoroughly.[55] Nonetheless, it is vital to Bebbington's reading of evangelical origins that Edwards was decisively influenced by Locke, a claim that is at the centre of this controversy. Some kind of assessment is thus unavoidable.

In short, I find that there are two insuperable problems with the attempt to class Edwards as in any significant way a Lockean. First, he disagrees with Locke on a number of philosophical issues central to both their intellectual projects. Second, as with Wesley, recent work has shown conclusively that the language and even the key concepts used by Edwards are explicable in terms of his Augustinian–Reformed theological heritage without appeal to Locke, except at a few isolated and insubstantial points, and for apologetic purposes.

First, we turn to the disagreements with Locke. Many examples of clear divergence between Edwards and Locke could be cited, but two brief and pointed instances will suffice to show the extent of the problem. With Locke, Edwards speaks of simple ideas generated by perceiving a particular content and reflecting on that content with reason. And yet, going far beyond and against Locke, he understands the content of spiritual perception to be divine excellency and holds that it can be perceived only through the illuminating work of the Holy Spirit in the individual creating a new sense. This particular supernatural claim would have been entirely unacceptable to the philosopher. Consequently, even here, where Edwards is using language definitely attributable to Locke, he is giving it a quite contradictory meaning. As Brad Walton comments in his recent work, 'On the rare occasion he uses a Lockean technical term, such as "simple idea," he does so metaphorically, in an un-Lockean sense, for the purposes of illustration by analogy.'[56] Second, the whole aim of the *Religious Affections* can be understood as a rejection of Lockean-style hostility to religious enthusiasm. Edwards sets out to establish the centrality of affections in perception and thus disagrees with Locke and his own contemporaries such as Charles Chauncy in arguing that the Christian individual is strongly *inclined to* the divine excellency that is spiritually perceived. These and many other examples show that, as Walton puts it, Edwards has 'a panoply of un-Lockean concepts' deployed at crucial points in the *Religious Affections*.[57]

Second, there is sufficiency of the Augustinian–Reformed theological heritage as an explanation for the language and concepts used by Edwards.

---

55. For a survey of the debate in relation to the *Religious Affections*, see Walton, *Jonathan Edwards*, ch. 1.

56. Ibid., p. 218.

57. Ibid., p. 216.

Edwards himself would have been troubled to think that his ideas were novel and based on a recent philosophical development. It is no surprise that he takes us to the Scriptures to show the origin of his concept of spiritual sense:

> Hence the work of the Spirit of God in regeneration is often in Scripture compared to the giving a new sense, giving eyes to see, and ears to hear, unstopping the ears of the deaf, and opening the eyes of them that were born blind, and turning from darkness unto light.[58]

In terms of his more immediate background, Edwards repeatedly cites long passages from Puritan writers in his footnotes. These passages and others from texts Edwards had read contain the concepts he is meant to have acquired from his adherence to Locke. For example, Edwards cites the following passage from John Owen on spiritual perception:

> The true nature of saving illumination consists in this, that it give the mind such a direct intuitive insight and prospect into spiritual things, as that in their own spiritual nature they suit, please, and satisfy it; so that it is transformed into them, cast into the mould of them, and rests in them.[59]

Edwards is here defending his second authentic sign, and uses this text from Owen's *Pneumatologia* to expand on his own point that in a saving work of the Spirit the true saint delights affectively in the spiritual sense of who God is.

At this point it is important to note the recent work of Walton on the *Religious Affections*.[60] Walton has done something that, in the light of the footnotes in the *Religious Affections*, ought to have been a very obvious move to make long ago to advance the scholarly deadlock over Edwards. That is, he has worked his way through a long list of Puritan writers to search for the kind of religious psychology we find in Edwards. And he has found it abundantly. He carefully traces the prehistory of the Edwardsean conceptions of, *inter alia*, assurance, illumination, spiritual sense, the affections, authentic signs, and the heart. His focus is on writers of the seventeenth century, but he goes back through the medieval period to the Scriptures and classical philosophy. I do not have the space to detail his findings, but it is hard to see how his work will not prove to be an insurmountable challenge to anyone who wishes to cling

---

58. *WJE* 2:206.

59. Ibid., 250. See Owen, *Works of John Owen*, vol. 3, p. 238.

60. See n. 50 above.

to Miller's understanding of Edwards, or to any view that sees the wellspring of Edwardsean theology in the Enlightenment.

I cite just two of Walton's more apposite Puritan examples to supplement my own reference to Owen. First is Thomas Goodwin (1600–80), sounding just like Edwards on a new sense: 'whereas God regenerateth any man, and constitutes him a new creature, lo, that man hath a new eye to see, an ear to hear, and all sorts of new senses to take in all sorts of spiritual things'.[61] Just as sensual in his language is John Flavel (1630–91), commenting that among true believers

> you will find also tasting as well as enlightening: so that they seem to abound not only in knowledge, but in sense also; i.e., in some kind of experience of what they know: for experience is the bringing of things to the test of the spiritual sense.[62]

With page upon page of such evidence carefully detailed and expounded, Walton has further undermined any conception of an Edwards decisively shaped by Locke. But he has also raised serious questions about any attempts to make other Enlightenment thinkers decisive for the shape of Edwards's thought.

Perhaps the most accurate assessment of the Enlightenment influence on Edwards is that he was engaged in an apologetic project in which he used the language and concepts of his opponents to his own theological ends. There are pointers in this direction in various commentators. Fiering, who is eager to make the case for Malebranche as an important influence, agrees that Edwards aimed 'to give seventeenth-century Puritan pietism a respectable philosophical structure, which would make it rationally credible and more enduring than it could be without the aid of philosophy'.[63] Michael McClymond pursues a similar line of argument in his recent work, arguing that Edwards used contemporary conceptions for an apologetic purpose.[64]

Having commented on Walton's work, it is only fair to point out that he himself would probably eschew even this concession to the claim of Enlightenment influence, since he avers that nearly all of the terminology used by Edwards in his discussion of conversion is wholly traditional.[65] Fortunately, we do not have to adjudicate here on the precise extent of the

---

61. *Jonathan Edwards*, p. 85.

62. Ibid., p. 120.

63. *Jonathan Edwards's Moral Thought*, p. 60.

64. Michael J. McClymond, *Encounters with God: An Approach to the Theology of Jonathan Edwards* (New York: Oxford University Press, 1998), pp. 7, 115, n. 17.

65. *Jonathan Edwards*, p. 218.

terminological influence of the Enlightenment. It is enough to note that at the least Walton has shown that the substance of Edwards's thought is not derived from the Enlightenment, while at the most he has shown that even its language was derived from elsewhere. Either way, following earlier work against the Lockean hypothesis, his research undermines the conception of Edwards on which Bebbington's assessment of the origins of evangelicalism depends.

Edwards on imagination and assurance

When, in the *Religious Affections*, Edwards considers how an individual can discern saving spiritual affections, he again employs the concept of spiritual sense. Here he is concerned to show how true sense and affection can be distinguished from false. It is this discussion of subjective self-knowledge that is germane to the doctrine of assurance, rather than his other work on the knowledge of the objective truth of the gospel. Edwards gives an account of assurance quite distinct from that held by Wesley, with the result that the two men taught strongly opposed doctrines. This disagreement undermines the idea that there was a coherent new doctrine at the heart of nascent evangelicalism.

Specifically, Edwards refuses to count as evidence for authentic spiritual sense and affection any phenomenon that pertains to the imagination, which he defines as

> that power of the mind, whereby it can have a conception, or idea of things of an external or outward nature (that is, of such sort of things as are the objects of the outward senses), when those things are not present, and be not perceived by the senses.[66]

This definition leads him to reject the same phenomena attesting the direct witness by the Spirit that Wesley endorses (and that were relied on by many in New England). As we saw above, Wesley favourably cites the example of a man hearing the statement 'Thy sins are forgiven thee.'[67] Edwards cites this as just the kind of thing that someone deluded by Satan might use as the basis for his assurance.[68] It is not just that this may be either a good or bad basis for assurance (which Wesley himself seems prepared to admit). It is that such a

---

66. *WJE* 2:210–211.

67. *Works of John Wesley*, vol. 1, p. 282.

68. *WJE* 2:149.

supposedly direct witness can *never* be any ground for a Christian's assurance. Edwards holds that anything which could be emulated by the devil is automatically excluded as a ground of assurance. It may not necessarily be a satanic witness; it may even be a work of the Spirit. But, if it is a work of the Spirit, it is not a witness to the salvation of the individual concerned:

> So if the Spirit of God impresses on a man's imagination, either in a dream, or when he is awake, any outward ideas of any of the senses, either voices, or shapes and colors, 'tis only exciting ideas of the same kind that he has by natural principles and senses.[69]

The difference can be set out with an example Bebbington himself uses when he asserts the novelty of the evangelical epistemology. In the middle of an account that makes no distinction between Edwards and Wesley, Bebbington tells us that the rank and file 'formulated their experience in the same way' as their leaders. He provides this example:

> 'By the eye of faith', wrote an early Methodist about his sense of pardon through the work of Christ, 'I had as real a view of His agony on Calvary as ever I had of any object by the eye of sense'. The understanding of faith in terms of self-validating sense impressions was a striking novelty.[70]

Edwards refers to just such an instance:

> Some have had ideas of Christ's hanging on the cross, and his blood running from his wounds; and this they call a spiritual sight of Christ crucified, and the way of salvation by his blood. . . . These things they have called having the inward call of Christ, hearing the voice of Christ spiritually in their hearts, having the witness of the Spirit, and the inward testimony of the love of Christ, etc.[71]

Does Edwards affirm such a witness? On the contrary, he speaks of it in strongly disparaging terms. The idea that the man has of Christ 'is no better in itself, than the external idea that the Jews his enemies had, who stood round his cross and saw this with their bodily eyes'.[72] Any kind of man can have such images: 'A natural man is capable of having an idea, and a lively idea of shapes

---

69. Ibid., 207.
70. 'Revival and Enlightenment', pp. 23–24.
71. *WJE* 2:211–212.
72. Ibid., 214.

and colors and sounds when they are absent, and as capable as a regenerate man is: so there is nothing supernatural in them.'[73]

Edwards is prepared to use strong language of this experience: 'There appears to be nothing in their nature above the power of the devil.'[74] Indeed, 'it is certain also that the devil can excite, and often hath excited such ideas'.[75] Edwards has by this point already used language of an even stronger nature, describing the way in which such visions denigrate Jesus Christ. They make the spiritual sense no better than the senses even the beasts of the field have, 'as it were, a turning Christ, or the divine nature in the soul, into a mere animal'.[76]

Behind this rejection of such experiences lies Edwards's hostility to imagination as the source of religious knowledge. He repeatedly attacks any source of assurance that could have been produced by the imagination, including ideas of shapes, words spoken and bodily sensations. For Edwards, imagination is the prime instrument Satan uses in deceiving people about their spiritual status. It is frequently a source of false knowledge, contrasted with the true enlightenment that is the fourth sign of gracious affections.

Edwards explains that the devil has no access to the thoughts in an individual's mind, unlike God to whom such knowledge is reserved. Hence 'it must be only by the imagination, that Satan has access to the soul, to tempt and delude it, or suggest anything to it'.[77] Persons who do not keep a close guard will be highly susceptible to the devil when he masquerades as an angel of light with 'inward whispers, and immediate suggestions of facts and events, pleasant voices, beautiful images, and other impressions on the imagination'.[78] True affections may produce lively imaginations, but lively imaginations are no assurance of true affections. Under the discussion of the fifth authentic sign, Edwards again describes imaginings as one of the types of false conviction:

> The extraordinary impressions which are made on the imaginations of some persons, in the visions, and immediate strong impulses and suggestions that they have, as though they saw sights, and had words spoken to 'em, may, and often do beget a strong persuasion of the truth of invisible things.[79]

---

73. Ibid., 213.
74. Ibid., 215.
75. Ibid., 216.
76. Ibid., 213.
77. Ibid., 289.
78. Ibid., 290.
79. Ibid., 309.

Edwards on perseverance in good works as the witness of the Spirit

The feeling one gets when reading the *Religious Affections* as a Christian is a feeling of gradual, painful deconstruction. Piece by piece Edwards removes the spiritual props so many rely on. We take a sharp intake of breath as yet another part of the evidence we have trusted in to show the genuineness of our profession is dismantled. The reader is beginning to wonder exactly what sound basis for assurance will be left to Edwards. The New England theologian is aware of this dynamic; indeed it is deliberate and accounts for much of the spiritual power of the work. Just after his dismissal of images, voices and even the spontaneous recollection of scriptural texts, he anticipates the reader's growing concern: 'But here, some may be ready to say, what, is there no such thing as any particular spiritual application of the promises of Scripture by the Spirit of God?'[80]

His reply unmistakably affirms such an application, but in a way that contradicts what will be Wesley's doctrine of assurance and Bebbington's picture of Edwards himself. The application of the promises is to be found in the fruit of the Spirit: 'A spiritual application of the Word of God consists in applying it to the heart, in spiritually enlightening, sanctifying influences.' The application of the offer of the gospel entails a sequence of stages. It means giving a spiritual sense of the blessings offered, of the grace of the one offering, of his excellency, faithfulness and sufficiency for it, eliciting a response, and 'thus giving the man evidence of his title to the thing offered'.[81]

We must consider carefully the use of the term 'evidence' here under the account of the first authentic sign. Where Wesley posits a direct, unmediated witness, Edwards routes all assurance via evidence considered by the individual's conscience, in these cases the sanctifying influences of the Spirit and an obedient response to the gospel. Edwards is adamant that because there is no statement in the Scriptures about any individual Christian believer being saved, no one can have a direct communication that *they themselves* are forgiven: 'there are no propositions to be found in the Bible declaring that such and such particular persons, independent on any previous knowledge of any qualifications, are forgiven and beloved of God'. Anyone who is comforted by such a statement is actually comforted 'by another word, a word newly coined, and not any Word of God contained in the Bible. And thus many persons are vainly affected and deluded.'[82]

---

80. Ibid., 224.

81. Ibid., 225.

82. Ibid., 226.

Edwards finds that people have been misled by the term 'witness' into denying that the Spirit uses evidence. They have done this by failing to note how the words 'witness' and 'testimony' are used in the New Testament. He points out, using Hebrews 2:4 as an example, that 'such terms often signify, not only a mere declaring and asserting a thing to be true, but holding forth evidence from whence a thing may be argued and proved to be true'.[83]

Edwards explicates his own conception of the witness of the Spirit by using what he deems to be the biblical equivalents 'seal' (*sphragis*) and 'earnest' (*arrabōn*). Both point to the role of fruit as evidence in the Spirit's witness. The seal denotes 'not an immediate voice or suggestion, but some work or effect of the Spirit, that is left as a divine mark upon the soul, to be an evidence, by which God's children might be known'.[84] This mark assures by 'exhibiting clear evidence to the conscience'. The seal, which Edwards compares to a royal signet, is thus 'enstamped in so fair and clear a manner, as to be plain to the eye of conscience'.[85] The earnest of the Spirit means the same thing.[86] In sum, the seal is understood by Edwards as the 'sanctifying communication and influence of the Spirit'.[87]

Edwards draws these comments together by turning to Romans 8:16. Discussing Paul's description of the Spirit as the 'Spirit of adoption', he explains that the Spirit works in 'disposing us to behave towards God as to a Father'.[88] The troubled Christian must therefore turn his conscience to look for evidence of childlike obedience to the Father if he wants assurance that his affections are genuine. Against the position later taken by Wesley, Edwards argues that a believer should not expect a twofold witness: 'When the apostle Paul speaks of the Spirit of God bearing witness with our spirit, he is not to be understood of two spirits, that are two separate, collateral, independent witnesses.'[89]

The position Edwards takes on evidence emerges most clearly in the treatment of the twelfth authentic sign, defined by the claim that 'gracious and holy affections have their exercise and fruit in Christian practice'.[90] The treatment of

---

83. Ibid., 231.
84. Ibid., 232.
85. Ibid., 233.
86. Ibid., 234ff.
87. Ibid., 237.
88. Ibid.
89. Ibid., 239.
90. Ibid., 383.

this sign occupies much of Part 3 of the *Religious Affections*, and Edwards explains that the other eleven aspects of gracious affections show why they will always culminate in Christian practice. In terms of the structure of the book and the direction of the argument, this sign is the centrepiece. Edwards takes great care in explaining it. He argues that Christian practice has three features. It entails a universal conformity to Christian rules (by which he means a full range of obedience, not perfect obedience). It takes priority over all other things in an individual's life, and it persists through trials and testing until the end.

This last point is very important, since Edwards holds that it is in trials that the true nature of an individual's affections is revealed: perseverance is defined as 'the continuance of professors in the practice of their duty, and being steadfast in an holy walk, through the various trials that they meet with'.[91]

Having explained what he means by 'Christian practice', Edwards distinguishes two aspects of its evidentiary function. On the one hand, it serves as a sign by which others can discern the authenticity of a professor's affections. In so doing they will consider only the external good works an individual does, since they have no direct access to his inner life. Despite the fact that their conclusions will thus never attain infallibility, 'practice is the best evidence of the sincerity of professing Christians'.[92] On the other hand, an individual's *own* conscience can perceive his inner life as well as his outward actions. This means that the individual's self-scrutiny involves the consideration of a whole range of evidence not available to others, namely the acts of the soul.

Edwards explains that practice is the culmination of a process which begins in the soul. Therefore, the entire activity of the soul that precedes the action of the body must be considered: 'the whole exercise of the spirit of the mind, in the action, must be taken in, with the end acted for, and the respect the soul then has to God, etc'.[93] Here we glimpse a sight of the vista that unfolds in *The Freedom of the Will*. There, Edwards is clear that any genuinely free external act of the body will be united to an internal act of the will that will be available to the conscience for scrutiny.[94] Just as Christian practice is the best evidence for another to discern genuine affections, so for the individual: it is 'the chief of all the evidences of a saving sincerity in religion, to the consciences of the professors of it'.[95] Edwards reaches a crescendo of praise for

---

91. Ibid., 389.
92. Ibid., 409.
93. Ibid., 423.
94. Ibid., 425–426.
95. Ibid., 426.

Christian practice:

> Now from all that has been said, I think it to be abundantly manifest, that
> Christian practice is the most proper evidence of the gracious sincerity of
> professors, to themselves and others; and the chief of all the marks of grace, the
> sign of signs, and evidence of evidences, that which seals and crowns all other
> signs.[96]

At the end of *Religious Affections*, Edwards anticipates the objection that
his position negates the role of Christian experience. In reply he makes a
move that further highlights how different his view is from that of Wesley.
Where Wesley speaks of a directly communicated spiritual sense, Edwards
subsumes spiritual sense itself within his account of assurance based on good
works. He defends his position by showing that his account makes much of
experience when experience is rightly understood as including holy practice;
indeed, 'nothing is so properly called by the name of experimental religion'.[97]
In particular, he affirms the evidentiary role of the experience of endurance in
the midst of trials:

> To have at such a time that sense of divine things, that apprehension of the truth,
> importance and excellency of the things of religion, which then sways and prevails,
> and governs his heart and hands; this is the most excellent spiritual light, and these
> are the most distinguishing discoveries.[98]

This statement reflects the earlier point that Edwards sees a continuity
between inner and outer actions, actions of the soul and the body. The true
'spiritual light' here works through from the grasp of divine things all the way
to the bodily deeds done by the hands.

At one point Edwards turns to address the question of instant assurance,
aware that his view might be taken to exclude even its possibility. In a statement, the tone of which hardly suggests a new, bold evangelicalism, he allows
that early assurance can be experienced: "'Tis possible that a man may have
a good assurance of a state of grace, at his first conversion, before he has had
opportunity to gain assurance, by this great evidence I am speaking of.'[99] This

---

96. Ibid., 443.
97. Ibid., 452.
98. Ibid., 453.
99. Ibid., 443.

experience is compared to a man setting off on a journey to claim a promised treasure. The man can know that he is determined to arrive as soon as the offer is first made. But quickly Edwards moves on to assert that this does not 'hinder but that his actual going for it is the highest and most proper evidence of his being willing'.[100]

In the light of such arguments it is no surprise that in the course of the work Edwards urges a thorough, suspicious and relentless self-examination, most notably on the issue of pride and humility. His advice needs to be cited at length to show just how committed to radically searching self-examination he was:

> Let not the reader lightly pass over these things in application to himself. If you once have taken it in, that it is a bad sign for a person to be apt to think himself a better saint than others, there will arise a blinding prejudice in your own favor; and there will probably be need of a great strictness of self-examination, in order to determine whether it be so with you. If on the proposal of the question, you answer, 'No, it seems to me, none are so bad as I'. Don't let the matter pass off so; but examine again, whether or no you don't think yourself better than others on this very account, because you imagine you think so meanly of yourself. Haven't you a high opinion of this humility? And if you answer again, 'No; I have not a high opinion of my humility; it seems to me I am as proud as the devil'; yet examine again, whether self-conceit don't rise up under this cover; whether on this very account, that you think yourself as proud as the devil, you don't think yourself to be very humble.[101]

This sounds far more like the voice of the Puritan of Puritans than of a carefree evangelical ready for action.

In the *Religious Affections* we therefore find a doctrine of assurance based not on Enlightenment epistemology but on a close attention to the language of Scripture. We find a doctrine concerned to urge not reliance on a direct witness, but careful scrutiny of ongoing good works done in a filial disposition amid trials and temptations. It is notable that it was *after* writing this treatise, perhaps a more cautious treatment than his earlier revival writings, that Edwards himself worked among the Indians in the frontier town of Stockbridge. Where we would expect from Bebbington to find the earlier, possibly more confident theology fuelling evangelistic activism, we find that Edwards's activism followed

---

100. Ibid.
101. Ibid., 336.

his attack on the idea of a direct witness. Perhaps the opposite of Bebbington's view is the case: that a more reserved view of assurance encourages activism in an attempt to provide the evidence that comforts the conscience.

If we have not already seen enough to demonstrate that there was not a new carefree view of early assurance, let alone a consensus on the subject, we shall attend briefly to the treatment that the *Religious Affections* received at the hands of John Wesley. Wesley produced abridged editions of many works as part of his *Christian Library*, one of which was the *Religious Affections*. Only a sixth of the work survived his editorial knife, with the twelve signs of Part 3 being reduced to eight. While many of Wesley's excisions in other works were purely for brevity and ease of reading, this was nothing short of a consistent theological programme, designed to purge the work of its errors. In introducing the work, Wesley himself admitted that this was his strategy. It is plain that he did not like the treatise as he found it because he thought it was a defence of the doctrine of the final perseverance of all believers. Edwards, he judged, wrote in order to explain why, since the Revival, so many 'believers' seemed to have fallen away. Wesley judges that Edwards goes to great lengths to reach his goal:

> He heaps together so many curious, subtile [subtle], metaphysical distinctions, as are sufficient to puzzle the brain, and confound the intellects, of all the plain men and women in the universe; and to make them doubt of, if not wholly deny, all the work which God had wrought in their souls.

In all, Wesley found the treatise a 'dangerous heap, wherein much wholesome food is mixed with much deadly poison'.[102] As we would expect from what we have seen of their respective positions, Wesley was quite happy to maintain Edwards's defence of works as authenticating signs, but cut out the strongest material that explained supposed examples of the direct witness as the fruit of delusory imagination. Gone is the attack on the idea of an immediate direct witness alongside Christian practice, which we find when Edwards describes the first sign of authentic affections. Wesley's opening fulmination and his strategic omission confirm that there was no uniform early evangelical doctrine of assurance, while his inclusion of Edwards's material on the centrality of works shows that there was no uniform rejection of the Puritan emphasis on self-examination.

---

102. *The Work of the Holy Spirit in the Human Heart, by the Rev. Jonathan Edwards M. A. [...] Being Two Tracts on That Subject Abridged by Rev. John Wesley, A. M.*, ed. T. O. Summers (Salem, Ohio: Schmul, 1998), p. 49.

John Newton on assurance

The lack of early evangelical uniformity on assurance is further highlighted by the teaching of John Newton. Bebbington cites Newton as an example of an evangelical who departed from traditional Puritan theological distinctions. These, Bebbington quotes Newton saying, were 'not Scriptural modes of expression, nor do they appear to me to throw light upon the subject'.[103] Newton functions for Bebbington as an example of evangelical dependence on the Enlightenment in that he favoured the empirical method rather than Puritan systematization in his theological reasoning. For our purposes, Newton is of interest not because of his method, but because of his doctrine of assurance as it is found in his sermon *Of the Assurance of Faith*.

Like Wesley, Newton speaks of assurance as a common privilege of Christians, though in context he may mean simply to assert that assurance is not exclusively apostolic, an observation he makes since he is discussing an apostolic text, 1 John 5:19.[104] But Newton's view of who has had assurance in the history of the church is distinctly reserved. Even in the apostolic period it was only 'some' who could say they were children of God, 'some' who had such assurance.[105] In the later history of the church there have been 'many' who could echo the apostle's words, and in his own day he trusts that 'there are more than a few' in such a position, though there are hindrances 'which keep so many who are interested in the Gospel salvation from enjoying their privilege'.[106] Indeed, he finds that the 'the greater part . . . live far below their just right and privilege'.[107]

The reason for Newton's hesitation becomes clear when he discusses the stage at which assurance is given and the ground on which it is established. The young believer is unlikely to have much hope in God's mercy, since hope depends on the knowledge of Christ, which in turn 'in a measure depends on our knowledge of the Scriptures, which testify of him, and on the proofs we have had of his wisdom, grace, and love to ourselves'. The young convert lacks these. Hence, Newton says, with a significant choice of words, 'though

---

103. 'Revival and Enlightenment', p. 24, quoting from *The Works of the Rev. John Newton* (London, 1808), vol. 2, p. 587.
104. *Works of the Rev. John Newton*, 6 vols. (London: Hamilton, Adams, 1824³), vol. 2, p. 585.
105. Ibid.
106. Ibid., pp. 585, 586.
107. Ibid., p. 586.

his eyes are opened, his sight is not yet confirmed, nor his spiritual senses exercised'.[108] The new believer has underdeveloped spiritual senses, which are not yet functioning to give him assurance. He is also tempted to legalism, which further weakens assurance. To make his point, Newton quotes Paul's persuasion that he will be rewarded (2 Tim. 1:12), a persuasion that he notes is expressed at the *end* of his life.

Newton's definition of the ground of assurance is also interestingly distinct from Wesley's account of the two witnesses: 'Assurance is the result of a competent spiritual knowledge of the person and work of Christ as revealed in the Gospel, and a consciousness of dependence on him and his work alone for salvation.'[109] This process of knowledge and dependence is expressly distinguished from three false grounds: from (1) an 'instantaneous impression of the Spirit of God upon the mind, independent of his word', from (2) the 'powerful application of a particular text of Scripture', and from (3) the consideration of 'inherent sanctification, or a considerable increase of it'. In other words, it is distinct from Wesley's immediate direct and indirect witness, as well as from Edwards's indirect witness. Nonetheless, at the end of his sermon, even Newton cannot avoid some appeal to works as negative evidence, warning that 'if your love and dependence are not fixed on the Lord Jesus Christ, if your tempers and practice are not governed by his commands, you are not of God'.[110]

As a result of basing assurance on the knowledge of the person and work of Christ, Newton speaks of a growing assurance, growing in proportion to increasing knowledge of Scripture and decreasing self-reliance. He sounds more like one of Bebbington's Puritans than one of his evangelicals: 'Remember that the progress of faith to assurance is gradual. Expect it not suddenly; but wait upon the Lord for it in the ways of his appointment.'[111] At least this evangelical did not believe assurance to be 'general, normally given at conversion and the result of simple acceptance of the gift of God'.[112]

With such evidence the picture of a shift from the Puritan view (a late works-based witness) to the new evangelical view (an early direct witness) will not hold. In his work on Newton, D. Bruce Hindmarsh is also uneasy with the idea of a new evangelical doctrine of assurance. He quotes Bebbington's

---

108. Ibid., p. 589.
109. Ibid., p. 593.
110. Ibid., p. 599.
111. Ibid., p. 598.
112. Bebbington, *Evangelicalism in Modern Britain*, p. 43.

characterization and states that 'It would perhaps be well to add that there was a spectrum of opinion on assurance among evangelicals as surely as there was among Puritans.'[113] I would go further and aver that there comes a point where the whole idea of a marked distinction between Puritanism and evangelicalism must be re-examined.

Activism before the 1730s

Finally, some more general remarks are necessary on the idea of evangelical activism. As we have seen, Bebbington ties the origins of evangelicalism to the emergence of activism. This activism was based on the evangelical doctrine of assurance. Given that we find much in the Reformers on assurance that is akin to Bebbington's picture of the evangelicals, it is odd that he does not trace the emergence of evangelicalism to the Reformation. The reason is that, though they had the doctrine of assurance, they did not have the activism. The Puritans had neither.[114]

Such claims highlight the importance of ascertaining exactly what the activism in question entailed. In many of Bebbington's publications he deploys the four characteristics of evangelicalism with a number of examples of each. Detailing some of these examples suggests a wide array of evangelical activism from across the centuries. In 'The Gospel in the Nineteenth Century' he speaks of preaching, visiting, distributing tracts, prayer meetings and Sunday schools. In the defining section of *Evangelicalism in Modern Britain* he mentions evangelism, pastoral care, preaching, missionary work and general philanthropy. In 'Evangelicalism in Modern Britain and America' he refers to missionary activity at home and abroad. In 'Evangelical Christianity and the Enlightenment' he cites spreading the gospel, philanthropy and preaching. In 'Revival and Enlightenment in Eighteenth-Century England' 'spreading the gospel where it was not yet known' is mentioned. In 'Towards an Evangelical Identity' a range of activities, including evangelism, preaching, missionary work, organized philanthropy and social reform, are referenced. And in

---

113. *John Newton and the English Evangelical Tradition* (Oxford: Clarendon, 1996), p. 66. See also pp. 250–256 for a discussion of three letters by Newton that confirm the analysis given here; assurance is traced to the second stage of three in the Christian life, to the wilderness between the exodus and Canaan (*Works*, vol. 1, p. 204).

114. 'Evangelical Christianity and the Enlightenment', in M. Eden and D. F. Wells (eds.), *The Gospel in the Modern World* (Leicester: IVP, 1991), p. 71.

'Scottish Cultural Influences on Evangelicalism' reference is made principally to the 11,000 visitations made in one year by Thomas Chalmers.[115]

Surely here Bebbington grants too much in his definition of activism. Allowing such breadth to the acceptable types of activity will result in finding the beginning of evangelicalism not in the eighteenth but the sixteenth century. The Reformers themselves were undeniably activists on these terms.

John Calvin and the Huguenots provide an excellent example of the Reformation concern for evangelism. The list drawn up for Admiral de Coligny in 1562 indicates that there were by then 2,150 Huguenot churches in France, and McGrath estimates a total membership above two million (more than a tenth of the population).[116] This was within thirty years of Calvin's own conversion. In England we need only think of a John Bradford preaching in the north of England, or the commonwealth thinkers with leaders such as Hugh Latimer urging practical reform on the young King Edward. Into the seventeenth century we find the quest for souls amply represented among the Puritans. Even in a writing that represents the height of John Owen's Reformed Scholasticism, his *Dissertation on Divine Justice*, we find a conclusion on the uses of the doctrine that directly addresses 'you who live, or rather are dead, under the guilt, dominion, power, and law of sin' and urges self-surrender to Christ.[117] Richard Baxter held to as complex a theological system as any of the Puritans, but from his work in Kidderminster he could hardly be thought of except as an activist.

It is no surprise then that when Bebbington denies the activism of the Puritans, he immediately specifies the absence of foreign missions: 'There was, for example, a remarkable absence of Protestant missions in the sixteenth and seventeenth centuries.'[118] This is a much tighter definition of activism than he suggests elsewhere, but it is the only one that will sustain his argument. The dating of evangelicalism to the 1730s will work only if we say that preaching, pastoring, evangelism and social concern do not count as examples

---

115. 'The Gospel in the Nineteenth Century', *Vox evangelica* 13 (1983), pp. 22–23; *Evangelicalism in Modern Britain*, pp. 10–12; 'Evangelicalism in Modern Britain and America', pp. 185–186; 'Evangelical Christianity and the Enlightenment', p. 67; 'Revival and Enlightenment', p. 21; 'Towards an Evangelical Identity', in S. Brady and H. Rowdon (eds.), *For Such a Time as This* (London: Scripture Union, 1996), pp. 44–45; 'Scottish Cultural Influences on Evangelicalism', *Scottish Bulletin of Evangelical Theology* 14.1 (1996), p. 23.

116. Alister E. McGrath, *A Life of John Calvin* (Oxford: Blackwell, 1990), pp. 191–192.

117. *Works of John Owen*, vol. 10, pp. 620–621.

118. 'Evangelical Christianity and the Enlightenment', p. 71.

of evangelical activism. To my mind, and it would seem from Bebbington's other examples, this is far too specific, and would be a better designation for a particular expression of evangelicalism than for the movement per se.

Evangelical origins and self-understanding

If my argument in this chapter is correct, then the way is opened to reconsidering the case for the Reformation and Puritanism being authentically evangelical movements. Whatever differences pertained between the various evangelical movements would then be understood as differences of accidents rather than substance. This would not be to deny that there were differences. But while they would be significant, they would not be defining, much as Bebbington finds with his account of evangelical variety, yet continuity, after the 1730s.

In closing, I wish to step out of the realm of history by commenting briefly on the consequences of this possibility for evangelical self-understanding. If we think that evangelicalism began in the 1730s, then Wesley and Edwards become its most important fathers. This means that evangelicalism was from its origin equally divided between Reformed and Arminian theology. Neither could claim to be the mainstream doctrinal position. In this sense it is easy to see how Bebbington's analysis serves to give a strong foothold to Arminianism within the evangelical movement by making foundational one of its most noted proponents. If, however, we reconsider the origins of evangelicalism and find that it is a Reformational and Puritan phenomenon, then the picture looks very different.

The magisterial Reformers on the Continent and in England during the sixteenth century and the Puritans of the seventeenth were almost without exception committed to a Reformed account of the doctrine of election. Evangelicalism then becomes aboriginally Reformed on the doctrine of election rather than divided. The position taken by John Wesley on election becomes a deviation along with that of Philip Melanchthon and his Lutheran followers, and Jacobus Arminius and the Remonstrants. With such a historical perspective, Reformed theology becomes the authentic evangelical mainstream of three centuries, and the historical case for the foundational status of Arminianism is undermined.[119]

© Garry J. Williams, 2008

---

119. This chapter was previously published as 'Was Evangelicalism Created by the Enlightenment?', *Tyndale Bulletin* 53.2 (2002), pp. 283–312.

16. EVANGELICAL ESCHATOLOGY AND 'THE PURITAN HOPE'

Crawford Gribben

Since the revival of Reformed theology in the late 1950s, evangelicals have debated the continuities and discontinuities that exist between their movement
and that of the seventeenth-century Puritans they have come to admire. Within
circles most influenced by this neo-Puritan theology, participants in the debate
have agreed that strong continuity ought to exist, but have disputed which of
their various constituencies or denominations best represents the tradition. One
of the debate's most important contributions has been its promotion of historical awareness within a subculture of popular religiosity that is often ahistorical
in its preoccupations. But many arguments advanced in the debate about Puritan–evangelical continuity have themselves been insufficiently historicized, not
paying proper attention to the series of discontinuities that separate Puritans
from those they succeeded, and from those who succeeded them.

Of course, there are obvious difficulties in this statement's assumption of
discrete historical periods, and in its implied distinction between 'Reformers',
'Puritans' and 'evangelicals'. But these qualifications cannot negate the obvious differences between the eschatological interests of Puritans, however they
are defined, and their sixteenth-century Protestant forebears.[1] Puritans read

---

1. On the eschatology of the Reformers, see T. F. Torrance, 'The Eschatology of
   the Reformation', *Eschatology: Scottish Journal of Theology Occasional Papers* 2 (1953),

Revelation in sharp discontinuity from the magisterial Reformers. Many of the leading advocates of reformation adopted an 'apocalyptic sense of urgency' about the programme of renewal they endorsed;[2] but, alarmed by the excesses of Anabaptists, many also turned against eschatological speculation and regarded Revelation with a passionate apathy.[3] Martin Luther disputed whether Revelation should be included in the canon, and Lutheranism, most famously, defined itself in opposition to the millennialism that seemed to fuel Anabaptist revolts.[4] John Calvin omitted Revelation from expositions

pp. 36–62; H. Quistorp, *Calvin's Doctrine of the Last Things* (London: Lutterworth, 1955); Paul Christianson, *Reformers and Babylon: English Apocalyptic Visions from the Reformation to the Eve of the Civil War* (Toronto: University of Toronto Press, 1978); Richard Bauckham, *Tudor Apocalypse: Sixteenth-Century Apocalypticism, Millenarianism and the English Reformation: From John Bale to John Foxe and Thomas Brightman* (Appleford: Sutton Courtenay, 1978); Katherine Firth, *The Apocalyptic Tradition in Reformation Britain, 1530–1645* (Oxford: Oxford University Press, 1979); and, more recently, Irena Backus, *Reformation Readings of the Apocalypse: Geneva, Zurich, and Wittenberg* (Oxford: Oxford University Press, 2000). On the eschatology of Puritans, see William Lamont, *Godly Rule: Politics and Religion, 1603–60* (London: Macmillan, 1969); Peter Toon (ed.), *Puritans, the Millennium and the Future of Israel: Puritan Eschatology 1600 to 1660* (Cambridge: James Clarke, 1970); J. A. de Jong, *As the Waters Cover the Sea: Millennial Expectations in the Rise of Anglo-American Missions 1640–1810* (Kampen: Kok, 1970); Bernard Capp, 'Godly Rule and English Millenarianism', *Past and Present* 52 (1971), pp. 106–117; Christopher Hill, *Antichrist in Seventeenth-Century England* (London: Oxford University Press, 1971); B. S. Capp, *The Fifth Monarchy Men: A Study in Seventeenth-Century Millenarianism* (London: Faber & Faber, 1972); Brian W. Ball, *A Great Expectation: Eschatological Thought in English Protestantism to 1660* (Leiden: E. J. Brill, 1975); William Lamont, *Richard Baxter and the Millennium: Protestant Imperialism and the English Revolution* (London: Croom Helm, 1979); Crawford Gribben, *The Puritan Millennium: Literature and Theology, 1550–1682* (Dublin: Four Courts, 2000); and Richard W. Cogley, 'The Fall of the Ottoman Empire in the "Judeo-Centric" Strand of Puritan Millenarianism', *Church History* 72.2 (2003), pp. 304–332.

2. Andrew Pettegree, *Reformation and the Culture of Persuasion* (Cambridge: Cambridge University Press, 2005), p. 212.

3. The Anabaptist revolution in Münster is described in Norman Cohn, *The Pursuit of the Millennium* (London: Secker & Warburg, 1957; repr. London: Mercury, 1962), pp. 278–306.

4. Augsburg Confession (1530), cited in Gribben, *Puritan Millennium*, p. 34.

that otherwise commented on almost every book in Scripture. One historian of the period has noted Roman Catholic assumptions that a rejection of the canonicity of Revelation was a staple component of the Protestant 'heresy'.[5] There is a chasm between the millennial apathy of the mid-sixteenth century and the millennial fascinations of the mid-seventeenth.

But there is some debate as to whether a similar gulf does or ought to exist between the millennialism of the seventeenth and twenty-first centuries. Part of the difficulty is that modern neo-Puritans have tended to measure (and, often, critique) contemporary evangelicalism by three-hundred-year-old doctrinal standards of doctrine and piety. This has been matched by a complementary tendency to interpret that doctrine and piety through paradigms derived from later developments in evangelical history and thought. Contemporary differences or recent exegetical traditions are read back into the earlier literature in anachronistic attempts to elucidate its meaning. The results have been confusing—and no wonder, when the past has been investigated in terms of the present, at the same time as the present has been assessed by the alleged evidence of the past. Whatever this trend may have done to benefit the theological recovery of sections of the evangelical church, it has certainly not led to a greater sensitivity to nor understanding of the theology and religious experience of the early modern period. Evangelicals may benefit from this attempt to create Puritans in their own image, but this is not the path to greater historical awareness, or an authentic renewal of Puritan piety and thought.

This confusion in methodology and results is most obvious in the debate about Puritan eschatology. A great deal of this recent discussion has been stimulated by Iain H. Murray's classic account *The Puritan Hope: Revival and the Interpretation of Prophecy* (1971). Murray's text was an early publication of the Banner of Truth, the publishing company that did, perhaps, most to advance the early stages of the neo-Puritan revival and its implicit critique of prevailing eschatological norms.[6]

Murray's text attempted to undermine the 'pessimistic' premillennialism that seemed to prevail in large parts of the mid-twentieth-century conservative evangelical movement. Murray wrote of his own earlier absorption in prophetic pessimism, and argued that its limited expectation of gospel blessing in

5. Irena Backus, 'The Church Fathers and the Canonicity of the Apocalypse in the Sixteenth Century: Erasmus, Frans Titelmans, and Theodore Beza', *Sixteenth Century Journal* 29 (1998), pp. 651–665.

6. See also Gary North, 'Towards the Recovery of Hope', *Banner of Truth* 88 (1971), pp. 12–16.

the future was quite different from the eschatological vitality of Puritans and earlier evangelicals. *The Puritan Hope* strongly implied that prophetic optimism (expectations of mass conversions among Jews and Gentiles as the end of the age approached) had been central in conservative Protestant eschatology until the nineteenth-century premillennial revival introduced the idea that little but decay could be expected before the coming of Jesus Christ.

While Murray was clearly rejecting most varieties of premillennialism, he was careful not to specify whether some variant of postmillennialism or optimistic amillennialism was his preferred alternative. But others who followed in Murray's wake were less cautious. In the USA, in particular, neo-Puritans (from pietists to theonomists) have argued that a robust postmillennialism had clearly been (in the singular and with a definite article) 'the Puritan hope'.[7] Puritan eschatology was widely assumed to be postmillennial in character.

Murray's text was published at the same time as a number of other histories of early modern eschatology. Often examining the same seventeenth-century evidence, these texts were generally less reluctant to embrace the apparent ambiguity of Murray's text. Their confusion has been highlighted in competing assessments of the most influential eschatological formulation of mid-seventeenth-century Puritanism, the paragraphs recorded in the Westminster Confession of Faith, 33:1–3.

Scholars of early modern eschatology have agreed on the importance of these paragraphs, but there is less unanimity as to their meaning. Their contents have been described as promoting a 'mild, unsystemized' postmillennialism;[8] as being 'clearly' amillennial, with 'no suggestion of a period of latter-day glory or of a millennium connected with the conversion of the Jews';[9] and as 'the strongest premillennialist symbol of Protestantism'.[10] While some of these descriptions must be more accurate than others, none is ultimately tenable. The grounding assumption of the prophetic schema of a-, pre- and post-millennialism (the assumption that Revelation 20 points to one period of one thousand years) was not universally shared among the most influential of seventeenth-century expositors. Definitions of a-, pre- and postmillennialism

---

7. See e.g. articles in the *Journal of Christian Reconstruction* 15 (1998), 'Symposium on Eschatology'.

8. De Jong, *As the Waters Cover the Sea*, p. 38, n. 11.

9. R. G. Clouse, 'The Rebirth of Millenarianism', in Toon, *Puritans*, p. 60.

10. L. E. Froom, *The Prophetic Faith of Our Fathers: The Historical Development of Prophetic Interpretation*, 4 vols. (Washington, D. C.: Review & Herald, 1946–54), vol. 2, p. 553.

were formulated two centuries after the composition of the Westminster Confession.

According to the *Oxford English Dictionary*, 'millenarian' dates back to 1626, 'millenarianism' dates to 1650 and 'millennial' dates to 1664. The description of a millennial believer as a 'millennist' (1664) or 'millennianite' (1834) never seemed to catch on. The *Oxford English Dictionary* notes that millennialism exists in two species, pre- and post-. 'Premillennian' first occurs in 1828, used by G. S. Faber; 'premillenarian' first occurs in 1844, and, again, is introduced by G. S. Faber; 'premillennial' first occurs in 1846, in the title of a work by G. Ogilvy; and 'postmillennial', as if to seal his dominance of eschatological neologism, is first used as an adjective by G. S. Faber in 1851.[11] The term 'amillennial', though it does not appear in the *Oxford English Dictionary*, actually has its origins in early twentieth-century theological discussion. These terms, a-, pre- and postmillenialism, cannot usefully be brought to bear on an exegetical tradition whose complexity and variety often seem broader than the limited options they represent.[12]

Nevertheless, the use of these competing categorizations ably illustrates the Westminster Confession's success in constructing a politic ambiguity, coining statements broad enough to carry a wide range of theological sympathies. The Westminster Confession, like other confessions of faith from the period, was the negotiated centre of a disparate movement.[13] The Confession stated truths to which the majority of the Assembly's delegates adhered, without preventing them from moving beyond its conservative formulations into overt, intense and often controversial eschatological speculation.

The debate about the meaning of the Westminster Confession of Faith 33:1–3 illustrates the disparity between the collective negotiation of a confession of faith and the individual pursuit of knowledge. Among the most influential of the delegates at the Westminster Assembly were the Presbyterian George Gillespie and the Independent Thomas Goodwin. In public preaching and publications, they variously argued that the fall of Babylon had begun with the calling of the

---

11. *Oxford English Dictionary*, under each word.

12. See Crawford Gribben, 'The Eschatology of the Puritan Confessions', *Scottish Bulletin of Evangelical Theology* 20.1 (2002), pp. 51–78. The first edition of *The Puritan Millennium* erred in making too much of these distinctions in the early modern period. A second edition is forthcoming from Paternoster.

13. See, for powerful evidence of this, Chad B. Van Dixhoorn, 'Reforming the Reformation: Theological Debate at the Westminster Assembly' (PhD thesis, University of Cambridge, 2004).

Assembly in 1643[14] and that the commencement of the millennium could be expected by 1700.[15] These conclusions did not characterize the moderate content of the Confession itself. Plainly, the Confession did not act to set boundaries for their eschatological research. But it is often believed to have done exactly that.

This misunderstanding of the Confession's authority is related to a wider tendency to read the Confession outside the textual culture of the Assembly's delegates. This misunderstanding has occluded the fact that the opinion of delegates often ranged far beyond the negotiated centre of the final confessional statement, and, perhaps, more widely in eschatology than in any other of the loci the Confession defined.[16] Recent research in Puritan eschatology has concluded that millennialism, in particular, was a central component of mainstream Puritan thinking. Nevertheless, while it drove a great deal of Puritan visions for reform, even leading the movement's adherents into violent disagreement, it hardly characterized the confessional tradition they shared.[17]

Puritans therefore embraced a wide range of eschatological conclusions within the confessional mainstream, and so have those evangelicals who have followed them. The eschatological speculation of evangelicals, like that of Puritans, has included both apocalyptic and millennial themes. In the seventeenth century, and long afterwards, apocalypticism has regularly given way to millennial hope. And yet, as the emergence of the a-, pre- and postmillennial taxonomies suggests, evangelical interpretations of Revelation 20 have tended to be narrower in range than those often articulated in the seventeenth century.

At the same time, however, evangelicals have gone far beyond Puritans in other areas of eschatological speculation. The nineteenth-century 'Plymouth' Brethren movement witnessed a wholesale revision of eschatological motifs as its early leaders abandoned traditional millennial teaching to endorse an innovative dispensational version of premillennialism, while at least one of their number, the popular devotional writer Andrew Jukes, drifted off into universalism with the financial assurance of a private patron. Some years later, the

14. George Gillespie, *The Presbyterian's Armoury* in *The Works of George Gillespie*, ed. W. M. Hetherington (Edinburgh: Robert Ogle and Oliver & Boyd, 1846), vol. 1, p. 23.

15. Thomas Goodwin, *The Works of Thomas Goodwin* (Edinburgh: James Nichol, 1861–6), vol. 3, pp. 158, 198.

16. This is evident even in the Assembly's debates about justification, according to Chad Van Dixhoorn, *A Day at the Westminster Assembly: Justification and the Minutes of a Post-Reformation Synod* (London: Congregational Memorial Hall Trust, 2005).

17. See Gribben, "The Eschatology of the Puritan Confession", pp. 51–78.

popular Baptist preacher F. B. Meyer explained in his biography that the resurrection had occurred at the end of the first century. This explained why there were so few Christians in the second century, compared with the first.[18]

More recently, and more controversially, John Stott, listed by *Time* magazine as among the one hundred most influential people in the world,[19] briefly followed his fellow Anglican scholar John Wenham into an adherence to conditional immortality.[20] The cautious ambivalence of the broader British evangelical community was reflected in a report published by the Evangelical Alliance. The report confirmed the church's traditional teaching on the torment of the damned, but did not insist that the torment was eternal.[21] Nevertheless, the fact that evangelical leaders could even consider alternatives to traditional teaching on hell sent shockwaves through conservative evangelical communities on both sides of the Atlantic.

The debate about conditional immortality highlighted one aspect of evangelicalism's discontinuity from the past. The rise of the a-, pre- and postmillennial taxonomies and the debate about conditional immortality indicate that evangelicalism is at once narrower and broader than the Puritan movement it followed, and new formulations of its eschatological hope continue to spring up in the most unexpected locations. Eschatological speculation has continued, but, in the UK at least, its focus has largely shifted from the communal consequences of the millennium to the individual consequences of soteriology.

This chapter will therefore assess the degree of continuity that exists between Puritanism and evangelicalism by tracing the development of a number of central themes in the eschatological thinking of their movements. Its conclusions will argue for both continuity and discontinuity, and will note that the discontinuities cannot always be explained by the Enlightenment influences that much of the current historiography links to the emergence of evangelicalism.[22] In eschatology, at least, the movement from 'Puritanism' to 'evangelicalism' is more gradual than many might expect.

18. W. Y. Fullerton, *No Ordinary Man: The Remarkable Life of F. B. Meyer* (London: Marshall, Morgan & Scott, 1929; repr. Belfast: Ambassador, 1993).

19. Billy Graham, 'Teacher of the Faith: John Stott', *Time* (18 Apr. 2005), p. 80.

20. John Wenham, *Facing Hell: The Story of a Nobody: An Autobiography, 1913–1996* (Carlisle: Paternoster, 1998); David L. Edwards and John Stott, *Evangelical Essentials: A Liberal–Evangelical Dialogue* (Leicester: IVP, 1989).

21. Evangelical Alliance, *The Nature of Hell* (Carlisle: Paternoster, 2000).

22. This is the thesis of David Bebbington, *Evangelicalism in Modern Britain: A History from the 1730s to the 1980s* (London: Unwin Hyman, 1989).

Hermeneutics

The slow pace of eschatological development is perhaps most obvious in the area of hermeneutics. While Enlightenment categories of interpretation fostered new approaches to biblical interpretation, a series of basic hermeneutical assumptions have governed the conclusions that expositors have reached from the seventeenth century to the present day. Other hermeneutical assumptions have been left behind.

One of the grounding assumptions of prophetic exegesis in the early post-Reformation period, for example, has been described as 'historicism', the assumption that large parts of Scriptural prophecy referred to the history of the church, from its inception to the second coming of Jesus Christ. Early attempts at commentary often combined historical and exegetical labours. This approach elevated historical writing almost to the status of Scripture. John Bale, Reformation Bishop of Ossory, claimed that the writing of history was second in importance only to the translation of Scripture itself: history was necessary for Scripture's proper interpretation.[23]

Bale's approach was closely followed by two of the most important and influential ecclesiastical historians of the sixteenth and seventeenth centuries: John Foxe, author of *Acts and Monuments* (1563), and James Ussher, author of *Gravissimae questionis de christianiarum ecclesiarum* (The most important questions concerning the Christian churches)[24] (1613), though better known among evangelicals for his chronological endeavours. Both Foxe and Ussher began their histories with an exegesis of Revelation 20, but while Foxe adhered to a fairly traditional location of the 'thousand years' in the Christian past, Ussher understood the chapter to teach two periods of one thousand years, the second of which had recently begun in the 'new binding of Satan' at the Reformation.[25] Nevertheless, they (and many like them) agreed that the seal, bowl and trumpet judgments could be allocated specific instances of fulfilment within the past history of the church. As Puritan exegesis developed through the seventeenth century, this historicist approach governed the developing eschatology. God was active in history, historicists believed, and prophecy gave an indication of his role.

23. Katharine R. Frith, *The Apocalyptic Tradition in Reformation Britain, 1530–1645* (Oxford: Oxford University Press, 1979), p. 60. For Bale, see Gribben, *Puritan Millennium*, pp. 37–38.

24. I am grateful to Dr Daniel Hill for supplying this translation.

25. For a recent discussion of the eschatology of Foxe and Ussher, see Gribben, *Puritan Millennium*, pp. 57–66, 80–100.

But, while it was certainly popular, the Foxe and Ussher histories demonstrate that Puritan historicism was never monolithic. While most historicists used Revelation to trace the entire history of the church, certain among their number nodded towards the opinion that the book's content was primarily concerned with events surrounding the fall of Jerusalem in AD 70 and political developments in the first century after Christ.

This emerging 'preterism' was voiced, for example, in later editions of the Geneva Bible and in some of the Parliamentary sermons of John Owen. It was always a minority position, however, and it took more than a century for preterist expositors to advance to the more radical claims that, as the British Congregationalist J. Stuart Russell claimed in *The Parousia: A Critical Inquiry into the New Testament Doctrine of our Lord's Second Coming* (1878, 2nd ed. 1887), the return of Jesus had already been symbolically completed with the destruction of Jerusalem in AD 70. Russell was a Unitarian, and, with links like this, preterism grew to be associated with the radical fringe of Protestantism.[26] But while moderate preterist ideas exercised some influence on the evangelical mainstream, the historicist approach outlined in the sixteenth and seventeenth centuries set an agenda that remained current within evangelical circles until its moment of disjunction in the immediate aftermath of the French Revolution.

The historicist consensus was interrupted by the sudden popularity of prophetic 'futurism'. This interpretative approach, which insisted that Revelation dealt mainly with events at the end of the age, gained in popularity after the French Revolution generated evangelicalism's moment of profound discontinuity with its prophetic past. The widespread adoption of futurism was one of the most radical developments in nineteenth-century evangelical eschatology, and reflected to some extent the increasing popularity of an innovative premillennialism.

Historicism had not required the adoption of any particular millennial theory: Jonathan Edwards had advanced a postmillennial historicism, while Isaac Newton, in the late seventeenth century, and Edward Irving, in the early nineteenth century, had preferred its premillennial equivalent. But the rise of a new variety of premillennialism, the 'dispensationalism' advanced by John Nelson Darby, premised the rejection of historicism as an outworking of its complex distinction between Israel and the mainly Gentile church. Darby, in the years

---

26. R. C. Sproul gave Russell's arguments a controversial new lease of life in *The Last Days According to Jesus: When Did Jesus Say He Would Return?* (Grand Rapids: Baker, 1998).

before his secession, cut his literary teeth in publishing rejections of the futurism that was being promoted by some of his most articulate colleagues in the Church of Ireland.[27] Before long, however, his rapidly developing dispensational premillennialism had been widely disseminated, and Darbyite theology severed one important link between nineteenth-century evangelicals and the majority of their post-Reformation forebears.[28]

In its most radical form, this new premillennialism contested that there could be no expected fulfilments of prophecy before the 'rapture'—not even the emergence of the Antichrist. The next event on the prophetic calendar was therefore the catching away of all true believers at the secret coming of Christ. This rapture would be followed by a seven-year tribulation, in which both Jews and those Gentiles who had come to faith after the rapture would face the persecution of the Antichrist. His tyranny would be ended by the second coming proper, when Jesus Christ would return to set up his millennial kingdom.

This futurism was popularized through prophetic conferences and journals on both sides of the Atlantic, and, despite its repudiation of the papal Antichrist motif, a founding assumption of Reformation eschatology, soon became the hermeneutic of choice for the emerging fundamentalist movement at the century's end. For futurists, the new century looked bleak.

Curiously, however, the century that seemed most to validate futurism's pessimistic prophetic scenarios actually witnessed the widespread reversal of this hermeneutical approach. Twentieth-century evangelicals did continue to adhere to premillennial options, at a popular level at least, and particularly within North America. The eschatological preferences of Anglo-American fundamentalists reiterated the basic themes of nineteenth-century futurism, and the dispensational approach was provided with classic expression in *The Scofield Reference Bible* (1909, 1917). The Scofield Bible sold several million copies and gained a degree of academic kudos from its association with Oxford University Press, going through several new editions as the century progressed.

The Scofield Bible's relative sobriety degenerated into an excessive pop-dispensationalism, however, that was most marked by the success of Hal

---

27. Jonathan D. Burnham, *A Story of Conflict: The Controversial Relationship between Benjamin Wills Newton and John Nelson Darby* (Milton Keynes: Paternoster, 2004).
28. See the relevant chapters in Crawford Gribben and Timothy C. F. Stunt (eds.), *Prisoners of Hope? Aspects of Evangelical Millennialism in Britain and Ireland, 1800–1880*, Studies in Evangelical History and Thought (Milton Keynes: Paternoster, 2004); and Crawford Gribben and Andrew R. Holmes (eds.), *Protestant Millennialism, Evangelicalism and Irish Society, 1790–2005* (Basingstoke: Palgrave, 2006).

Lindsey's *The Late Great Planet Earth* (1970). Lindsey's 'dispen-sensationalism' modified the futurist tradition to incorporate specific references to historical fulfilments of prophecy.[29] He grounded his expectations in the significance of the establishment of the state of Israel in 1948, and hinted darkly that great events could be expected within forty years of that date: 'Many scholars who have studied Bible prophecy all their lives believe that this is so.'[30] Events would, of course, disprove Lindsey's suggestions. But the flood of popular eschatological writing, almost always from a dispensational perspective, has not reversed his trend back towards a limited historicism with a specific interest in the setting of dates, or the identification of events in the 'church age' before the rapture as specific fulfilments of prophecy.

Lindsey's career suggests that dispensational futurists are happy to turn back to historicism if they believe a specific event can be identified as the fulfilment of prophecy and, ironically, as confirmation of the wider futurist perspective. At a popular level, at least, dispensational writers rarely explain how purported historical fulfilments of prophecy can cohere with their repeated statements that Christ could return at any moment, and that nothing more need be fulfilled before the rapture can take place.

More generally, at a scholarly level, evangelicals have tended not to be impressed by popular futurism or its revival of a limited historicism. Premillennialists in the academy, such as George E. Ladd and Robert H. Gundry, have responded to this mood of 'dispensensationalism' by articulating a confident, conservative and exegetical eschatology without pandering to the mass-market expectations exploited by some of their peers.[31] But, ironically, it is in the limited historicism of these pop-dispensational writers that contemporary evangelicalism shows greatest continuity with the Puritan past.

Outside the ranks of premillennialists, throughout the twentieth century, scholars in universities and mainstream seminaries moved steadily towards the 'idealism' of the Dutch amillennial tradition. This approach, perhaps best

---

29. Gary North coined the expression 'dispen-sensationalism', Gary North, 'Publisher's Preface', in Dwight Wilson, *Armageddon Now! The Premillenarian Response to Russia and Israel since 1917* (Tyler, Tex.: Institute for Christian Economics, 1991), p. x.

30. Hal Lindsey, *The Late Great Planet Earth* (Grand Rapids: Zondervan, 1970), p. 54.

31. This is most evident in George E. Ladd, *A Theology of the New Testament* (London: Lutterworth, 1975); and Robert H. Gundry, *The Church and the Tribulation: A Biblical Examination of Posttribulationism* (Grand Rapids: Zondervan, 1973).

summarized in William Hendricksen's *More than Conquerors* (1940), understands Revelation to be organized as a series of pictures that teach timeless
truths about the relationship between the church and the world, and that
resist specific historical applications. Perhaps this modern evangelical hermeneutic has less in common with the interpretative schemes of Puritans than
the historicism, preterism or futurism the movement had earlier preferred. At
popular level, at least, this idealism has been most marked by the reluctance
of its adherents to embrace a specifically millennial hope, a reluctance, many
evangelicals might assume, that puts them at some distance from the confident postmillennialism of 'the Puritan hope'. In a sense, if pop-dispensation-
alists take evangelicals back to the exegetical style of wild-eyed Puritans, this
idealism takes evangelicals back to the relative sobriety of sixteenth-century
Reformers.

The millennium

And yet the differences may not be as great as some evangelicals imagine. Despite widespread assumptions about the singularity of 'the Puritan hope', seventeenth-century Protestants enjoyed a great deal of liberty in expounding references to the period or periods of one thousand years in Revelation 20. That
liberty stood in sharp contrast to the apathy of most mid-sixteenth-century
Reformers, an apathy that was, as we have seen, institutionalized in a number
of their confessions of faith. Nevertheless, the millennialism of British Puritans
was probably most influenced by a series of texts that emerged from exactly
this early Reformation period, the texts known collectively, if inaccurately, as
the Geneva Bible.[32]

The first editions of the Geneva Bible were produced by a team of translators, many of whose members had fled England and the persecutions of Mary
Tudor. Based in the city John Knox described as 'the most perfect school of
Christ since the Apostles',[33] the translators embarked on a project that was
to have incalculable influence for the ensuing century. Developing a New
Testament in 1557, they quickly moved on to the production of a full Bible in
1560, a Bible that contained a number of innovations, including verse divisions

---

32. On the eschatological importance of the Geneva Bible, see Gribben, *Puritan
     Millennium*, pp. 67–79.
33. Quoted in Gordon Donaldson, 'Knox the Man', in Duncan Shaw (ed.), *John Knox:
     A Quartercentenary Reappraisal* (Edinburgh: St Andrew, 1975), p. 26.

and Roman type, and copious annotations in some three hundred thousand words of textual commentary.

As a number of scholars have recently noted, the notes published in the 1560 Geneva Bible were fairly conservative, designed to guide an imagined 'simple reader' rather than attempting to educate someone who was already a biblical specialist. But some dissatisfaction was felt with the text and commentary of the New Testament, and in 1576 Laurence Thomson, a Puritan Member of Parliament, oversaw the publication of a second edition of the full Bible, with a new text of the New Testament and with updated annotations, based on Beza's earlier work.

This Geneva–Thomson text had fewer annotations on Revelation, and eventually it too was replaced. In 1599, a third edition of the Geneva Bible appeared. Its only substantial novelty was its inclusion of a commentary on Revelation that had been prepared from an earlier publication of Franciscus Junius, a French Reformed minister. This Geneva–Thomson–Junius edition grew to be one of the most influential English-language biblical translations. Its production quickly outpaced that of the second edition, and it regularly appeared in fresh editions on booksellers' stalls until the final edition was published in 1644.

Franciscus Junius' notes exercised immense influence on the millennial development of British Puritans, emphasizing the literary structures and theological meaning of Revelation and suggesting interpretations that were sometimes at odds with earlier citations' glosses, or indeed annotations by other authors within the same edition of the Bible. This eschatological tension was most obvious in the emphasis on the conversion of the Jews, developed at length in Beza's notes on Romans and almost entirely overlooked in Junius' notes on Revelation. The annotations on Romans had immediate impact. Explaining chapters 9–11, they anticipated an unimaginable mass conversion of Jewish people to Christian faith, which, the notes argued, would be a convincing sign of the approach of the end of the age. In England, the idea was picked up by William Perkins, who from his influential Cambridge pulpit would go on to convince generations of Puritans that better days for the church lay in the near future. A widespread conversion of Jews would lead the Christian church into a period of unimaginable peace.

This combination of interest in Revelation 20 and anticipation of future blessing combined in the publications of an English Presbyterian minister, Thomas Brightman. Brightman advanced a radical rethinking of the significance of Revelation 20. Most basically, he argued, the chapter referred to two periods of one thousand years, the first of which ended around 1300, and the second of which began with the Protestant Reformation. In the first two decades after their publication, Brightman's works did not circulate as widely as they would have when censorship collapsed in the 1640s. By then, his calculation that Turkish power would collapse in 1650, as a signal of impending apocalyptic changes, loomed on the very near horizon. But Brightman's ideas were influencing Puritan expositors long before the 1640s.

James Ussher, Professor of Theology at Trinity College, Dublin, and later Archbishop of Armagh, seems to have been among Brightman's earliest disciples. In 1613, as we have seen, Ussher published the first volume of an ecclesiastical history that also discovered two periods of one thousand years in Revelation 20, and signalled the importance of the years around 1370 for the transition from the first millennium to the second. Finding himself at the cusp of a theological revolution, projecting the possibility of a millennial period in the future, Ussher retreated from uncharacteristic radicalism into a more conventional apocalyptic world view.

As the century progressed, the bimillennialism Ussher had shared with Brightman fell out of fashion as Puritan expositors developed a more forthright and almost entirely futuristic millennial consensus. Brightman was still being cited, but his bimillennialism was rapidly disappearing as scholars across the Puritan spectrum agreed that the future of the church involved the destruction of her Catholic and Islamic enemies, the conversion of the Jews, the reign of the saints, and the personal appearing of Jesus Christ, all somewhere in relation to a single period of one thousand years.

This single-millennial future was maintained, with various qualifications, by Joseph Mede, John Cotton, Thomas Goodwin, John Owen, John Milton, Increase Mather and John Bunyan, though its exponents differed as to whether the return of Christ should be expected at its beginning or its end. This millennialism led some radical Puritans into militaristic aggression. Fifth Monarchists and other extremists drew heavily on eschatological motifs to justify their rebellion against Cromwellian authorities. But it also led others into quietist dissent, after the Restoration clampdown on Nonconformity. Only at the Glorious Revolution were Puritan hopes for the inauguration of the millennial kingdom raised again in any significant way.[34] Whatever the political impact of their competing systems, Puritans increasingly agreed that Revelation 20 referred only to one period of a thousand years, and agreed that its beginning lay somewhere in the future.

By the early eighteenth century, the ambiguous millennialism of Puritan expositors seems to have been eclipsed by an emerging postmillennial

---

34. Barry Howson, 'Eschatology in Sixteenth- and Seventeenth-Century England', *Evangelical Quarterly* 70.4 (1998), p. 331.

consensus. While the new movement may or may not have been influenced by Enlightenment ideas of rationalism, it certainly developed the eschatological preoccupations of its Puritan adherents in a rationalistic and progressive direction.

Jonathan Edwards, whom Professor Bebbington cites as a progenitor of the evangelical movement, drew his eschatology, like his soteriology, from the seventeenth-century writers he knew so well. Edwards's eschatology drew heavily on the providential historicism earlier writers had favoured. George Marsden's biography describes Edwards's fascination with contemporary history, and his attempts to relate current affairs, particularly relating to the tremors of European Catholicism, to the prophetic paradigms he had inherited. But Edwards's millennialism was set alight by his experience of revival. Documenting the events of the 1730s and 1740s, he wondered whether a century of Puritan praying was finally bearing fruit. The unprecedented outpouring of the Spirit, he felt, was very possibly a signal that the millennium was about to commence.

Edwards's postmillennialism was stripped of its 'enthusiasm' by Daniel Whitby, and was occasionally challenged within the community of evangelicals. Charles Wesley's brief dalliance with premillennialism was paralleled by the more enduring commitments of some of those who publicly attacked his movement.

In the eighteenth century, premillennialism was regularly linked to a very high species of Calvinistic theology. Augustus Toplady and John Gill were both significant voices in eighteenth-century British church life. Both were accused of hyper-Calvinism, and both maintained systems of premillennialism that refused to concede to the Enlightened progressivism of their day. Their eschatology looked unusual by eighteenth-century standards, and was perhaps a reflection of their strongly interventionist soteriology, that downplayed human cooperation with the divine will and emphasized God's monergistic activity. But their promotion of high Calvinism, and the public debates they entered in its defence, made their premillennialism easy to dismiss. Postmillennialism was gaining ground.

Nevertheless, Gill's lonely scholarship cast a long shadow through the nineteenth century, as the life and opinions of his most famous pastoral successor would demonstrate. It was, significantly, among British Calvinists that premillennialism experienced its revival. Charles Haddon Spurgeon was a vocal proponent of a premillennialism that developed from its roots in Gill to reflect nineteenth-century concerns. Spurgeon's eschatology, most obviously in his speculation about the prospects of children dying in infancy, clearly reflected the sentimentalism of his age. He may have published more than any other writer in English, but the premillennialism that came to exercise such influence in transatlantic evangelicalism was quite different from his simple futurism.

The premillennial revival of the nineteenth century is most often associated with another seceding Calvinist, John Nelson Darby, a Church of Ireland priest who left the establishment as he developed his characteristic theory of 'dispensational' premillennialism. Dispensations had always been used to reflect the soteriological development of redemptive history: the Westminster Confession of Faith, for example, had referred to dispensations in explaining how the administration of the covenant of grace differed in the Old and New Testaments. But Darby's dispensationalism differed from historic premillennialism in sharply contrasting the place and purposes of Israel and the church in its scheme of redemptive history.

Darby's theory remained largely undefined throughout most of his life, and is related to, though cannot really be compared with, the systems of dispensationalism developed in the Scofield Bible and in the rise of dispensational scholasticism in the twentieth century. Nevertheless, the premillennial revival he inaugurated startled ecclesiastical observers, and grew rapidly in favour in the establishment he had left behind. In the 1840s, the *British and Foreign Review*, for example, noted that half the clergy of the Church of England were now adherents of the new eschatological faith. Its impact in North America was even more pronounced through the widespread activity of D. L. Moody and the development of the transdenominational prophetic conferences. But premillennialism could not sustain this growth.

With the emergence of a discrete fundamentalist movement in the 1920s and 30s, those evangelicals who wanted to distance themselves from the perceived excesses of conservatives frequently abandoned the eschatological systems to which they adhered. As evangelicals and fundamentalists drew apart, their eschatological preferences tended to become more distinct, reflecting, for the former, their generally optimistic social and political engagement, and, for the latter, their generally pessimistic withdrawal from a perishing world. This divergence was most obvious in North America. The preaching and writing of Billy Graham, the most famous evangelical of the twentieth century, reflected this trend, moving from the apocalyptic denunciations of his early Cold War publications to genuine engagement with some late Communist regimes.

In the world of academe, George E. Ladd also came to typify the eschatology of the moderate evangelicals. He retained premillennial convictions, but withdrew from dispensationalism to promote a system that, in his *Theology of the New Testament*, was to interact constructively with the interests of 'liberal' scholarship and would influence several generations of students at Fuller Seminary, where he taught, and far beyond. Ladd's *Theology of the New Testament* was ranked alongside Calvin's *Institutes* as one of the books most influential on late twentieth-century American evangelicals in polls published in *Christianity Today*. But outside North America, this renewed premillennialism struggled to survive.

British fundamentalism was always less vigorous and much less numerous than its North American counterpart, and the effective eclipse of its premillennialism has yet to be satisfactorily explained. While premillennialism is a respected and mainstream variant of belief among North American Protestants, it has again become a fringe concern in the generally amillennial cultures of British evangelicalism.

Contemporary evangelicals largely agree that Revelation 20 refers to one period of a thousand years. In that sense, they are clearly the heirs of mid-seventeenth-century Puritan exegesis. But, in their sustained interest in a millennial future, North American evangelicals are closer to their Puritan forebears than are their British brethren, who, in their widespread millennial apathy, are closer to the cautious moderation of the sixteenth-century Reformers. Once again, it seems, the British Reformed constituency that started the quest for 'the Puritan hope' may have much less in common with it than those dispensationalists whose opinions they hoped to change.

Conclusion

The quest for 'the Puritan hope', therefore, is far from complete. While this survey chapter has concentrated on the two most fundamental of eschatological themes, a fuller examination of the topic would also draw attention to continuities and discontinuities in a number of other areas. Puritans and evangelicals have variously constructed the relationship between the church and eschatology, the 'now' and the 'not yet', discussing the possibility of progressive revelation and the provision of extraordinary gifts as the end of the age approached. Within this context, the twentieth-century turn to biblical theology, and the influence of Ladd and Geerhardus Vos, has emphasized the church's current position in the overlapping of the ages, a variant of Reformed theology now controversially developed in some of the 'kingdom now' perspectives of the charismatic movement.

The development of a theology of prophetic Israel and the emergence of political Zionism would also be a component of this larger discussion. While the Geneva Bible emphasized the 'conversion of the Jews' motif, Puritans increasingly theorized the physical return of Jews to the Promised Land, in a discourse that has dominated recent discussions of the relationship between certain varieties of evangelical eschatology and the foreign policies of successive US administrations.

In a parallel concern, Puritans and evangelicals have also theorized the prophetic future of Islam. The threat of Islam in Puritan writing mirrored the geopolitical tensions of the early modern period. The increasing security of western Europe in recent centuries precipitated a waning interest in the threat of Islam, which has recently revived with the 'war on terror' at the start of the twenty-first century.

A sense of the danger of the Roman Catholic Church has experienced similar ebbs and flows. While Catholicism represented the Antichristian nadir of the Reformation, Puritans repeatedly dismissed it in apocalyptic terms. With the rise of secularism, however, and increasing attention on the 'culture wars' in the North American political landscape, evangelicals are rethinking their traditional hostility to Rome. In the recent *Left Behind* novels, perhaps most significantly, the Pope and apparently non-evangelical Catholic laity are included among the raptured.[35] Each of these themes demonstrates both continuity and discontinuity between Puritan and evangelical believers.

But what of their distinction? This chapter has not disputed Professor Bebbington's dating of the emergence of evangelicalism in the 1730s and 1740s. It has not disputed his claim that evangelicalism added a new epistemological confidence to the theological structures of the seventeenth century, although this has been challenged in other chapters of this book. But this chapter has noted the existence of a series of continuities and discontinuities between the eschatologies developed in the sixteenth and seventeenth centuries and those popular among evangelicals thereafter. Puritan eschatology was grounded in hermeneutical approaches and a political context that looked increasingly old-fashioned as the eighteenth century waned. Yet, at the beginning of the twenty-first century, the urgent and often political prophetic enquiry of North American premillennialists can seem closer to the Puritan legacy than the passive apathy of many of their British Reformed cousins.

But the greatest challenge in the writing of this chapter, the sheer diversity of Puritan and evangelical eschatological options, is perhaps the strongest

---

35. The earliest printing of *Left Behind* (1995) included Mother Theresa among the raptured, but the idea was so controversial that it was rapidly omitted from subsequent editions of the same text. I owe this information to Dr Thomas Ice, personal conversation, 14 July 2006.

evidence that in many constituencies within the modern movement, end-times thinking remains the secondary issue that Puritans agreed it was. As in the seventeenth century, so in the twenty-first: eschatology has been generally reduced to a secondary status, and evangelicals have felt free to adopt a range of eschatological perspectives without believing themselves to have overstepped the boundaries of the movement. That variety is as much a characteristic of contemporary evangelicalism as it was of early modern Puritanism. For some modern neo-Puritans this may not be welcome news, but perhaps this is the greatest evidence for seeing both movements as participating in a single eschatological tradition.

© Crawford Gribben, 2008

17. THE EVANGELICAL DOCTRINE OF SCRIPTURE, 1650–1850: A RE-EXAMINATION OF DAVID BEBBINGTON'S THEORY

Kenneth J. Stewart

Prolegomena

When, in 1989, David Bebbington released his impressive volume *Evangelicalism in Modern Britain: A History from the 1730s to the 1980s*, he was providing not simply an account of British evangelical origins but of the origins of the movement across the English-speaking world. Notably, this acclaimed volume put forward a novel interpretation of the genesis of evangelicalism, that is, that it had emerged around 1730 through a coalescing of factors, such as biblicism, crucicentrism and conversionism, which had hitherto existed individually, and in isolation from one another.

The book also posited hypotheses regarding theological developments within evangelical Christianity at or around 1830: (1) that an until–then 'moderating' pan-evangelical Calvinism rapidly grew more belligerent, (2) that expectations of a non-material, spiritual second advent gave way to a firm belief that Christ's return would be physical and visible, and (3) that somewhat elastic views of biblical inspiration associated with the earlier usage of the term 'plenary' subsequently gave way to the stricter views associated with the term 'verbal', a concomitant element of which was a belief in scriptural inerrancy.[1]

---

1. David W. Bebbington, *Evangelicalism in Modern Britain: A History from the 1730s to the 1980s* (London: Unwin Hyman, 1989), pp. 77–91.

The purview of this chapter is purely the third of these suggested theological developments within evangelicalism. Here, I shall aim to show the following:

1. The view of inspiration termed 'verbal', rather than *following* the 'plenary' view as an early nineteenth-century development (so, Bebbington), in fact coexisted with it from the seventeenth century and then had a parallel existence with it into the nineteenth century.
2. That the genius of the plenary view of inspiration (as opposed to the verbal) was *not* that it could, by design, countenance scriptural inexactitude or error, but that it took seriously the observable phenomena of Scripture related to the multiple authors, eras, and literature encompassed within the biblical canon.
3. That, in consequence, we are left to ponder the nineteenth-century developments of the verbal and plenary views of inspiration on another basis than that provided in *Evangelicalism in Modern Britain*, that is, that the upsurge of interest in verbal inspiration represented something novel and provided a basis for the first substantive defence of an errorless Bible.

I should make it plain, at the outset, that I have no particular vested interest in seeing one of these conceptions of inspiration 'trump' the other. I have elsewhere indicated that the verbal-inspiration view, which, as Bebbington has indicated, received forceful elaboration in the 1815–40 period, did not deal very fairly with its rival.[2] Each view, in my mind, has proved a tenable way of stating a doctrine of inspiration—though conservative evangelicalism probably misjudged matters in the twentieth century when it was so often ready to treat 'plenary' and 'verbal' as synonymous terms.[3] With this much acknowledged, let us begin.

From Ames to Pictet

Leaving aside the extensive debate about the views on inspiration characteristic of the century of the Reformation,[4] it is evident that views on inspiration

---

2. See my 'A Bombshell of a Book: Gaussen's *Theopneustia* (1841) and its Subsequent Influence on Evangelical Theology', *Evangelical Quarterly* 85.3 (2003), pp. 235–257.
3. This is the impression created by reference to the two as a hyphenated pair, plenary-verbal, in numerous sets of doctrinal articles. Any Internet search engine will provide numerous examples once the hyphenated set of terms is inserted.
4. See e.g. R. E. Davies, *The Problem of Authority in the Continental Reformers: Luther,*

that might be classified as 'verbal' (i.e. the divine involvement is understood to extend uniformly to the provision of the very words utilized) were widespread by the mid-seventeenth century.

William Ames (1576–1633), the refugee English Puritan divine dwelling in the Netherlands, so impressed Dutch delegates at the Synod of Dordt (1618–19) that he was appointed to a theological chair at the University of Franeker in 1622. The author of a major treatise on Scripture never translated from Latin, *Disputatio theologicae de perfectione ss scriptura* (Theological Discussions on the Perfection of the Holy Scriptures), I here make reference purely to Ames's *The Marrow of Theology*.[5] He is a transitional figure in handling this doctrine. Familiar with the fact that sixteenth-century Reformed writers had tended to see divine inspiration active primarily in the prophets and heralds who both received and relayed divine revelation,[6] he emphasizes the variety of the divine working in them. In this way, he anticipates (yet without advocating) what will come to be called the 'plenary' view:

> Divine inspiration was present among these writers in different ways. Some things were utterly unknown to the writer in advance, as appears in the history of creation or in the foretelling of things to come. But some things were previously known to the writers . . . Some things were known by a natural knowledge and some by a supernatural. In those things that were hidden and unknown, divine inspiration was at work by itself.[7]

Thus, in principle, Ames is granting that inspiration has not functioned identically in all writers and all parts of Scripture. However, if Ames can anticipate what a century later would be called 'plenary' inspiration, he is simultaneously found striking notes that have recognizably to do with 'verbal' understandings of inspiration. He writes:

Zwingli and Calvin (London: Epworth, 1946); Robert Preus, *The Inspiration of Scripture: A Study of the Theology of the Seventeenth Century Lutheran Dogmaticians* (Edinburgh: Oliver & Boyd, 1955); H. Jackson Forstman, *Word and Spirit: Calvin's Doctrine of Biblical Authority* (Palo Alto: Stanford University Press, 1962); and, more recently, John Warwick Montgomery (ed.), *God's Inerrant Word: An International Symposium on the Trustworthiness of the Scriptures* (Minneapolis: Bethany House, 1974).

5. William Ames, *The Marrow of Theology* (1623), ed. and trans. from the 3rd London edition (1629) by John D. Eusden (Boston: Beacon Hill, 1968).

6. A point stressed by Heinrich Heppe, *Reformed Dogmatics Set out from the Sources* (English trans. London: Allen & Unwin, 1950; repr. Grand Rapids, Baker, 1978), ch. 2.

7. Ames, *Marrow of Theology*, p. 186.

> Only those could set down the rule of faith and conduct in writing who in that
> matter were free from all error because of the direct and infallible direction they had
> from God . . . They also wrote by the inspiration and guidance of the Holy Spirit,
> so that the men themselves were, at that point, so to speak, instruments of the
> Spirit.[8]

Anticipating future developments, though in a different way, was the Irish Archbishop of Armagh, James Ussher (1581–1656). As though each part, each genre, of Scripture had been furnished through a process akin to prophecy, Ussher contended for an 'oracular' view of inspiration, extending to the very words, in his *A Bodie of Divinitie*. It was this predominating divine influence upon the writers which ensured that though 'subject to infirmities', their writings could nevertheless be considered the 'Word of God'. Inspiration,

> because it proceeded not from the will or mind of man, but holy men, set apart for
> that work by God, spake and wrote as they were moved by the Holy Ghost.
> Therefore, God alone is to be accounted the author thereof, who inspired the hearts
> of these holy men whom he chose to be his secretaries, who are to be held only the
> instrumental causes thereof.[9]

The viewpoint implicit in Ussher's conviction, that a divine governance extending to the supplying of words of the text had kept the fallible human writers from floundering at their task, was made explicit later in the century by the Swiss compilers of the *Formula consensus helvetica* (1675). In it, there was a readiness to posit a view of verbal inspiration extending not only to the consonants, but to the vowel points in the Hebrew script.[10]

---

8. Ibid., p. 186, theses 2, 4.

9. James Ussher, *A Bodie of Divinitie* (London, 1647), pp. 7, 8. A survey of the fascinating volume of James T. Burtchaell, *Catholic Theories of Biblical Inspiration Since 1810* (Cambridge: Cambridge University Press, 1969), esp. ch. 2, 'Theories Dead and Buried', illustrates considerable overlap of categories between evangelical Protestant and Roman Catholic theories of inspiration in the eighteenth century.

10. The *Formula consensus helvetica* is reprinted with commentary in Philip Schaff (ed.), *The Creeds of Christendom*, 3 vols. (New York: Harper, 1877; repr. Grand Rapids, Baker, 1977), vol. 1, pp. 477–489. The text is also reprinted in A. A. Hodge, *Outlines of Theology* (New York: R. Carter, 1860; repr. Edinburgh: Banner of Truth, 1972), pp. 656–663. The relevant heads are II and III.

Francis Turretin (1623–87), venerated so long after his death as a giant of Reformed orthodoxy,[11] had collaborated in the preparation of the *Formula consensus helvetica*. As he contended that a divine revelation in words was essential for the salvation of the human race, so he also insisted that this word-revelation had, of necessity, been committed to writing. 'Without it, the Church could not stand.'[12] Alluding to the indications of Hebrews 1:1 that God's saving revelation was given variously at different times, he allowed that the original recipients of the revelation had sometimes heard a clear voice and a disclosure delivered in words, on other occasions been given to understand through 'mental discourse' and in other cases received revelation through dreams, visions, theophanies and the ministry of angels. Yet, these admittedly different modes of revelation did not alter the fact that the saving revelation was preserved through verbal inspiration.[13] Turretin, in consequence of his confidence in a past multiform revelation preserved in inspired words, would have no patience with those who posited the view that 'the sacred writers could slip or err in smaller things'. To him, such concessions were 'an abandonment of the cause'. 'Are there real and true, and not merely apparent contradictions?' 'We deny the former.'[14]

His British contemporary John Owen (1616–83) held highly similar views. Owen, writing in his *The Office and Work of the Holy Spirit* (1674) would affirm that the Holy Spirit 'prepared and elevated' the intellectual faculties of those who were to receive divine revelation, all the while affirming that as to what was actually received, the Spirit 'himself *acted* their faculties, making use of them to express his words not their own conceptions'.[15] Owen

11. Donald D. Grohman, 'Turretin, Francis', in Donald McKim (ed.), *Encyclopedia of the Reformed Faith* (Philadelphia: Westminster John Knox; Edinburgh: T. & T. Clark, 1992), p. 377.

12. Francis Turretin, *Institutes of Elenctic Theology*, trans. George Musgrave Giger, 3 vols. (Geneva, 1679–85; Phillipsburg: Presbyterian & Reformed, 1992), vol. 1, pp. 56–57.

13. Ibid., vol. 1, p. 58.

14. Ibid., pp. 70–71. The wide circulation of the writings of Turretin and his successor, Pictet, within English Nonconformist ministerial academies in the late seventeenth and early eighteenth centuries is described by David Bogue and James Bennett, *History of Dissenters* (London: Westly & Davis, 1808), vol. 3, pp. 215ff.; H. McLachlan, *English Education under the Test Acts* (Manchester: Manchester University Press, 1931), p. 300; and E. G. Rupp, *Religion in England 1688–1791* (Oxford: Oxford University Press, 1986), p. 172.

15. John Owen, *The Office and Work of the Holy Spirit* in *The Works of John Owen*, ed. W. H. Goold, 16 vols. (1674; repr. London: Banner of Truth, 1965–8), vol. 3, p. 132.

was clearly in the camp of those insisting not upon the creative individuality of the writers, but upon the overarching divine control of the process.
'The Spirit used them (the writers) as his organs,' wrote Owen. 'He left
them liable to no suspicion whether their minds were under his conduct
and influence or no.'[16] The human writers were 'but pipes through which
the waters (of revelation) were conveyed, without the least mixture with any
alloy from their frailties or infirmities'.[17] Here, articulated by both a Genevan
and an English Reformed theologian of renown was the precursor of what
the Bebbington theory would convince us arose only in the early decades of
the nineteenth century.[18]

Benedict Pictet (1655–1724), successor to Turretin,[19] is credited with
being the last Genevan theologian to have upheld the high Calvinist
orthodoxy characteristic of the seventeenth century. In Pictet's *Christian
Theology* (1696), the emphases already present in Turretin are developed
in new directions. Concurring with Turretin that God has given fallen
humanity a verbal revelation, he nevertheless demurs at a point where
Turretin had made haste. The latter, while granting the multiformity of
special revelation, inferred nothing about variegated divine action in inspiration from this multiformity. Pictet, by contrast, introduces for the first
time known to the present writer the notion that a comprehensive divine
inspiration has functioned in distinguishable ways in the various Scripture
writers. He notes as follows.

> First, it is unnecessary to suppose that the Holy Spirit always dictated to the prophets
> and apostles every word they used. Nevertheless, these holy men wrote many things
> under the immediate suggestion of the Spirit, such as prophecies. Hence, Paul says
> 'Now the Spirit speaketh expressly' (1 Tim. 4.1) and many other things. Again: they
> wrote some things in which there was no need of the Spirit's suggestion: such as those
> things with which they were already acquainted, which they had seen and heard or
> those which related to their own private affairs.[20]

---

16. Ibid., p. 133.
17. Ibid., p. 134.
18. Bebbington, *Evangelicalism in Modern Britain*, pp. 90–91.
19. Robert D. Linder, 'Pictet, Benedict', in McKim, *Encyclopedia of the Reformed Faith*,
     p. 228.
20. Benedict Pictet, *Christian Theology*, trans. Frederick Reyroux (1696; London: Seeley,
     1834), p. 53.

And Pictet, perhaps anticipating that some contemporary reader would draw from such distinctions the possible inference that the Spirit's variegated activity rendered some parts of Scripture more trustworthy than others, emphatically closed the door on such a hypothesis. 'Yet, they wrote nothing without the Spirit either inspiring them, or influencing them to write, or directing them, so as not to suffer them, while writing, to commit even the least error or mistake.'[21]

What has moved Pictet to pass beyond the bare granting of the diverse modes of divine revelation (a concept certainly present in Ames and Turretin) to acknowledging a likely variation of intensity in the Spirit's operation in the Scripture writers? Not the discovery of apparent error, for this Pictet denies as stoutly as they. On the contrary, it would seem warranted to suppose that a changing intellectual climate in which miracle is questioned has moved Pictet to build his doctrine of inspiration more inductively than they. He is wrestling with questions such as 'What kind of intensity of the Spirit's operation is necessary to explain the composition of the contents of the Bible as we have it?' His answer is that a discernible variety of divine inspiration was required.

From Ridgley to Bogue

This same emphasis upon an inductive method in framing a right understanding of biblical inspiration is a characteristic of the English Independent theologian Thomas Ridgley (1667–1734).[22] His *A Body of Divinity* (London, 1731) was structured around the questions of the Westminster Larger Catechism. Whereas seventy-five years earlier James Ussher was certain that the 'in divers manners' of Hebrews 1:1 implied no more than the Spirit's customary granting of oracles and visions to the writers of Scripture,[23] Ridgley has plainly reflected more deeply on the question. He points to the diversity of terminology within the biblical writings bearing on the question of how inspiration operated. The nineteenth psalm, for instance, speaks of written Scripture as 'statutes', 'laws', 'testimonies' and 'precepts'. Surely these imply *something* about a varied process of revelation and inspiration? He finds the same hinted at in the distinctions

21. Ibid., p. 34.

22. Basic biographical data regarding Ridgley are provided in H. C. G. Matthew and Brian Harrison (eds.), *Oxford Dictionary of National Biography*, 60 vols. (Oxford: Oxford University Press, 2004), vol. 46, p. 934.

23. Ussher, *Bodie of Divinitie*, p. 6.

that can be drawn between Scripture's historical books and those scriptural writings that comprise poetry or wisdom.[24]

But if Ridgley was taking small steps down a path cleared by Pictet, the eighteenth century would demonstrate that Ussher, Turretin and Owen's emphasis upon oracular inspiration also had its loyal supporters. Thomas Boston of Ettrick (1676–1732) left in manuscript a *Body of Divinity*,[25] which left no doubt that divine inspiration consistently extended to the very words. On the key text of 2 Timothy 3:16 he wrote:

> It principally here aims at the Scriptures of the Old Testament, which were written by men of a prophetic spirit; but seeing that the New Testament was written by such as were endowed with the same Spirit for writing, upon that reason, what is applied to the Old Testament belongs also to the New Testament. It is said to be of divine inspiration because the writers were inspired by the Spirit who guided their hearts and pens; he dictated and they wrote so that it is his word and not theirs, and that is extended to the whole Scriptures.[26]

In a similar vein, the Scottish seceding Presbyterian James Fisher (1697–1775), explaining inspiration in 1753, maintained that while revelation had been furnished by a variety of methods, including immediate revelation, theophany and the ministry of angels, inspiration was of one kind only: all Scripture was 'immediately indited by God'.[27] Here, manifestly, the emphasis is upon a common canon-wide inspiration, the nature of which is to be deduced from 'pillar' passages. But clearly the dominant personality in evangelical theology on these questions for the balance of the eighteenth century was Philip Doddridge of Northampton (1702–51). His *Lectures on Pneumatology and Ethics* (published posthumously from a manuscript) relay to us not only the skeleton outlines of his lectures, but an indication of what he had read and expected his students to read relative to each class session.

---

24. Ridgely, *Body of Divinity* (London: Daniel Midwinter, 1731), vol. 1, pp. 19, 20.

25. Seen through the press by his son, Thomas Boston, Jr. I refer here to a later edition, *A Complete Body of Divinity*, 2 vols. (Aberdeen: G. & R. King, 1848), vol. 1. No precise dating is offered for the year in which Boston composed the work.

26. Ibid., p. 10.

27. James Fisher, *The Westminster Shorter Catechism Explained* (Philadelphia: Presbyterian Board of Publication, 1753; repr. n. d.), p. 17. Fisher, a Glaswegian, was the theological tutor under whom John Brown (1722–87), treated below, trained for the ministry.

While we can acknowledge that in certain limited respects, Doddridge's doctrine of Scripture builds upon insights displayed earlier in Pictet and Ridgley, one is at the same time driven to the impression that Doddridge is striking out in new territory. His argument is very often that of a historian who is weighing various possible explanations for a phenomenon. He does not resolve questions about inspiration deductively, by citing key texts as determinative, but in an inductive and evidentiary way. His use of the historical method carries limitations with it: absolute certainty cannot be yielded by its use. Thus, it is the employment of an evidentiary method that compels Doddridge to halt by making such assertions as 'The Old Testament is, *in the main*, worthy of credit,' and 'The system of doctrines delivered to the world in the New Testament is, *in the main*, worthy of being received as true and divine'[28] (emphasis added). Doddridge is not himself insinuating error or shortcoming in the Scripture record. He is simply in this way acknowledging the limitations of the evidentiary method in establishing certainty. His overall aim is to present the claims of theology in terms comprehensible to that 'Age of Reason'.

With Doddridge's name and reputation, there has come to be very justifiably associated the proposal that divine inspiration might take the form of *superintendence*, 'in which God does so influence and direct the mind of any person as to keep him more secure from error in some various and complex discourse than he would have been merely by the use of his natural faculties'. He posited also an inspiration of *elevation*, by which the human faculties are raised to an extraordinary degree so that they grasp 'more of the true sublime, or pathetic than natural genius could have given'. He posited also an inspiration of *suggestion* under which 'God speaks directly to the mind making such discoveries to it as it could not otherwise have obtained and dictating the very words'.[29]

---

28. Doddridge, 'Lectures on Pneumatology and Ethics' (Lectures 127 and 136), in *Miscellaneous Works* (London: Joseph Robinson, 1839), vol. 1, pp. 373, 386.

29. Doddridge, Lecture 137 (ibid., pp. 388, 389). These concepts are developed in some greater detail in Doddridge's separate treatise *A Dissertation on the Inspiration of the New Testament* (ibid., pp. 1095–1109). There, Doddridge makes plain that the most general conception of inspiration (that taking place under divine superintendence) operated universally in *all* parts of Scripture, with 'elevation' and 'suggestion' operating only in select instances. To the first and most general conception he awarded the name 'plenary superintending inspiration' or, to be more brief, 'full inspiration' (ibid., p. 1096).

One is struck, on the one hand, by the fact that Doddridge does not illustrate these gradations of inspiration by reference to actual portions or units of Scripture (this is not to say that he could not have so illustrated them);[30] admittedly, this leaves his distinctions somewhat in the abstract. On the other hand, one is driven to grant that Doddridge is plainly *not* employing these distinctions to explain how portions of the Bible have come to be unworthy of our confidence (with the less intensive mode of inspiration leaving a wider scope for error), but rather in the light of the incontestable fact that Scripture records a range of events, sayings and thoughts ranging from the sublime and hidden to the ordinary and everyday. The 'degrees of inspiration' scheme is meant to explain the writing of a wide range of things, all of which are true, and not to explain the presence of alleged error or even inconsistency.[31]

Yet Doddridge was not necessarily understood to give adequate assurances on this score. And thus two prominent writers who explored the doctrine of inspiration in the decades subsequent to Doddridge's premature death can be observed to have maintained the earlier 'oracular' ideas of inspiration. The Baptist theologian John Gill (1697–1771) and the seceding Presbyterian theological tutor John Brown (1722–87) both show familiarity with the matters Doddridge had weighed, and claimed to find a solution for, in the concept of degrees of inspiration.

Gill, despite his reputation for being a theological high-flyer, can show himself to be disarming in his approach to biblical inspiration; his perspective is at least seasoned with an attempt at induction from scriptural phenomena. His insistence that the Scriptures *are* the word of God is not to be construed as meaning that God himself spoke or wrote them immediately. It was enough that the biblical writers wrote 'what they were bid to write . . . it was the same as if it was written by himself'.[32] Gill is prepared to speak of the contents of the Scripture being 'suggested' to the writers, and yet when elaborating what he means by this, adds that 'they wrote as they were directed, dictated,

30. Doddridge does supply examples in the fuller *Dissertation on the Inspiration*. There, he maintains that the final book of the New Testament, Revelation, was composed under an inspiration of suggestion (*Miscellaneous Works*, vol. 1, p. 1097).

31. Doddridge plainly believed that even the lesser degrees of inspiration (superintendence and elevation) could as surely as the greater (suggestion) be exercised by the Spirit in a way that eliminated the possibility of error. See ibid., p. 389.

32. John Gill, *Body of Divinity* (London: Thomas Tegg, 1839; repr. Baker: Grand Rapids, 1978), vol. 1, p. 16.

and inspired' to do.[33] Again, Gill did not insist that everything contained in
the Scriptures was 'of God', illustrating his meaning by allusions to recorded
speeches of Satan, and the apostle Paul's readiness to quote pagan poets.[34]

Yet what Gill seemed to give with one hand, he withdrew with another. He
explicitly repudiated the efforts of those theological writers who think that the
sacred writers were only furnished of God with matter, and had general

> ideas of things given them, and were left to clothe them with their own words, and
> to use their own style, which they suppose accounts for the difference of style to be
> observed in them; but if this was the case, as it sometimes is with men, that they have
> clear and satisfactory ideas of things in their own minds, and yet are at a loss for
> proper words to express and convey the sense of them to others, so it might be with
> the sacred writers if the words were not suggested to them, as well as matter . . . it
> seems therefore most agreeable that words also, as well as matter, were given by divine
> inspiration; and as for difference of style, as it was easy with God to direct to the use
> of proper words, so he could accommodate himself to the style such persons were
> wont to use, and which was natural to them and agreeable to their genius and
> circumstances.[35]

Here I think we may say that we see Gill awake to the issues raised by Doddridge and yet choosing the familiar path of verbal inspiration as he had received it from writers of the preceding century.

Brown, author of *A Compendious View of Natural and Revealed Religion* (1782),
names two of Doddridge's three 'degrees' before setting them aside as unsat-
isfactory.[36] The bone of contention? Brown cannot bring himself to accept
the notion that a mere divine superintendence (allegedly the most prevalent
'degree' of inspiration behind the biblical writings) was adequate to guide Bible
writers to keep them from major blunders. He reiterated the older theological conviction that only an inspiration extending to the words was adequate

---

33. Ibid., pp. 16–17.

34. Ibid., p. 17. Gill cited the speeches of Satan recorded in Job 1:9–11 and 2:4–6,
    and Paul's use of Aratus in Acts 17:28.

35. Ibid., p. 18.

36. Brown, *A Compendious View of Natural and Revealed Religion* (Glasgow: James Bryce,
    1782; repr. Grand Rapids, Christian Heritage, 2002). The introduction (p. l)
    indicates that Brown's own theological education was reliant on the use of
    Turretin's *Institutes of Elenctic Theology*. See Brown's allusion to the degrees of
    inspiration question at p. 71.

to the task. The writers were 'penmen who concurred in exercising their own reason and judgement . . . and were stirred up by the Spirit to write'.[37]

Yet the beachhead claimed by the innovative but short-lived Doddridge was not abandoned in the late eighteenth century. David Bogue (1750–1825), the Edinburgh-trained expatriate Scot whose theological academy at Gosport, England, trained many scores of English Independent ministers and 115 agents of the London Missionary Society,[38] happily employed the degrees of inspiration scheme over the decades in which he taught.[39] Doddridge's *Lectures on Pneumatology and Ethics* had been published in 1763, and his views were steadily disseminated thereafter; it is plausible to believe that Bogue encountered this viewpoint in his own Edinburgh studies in the 1770s.

The somewhat uneasy coexistence of these alternative understandings of biblical inspiration in the eighteenth century is nowhere better illustrated than in the 'Notes of the Discussions of the Eclectic Society, London, during

---

37. Brown surely cannot be accused, in his preference for a uniform inspiration extending to the words, of proceeding by simplistic deduction. An examination of his *Compendious View* immediately impresses one with its copious use of Scripture—quite in contrast to Doddridge. Brown plainly does not accept that the actual phenomena of Scripture are congruent with the framework Doddridge has developed. I believe that Brown has broken new ground here by his introduction of the term 'concurred' in recognition that the Scripture writers each brought something individual and unique to the inspiration process. Their individuality had been recognized earlier, but with an insistence that it was somehow engulfed in the divine action of inspiration.

38. S. Piggin, 'Bogue, David', in Nigel M. de S. Cameron (ed.), *Scottish Dictionary of Church History and Theology* (Downers Grove: IVP, 1996), p. 83.

39. See Bogue, *Theological Lectures* (New York: R. Carter, 1848), p. 371. Significantly, Bogue discussed with his students the vexed question of 'How far did inspiration extend to things or words?' That Bogue's reliance on the 'degrees' framework was considered mainstream may be inferred both from the readiness of the London Missionary Society to refer its missionary candidates to Bogue for training and the same society's preparedness to circulate a translation of Bogue's essay on *The Divine Authority of the New Testament* (1801) in Francophone Europe from 1805 onwards. See Kenneth J. Stewart, *Restoring the Reformation: British Evangelicalism and the Francophone Réveil 1816–49* (Milton Keynes: Paternoster, 2006), ch. 2. Bogue's treatment of inspiration in his *Lectures* is remarkable only in this: he deals with inspiration almost at the end of the topics rather than, as was customary, in a foundational lecture.

the years 1798–1814'.[40] That Society, meeting on 19 January 1800 to discuss the theme 'What is the nature of the inspiration of the Scriptures?', heard both opinions enunciated. The majority, led by the Revd John Venn, urged views very similar to those popularized by Doddridge. 'Superintendence varied in its character according to circumstances,' opined Venn. 'There is some danger in considering *all* Scripture as equally inspired; God undertakes to furnish man with truth; but he does not undertake to work miracles where no miracle is necessary,' added the Revd Richard Cecil. Yet their companion the Revd H. Foster insisted, on the contrary, 'I believe the writers were influenced not only as to *matter*, but as to *words*.' The senior clergyman present, the Revd John Newton, seemed to adhere to Foster's view when he insisted, 'Exceptions prove the rule. When St. Paul says he speaks by *permission*, he implies strongly that on all other occasions, it is by *direction*.'[41] It should be clear that each viewpoint articulated had, by then, a long pedigree.

From Dick to Gaussen

If Doddridge's views, once disseminated, proved acceptable both to English Anglicans and to Independents, John Dick (theological tutor of the United Secession Church between 1820 and 1833) showed their influence north of the Tweed. Already while serving a congregation of his denomination in 1800, he had published his *Essay on the Inspiration of the Holy Scriptures of the Old and New Testaments*, which employed the degrees of inspiration schema to account for the identifiable literary genre represented by the books of Scripture.[42]

Writing as the new century dawned, Dick insisted that a distinction of degrees of inspiration had long been present in rabbinic thought regarding the Old Testament. While there was every reason to think along such lines also regarding the Christian Scriptures, he reserved the right to modify the

40. Published as John H. Pratt (ed.), *The Thought of the Evangelical Leaders* (London: James Nisbet, 1856; repr. Edinburgh: Banner of Truth, 1978).
41. Ibid., pp. 152–154. Bebbington refers to this episode in *Evangelicalism in Modern Britain*, p. 87.
42. J. R. McIntosh, 'Dick, John', in de S. Cameron, *Scottish Dictionary*, p. 242; and the most judicious article by D. MacLeod, 'Systematic Theology', in the same volume, pp. 809–812. I have seen Dick's utilization of the degrees of inspiration scheme demonstrated also in his *Lectures on Theology* (Edinburgh: Oliphant, 1834; repr. New York: R. Carter, 1855), vol. 1, pp. 114–118.

scheme handed down from Doddridge, half a century before, as it was 'liable to material objections'.[43] To the Doddridgean idea of 'superintendence' (taken to mean a bare guarding from error in the recording of eyewitness events) the judicious Dick insisted that there be added a clear understanding that such writers were 'moved and excited' to record what they had plainly seen. This enlarged conception of superintendence, Dick maintained, provided a kind of pyramid base undergirding *every* type of biblical inspiration. As for the received category of 'elevation', Dick insisted that it was necessary to perceive this type of inspiration at work even in the chronicling of Christ's life by the Gospel writers; how else could a Matthew or a John, at the distance of considerable years from the ascension of Jesus, so carefully have recalled the events and utterances of his career?[44] He deemed the third category, 'suggestion', to be too weak a term to do justice to the disclosure of things unseen, things future, things heavenly. This he insisted be termed 'revelation', as with the last book of the New Testament.[45]

Yet having put such qualifications in place, regarding the Doddridgean scheme of 'degrees', the judicious Dick could still conclude:

> From the preceding statement it appears, that we do not apply the term, inspiration, in the same sense to the whole of Scripture, because the same degree of divine assistance was not necessary in the composition of every part of it. In some parts, if I may speak so, there is more of God than in others. When a prophet predicts an event of futurity, or an apostle makes known the mysteries of redemption, it is God alone who speaks; and the voice or the pen of a man is merely the instrument employed . . . When Moses relates the miracles of Egypt . . . or the evangelists relate the history of Christ, they tell nothing but what they formerly knew.[46]

John Dick's contemporary George Hill (1750–1819), Church of Scotland divinity professor at St Andrews,[47] was all the while taking a highly similar stance.

---

43. *Lectures on Theology*, vol. 1, p. 115.

44. Ibid., p. 116.

45. Ibid., p. 117.

46. Ibid., pp. 117–118.

47. H. R. Sefton, 'Hill, George', in de S. Cameron, *Scottish Dictionary*, pp. 407–408. See also H. R. Sefton, '"Neu-lights and Preachers Legall": Some Observations on the Beginnings of Moderatism in the Church of Scotland', in Norman MacDougall (ed.), *Church, Politics and Society: Scotland 1408–1929* (Edinburgh: John Donald, 1993), pp. 186–196. Also worthy of consideration on this era is the article

His *Theological Institutes* (1803), reissued after his death as the more extensive *Lectures in Divinity* (1821), simply takes up and utilizes the Doddridgean scheme. Even in Hill, by all standards a leader in the Church of Scotland 'moderate' party,[48] there is an explicit insistence that even the least intensive form of inspiration, superintendence, was used by God 'to prevent the possibility of error in their writings'. 'No sound theist will deny that all three degrees are possible,' he opined.[49] The judicious and painstaking use of Doddridge's framework to make a culturally informed defence of biblical integrity, by one in no way aligned with evangelical movements of the period, should serve to impress on us that the degrees of inspiration schema enjoyed very wide acceptance in the theological world of that day.

The same judicious use of Doddridge's schema is evident in the Anglican evangelical writer Daniel Wilson (1778–1858), London rector and eventual Bishop of Calcutta. Wilson's *Evidences of Christianity Stated in a Popular and Practical Manner* (1828) gives a highly nuanced and extensively inductive approach to questions of biblical inspiration and accuracy, in which he surveys the New Testament writings individually to ascertain what contribution they can make to the construction of an adequate understanding. In the process of making good his endorsement of a variegated biblical inspiration (along Doddridgean lines), a framework that, he urges, requires no 'superfluous miracle',[50] he also, like Doddridge, repeatedly and emphatically insists that views such as these make no room for insinuations of error in Scripture. In the space of forty pages he asserts in a variety of ways one theme:[51] even if undergirded by the mildest form of inspiration, that is, superintendence, 'the inspiration of superintendence reached even to the least circumstances and most casual allusions of the sacred writers . . . In all parts . . . the operations

---

of Colin Kidd, 'Scotland's Invisible Enlightenment: Subscription and Heterodoxy in the Eighteenth-Century Kirk', *Records of the Scottish Church History Society* 30 (2000), pp. 28–59.

48. H. R. Sefton, 'Moderates', in de S. Cameron, *Scottish Dictionary*, p. 595.

49. George Hill, *Lectures in Divinity*, 3 vols. (Edinburgh: Waugh & Innes, 1821; repr. Philadelphia: Herman Hooker, 1844), vol. I, p. 156.

50. Daniel Wilson, *Evidences of Christianity Stated in a Popular and Practical Manner* (London: George Wilson, 1828²; repr. New York: Leavitt, 1833), p. 284.

51. See Wilson's unwillingness to countenance biblical error, enunciated at ibid., pp. 255, 256, 265, 271, 279, 281, 282, 284, 290, 293, 294. It does not seem to me that Bebbington's single allusion to the sentiments of Wilson (*Evangelicalism in Modern Britain*, p. 87) is representative of this overall view.

of the mind and habits of the writers appear to act, but were exempted from error and mistake.'[52]

And in America, the original Professor of Theology in the recently founded Princeton Seminary, Archibald Alexander,[53] was still extolling the merits of the 'degrees of inspiration' schema when he wrote *Evidences of the Authenticity, Inspiration and Canonical Authority of the Holy Scriptures* in 1835. Explicitly acknowledging Doddridge and Dick, who had gone before him, Alexander exerted himself to place the conception of the 'degrees' in an entirely wholesome framework. Even the most general operation of inspiration, that of superintendence, was used by the Holy Spirit so that a Bible historian was 'to be preserved from error and mistake'.[54] As to the oft-debated question of whether divine inspiration provided 'the words of Scripture, as well as the ideas', Alexander insisted that 'advocates for both parties are right; . . . the truth will be fully possessed by adopting the views entertained on both sides'.[55] He also chastised certain unnamed contemporary holders of this plenary inspiration view for allowing that the Scripture writers were 'left to their own unassisted powers in trivial matters . . . and therefore have fallen into mistakes in regard to trivial circumstances'. Since no Christian can infallibly identify which, and which only, are the instances of this tendency to lapse, 'the effect of this opinion is to introduce uncertainty and doubt in a matter concerning which assurance is of the utmost importance'.[56] No, for Alexander the plenary understanding of inspiration led to no such uncertain end, as for him the true definition of plenary inspiration is 'Such a divine influence upon the minds of the sacred writers as rendered them exempt from error, both in regard to the ideas and words.'[57]

With such a phalanx of circumspect and noteworthy advocates of the plenary inspiration view, all careful to guard the viewpoint against any appearance of laxity, it might be thought that the plenary view had established itself in an invulnerable position. But in fact, the very cautions sounded out by Dick and Alexander, noted above, contained in them the admission that some

---

52. Wilson, *Evidences*, pp. 284–285.

53. The seminary had a separate existence from the College of New Jersey as of 1812.

54. Archibald Alexander, *Evidences of the Authenticity, Inspiration and Canonical Authority of the Holy Scriptures* (Philadelphia: Presbyterian Board of Publication, 1836), p. 225. This was precisely Hill's emphasis (above).

55. Ibid., pp. 225–226.

56. Ibid., pp. 226–227.

57. Ibid., p. 230.

contemporary writers were drawing unsettling implications from an allowance that divine inspiration had functioned with variegations. And in this climate, there were those, standing in continuity with the earlier champions of verbal inspiration (Boston, Brown, Fisher, Gill, and before them, Turretin, Owen and Ussher), who were ready to charge the Doddridgean scheme of degrees of inspiration with having blazed the trail over which current suggestions of biblical inexactitude and error in trivial matters now advanced.

This was the concern of the Scot Robert Haldane, who in 1816 saw through the press his *The Evidence and Authority of Divine Revelation*.[58] Haldane had sat for a period in the lecture hall of David Bogue at Gosport; there he had heard the degrees of inspiration scheme warmly espoused by Bogue, his countryman and fast friend. But by 1816, if not earlier, he had come emphatically to reject the scheme and the consequences for which it had seemed to prepare the way:

> It has been contended that different degrees of inspiration are to be attributed to different parts of the Word of God. To some places belongs, as is supposed, an inspiration of superintendance, to others of elevation, and to the rest of suggestion. To this view of the matter, though very generally adopted, the writers of the Scriptures give no countenance whatsoever. This being the case, and as the question of inspiration can be determined only by the Scriptures themselves, all the distinctions that have been introduced are mere theories and unsupported by any evidence. The Scriptures uniformly assert the highest degree of inspiration and give no intimation of any part of them being written under an inspiration of any kind but one.

In sum, Haldane's position was reducible to this one proposition: 'Our knowledge of the inspiration of the Bible, like every other doctrine that it contains, must be collected from itself.'[59] Haldane was breaking no new ground here; he was 'plumping' for a return to a consideration of inspiration carried out deductively from 'pillar' passages. The method, if not the particular elaboration, was there to be inspected in Turretin, Owen, Boston, Fisher and Brown. What Haldane had no curiosity for was building a conception of inspiration

---

58. For lack of attention to the advocates of verbal inspiration throughout the seventeenth and eighteenth centuries, described above, Bebbington (*Evangelicalism in Modern Britain*, p. 87) portrays Haldane as the theological innovator.

59. Haldane, *The Evidence and Authority of Divine Revelation* (Edinburgh: W. Whyte, 1816), vol. I, pp. 134–135.

from induction from the genre and phenomena of Scripture, as well as deduction from major passages. Advocates of plenary inspiration had been attempting to do justice to both considerations for at least a century.

Robert Haldane's two-volume work had just been issued from Edinburgh printing presses when he embarked for Europe. His sojourn in France and Switzerland would occupy him until 1819. It would be a period of expounding Paul's *Letter to the Romans*, and of conducting personal and theological conferences with students at Geneva and Montauban. Before returning to Edinburgh, he worked to consolidate the achievements of his Francophone ministry through assisting in the foundation of Independent churches, of funding the publication of books and Bibles, and launching schemes for the training and deployment of Christian workers.

While numerous theological students at Geneva experienced religious conversion in connection with Haldane's labours, one minister, already an evangelical believer, found in Haldane a kind of kindred spirit in their common preference for the theology of a previous century. F. S. L. Gaussen, Reformed minister of Satigny, canton of Geneva, would soon come to the forefront of the evangelical cause there. He would be the champion of the founding of a Genevan Mission Society; he would stand up for continued recognition of the Second Helvetic Confession (1566); he would be a founder in 1831 of the Geneva Evangelical Society and professor of dogmatics in its agency, the Evangelical School of Theology.

In 1840 Gaussen's volume *Theopneustia* (English trans. 1841: *The Divine Inspiration of the Bible*) came forth from Paris printing presses: it expanded upon the very themes Robert Haldane, Gaussen's senior comrade, had enunciated in 1816. But Gaussen went farther. Whereas in 1816, Haldane had refrained from naming contemporary advocates of Doddridge's allegedly harmful degrees-of-inspiration view (one had been his own teacher, Bogue), Gaussen named names. He named Germans who taught only a partial inspiration; he also cited three contemporary Brits, John Dick, Daniel Wilson and John Pye Smith,[60] whom he believed to be sowing confusion by their continued espousal of the degrees of inspiration view.

---

60. F. S. L. Gaussen, *Theopneustia* (London: Bagster, 1841), pp. 26–28. Had David Bogue's posthumously published *Theological Lectures* (1848) been in print in 1840, no doubt Gaussen would have shown disapprobation towards his views of inspiration also. And Bogue was just as stalwart a friend of evangelicalism in Switzerland and France as had been Daniel Wilson and John Pye Smith. See Stewart, *Restoring the Reformation*, ch. 2.

That the Holy Spirit might have dealt variously with the biblical writers, Gaussen could conceive as plausible; but that the Scriptures taught anything other than a uniform inspiration extending to the very words, he denied as emphatically as Haldane had.[61] Gaussen was a polished and very learned Swiss pastor-theologian, and thus it was he rather than Haldane who was soon established as the international figurehead of the evangelical movement in favour of a return to the conception of verbal inspiration. There was little that was new about this viewpoint, other than the open disdain for those favouring what was now written off as the 'concessive' plenary view. In Gaussen's case, two of his three British 'targets' had personally visited Geneva and had openly aligned themselves with the cause of Genevan evangelicalism. Through such contacts he was personally acquainted with Daniel Wilson, and had in all likelihood met Pye Smith when this London theological professor had visited Geneva. But it did not matter.

By 1842, evidence was accumulating that the renewed case for verbal inspiration was in the ascendant. A nameless reviewer for the *Princeton Review* praised Gaussen's book, and by implication dispatched to oblivion Archibald Alexander's 1835 defence of the plenary view.[62] Expounding the doctrines of the Westminster Confession of Faith in 1845, the Scottish Associate Presbyterian theologian Robert Shaw, in reliance on Gaussen, dispatched the degrees of inspiration view, and extolled verbal inspiration, all the while co-opting the terminology of 'plenary' for a view that had stood distinguished from it for over a century.[63]

Did the early Victorian upsurge of conviction about verbal inspiration and biblical inerrancy represent a change? Not in the sense proposed by David Bebbington. The new preference for verbal inspiration as the safeguard of inerrancy was in fact indicative of some loss of evangelical confidence in that

---

61. Gaussen, *Theopneustia*, pp. 24–25.

62. *Princeton Review* 14 (1842), p. 525, suggestively commented, 'It will be read, understood, and felt by those who would throw aside with a sneer the productions of a Scottish or American author.'

63. Robert Shaw, *Exposition of the Westminster Confession of Faith* (Edinburgh: J. Johnstone, 1845), repr. as *The Reformed Faith* (Tain: Christian Focus, 1972), pp. 11–12. On Shaw, see Sherman Isbell, 'Shaw, Robert', in de S. Cameron, *Scottish Dictionary*, p. 770. Gaussen himself had unwittingly fuelled the confusion of terminology by using the French adjective *pleine* (full) to describe his own view. Translators of his work infelicitously rendered *pleine* as 'plenary' and so sowed the seeds of the blurring of the distinction between two distinct long-standing views.

new and changing century, and represented a determination to regroup theologically by resorting again to respectable and venerable assertions about biblical inspiration that had never lacked evangelical advocates through the 1780s. Judicious advocates of the plenary view had defended the Scripture against insinuations of error as assuredly as their verbal-inspirationist contemporaries, and done so while following an admirable inductive method. Yet only in the mid-twentieth century would there be a rehabilitation of the evangelical quest to build a doctrine of inspiration as informed by induction from the genre and phenomena of Scripture as by deduction from pillar passages.[64]

© Kenneth J. Stewart, 2008

---

64. I have elsewhere drawn attention to the significance of Everett F. Harrison's chapter 'The Phenomena of Scripture', in Carl F. Henry (ed.), *Revelation and the Bible* (Grand Rapids: Baker, 1959), pp. 235–250. See my 'Bombshell of a Book' (n. 2 above).

PART 5: RESPONSE

18. RESPONSE

David W. Bebbington

The novelist William Hale White, who specialized in depicting the English Dissenting tradition from which he sprang, was acutely aware of the processes of change that had moulded it over time. In his book *The Revolution in Tanner's Lane* (1887), Hale White recounts a sermon by Thomas Bradshaw, the minister of a London meeting house at the start of the nineteenth century who claimed descent from the family of a Puritan regicide and who himself upheld the full range of Calvinist belief. The sermon, on Jephthah's daughter, a moving but sternly cerebral discourse, asserts the doctrine of absolute predestination. It was, says the author, 'utterly unlike the simple stuff which became fashionable with the Evangelistic movement'.[1] The book is designed to lay bare what Hale White sees as the decay of the Dissenting interest. Dissenters had once upheld Puritan views that were, in the author's eyes, totally untenable, but they had done so with admirable consistency. However, the 'Evangelistic movement', by which the author means the Evangelical Revival, had combined with subtle social influences to rob them of their inheritance. By the 1840s, as he goes on to suggest, they were shallow, affected gentility and lacked intellectual rigour. For this jaundiced observer of the impact of evangelicalism, the movement was

---

1. Mark Rutherford (William Hale White), *The Revolution in Tanner's Lane* (London: T. Fisher Unwin, n. d., 9th ed.), p. 96.

partly responsible for a transformation in the Dissenting tradition that left it impoverished. That was part of what he was portraying as a *revolution* in Tanner's Lane.

The effect of the Evangelical Revival on the inherited Calvinism of Britain is the central theme of the chapters that have formed this book. Nearly all ask whether the revival was revolutionary or whether, on the whole, it maintained characteristics displayed by the Reformers of the sixteenth century and the Puritans of the seventeenth. A related question is how far the revival was bound up with the Enlightenment that flowered in the eighteenth century. These issues were raised in chapter 2 of *Evangelicalism in Modern Britain*, a book published in 1988, fully two decades ago, and it is gratifying that they are now thought worthy of discussion. Hale White had little if anything to say about the Enlightenment, but in answer to the main question he had no doubt that there was a major shift from Puritanism to evangelicalism. Intellectual depth, together with other qualities such as a commitment to radical politics, had been sacrificed. His account, however, suggests that the erosion of the Puritan virtues was a protracted process. They were still in evidence, according to his story, in the early years of the nineteenth century. Hale White wrote fiction, and was notably unfriendly to evangelicalism, but his point of view is worth pondering. In this response to the various evaluations of the case set out in *Evangelicalism in Modern Britain*, it will be argued that, notwithstanding the sometimes legitimate criticism of the book, the rise of the movement did represent much that was new but that the chronology of change needs adjustment. The chief specific critiques will be considered in turn before some main contentions of the book are restated in modified form. What, then, were the continuities, and the discontinuities, in evangelical history?

In the first place there is the question of activism. Several contributors to this volume, following in the wake of an essay by Carl Trueman, contend that activism was no novelty in the eighteenth century.[2] At an earlier date there had existed zealous preaching, energetic evangelism and dedicated catechizing, all epitomized in the career of Richard Baxter.[3] There were activists in seventeenth-

---

2. Carl R. Trueman, 'Reformers, Puritans and Evangelicals: The Lay Connection', in Deryck W. Lovegrove (ed.), *The Rise of the Laity in Evangelical Protestantism* (London: Routledge, 2002), p. 31.

3. In this volume, John Coffey, 'Puritanism, Evangelicalism and the Evangelical Protestant Tradition', p. 266; Garry J. Williams, 'Enlightenment Epistemology and Eighteenth-Century Evangelical Doctrines of Assurance', p. 373.

century Welsh Dissent and among New England Congregationalists in the
1710s, before the received dating of the start of evangelicalism.[4] All this is true,
but nevertheless there were innovations in the Evangelical Revival. There were
fresh techniques such as magazines and coordinating organizations; equally
there were other methods, such as the printing of books and international
correspondence, that were greatly expanded.[5] Field preaching, though not
entirely novel, became for the first time a standard form of outreach. Itinerant
preachers, with George Whitefield at their head, became star personalities
in a way that was alien to an earlier age.[6] Many of these developments were
possible because of the commercial growth of the eighteenth century, and one
of its chief motors, the joint stock company, became the model for the voluntary societies that best embodied the intensified outreach flowing from the
revival. The innovations, and especially the societies, were justified in terms
of a particular teaching that came to prominence. The Almighty, rather than
habitually exercising his capacity for divine fiat, deigned to employ 'means'
(a key word) for the furtherance of his purposes. Christians, it was insisted,
had licence to use the same 'means' to spread the gospel. Here was an ideological rationale for the extra-ecclesiastical agencies, many of them interdenominational, that marked the evangelical era. In such bodies the prominence
of laypeople in promoting Christian enterprise was unprecedented, another
feature that tended to distinguish eighteenth-century (and later) evangelicals
from their Protestant predecessors. The extensive deployment of lay preachers (though not wholly new) was just one symptom of a different attitude to
non-ministerial endeavour.[7] So it is undoubtedly true that activism had existed
before the 1730s, but it is also true that its scale and dimensions altered significantly after around that point.

That is most obvious in the case of transcultural missions, a second topic that
has prompted considerable comment in the present volume. The Reformers and
many of their successors assumed that a Protestant government needed to exist

4. In this volume, D. Densil Morgan, 'Continuity, Novelty and Evangelicalism
   in Wales, c. 1640–1850', pp. 91–92, 96–97; Thomas S. Kidd, '"Prayer for a
   Saving Issue": Evangelical Development in New England before the Great
   Awakening', pp. 140–141.
5. In this volume, David Ceri Jones, 'Calvinistic Methodism and the Origins of
   Evangelicalism in England', pp. 116–123.
6. Harry S. Stout, *The Divine Dramatist: George Whitefield and the Rise of Modern
   Evangelicalism* (Grand Rapids: Eerdmans, 1991).
7. Lovegrove, *Rise of the Laity*.

in particular lands before they could be effectively evangelized. Although there
were expressions of aspiration to carry the gospel beyond Christendom during the seventeenth century and even instances of Puritans undertaking such
ventures,[8] they had nothing of the sustained character that arose in the classic
missionary societies from the 1790s onwards. Because those organizations did
not arise from around the 1730s or 40s, doubt has been expressed about whether
they should be seen as intrinsic to the evangelical impulse.[9] Yet there was support before the 1790s for missions to lands where the gospel was not yet known.
The rising tide of postmillennial teaching encouraged a missionary interest. In
1747 Jonathan Edwards recommended concerted prayer 'for the advancement
of Christ's kingdom on earth' and his biography of David Brainerd, published
two years later, inspired subsequent missionary efforts.[10] Many evangelicals
concentrated their support on the Moravian efforts that pioneered the global
missionary movement in the eighteenth century.[11] The involvement of evangelicals in foreign missions, it has been proposed, has more to do with empire,
together with the rise of voluntary societies, than with any change in theory
or practice since the seventeenth century.[12] Yet, though the missionary effort
was never restricted to empire, the seizure of the opportunities it offered was
a result of the pragmatic temper of evangelicalism.[13] Missions illustrate that
evangelicals, possessing a rather different mindset from their Protestant predecessors, were willing to undertake ventures of an altogether unprecedented
magnitude.

Assurance, in the third place, has aroused a good deal of discussion in this
book. It has been shown that the eighteenth-century evangelical expectation
that converts would receive a sense of their acceptance by God was anticipated by some early adherents of the Reformation who were swayed by late

---

8. In this volume, Michael A. G. Haykin, 'Evangelicalism and the Enlightenment:
   A Reassessment', pp. 52–54.

9. Ibid., p. 54.

10. In this volume, Douglas A. Sweeney and Brandon G. Withrow, 'Jonathan
    Edwards: Continuator or Pioneer of Evangelical History?', pp. 298–299.

11. J. C. S. Mason, *The Moravian Church and the Missionary Awakening in England, 1760–
    1800* (London: Royal Historical Society, 2001).

12. Coffey, 'Puritanism, Evangelicalism', p. 267.

13. Brian Stanley, 'Christianity and Civilization in English Evangelical Mission
    Thought', in Brian Stanley (ed.), *Christian Missions and the Enlightenment* (Grand
    Rapids: Eerdmans, 2001), pp. 195–196.

medieval affective piety.[14] The richness of Puritan and Dutch teaching about full assurance, a specialist explains, was lost in subsequent revivalism.[15] It has also been proposed that in Scotland there was substantial consistency of teaching about assurance between the Reformers and the mid-nineteenth century.[16] It has equally been suggested, however, that there was great variation in Puritan teaching on the subject, with some expounding a system in which confidence of one's salvation was difficult to attain and others claiming that it was easy.[17] Because of the close relationship between Scottish and English Reformed theologians in the seventeenth century, it would be surprising if both these views turn out to be correct. In the case of Edwards, it has been demonstrated that he receded from his earlier confidence in the experience of converts to a much more circumspect view that echoed Puritan questionings.[18] Yet evidence has also been brought forward to show that Edwards abandoned his grandfather's preparationism, a wrestling through specified stages of experience in order to reach an assured faith. Because of his awareness that he had not passed through the steps experienced by 'the Dissenters of Old England', Edwards was initially inclined to question whether he had been truly converted.[19] The traditional way, as taught by the authoritative voice of Puritans in the Church of England as well as Dissent, seems to have encompassed a great deal of doubt. Even while drawing attention to the diversity of Puritan views, John Coffey acknowledges this belief as the 'mainstream' Puritan opinion.[20] This was the phase of Reformed teaching that was so arresting as to persuade the pioneer sociologist Max Weber about the habitual self-questioning of Protestants. Their doubts about salvation drove them, according to Weber, to demonstrate their faith by works, not least the qualities that gave rise to capitalism.[21] Assurance was therefore a more complex matter than *Evangelicalism*

---

14. In this volume, Ashley Null, 'Thomas Cranmer and Tudor Evangelicalism', pp. 238–246.

15. In this volume, Joel R. Beeke, 'Evangelicalism and the Dutch Second Reformation', pp. 166–167.

16. In this volume, A. T. B. McGowan, 'Evangelicalism in Scotland from Knox to Cunningham', pp. 63–83.

17. Coffey, 'Puritanism, Evangelicalism', pp. 265–266.

18. Haykin, 'Evangelicalism and the Enlightenment', pp. 56–57.

19. Sweeney and Withrow, 'Jonathan Edwards', p. 290.

20. Coffey, 'Puritanism, Evangelicalism', pp. 265–266.

21. Max Weber, *The Protestant Ethic and the Spirit of Capitalism* (London: G. Allen & Unwin, 1930), ch. 4A.

in Modern Britain allows. Nevertheless, on the evidence so far available it seems likely that the predominant view on the subject in the seventeenth century was less confident than what was normally professed in the eighteenth.

What, fourthly, was the relationship of assurance to the Enlightenment? The careful textual study by Garry Williams shows that the spiritual sense giving knowledge of God in John Wesley is more deeply indebted to earlier Christian thought than *Evangelicalism in Modern Britain* supposed. Williams's contention that Jonathan Edwards was untouched by the thought of John Locke, however, is called into some question by the evidence of Douglas Sweeney and Brandon Withrow that Locke admitted a spiritual sense; and Williams's view that Edwards would have been troubled to think that his ideas were novel is undermined by Sweeney and Withrow's evidence that he saw his age, a different one from that of the Reformers, having as its particular task the unravelling of doctrine. Sweeney and Withrow conclude that Edwards, though not a thoroughgoing empiricist, nevertheless used the Lockean language of his day more than was necessary for apologetic purposes. Like Wesley, however, he owed more to inherited Christian beliefs than to contemporary philosophical opinion.[22] John Newton, as Garry Williams explains here and Bruce Hindmarsh has shown in his study of Newton, spoke more like a Puritan on assurance than *Evangelicalism in Modern Britain* would suggest.[23] So the balance of sources for the thought of the early evangelicals on the doctrine of assurance has to be adjusted. The Enlightenment was less their inspiration than was previously argued. A type of assurance deriving from contemporary thought was not the single hinge of the door into evangelicalism. Nevertheless, even if the mechanism of the transition from Puritanism to evangelicalism described in the book of 1988 turns out to be invalid, it does not necessarily follow that there was no such evolution. More will be said about the overall relationship between the evangelical movement and the Enlightenment below.

A fifth subject raised by the discussions in this volume is the question of revival. In this area the evidence points to a fresh dimension of novelty that was not highlighted in *Evangelicalism in Modern Britain*. The phenomenon of revival, Thomas Kidd shows, arose in its Congregational form in New England. Because the churches began to permit a form of halfway membership, there were many unconverted individuals in the pews ready to respond to stirring

---

22. Williams, 'Enlightenment Epistemology', pp. 351–361; Sweeney and Withrow, 'Jonathan Edwards', pp. 284–294.

23. Williams, 'Enlightenment Epistemology', pp. 370–372; D. Bruce Hindmarsh, *John Newton and the English Evangelical Tradition* (Oxford: Clarendon, 1996), ch. 6.

appeals from the pulpit. Periodic ingatherings of such souls took place even before the 1730s.[24] Again, as Leigh Schmidt has demonstrated and as Douglas Sweeney and Brandon Withrow point out in this volume, the Presbyterian pattern of revival, closely associated with the Communion season, went back to the early years of the seventeenth century in Scotland.[25] So an awareness of the possibilities of revival had been kindled long before the conventional date for the commencement of evangelicalism. However, the discourse of revival was popularized, John Coffey suggests, only from the 1730s. So the expectation of regular revival that has been so prominent a mark of modern evangelicalism was born.[26] It was this revivalist atmosphere, Crawford Gribben notes, that set alight the postmillennial hopes of Jonathan Edwards.[27] Although revivals of the type experienced from the 1730s onwards were known in previous years, showing a tangible continuity, the Evangelical Revival was novel both because of its scale and because it created an eager anticipation of more awakenings.

The sixth topic, the Bible, is unique among the subjects discussed here in relating to an issue considered outside chapter 2 of *Evangelicalism in Modern Britain*. In chapter 3 of that book there is an account of the rise of a new attitude to Scripture in the middle years of the nineteenth century. Assumptions about the Bible based on an Enlightenment outlook gave way to premises associated with Romanticism.[28] In the present volume, however, Kenneth Stewart demonstrates that it was mistaken to claim that Louis Gaussen, the leading exponent of the Romantic approach to inspiration, was the first to offer a carefully argued case for biblical inerrancy. There were previous defences of the absence of error from the Scriptures.[29] Nevertheless, it has to be restated that the Enlightenment stance towards inspiration did often foster a broader outlook, so that the leading Anglican evangelical of the early nineteenth century, Charles Simeon, could remark that the Bible includes

24. Kidd, "'Prayer for a Saving Issue'", pp. 129–145.
25. L. E. Schmidt, *Holy Fairs: Scotland and the Making of American Revivalism* (Grand Rapids: Eerdmans, 1989). Sweeney and Withrow, 'Jonathan Edwards', pp. 295–296.
26. Coffey, 'Puritanism, Evangelicalism', p. 275.
27. In this volume, Crawford Gribben, 'Evangelical Eschatology and "the Puritan Hope"', p. 389.
28. D. W. Bebbington, *Evangelicalism in Modern Britain: A History from the 1730s to the 1980s* (London: Unwin Hyman, 1989 [sc. 1988]), pp. 86–88.
29. Kenneth J. Stewart, 'The Evangelical Doctrine of Scripture, 1650–1850: A Re-examination of David Bebbington's Theory', pp. 405, 408, 409.

'inexactnesses in reference to philosophical and scientific matters'.[30] Only the religious message of the Scriptures, he supposed, was immune to error. Furthermore, the revolution in attitudes to the Bible of the mid-nineteenth century sketched in *Evangelicalism in Modern Britain* did take place. There was a shift from an inductive approach to a deductive understanding of the nature of Scripture. How much there was an equivalent alteration in attitudes to the Bible around the middle years of the eighteenth century would be an instructive study. It would go some way towards resolving the question of how far evangelicals were in continuity with their Puritan predecessors.

Then, in the seventh place, there is the place of Methodism. The movement spearheaded by John Wesley, notwithstanding his predilection for antiquity, was undoubtedly novel. The historian cannot dismiss it as an aberration, because it was numerically the largest sector of the evangelical movement in Britain. Nineteenth-century commentators of Calvinist conviction, whether Anglican or Dissenting, may have downplayed the place of Methodism,[31] but twentieth-century historians, generally much more sympathetic to Arminian theology, conversely tended to exaggerate the role of Methodism in the Evangelical Revival. In his volume in the Pelican history of the church, for example, G. R. Cragg has a chapter entitled 'Methodism and the Evangelical Revival', with the former occupying twice as much space as the latter.[32] In the present volume, by contrast, there are no chapters on Methodism. Wesley is discussed in two chapters[33] and mentioned in several others, but there is no coverage of his movement. The omission of the sector of evangelicalism that displayed most theological and practical innovation, together with the greatest debt to non-Reformed sources, unduly skews the evidence of this volume in favour of continuity between the seventeenth and eighteenth centuries. It could be replied that evangelicals in the Church of England and orthodox Dissent saw Methodism as an alien force. Paul Helm shows that Augustus Toplady viewed Wesley and all his works in exactly this

---

30. A. W. Brown, *Recollections of the Conversation Parties of the Rev. Charles Simeon* (London: Hamilton, Adams, 1863), p. 100.

31. In this volume, Ian J. Shaw, 'The Evangelical Revival through the Eyes of the "Evangelical Century": Nineteenth-Century Perceptions of the Origins of Evangelicalism', p. 320.

32. G. R. Cragg, *The Church and the Age of Reason, 1648–1789* (Harmondsworth: Penguin, 1966, rev. ed.), ch. 10.

33. Null, 'Thomas Cranmer', pp. 246–251; and Williams, 'Enlightenment Epistemology', pp. 351–356.

light,[34] and equivalent Dissenters would not be hard to find. Yet Toplady, the author of *The Historic Proof of the Doctrinal Calvinism of the Church of England* (1774), was probably the sternest opponent of Arminian theology within his church. His degree of hostility to Wesley was quite exceptional. Despite the theological polarity over free will, there was generally a remarkable degree of mutual respect within the diverse ranks of the evangelicals. They had a sense of belonging to a common movement in which their united proclamation of the new birth transcended doctrinal differences. 'Insignificant indeed', declared Joseph Milner, a prominent Anglican evangelical, 'are all the distinctions of another kind compared with these, converted or unconverted . . . heirs of heaven or heirs of hell.'[35] Methodists were full participants in the Evangelical Revival. Their contribution ensured that the movement as a whole was in many respects discontinuous with earlier Protestantism as well as in other ways continuous with it.

What, then, can be reaffirmed in the light of the conversation represented by this book? Again seven points can be made. The first is that the nature of evangelicalism appears to be more or less agreed. Evangelicals believed the Bible, returning to its pages for teaching, consolation and guidance. They saw the cross of Christ as central to their faith, for the atonement saved them from their sins. They held that individuals must be converted so as to begin changed lives of allegiance to Christ. And they displayed an activism that carried the gospel to others and brought them help in their suffering. For all the enormous differences between evangelicals, emphases on the Bible, the cross, conversion and activism are together the features they have displayed down the ages. The most critical commentators on chapter 2 of *Evangelicalism in Modern Britain* do not dispute this characterization in chapter 1. The so-called quadrilateral contrasts with the five-point description of Luther's convictions set out by Cameron Mackenzie in this volume. There is evidently a family likeness, but evangelicals would normally have hotly repudiated the belief of Luther that infants become Christians at their baptism.[36] Evangelicalism has been distinct from higher systems of Christian faith upholding such teachings

---

34. In this volume, Paul Helm, 'Calvin, A. M. Toplady and the Bebbington Thesis', pp. 199–220.

35. Joseph Milner, *Practical Sermons*, 3 vols. (London: Cadell & Davies, 1821⁴), vol. 2, p. 250, quoted by R. H. Martin, *Evangelicals United: Ecumenical Stirrings in Pre-Victorian Britain, 1795–1830* (Metuchen, N. J.: Scarecrow, 1983), p. 4.

36. In this volume, Cameron A. Mackenzie, 'The Evangelical Character of Martin Luther's Faith', p. 188.

as baptismal regeneration as well as broader systems professing looser theological notions, especially in the area of soteriology. Whatever the date of the
beginning of evangelicalism, its identity is known.[37]

A second aspect of *Evangelicalism in Modern Britain* that has not been challenged is its contention that the evangelical movement has been strongly tinc-
tured by its cultural setting. It had long been appreciated that other phases of
Christian history, such as the theology of the high Middle Ages or the liberal
views of the Victorian era, were deeply affected by the intellectual atmosphere
of the times, but it was commonly supposed that evangelicals, in clinging to
their unyielding convictions, maintained a constant protest against cultural
assimilation. It is true that many evangelicals have been persistently hostile
to 'the world', shunning the beershop and the theatre alike, but they could
hardly escape the common assumptions of their age. So their attitudes to art
and recreation, family life and public affairs, the Bible and even the nature
of God have altered over time in perceptible relationship with the changing
opinions of their contemporaries. Religion is normally moulded less by the
class determinants isolated for scrutiny by many social historians than by the
broad outlines of how people think. Consequently, evangelicals habitually
used concepts provided by the Enlightenment during a long epoch beginning
in the eighteenth century. Many of them, however, subsequently adopted
ways of looking about them derived from the Romantic reaction against
the Enlightenment. In the twentieth century, again, some of them took up
expressivist views (called 'Modernist' in *Evangelicalism in Modern Britain*) that
are continuous with the postmodernist attitudes of the twenty-first century.
This general process of the assimilation of influences from the host culture has
proceeded throughout evangelical history.

Consequently, and in the third place, the early evangelicals shared much
common ground with the Enlightenment. This proposition would not be
accepted by all the contributors to this volume. Andrew McGowan in particular regards the Enlightenment as having exerted little influence over evangelicals (common sense philosophy apart) other than setting in train a baneful
subversion of Christian orthodoxy.[38] It was not, however, the legacy of Kant
that formed the groundwork of the discourse of eighteenth-century progressive
thinkers. Rather, it was the set of values surrounding reason and happiness,

---

37. This case is developed in D. W. Bebbington, 'Towards an Evangelical Identity',
    in Steve Bruce and Harold Rowdon (eds.), *For Such a Time as This: Perspectives on
    Evangelicalism Past, Present and Future* (London: Scripture Union, 1996), pp. 37–48.

38. McGowan, 'Evangelicalism in Scotland', pp. 79–80.

benevolence and liberty. There was an aversion to systems and metaphysics, a preference for clarity and simplicity. These principles suffused the ideas of the early evangelicals. Michael Haykin, in writing on the relationship of evangelicalism to the Enlightenment in this volume, acknowledges this permeation.[39] The consequence, as he and others appreciate, is that evangelicalism cannot be seen as an anti-intellectual, or proto-Fundamentalist, reaction against the age of reason. The evangelical movement was aligned with the modern, a circumstance that greatly enhanced its appeal. It shared the empiricist approach of the age, and so was bound up with the rising spirit of scientific enquiry. Equally it upheld an optimistic providentialism, frequently reinforced by a postmillennial hope of steady advance in the human lot on earth that was a close Christian equivalent of the secular idea of progress. Despite the justified criticism of the treatment of assurance in *Evangelicalism in Modern Britain*, it may still be the case that the common (though not universal) greater confidence in knowing God among evangelicals, for example in the Wesleyan doctrine of the witness of the Spirit, was a counterpart of the characteristic quest of the age for greater certainty. So many of the features of evangelical faith and practice during the eighteenth century, and for long afterwards, bore the stamp of the Enlightenment. Though not created by the Enlightenment, evangelicalism was embedded in it.

The relation of the evangelical movement to earlier expressions of Protestantism, fourthly, was one of continuity as well as discontinuity. That was the position of *Evangelicalism in Modern Britain* and the evidence marshalled in this volume often confirms the verdict. Thus Densil Morgan perceives both continuity and novelty in Wales; and Sweeney and Withrow see Jonathan Edwards as continuator and pioneer.[40] Two major qualifications, however, are now required. One is that there was a higher degree of continuity with the Puritans than the book of 1988 recognized. Bruce Hindmarsh, who describes the prehistory of conversion narratives in this volume, has previously shown their emergence in seventeenth-century Dissent and development in the Evangelical Revival.[41] John Coffey has listed other symptoms of continuity such

39. Haykin, 'Evangelicalism and the Enlightenment', pp. 48.

40. Morgan, 'Continuity, Novelty', pp. 84–102; Sweeney and Withrow, 'Jonathan Edwards', pp. 278–301.

41. D. Bruce Hindmarsh, 'The Antecedents of Evangelical Conversion Narrative: Spiritual Autobiography and the Christian Tradition', pp. 327–344; see also D. Bruce Hindmarsh, *The Evangelical Conversion Narrative: Spiritual Autobiography in Early Modern England* (Oxford: Oxford University Press, 2005).

as study Bibles, hymn-singing, controversies over imputation, moral reform and sabbatarianism.[42] At the same time, Reg Ward has strengthened the case for continental Pietist influence in two weighty books.[43] Ward has no qualms about calling Pietism a species of evangelicalism, and so dating the origins of the movement to circa 1670.[44] That leads on to the second qualification. The chronology of the early stages of evangelicalism needs to be extended in both directions. The New England exhortations to revival of the late seventeenth century imply that at least one typical feature of the later movement was already in place.[45] At the other end of the period it is evident that estimates of assurance as hard to gain persisted in mainstream Calvinistic Dissent into the nineteenth century, though fading as the century wore on.[46] That suggests that the changes wrought by the Evangelical Revival were in some quarters more delayed than the book of 1988 proposed. Hale White's *Revolution in Tanner's Lane*, though no transcription from life, is not mistaken in positing the survival of aspects of Puritanism beyond the eighteenth century. Primarily because published works from previous generations were habitually read and reread, early modern religion proved a persistent force.

Yet the discontinuities should not be underestimated. The ablest nineteenth-century commentator on the history of English Congregationalism, R. W. Dale, contended that there had been a transformation in the ethos of his denomination as a result of the onset of the eighteenth-century revival. Dale makes a point that can constitute the fifth in the list of affirmations: evangelicalism was responsible for a substantial shift in churchmanship. The Puritans, as Morgan and Coffey note here, were preoccupied with correct order and discipline.[47] Traditionalists in the eighteenth century remained so. The Secession in Scotland, beginning in the 1730s, divided as early as 1747 over whether a member could legitimately take an oath implying recognition of the established church of Scotland. In America the Presbyterian Old Sides,

---

42. Coffey, 'Puritanism, Evangelicalism', p. 274.

43. W. R. Ward, *The Protestant Evangelical Awakening* (Cambridge: Cambridge University Press, 1992); *Early Evangelicalism: A Global Intellectual History* (Cambridge: Cambridge University Press, 2006).

44. Ward, *Early Evangelicalism*, p. 1.

45. Kidd, '"Prayer for a Saving Issue"', pp. 130–131.

46. D. W. Bebbington, 'Evangelical Conversion, c. 1740–1850', *Scottish Bulletin of Evangelical Theology* 18 (2000), pp. 122–124.

47. Morgan, 'Continuity, Novelty', pp. 91–92; Coffey, 'Puritanism, Evangelicalism', p. 277.

the Congregational Old Lights and eventually the Primitive Baptists similarly insisted, against the revivalists, on matters of ecclesiastical punctilio. These groups were resisting the alteration brought about by the spirit of the Great Awakening. Dale described it thus:

> The Evangelical movement encouraged what is called an undenominational temper. It emphasized the vital importance of the Evangelical creed, but it regarded almost with indifference all forms of Church polity that were not in apparent and irreconcilable antagonism to that creed.[48]

The gospel was so precious that it eclipsed all other concerns, churchly issues included. The 'Catholic spirit' displayed in the beginnings of the undenominational London Missionary Society of 1795 was a quintessential expression of evangelicalism. Even some Anglicans, though members of an established church, were content to join Dissenters in the venture. There was a discarding of inherited inhibitions for the sake of bold outreach.[49] Here was a definite symptom of discontinuity.

Similarly, and in the sixth place, there was a difference between early evangelicals and their predecessors over their attitude to matters of public concern. Dale put it like this in his account of evangelicalism:

> Although its leaders insisted very earnestly on the obligation of individual Christian men to live a devout and godly life, they had very little to say about the relations of the individual Christian to the general order of human society, or about the realization of the Kingdom of God in all the various regions of human activity.[50]

Evangelicals lacked any concerted social or political theory. That is hardly surprising, since in England and Wales they were divided between adherents of an established church and members of Dissenting bodies. The sociopolitical ideas of the churches were so bound up with the question of establishment that it would have been hard for a distinctive evangelical view to command anything like general assent. There was a contrast here with their Puritan predecessors. Calvin had aspired to foster the creation of a Christian city-state in Geneva,

---

48. R. W. Dale, *The Old Evangelicalism and the New* (London: Hodder & Stoughton, 1889), p. 17.
49. Martin, *Evangelicals United*, chs. 3–4.
50. Dale, *Old Evangelicalism and the New*, p. 18.

and the establishment of a godly commonwealth was a perennial aim of Puritan groups. Their paradigm of Reformation entailed almost as much attention to the state as to the church, as Oliver Cromwell's career illustrates. The
revolutionary fervour of the British Civil Wars, however, had cooled by the
eighteenth century. Although the transformation was at least partly the result
of altered political circumstances, evangelicals believed in toleration, not ascendancy. They were normally content, at least down to the 1820s, if they avoided
state harassment of their evangelistic efforts. In Presbyterian Scotland there
may have been greater persistence of the older aim, for Thomas Chalmers,
the early nineteenth-century leader of evangelicals in the Church of Scotland,
hoped to establish a communitarian ideal in his native land.[51] But elsewhere
evangelicalism induced a withdrawal from the ambition to control the state.
Again there was a palpable change between the attitudes of the seventeenth
century and of the later epoch.

A further contrast, seventhly, lies in the area of theology. Evangelicals,
according to Dale, lacked 'a disinterested love of truth'. They did champion
doctrines that related directly to salvation, but the beliefs were appreciated
chiefly as necessary instruments for converting people to Christ: 'They cared
for their truth', wrote Dale, 'as a general cares for his guns and ammunition,
or as a mechanic cares for his tools; not as an artist of genius cares for his
canvas.'[52] This instrumentalist stance contrasted with the theological precision of the seventeenth century that gave rise to extensive doctrinal treatises,
multiple points in sermons and elaborate works of casuistry. Puritans were
part of the European university culture that dealt with theology as a rigorous academic discipline; evangelicals in Scotland remained so, but those in
England and Wales did not.[53] The Anglicans among them might attend university, but theology was not studied as a separate discipline; Dissenters might
have their academies, but they were designed to multiply gospel preachers,
not advance learning. The love of the Bible professed by evangelicals, together
with their aversion to metaphysics, often induced them to neglect the theological issues that had preoccupied earlier generations. The catechism issued
by Dan Taylor for the New Connexion of General Baptists, an enthusiastic
evangelistic body, contains two sections on God, specifying his various attributes with appropriate Scripture proofs, but entirely omitting mention of the

---

51. S. J. Brown, *Thomas Chalmers and the Godly Commonwealth in Scotland* (Oxford:
     Oxford University Press, 1982).
52. Dale, *Old Evangelicalism and the New*, pp. 19–20.
53. Trueman, 'Reformers, Puritans and Evangelicals', p. 32.

doctrine of the Trinity.[54] Taylor had confessed that he did not understand the dogma, seeing difficulties in all the explanations of how God could simultaneously be three and one.[55] There was no need to wrestle with complex and mysterious questions. Here was a striking dissimilarity between the prevailing ethos among the seventeenth-century Puritans and the atmosphere of the eighteenth-century Evangelical Revival.

The contributions to this volume go a long way towards advancing our understanding of the relationship between the evangelicalism of the eighteenth century and its antecedents. Yet some of the contentions call for qualification. Activism had existed among Puritans, but its scope, extending to the launching of global missions, greatly expanded among evangelicals. The doctrine of assurance did not have so uniform a character at any stage as *Evangelicalism in Modern Britain* proposed and among evangelicals its form was more rooted in the Christian past than in the Enlightenment; nevertheless, it does seem to have altered significantly over time, with a mainstream view encouraging sustained anxiety giving way very gradually to expectation of more confident experience. Revivals formed a thread of continuity between the periods before and after the appearance of Whitefield and Wesley as travelling evangelists, but, with the mushrooming of the awakening from that point, expectation of further revival emerged as a novelty. Although inspiration was understood to exclude error from the Bible before the Romantic era, there was a widespread firming up of attitudes to Scripture in the mid-nineteenth century. And what is missing from the volume is a sustained treatment of Wesleyan Methodism, which would make for greater discontinuity than might otherwise appear. There is agreement, however, about the nature of evangelicalism as biblicist, crucientric, conversionist and activist, about its being moulded by its cultural setting and, among many contributors, about there being much common ground between early evangelicals and the Enlightenment. It is also generally accepted that there were both continuity and discontinuity between the Evangelical Revival and what preceded it, though there were more features of continuity than *Evangelicalism in Modern Britain* itemized and the process of change was more gradual than the book proposed. Nevertheless, there were major novelties in the areas of churchmanship, public affairs and

---

54. Dan Taylor, *A Catechism* (London: for the author, 1805[6]), pp. 5–6; repr. in D. W. Bebbington et al. (eds.), *Protestant Nonconformist Texts*, vol. 3: *The Nineteenth Century* (Aldershot: Ashgate, 2006), pp. 35–36.

55. Dan Taylor to William Thompson, 9 July 1770, in Adam Taylor, *Memoirs of the Rev. Dan Taylor* (London: for the author, 1820), pp. 140–141.

theological precision. Notwithstanding the weighty legacy from the past, the emergence of evangelicalism did represent a revolutionary development in Protestant history.

© David W. Bebbington, 2008